CCNA Self-Study
CCNA INTRO
Exam Certification Guide

Wendell Odom, CCIE No. 1624

Cisco Press

Cisco Press
800 East 96th Street
Indianapolis, IN 46240 USA

CCNA INTRO Exam Certification Guide

Wendell Odom

Copyright© 2004 Cisco Systems, Inc.

Published by:
Cisco Press
800 East 96th Street
Indianapolis, IN 46240 USA

Printed in the United States of America 7 8 9 0

Seventh Printing September 2004

Library of Congress Cataloging-in-Publication Number: 2003104998

ISBN: 1-58720-094-5

Warning and Disclaimer

This book is designed to provide information about selected topics for the Introduction to Cisco Networking Technologies (INTRO) exam for the CCNA certification. Every effort has been made to make this book as complete and as accurate as possible, but no warranty or fitness is implied.

The information is provided on an "as is" basis. The authors, Cisco Press, and Cisco Systems, Inc., shall have neither liability nor responsibility to any person or entity with respect to any loss or damages arising from the information contained in this book or from the use of the discs or programs that may accompany it.

The opinions expressed in this book belong to the author and are not necessarily those of Cisco Systems, Inc.

Feedback Information

At Cisco Press, our goal is to create in-depth technical books of the highest quality and value. Each book is crafted with care and precision, undergoing rigorous development that involves the unique expertise of members from the professional technical community.

Readers' feedback is a natural continuation of this process. If you have any comments regarding how we could improve the quality of this book or otherwise alter it to better suit your needs, you can contact us through e-mail at feedback@ciscopress.com. Please make sure to include the book title and ISBN in your message.

We greatly appreciate your assistance.

Trademark Acknowledgments

All terms mentioned in this book that are known to be trademarks or service marks have been appropriately capitalized. Cisco Press or Cisco Systems, Inc., cannot attest to the accuracy of this information. Use of a term in this book should not be regarded as affecting the validity of any trademark or service mark.

Corporate and Government Sales

Cisco Press offers excellent discounts on this book when ordered in quantity for bulk purchases or special sales. For more information, please contact:

U.S. Corporate and Government Sales 1-800-382-3419 corpsales@pearsontechgroup.com

For sales outside of the U.S. please contact:

International Sales 1-317-581-3793 international@pearsontechgroup.com

Publisher: John Wait

Editor-In-Chief: John Kane

Executive Editor: Brett Bartow

Managing Editor: Patrick Kanouse

Development Editor: Christopher Cleveland

Project Editor: Marc Fowler

Copy Editor: Krista Hansing

Team Coordinator: Tammi Barnett

Book Designer: Louisa Adair

Cover Designer: Louisa Adair

Compositor: Mark Shirar

Indexer: Tim Wright

Cisco Representative: Anthony Wolfenden

Cisco Press Program Manager:Sonia Torres Chavez

Cisco Marketing Communications Manager:Scott Miller

Cisco Marketing Program Manager:Edie Quiroz

Technical Editors:Elan Beer, Lynn Maynes, Martin Walshaw

CISCO SYSTEMS

Corporate Headquarters	European Headquarters	Americas Headquarters	Asia Pacific Headquarters
Cisco Systems, Inc.	Cisco Systems International BV	Cisco Systems, Inc.	Cisco Systems, Inc.
170 West Tasman Drive	Haarlerbergpark	170 West Tasman Drive	Capital Tower
San Jose, CA 95134-1706	Haarlerbergweg 13-19	San Jose, CA 95134-1706	168 Robinson Road
USA	1101 CH Amsterdam	USA	#22-01 to #29-01
www.cisco.com	The Netherlands	www.cisco.com	Singapore 068912
Tel: 408 526-4000	www-europe.cisco.com	Tel: 408 526-7660	www.cisco.com
800 553-NETS (6387)	Tel: 31 0 20 357 1000	Fax: 408 527-0883	Tel: +65 6317 7777
Fax: 408 526-4100	Fax: 31 0 20 357 1100		Fax: +65 6317 7799

Cisco Systems has more than 200 offices in the following countries and regions. Addresses, phone numbers, and fax numbers are listed on the
Cisco.com Web site at www.cisco.com/go/offices.

Argentina • Australia • Austria • Belgium • Brazil • Bulgaria • Canada • Chile • China PRC • Colombia • Costa Rica • Croatia • Czech Republic
Denmark • Dubai, UAE • Finland • France • Germany • Greece • Hong Kong SAR • Hungary • India • Indonesia • Ireland • Israel • Italy
Japan • Korea • Luxembourg • Malaysia • Mexico • The Netherlands • New Zealand • Norway • Peru • Philippines • Poland • Portugal
Puerto Rico • Romania • Russia • Saudi Arabia • Scotland • Singapore • Slovakia • Slovenia • South Africa • Spain • Sweden
Switzerland • Taiwan • Thailand • Turkey • Ukraine • United Kingdom • United States • Venezuela • Vietnam • Zimbabwe

About the Author

Wendell Odom, CCIE No. 1624, is a senior instructor with Skyline Computer (www.skylinecomputer.com), where he currently teaches courses on QoS, CCNA, and CCIE lab preparation. Wendell has worked in the networking arena for 20 years, with jobs in pre- and post-sales technical consulting, teaching, and course development. He has authored portions of more than 12 courses, including topics such as IP routing, MPLS, Cisco WAN switches, SNA protocols, and LAN troubleshooting. He is author of three previous editions of the *CCNA Exam Certification Guide* as well as the *Cisco Press DQOS Exam Certification Guide*.

About the Technical Reviewers

Elan Beer, CCIE No. 1837, CCSI No. 94008, is a Senior Consultant and Certified Cisco Instructor. Elan's internetworking expertise is recognized internationally through his global consulting and training engagements. As one of the industry's top internetworking consultants and Cisco instructors, Elan has utilized his expertise to design, implement, and deploy multiprotocol networks for a wide range of international clientele. As a senior instructor and course developer, Elan has designed and presented public and implementation-specific technical courses spanning many of today's top technologies. Elan can be reached via e-mail at elan@CiscoConsultants.com.

Lynn Maynes, CCIE No. 6569, is a senior network engineer with Sprint Managed Network Services specializing in network design, architecture and security for large-scale networks worldwide. He has more than 9 years of experience in computer networking and is a co-author of the Cisco Press book *CCNA Practical Studies*. He holds a bachelor's degree in international business from Westminster College.

Martin Walshaw, CCIE No. 5629, CISSP, CCNP, CCDP, is a systems engineer working for Cisco Systems in the Enterprise Line of Business in South Africa. His areas of specialty include convergence, security, and content delivery networking, which keeps him busy both night and day. During the last 15 years or so, Martin has dabbled in many aspects of the IT industry, ranging from programming in RPG III and COBOL to PC sales. When Martin is not working, he likes to spend all of his available time with his patient wife, Val, and his sons, Joshua and Callum. Without their patience, understanding, and support, projects such as this would not be possible.

Dedications

Chris Cleveland is the best Development Editor I could imagine working with. So, instead of just the usual "Thanks Chris for doing an excellent job," I'd like to dedicate this book to Chris. Chris, it's an absolute pleasure to work with the best in the business —thanks for your fantastic help and support!

Acknowledgments

The technical editing team for this book and its companion volume was fantastic! Not only did they find where I had simply written the wrong technical facts, but they also helped me find new, more interesting, and clearer ways to convey certain facts about networking. Lynn was particular helpful with comments that helped keep small sections in line with the overall theme of the chapter—a skill I'm sure he developed as a result of having written books himself. Martin helped a lot with technical detail and perspectives from what customers see every day today. And Elan excelled in noticing both the small nit-picky errors and the significant technical problems. (And that's not an insult—every technical author loves help in finding the small problems!) Together, these three gentlemen formed a great team, with complementary skills. Thanks so much, guys!

The production team, headed by Patrick Kanouse, did its usual excellent job. Like the behind-the-scenes people in many businesses, their specific efforts may not be obvious to the public, but it's no less appreciated by me. In particular, Marc Fowler, the project editor, did an incredible job working through these two books on a very tight schedule, with his usual excellent work. You folks make me look good on paper all the time—if only you could be in charge of my wardrobe, too—I'd look good all the time!

Brett Bartow, executive editor, did his usual New-York-Yankees-like job in helping steer these two projects to completion. In between talking about sports, Brett worked through the many changes in direction with this book and helped guide us to the right product. And, yes, so the whole world knows, he did pick an Atlanta Braves player, John Smoltz, for his fantasy league baseball team—again proving he's a really smart guy.

Chris "develops" books for Cisco Press. What does that mean? Well, it means that he takes the Word documents and figures from geeky authors, and makes their writing become understandable. He takes the input from technical editors, and combines all the comments into a single word document, making the author's life easier. He constantly finds ways to rephrase, reword, and improve the manuscript. He manages all the work with the authors. And he always works to optimize the author's time, taking away some of the unpleasant part of the work, so that the author can worry about the technical details. Chris has worked with me on 6 projects now, and every time, he has done an excellent job. His work ethic goes far beyond the call of duty, and his performance is consistently excellent. To quote a few other authors as well: "Chris has taken all of the difficulty (of writing) out of the picture", "Chris has absolutely spoiled me and completely amazes me", and "He even helped me with my daughter's homework". Whatever, however, to make the book better, with an eye towards the least pain for the author, Chris is on top of it. Thanks, Chris, for all you do!

Contents at a Glance

Contents

Icons Used in This Book

Router

Bridge

Hub

DSU/CSU

Catalyst
Switch

Multilayer
Switch

ATM
Switch

ISDN/Frame Relay
Switch

Communication
Server

Gateway

Access
Server

PC

PC with
Software

Sun
Workstation

Macintosh

Terminal

File
Server

Web
Server

Cisco Works
Workstation

Modem

Printer

Laptop

IBM
Mainframe

Front End
Processor

Cluster
Controller

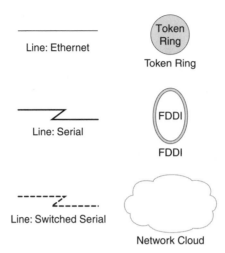

Command Syntax Conventions

The conventions used to present command syntax in this book are the same conventions used in the Cisco IOS Command Reference. The Command Reference describes these conventions as follows:

- Vertical bars (|) separate alternative, mutually exclusive elements.

- Square brackets [ ] indicate optional elements.

- Braces { } indicate a required choice.

- Braces within brackets [{ }] indicate a required choice within an optional element.

- **Boldface** indicates commands and keywords that are entered literally as shown. In actual configuration examples and output (not general command syntax), boldface indicates commands that are manually input by the user (such as a **show** command).

- *Italics* indicate arguments for which you supply actual values.

Introduction: Overview of Certification and How to Succeed

Congratulations! If you're reading far enough to look at the introduction to this book, then you've probably already decided to go for your Cisco Certified Network Associate (CCNA) certification. Cisco System's entry-level certification, CCNA, has a reputation as one of the most valuable entry-level certifications in the computing industry. Although getting your CCNA does not guarantee you a first networking job or a new job, it will certainly help convince others that you know what you are talking about.

Cisco's CCNA certification proves that you have a firm foundation in the most important components of the Cisco product line—namely, routers and switches. It also proves that you have a broad knowledge of protocols and networking technologies. CCNA is not an easy certification to get, but it is well worth the effort. In a booming economy, CCNA is the first step toward getting a higher salary than your noncertified peers. In a difficult economy, it could be the difference between whether a prospective employer even looks at your résumé. Regardless of your local economy, CCNA does improve how people in the marketplace view your skill level.

People ask me for career advice from time to time, and my answer is typically the same: If you want to be in the networking industry at all, you need to know Cisco. Cisco has some ridiculous market shares in the router and switch marketplace, with more than 80% market share in some markets. In many geographies and many markets, networking equals Cisco. If you want to be taken seriously as a network engineer, you need a CCNA certification. Frankly, you probably also need to be working toward a more advanced Cisco certification as well—but first things first! CCNA requires some time and effort.

Cisco's Motivation: Certifying Partners

Cisco's primary motivation for creating CCNA and most of the other Cisco certifications is to help determine the skill levels of its partners. Cisco fulfills only a small portion of its orders through direct sale from Cisco; most often, a Cisco reseller is involved. (Cisco calls resellers channel partners.) Also, Cisco encourages partners to perform most consulting and implementation services relating to Cisco products. While working heavily with partners, Cisco needed to know which partners truly had the right skills. So, Cisco created many certifications, including CCNA.

Cisco measures the technical readiness of channel partners (resellers) and professional services partners in part by requiring specific numbers of Cisco certified employees. For instance, Premier, Silver, and Gold Channel Partners are required to have either two or four CCNAs on staff, along with Cisco professional- and expert-level certified individuals.

So, what does that mean to you? Well, if you already have some Cisco certifications on your résumé, you are more valuable to Cisco partners. In today's competitive environment, every edge counts—so having the right Cisco certifications can help you get that next job. In particular, the CCNA certification is a prerequisite for almost every Cisco certification, so it is the right place to start.

The CCNA Certification Exams: What, There's More than One Exam?

For the first time since Cisco announced CCNA in 1998, the CCNA certification has an option for multiple exams. Before Cisco announced these latest changes around summer of 2003, to get your CCNA certification, you just passed a single "CCNA exam." With this latest generation of the CCNA, you can either take a single exam to get your CCNA, or you can take two exams, with each of these exams covering a subset of the CCNA exam topics. Table I-1 lists the exams.

Table I-1   *CCNA Exam Names and Numbers*

Exam Name	Exam Number	Comment
Introduction to Cisco Networking Technologies (INTRO) exam	640-821	A subset of the CCNA topics; should be taken before the ICND exam
Interconnecting Cisco Network Devices (ICND) Exam	640-811	A subset of the CCNA topics; should be taken after the INTRO exam
CCNA Exam	640-801	Can be taken instead of INTRO and ICND exams; covers the same content as the other two exams combined

So, you either take the CCNA exam or you take both the INTRO and the ICND exam to pass CCNA.

Like most Cisco certification exams, the names of the INTRO and the ICND exams come from two Cisco Authorized courses. Cisco's INTRO course covers a broad range of topics, from Ethernet cabling to virtual private networks (VPNs). The Interconnecting Cisco Network Devices (ICND) course dives more deeply into core Cisco technology and protocols, in particular, switching and routing. Whereas the INTRO course covers a broader range of topics to a small amount of depth, the ICND course covers fewer topics but to more depth. Like their namesakes, the INTRO and ICND exams cover similar depth and breadth.

The CCNA exam simply covers everything on both the INTRO and ICND exams. So, if you want to save some cash and you are confident that you are ready to answer questions across the whole range of topics for CCNA, you can take just the CCNA exam itself. Alternately, you can focus on the INTRO exam first, master those topics, pass the exam, and then move on to the ICND exam.

Format of the CCNA Exams

The INTRO, ICND, and CCNA exams all follow the same general format. When you get to the testing center and check in, the proctor will give you some general instructions and then take you into a quiet room with a PC. When you're at the PC, you have a few things to do before the timer starts on your exam—for instance, you can take a sample quiz, just to get accustomed to the PC and to the testing engine. Anyone who has user-level skills in getting around a PC will have no problems with the testing envinronment.

When you start the exam, you will be asked a series of questions. You answer the question and then move on to the next question. *The exam engine does not let you go back and change your answer.* Yes, that's true—when you move on to the next question, that's it for the earlier question.

The exam questions can be in the following format:

- Multiple choice
- Fill-in-the-blank
- Drag-and-drop
- Simulated lab

The multiple choice format simply requires that you point and click on a circle beside the correct answer(s). If more than one answer is required, the questions traditionally have told you how many answers to choose. Fill-in-the-blank questions require that you type in the answer, so you must get the answer exactly correct.

Drag-and-drop questions require you to left-click and hold, move a button or icon to another area, and release the clicker to place the object somewhere else—typically into a list. So, for some questions, to get the question correct, you might need to put a list of five things into the proper order.

Finally, the type of question that gives most people a scare before the exam is the simulated lab question. The exam engine actually gives you an interface into a network with several routers, and you must log in and troubleshoot a scenario. To solve the problem, you need to be able to navigate through the user interface, know several commands, and possibly configure something that has been misconfigured. You should also save your configurations, unless the question tells you not to save it, just in case.

The best way to prepare for simulated lab questions is to practice with real gear. You can actually find sites where CCNA lab access is free over the Internet—I did a search from www.google.com tonight, searching for "free CCNA labs," and the first three hits were (seemingly) legitimate offers for free lab access for CCNA study. You can also use a simulator product, such as Cisco Press's CCNA Router and Switch eSIM. A special version of Boson's Netsim product, compiled specifically for this book, is also included on the CD that comes with this book.

What's on the CCNA Exam(s)?

Ever since I was in grade school, whenever the teacher announced that we were having a test soon, someone would always ask, "What's on the test?" Even in college, people would try to get more infomrmation about what would be on the exams. At heart, the goal is to know what to study hard, what to study a little, and what to not study at all.

Cisco does want you to know what topics to study and wants you to be well prepared for your exams. However, Cisco does not want to be so specific that you could just memorize a certain set of facts and pass the exams. In short, Cisco wants you to pass the exams because you know your stuff, not because you memorized a set of questions that someone posted (possibly illegally) on an Internet site.

So, what can be said about the content of the exams? First, Cisco posts exam topics for each exam. This official posting is the basis for what Cisco intends to put on the exams, so you should pay particularly close attention to this list. Also, the breadth and depth of topics on the exams tend to match the Cisco Authorized courses with which they are associated, so it is useful to know the outlines for those courses. Finally, Cisco designs the Cisco Networking Academy Program (CNAP) course materials with CCNA in mind. Looking at all these sources can help give you insight into CCNA.

INTRO Exam Topics

Carefully consider the exam topics posted by Cisco on its web site as you study, particularly for clues as to how deeply you should know each topic. The exam topics use action words that follow a quasi-standard called Bloom's Taxonomy of the Cognitive Domain. Bloom's taxonomy defines a standard for word usage for when educators create objectives for courses. Objectives written according to Bloom's taxonomy define what the learner (student) should be able to accomplish after taking the class. So, when you look at an exam topic, look for the action word. If you want to see a description of Bloom's taxonomy, search the Internet, and you will find a lot of matches. My favorite quick list of terms is at http://chiron.valdosta.edu/whuitt/col/cogsys/bloom.html.

The action word in the exam topic gives you a good hint about the level of knowledge and skill you will need to have before taking the exam. For instance, a course objective that uses the word *list* as the action word then means that you should be able to list the features, but an action word such as *configure* means that you should know all the related configuration commands and how to use them. *Troubleshoot* might mean that you need to know what all the **show** and **debug** commands do for a particular topic.

So, what does Bloom's taxonomy mean in terms of how you study for the exam? It means that you should focus on the action words in the exam topics and make sure that you can do those things for the stated topics. For instance, if an exam topic says something like "Configure RIP," then do not study just RIP concepts, but also study the configuration details because the exam topic specifically tells you that you need to know how to perform configuration.

In addition, Cisco adds a disclaimer that the posted exam topics for all of its certification exams are *guidelines*. Cisco makes the effort to keep the exam questions within the confines of the stated exam objectives, but doing this for every question and every exam is difficult. Thus, you could see questions that fall outside both the scope and the depth implied by the exam topics. However, if you follow the Cisco exam topic "guidelines," you should have a good understanding of the breadth and depth of topics on the exam.

Table I-2 lists the exam topics for the INTRO exam. You can find the ICND exam topics in the Introduction to the *CCNA ICND Exam Certification Guide* and on www.cisco.com. Note that although Cisco's posted exam topics are not numbered, we do number them in the *Cisco Press Exam Certification Guide* series for easier reference. Also note that Cisco has historically changed exam topics without changing the exam number, so do not be alarmed if small changes in the exam topics occur over time. When in doubt, go to www.cisco.com, click Learning and Events, and select Career Certifications and Paths.

Table I-2 *INTRO Exam Topics*

Exam Topic Reference Number	Exam Topic
	Design & Support
1	Use a subset of Cisco IOS commands to analyse and report network problems
2	Use embedded layer 3 through layer 7 protocols to establish, test, suspend or disconnect connectivity to remote devices from the router console
3	Determine IP addresses
	Implementation & Operation
4	Establish communication between a terminal device and the router IOS, and use IOS for system analysis
5	Manipulate system image and device configuration files

continues

Table I-2 *INTRO Exam Topics (Continued)*

Exam Topic Reference Number	Exam Topic
6	Perform an initial configuration on a router and save the resultant configuration file
7	Use commands incorporated within IOS to analyse and report network problems
8	Assign IP addresses
9	Describe and install the hardware and software required to be able to communicate via a network
10	Use embedded data link layer functionality to perform network neighbor discovery and analysis from the router console
11	Use embedded layer 3 through layer 7 protocols to establish, test, suspend or disconnect connectivity to remote devices from the router console
	Technology
12	Demonstrate the mathematical skills required to work seamlessly with integer decimal, binary and hexadecimal numbers and simple binary logic (AND)
13	Define and describe the structure and technologies of computer networks
14	Describe the hardware and software required to be able to communicate via a network
15	Describe the physical, electrical and mechanical properties and standards associated with optical, wireless and copper media used in networks
16	Describe the topologies and physical issues associated with cabling common LANs
17	Identify the key characteristics of common wide area networking (WAN) configurations and technologies , and differentiate between these and common LAN technologies.
18	Describe the purpose and fundamental operation of the internetwork operating system (IOS)
19	Describe the role of a router in a WAN.
20	Identify the major internal and external components of a router, and describe the associated functionality
21	Identify and describe the stages of the router boot-up sequence
22	Describe how the configuration register and boot system commands modify the router boot-up sequence

Table I-2 *INTRO Exam Topics (Continued)*

Exam Topic Reference Number	Exam Topic
23	Describe the concepts associated with routing, and the different methods and protocols used to achieve it
24	Describe how an IP address is associated with a device interface, and the association between physical and logical addressing
25	Employ IP addressing techniques
26	Compare and contrast collision and broadcast domains, and describe the process of network segmentation
27	Describe the principles and practice of switching in an Ethernet network
28	Explain how collisions are detected and handled in an Ethernet system
29	Explain the fundamental concepts associated with the Ethernet media access technique
30	Describe how the protocols associated with TCP/IP allow host communication to occur
31	Describe the operation of the Internet Control Message Protocol (ICMP) and identify the reasons, types and format of associated error and control messages
32	Describe the principles and practice of packet switching utilizing the Internet Protocol (IP)
33	Describe, compare and contrast network communications using **two** examples of layered models (OSI and IETF)
34	Describe the fundamental concepts associated with transport layer protocols, and compare the connectionless approach to transport with the connection oriented one
35	List the major TCP/IP application protocols, and briefly define their features and operation
36	Describe the operation of the major transport layer protocols TCP and UDP and the interaction and carriage of application layer data
37	Perform an initial configuration on a switch and save the resultant configuration file

Cross-Reference Between Exam Topics and Book Parts

Table I-3 provides a cross-reference between the exam topics and the book parts in which they are covered.

Table I-3 *INTRO Exam Topics Cross-Reference to Parts in the CCNA INTRO Exam Certification Guide*

Exam Topic	Part		Exam Topic	Part
1	2, 3, 4		19	1, 5
2	2		20	2
3	4		21	2
4	2		22	2
5	2		23	4
6	2		24	4
7	2, 3, 4		25	4
8	2, 4		26	1, 3
9	2, 3, 4, 5		27	3
10	2, 4		28	1
11	4		29	1
12	4		30	1
13	1 – 5		31	4
14	1 - 5		32	1, 4
15	1		33	1
16	1, 3		34	1
17	1, 5		35	1
18	2		36	1
			37	2

CCNA Exam Topics

Interestingly, the CCNA (640-801) exam topics posted by Cisco are not simply the combination of the INTRO exam topics and the ICND exam topics. If you look closely, the CCNA exam topics match more closely to the ICND exam topics than they do to the INTRO exam topics.

So, for those of you planning to take the single CCNA exam, what does that mean? Well, for practical purposes, the CCNA exam covers all the topics covered on both the INTRO and ICND exams. However, the length of the CCNA exam does not allow Cisco to ask you about every possible fact. So, you should expect the CCNA exam to include questions that cover more advanced topics, many of which require that you know the more basic facts. For instance, rather than ask a question about how to do binary math, which is specifically mentioned for the INTRO exam topics, you might have to derive subnet numbers – which requires you to use binary math. Another example: instead of describing LAN cabling, you might have a question about troubleshooting a LAN topology, and need to decide if an incorrect type of cable was used. So, while the exam topics do not exactly match up, but you essentially need to know all the same concepts on both the INTRO and ICND exams in order to succeed on the CCNA exam.

Table I-4 lists the CCNA exam topics at time of publication. As always, look to www.cisco.com for the latest posted information about the CCNA, INTRO, and ICND exams!

Table I-4 *CCNA Exam Topics*

Exam Topic Reference Number	Exam Topic
	Planning and Design
1	Design a simple LAN using Cisco Technology
2	Design an IP addressing scheme to meet design requirements
3	Select an appropriate routing protocol based on user requirements
4	Design a simple internetwork using Cisco technology
5	Develop an access list to meet user specifications
6	Choose WAN services to meet customer requirements
	Implementation and Operation
7	Configure routing protocols given user requirements
8	Configure IP addresses, subnet masks, and gateway addresses on routers and hosts
9	Configure a router for additional administrative functionality
10	Configure a switch with VLANS and inter-switch communication
11	Implement a LAN
12	Customize a switch configuration to meet specified network requirements
13	Manage system image and device configuration files
14	Perform an initial configuration on a router
15	Perform an initial configuration on a switch
16	Implement access lists
17	Implement simple WAN protocols

continues

Table I-4 *CCNA Exam Topics (Continued)*

Exam Topic Reference Number	Exam Topic
	Troubleshooting
18	Utilize the OSI model as a guide for systematic network troubleshooting
19	Perform LAN and VLAN troubleshooting
20	Troubleshoot routing protocols
21	Troubleshoot IP addressing and host configuration
22	Troubleshoot a device as part of a working network
23	Troubleshoot an access list
24	Perform simple WAN troubleshooting
	Technology
25	Describe network communications using layered models
26	Describe the Spanning Tree process
27	Compare and contrast key characteristics of LAN environments
28	Evaluate the characteristics of routing protocols
29	Evaluate TCP/IP communication process and its associated protocols
30	Describe the components of network devices
31	Evaluate rules for packet control
32	Evaluate key characteristics of WANs

INTRO and ICND Course Outlines

Another way to get some direction about the topics on the exams is to look at the course outlines for the related courses. Cisco offers the Introduction to Cisco Networking (INTRO) and Interconnection Cisco Network Devices (ICND) courses through its Certified Learning Solutions Providers (CLSP); CLSPs, in turn, work with other learning partners as well.

The INTRO course covers a much broader set of topics than does ICND, but for the topics it covers, ICND covers the topics to much greater detail. In particular, ICND includes a lot more information about commands used on routers and switches to configure and troubleshoot the various features.

These outlines can be found at www.cisco.com.

About the *CCNA INTRO Exam Certification Guide* and *CCNA ICND Exam Certification Guide*

As mentioned earlier in this introduction, you can take both the INTRO and ICND exams to acquire CCNA certification, or you can take a single CCNA exam. Because of the significantly expanded topics as compared with the previous CCNA exam, there was simply too much material for a single book. So, we simply created two books—one for the INTRO exam and one for the ICND exam.

The contents of the two books, however, were actually designed for both the single-exam and dual-exam audience. For those of you preparing just for the INTRO exam, you can read just this book. Similarly, if you have passed the INTRO exam and you want to study for the ICND exam, you can use just the other book. However, if you are studying for the CCNA exam, you can use both books, and alternate between reading different parts of each book to optomize your effort in preparing for the exam. This introduction includes a reading plan for anyone taking the CCNA exam, directing you on the order in which to read the chapters in the two books. Essentially, you would read the first three parts of this book and then start alternating, reading an entire part of the other book, coming back here for a part, going back to the other book, and so on, for most of the parts of both books. The parts are named so that it is obvious which sections to read as you move between the books. By doing so, you complete all the coverage in a particular technical area before moving on to another.

Objectives and Methods

The most important and somewhat obvious objective of this book is to help you pass the INTRO exam or the CCNA exam. In fact, if the primary objective of this book were different, the book's title would be misleading! However, the methods used in this book to help you pass the exams are also designed to make you much more knowledgeable about how to do your job.

This book uses several key methodologies to help you discover the exam topics on which you need more review, to help you fully understand and remember those details, and to help you prove to yourself that you have retained your knowledge of those topics. So, this book does not try to help you pass the exams only by memorization, but by truly learning and understanding the topics. The CCNA certification is the foundation for many of the Cisco professional certifications, and it would be a disservice to you if this book did not help you truly learn the material. Therefore, this book helps you pass the CCNA exam by using the following methods:

- Helping you discover which exam topics you have not mastered
- Providing explanations and information to fill in your knowledge gaps

- Supplying exercises that enhance your ability to recall and deduce the answers to test questions
- Providing practice exercises on the topics and the testing process via test questions on the CD

Book Features

To help you customize your study time using these books, the core chapters have several features that help you make the best use of your time:

- **"Do I Know This Already?" Quizzes**—Each chapter begins with a quiz that helps you determine the amount of time you need to spend studying that chapter. If you follow the directions at the beginning of the chapter, the "Do I Know This Already?" quiz directs you to study all or particular parts of the chapter.

- **Foundation Topics**—These are the core sections of each chapter. They explain the protocols, concepts, and configuration for the topics in that chapter. If you need to learn about the topics in a chapter, read the "Foundation Topics" section.

- **Foundation Summary**—Near the end of each chapter, a summary collects the most important information from the chapter summarized in lists, tables, and figures. The "Foundation Summary" section is designed to help you review the key concepts in the chapter if you scored well on the "Do I Know This Already?" quiz. This section is an excellent tool for last-minute review.

- **Q&A**—Each chapter ends with a Q&A section that forces you to exercise your recall of the facts and processes described inside that chapter. The questions are generally harder than the actual exam, partly because the questions are in short-answer format instead of multiple choice. These questions are a great way to increase the accuracy of your recollection of the facts.

- **CD-based practice exam**—The companion CD contains a large number of questions not included in the book, as well as all the questions from the "Do I Know This Already" quizzes. You can answer these questions by using the simulated exam feature or the topical review feature. This is the best tool for helping you prepare for the test-taking process.

- **Hands-on practice using Boson Netsim™ LE**—The CD also includes the Boson Netsim for CCNA INTRO Learning Edition network simulator, supporting the ability to perform many of the commands covered in the book. In particular, you can perform many of the practice scenarios and hands-on lab exercises also included on the CD, as well as several from the book. Appendix C details how to access the simulator, and what lab exercises can be performed. (The version of the Boson NetSim software included with this book is a limited functionality version. In order to access all functions and features of the software, you must purchase a full license for the software from Boson Software, Inc.)

- **CD-based practice scenarios**—The companion CD contains a CD-only appendix B (which is a totally different appendix as compared with the printed appendix B in the book) which has several practice scenarios. These scenarios include several problem statements, with solutions, in order to help you pull both concepts and configuration commands together. These scenarios are useful for building your hands-on skills, even if you do not have lab gear. You can also perform some of these scenarios using the Boson NetSim LE network simulator, or using your own lab gear.

- **CD-based lab exercises**—The companion CD contains a CD-only appendix C (which is a totally different appendix as compared with the printed appendix C in the book) which has several lab exercises. These lab exercises guide you through the steps used to perform the most popular configuration tasks. Like the scenarios, CD-only appendix C includes the answers to the labs, making it useful to just read the materials for extra reinforcement of the commands. You can also perform these labs using the Boson NetSim LE network simulator, or using your own lab gear.

- **CD-based subnetting practice**—The companion CD contains an appendix that has 25 additional subnetting practice problems. Each problem shows the solutions for the subnet number, broadcast address, and valid IP addresses in each subnet. With this extra practice, you can be ready to answer subnetting questions quickly and accurately on the INTRO, ICND, and CCNA exams.

How This Book Is Organized

This book contains 15 core chapters—Chapters 1 through 15, with Chapter 16 including some summary materials and suggestions for how to approach the actual exams. Each core chapter covers a subset of the topics on the INTRO exam. The core chapters are organized into sections. The core chapters cover the following topics:

Part I: Networking Fundamentals

- **Chapter 1, "Introduction to Computer Networking Concepts"**—This chapter provides a very basic introduction for those who are brand new to networking.

- **Chapter 2, "The TCP/IP and OSI Networking Models"**—Chapter 2 introduces the terminology surrounding two different networking architectures, namely Transmission Control Protocol/Internet Protocol (TCP/IP) and Open Systems Interconnection (OSI). This chapters also compares the new protocol architectural models.

- **Chapter 3, "Data Link Layer Fundamentals: Ethernet LANs"**—TCP/IP and OSI both have several protocols and functions performed at the data link layer. This chapter covers the concepts and terms used for the most popular option for the data link layer for local-area networks (LANs), namely Ethernet.

- **Chapter 4, "Fundamentals of WANs"**—TCP/IP and OSI both have several protocols and functions performed at the data link layer. This chapter covers the concepts and terms used for the most popular options for the data link layer for wide-area networks (WANs), including High-Level Data Link Control (HDLC), the Point-to-Point Protocol (PPP), and Frame Relay.

- **Chapter 5, "Fundamentals of IP"**—The Internet Protocol (IP) is the main network layer protocol for TCP/IP. This chapter introduces the basics of IP, including IP addressing.

- **Chapter 6, "Fundamentals of TCP and UDP"**—The Transmission Control Protocol (TCP) and User Datagram Protocol (UDP) are the main transport layer protocols for TCP/IP. This chapter introduces the basics of TCP and UDP.

Part II: Operating Cisco Devices

- **Chapter 7, "Operating Cisco Routers"**—The basic navigation around the user interface of a Cisco router is covered here. Also, some of the more common administrative tasks—upgrading the router's software, deleting configurations, adding configurations, and so on—are covered here.

- **Chapter 8, "Operating Cisco LAN Switches"**—Chapter 8 is like Chapter 7, except that it covers details for the Cisco 2950 series of LAN switches. Given the many similarities with routers, the chapter points out the similarities briefly and then explains the differences more fully.

Part III: LAN Switching

- **Chapter 9, "Cisco LAN Switching Basics"**—This chapter focuses on the internal operation of a LAN switch, as well as configuration of LAN switches.

- **Chapter 10, "Virtual LANs and Trunking"**—Most campus networks of any size use virtual LANs, and if more than one VLAN is used, those same networks also use VLAN trunking. This chapter explains the concepts.

- **Chapter 11, "LAN Cabling, Standards, and Topologies"**—The final LAN-specific chapter in this book details LAN standards, including the cabling media, for Ethernet. Many of the details in this chapter are not very glamorous, but they are important.

Part IV: TCP/IP

- **Chapter 12, "IP Addressing and Subnetting"**—This chapter gets into the depths of IP addressing and subnetting. The Boolean math operations required for analyzing IP addresses are explained, and several examples are used to detail how IP subnets are created, what IP addresses are in the same subnet, and the math required to answer exam questions about subnetting.

- Chapter 13, "Basic Router Configuration and Operation"—The most common commands for configuring IP and examining the status of IP routing in a router are outlined in this chapter.

- Chapter 14, "Introduction to Dynamic Routing Protocols"—Routing Protocols dynamically learn and advertise the routes in a network. This chapter introduces the TCP/IP routing protocols.

Part V: Wide-Area Networking

- Chapter 15, "Remote Access Technologies"—Many options exist today for accessing the Internet. This chapter introduces the basics of four of these—analog dial using modems, Integrated Services Digital Network (ISDN), Digital Subscriber Line (DSL), and cable modems.

Part VI: Final Preparation

- Chapter 16, "Final Preparation"—This chapter covers a variety of suggestions for taking the exam, and it provides a scenario that helps you review some of the material in the book.

Part VII: Appendixes

- Appendix A, "Answers to the "Do I Know This Already" Quizes and Q&A Sections"—Includes the answers to all the questions from chapters 1 through 15.

- Appendix B, "Binary to Decimal Conversion Table"—Lists decimal values 0 through 255, along with the binary equivalents.

- Appendix C, "Using the Simulation Software for the Hands-on Exercises"—Provides instructions for accessing the NetSim network simulator that comes with the book. This appendix also lists the labs and scenarios from this book that can be performed using NetSim.

When you are finished with the core chapters, you have several options on how to finish your exam preparation. Additional exercises in Chapter 16 provide a method of final preparation with more questions and exercises. You can review the questions at the end of each chapter, and you can use the CD's testing software to practice the exam.

How to Use This Book to Prepare for the INTRO Exam

To study for the INTRO exam, you can simply use this book and start reading. The study plan is simple. However, if you have some experience or knowledge of Cisco products and networking protocols already, you might be able to save a little study time while taking only small risks. Figure I-1 shows the progression you should take through the books as you prepare for the INTRO exam.

Figure I-1 *How to Approach Each Chapter of This Book*

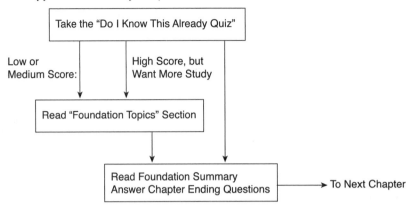

In each chapter, an assessment quiz, called the "Do I Know This Already? Quiz," helps you decide whether you already know a lot of the material in the chapter. The DIKTA quiz does not quiz you on every topic in the chapter, but it does focus on a representative sample from each chapter. If you do well on the DIKTA quiz, it is an indication of how much you already know about the topic.

Based on your DIKTA score and your confidence level, you can choose to either skip the "Foundation Topics" section of the chapter or not. Regardless, everyone should at least read the "Foundation Summary" section and answer all the questions at the end of the chapter. If you get a good score on DIKTA and then miss a lot of the open-ended questions at the end of the chapter, you might still consider reading the "Foundations Topics" section of that chapter.

When you have completed Chapters 1–15, you can move on to your final preparation. Several activities can help you make your final preparations:

- Read Chapter 16. It contains some exam-taking tips and some exercises that help to reinforce materials from all parts of the book.

- Answer the chapter-ending questions again. These questions are generally harder than those on the CD because they are all open-ended questions.

- Review the "Foundation Summary" sections of each chapter.

- Prepare for hands-on questions on the exam. You should definitely perform all simluated questions using the exam engine on the CD. Also, you may want to either read or perform the scenario in chapter 16, the scenarios in CD-only appendix B, and the labs in CD-only appendix C. Appendix C in this book (not the CD-only appendix C), titled, "Using the Simulation Software for Hands-on Exercises", both summarizes all the hands-on exercises included with the book that can be performed on the simulator.

- Practice subnetting. If needed, use the subnetting appendix on the CD. You get 25 more full subnetting questions with answers worked out, most using difficult subnet masks.

- Using the exam engine on the CD, select Questions from the Book instead of Questions Only on the CD. By doing so, you will just be quizzed from the CD, but with questions that appeared in the DIKTA quizzes in the chapters. Use practice mode, and drill on these questions until it is automatic.

- Finally, using the CD, deselect Book Questions, and select New Questions. Then use exam mode and take a couple of simulated exams. This should be the final step in preparation.

For any questions that you miss, make sure you read the relavent sections of the book for a refresher.

By this point, you should be well prepared for the INTRO exam.

How to Use These Books to Prepare for the CCNA Exam

If you are using this book to study for the INTRO exam, just follow the plan outlined in the last few pages. However, to use this book to study for the CCNA exam, you really should use both this book and the *CCNA ICND Exam Certification Guide*. (By the way, if you've not bought this book yet and you want both, you can generally get the pair cheaper by buying a set, called the *CCNA Certification Library*.) These two books were designed to be used together to help those who want to get their CCNA certification by taking a single exam.

Notice that the names of four of the six parts in the *CCNA INTRO Exam Certification Guide* match the names of all five parts in the *CCNA ICND Exam Certification Guide*. Essentially, when you complete a section of the first book, if there is a like-named section of the second book, you move over and read that section. After finishing that section in the *CCNA ICND Exam Certification Guide*, you move back to the *CCNA INTRO Exam Certification Guide*. Figure I-2 outlines the process.

Figure I-2 *Reading Plan When Studying for CCNA Exam*

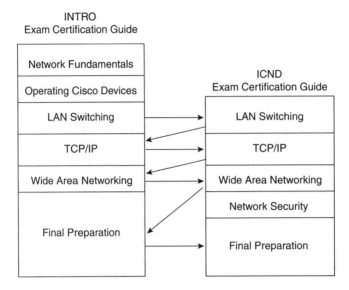

Moving back and forth between books will help you to focus on one general topic at a time. Each time you transition to the ICND book, you will read about a lot of additional material about the general topic, plus a few things that seem like review. (Those review items are included for the readers who are using the ICND book for their ICND exam preparation.) As a result, you will complete the coverage of each major topic before moving on to the next.

There is one point in this reading plan for the CCNA exam for which you should consider a couple of options. Cisco includes one major topic, IP addressing and subnetting, on both the INTRO and ICND exams. So, that topic is covered in both books for those readers who are studying for the INTRO and ICND exams. Chapter 12 in the *CCNA INTRO Exam Certification Guide* covers subnetting, and Chapter 4 in the *CCNA ICND Exam Certification Guide* does so as well. If you are studying for the CCNA exam, you should keep in mind that the "Foundation Topics" of the ICND book's Chapter 4—the core part of the chapter—is a subset of the INTRO book's Chapter 12. So, there's no need to read it twice!

When reading the books, you should take a few minutes to look at the ICND book's Chapter 4, however. There are some new questions in the DIKTA quiz and some new questions at the end of the chapter, which are different from the INTRO book's Chapter 12. You might also make some adjustments in the order that you read the chapters. Figure I-3 outlines two suggested options for your IP subnetting study with these two books'

Figure I-3 *Study Plan Options for Studying IP Addressing When Studying for the CCNA Exam*

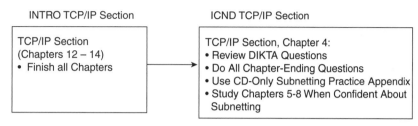

Option 1 – Follow Normal CCNA Reading Plan

INTRO TCP/IP Section | ICND TCP/IP Section

TCP/IP Section
(Chapters 12 – 14)
• Finish all Chapters

TCP/IP Section, Chapter 4:
• Review DIKTA Questions
• Do All Chapter-Ending Questions
• Use CD-Only Subnetting Practice Appendix
• Study Chapters 5-8 When Confident About
  Subnetting

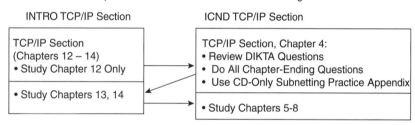

Option 2 – Follow Alternative CCNA Reading Plan

INTRO TCP/IP Section | ICND TCP/IP Section

TCP/IP Section
(Chapters 12 – 14)
• Study Chapter 12 Only

• Study Chapters 13, 14

TCP/IP Section, Chapter 4:
• Review DIKTA Questions
• Do All Chapter-Ending Questions
• Use CD-Only Subnetting Practice Appendix

• Study Chapters 5-8

By taking the first of the two options in the figure, you can review IP subnetting after you have finished all the TCP/IP topics from the first book. If you follow the second option, you can inundate yourself with IP addressing all at once, then finish all the TCP/IP specific coverage in the first book, and then move back to the second book for the rest of the TCP/IP coverage. Either plan can work well; it's just a matter of personal preference.

For More Information

If you have any comments about the book, you can submit those via the www.ciscopress.com web site. Just go to the web site, select Contact Us, and type in your message.

Cisco might make changes that affect the CCNA certification from time to time. You should always check www.cisco.com for the latest detail. Also, you can look to www.ciscopress.com/1587200945, where we will publish any information pertinent to how you might use this book differently in light of Cisco's future changes. For instance, if Cisco decided to remove a major topic from the exam, they might post it on their web site; Cisco Press would make an effort to list that information as well.

The CCNA certification is arguably the most important Cisco certification. It certainly is the most popular, is required for several other certifications, and is the first step in distinguishing yourself as someone who has proven knowledge of Cisco.

The *CCNA INTRO Exam Certification Guide* is designed to help you attain CCNA certification. This is the CCNA INTRO certification book from the only Cisco-authorized publisher. We at Cisco Press believe that this book certainly can help you achieve CCNA certification—but the real work is up to you! I trust that your time will be well spent.

Cisco Published INTRO Exam Topics*
Covered in This Part:

13 Define and describe the structure and technologies of computer networks

14 Describe the hardware and software required to be able to communicate via a network

15 Describe the physical, electrical and mechanical properties and standards associated with optical, wireless and copper media used in networks

16 Describe the topologies and physical issues associated with cabling common LANs

17 Identify the key characteristics of common wide area networking (WAN) configurations and technologies, and differentiate between these and common LAN technologies

19 Describe the role of a router in a WAN

26 Compare and contrast collision and broadcast domains, and describe the process of network segmentation

28 Explain how collisions are detected and handled in an Ethernet system

29 Explain the fundamental concepts associated with the Ethernet media access technique

30 Describe how the protocols associated with TCP/IP allow host communication to occur

32 Describe the principles and practice of packet switching utilizing the Internet Protocol (IP)

33 Describe, compare and contrast network communications using two examples of layered models (OSI and IETF)

34 Describe the fundamental concepts associated with transport layer protocols, and compare the connectionless approach to transport with the connection oriented one

35 List the major TCP/IP application protocols, and briefly define their features and operation

36 Describe the operation of the major transport layer protocols TCP and UDP and the interaction and carriage of application layer data

37 Perform an initial configuration on a switch and save the resultant configuration file

* Always re-check www.cisco.com for the latest posted exam topics

PART I: Networking Fundamentals

CHAPTER 1

Introduction to Computer Networking Concepts

This chapter gives you a light-hearted perspective about networks, how they were originally created, and why networks work the way they do. Although no specific fact from this chapter happens to be on either of the CCNA exams, this chapter helps you prepare for the depth of topics you will start to read about in Chapter 2, "The TCP/IP and OSI Networking Models." If you are brand new to networking, this short introductory chapter will help you get ready for the details to follow. If you already understand the basics of TCP/IP, Ethernet, switches, routers, IP addressing, and the like, go ahead and skip on to Chapter 2. The rest of you will probably want to read through this short introductory chapter before diving into the details.

Perspectives on Networking

So, you are new to networking. You might have seen or heard about different topics relating to networking, but you are only just now getting serious about learning the details. Like many people, your perspective about networks might be that of a user of the network, as opposed to the network engineer who builds networks. For some, that perspective is as a dialup user of the Internet. Others might use a computer at a job or at school; that computer is typically connected to a network via some cable. Figure 1-1 shows the basic end-user perspective of networking.

Figure 1-1 *End-User Perspective on Networks*

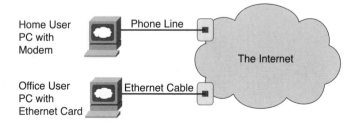

The top part of the figure shows a typical dialup user of the Internet. The user has a PC, and the user plugs in the phone line from the wall into a modem in a PC. By dialing the right phone number, the user connects to the Internet. After connecting, the user can send e-mail, browse web sites, and use other tools and applications as well.

Similarly, an employee of a company or a student at a university views the world as a connection through a wall plug. Typically, this connection uses a type of local-area network (LAN) called Ethernet. Instead of a phone cord between a PC modem and the wall plug at your house, you have an Ethernet cable between a PC Ethernet card and a wall plug near where you are sitting at work or at school. The Ethernet connection does not require the PC to "dial" a phone number—it's always there waiting to be used, similar to the power outlet.

From the end-user perspective, whether at home, at work, or at school, what happens behind the wall plug is magic. Just as most people do not really understand how cars work, how TVs work, and so on, most people who use networks do not understand how they work. Nor do they want to! But if you have read this much into Chapter 1, you obviously have a little more interest in networking than an end user. By the end of this book, you will have a pretty thorough understanding of what's behind that wall plug.

The concepts, protocols, and devices covered on the CCNA exam are used to help build the network cloud shown in Figure 1-1. However, the CCNA exam focuses on technology that is used to build a network at a single company or school. These same technologies are used to build the Internet, but the CCNA exam topics focus on things that matter most to what Cisco calls "enterprise" networks—networks owned by a single enterprise or company. Figure 1-2 shows an alternative view of the world of networking, with several enterprise networks.

Figure 1-2 *Enterprise Networks and the Internet*

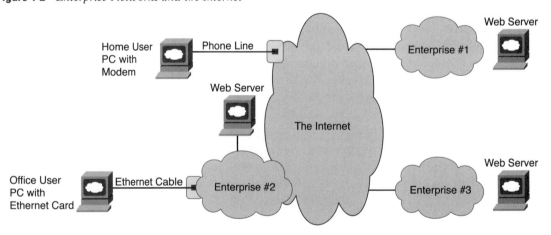

When you go to your school or your job and connect to "the network," you are most likely connecting to the private network, or enterprise network, for that school or company. That network, in turn, is connected to the Internet. Conversely, if you dial into some Internet service provider (ISP) from home, you are not connected to an Enterprise network, but you are connected directly to the Internet. However, if you then use a web browser to browse some web site, the web site itself might be inside that company's enterprise network.

In either case, practically every company or school that uses computers also has an enterprise network. To communicate, many enterprise networks connect to the Internet. The Internet itself is really a collection of ISPs that, in turn, connect to each other. By having the various enterprise networks connect to the Internet, most computer users around the world can use applications to communicate with each other—worldwide.

The CCNA exams focus on the technology used to build enterprise networks, with some coverage of technology more often used in the Internet. However, a lot of the protocols and concepts used in an enterprise network also happen inside the Internet. Because CCNA topics encompass the typical features found in enterprise networks, and because a much larger number of people work on enterprise networks than ISP networks, most of the examples in this book focus on enterprise networks.

Most of the details about standards for enterprise networks were created in the last quarter of the 20th century. You might have gotten interested in networking after most of the conventions and rules used for basic networking were created—if so, you missed out on the opportunity to help create the standards. However, taking the time to pause and think about what you would do if you were creating these standards can be helpful. The next section takes you through a somewhat silly example, but with real value in terms of thinking through some of the basic concepts behind enterprise networking and some of the design trade-offs.

The Flintstones Network: The First Computer Network?

The Flintstones are a cartoon family that, according to the cartoon, lived in prehistoric times. Because I want to discuss the thought process behind some imaginary initial networking standards, the Flintstones seem to be the right group of people to put in the example.

Fred is the president of FredCo, where his wife (Wilma), buddy (Barney), and buddy's wife (Betty) all work. They all have phones and computers, but they have no network because no one has ever made up the idea of a network before. Fred sees all his employees running around giving each other disks with files on them, and it seems inefficient. So, Fred, being a visionary, imagines a world in which people can connect their computers somehow and exchange files, without having to leave their desks. The (imaginary) first network is about to be born.

Fred's daughter, Pebbles, has just graduated from Rockville University and wants to join the family business. Fred gives her a job, with the title First-Ever Network Engineer. Fred says to Pebbles, "Pebbles, I want everyone to be able to exchange files without having to get up from their desks. I want them to be able to simply type in the name of a file and the name of the person, and poof! The file appears on the other person's computer. And because everyone changes departments so often around here, I want the workers to be able to take their PCs with them and just have to plug the computer into a wall socket so that they can send and receive files from the new office they moved to. I want this network thing to be like the electrical power thing your boyfriend, Bam Bam, created for us last year—a plug in the wall near every desk, and if you plug in, you're on the network!"

Pebbles first decides to do some research and development. If she can get two PCs to transfer files in a lab, then she ought to be able to get all the PCs to transfer files, right? She writes a program called Fred's Transfer Program, or FTP, in honor of her father.

The program uses a new networking card that Pebbles built in the lab. This networking card uses a cable with two wires in it—one wire to send bits and one to receive bits. Pebbles puts one card in each of the two computers and cables the computers together with a cable with two wires in it. The FTP software on each computer sent the bits that comprised the files using the networking cards. If Pebbles types a command like **ftp send filename,** the software transfers the file called filename to the computer at the other end of the cable. Figure 1-3 depicts the first network test at FredCo.

Figure 1-3 *Two PCs Transfer Files in the Lab*

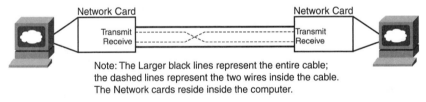

Note that because each networking card uses wire 1 to send bits and wire 2 to receive bits, the cable used by Pebbles connects wire 1 on PC1 to wire 2 on PC2, and vice versa. That way, both cards can send using wire 1, and it will enter the other PC on the other PC's wire 2.

Bam Bam happens by to give Pebbles some help after hearing about the successful test. "I'm ready to start deploying the network!" she claims. Bam Bam, the wizened one-year veteran of FredCo who graduated from Rockville U. a year before Pebbles, starts asking some questions. "What happens when you want to connect three computers together?" he asks. Pebbles explains that she can put two networking cards in each computer and cable each computer to each other. "So what happens when you connect 100 computers to the network—in each building?" Hmmm…. Pebbles then realizes that she has a little more work to do. She needs a scheme that allows her network to scale to more than two users. Bam Bam goes on, "We ran all the electrical power cables from the wall plug at each cube back to the broom closet. We just send electricity from the closet out to the wall plug near every desk. Maybe if you did something similar, you can find a way to somehow make it all work."

With that bit of input, Pebbles has all the inspiration she needs. Emboldened by the fact that she had already created the world's first PC networking card, she decides to create a device that will allow cabling similar to Bam Bam's electrical cabling plan. Pebble's solution to this first major hurdle is shown in Figure 1-4.

Figure 1-4   *Star Cabling to a Repeater*

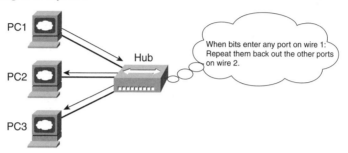

Pebbles follows Bam Bam's advice about the cabling. However, she needs a device into which she can plug the cables—something that will take the bits sent by a PC, and reflect, or repeat, the bits back to all the other devices connected to this new device. Because the networking cards send bits using wire 1, Pebbles builds this new device so that when it receives bits coming in wire 1 on one of its ports, it will repeat the same bits—but out wire 2 on all the other ports, so the other PCs get those bits on the receive wire. (Therefore, the cabling does not have to swap wires 1 and 2—this new device takes care of that.) And because she is making this up for the very first time in history, she needs to decide on a name for this new device: She names the device a hub.

Before deploying the first hub and running a bunch of cables, Pebbles does the right thing: She tests it in a lab, with three PCs connected to the world's first hub. She starts FTP on PC1, transfers the file called recipe.doc, and sees a window pop up on PC2 saying that the file was received, just like normal. "Fantastic!" she thinks—until she realizes that PC3 also has the same pop-up window on it. She has transferred the file to both PC2 and PC3! "Of course!" she thinks. "If the hub repeats everything out every cable connected to it, then when FTP sends a file, everyone will get it. I need a way for FTP to send a file to a specific PC!"

At this point, Pebbles thinks of a few different options. First, she thinks that she will give each computer the same name as the first name of the person using the computer. She will then change FTP to put the name of the PC that the file was being sent to in front of the file contents. In other words, to send her mom a recipe, she will use the **ftp Wilma recipe.doc** command. So, each PC will receive the bits because the hub repeats the signal to everyone connected to it, but only the PC whose name is the one in front of the file should actually create the file. Then her Dad walks in: "Pebbles, I want you to meet Barney Fife, our new head of security. He'll need a network connection as well—you are going to be finished soon, right?"

So much for using first names for the computers: There are now two people named Barney at FredCo. Pebbles, being mathematically inclined and in charge of creating all the hardware, decides on a different approach. "I'll put a unique address on each networking card—a 4-digit decimal number," she exclaims. Because Pebbles created all the cards, she will make sure that the number used on each card is unique. Also, with a 4-digit number, she will never run out of unique numbers—she has 10,000 (10^4) to choose from and only 200 employees at FredCo.

By the way, because she's making all this up for the very first time, she calls these built-in numbers on the cards *addresses*. When anyone wants to send a file, they can just use the **ftp** command, but with a number instead of a name. For instance, **ftp 0002 recipe.doc** will send the recipe.doc file to the PC whose network card has the address 0002. Figure 1-5 depicts the new environment in the lab.

Figure 1-5 *The First Network Addressing Convention*

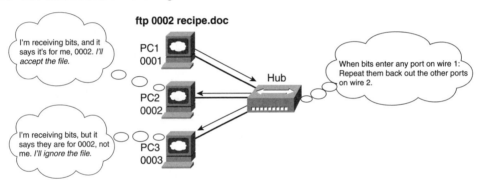

Now, with some minor updates to the Fred Transfer Program, the user can type **ftp 0002 recipe.doc** to send the file recipe.doc to the PC with address 0002. Pebbles tests the software and hardware in the lab again, and only PC2 receives the file when it is sent to PC2. When she sends the file to 0003, only PC3 receives the file. She's now ready to deploy the first computer network.

Pebbles now needs to build all the hardware needed. She first creates 200 network cards, each with a unique address. She installs the FTP program on all 200 PCs and installs the cards in each PC. Then she goes back to the lab and starts planning how many cables she will need and how long each cable should be. Then she realizes that she will need to run some cables a long way. Even if she puts the hub in the bottom floor of building A, the PCs on the fifth floor of building B will need a really long cable to connect to the hub. Cables cost money, and the longer the cable is, the more expensive the cable is. Besides, she has not yet tested the network with longer cables; she has been using cables that are only a couple of meters long.

Bam Bam happens by and sees that Pebbles is stressed. Pebbles vents a little: "Daddy wants this project finished, and you know how demanding he is. And I didn't think about how long the cables will be—I'll be way over budget. And I'll be running cables for weeks!" Bam Bam, being a little less stressed, having just come from a workout during lunch break at the club, knows that Pebbles already has the solution—she was too stressed to see it. Of course, the solution is not terribly different from how Bam Bam solved a similar problem with the electrical cabling last year. "Those hubs repeat everything they hear, right? So, why not make a bunch of hubs. Put one hub on each floor, and run cables from all the PCs. Then run a cable from the hub on each floor to a hub on the first floor Then, run one cable between the two main hubs in the two buildings. Because they repeat everything, every PC should receive the signal when just one PC sends, whether they are attached to the same hub or are four hubs away." Figure 1-6 depicts Bam Bam's suggested design.

Figure 1-6 *Per-Floor Hubs, Connected Together*

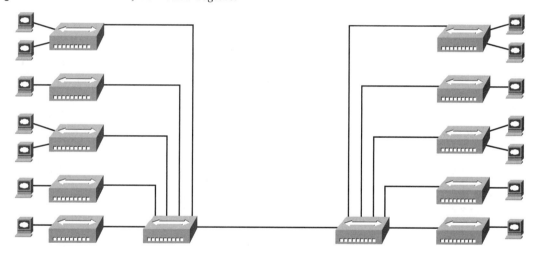

Pebbles loves the idea. She builds and connects the new hubs in the lab, just to prove the concept. It works! She makes the (now shorter) cables, installs the hubs and cables, and is ready to test. She goes to a few representative PCs and tests, and it all works! The first network has now been deployed.

Wanting to surprise Poppa Fred, Pebbles writes a memo to everyone in the company, telling them how to use the soon-to-be-famous Fred Transfer Program to transfer files. Along with the memo, she puts a list of names of people and the four-digit network address to be used to send files to each PC. She puts the memos in everyone's mail slot and waits for the excitement to start.

Amazingly, it all works. The users are happy. Fred treats Pebbles and Bam Bam to a nice dinner—at home, cooked by Wilma, but a good meal nonetheless.

Pebbles thinks she did it—created the world's first computer network, with no problems—until a few weeks pass. "I can't send files to Fred anymore!" exclaims Barney Rubble. "Ever since Fred got that new computer, he's too busy to go bowling, and now I can't even send him files telling him how much we need him back on the bowling team!" Then it hits Pebbles—Fred had just gotten a new PC and a new networking card. Fred's network address had changed. Or what happens if the card fails and it has to be replaced? The address changes.

About that time, Wilma comes in to say hi. "I love that new network thing you built. Betty and I can type each other notes, put them in a file, and send them anytime. It's almost like working on the same floor!" she says. "But I really don't remember the numbers so well. Couldn't you make that FTP thing work with names instead of addresses?"

In a fit of inspiration, Pebbles sees the answer to the first problem in the solution to her mom's problem. "I'll change FTP to use names instead of addresses. I'll make everyone tell me what name they want to use—maybe Barney Rubble will use BarneyR, and Barney Fife will use BarneyF, for instance. I'll change FTP to accept names as well as numbers. Then I'll tell FTP to look in a table that I will put on each PC that correlates the names to the numeric addresses. That way, if I ever need to replace a LAN card, all I have to do is update the list of names and addresses and put a copy on everyone's PC, and no one will know that anything has changed!" Table 1-2 lists Pebbles first name table.

Table 8-1   *Pebble's First Name/Address Table*

Person's Name	Computer Name	Network Address
Fred Flintstone	Fred	0001
Wilma Flintstone	Wilma	0002
Barney Rubble	BarneyR	0011
Betty Rubble	Betty	0012
Barney Fife	BarneyF	0022
Pebbles Flintstone	Netguru	0030
Bam Bam Rubble	Electrical-guy	0040

Pebbles tries out the new FTP program and name/address table in the lab, and it works. She deploys the new FTP software, puts the name table on everyone's PC, sends another memo—and now she can accommodate changes easily by separating the physical details, such as addresses on the networking cards, from what the end users need to know.

Like all good network engineers, Pebbles thought through the design and tested in a lab before deploying the network. For the problems she did not anticipate, she found a reasonable solution to get around the problem.

So ends the obviously contrived imaginary first computer network. What purpose did this silly example really serve? First, you have now been forced to think about some basic design issues that confronted the people who created the networking tools that you will be learning about for the CCNA exams. Although the example with Pebbles might have been fun, the problems that she faced are the same problems faced—and solved—by the people who created the original networking protocols and products.

The other big benefit to this story, particularly for those of you brand new to networking, is that you already know some of the more important concepts in networking:

Ethernet networks use cards inside each computer.

The cards have unique addresses, similar to Pebble's networking cards.

Ethernet cables connect PCs to Ethernet hubs—hubs that repeat each received signal out all other ports.

The cabling is typically run in a star configuration—in other words, all cables run from a cubicle to a wiring (not broom!) closet.

Applications such as the contrived Fred Transfer Program or the real-life File Transfer Protocol (FTP) ask the underlying hardware to transfer the contents of files. Users can use names—for instance, you might surf a web site called www.myfavoritewebsite.org—but the name gets translated into the correct address.

Now on to the real chapters, with real protocols and devices, with topics that you could see on the CCNA INTRO exam.

This chapter covers the following subjects:

- The TCP/IP Protocol Architecture

- OSI Reference Model

CHAPTER 2

The TCP/IP and OSI Networking Models

The term *networking model*, or *networking architecture*, refers to an organized description of all the functions needed for useful communications to occur. Individual protocols and hardware specifications then are used to implement the functions described in the networking model. When multiple computers and other networking devices implement these protocols, which, in turn, implement the functions described by the networking model, the computers can successfully communicate.

You can think of a networking model like you think of a set of architectural plans for building a house. Sure, you can build a house without the architectural plans, but it will work better if you follow the plans. And because you probably have a lot of different people working on building your house, such as framers, electricians, bricklayers, painters, and so on, it helps if they can all reference the same plan. Similarly, you could build your own network, write your own software, build your own networking cards, and create a network without using any existing networking model. However, it is much easier to simply buy and use products that already conform to some well-known networking model. And because the products from different vendors conform to the same networking architectural model, the products should work well together.

The CCNA exams include detailed coverage of one networking model—the Transmission Control Protocol/Internet Protocol, or TCP/IP. TCP/IP is the most pervasive networking model in the history of data networking. You can find support for TCP/IP on practically every computer operating system in existence today, from mobile phones to mainframe computers. Almost every network built using Cisco products today supports TCP/IP. Not surprisingly, the CCNA exams focus on TCP/IP.

The INTRO exam, and the ICND exam to a small extent, also covers a second networking model, called the Open Systems Interconnection (OSI) model. Historically, OSI was the first large effort to create a vendor-neutral networking model that could be added to any and every computer in the world. Ironically, OSI might be the least-pervasive networking model deployed today. However, because OSI was the first major effort to create a vendor-neutral networking architectural model, many of the terms used in networking today come from the OSI model.

"Do I Know This Already?" Quiz

The purpose of the "Do I Know This Already?" quiz is to help you decide whether you really need to read the entire chapter. If you already intend to read the entire chapter, you do not necessarily need to answer these questions now.

The ten-question quiz, derived from the major sections in "Foundation Topics to portion of the chapter, helps you determine how to spend your limited study time.

Table 2-1 outlines the major topics discussed in this chapter and the "Do I Know This Already?" quiz questions that correspond to those topics.

Table 2-1 *"Do I Know This Already?" Foundation Topics Section-to-Question Mapping*

Foundations Topics Section	Questions Covered in This Section
The TCP/IP Protocol Architecture	1, 2, 7, 8, 9, 10
The OSI Reference Model	3, 4, 5, 6

CAUTION   The goal of self-assessment is to gauge your mastery of the topics in this chapter. If you do not know the answer to a question or are only partially sure of the answer, you should mark this question wrong for purposes of the self-assessment. Giving yourself credit for an answer that you correctly guess skews your self-assessment results and might provide you with a false sense of security.

1. Which of the following protocols are examples of TCP/IP transport layer protocols?

    a. Ethernet

    b. HTTP

    c. IP

    d. UDP

    e. SMTP

    f. TCP

    g. PPP

2. Which of the following protocols are examples of TCP/IP network interface layer protocols?

    a. Ethernet

    b. HTTP

    c. IP

    d. UDP

    e. SMTP

    f. TCP

    g. PPP

3. Which OSI layer defines the functions of logical network-wide addressing and routing?

    a. Layer 1

    b. Layer 2

    c. Layer 3

    d. Layer 4

    e. Layer 5

    f. Layer 6

    g. Layer 7

4. Which OSI layer defines the standards for cabling and connectors?

    a. Layer 1

    b. Layer 2

    c. Layer 3

    d. Layer 4

    e. Layer 5

    f. Layer 6

    g. Layer 7

5. Which OSI layer defines the standards for data formats and encryption?

    a. Layer 1

    b. Layer 2

    c. Layer 3

    d. Layer 4

    e. Layer 5

    f. Layer 6

    g. Layer 7

6. Which of the following terms are not valid terms for the names of the seven OSI layers?

   a. Application

   b. Data link

   c. Transmission

   d. Presentation

   e. Internetwork

   f. Session

7. The process of HTTP asking TCP to send some data and make sure that it is received correctly is an example of what?

   a. Same-layer interaction

   b. Adjacent-layer interaction

   c. The OSI model

   d. All of the above

   e. None of the above

8. The process of TCP on one computer marking a segment as segment 1, and the receiving computer then acknowledging the receipt of segment 1, is an example of what?

   a. Data encapsulation

   b. Same-layer interaction

   c. Adjacent-layer interaction

   d. The OSI model

   e. None of the above

9. The process of a web server adding a TCP header to a web page, followed by adding a TCP header, then an IP header, and then data link header and trailer is an example of what?

   a. Data encapsulation

   b. Same-layer interaction

   c. The OSI model

   d. All of the above

   e. None of the above

10. Which of the following terms is used specifically to identify the entity that is created when encapsulating data inside data-link headers and trailers?

    a. Data

    b. Chunk

    c. Segment

    d. Frame

    e. packet

    f. None—there is no encapsulation by the data link layer

The answers to the "Do I Know This Already?" quiz are found in Appendix A, "Answers to the 'Do I Know This Already?' Quizzes and Q&A Sections." The suggested choices for your next step are as follows:

■ **8 or less overall score**—Read the entire chapter. This includes the "Foundation Topics" and "Foundation Summary" sections and the Q&A section.

■ **9 or 10 overall score**—If you want more review on these topics, skip to the "Foundation Summary" section and then go to the Q&A section. Otherwise, move to the next chapter.

Foundation Topics

It is practically impossible to find a computer today that does not support the set of networking protocols called TCP/IP. Every Microsoft, Linux, and UNIX operating system includes support for TCP/IP. Hand-held digital assistants and cell phones support TCP/IP. Even IBM Mainframe operating systems support TCP/IP. And because Cisco sells products that create the infrastructure that allows all these computers to talk with each other using TCP/IP, Cisco products also include extensive support for TCP/IP.

The world has not always been so simple. Once upon a time, there were no networking protocols, including TCP/IP. Vendors created the first networking protocols; these protocols supported only that vendor's computers, and the details were not even published to the public. As time went on, vendors formalized and published their networking protocols, enabling other vendors to create products that could communicate with their computers. For instance, IBM published its Systems Network Architecture (SNA) networking model in 1974. After SNA was published, you could buy computers from other vendors as well as IBM, and they could communicate—as long as they supported IBM's proprietary SNA.

Using only vendor-proprietary networking models allowed a business to successfully communicate between computers from multiple vendors. However, to talk to a computer using the hardware or software from vendor X, you needed to use the networking protocols created by vendor X. Imagine sitting at your desk in the late 1980s and needing to work with an IBM mainframe using SNA, a DEC minicomputer using DECnet, and a Novell server using NetWare, and having to transfer files with an Apple computer using AppleTalk. Believe it or not, it actually worked, and networks using all these different protocols were not at all uncommon.

A better solution was to create a standardized networking model that all vendors would support. The International Organization for Standardization (ISO) took on this task starting as early as the late 1970s, beginning work on what would become known as the Open Systems Interconnection (OSI) networking model. The ISO had a noble goal for the OSI: to standardize data networking protocols to allow communication between all computers across the entire planet. The OSI worked toward this ambitious and noble goal, with participants from most of the technologically developed nations on Earth participating in the process.

A second, less formal effort to create a standardized, public networking model sprouted forth from a U.S. Defense Department contract. Researchers at various universities volunteered to help further develop the protocols surrounding the original department's work. These efforts resulting in a competing networking model called TCP/IP.

The world now had many competing vendor networking models and two competing standardized networking models. So what happened? TCP/IP won the war. Proprietary protocols are still in use today in many networks, but much less so than in the 1980s and 1990s. OSI, whose development suffered in part because of the slow formal standardization processes of the ISO, never succeeded in the marketplace. And TCP/IP, the networking model created almost entirely by a bunch of volunteers, has become the most prolific set of data networking protocols ever.

In this chapter, you will read about some of the basics of TCP/IP. Although you will learn some interesting facts about TCP/IP, the true goal of this chapter is to help you understand what a networking model or networking architecture really is and how one works.

Also in this chapter, you will learn about some of the jargon used with OSI. Will any of you ever work on a computer that is using the full OSI protocols instead of TCP/IP? Probably not. However, you will often use terms relating to OSI. Also, the INTRO exam covers the basics of OSI, so this chapter also covers OSI to prepare you for questions about it on the exam.

The TCP/IP Protocol Architecture

TCP/IP defines a large collection of protocols that allow computers to communicate. TCP/IP defines the details of each of these protocols inside document called Requests For Comments (RFCs). By implementing the required protocols defined in TCP/IP RFCs, a computer can be relatively confident that it can communicate with other computers that also implement TCP/IP.

An easy comparison can be made between telephones and computers that use TCP/IP. I can go to the store and buy a phone from one of a dozen different vendors. When I get home, I plug the phone in to the wall socket, and it works. The phone vendors know the standards for phones in their country and build their phones to match those standards. Similarly, a computer that implements the standard networking protocols defined by TCP/IP can communicate with other computers that also use the TCP/IP standards.

Like other networking architectures, TCP/IP classifies the various protocols into different categories. Table 2-2 outlines the main categories in the TCP/IP architectural model.

Table 2-2   *TCP/IP Architectural Model and Example Protocols*

TCP/IP Architecture Layer	Example Protocols
Application	HTTP, POP3, SMTP
Transport	TCP, UDP
Internetwork	IP
Network interface	Ethernet, Frame Relay

The TCP/IP model represented in column 1 of the table lists the four layers of TCP/IP, and column 2 of the table lists several of the most popular TCP/IP protocols. If someone makes up a new application, the protocols used directly by the application would be considered to be application layer protocols. When the World Wide Web (WWW) was first created, a new application layer protocol was created for the purpose of asking for web pages and receiving the contents of the web pages. Similarly, the network interface layer includes protocols and standards such as Ethernet. If someone makes up a new type of LAN, those protocols would be considered to be a part of the networking interface layer. In the next several sections, you will learn the basics about each of these four layers in the TCP/IP architecture and how they work together.

TCP/IP application layer protocols provide services to the application software running on a computer. The application layer does not define the application itself, but rather it defines services that applications need - like the ability to transfer a file in the case of HTTP. In short, the application layer provides an interface between software running on a computer and the network itself.

The TCP/IP Application Layer

Arguably, the most popular TCP/IP application today is the web browser. Many major software vendors either have already changed or are changing their software to support access from a web browser. And thankfully, using a web browser is easy—you start a web browser on your computer and select a web site by typing in the name of the web site, and the web page appears.

What really happens to allow that web page to appear on your web browser? These next few sections take a high-level look at what happens behind the scene.

Imagine that Bob opens his browser. His browser has been configured to automatically ask for web server Larry's default web page, or *home page*. The general logic looks like that in Figure 2-1.

Figure 2-1   *Basic Application Logic to Get a Web Page*

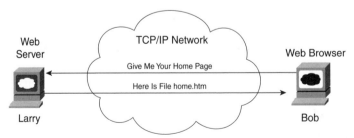

So what really happened? Bob's initial request actually asks Larry to send his home page back to Bob. Larry's web server software has been configured to know that Larry's default web page is contained in a file called home.htm. Bob receives the file from Larry and displays the contents of the file in the web browser window.

Taking a closer look, this example uses two TCP/IP application layer protocols. First, the request for the file and the actual transfer of the file are performed according to the Hypertext Transfer Protocol (HTTP). Many of you have probably noticed that most web sites' URLs (Universal Resource Locators, the text that identifies a web server and a particular web page) begin with the letters "http," to imply that HTTP will be used to transfer the web pages.

The other protocol used is the Hypertext Markup Language (HTML). HTML defines how Bob's web browser should interpret the text inside the file he just received. For instance, the file might contain directions about making certain text be a certain size, color, and so on. In most cases, it also includes directions about other files that Bob's web browser should get—things such as graphics images and animation. HTTP would then be used to get those additional files from Larry, the web server.

A closer look at how Bob and Larry cooperate in this example reveals some details about how networking protocols work. Consider Figure 2-2, which simply revises Figure 2-1, showing the locations of HTTP headers and data.

Figure 2-2   *HTTP Get Request and HTTP Reply*

To get the web page from Larry, Bob sends something called an HTTP header to Larry. This header includes the command to "get" a file. The request typically contains the name of the file (home.htm in this case), or, if no filename is mentioned, the web server assumes that Bob wants the default web page.

The response from Larry includes an HTTP header as well, with something as simple as "OK" returned in the header. In reality, it includes an HTTP return code. For instance, if you have ever used the web, and a web page that you looked for was not found, then you received an HTTP 404 "not found" error, which means that you received an HTTP return code of 404. When the requested file is found, the return code is 0, meaning that the request is being processed.

This simple example between Bob and Larry introduces one of the most important general concepts behind networking models: When a particular layer wants to communicate with the same layer on another computer, the two computers use headers to hold the information that they want to communicate. The headers are part of what is transmitted between the two computers. This process is called *same-layer interaction*.

The application layer protocol (HTTP, in this case) on Bob is communicating with Larry's application layer. They each do so by creating and sending application layer headers to each other—sometimes with application data following the header and sometimes not, as seen in Figure 2-2. Regardless of what the application layer protocol happens to be, they all use the same general concept of communicating with the same layer on the other computer using application layer headers.

TCP/IP application layer protocols provide services to the application software running on a computer. The application layer does not define the application itself, but rather it defines services that applications need—like the ability to transfer a file in the case of HTTP. In short, the application layer provides an interface between software running on a computer and the network itself.

The TCP/IP Transport Layer

The TCP/IP application layer includes a relatively large number of protocols, with HTTP being only one of those. The TCP/IP transport layer consists of two main protocol options—the Transmission Control Protocol (TCP) and the User Datagram Protocol (UDP). To get a true appreciation for what TCP/IP transport layer protocols do, read Chapter 6, "Fundamentals of TCP and UDP." However, in this section, you will learn about one of the key features of TCP, which enables us to cover some more general concepts about how networking models behave.

To appreciate what the transport layer protocols do, you must think about the layer above the transport layer, the application layer. Why? Well, each layer provides a service to the layer above it. For example, in Figure 2-2, Bob and Larry used HTTP to transfer the home page from Larry to Bob. But what would have happened if Bob's HTTP get request was lost in transit through the TCP/IP network? Or, what would have happened if Larry's response, which includes the contents of the home page, was lost? Well, the page would not show up in Bob's browser, as you might expect.

So, TCP/IP needs a mechanism to guarantee delivery of data across a network. TCP provides that feature by using acknowledgments. Figure 2-3 outlines the basic acknowledgment logic.

As Figure 2-3 shows, the HTTP software asks for TCP to reliably deliver the HTTP get request. TCP sends the HTTP data from Bob to Larry, and the data arrives successfully. Larry's TCP software acknowledges receipt of the data and also gives the HTTP get request to the web server software. The reverse happens with Larry's response, which also arrives at Bob successfully.

Figure 2-3 *TCP Services Provided to HTTP*

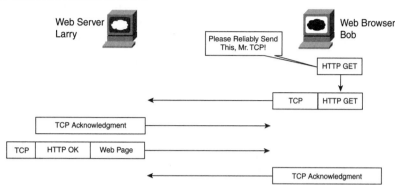

Of course, the benefits of TCP error recovery cannot be seen unless the data is lost. Chapter 6 covers TCP, including error recovery, in detail. For now, assume that if either transmission had been lost, that HTTP would not be concerned, and that TCP would resend the data and ensure that it was received successfully.

This example outlines the concepts of how adjacent layers in a networking model work together on the same computer. The higher-layer protocol (HTTP) needs to do something it cannot do (error recovery). So, the higher layer asks for the next lower-layer protocol (TCP) to perform the service, and the next lower layer performs the service. The lower layer provides a service to the layer above it.

Table 2-3 summarizes the key points about how adjacent layers work together on a single computer and how one layer on one computer works with the same networking layer on another computer.

Table 2-3 *Summary: Same-Layer and Adjacent-Layer Interactions*

Concept	Description
Same-layer interaction on different computers	The two computers use a protocol to communicate with the same layer on another computer. The protocol defined by each layer uses a header that is transmitted between the computers, to communicate what each computer wants to do.
Adjacent-layer interaction on the same computer	On a single computer, one layer provides a service to a higher layer. The software or hardware that implements the higher layer requests that the next lower layer perform the needed function.

The TCP/IP transport layer provides services to the various application layer protocols. Error recovery, as performed by TCP, is one feature. This layer also provides other functions, as detailed in Chapter 6.

All the examples describing the application and transport layers ignored many details relating to the physical network. The application and transport layers purposefully were defined to work the same, way whether the endpoint host computers were on the same LAN or were separated by the Internet. The lower two layers of TCP/IP, the internetwork layer and the network interface layer, must understand the underlying physical network because they define the protocols used to deliver the data from one host to another.

The TCP/IP Internetwork Layer

Imagine that you just wrote a letter to your favorite person on the other side of the country and that you also wrote a letter to someone on the other side of town. It's time to send the letters. Is there much difference in how you treat each letter? Not really. You put different addresses on the envelope for each letter because the letters need to go to two different places. You put stamps on both letters and put them in the same mailbox. The postal service takes care of all the details of figuring out how to get each letter to the right place—whether it is across town or across the country.

Inside the postal service, both letters are processed. One letter gets sent to another post office, then another, and so on, until the letter gets delivered across the country. The local letter might go to the post office in your town and then simply be delivered to your friend across town, without going to another post office.

So what does this all matter to networking? Well, the internetwork layer of the TCP/IP networking model, the Internet Protocol (IP), works much like the postal service. IP defines addresses so that each host computer can have a different IP address, just like the postal service defines addressing that allows unique addresses for each house, apartment, and business. Similarly, IP defines the process of routing so that devices called routers (ingenious name, huh?) can choose where to send packets of data so that they are delivered to the correct destination. Just like the postal service created the necessary post offices, sorting machines, trucks, and personnel to deliver the mail, the internetwork layer defines much of the details needed to implement the necessary networking infrastructure.

Chapter 5, "Fundamentals of IP," describes the TCP/IP Internetwork layer further, with other details scattered throughout the book. But to help you understand the basics of the internetwork layer, take a look at Bob's request for Larry's home page, now with some information about IP, in Figure 2-4.

First, some basic information about the figure will help. The LAN cabling details are not important for this example, so both LANs simply are represented by the lines shown near Bob and Larry, respectively. When Bob sends the data, he is sending an IP packet, which includes the IP header, the transport layer header (TCP, in this example), the application header (HTTP, in this case), and any application data (none, in this case). The IP header includes both a source and a destination IP address field, with Larry's IP address as the destination address and Bob's as the source.

Figure 2-4   *IP Services Provided to TCP*

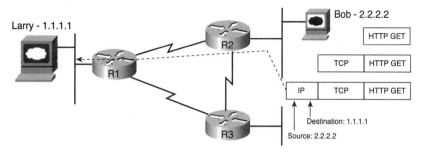

Bob sends the packet to R2, which makes a routing decision. R2 chooses to send the packet to R1 because the destination address of the packet is 1.1.1.1, and R1 knows enough about the network topology to know that 1.1.1.1 (Larry) is on the other side of R1. Similarly, when R1 gets the packet, it forwards the packet over the Ethernet to Larry. And if the link between R2 and R1 fails, IP allows R2 to learn of the alternate route through R3 to reach 1.1.1.1.

IP defines logical addresses, called *IP addresses*, that allow each TCP/IP speaking device (called IP hosts) to communicate. It also defines routing—the process of how a router should forward, or route, packets of data. Other protocol specifications, like OSI, have different protocols that also define addressing and routing.

Both CCNA exams cover IP fairly deeply. For the INTRO exam, this book's Chapter 5 covers more of the basics, and Chapters 12, "IP Addressing and Subnetting," through 14, "Introduction to Dynamic Routing Protocols," cover many of the details.

The TCP/IP Network Interface Layer

The network interface layer defines the protocols and hardware required to deliver data across some physical network. The term *network interface* refers to the fact that this layer defines how to connect the host computer, which is not part of the network, to the network; it is the interface between the computer and the network. For instance, Ethernet is one example protocol at the TCP/IP network interface layer. Ethernet defines the required cabling, addressing, and protocols used to create an Ethernet LAN. Likewise, the connectors, cables, voltage levels, and protocols used to deliver data across WAN links are defined in a variety of other protocols that also fall into the network interface layer.

Chapter 3, "Data Link Layer Fundamentals: Ethernet LANs," and Chapter 4, "Fundamentals of WANs," cover more details about the TCP/IP network interface layer.

Just like every layer in any networking model, the TCP/IP network interface layer provides services to the layer above it in the model. The best way to understand the basics of the TCP/IP network interface layer is to examine the services that it provides to IP.

IP relies on the network interface layer to deliver IP packets across each physical network. IP understands the overall network topology, things such as which routers are connected to each other, which host computers are connected to which networks, and what the IP addressing scheme looks like. However, the IP protocol purposefully does not include the details about each of the underlying physical networks. Therefore, the Internet layer, as implemented by IP, uses the services of the network interface layer to deliver the packets over each physical network, respectively.

The network interface layer includes a large number of protocols. For instance, the network interface layer includes all the variations of Ethernet protocols and other LAN standards. This layer also includes the popular WAN standards, such as the Point-to-Point Protocol (PPP) and Frame Relay. The same familiar network is shown in Figure 2-5, with Ethernet and PPP used as the two network interface layer protocols.

Figure 2-5   *Ethernet and PPP Services Provided to IP*

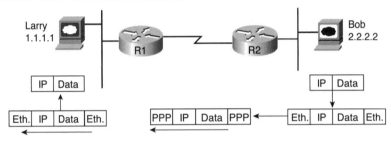

To fully appreciate Figure 2-5, first think a little more deeply about how IP accomplishes its goal of delivering the packet from Bob to Larry. Bob wants to send the IP packet to Larry, but it must first do so by sending the packet to R2. Bob uses Ethernet to get the packet to R2. At R2, R2 strips the Ethernet header and trailer from the IP packet. To get the IP packet from R2 to R1, R2 does not need to use Ethernet—it instead needs to use the PPP serial link. To send the IP packet from R2 to R1, R2 needs to place a PPP header in front of the IP packet and a PPP trailer at the end. Similarly, after the packet is received by R1, R1 removes the PPP header and trailer because PPP's job is to get the IP packet across the serial link. R1 then decides that it should forward the packet over the Ethernet to Larry. To do so, R1 adds a brand-new Ethernet header and trailer to the packet and forwards it to Larry.

In effect, IP uses the network interface layer protocols to deliver the IP packet to the next router or host, with each router repeating the process until the packet arrives at the destination. Each network interface protocol uses headers to encode the information needed to successfully deliver the data across the physical network, much like other layers use headers to achieve their goals.

CAUTION Many people describe the network interface layer of the TCP/IP model as two layers, the data link layer and the physical layer. The reasons for the popularity of these alternate terms are explained in the section covering OSI because the terms originated with the OSI model.

In short, the TCP/IP Network Interface layer includes the protocols, cabling standards, headers and trailers that define how to send data across a wide variety of types of physical networks.

Data Encapsulation

The term *encapsulation* describes the process of putting headers and trailers around some data. A computer that needs to send data encapsulates the data in headers of the correct format so that the receiving computer will know how to interpret the received data.

You have seen several examples of encapsulation in this chapter already. The web server encapsulated the home page inside an HTTP header in Figure 2-2. The TCP layer encapsulated the HTTP headers and data inside a TCP header in Figure 2-3. IP encapsulated the TCP headers and the data inside an IP header in Figure 2-4. Finally, the network interface layer encapsulated the IP packets inside both a header and a trailer in Figure 2-5.

You can think about the complete process of data encapsulation with TCP/IP as a five-step process. In fact, previous CCNA exams referred to a specific five-step process for encapsulation. This included the typical encapsulation by the application, transport, network, and network interface (referred to as data link) layers as Steps 1 through 4 in the five-step process. The fifth step was the physical layer's transmission of the bit stream. In case any questions remain in the CCNA question database referring to a five-step encapsulation process, the following list provides the details and explanation. Regardless, the ideas behind the process apply to any networking model and how it encapsulates data:

Step 1   **Create the application data and headers**—This simply means that the application has data to send.

Step 2   **Package the data for transport**—In other words, the transport layer (TCP or UDP) creates the transport header and places the data behind it.

Step 3   **Add the destination and source network layer addresses to the data**— The network layer creates the network header, which includes the network layer addresses, and places the data behind it.

Step 4   **Add the destination and source data link layer addresses to the data**— The data link layer creates the data link header, places the data behind it, and places the data link trailer at the end.

Step 5   Transmit the bits—The physical layer encodes a signal onto the medium to transmit the frame.

This five-step process happens to match the TCP/IP network model very well. Figure 2-6 depicts the concept; the numbers shown represent each of the five steps.

Figure 2-6 *Five Steps of Data Encapsulation—TCP/IP*

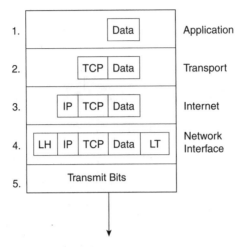

* The letters LH and LT stand for link header and link trailer, respectively, and refer to the data link layer header and trailer.

When each layer encapsulates data given to it from the next higher layer, that layer does not really care about the details of the data. Figure 2-7 shows the encapsulated data from the perspective of the transport, internetwork, and data link (network interface) layers.

Figure 2-7 *Perspectives on Encapsulation and "Data"*

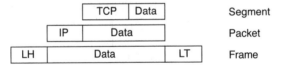

Each layer treats the data given to it by the next higher layer simply as "data." For instance, IP just wants to transport what TCP gives it—IP does not really care what is inside the data. So, the IP packet shown in the figure shows the rest of the bits as data, meaning that IP does not care that the data field looks like the TCP segment above it in the figure.

Also notice the specific terms used for the framing as it exists at each layer, as shown in the figure. Throughout this book and on the CCNA exams, the term *frame* defines all the encapsulated data. The term *packet* includes the IP header but not any data link headers. Finally, the term *segment* includes the TCP or UDP header but not the IP header or data link header or trailer.

OSI Reference Model

To pass the INTRO exam, you must be conversant in a protocol specification with which you are very unlikely to ever have any hands-on experience—the OSI reference model. The difficulty these days when discussing the OSI protocol specifications is that you have no point of reference—you simply cannot typically walk down the hall and use a computer whose main, or even optional, networking protocols conform to OSI.

OSI is the Open System Interconnection reference model for communications. Some participants in OSI's creation and development wanted OSI to become *the* networking protocol used by all applications on all computers in the world. The U.S. government went so far as to require OSI support on every computer that it purchased, as of a certain date in the early 1990s, which certainly gave vendors some incentive to write OSI code. In fact, in my old IBM days, they even had charts showing how the TCP/IP-installed base would start declining by 1994, how OSI installations would increase, and how OSI would be the protocol from which the 21st-century Internet was built.

What is OSI today? Well, OSI never succeeded in the marketplace. Some of the original protocols that comprised OSI are still used. The U.S. government reversed its decision to require OSI support on computers that it bought, which was probably the final blow to the possibility of pervasive OSI implementations. So, why do you even need to think about OSI for the CCNA exam? Well, the OSI model now is mainly used as a point of reference for discussing other protocol specifications. And because being a CCNA requires you to understand some of the concepts and terms behind networking architecture and models, and because other protocols are almost always compared to OSI, you need to know some things about OSI.

OSI Layers

The OSI reference model consists of seven layers. Each layer defines a set of typical networking functions. When OSI was in active development in the 1980s and 1990s, the OSI committees created new protocols and specifications to implement the functions specified by each layer. In other cases, the OSI committees did not create new protocols or standards, but instead referenced other protocols that were already defined. For instance, the IEEE defines Ethernet standards, so the OSI committees did not waste time specifying a new type of Ethernet; it simply referred to the IEEE Ethernet standards.

Today the OSI model can be used as a standard of comparison to other networking models. Figure 2-8 shows OSI, as compared with TCP/IP and Novell NetWare.

Figure 2-8 *Comparing OSI, TCP/IP, and NetWare*

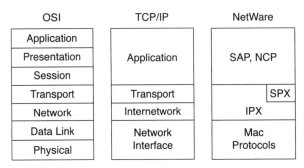

Because OSI does have a very well-defined set of functions associated with each of its seven layers, you can examine any networking protocol or specification and make some determination of whether it most closely matches OSI Layer 1, 2, or 3, and so on. For instance, TCP/IP's internetworking layer, as implemented by IP, equates most directly to the OSI network layer. So, most people say that IP is a network layer, or Layer 3, protocol, using OSI terminology and numbers for the layer. Of course, if you numbered the TCP/IP model, starting at the bottom, IP would be in Layer 2—but, by convention, everyone uses the OSI standard when describing other protocols. So, using this convention, IP is a network layer protocol.

Cisco requires that CCNAs demonstrate an understanding of the functions defined by OSI for each layer, as well as some example protocols that correspond to each OSI layer. The names of the OSI reference model layers, a few of the typical protocols at each layer, and the functions of each layer are simply good things to memorize for the INTRO exam. And frankly, if you want to pursue your Cisco certifications beyond CCNA, these names and functional areas will come up continually.

The upper layers of the OSI reference model (application, presentation, and session—Layers 7, 6, and 5) define functions focused on the application. The lower four layers (transport, network, data link, and physical—Layers 4, 3, 2, and 1) define functions focused on end-to-end delivery of the data. Both CCNA exams focus on issues in the lower layers—in particular, with Layer 2, upon which switching is based, and Layer 3, upon which routing is based. Table 2-4 defines the functions of the seven layers, and Table 2-5 lists typical protocols considered to be comparable to the OSI layers.

Table 2-4 *OSI Reference Model Layer Definitions*

Layer	Functional Description
7	Layer 7 defines the interface between the communications software and any applications that need to communicate outside the computer on which the application resides. For example, a web browser is an application on a computer. The browser needs to get the contents of a web page; OSI Layer 7 defines the protocols used on behalf of the application to get the web page.
6	This layer's main purpose is to define data formats, such as ASCII text, EBCDIC text, binary, BCD, and JPEG. Encryption also is defined by OSI as a presentation layer service. For example, FTP enables you to choose binary or ASCII transfer. If binary is selected, the sender and receiver do not modify the contents of the file. If ASCII is chosen, the sender translates the text from the sender's character set to a standard ASCII and sends the data. The receiver translates back from the standard ASCII to the character set used on the receiving computer.
5	The session layer defines how to start, control, and end conversations (called sessions). This includes the control and management of multiple bidirectional messages so that the application can be notified if only some of a series of messages are completed. This allows the presentation layer to have a seamless view of an incoming stream of data. The presentation layer can be presented with data if all flows occur in some cases. For example, an automated teller machine transaction in which you withdraw cash from your checking account should not debit your account and then fail before handing you the cash, recording the transaction even though you did not receive money. The session layer creates ways to imply which flows are part of the same session and which flows must complete before any are considered complete.
4	Layer 4 protocols provide a large number of services, as seen in Chapter 5 of this book. Although Layers 5 through 7 focus on issues related to the application, Layer 4 focuses on issues related to data delivery to the other computer—for instance, error recovery, segmentation of large application data blocks into smaller ones for transmission, and reassembly of those blocks of data on the receiving computer.
3	This layer defines end-to-end delivery of packets. To accomplish this, the network layer defines logical addressing so that any endpoint can be identified. It also defines how routing works and how routes are learned so that the packets can be delivered. Chapter 4 of this book examines Layer 3 concepts in detail. The network layer of OSI defines most of the details that a Cisco router considers when routing. For example, IP running in a Cisco router is responsible for examining the destination IP address of a packet, comparing that address to the IP routing table, fragmenting the packet if the outgoing interface requires smaller packets, and queuing the packet to be sent out to the interface.
2	The data link layer (Layer 2) specifications deliver data across one particular link or medium. These protocols are necessarily concerned with the type of media in question; for example, 802.3 and 802.2 define Ethernet for the IEEE, which are referenced by OSI as valid data link layer (Layer 2) protocols. Other protocols, such as High-Level Data Link Control (HDLC) for a point-to-point WAN link, deal with the different details of a WAN link.

continues

Table 2-4 *OSI Reference Model Layer Definitions (Continued)*

Layer	Functional Description
1	These physical layer (Layer 1) specifications, which are also typically standards from other organizations that are referred to by OSI, deal with the physical characteristics of the transmission medium. Connectors, pins, use of pins, electrical currents, encoding, and light modulation are all part of different physical layer specifications. Multiple specifications sometimes are used to complete all details of the physical layer. For example, RJ-45 defines the shape of the connector and the number of wires or pins in the cable. Ethernet and 802.3 define the use of wires or pins 1, 2, 3, and 6. So, to use a Category 5 cable with an RJ-45 connector for an Ethernet connection, Ethernet and RJ-45 physical layer specifications are used.

Table 2-5 *OSI Reference Model—Example Protocols*

Layer Name	Examples
Application (Layer 7)	Telnet, HTTP, FTP, WWW browsers, NFS, SMTP gateways (Eudora, CC:mail), SNMP
Presentation (Layer 6)	JPEG, ASCII, EBCDIC, TIFF, GIF, PICT, encryption, MPEG, MIDI
Session (Layer 5)	RPC, SQL, NFS, NetBIOS names, AppleTalk ASP, DECnet SCP
Transport (Layer 4)	TCP, UDP, SPX
Network (Layer 3)	IP, IPX, AppleTalk DDP
Data link (Layer 2)	IEEE 802.3/802.2, HDLC, Frame Relay, PPP, FDDI, ATM, IEEE 802.5/802.2
Physical (Layer 1)	EIA/TIA-232, V.35, EIA/TIA-449, RJ-45, Ethernet, 802.3, 802.5, B8ZS

OSI Layering Concepts and Benefits

Many benefits can be gained from the process of breaking up the functions or tasks of networking into smaller chunks, called *layers*, and defining standard interfaces between these layers. The layers break a large, complex set of concepts and protocols into smaller pieces, making it easier to talk about, easier to implement with hardware and software, and easier to troubleshoot. The following list summarizes the benefits of layered protocol specifications:

- **Easier to learn**—Humans can more easily discuss and learn about the many details of a protocol specification.

- **Easier to develop**—Reduced complexity allows easier program changes and faster product evolution.

- **Multivendor interoperability**—Creating products to meet the same networking standards means that computers and networking gear from multiple vendors can work in the same network.

■ **Modular engineering**—One vendor can write software that implements higher layers—for example, a web browser—and another can write software that implements the lower layers—for example, Microsoft's built-in TCP/IP software in its operating systems.

The benefits of layering can be seen in the familiar postal service analogy. A person writing a letter does not have to think about how the postal service will deliver a letter across the country. The postal worker in the middle of the country does not have to worry about the contents of the letter. Likewise, layering enables one software package or hardware device to implement functions from one layer, assuming that other software/hardware will perform the functions defined by the other layers. For instance, a web browser does not need to think about what the network topology looks like, the Ethernet card in the PC does not need to think about the contents of the web page, and a router in the middle of the network does not need to worry about the contents of the web page or whether the computer that sent the packet was using an Ethernet card or some other networking card.

OSI Terminology

First, remembering the names of the OSI layers is just an exercise in memorization. You might benefit from the following list of mnemonic phrases, with the first letters in each word being the same as the first letters of the OSI layer names, in order:

■ All People Seem To Need Data Processing (Layers 7 to 1)

■ Please Do Not Take Sausage Pizzas Away (Layers 1 to 7)

■ Pew! Dead Ninja Turtles Smell Particularly Awful (Layers 1 to 7)

You also should know how to use the names of the layers when discussing other networking models. An example definitely helps make sense of this concept. In Figure 2-9, you see the OSI model, the TCP/IP model, and a third figure with some sample TCP/IP protocols shown at their respective layers.

Figure 2-9 *Using OSI Layers for Referencing Other Protocols*

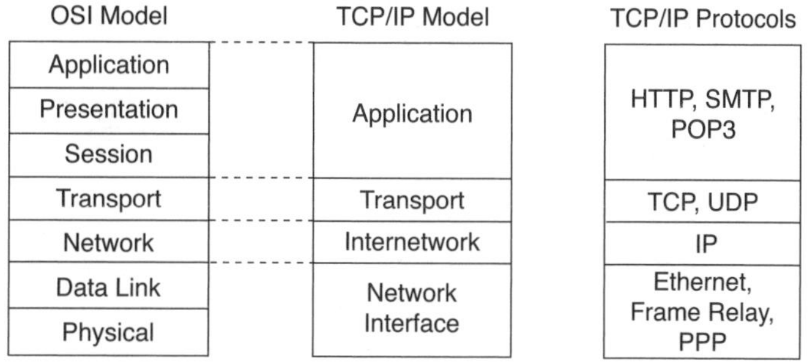

OSI Model	TCP/IP Model	TCP/IP Protocols
Application	Application	HTTP, SMTP, POP3
Presentation		
Session		
Transport	Transport	TCP, UDP
Network	Internetwork	IP
Data Link	Network Interface	Ethernet, Frame Relay, PPP
Physical		

As shown in the figure, the layers in the TCP/IP model correlate to particular layers in the OSI model. For instance, the TCP/IP internetwork layer corresponds to the OSI network layer. Why? Well, the OSI network layer defines logical addressing and routing, as does the TCP/IP internetwork layer. So, IP is called a *network layer*, or *Layer 3*, protocol. Similarly, the TCP/IP transport layer defines many functions, including error recovery, as does the OSI transport layer—so TCP is called a *transport layer*, or *Layer 4*, protocol.

Not all TCP/IP layers correspond to a single OSI layer. For instance, the TCP/IP network interface layer defines both the physical network specifications and the protocols used to control the physical network. OSI separates the physical network specifications into the physical layer and the control functions into the data link layer.

Ethernet includes functions defined by OSI Layers 1 and 2. So, depending on the context, you can refer to Ethernet as a Layer 1 or Layer 2 protocol.

The final OSI terms covered here all use the base term *protocol data unit*, or *PDU*. A PDU represents the bits that include the headers and trailers for that layer, as well as the encapsulated data. For instance, an IP packet, as shown in Figure 2-7, is a protocol data unit. In fact, an IP packet is a Layer 3 PDU because IP is a Layer 3 protocol. The term *L3PDU* is a shorter version of the phrase *Layer 3 PDU*. Figure 2-10 represents the typical encapsulation process, this time for the OSI model, with the terms used for the PDUs listed at each layer.

Figure 2-10   *OSI Encapsulation and Protocol Data Units*

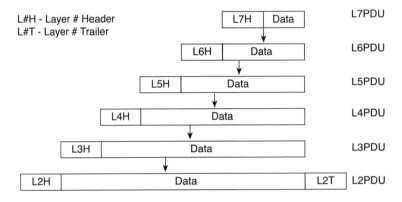

OSI Summary

In the first part of this chapter, you learned about how TCP/IP protocols at the various layers work with each other and how TCP/IP encapsulates data. Those same concepts are true of OSI, as well as other networking models. The basic ideas can be summed up as follows:

- Each layer provides a service to the layer above it in the protocol specification.
- Each layer communicates with the same layer's software or hardware on other computers.
- To accomplish these tasks, the data is encapsulated progressively with new headers when sending the data and is de-encapsulated when receiving the data.

Foundation Summary

The "Foundation Summary" section of each chapter lists the most important facts from the chapter. Although this section does not list every fact from the chapter that will be on your INTRO exam, a well-prepared CCNA candidate should know, at a minimum, all the details in each "Foundation Summary" section before going to take the exam.

Table 2-6 summarizes the key points about how adjacent layers work together on a single computer and how one layer on one computer works with the same networking layer on another computer. These concepts are some of the most important concepts in this chapter.

Table 2-6   *Summary: Same-Layer and Adjacent-Layer Interactions*

Concept	Description
Same-layer interaction on different computers	Each layer of a networking model works with the same layer on another computer with which it wants to communicate. The protocol defined by each layer uses a header that is transmitted between the computers to communicate what each computer wants to do.
Adjacent-layer interaction on the same computer	A higher layer might need a particular service that is not included in that layer. To perform the missing function, the protocol at the higher layer requests that the next lower layer perform the needed function.

Data encapsulation is another key concept discussed throughout this chapter. You can think about the complete process generically or with the example five-step TCP/IP encapsulation process shown in the following list and in Figure 2-11:

Step 1   Create the application data and headers—This simply means that the application has data to send.

Step 2   Package the data for transport—In other words, the transport layer (TCP or UDP) creates the transport header and places the data behind it.

Step 3   Add the destination and source network layer addresses to the data—The network layer creates the network header, which includes the network layer addresses, and places the data behind it.

Step 4   Add the destination and source data link layer addresses to the data—The data link layer creates the data link header, places the data behind it, and places the data link trailer at the end.

Step 5 **Transmit the bits**—The physical layer encodes a signal onto the medium to transmit the frame.

Figure 2-11 *Five Steps of Data Encapsulation—TCP/IP*

1.
Data
Application
2.
TCP
Data
Transport
3.
IP
TCP
Data
Internet
4.
LH
IP
TCP
Data
LT
Network interface
5.
Transmit bits

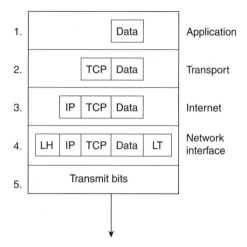

* The letters LH and LT stand for link header and link trailer, respectively, and refer to the data link layer header and trailer.

You should know the names of all the OSI and TCP/IP layers, as shown in Figure 2-12.

Figure 2-12 *Comparing OSI, TCP/IP, and NetWare*

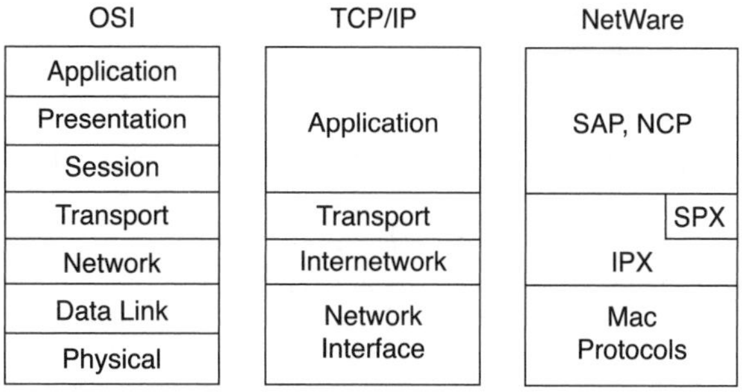

OSI
Application
Presentation
Session
Transport
Network
Data Link
Physical
TCP/IP
Application
Transport
Internetwork
Network Interface
NetWare
SAP, NCP
SPX
IPX
Mac Protocols

You should memorize the names of the layers of the OSI model. Table 2-7 lists a summary of OSI functions at each layer, along with some sample protocols at each layer.

Table 2-7   *OSI Functional Summary*

OSI Layer Name	Functional Description	Examples
Application (Layer 7)	Interface between network and application software.	Telnet, HTTP
Presentation (Layer 6)	How data is presented. Special processing, such as encryption.	JPEG, ASCII, EBCDIC
Session (Layer 5)	Establishing and maintaining end-to-end bidirectional flows between endpoints. Includes managing transaction flows.	Operating systems and application access scheduling RPC
Transport (Layer 4)	Reliable or unreliable delivery. Multiplexing.	TCP, UDP, SPX
Network (Layer 3)	Logical addressing, which routers use for path determination.	IP, IPX
Data link (Layer 2)	Combination of bits into bytes, and bytes into frames. Access to the media using MAC address. Error detection and error recovery.	802.3/802.2, HDLC
Physical (Layer 1)	Moving of bits between devices. Specification of voltage, wire speed, and cable pinouts.	EIA/TIA-232, V.35

The following list summarizes the benefits of layered protocol specifications:

■ **Easier to learn**—Humans can more easily discuss and learn about the many details of a protocol specification.

■ **Easier to develop**—Reduced complexity allows easier program changes and faster product evolution.

■ **Multivendor interoperability**—Creating products to meet the same networking standards means that computers and networking gear from multiple vendors can work in the same network.

■ **Modular engineering**—One vendor can write software that implements higher layers—for example, a web browser—and another can write software that implements the lower layers—for example, Microsoft's built-in TCP/IP software in its operating systems.

Q&A

As mentioned in the introduction, you have two choices for review questions. The questions that follow give you a bigger challenge than the exam itself by using an open-ended question format. By reviewing now with this more difficult question format, you can exercise your memory better and prove your conceptual and factual knowledge of this chapter. The answers to these questions are found in Appendix A.

For more practice with exam-like question formats, including questions using a router simulator and multiple-choice questions, use the exam engine on the CD.

1. Name the seven layers of the OSI model.

2. What is the main purpose(s) of Layer 7?

3. What is the main purpose(s) of Layer 6?

4. What is the main purpose(s) of Layer 5?

5. What is the main purpose(s) of Layer 4?

6. What is the main purpose(s) of Layer 3?

7. What is the main purpose(s) of Layer 2?

8. What is the main purpose(s) of Layer 1?

9. Describe the process of data encapsulation as data is processed from creation until it exits a physical interface to a network. Use the OSI model as an example.

10. Name three benefits to layering networking protocol specifications.

11. What header or trailer does a router discard as a side effect of routing?

12. What OSI layer typically encapsulates using both a header and a trailer?

13. What terms are used to describe the contents of the data encapsulated by the data link, network, and transport layers, respectively?

14. Explain the meaning of the term L5PDU.

15. Explain how Layer x on one computer communicates with Layer x on another computer.

16. List the terms behind the acronym TCP/IP.

17. List the terms behind the acronym OSI.

This chapter covers the following subjects:

- OSI Perspectives on Local-Area Networks

- Early Ethernet Standards

- Ethernet Data-Link Protocols

- Recent Ethernet Standards

Data Link Layer Fundamentals: Ethernet LANs

As you learned in the previous chapter, OSI Layers 1 and 2 map closely to the network interface layer of TCP/IP. In this chapter, you will learn more details about the functions of each of the two lowest layers in the OSI reference model, with specific coverage of Ethernet local-area networks (LANs).

The introduction to this book mentioned that the INTRO exam covers some topics lightly and covers others to great depth. As implied in the title, this chapter hits the fundamentals of Ethernet, paving the way for deeper coverage of other topics later in the book. Chapter 9, "Cisco LAN Switching Basics," and Chapter 10, "Virtual LANs and Trunking," delve into a much deeper examination of LAN switches and virtual LANs. Chapter 11, "LAN Cabling, Standards, and Topologies," increases your breadth of knowledge about Ethernet, including a lot of broad details about Ethernet standards, cabling, and topologies—all of which can be on the exam.

"Do I Know This Already?" Quiz

The purpose of the "Do I Know This Already?" quiz is to help you decide whether you really need to read the entire chapter. If you already intend to read the entire chapter, you do not necessarily need to answer these questions now.

The ten-question quiz, derived from the major sections in "Foundation Topics" portion of the chapter, helps you determine how to spend your limited study time.

Table 3-1 outlines the major topics discussed in this chapter and the "Do I Know This Already?" quiz questions that correspond to those topics.

Table 3-1 *"Do I Know This Already?" Foundation Topics Section-to-Question Mapping*

Foundations Topics Section	Questions Covered in This Section
OSI Perspectives on Local-Area Networks	1, 5
Early Ethernet Standards	3, 7, 8
Ethernet Data Link Protocols	2, 4, 6, 9
Recent Ethernet Standards	10

> **CAUTION** The goal of self-assessment is to gauge your mastery of the topics in this chapter. If you do not know the answer to a question or are only partially sure of the answer, you should mark this question wrong for purposes of self-assessment. Giving yourself credit for an answer that you correctly guess skews your self-assessment results and might provide you with a false sense of security.

1. Which of the following best describes the main function of OSI Layer 1 protocols?

   a. Framing

   b. Delivery of bits from one device to another

   c. Addressing

   d. CSMA/CD

   e. Defining the size and shape of Ethernet cards

2. Which of the following are part of the functions of OSI Layer 2 protocols?

   a. Framing

   b. Delivery of bits from one device to another

   c. Logical addressing

   d. Error recovery

   e. Defining the size and shape of Ethernet cards

3. Which of the following is true about Ethernet crossover cables?

   a. Pins 1 and 2 are reversed on the other end of the cable.

   b. Pins 1 and 2 connect to pins 3 and 6 on the other end of the cable.

   c. Pins 1 and 2 connect to pins 3 and 4 on the other end of the cable.

   d. The cable can be up to 1000 m to cross over between buildings.

   e. None of the above.

4. Which of the following are true about the format of Ethernet addresses?

   a. Each manufacturer puts a unique code into the first 2 bytes of the address.

   b. Each manufacturer puts a unique code into the first 3 bytes of the address.

   c. Each manufacturer puts a unique code into the first half of the address.

   d. The part of the address that holds this manufacturer's code is called the MC.

   e. The part of the address that holds this manufacturer's code is called the OUI.

   f. The part of the address that holds this manufacturer's code has no specific name.

5. Which of the following is true about the Ethernet FCS field?

    a. It is used for error recovery.

    b. It is 2 bytes long.

    c. It resides in the Ethernet trailer, not the Ethernet header.

    d. It is used for encryption.

    e. None of the above.

6. Which of the following fields can be used by Ethernet as a "type" field, to define the type of data held in the "data" portion of the Ethernet frame?

    a. The DIX Ethernet DSAP field

    b. The IEEE 802.2 Ethernet Type field

    c. The IEEE 802.2 Ethernet DSAP field

    d. The SNAP header Protocol Type field

    e. None of the above.

7. Which of the following are true about the CSMA/CD algorithm?

    a. The algorithm never allows collisions to occur.

    b. Collisions can happen, but the algorithm defines how the computers should notice a collision and how to recover.

    c. The algorithm works only with two devices on the same Ethernet.

    d. None of the above.

8. Which of the following would be a collision domain?

    a. All devices connected to an Ethernet hub

    b. All devices connected to an Ethernet switch

    c. Two PCs, with one cabled to a router Ethernet port with a crossover cable, and the other PC cabled to another router Ethernet port with a crossover cable.

    d. None of the above

9. Which terms describe Ethernet addresses that can be used to communicate with more than one device at a time?

    a. Burned-in address

    b. Unicast address

    c. Broadcast address

    d. Multicast address

    e. None of the above

10. With autonegotiation on a 10/100 card, what characteristics are negotiated if the device on the other end does not perform negotiation at all?

   a. 100 Mbps, half duplex

   b. 100 Mbps, full duplex

   c. 10 Mbps, half duplex

   d. 10 Mbps, full duplex

The answers to the "Do I Know This Already?" quiz are found in Appendix A, "Answers to the 'Do I Know This Already?' Quizzes and Q&A Sections." The suggested choices for your next step are as follows:

- **8 or less overall score**—Read the entire chapter. This includes the "Foundation Topics" and "Foundation Summary" sections and the Q&A section.

- **9 or 10 overall score**—If you want more review on these topics, skip to the "Foundation Summary" section and then go to the Q&A section. Otherwise, move to the next chapter.

Foundation Topics

Ethernet is the undisputed king of LAN standards today. Fifteen years ago, people wondered whether Ethernet or Token Ring would become win the battle of the LANs. Eight years ago, it looked like Ethernet would win that battle, but it might lose to an upstart called Asynchronous Transfer Mode (ATM) in the LAN. Today when you think of LANs, no one even questions what type—it's Ethernet.

Ethernet has remained a viable LAN option for many years because it has adapted to the changing needs of the marketplace while retaining some of the key features of the original protocols. From the original commercial specifications that transferred data 10 megabits per second (Mbps) to the 10 gigabits per second (Gbps) rates today, Ethernet has evolved and become the most prolific LAN protocol ever.

Ethernet defines both Layer 1 and Layer 2 functions, so this chapter starts with some basic concepts in relation to OSI Layers 1 and 2. After that, the three earliest Ethernet standards are covered, focusing on the physical layer details. Next, this chapter covers data link layer functions, which are common among all the earlier Ethernet standards as well as the newer standards. Finally, two of the more recent standards, Fast Ethernet and Gigabit Ethernet, are introduced.

OSI Perspectives on Local-Area Networks

The OSI physical and data link layers work together to provide the function of delivery of data across a wide variety of types of physical networks. Some obvious physical details must be agreed upon before communication can happen, such as the cabling, the types of connectors used on the ends of the cables, and voltage and current levels used to encode a binary 0 or 1.

The data link layer typically provides functions that are less obvious at first glance. For instance, it defines the rules (protocols) to determine when a computer is allowed to use the physical network, when the computer should not use the network, and how to recognize errors that occurred during transmission of data. Part II, "Operating Cisco Devices," and Part III, "LAN Switching," cover a few more details about Ethernet Layers 1 and 2.

Typical LAN Features for OSI Layer 1

The OSI physical layer, or Layer 1, defines the details of how to move data from one device to another. In fact, many people think of OSI Layer 1 as "sending bits." Higher layers encapsulate the data and decide when and what to send. But eventually, the sender of the data needs to actually transmit the bits to another device. The OSI physical layer defines the standards used to send and receive bits across a physical network.

To keep some perspective on the end goal, consider the example of the web browser requesting a web page from the web server. Figure 3-1 reminds you of the point at which Bob has built the HTTP, TCP, IP, and Ethernet headers, and is ready to send the data to R2.

Figure 3-1 *Data Link Frames Sent Using Physical Layer*

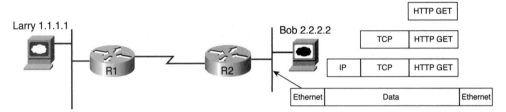

In the figure, Bob's Ethernet card uses the Ethernet physical layer specifications to transmit the bits shown in the Ethernet frame across the physical Ethernet. The OSI physical layer and its equivalent protocols in TCP/IP define all the details that allow the transmission of the bits from one device to the next. For instance, the physical layer defines the details of cabling—the maximum length allowed for each type of cable, the number of wires inside the cable, the shape of the connector on the end of the cable, and other details. Most cables include several conductors (wires) inside the cable; the endpoint of these wires, which end inside the connector, are called *pins*. So, the physical layer also must define the purpose of each pin, or wire. For instance, on a standard Category 5 (CAT5) unshielded twisted-pair (UTP) Ethernet cable, pins 1 and 2 are used for transmitting data by sending an electrical signal over the wires; pins 3 and 6 are used for receiving data. Figure 3-2 shows an example Ethernet cable, with a couple of different views of the RJ-45 connector.

Figure 3-2 *CAT5 UTP Cable with RJ-45 Connector*

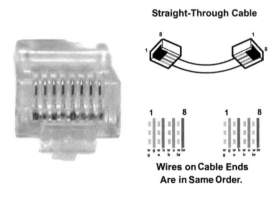

The picture on the left side of the figure shows a Regulated Jack 45 (RJ-45) connector, which is a typical connector used with Ethernet cabling today. The right side shows the pins used on the cable when supporting some of the more popular Ethernet standards. One pair of wires is used for transmitting data, using pins 1 and 2, and another pair is used for receiving data, using pins 3 and 6. The Ethernet shown between Bob and R2 in Figure 3-1 could be built with cables, using RJ-45 connectors, along with hubs or switches. (Hubs and switches are defined later in this chapter.)

The cable shown in Figure 3-2 is called a *straight-through cable*. A straight-through cable connects pin 1 on one end of the cable with pin 1 on the other end, pin 2 on one end to pin 2 on the other, and so on. If you hold the cable so that you compare both connectors side by side, with the same orientation for each connector, you should see the same color wires for each pin with a straight-through cable.

One of the things that surprises people who have never thought about network cabling is the fact that many cables use two wires for transmitting data and that the wires are twisted around each other inside the cable. When two wires are twisted inside the cable, they are called a *twisted pair* (ingenious name, huh?). By twisting the wires, the electromagnetic interference caused by the electrical current is greatly reduced. So, most LAN cabling uses two twisted pairs—one pair for transmitting and one for receiving.

The OSI physical layer and its equivalent protocols in TCP/IP define all the details that allow the transmission of the bits from one device to the next. In later sections of this chapter, you will learn more about the specific physical layer standards for Ethernet. Table 3-2 summarizes the most typical details defined by physical layer protocols.

Table 3-2 *Typical Physical Layer Functions*

Function	Description
Cabling	Defines the number of wires and the type of shielding used (or not used).
Connectors	Defines the shape of the connectors and the number of pins.
Pins	Defines the purpose of the pins. For instance, one pin might be used to signal to the other device whether it is allowed to send.
Voltage and current	Defines the electrical characteristics of the endpoint devices that use a cable.
Encoding	Defines how a device signals a binary 0 or 1 onto the transmit pin(s). For instance, +5V might mean 1, and –5V might mean 0. (Many encoding schemes exist and are beyond the scope of CCNA.)

Typical LAN Features for OSI Layer 2

OSI Layer 2, the data link layer, defines the standards and protocols used to control the transmission of data across a physical network. If you think of Layer 1 as "sending bits," you can think of Layer 2 as meaning "knowing when to send the bits, noticing when errors occurred when sending bits, and identifying the computer that needs to get the bits."

Similar to the section about the physical layer, this short section describes the basic data link layer functions. Later, you will read about the specific standards and protocols for Ethernet.

Data link protocols perform many functions, with a variety of implementation details. Because each data link protocol "controls" a particular type of physical layer network, the details of how a data link protocol works must include some consideration of the physical network. However, regardless of the type of physical network, most data link protocols perform the following functions:

- **Arbitration**—Determines when it is appropriate to use the physical medium
- **Addressing**—Ensures that the correct recipient(s) receives and processes the data that is sent
- **Error detection**—Determines whether the data made the trip across the physical medium successfully
- **Identification of the encapsulated data**—Determines the type of header that follows the data link header

Data Link Function 1: Arbitration

Imagine trying to get through an intersection in your car when all the traffic signals are out—you all want to use the intersection, but you had better use it one at a time. You finally get through the intersection based on a lot of variables—on how tentative you are, how big the other cars are, how new or old your car is, and how much you value your own life! Regardless, you cannot allow cars from every direction to enter the intersection at the same time without having some potentially serious collisions.

With some types of physical networks, data frames can collide if devices can send any time they want. When frames collide in a LAN, the data in each frame is corrupted and the LAN is unusable for a brief moment—not too different from a car crash in the middle of an intersection. The specifications for these data-link protocols define how to arbitrate the use of the physical medium to avoid collisions, or at least to recover from the collisions when they occur.

Ethernet uses the *carrier sense multiple access with collision detection (CSMA/CD)* algorithm for arbitration. The CSMA/CD algorithm is covered in the upcoming section on Ethernet.

Data Link Function 2: Addressing

When I sit and have lunch with my friend Gary, and just Gary, he knows I am talking to him. I don't need to start every sentence by saying "Hey, Gary...." Now imagine that a few other people join us for lunch—I might need to say something like "Hey, Gary..." before saying something so that Gary knows I'm talking to him.

Data-link protocols define addresses for the same reasons. Many physical networks allow more than two devices attached to the same physical network. So, data-link protocols define addresses to make sure that the correct device listens and receives the data that is sent. By putting the correct address in the data-link header, the sender of the frame can be relatively sure that the correct receiver will get the data. It's just like sitting at the lunch table and having to say "Hey Gary..." before talking to Gary so that he knows you are talking to him and not someone else.

Each data-link protocol defines its own unique addressing structure. For instance, Ethernet uses Media Access Control (MAC) addresses, which are 6 bytes long and are represented as a 12-digit hexadecimal number. Frame Relay typically uses a 10-bit-long address called a data-link connection identifier (DLCI)—notice that the name even includes the phrase *data link*. This chapter covers the details of Ethernet addressing. You will learn about Frame Relay addressing in the *CCNA ICND Exam Certification Guide*.

Data Link Function 3: Error Detection

Error detection discovers whether bit errors occurred during the transmission of the frame. To do this, most data-link protocols include a *frame check sequence (FCS)* or *cyclical redundancy check (CRC)* field in the data-link trailer. This field contains a value that is the result of a mathematical formula applied to the data in the frame.

An error is detected when the receiver plugs the contents of the received frame into a mathematical formula. Both the sender and the receiver of the frame use the same calculation, with the sender putting the results of the formula in the FCS field before sending the frame. If the FCS sent by the sender matches what the receiver calculates, the frame did not have any errors during transmission.

Error detection does not imply recovery; most data links, including IEEE 802.5 Token Ring and 802.3 Ethernet, do not provide error recovery. The FCS allows the receiving device to notice that errors occurred and then discard the data frame. Error recovery, which includes the resending of the data, is the responsibility of another protocol. For instance, TCP performs error recovery, as described in Chapter 6, "Fundamentals of TCP and UDP."

Data Link Function 4: Identifying the Encapsulated Data

Finally, the fourth part of a data link identifies the contents of the Data field in the frame. Figure 3-3 helps make the usefulness of this feature apparent. The figure shows a PC that uses both TCP/IP to talk to a web server and Novell IPX to talk to a Novell NetWare server.

Figure 3-3   *Multiplexing Using Data-Link Type and Protocol Fields*

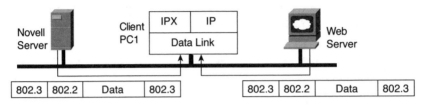

When PC1 receives data, should it give the data to the TCP/IP software or the NetWare client software? Of course, that depends on what is inside the Data field. If the data came from the Novell server, PC1 hands off the data to the NetWare client code. If the data comes from the web server, PC1 hands it off to the TCP/IP code. But how does PC1 make this decision? Well, IEEE Ethernet 802.2 Logical Link Control (LLC) uses a field in its header to identify the type of data in the Data field. PC1 examines that field in the received frame to decide whether the packet is an IP packet or an IPX packet.

Each data-link header has a field, generically with a name that has the word *Type* in it, to identify the type of protocol that sits inside the frame's data field. In each case, the Type field has a code that means IP, IPX, or some other designation, defining the type of protocol header that follows.

Early Ethernet Standards

Now that you have a little better understanding of some of the functions of physical and data link standards, the next section focuses on Ethernet in particular. This chapter covers some of the basics, while Chapters 9 through 11 cover the topics in more detail.

In this section of the chapter, you learn about the three earliest types of Ethernet networks. The term *Ethernet* refers to a family of protocols and standards that together define the physical and data link layers of the world's most popular type of LAN. Many variations of Ethernet exist; this section covers the functions and protocol specifications for the more popular types of Ethernet, including 10BASE-T, Fast Ethernet, and Gigabit Ethernet. Also, to help you appreciate how some of the features of Ethernet work, this section covers historical knowledge on two older types of Ethernet, 10BASE2 and 10BASE5 Ethernet.

Standards Overview

Like most protocols, Ethernet began life inside a corporation that was looking to solve a specific problem. Xerox needed an effective way to allow a new invention, called the personal computer, to be connected in its offices. From that, Ethernet was born. (Look at inventors.about.com/library/weekly/aa111598.htm for an interesting story on the history of Ethernet.) Eventually, Xerox teamed with Intel and Digital Equipment Corp. (DEC) to further develop Ethernet, so the original Ethernet became known as *DIX Ethernet*, meaning DEC, Intel, and Xerox.

The IEEE began creating a standardized version of Ethernet in February 1980, building on the work performed by DEC, Intel, and Xerox. The IEEE Ethernet specifications that match OSI Layer 2 were divided into two parts: the *Media Access Control (MAC)* and *Logical Link Control (LLC)* sublayers. The IEEE formed a committee to work on each part—the 802.3 committee to work on the MAC sublayer, and the 802.2 committee to work on the LLC sublayer.

Table 3-3 lists the various protocol specifications for the original three IEEE LAN standards, plus the original prestandard version of Ethernet.

Table 3-3   *MAC and LLC Standards for Three Types of LANs*

Name	MAC Sublayer Spec	LLC Sublayer Spec
Ethernet Version 2 (DIX Ethernet)	Ethernet	—
IEEE Ethernet	IEEE 802.3	IEEE 802.2
IEEE Token Ring	IEEE 802.5	IEEE 802.2
ANSI FDDI	ANSI X3T9.5	IEEE 802.2

The Original Ethernet Standards: 10BASE2 and 10BASE5

Ethernet is best understood by first considering the early DIX Ethernet specifications, called *10BASE5* and *10BASE2*. These two Ethernet specifications defined the details of the physical layer of early Ethernet networks. (10BASE2 and 10BASE5 differ in the cabling details, but for the discussion included in this chapter, you can consider them as behaving identically.) With these two specifications, the network engineer installs a series of coaxial cables, connecting each device on the Ethernet network—there is no hub, switch, or wiring panel. The Ethernet consists solely of the collective Ethernet cards in the computers and the cabling. The series of cables creates an electrical bus that is shared among all devices on the Ethernet. When a computer wants to send some bits to another computer on the bus, it sends an electrical signal, and the electricity propagates to all devices on the Ethernet.

Because it is a single bus, if two or more signals were sent at the same time, the two would overlap and collide, making both signals unintelligible. So, not surprisingly, Ethernet also defined a specification for how to ensure that only one device sends traffic on the Ethernet at one time—otherwise, the Ethernet would have been unusable. The algorithm, known as the *carrier sense multiple access with collision detection (CSMA/CD)* algorithm, defines how the bus is accessed. In human terms, CSMA/CD is similar to what happens in a meeting room with many attendees. Some people talk much of the time. Some do not talk, but they listen. Others talk occasionally. Being humans, it's hard to understand what two people are saying at the same time, so generally, one person is talking and the rest are listening. Imagine that Bob and Larry both want to reply to the current speaker's comments. As soon as the speaker takes a breath, Bob and Larry might both try to speak. If Larry hears Bob's voice before Larry actually makes a noise, Larry might stop and let Bob speak. Or, maybe they both start at almost the same time, so they talk over each other and many others in the room can't hear what was said. Then there's the proverbial "Excuse me, you talk next," and eventually Larry or Bob talks. Or, in some cases, another person jumps in and talks while Larry and Bob are both backing off. These "rules" are based on your culture; CSMA/CD is based on Ethernet protocol specifications and achieves the same type of goal.

Figure 3-4 shows the basic logic of an old Ethernet 10BASE2 network, which literally uses a single electrical bus, created with coaxial cable and Ethernet cards.

Figure 3-4   *Small Ethernet 10BASE2 Network*

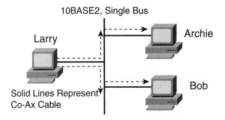

The solid lines in the figure represent the physical network cabling. The dashed lines with arrows represent the path that Larry's transmitted frame takes. Larry sends a signal across out his Ethernet card onto the cable, and both Bob and Archie receive the signal. The cabling creates a physical electrical bus, meaning that the transmitted signal is received by all stations on the LAN. Just like a school bus stops at everyone's house along a route, the electrical signal on a 10BASE2 or 10BASE5 network is propagated to each station on the LAN.

Because the transmitted electrical signal travels along the entire length of the bus, when two stations send at the same time, a collision occurs. The collision first occurs on the wire, and then some time elapses before the sending stations hear the collision—so technically, the stations send a few more bits before they actually notice the collision. CSMA/CD logic helps prevent collisions and also defines how to act when a collision does occur. The CSMA/CD algorithm works like this:

1. A device with a frame to send listens until the Ethernet is not busy.

2. When the Ethernet is not busy, the sender begins sending the frame.

3. The sender listens to make sure that no collision occurred.

4. Once the senders hear the collision, they each send a jamming signal, to ensure that all stations recognize the collision.

5. After the jamming is complete, each sender randomizes a timer and waits that long.

6. When each timer expires, the process starts over with Step 1.

So, all devices on the Ethernet need to use CSMA/CD to avoid collisions and to recover when inadvertent collisions occur.

Repeaters

Like any type of network, 10BASE5 and 10BASE2 had limitations on the total length of a cable. With 10BASE5, the limit was 500 m; with 10BASE2, it was 185 m. Interestingly, these two types of Ethernet get their name from the maximum segment lengths—if you think of 185 m as being close to 200 m, then the last digit of the names defines the multiple of 100 m that is the maximum length of a segment. That's really where the 5 and the 2 came from in the names.

In some cases, the length was not enough. So, a device called a *repeater* was developed. One of the problems with using longer segment lengths was that the signal sent by one device could attenuate too much if the cable was longer that 500 m or 185 m, respectively. *Attenuation* means that when electrical signals pass over a wire, the strength of the signal gets smaller the farther along the cable it travels. It's the same concept behind why you can hear someone talking right next to you, but if that person speaks at the same volume and you are across the room, you might not hear her because the sound waves have attenuated.

Repeaters allow multiple segments to be connected by taking an incoming signal, interpreting the bits as 1s and 0s, and generating a brand new, clean signal. A repeater does not simply amplify the signal because amplifying the signal might also amplify any noise picked up along the way.

NOTE Because the repeater does not interpret what the bits mean, but does examine and generate electrical signals, a repeater is considered to operate at Layer 1.

So, why all this focus on standards for Ethernets that you will never work with? Well, these older standards provide a point of comparison to how things work today, with several of the features of these two early standards being maintained today. Now, on to an Ethernet standard that is still found occasionally in production networks today—10BASE-T.

10BASE-T Ethernet

10BASE-T solved several problems with the early Ethernet specifications. 10BASE-T allowed the use of telephone cabling that was already installed, or simply allowed the use of cheaper, easier-to-install cabling when new cabling was required. 10BASE-T networks make use of devices called *hubs*, as shown in Figure 3-5.

Figure 3-5   *Small Ethernet 10BASE-T Network*

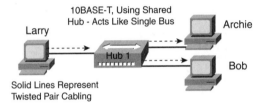

The physical 10BASE-T Ethernet uses Ethernet cards in the computers, cabling, and a hub. The hubs used to create a 10BASE-T Ethernet are essentially multiport repeaters. That means that the hub simply regenerates the electrical signal that comes in one port and sends the same signal out every other port. By doing so, 10BASE-T creates an electrical bus, just like 10BASE2 and 10BASE5. Therefore, collisions can still occur, so CSMA/CD access rules continue to be used.

The use of 10BASE-T hubs gives Ethernet much higher availability compared with 10BASE2 and 10BASE5 because a single cable problem could, and probably did, take down those types of LANs. With 10BASE-T, a cable is run from each device to a hub, so a single cable problem affects only one device.

The concept of cabling each device to a central hub, with that hub creating the same electrical bus as in the older types of Ethernet, was a core fact of 10BASE-T Ethernet. Because hubs continued the concept and physical reality of a single electrical path that is shared by all devices, today we call this *shared Ethernet*: All devices are sharing a single 10-Mbps bus.

A variety of terms can be used to describe the topology of networks. The term *star* refers to a network with a center, with branches extended outward—much like how a child might draw a picture of a star. 10BASE-T network cabling uses a star topology, as seen in Figure 3-5. However, because the hub repeats the electrical signal out every port, the effect is that the network acts like a bus topology. So, 10BASE-T networks are a physical *star* network design, but also a logical *bus* network design. (Chapter 11 covers the types of topologies and their meaning in more depth.)

Ethernet 10BASE-T Cabling

The PCs and hub in Figure 3-5 typically use Category 5 UTP cables with RJ-45 connectors, as shown in Figure 3-2. The Ethernet cards in each PC have an RJ-45 connector, as does the hub; these connectors are larger versions of the same type of connector used for telephone cords between a phone and the wall plate in the United States. So, connecting the Ethernet cables is as easy as plugging in a new phone at your house.

The details behind the specific cable used to connect to the hub are important in real life as well as for the INTRO exam. The detailed specifications are covered in Chapter 11, and the most typical standards are covered here. You might recall that Ethernet specifies that the pair of wires on pins 1 and 2 is used to transmit data, and pins 3 and 6 are used for receiving data. The PC Ethernet cards do indeed use the pins in exactly that way.

The cable used to connect the PCs to the hub is called a *straight-through* cable, as shown back in Figure 3-2. In a straight-through cable, the wire connected to pin 1 on one end of the cable is connected to pin 1 on the other side, pin 2 is connected to pin 2 on the other end, and so on. Therefore, when Larry sends data on the pair on pins 1 and 2, the hub receives the electrical signal over the straight-through cable on pins 1 and 2. So, for the hub to correctly receive the data, the hub must think oppositely, as compared to the PC—in other words, the hub receives data on pins 1 and 2, and transmits on pins 3 and 6. Figure 3-6 outlines how it all works.

Figure 3-6 *Straight-Through Ethernet Cable with Exaggerated RJ-45 Connectors*

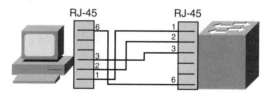

For example, Larry might send data on pins 1 and 2, with the hub receiving the signal on pins 1 and 2. The hub then repeats the electrical signal out the other ports, sending the signal to Archie and Bob. The hub transmits the signal on pins 3 and 6 on the cables connected to Archie and Bob because Archie and Bob expect to receive data on pins 3 and 6.

In some cases, you need to cable two devices directly together with Ethernet, but both devices use the same pair for transmitting data. For instance, you might want to connect two hubs, and each hub transmits on pins 3 and 6, as just mentioned. Similarly, you might want to create a small Ethernet between two PCs simply by cabling the two PCs together—but both PCs use pins 1 and 2 for transmitting data. To solve this problem, you use a special cable called a *crossover* cable. Instead of pin 1 on one end of the cable being the same wire as pin 1 on the other end of the cable, pin 1 on one end of the cable becomes pin 3 on the other end. Similarly, pin 2 is connected to pin 6 at the other end, pin 3 is connected to pin 1, and pin 6 is connected to pin 2. Figure 3-7 shows an example with two PCs connected and a crossover cable.

Figure 3-7   *Crossover Ethernet Cable*

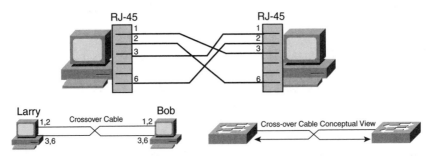

Both Bob and Larry can transmit on pins 1 and 2—which is good because that's the only thing an Ethernet card for an end user computer can do. Because pins 1 and 2 at Larry connect to pins 3 and 6 at Bob, and because Bob receives frames on pins 3 and 6, the receive function works as well. The same thing happens for frames sent by Bob to Larry—Bob sends on his pins 1 and 2, and Larry receives on pins 3 and 6.

Most of the time, you will not actually connect two computers directly with an Ethernet cable. However, you typically will use crossover cables for connections between switches and hubs. An Ethernet cable between two hubs or switches often is called a *trunk*. Figure 3-8 shows a typical network with two switches in each building and the typical cable types used for each connection.

Figure 3-8   *Typical Uses for Straight-Through and Crossover Ethernet Cables*

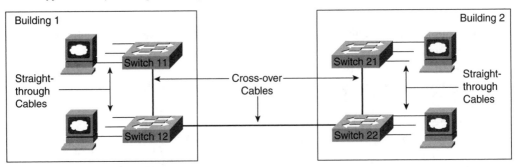

10BASE-T Hubs

Compared to 10BASE2 and 10BASE5, hubs solved some cabling and availability problems. However, the use of hubs allowed network performance to degrade as utilization increased, just like when 10BASE2 and 10BASE5 were used, because 10BASE-T still created a single electrical bus shared among all devices on the LAN. Ethernets that share a bus cannot reach 100 percent utilization because of collisions and the CSMA/CD arbitration algorithm. To solve the performance problems, the next step was to make the hub smart enough to ensure that collisions simply did not happen—which means that CSMA/CD would no longer be needed.

First, you need a deeper knowledge of 10BASE-T hubs before the solution to the congestion problem becomes obvious. Figure 3-9 outlines the operation of half-duplex 10BASE-T with hubs.

Figure 3-9 *10BASE-T Hub Re-Creates One Electrical Bus, Similar to 10BASE2*

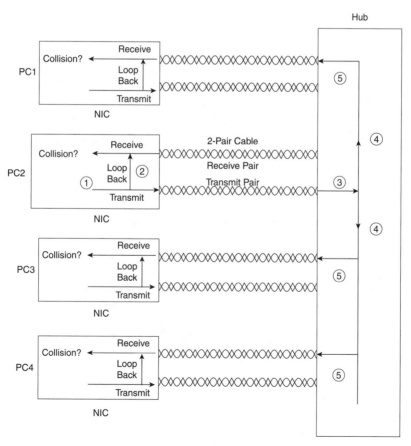

The figure outlines how a 10BASE-T hub creates an electrical bus. The chronological steps illustrated in Figure 3-9 are as follows:

1. The network interface card (NIC) sends a frame.

2. The NIC loops the sent frame onto its receive pair internally on the card.

3. The hub receives the frame.

4. The hub's internal wiring propagates the signal to all other ports, but not back to the port that the signal was received upon.

5. The hub repeats the signal to each receive pair to all other devices.

The figure details how the hub works, with one device sending and no collision. If PC1 and PC2 sent a frame at the same time, a collision would occur. At Steps 4 and 5, the hub would forward both electrical signals, which would cause the overlapping signals to be sent to all the NICs. So, because collisions can occur, CSMA/CD logic still is needed to have PC1 and PC2 wait and try again.

NOTE PC2 would sense a collision because of its loopback circuitry on the NIC. The hub does not forward the signal that PC2 sent to the hub back to PC2. Instead, each NIC loops the frame that it sends back to its own receive pair on the NIC, as shown in Step 2 of the figure. Then, if PC2 is sending a frame and PC1 also sends a frame at the same time, the signal sent by PC1 is forwarded by the hub to PC2 on PC2's receive pair. The incoming signal from the hub, plus the looped signal on PC2's NIC, lets PC2 notice that there is a collision. Who cares? Well, to appreciate full-duplex LAN operation, you need to know about the NIC's loopback feature.

Performance Issues: Collisions and Duplex Settings

10BASE2, 10BASE5, and 10BASE-T Ethernet would not work without CSMA/CD. However, because of the CSMA/CD algorithm, Ethernet becomes more inefficient under higher loads. In fact, during the years before LAN switches made these types of phenomena go away, the rule of thumb was that an Ethernet began to degrade when the load began to exceed 30 percent utilization.

In the next section, you will read about two things that have improved network performance, both relating to the reduction or even elimination of collisions: LAN switching and full-duplex Ethernet.

Reducing Collisions Through LAN Switching

The term *collision domain* defines the set of devices for which their frames could collide. All devices on a 10BASE2, 10BASE5, or 10BASE-T network using a hub risk collisions between the frames that they send, so all devices on one of these types of Ethernet networks are in the same collision domain. For instance, all the devices in Figure 3-9 are in the same collision domain.

LAN switches overcome the problems created by collisions and the CSMA/CD algorithm by removing the possibility of a collision. Switches do not create a single shared bus, like a hub; they treat each individual physical port as a separate bus. Switches use memory buffers to hold incoming frames as well, so when two attached devices send a frame at the same time, the switch can forward one frame while holding the other frame in a memory buffer, waiting to forward one frame until after the first one has been forwarded. So, as Figure 3-10 illustrates, collisions can be avoided.

Figure 3-10 *Basic Switch Operation*

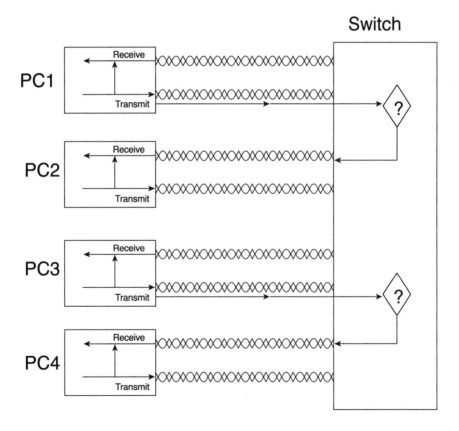

In Figure 3-10, both PC1 and PC3 are sending at the same time. The switch looks at the destination Ethernet address and sends the frame sent from PC1 to PC2 at the same instant as the frame is sent by PC3 to PC4. The big difference between the hub and the switch is that the switch interpreted the electrical signal as an Ethernet frame and processed the frame to make a decision. (The details of Ethernet addressing and framing are coming up in the next two sections.) A hub simply repeats the electrical signal and makes no attempt to interpret the electrical signal (Layer 1) as a LAN frame (Layer 2). So, a hub actually performs OSI Layer 1 functions, repeating an electrical signal, whereas a switch performs OSI Layer 2 functions, actually interpreting Ethernet header information, particularly addresses, to make forwarding decisions.

Buffering also helps prevent collisions. Imagine that PC1 and PC3 both sent a frame to PC4 at the same time. The switch, knowing that forwarding both frames to PC4 would cause a collision, would buffer one frame until the first one has been completely sent to PC4.

Two features of switching bring a great deal of improved performance to Ethernet, as compared with hubs:

■ If only one device is cabled to each port of a switch, no collisions occur. If no collisions can occur, CSMA/CD can be disabled, solving the Ethernet performance problem.

■ Each switch port does not share the bandwidth, but it has its own separate bandwidth, meaning that a switch with a 10-Mbps ports has 10 Mbps of bandwidth *per port*.

So, LAN switching brings significant performance to Ethernet LANs. The next section covers another topic that effectively doubles Ethernet performance.

Eliminating Collisions to Allow Full-Duplex Ethernet

The original Ethernet specifications used a shared bus, over which only one frame could be sent at any point in time. So, a single device could not be sending a frame and receiving a frame at the same time because it would mean that a collision was occurring. So, devices simply chose not to send a frame while receiving a frame. That logic is called *half-duplex* logic.

Ethernet switches allow multiple frames to be sent over different ports at the same time. Additionally, if only one device is connected to a switch port, there is never a possibility that a collision could occur. So, LAN switches with only one device cabled to each port of the switch allow the use of *full-duplex* operation. Full duplex means that an Ethernet card can send and receive concurrently. Consider Figure 3-11, which shows the full-duplex circuitry used with a single PC cabled to a LAN switch.

Figure 3-11 *10BASE-T Full-Duplex Operation Using a Switch*

Full duplex allows the full speed—10 Mbps, in this example—to be used in both directions simultaneously. For this to work, the NIC must disable its loopback circuitry.

So far in this chapter, you have read about the basics of 12 years of Ethernet evolution. Table 3-4 summarizes some of the key points as they relate to what is covered in this initial section of the chapter.

Table 3-4 *Summary of Some Basic Ethernet Features*

Ethernet Environment	Description
10BASE2, 10BASE5	Single bus cabled serially between devices using coaxial cable. Neither is used much today.
10BASE-T with a Hub	One electrical bus shared among all devices creating a single collision domain, cabled in a star topology using twisted-pair cabling.
10BASE-T with a Switch	One electrical bus per switch port creating multiple collision domains, cabled in a star physical topology but a logical bus topology using twisted-pair cabling.
Half Duplex	Logic that requires a card to only send or receive at a single point in time. Used to avoid collisions.
Full Duplex	Logic that enables concurrent sending and receiving, allowed when one device is attached to a switch port, ensuring that no collisions can occur.

Ethernet Data-Link Protocols

One of the most significant strengths of the Ethernet family of protocols is that these protocols use the same small set of data-link protocols. For instance, Ethernet addressing works the same on all the variations of Ethernet, even back to 10BASE5. This section covers most of the details of the Ethernet data-link protocols.

Ethernet Addressing

Ethernet LAN addressing identifies either individual devices or groups of devices on a LAN. *Unicast* Ethernet addresses identify a single LAN card. Each address is 6 bytes long, is usually written in hexadecimal, and, in Cisco devices, typically is written with periods separating each set of four hex digits. For example, 0000.0C12.3456 is a valid Ethernet address. The term *unicast addresses*, or *individual addresses*, is used because it identifies an individual LAN interface card. (The term *unicast* was chosen mainly for contrast with the terms *broadcast*, *multicast*, and *group addresses*.)

Computers use these addresses to identify the sender and receiver of an Ethernet frame. For instance, imagine that Fred and Barney are on the same Ethernet, and Fred sends Barney a frame. Fred puts his own Ethernet MAC address in the Ethernet header as the source address and uses Barney's Ethernet MAC address as the destination. When Barney receives the frame, he notices that the destination address is his own address, so Barney processes the frame. If Barney receives a frame with some other device's unicast address in the destination address field, Barney simply does not process the frame.

The IEEE defines the format and assignment of LAN addresses. The IEEE requires globally unique unicast MAC addresses on all LAN interface cards. (IEEE calls them MAC addresses because the MAC protocols such as IEEE 802.3 define the addressing details.) To ensure a unique MAC address, the Ethernet card manufacturers encode the MAC address onto the card, usually in a ROM chip. The first half of the address identifies the manufacturer of the card. This code, which is assigned to each manufacturer by the IEEE, is called the *organizationally unique identifier (OUI)*. Each manufacturer assigns a MAC address with its own OUI as the first half of the address, with the second half of the address being assigned a number that this manufacturer has never used on another card.

Many terms can be used to describe unicast LAN addresses. Each LAN card comes with a *burned-in address (BIA)* that is burned into the ROM chip on the card. BIAs sometimes are called *universally administered addresses (UAAs)* because the IEEE universally (well, at least worldwide) administers address assignment. Regardless of whether the BIA is used or another address is configured, many people refer to unicast addresses as either LAN addresses, Ethernet addresses, or MAC addresses.

Group addresses identify more than one LAN interface card. The IEEE defines two general categories of group addresses for Ethernet:

■ **Broadcast addresses**—The most often used of IEEE group MAC addresses, the broadcast address, has a value of FFFF.FFFF.FFFF (hexadecimal notation). The broadcast address implies that all devices on the LAN should process the frame.

■ **Multicast addresses**—Multicast addresses are used to allow a subset of devices on a LAN to communicate. Some applications need to communicate with multiple other devices. By sending one frame, all the devices that care about receiving the data sent by that application can process the data, and the rest can ignore it. The IP protocol supports multicasting. When IP multicasts over an Ethernet, the multicast MAC addresses used by IP follow this format: 0100.5e*xx.xxxx*, where any value can be used in the last half of the addresses.

Table 3-5 summarizes most of the details about MAC addresses.

Table 3-5 *LAN MAC Address Terminology and Features*

LAN Addressing Terms and Features	Description
MAC	Media Access Control. 802.3 (Ethernet) and 802.5 (Token Ring) are the MAC sublayers of these two LAN data-link protocols.
Ethernet address, NIC address, LAN address, Token Ring address, card address	Other names often used instead of MAC address. These terms describe the 6-byte address of the LAN interface card.
Burned-in address	The 6-byte address assigned by the vendor making the card. It usually is burned into a ROM or EEPROM on the LAN card and begins with a 3-byte organizationally unique identifier (OUI) assigned by the IEEE.
Unicast address	Fancy term for a MAC that represents a single LAN interface.
Broadcast address	An address that means "all devices that reside on this LAN right now."
Multicast address	Not valid on Token Ring. On Ethernet, a multicast address implies some subset of all devices currently on the LAN.

Ethernet Framing

Framing defines how a string of binary numbers is interpreted. In other words, framing defines the meaning behind the bits that are transmitted across a network. The physical layer helps you get a string of bits from one device to another. When the receiving device gets the bits, how should they be interpreted? The term *framing* refers to the definition of the fields assumed to be in the data that is received. In other words, framing defines the meaning of the bits transmitted and received over a network.

For instance, you just read an example of Fred sending data to Barney over an Ethernet. Fred put Barney's Ethernet address in the Ethernet header so that Barney would know that the Ethernet frame was meant for Barney. The IEEE 802.3 standard defines the location of the destination address field inside the string of bits sent across the Ethernet. Figure 3-12 shows the details of several types of LAN frames.

Figure 3-12 *LAN Header Formats*

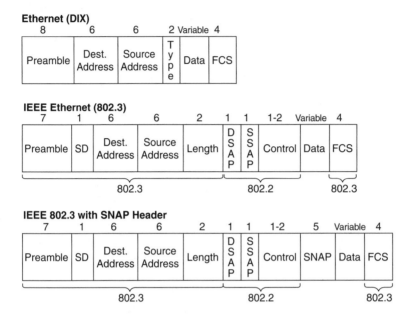

Every little field in these frames might not be interesting, but you should at least remember some details about the contents of the headers and trailers. In particular, the addresses and their location in the headers are important. Also, the names of the fields that identify the type of data inside the Ethernet frame—namely, the Type, DSAP, and SNAP fields—are important. Finally, the fact that a FCS exists in the trailer is also vital.

The IEEE 802.3 specification limits the data portion of the 802.3 frame to a maximum of 1500 bytes. The Data field was designed to hold Layer 3 packets; the term *maximum transmission unit (MTU)* defines the maximum Layer 3 packet that can be sent over a medium. Because the Layer 3 packet rests inside the data portion of an Ethernet frame, 1500 bytes is the largest IP packet allowed over an Ethernet.

Identifying the Data Inside an Ethernet Frame

Each data-link header has a field in its header with a code that defines the type of protocol header that follows. For example, in the first frame in Figure 3-13, the Destination Service Access Point (DSAP) field has a value of E0, which means that the next header is a Novell IPX header. Why is that? Well, when the IEEE created 802.2, it saw the need for a protocol type field that identified what was inside the field called "data" in an IEEE Ethernet frame.

Figure 3-13 *802.2 SAP and SNAP Type Fields*

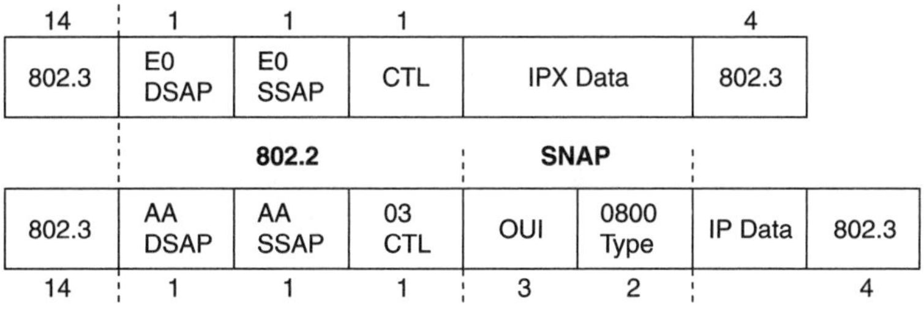

The IEEE called its Type field the destination service access point (DSAP). When the IEEE first created the 802.2 standard, anyone with a little cash could register favorite protocols with the IEEE and receive a reserved value with which to identify those favorite protocols in the DSAP field. For instance, Novell registered IPX and was assigned hex E0 by the IEEE. However, the IEEE did not plan for a large number of protocols—and it was wrong. As it turns out, the 1-byte-long DSAP field is not big enough to number all the protocols.

To accommodate more protocols, the IEEE allowed the use of an extra header, called a *Subnetwork Access Protocol (SNAP)* header. In the second frame of Figure 3-13, the DSAP field is AA, which implies that a *SNAP* header follows the 802.2 header, and the SNAP header includes a 2-byte protocol type field. The SNAP protocol type field is used for the same purpose as the DSAP field, but because it is 2 bytes long, all the possible protocols can be identified. For instance, in Figure 3-13, the SNAP type field has a value of 0800, signifying that the next header is an IP header. RFC 1700, "Assigned Numbers" (www.isi.edu/in-notes/rfc1700.txt), lists the SAP and SNAP Type field values and the protocol types that they imply.

Table 3-6 summarizes the fields that are used for identifying the types of data contained in a frame.

Table 3-6 *Protocol Type Fields in LAN Headers*

Field Name	Length	LAN Type
Ethernet Type	2 bytes	DIX Ethernet
802.2 DSAP and SSAP	1 byte each	IEEE Ethernet, IEEE Token Ring, ANSI FDDI
SNAP Protocol	2 bytes	IEEE Ethernet, IEEE Token Ring, ANSI FDDI

Some examples of values in the Ethernet Type and SNAP Protocol fields are 0800 for IP and 8137 for NetWare. Examples of IEEE SAP values are E0 for NetWare, 04 for SNA, and AA for SNAP. Interestingly, the IEEE does not have a reserved DSAP value for TCP/IP; SNAP headers must be used to support TCP/IP over IEEE Ethernet.

Layer 2 Ethernet Summary

As mentioned earlier in this chapter, physical layer protocols define how to deliver data across a physical medium. Data-link protocols make that physical network useful by defining how and when the physical network is used. Ethernet defines the OSI Layer 1 functions for Ethernet, including cabling, connectors, voltage levels, and cabling distance limitations, as well as many important OSI Layer 2 functions. In this section, four of these data link features were emphasized, as shown in Table 3-7.

Table 3-7 *OSI Layer 2 Feature Summary: Ethernet*

OSI Layer 2 Function	Ethernet Implementation
Arbitration	CSMA/CD algorithm
Addressing	6-byte-long MAC addresses
Error detection	FCS in Ethernet trailer
Identifying the type of packet inside the frame	Protocol Type (2 bytes)—DIX Ethernet DSAP (1 byte)—IEEE 802.2 SNAP Protocol Type (2 bytes)—IEEE 802.2 with SNAP header

Recent Ethernet Standards

In most networks today, you would not use 10BASE2 or 10BASE5—in fact, you probably might not have many 10BASE-T hubs still in your network. More recently created alternatives, such as Fast Ethernet and Gigabit Ethernet, provide faster Ethernet options at reasonable costs. Both have gained widespread acceptance in networks today, with Fast Ethernet most likely being used on the desktop and Gigabit Ethernet being used between networking devices or on servers. Additionally, 10 Gb provides yet another improvement in speed and performance and is covered briefly in Chapter 11.

Fast Ethernet

Fast Ethernet, as defined in IEEE 802.3u, retains many familiar features of 10-Mbps IEEE 802.3 Ethernet variants. The age-old CSMA/CD logic still exists, but it can be disabled for full-duplex point-to-point topologies in which no collisions can occur. The 802.3u specification calls for the use of the same old IEEE 802.3 MAC and 802.2 LLC framing for the LAN headers and trailers. A variety of cabling options is allowed—unshielded and shielded copper cabling as well as multimode and single-mode fiber. Both Fast Ethernet shared hubs and switches can be deployed.

Two of the key features of Fast Ethernet, as compared to 10-Mbps Ethernet, are higher bandwidth and autonegotiation. Fast Ethernet operates at 100 Mbps—enough said. The other key difference, autonegotiation, allows an Ethernet card or switch to negotiate dynamically to discover whether it should use either 10 or 100 Mbps. So, many Ethernet cards and switch ports are called 10/100 cards or ports today because they can autonegotiate the speed. The endpoints autonegotiate whether to use half duplex or full duplex as well. If autonegotiation fails, it settles for half-duplex operation at 10 Mbps.

The autonegotiation process has been known to fail. Cisco recommends that, for devices that seldom move, such as servers and switches, you should configure the LAN switch and the device to use the identical desired setting instead of depending on autonegotiation. Cisco recommends using autonegotiation for switch ports connected to end-user devices because these devices are moved frequently relative to servers or other network devices, such as routers.

Gigabit Ethernet

The IEEE defines Gigabit Ethernet in standards 802.3z for optical cabling and 802.3ab for electrical cabling. Like Fast Ethernet, Gigabit Ethernet retains many familiar features of slower Ethernet variants. CSMA/CD still is used and can be disabled for full-duplex support. The 802.3z and 802.3ab standards call for the use of the same old IEEE 802.3 MAC and 802.2 LLC framing for the LAN headers and trailers. The most likely place to use Gigabit is between switches, between switches and a router, and between a switch and a server.

Gigabit Ethernet is similar to its slower cousins in several ways. The most important similarity is that the same Ethernet headers and trailers are used, regardless of whether it's 10 Mbps, 100 Mbps, or 1000 Mbps. If you understand how Ethernet works for 10 and 100 Mbps, then you know most of what you need to know about Gigabit Ethernet.

Gigabit Ethernet differs from the slower Ethernet specifications in how it encodes the signals onto the cable. Gigabit Ethernet is obviously faster, at 1000 Mbps, or 1 Gbps.

Foundation Summary

The "Foundation Summary" section of each chapter lists the most important facts from the chapter. Although this section does not list every fact from the chapter that will be on your CCNA exam, a well-prepared CCNA candidate should know, at a minimum, all the details in each "Foundation Summary" section before going to take the exam.

Table 3-8 lists the various protocol specifications for the original three IEEE LAN standards.

Table 3-8 *MAC and LLC Details for Three Types of LANs*

Name	MAC Sublayer Spec	LLC Sublayer Spec
Ethernet Version 2 (DIX Ethernet)	Ethernet	—
IEEE Ethernet	IEEE 802.3	IEEE 802.2
IEEE Token Ring	IEEE 802.5	IEEE 802.2
ANSI FDDI	ANSI X3T9.5	IEEE 802.2

Figure 3-14 depicts the cabling and basic operation of an Ethernet network built with 10BASE-T cabling and an Ethernet hub.

Figure 3-14 *Small Ethernet 10BASE-T Network*

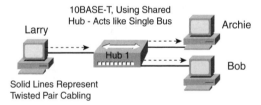

Figures 3-15 and 3-16 show Ethernet straight-through and crossover cabling.

Figure 3-15 *Straight-Through Ethernet Cable*

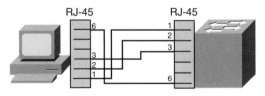

Figure 3-16 *Crossover Ethernet Cable*

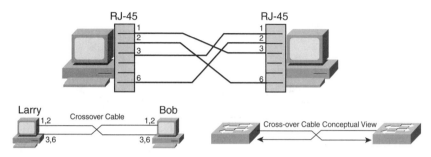

Full-duplex Ethernet cards can send and receive concurrently. Figure 3-17 shows the full-duplex circuitry used with a single PC cabled to a LAN switch.

Figure 3-17 *10BASE-T Full-Duplex Operation*

Table 3-9 summarizes some of the key points as they relate to what is covered in this initial section of the chapter.

Table 3-9 *Summary of Some Basic Ethernet Features*

Ethernet Environment	Description
10BASE2, 10BASE5	Single bus cabled serially between devices using coaxial cable.
10BASE-T with a Hub	One electrical bus shared among all devices creating a single collision domain, cabled in a star topology using twisted-pair cabling.
10BASE-T with a Switch	One electrical bus per switch port creating multiple collision domains, cabled in a star topology using twisted-pair cabling.
Half Duplex	Logic that requires a card to only send or receive at a single point in time. Used to avoid collisions.
Full Duplex	Logic that enables concurrent sending and receiving, allowed when one device is attached to a switch port, ensuring that no collisions can occur.

Figure 3-18 shows the details of several types of LAN frames.

Figure 3-18 *LAN Header Formats*

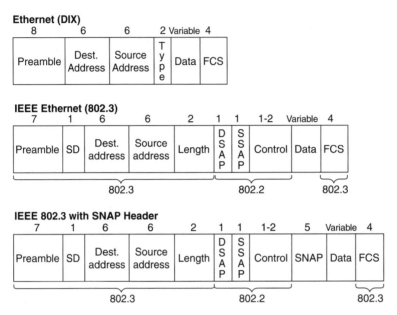

Table 3-10 summarizes the fields that are used for identifying the types of data contained in a frame.

Table 3-10 *Protocol Type Fields in LAN Headers*

Field Name	Length	LAN Type
Ethernet Type	2 bytes	Ethernet
802.2 DSAP and SSAP	1 byte each	IEEE Ethernet, IEEE Token Ring, ANSI FDDI
SNAP Protocol	2 bytes	IEEE Ethernet, IEEE Token Ring, ANSI FDDI

Ethernet also defines many important OSI Layer 2 functions. In this chapter, four of these features were emphasized, as shown in Table 3-11.

Table 3-11   *OSI Layer 2 Feature Summary: Ethernet*

OSI Layer 2 Function	Ethernet Implementation
Arbitration	CSMA/CD algorithm
Addressing	6-byte-long MAC addresses
Error detection	FCS in Ethernet trailer
Identifying the type of packet inside the frame	Protocol Type (2 bytes)—DIX Ethernet DSAP (1 byte)—IEEE 802.2 SNAP Protocol Type (2 bytes)—IEEE 802.2 with SNAP header

Q&A

As mentioned in the introduction, you have two choices for review questions. The questions that follow give you a bigger challenge than the exam itself by using an open-ended question format. By reviewing now with this more difficult question format, you can exercise your memory better and prove your conceptual and factual knowledge of this chapter. The answers to these questions are found in Appendix A.

For more practice with exam-like question formats, including questions using a router simulator and multiple-choice questions, use the exam engine on the CD.

1. What is the main purpose(s) of Layer 2?

2. What is the main purpose(s) of Layer 1?

3. What does MAC stand for?

4. Name three terms popularly used as a synonym for MAC address.

5. What portion of a MAC address encodes an identifier representing the manufacturer of the card?

6. Are MAC addresses defined by a Layer 2 or Layer 3 protocol?

7. How many bits are present in a MAC address?

8. Name the two main parts of a MAC address. Which part identifies which "group" this address is a member of?

9. What OSI layer typically encapsulates using both a header and a trailer?

10. If a Fast Ethernet NIC currently is receiving a frame, can it begin sending a frame?

11. What are the two key differences between a 10-Mbps NIC and a 10/100 NIC?

12. What is the distance limitation of a single cable for 10BASE-T? For 100 BASE-TX?

13. How fast is Fast Ethernet?

14. How many bytes long is a MAC address?

15. Define the difference between broadcast and multicast MAC addresses.

16. Explain the function of the loopback and collision-detection features of an Ethernet NIC in relation to half-duplex and full-duplex operations.

This chapter covers the following subjects:

- OSI Layer 1 for Point-to-Point WANs

- OSI Layer 2 for Point-to-Point WANs

- Packet-Switching Services

CHAPTER 4

Fundamentals of WANs

In the previous chapter, you learned more details about OSI Layers 1 and 2, and how Ethernet LANs perform the functions defined by the two lowest OSI layers. In this chapter, you will learn about how wide-area network (WAN) standards and protocols also implement OSI Layers 1 and 2. The OSI physical layer details are covered, along with two popular WAN data link layer protocols, High-Level Data Link Control (HDLC) and Frame Relay.

"Do I Know This Already?" Quiz

The purpose of the "Do I Know This Already?" quiz is to help you decide whether you really need to read the entire chapter. If you already intend to read the entire chapter, you do not necessarily need to answer these questions now.

The ten-question quiz, derived from the major sections in "Foundation Topics" portion of the chapter, helps you determine how to spend your limited study time.

Table 4-1 outlines the major topics discussed in this chapter and the "Do I Know This Already?" quiz questions that correspond to those topics.

Table 4-1   *"Do I Know This Already?" Foundation Topics Section-to-Question Mapping*

Foundations Topics Section	Questions Covered in This Section
OSI Layer 1 for Point-to-Point WANs	1–3, 6
OSI Layer 2 for Point-to-Point WANs	4, 5, 7
Packet-Switching Services	8–10

CAUTION   The goal of self-assessment is to gauge your mastery of the topics in this chapter. If you do not know the answer to a question or are only partially sure of the answer, you should mark this question wrong for purposes of the self-assessment. Giving yourself credit for an answer that you correctly guess skews your self-assessment results and might provide you with a false sense of security.

1. Which of the following best describes the main function of OSI Layer 1 protocols?

   a. Framing

   b. Delivery of bits from one device to another

   c. Addressing

   d. Local Management Interface (LMI)

   e. DLCI

2. Which of the following typically connects to a four-wire line provided by a telco?

   a. Router serial interface

   b. CSU/DSU

   c. Transceiver

   d. Switch serial interface

3. Which of the following typically connects to a V.35 or RS-232 end of a cable when cabling a leased line?

   a. Router serial interface

   b. CSU/DSU

   c. Transceiver

   d. Switch serial interface

4. Which of the following functions of OSI Layer 2 is specified by the protocol standard for PPP, but is implemented with a Cisco proprietary header field for HDLC?

   a. Framing

   b. Arbitration

   c. Addressing

   d. Error detection

   e. Identifying the type of protocol that is inside the frame

5. Which of the following WAN data link protocols on Cisco routers support multiple Layer 3 protocols by virtue of having some form of Protocol Type field?

   a. PPP

   b. HDLC

   c. LAPB

   d. LAPD

   e. SDLC

   f. None of the above

6. On a point-to-point WAN link between two routers, what device(s) are considered to be the DTE devices?

   a. The routers

   b. The CSU/DSUs

   c. The central office equipment

   d. A chip on the processor of each router

   e. None of the above

7. Imagine that Router1 has three point-to-point serial links, one link each to three remote routers. Which of the following is true about the required HDLC addressing at Router1?

   a. Router1 must use HDLC addresses 1, 2, and 3.

   b. Router1 must use any three unique addresses between 1 and 1023.

   c. Router1 must use any three unique addresses between 16 and 1000.

   d. Router1 must use three sequential unique addresses between 1 and 1023.

   e. None of the above.

8. What is the name of the Frame Relay field used to identify Frame Relay Virtual Circuits?

   a. Data-link connection identifier

   b. Data-link circuit identifier

   c. Data-link connection indicator

   d. Data-link circuit indicator

   e. None of the above

9. Which of the following is true about Frame Relay virtual circuits?

   a. Each VC requires a separate access link.

   b. Multiple VCs can share the same access link.

   c. All VCs sharing the same access link must connect to the same router on the other side of the VC.

   d. All VCs on the same access link must use the same DLCI.

10. Which of the following defines a SONET link speed around 155 Mbps?

   a. T1

   b. T3

   c. DS3

   d. DS155

   e. OC-3

   f. OC-12

   g. OC-48

   h. OC-155

The answers to the "Do I Know This Already?" quiz are found in Appendix A, "Answers to the 'Do I Know This Already?' Quizzes and Q&A Sections." The suggested choices for your next step are as follows:

■ **8 or less overall score**—Read the entire chapter. This includes the "Foundation Topics" and "Foundation Summary" sections and the Q&A section.

■ **9 or 10 overall score**—If you want more review on these topics, skip to the "Foundation Summary" section and then go to the Q&A section. Otherwise, move to the next chapter.

Foundation Topics

As you read in the previous chapter, the OSI physical and data link layers work together to deliver data across a wide variety of types of physical networks. LAN standards and protocols define how to network between devices that are relatively close together—hence the term *local* in the acronym *LAN*. WAN standards and protocols define how to network between devices that are relatively far apart—in some cases, even thousands of miles apart—hence the term *wide-area* in the acronym *WAN*.

LANs and WANs both implement the details of OSI Layers 1 and 2. Some details are different, but many of the concepts are the same. In this chapter, because you just finished reading about LANs, I will compare WANs to LANs whenever possible, to point out the similarities and differences.

In the *CCNA ICND Exam Certification Guide*, you will read more about the details of WANs, including the configuration details on Cisco routers.

OSI Layer 1 for Point-to-Point WANs

The OSI physical layer, or Layer 1, defines the details of how to move data from one device to another. In fact, many people think of OSI Layer 1 as "sending bits." Higher layers encapsulate the data, as described in Chapter 2, "The TCP/IP and OSI Networking Models." No matter what the other OSI layers do, eventually the sender of the data needs to actually transmit the bits to another device. The OSI physical layer defines the standards and protocols used to create the physical network and to send the bits across that network.

A point-to-point WAN link acts like a trunk between two Ethernet switches in many ways. For perspective, look at Figure 4-1, which shows a LAN with two buildings and two switches in each building.

As a brief review, remember that Ethernet uses a twisted pair of wires to transmit and another twisted pair to receive, to reduce electromagnetic interference. You typically use straight-through Ethernet cables between end user devices and the switches. For the trunk links between the switches, you use crossover cables because each switch transmits on the same pair, so the crossover cable connects one device's transmit pair to the other device's receive pair. The lower part of the figure reminds you of the basic idea behind a crossover cable.

Figure 4-1 *Example LAN, Two Buildings*

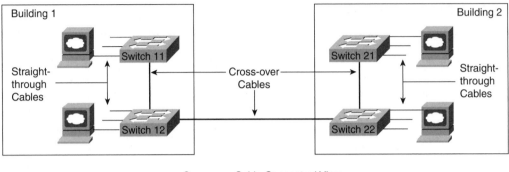

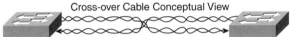

Now imagine that the buildings are 1000 miles apart instead of right next to each other. You are immediately faced with two problems:

■ Ethernet does not support any type of cabling that allows an individual trunk to run for 1000 miles.

■ Even if Ethernet supported a 1000-mile trunk, you do not have the rights of way needed to bury a cable over the 1000 miles of real estate between buildings.

The big distinction between LANs and WANs relates to how far apart the devices can be and still be capable of sending and receiving data. LANs tend to reside in a single building or possibly among buildings in a campus using optical cabling approved for Ethernet. WAN connections typically run longer distances than Ethernet, across town or between cities. Often, only one or a few companies even have the rights to run cables under the ground between the sites. So, the people who created WAN standards needed to use different physical specifications than Ethernet to send data 1000 km or more (WAN).

> **NOTE**   Besides LANs and WANs, the term *metropolitan-area network* (MAN) is sometimes used for networks that extend between buildings and through rights-of-ways. The term typically implies a network that does not reach as far as a WAN, generally in a single metropolitan area. The distinctions between LANs, MANs, and WANs are blurry—there is no set distance that means a link is a LAN, MAN, or WAN link.

To create such long links, or circuits, the actual physical cabling is owned, installed, and managed by a company that has the right of way to run cables under streets. Because a company that needs to send data over the WAN circuit does not actually own the cable or line, it is called a *leased line*. Companies that can provide leased WAN lines typically started life as the local telephone company, or telco. In many countries, the telco is still a government-regulated or government-controlled monopoly; these companies are sometimes called *public telephone and telegraph (PTT)* companies. Today many people use the generic term *service provider* to refer to a company that provides any form of WAN connectivity, including Internet services.

Point-to-point WAN links provide basic connectivity between two points. To get a point-to-point WAN link, you would work with a service provider to install a circuit. What the phone company or service provider gives you is similar to what you would have if you made a phone call between two sites but you never hung up. The two devices on either end of the WAN circuit could send and receive bits between each other any time they want, without needing to dial a phone number. And because the connection is always available, a point-to-point WAN connection sometimes is called a *leased circuit* or *leased line* because you have the exclusive right to use that circuit, as long as you keep paying for it.

Now back to the comparison of the LAN between two nearby buildings versus the two buildings that are 1000 miles apart. The physical details are different, but the same general functions need to be accomplished, as shown in Figure 4-2.

Figure 4-2 *Conceptual View of Point-to-Point Leased Line*

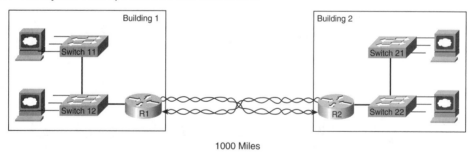

1000 Miles

Keep in mind that Figure 4-2 provides a conceptual view of a point-to-point WAN link. In concept, the telco installs a physical cable, with a transmit and a receive twisted pair, between the buildings. The cable has been connected to each router, and each router, in turn, has been connected to the LAN switches. As a result of this new physical WAN link and the logic used by the routers connected to it, data now can be transferred between the two sites. In practice, the telco does not actually run a cable between the two buildings. In the next section, you will learn more about the physical details of the WAN link.

NOTE   Ethernet switches have many different types of interfaces, but all the interfaces are some form of Ethernet. Routers provide the capability to connect many different types of OSI Layer 1 and 2 technologies. So, when you see a LAN connected to some other site using a WAN connection, you will see a router connected to each, as in Figure 4-2.

WAN Connections from the Customer Viewpoint

The concepts behind a point-to-point connection are simple. However, to fully understand what the service provider does to build his network to support your point-to-point line, you would need to spend lots of time studying and learning. However, most of what you need to know about WANs for the INTRO exam relates to how WAN connections are implemented between the telephone company and a customer site. Along the way, you will need to learn a little about the terminology used by the provider.

In Figure 4-2, you saw that a WAN leased line acts as if the telco gave you two twisted pairs of wires between the two sites on each end of the line. Well, it's not that simple. Of course, a lot more underlying technology must be used to create the circuit, and telcos use a lot of terminology that is different from LAN terminology. The telco seldom actually runs a 1000-mile cable for you between the two sites. Instead, it has built a large network already and even runs extra cables from the local central office (CO) to your building. (A CO is just a building where the telco locates the devices used to create its own network.) However the telco works out the details, what you receive is the equivalent of a four-wire leased circuit between two buildings.

Figure 4-3 introduces some of those key concepts and terms relating to WAN circuits.

Figure 4-3 *Point-to-Point Leased Line: Components and Terminology*

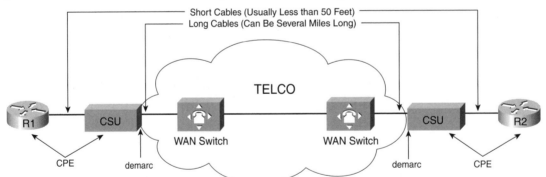

Typically, routers connect to a device called an external *channel service unit/data service unit (CSU/DSU)*. The router connects to the CSU/DSU with a relatively short cable, typically less than 50 feet, because the CSU/DSUs typically get placed in a rack near the router. The much longer four-wire cable from the telco plugs into the CSU/DSU. That cable leaves the building, running through the hidden (typically buried) cables that you always see phone company workers fixing by the side of the road. The other end of that cable ends up in something called a *central office (CO)*, which is simply a building where the phone company puts its equipment. The actual physical line terminates in a device generically called a *WAN switch*, of which there are many types.

The same general physical connectivity exists on each side of the point-to-point WAN link. In between the two COs, the service provider can build its network with several competing different types of technology, all of which is beyond the scope of either CCNA exam. However, the perspective in Figure 4-2 remains true—the two routers can send and receive data simultaneously across the point-to-point WAN link.

From a legal perspective, two different companies own the various components of the equipment and lines in Figure 4-3. For instance, the router cable and typically the CSU/DSU are owned by one company, and the wiring to the CO and the gear inside the CO are owned by the telco. So, the telco uses the term *demarc*, which is short for *demarcation point*, to refer to the point at which the telco's responsibility is on one side and the customer's responsibility is on the other. The demarc is not a separate device or cable, but instead a concept of where each company's responsibilities end.

In the United States, the demarc is typically where the telco physically terminates the set of two twisted pairs inside the customer building. Typically, the customer asks the telco to terminate the cable in a particular room, and most, if not all, the lines from the telco into that building terminate in the same room.

The term *customer premises equipment* (CPE) refers to devices that are at the customer site, from the telco's perspective. For instance, both the CSU/DSU and the router are CPE devices in this case.

The demarc does not always reside between the telco and all CPE. In some cases, the telco actually could own the CSU/DSU, and the demarc would be on the router side of the CSU/DSU. In some cases today, the telco even owns and manages the router at the customer site, again moving the point that would be considered the demarc. Regardless of where the demarc sits from a legal perspective, the term CPE still refers to the equipment at the telco customer's location.

WAN Cabling Standards

Cisco offers a large variety of different WAN interface cards for its routers, including synchronous and asynchronous serial interfaces. For any of the point-to-point serial links or Frame Relay links in this chapter, the router uses an interface that supports synchronous communication.

Synchronous serial interfaces in Cisco routers use a variety of proprietary physcial connector types, such as the 60-pin D-shell connector shown in Figure 4-4. The cable connecting the router to the CSU uses a connector that fits the router serial interface on the router side, and a standardized WAN connector type that matches the CSU/DSU interface on the CSU/DSU end of the cable. Figure 4-4 shows a typical connection, with some of the serial cabling options listed.

Figure 4-4 *Serial Cabling Options*

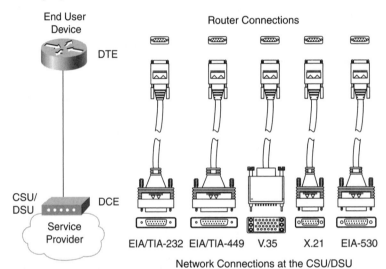

The engineer who deploys a network chooses the cable based on the connectors on the router and the CSU/DSU. Beyond that choice, engineers do not really need to think about how the cabling and pins work—they just work! Many of the pins are used for control functions, and a few are used for the transmission of data. Some pins are used for clocking, as described in the next section. Table 4-2 summarizes the variety of standards that define the types of connectors and physical signaling protocols used on WAN interfaces.

Table 4-2 *WAN Interface Cable Standards*

Standard Connectors (into CSU/DSU)	Standards Body	Number of Pins on the Connector
EIA/TIA-232	TIA	25
EIA/TIA-449	TIA	37
EIA/TIA-530	TIA	25
V.35	ITU	34
X.21	ITU	15

NOTE   The Telecommunications Industry Association (TIA) is accredited by the American National Standards Institute (ANSI) for the development of telecommunications standards. ANSI has the rights by U.S. federal law to represent the United States in work with international standards bodies, such as the International Telecommunication Union (ITU). For more information on these standards bodies, and for the opportunity to spend money to get copies of the standards, refer to the web sites www.tiaonline.org and www.itu.int.

These cables provide connectivity to the external DSU/CSU, as shown in Figure 4-4. The cable between the CSU/DSU and the telco CO typically uses an RJ-48 connector to connect to the CSU/DSU; the RJ-48 connector has the same size and shape as the RJ-45 connector used for Ethernet cables.

The cables and physical connector types each have differing limits on the speed of serial data transmission. Generally, the shorter the length of the cable is, the closer it can get to the maximum speed allowed for that cable and connector. From a practical perspective, this just means that you typically locate the CSU/DSU relatively close to the routers so that the cables can be kept short. Table 4-3 lists the speeds that can be used for certain cables and connectors, based on the lengths of the cables.

Table 4-3   *Maximum Speeds for Various Cables*

Data (bps)	Distance (Meters) EIA/TIA-232	Distance (Meters) EIA/TIA-449, V.35, X.21, EIA-530
2400	60	1250
4800	30	625
9600	15	312
19,200	15	156
38,400	15	78
115,200	3.7	—
T1 (1.544 Mbps)	—	15

Many Cisco routers support serial interfaces that have an integrated DSU/CSU. With an internal CSU/DSU, the router does not need a cable connecting it to the CSU/DSU because the CSU/DSU is internal to the router. The line from the telco is connected to a receptacle on the router, typically an RJ-48 receptacle, in the router serial interface card.

Clock Rates, DCE, and DTE

When a network engineer needs to add a point-to-point leased line between two routers, he contacts a service provider and orders the circuit. As part of that process, the customer specifies how fast the circuit should run, in kilobits per second (kbps). While the circuit is being set up by the telco, the engineer purchases two CSU/DSUs, installs one at each site, and configures each CSU/DSU. He also cables each router to the respective CSU/DSU using the cables shown in the previous section. Eventually, the telco installs the new line into the customer premises, and the line can be connected to the CSU/DSUs, as shown in Figure 4-3. (Note: In some countries, the telco owns the CSU/DSU, so it orders, installs, and configures the CSU/DSUs.)

The terms *clock rate* and *bandwidth* both refer to the speed of the circuit. You will also hear the speed referred to as the *link speed*. When you order a circuit that runs at a particular speed, the two CSU/DSUs are configured to operate at that same speed. The CSU/DSUs provide a clocking signal to the routers so that the routers simply react, sending and receiving data at the correct rate. So, the CSU/DSU is considered to be *clocking* the link.

A couple of other key WAN terms relate to the process of clocking. The device that provides clocking, typically the CSU, is considered to be the *data communications equipment (DCE)*. The device receiving clocking, typically the router, is referred to as *data terminal equipment (DTE)*.

On a practical note, when purchasing serial cables from Cisco, you can pick either a DTE or a DCE cable. You pick the type of cable based on whether the router is acting like a DTE or a DCE. If the router is a DTE, with the CSU providing the clocking, you need a DTE cable. If the router was clocking the CSU/DSU, which can be done, you would need a DCE cable—but that almost never happens.

However, DCE cables do have an important practical use. When building a lab to study for any of the Cisco exams, you do not need to buy DSU/CSUs. You can buy two routers, a DTE serial cable for one router, and a DCE serial cable for the other and connect the two cables together. The router with the DCE cable in it can be configured to provide clocking— meaning that you do not need a CSU/DSU. So, you can build a WAN in your home lab, saving hundreds of dollars by not buying CSU/DSUs. The DTE and DCE cables can be connected to each other and to the two routers. (The DCE cable has a female connector, and the DTE has a male connector, so they can be connected.) With one additional configuration command on one of the routers (the **clock rate** command), you have a point-to-point serial link. This type of connection between two routers sometimes is called a *back-to-back* serial connection.

Figure 4-5 shows the cabling for a back-to-back serial connection and also shows that the combined DCE/DTE cables reverse the transmit and receive pins, much like a crossover Ethernet cable allows two directly connected devices to communicate.

Figure 4-5 *Serial Cabling Uses a DTE and a DCE Cable*

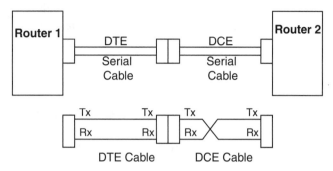

As you see in the figure, the DTE cable, the same cable that you typically use to connect to a CSU/DSU, does not swap the Tx and Rx pins. The DCE cable swaps transmit and receive, so the wiring with one router's Tx pin connected to the other router's Rx, and vice versa, remains intact.

Link Speeds Offered by Telcos

No matter what you call them—telcos, PTTs, service providers—these companies do not simply let you pick the exact speed of a WAN link. Instead, standards define how fast a point-to-point link can run.

For a long time, the telcos of the world made more money selling voice services. That is no longer the case for any of these companies in the United States, except for the companies that provide local residential telephone service. So, years ago, the telcos of the world developed a standard for sending voice using digital transmissions. Digital signaling inside their networks allowed for the growth of more profitable data services, such as leased lines. It also allowed better efficiencies, making the build-out of the expanding voice networks much less expensive.

The original standard for converting analog voice to a digital signal is called *pulse code modulation* (PCM). (There are alternatives, but for the exam, you should just be aware of PCM.) PCM defines that an incoming analog voice signal should be sampled 8000 times per second, and each sample should be represented by an 8-bit code. So, 64,000 bits were needed to represent 1 second of voice.

When the telcos of the world built their first digital networks, the baseline transmission speed was 64 kbps because that was the necessary bandwidth for a single voice call. The term *digital signal level 0 (DS0)* refers to the standard for a single 64-kbps line.

Later the telcos starting selling data services—in other words, leased lines. The phone companies could sell a DS0 service at 64 kbps. However, when it first came out, they typically offered 56-kbps service. Why? Well, it turned out that the telcos needed some bits for some management overhead. They found that if they used a bit inside the actual DS0 channel occasionally, the voice quality did not suffer, so they defined a standard in which a switch regularly could use one of every 8 bits in the DS0 channel for its own purposes. That worked fine for voice. But for data, having something else in the telco network change the bits that you sent does not work very well. At best, it can cause retransmissions; at worst, it doesn't work. So, the telco decided to just sell 7 of every 8 bits that could be sent over a DS0—and 7/8 of 64 kbps is 56 kbps. Today many telcos do not use that bit, so they can offer the full 64-kbps channel.

The telco offers specific increments of the DS0 channel. In the United States, the *digital signal level 1 (DS1)* standard defines a single line that supports 24 DS0s, plus an 8-kbps overhead channel, for a speed of 1.544 Mbps. (A DS1 is also called a T1 line.) It also defines a digital signal level 3 (DS3) service, also called a T3 line, which holds 28 DS1s. Other parts of the world use different standards, with Europe and Japan using standards that hold 32 DS0s; this type of line often is called an E1.

Table 4-4 lists some of the standards for WAN speeds. Included in the table are the type of line, plus the type of signaling (for example, DS1). The signaling specifications define the electrical signals that encode a binary 1 or 0 on the line. You should be aware of the general idea, and remember the key terms for T1 and E1 lines in particular, for the INTRO exam.

Table 4-4 *WAN Speed Summary*

Type of Line	Name of Signalling Type	Bit Rate
56	DS0*	56 kbps
64	DS0	64 kbps
T1	DS1	1.544 Mbps (24 DS0s, plus 8 kbps overhead
T3	DS3	44.736 Mbps (28 DS1s, plus management overhead)
E1	ZM	2.048 Mbps (32 DS0s)
E3	M3	34.064 Mbps (16 E1s, plus management overhead)
J1	Y1	2.048 Mbps (32 DS0s; Japanese standard)

*DS0, with 1 robbed bit out of 8

Later in the chapter, the text explains the Synchronous Optical Network (SONET) standards, which include yet another range of types of WAN lines and speeds.

OSI Layer 2 for Point-to-Point WANs

WAN protocols used on point-to-point serial links provide the basic function of data delivery across that one link. The two most popular data-link protocols used on point-to-point links are High-Level Data Link Control (HDLC) and Point-to-Point Protocol (PPP). You should also remember the names of some other serial data-link protocols.

HDLC

HDLC performs OSI Layer 2 functions, so a brief review of the OSI Layer 2 functions covered in Chapter 3, "Data Link Fundamentals: Ethernet LANs," will be helpful:

- **Arbitration**—Determines when it is appropriate to use the physical medium

- **Addressing**—Ensures that the correct recipient(s) receives and processes the data that is sent

- **Error detection**—Determines whether the data made the trip across the physical medium successfully

- **Identifying the encapsulated data**—Determines the type of header that follows the data-link header

HDLC is very simple as compared with Ethernet. For instance, with Ethernet, the CSMA/CD algorithm arbitrates which device gets to send a frame next and how to recover when frames collide. In a point-to-point serial link, each router can send over the four-wire (two-pair) circuit at any time, so there is no need for any kind of arbitration.

HDLC defines framing that includes an address field, a frame check sequence (FCS) field, and a protocol type field. These three fields in the HDLC frame help provide the other three functions of the data link layer. Figure 4-6 outlines the framing.

Figure 4-6   *HDLC Framing*

HDLC defines a 1-byte address field, although on point-to-point links, it is not really needed. Having an address field in HDLC is sort of like when I have lunch with my friend Gary, and only Gary. I don't need to start every sentence with "Hey Gary…"—he knows I'm talking to him. On point-to-point WAN links, the router on one end of the link knows that there is only one possible recipient of the data —the router on the other end of the link—so the address does not really matter.

Historically, HDLC includes an address field because, in years past, the telco would sell you a multidrop circuit. With a multidrop circuit, one central site device could send and receive frames with multiple remote sites. HDLC defined the address field to identify the different remote sites on a multidrop link. Because routers use HDLC only for point-to-point links, the address field really is not needed to identify the other router. However, because the address field still is defined by HDLC, it is included in the header by routers. By the way, routers put the decimal value of 3 in the address field.

HDLC performs error detection just like Ethernet—it uses an FCS field in the HDLC trailer. And just like Ethernet, if a received frame has errors in it, the frame is discarded, with no error recovery performed by HDLC.

HDLC performs the function of identifying the encapsulated data just like Ethernet as well. When a router receives an HDLC frame, it wants to know what type of packet is held inside the frame. Cisco's implementation of HDLC includes a *Protocol Type* field, as seen in Figure 4-6, that identifies the type of packet inside the frame. Cisco uses the same values in its 2-byte HDLC Protocol Type field as it does in the Ethernet Protocol Type field.

The original HDLC standards did not include a Protocol Type field, so Cisco added one; by adding something to the HDLC header, Cisco made its version of HDLC proprietary. So, Cisco's HDLC will not work when connecting a Cisco router to another vendor's router. Figure 4-6 does not show the Cisco proprietary protocol type field; it sits between the control field and the data field in the frame.

HDLC is very simple. There simply is not a lot of work for the point-to-point data link protocols to perform.

Point-to-Point Protocol

The International Telecommunications Union (ITU), then known as the Consultative Committee for International Telecommunications Technologies (CCITT), first defined HDLC. Later, the Internet Engineering Task Force (IETF) saw the need for another data-link protocol for use between routers over a point-to-point link. In RFC 1661, the IETF created the Point-to-Point Protocol (PPP).

Comparing the basics, PPP behaves exactly like HDLC. The framing looks identical. There is an address field, but the addressing does not matter. PPP does discard errored frames that do not pass the FCS check. And PPP uses a 2-byte Protocol Type field—although PPP's Protocol Type field is defined by the protocol, as opposed to being a Cisco proprietary feature added later.

PPP was defined much later than the original HDLC specifications. As a result, the creators of PPP included many additional features that had not been seen in WAN data-link protocols up to that time. As a result, PPP has become the most popular and feature-rich of WAN data link layer protocols.

PPP-unique features fall into two main categories:

■ Those needed regardless of the Layer 3 protocol sent across the link

■ Those specific to each Layer 3 protocol

So, the PPP specifications actually include several different protocols. One protocol, the PPP Link Control Protocol (LCP), focuses on the features that apply regardless of the Layer 3 protocol used. LCP performs most of its work when the line comes up, so it has a lot more work to do with dialed links, which come up and down a lot, versus leased lines, which hopefully seldom fail.

PPP also defines several control protocols (CPs), which are used for any special purposes for a particular Layer 3 protocol. For instance, the IP Control Protocol (IPCP) provides for IP address assignment over a PPP link. When a user dials a new connection to an ISP using a modem, PPP typically is used, with IPCP assigning an IP address to the remote PC.

Each link that uses PPP has one LCP per link and one CP for each Layer 3 protocol defined on the link. If a router is configured for IPX, AppleTalk, and IP on a PPP serial link, the router configured for PPP encapsulation automatically tries to bring up the appropriate control protocols for each Layer 3 protocol.

LCP provides a variety of optional features for PPP besides just managing the link. You should at least be aware of the concepts behind these features, as summarized in Table 4-5.

Table 4-5 *PPP LCP Features*

Function	LCP Feature	Description
Error detection	Link quality monitoring (LQM)	PPP can take down a link based on the percentage of errors on the link using LQM.
Looped link detection	Magic number	The telco might reflect the data that a router sends it back to the router, to test a circuit. PPP uses a feature called magic numbers to detect a looped link and takes down the link.
Multilink support	Multilink PPP	This allows multiple parallel serial links to be connected between the same two routers, balancing traffic across the links.
Authentication	PAP and CHAP	Particularly useful for dial-up links, PPP initiates an authentication process to verify the identity of the device on the other end of the serial link.

Other Point-to-Point WAN Data-Link Protocols

WAN data-link protocols can be compared relative to two main attributes. First, some protocols do support multiprotocol traffic by virtue of having a defined protocol type field. Also, some protocols actually perform error recovery—so when the receiving end notices that the received frame did not pass the FCS check, it causes the frame to be resent. Protocols that were developed more recently tend to have a protocol type field and do not perform error recovery. Instead, they expect a higher-layer protocol to perform recovery. Table 4-6 lists the protocols, with comments about each.

Table 4-6 *List of WAN Data-Link Protocols*

Protocol	Error Correction?	Type Field?	Other Attributes
Synchronous Data Link Control (SDLC)	Yes	No	SDLC supports multipoint links. It assumes that an SNA header occurs after the SDLC header.
Link Access Procedure Balanced (LAPB)	Yes	No*	LAPB is used mainly with X.25.
Link Access Procedure on the D Channel (LAPD)	No	No	LAPD is used by ISDN lines for signaling to set up and bring down circuits.
Link Access Procedure for Frame Mode Bearer Services(LAPF)	No	Yes	This is a data-link protocol used over Frame Relay links.
High-Level Data Link Control (HDLC)	No	No*	HDLC serves as Cisco's default on serial links.
Point-to-Point Protocol (PPP)	Supported but not enabled by default	Yes	PPP was meant for multiprotocol interoperability from its inception, unlike all the others.

*Cisco's implementation of LAPB and HDLC includes a proprietary Protocol Type field.

Synchronization

One additional feature of HDLC and PPP not mentioned so far is that they are both synchronous. *Synchronous* simply means that there is an imposed time ordering at the link's sending and receiving ends. Essentially, the sides agree to a certain speed, but it is expensive to build devices that truly can operate at exactly the same speed. So, the devices operate at close to the same speed and listen to the speed of the other device on the other side of the link. One side makes small adjustments in its rate to match the other side.

Synchronization occurs by having one CSU (the slave) adjust its clock to match the clock rate of the other CSU (the master). The process works almost like the scenes in spy novels in which the spies synchronize their watches; in this case, the watches or clocks are synchronized automatically several times per second.

Point-to-Point WAN Summary

Point-to-point WAN leased lines and their associated data-link protocols use another set of terms and concepts beyond those covered for LANs. Table 4-7 lists the terms.

Table 4-7 *WAN Terminology*

Term	Definition
Synchronous	The imposition of time ordering on a bit stream. Practically, a device tries to use the same speed as another device on the other end of a serial link. However, by examining transitions between voltage states on the link, the device can notice slight variations in the speed on each end and can adjust its speed accordingly.
Asynchronous	The lack of an imposed time ordering on a bit stream. Practically, both sides agree to the same speed, but there is no check or adjustment of the rates if they are slightly different. However, because only 1 byte per transfer is sent, slight differences in clock speed are not an issue. A start bit is used to signal the beginning of a byte.
Clock source	The device to which the other devices on the link adjust their speed when using synchronous links.
DSU/CSU	Data service unit/channel service unit. Used on digital links as an interface to the telephone company in the United States. Routers typically use a short cable from a serial interface to a DSU/CSU, which is attached to the line from the telco with a similar configuration at the other router on the other end of the link.
Telco	Telephone company.
Four-wire circuit	A line from the telco with four wires, comprised of two twisted-pair wires. Each pair is used to send in one direction, so a four-wire circuit allows full-duplex communication.
T1	A line from the telco that allows transmission of data at 1.544 Mbps.
E1	Similar to a T1, but used in Europe. It uses a rate of 2.048 Mbps and 32 64-kbps channels.

Packet-Switching Services

So far, this chapter has covered technologies related to a permanent point-to-point leased line. Service providers also offer services that can be categorized as *packet-switching services*. In a packet-switched service, physical WAN connectivity exists, similar to a leased line. However, the devices connected to a packet-switched service can communicate directly with each other, using a single connection to the service.

Two types of packet-switching service are very popular today—Frame Relay and ATM. Both are covered in this chapter. At the end of the chapter, a summary section compares these types of networks with other types of WAN connectivity.

Frame Relay

Point-to-point WANs can be used to connect a pair of routers at multiple remote sites. However, an alternative WAN service, Frame Relay, has many advantages over point-to-point links, particularly when you connect many sites via a WAN. To introduce you to Frame Relay, I focus on a few of the key benefits compared to leased lines. One of the benefits is seen easily by considering Figures 4-7.

Figure 4-7 *Two Leased Lines to Two Branch Offices*

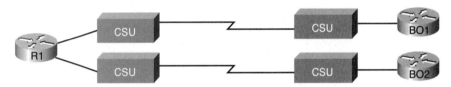

In Figure 4-7, a main site is connected to two branch offices, labeled BO1 and BO2. The main site router, R1, requires two serial interfaces and two separate CSUs. But what happens when the company grows to 10 sites? Or 100 sites? Or 500 sites? For each point-to-point line, R1 needs a separate physical serial interface and a separate CSU/DSU. As you can imagine, growth to hundreds of sites will take many routers, with many interfaces each and lots of rack space for the routers and CSU/DSUs.

Now imagine that the phone company salesperson talks to you when you have two leased lines, or circuits, installed as in Figure 4-7: "You know, we can install Frame Relay instead. You will need only one serial interface on R1 and one CSU/DSU. To scale to 100 sites, you might need two or three more serial interaces on R1 for more bandwidth, but that's it. And by the way, because your leased lines run at 128 kbps today, we'll guarantee that you can send and receive that much to and from each site. We will upgrade the line at R1 to T1 speed (1.544 Mbps). When you have more traffic than 128 kbps to a site, go ahead and send it! If we've got capacity, we'll forward it, with no extra charge. And by the way, did I tell you that it's cheaper than leased lines anyway?"

You consider the facts for a moment: Frame Relay is cheaper, it's at least as fast (probably faster) than what you have now, and it allows you to save money when you grow. So, you quickly sign the contract with the Frame Relay provider, before the salesman can change his mind, and migrate to Frame Relay. Does this story seem a bit ridiculous? Sure. But Frame Relay does compare very favorably with leased lines in a network with many remote sites. In the next few pages, you will see how Frame Relay works and realize how Frame Relay can provide functions claimed by the fictitous salesman.

Frame Relay Basics

Frame Relay networks provide more features and benefits than simple point-to-point WAN links, but to do that, Frame Relay protocols are more detailed. Frame Relay networks are multiaccess networks, which means that more than two devices can attach to the network, similar to LANs. To support more than two devices, the protocols must be a little more detailed.

Figure 4-8 introduces some basic connectivity concepts for Frame Relay.

Figure 4-8 *Frame Relay Components*

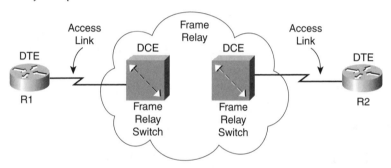

Figure 4-8 reflects the fact that Frame Relay uses the same Layer 1 features as a point-to-point leased line. For a Frame Relay services, a leased line is installed between each router and a nearby Frame Relay switch; these links are called *access links*. The access links run the same speeds and use the same signaling standards as do point-to-point leased lines. However, instead of extending from one router to the other, each leased line runs from one router to a Frame Relay switch.

The difference between Frame Relay and point-to-point links is that the equipment in the telco actually examines the data frames sent by the router. Each frame header holds an address field called a data-link connection identifier (DLCI). The WAN switch forwards the frame, based on the DLCI, through the provider's network until it gets to the router on the other side of the network.

Because the equipment in the telco can forward one frame to one remote site and another frame to another remote site, Frame Relay is considered to be a form of *packet switching*. However, Frame Relay protocols most closely resemble OSI Layer 2 protocols; the term usually used for the bits sent by a Layer 2 device is *frame*. So, Frame Relay is also called a *frame-switching service*.

The terms *DCE* and *DTE* actually have a second set of meanings in the context of any packet-switching or frame-switching service. With Frame Relay, the Frame Relay switches are called DCE, and the customer equipment—routers, in this case—are called DTE. In this case, *DCE* refers to the device providing the service, and the term *DTE* refers to the device needing the frame-switching service. At the same time, the CSU/DSU provides clocking to the router, so from a Layer 1 perspective, the CSU/DSU is still the DCE and the router is still the DTE. It's just two different uses of the same terms.

Figure 4-8 depicts the physical and logical connectivity at each connection to the Frame Relay network. In contrast, Figure 4-9 shows the end-to-end connectivity associated with a *virtual circuit*.

Figure 4-9   *Frame Relay PVC Concepts*

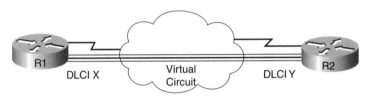

The logical path between each pair of routers is called a Frame Relay *virtual circuit (VC)*. In Figure 4-9, a single VC is represented by the trio of parallel lines. Typically, the service provider preconfigures all the required details of a VC; these VCs are called *permanent virtual circuits (PVCs)*. When R1 needs to forward a packet to R2, it encapsulates the Layer 3 packet into a Frame Relay header and trailer and then sends the frame. R1 uses a Frame Relay address called a DLCI in the Frame Relay header. This allows the switches to deliver the frame to R2, ignoring the details of the Layer 3 packet and caring to look at only the Frame Relay header and trailer. Just like on a point-to-point serial link, when the service provider forwards the frame over a physical circuit between R1 and R2, with Frame Relay, the provider forwards the frame over a logical virtual circuit from R1 to R2.

Frame Relay provides significant advantages over simply using point-to-point leased lines. The primary advantage has to do with virtual circuits. Consider Figure 4-10 with Frame Relay instead of three point-to-point leased lines.

Frame Relay creates a logical path between two Frame Relay DTEs. That logical path is called a VC, which describes the concept well. A VC acts like a point-to-point circuit, but physically it is not, so it's virtual. For example, R1 terminates two VCs—one whose other endpoint is R2 and one whose other endpoint is R3. R1 can send traffic directly to either of the other two routers by sending it over the appropriate VC, although R1 has only one physical access link to the Frame Relay network.

Figure 4-10   *Typical Frame Relay Network with Three Sites*

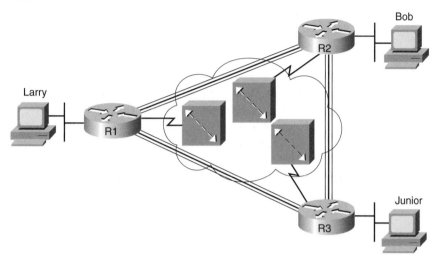

VCs share the access link and the Frame Relay network. For example, both VCs terminating at R1 use the same access link. So, with large networks with many WAN sites that need to connect to a central location, only one physical access link is required from the main site router to the Frame Relay network. If point-to-point links were used, a physical circuit, a separate CSU/DSU, and a separate physical interface on the router would be required for each point-to-point link. So, Frame Relay enables you to expand the WAN but add less hardware to do so.

Many customers of a single Frame Relay service provider share that provider's Frame Relay network. Originally, people with leased-line networks were reluctant to migrate to Frame Relay because they would be competing with other customers for the provider's capacity inside the cloud. To address these fears, Frame Relay is designed with the concept of a *committed information rate* (*CIR*). Each VC has a CIR, which is a guarantee by the provider that a particular VC gets at least that much bandwidth. You can think of CIR of a VC like the bandwidth or clock rate of a point-to-point circuit, except that it's the minimum value—you can actually send more, in most cases.

It's interesting that, even in this three-site network, it's probably less expensive to use Frame Relay than to use point-to-point links. Now imagine an organization with a hundred sites that needs any-to-any connectivity. How many leased lines are required? 4950! Besides that, you would need 99 serial interfaces per router. Or, you could have 100 access links to local Frame Relay switches—1 per router—and have 4950 VCs running over them. Also, you would need only one serial interface on each router. As a result, the Frame Relay topology is easier for the service provider to implement, costs the provider less, and makes better use of the core of the provider's network. As you would expect, that makes it less expensive to the Frame Relay customer as well. For connecting many WAN sites, Frame Relay is simply more cost-effective than leased lines.

ATM and SONET

Asynchronous Transfer Mode (ATM) and Synchronous Optical Network (SONET) together provide the capability for a telco to provide high-speed services for both voice and data over the same network. SONET defines a method for transmitting digital data at high speeds over optical cabling, and ATM defines how to frame the traffic, how to address the traffic so that DTE devices can communicate, and how to provide error detection. In short, SONET provides Layer 1 features, and ATM provides Layer 2 features over SONET. This short section introduces you to the basic concepts.

SONET

Synchronous Optical Network (SONET) defines an alternative Layer 1 signaling and encoding mechanism, as compared with the line types listed in Table 4-4. The motivation behind SONET was to allow the phone companies of the world to connect their COs with high-speed optical links. SONET provides the Layer 1 details of how to pass high-speed data over optical links.

Optical cabling has fiberglass in the middle, with a light signal being sent over the fiberglass. Optical cabling is more expensive than copper wire cables, and the devices that generate the light that crosses the cables are also more expensive—but they allow very high speeds.

During the same time frame of the development of SONET, the telcos of the world wanted a new protocol to support data and voice over the same core infrastructure. SONET was built to provide the Layer 1 high-speed links, and ATM was created to provide the capability to mix the voice and data. Both voice and data traffic could be broken into cells; by using small ATM cells, the delay-sensitive voice traffic could be interleaved with the data traffic, without letting any congestion caused by the bursty nature of data get in the way of high-quality voice.

Outside the United States, the term *Synchronous Digital Hierarchy* (*SDH*) represents the same standards as SONET. Also, the term *optical carrier* (*OC*) represents the prefix in the names for SONET links that use a variety of different link speeds. Table 4-8 lists the different speeds supported by SONET.

Table 4-8 *SONET Link Speeds*

Optical Carrier	Speed*
OC-1	52 Mbps
OC-3	155 Mbps
OC-12	622 Mbps
OC-48	2.4 Gbps
OC-192	9.6 Gbps
OC-768	40 Gbps

*Speeds rounded to commonly used values

ATM

Asynchronous Transfer Mode (ATM) provides data link layer services that run over SONET Layer 1 links. ATM has a wide variety of applications, but its use as a WAN technology has many similarities to Frame Relay. When using ATM, routers connect to an ATM service via an access link to an ATM switch inside the service providers network. For multiple sites, each router would need a single access link to the ATM network, with a VC between sites as needed. ATM can use use permanent VCs (PVCs) like Frame Relay. In fact, the basic concepts between Frame Relay and ATM are identical.

Of course, there are differences between Frame Relay and ATM—otherwise, you wouldn't need both! First, ATM relies on SONET for Layer 1 features instead of the traditional twisted-pair specifications such as T1 and DS0. The other big difference is that ATM does not forward frames—it forwards *cells*. Just like packets and frames refer to a string of bits that are sent over some network, cells are a string of bits sent over a network. Packets and frames can vary in size, but ATM cells are always a fixed 53-bytes in length.

ATM cells contain 48 bytes of payload and a 5-byte header. The header contains two fields that together act like the DLCI for Frame Relay by identifying each VC. The two fields are named *Virtual Path Identifier (VPI)* and *Virtual Channel Identifier (VCI)*. Just like Frame Relay switches forward frames based on the DLCI, devices called ATM switches, resident in the service provider network, forward cells based on the VPI/VCI pair.

The users of a network typically connect using Ethernet, and Ethernet devices do not create cells. So, how do you get traffic off an Ethernet onto an ATM network? When a router receives a packet and decides to forward the packet over the ATM network, the router creates the cells. The creation process involves breaking up a data link layer frame into 48-byte-long segments. Each segment is placed in a cell along with the 5-byte header. Figure 4-11 shows the general idea, as performed on R2.

Figure 4-11 *ATM Segmentation and Reassembly*

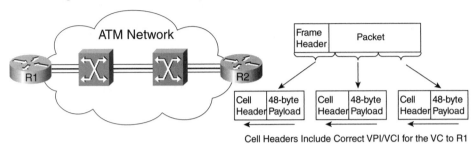

As you will read more about in Chapter 5, "Fundamentals of IP," routers forward IP packets, but they must add a data-link header and trailer to the packet before sending it. R2 takes the packet, adds a data-link header appropriate for ATM, and then also segments the frame into cells before sending any data. R2 takes the first 48 bytes of the frame and puts them in the payload field of a new cell. Next, it takes the next 48 bytes and puts them in another cell, and so on. The cell header includes the correct VPI/VCI pair so that the ATM switches in the ATM network know to forward the cells to R1.

R1 actually reverses the segmenation process after receiving all the cells—a process called *reassembly.* The entire concept of segmenting a frame into cells, and reassmebling them, is called *segmentation and reassembly (SAR).*

Cisco routers use specicalized ATM interfaces to support ATM. The ATM cards include special hardware to perform the SAR function quickly. They also often include specical hardware to support SONET.

Because of its similar function to Frame Relay, ATM also is considered to be a type of packet-switching service. However, because it uses fixed-length cells, it more often is called a *cell-switching* service.

WAN Terminology Related to Packet Switching

You have already read about how both Frame Relay and ATM are considered to be *packet-switching* services but how, more often, Frame Relay is called a *frame-switching* service and ATM is called a *cell-switching* service. Table 4-9 lists the key terms about WANs, plus a few related terms and a brief explanation.

Table 4-9 *Terms Describing Types of WAN Connections*

Dedicated Circuit	Another Term for a Leased Point-to-Point Line
Packet switching	Service in which each DTE device connects to a telco using a single physical line, with the possibility of being able to forward traffic to all other sites. The telco switch makes the forwarding decision based on an address in the packet header.
Frame switching	In concept, it is identical to packet switching. However, when the protocols match OSI Layer 2 more than any other layer, it is called frame switching. Frame Relay is a frame-switching technology.
Cell switching	In concept, it is identical to packet switching. However, because ATM DTEs break frames into small, fixed-length cells, these services are also called cell switching. ATM is a cell-switching technology.
Circuit switching	A circuit is a point-to-point link between only two sites, much like a leased line. However, circuit switching refers to the process of dialing, setting up a circuit, and then hanging up—in other words, the circuit is switched on and off. Dialed lines using modems and ISDN, as covered in Chapter 15, are examples of circuit switching.

*Speeds rounded to commonly used values

Foundation Summary

The "Foundation Summary" section of each chapter lists the most important facts from the chapter. Although this section does not list every fact from the chapter that will be on your CCNA exam, a well-prepared CCNA candidate should know, at a minimum, all the details in each "Foundation Summary" section before going to take the exam.

Figure 4-12 depicts some of those key concepts and terms used with point-to-point WAN leased lines.

Figure 4-12   *Point-to-Point Leased Line—Components and Terminology*

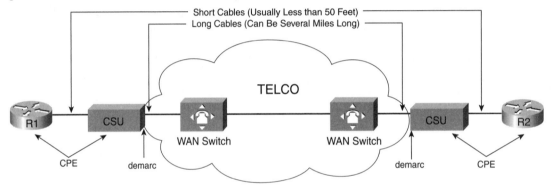

Table 4-10 lists some of the standards for WAN speeds.

Table 4-10   *WAN Speed Summary*

Type of Line	Name of Signaling Type	Bit Rate
56	DS0*	56 kbps
64	DS0	64 kbps
T1	DS1	1.544 Mbps (24 DS0s, plus 8-kbps overhead
T3	DS3	44.736 Mbps (28 DS1s, plus management overhead)
E1	ZM	2.048 Mbps (32 DS0s)
E3	M3	34.064 Mbps (16 E1s, plus management overhead)
J1	Y1	2.048 Mbps (32 DS0s; Japanese standard)

*DS0, with 1 robbed bit out of 8

Table 4-11 lists the WAN data-link protocols, with comments about each.

Table 4-11   *List of WAN Data-Link Protocols*

Protocol	Error Correction?	Type Field?	Other Attributes
Synchronous Data Link Control (SDLC)	Yes	No	SDLC supports multipoint links. It assumes that the SNA header occurs after the SDLC header.
Link Access Procedure Balanced (LAPB)	Yes	No	LAPB is used mainly with X.25.
Link Access Procedure on the D Channel (LAPD)	No	No	LAPD is used by ISDN lines for signaling to set up and bring down circuits.
Link Access Procedurefor Frame Mode Bearer Services (LAPF)	No	Yes	This is a data-link protocol used over Frame Relay links.
High-Level Data Link Control (HDLC)	No	No	HDLC serves as Cisco's default on serial links.
Point-to-Point Protocol (PPP)	Supported but not enabled by default	Yes	PPP was meant for multiprotocol interoperability from its inception, unlike all the others.

Figure 4-13 depicts some of the terms and ideas related to basic Frame Relay.

Figure 4-13   *Frame Relay Components*

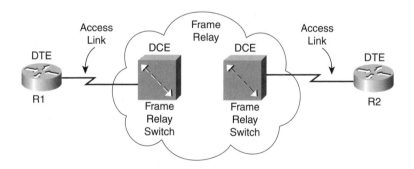

Q&A

As mentioned in the introduction, you have two choices for review questions. The questions that follow give you a bigger challenge than the exam itself by using an open-ended question format. By reviewing now with this more difficult question format, you can exercise your memory better and prove your conceptual and factual knowledge of this chapter. The answers to these questions are found in Appendix A.

For more practice with exam-like question formats, including questions using a router simulator and multiple-choice questions, use the exam engine on the CD.

1. Are DLCI addresses defined by a Layer 2 or Layer 3 protocol?

2. What OSI layer typically encapsulates using both a header and a trailer?

3. Define the terms *DCE* and *DTE* in the context of the physical layer and a point-to-point serial link.

4. Which layer or layers of OSI are most closely related to the functions of Frame Relay? Why?

5. What is the name of the field that identifies, or addresses, a Frame Relay virtual circuit?

6. True or False: "A leased line between two routers provides a constant amount of bandwidth—never more and never less." Defend your answer.

7. True or False: "Frame Relay VCs provide a constant amount of bandwidth between two devices, typically routers—never more and never less." Defend your answer.

8. Explain how many DS0 channels fit into a T1, and why the total does not add up to the purported speed of a T1, which is 1.544 Mbps.

9. Define the term synchronous.

10. Imagine a drawing with two routers, each connected to an external CSU/DSU, which each is connected with a four-wire circuit, as seen in this chapter. Describe the role of the devices in relation to clocking and synchronization.

11. Imagine a drawing with two routers, each connected to an external CSU/DSU, which each is connected with a four-wire circuit, as seen in this chapter. List the words behind the acronyms DTE and DCE, and describe which devices in this imagined network are DTE and which are DCE.

12. Imagine a drawing with two routers, each connected to a Frame Relay switch over a local access link. Describe which devices in this imagined network are Frame Relay DTEs and which are Frame Relay DCEs.

13. Do HDLC and PPP, as implemented by Cisco routers, support protocol type fields and error detection? Explain your answer.

14. Imagine a point-to-point leased line between two routers, with PPP in use. What are the names of the protocols inside PPP that would be used on this link? What are their main functions?

15. What are some of the main similarities between Frame Relay and ATM?

16. Compare and contrast ATM and SONET in terms of the OSI model.

17. Besides HDLC and PPP, list the other four serial point-to-point data-link protocols covered in this chapter.

18. List the speeds of a T1 line, E1, OC-3, and OC-12.

This chapter covers the following subjects:

- Typical Features of OSI Layer 3

- IP Addressing Fundamentals

- Network Layer Utilities

- IP Routing and Routing Protocols

CHAPTER 5

Fundamentals of IP

The OSI model assigns the functions of path selection and logical addressing to the OSI network layer (Layer 3). Path selection includes the process of learning all the paths, or routes, in a network and then forwarding packets based on those paths or routes. Often the terms *path selection* and *routing* are used interchangeably. In most Cisco documentation and in this book, *routing* is the more popular term.

In this chapter, you will learn about the core concepts behind OSI Layer 3. Because CCNA focuses on TCP/IP, you also will learn about the main Layer 3 protocol used by TCP/IP—namely, the Internet Protocol (IP). This coverage includes IP addressing, IP routing, and some protocols useful to IP's effort to deliver packets end to end through a network.

"Do I Know This Already?" Quiz

The purpose of the "Do I Know This Already?" quiz is to help you decide whether you really need to read the entire chapter. If you already intend to read the entire chapter, you do not necessarily need to answer these questions now.

The 12-question quiz, derived from the major sections in the "Foundation Topics" portion of the chapter, helps you determine how to spend your limited study time.

Table 5-1 outlines the major topics discussed in this chapter and the "Do I Know This Already?" quiz questions that correspond to those topics.

Table 5-1 *"Do I Know This Already?" Foundation Topics Section-to-Question Mapping*

Foundations Topics Section	Questions Covered in This Section
Typical Features of OSI Layer 3	1, 2, 4, 12
IP Addressing Fundamentals	5–9
Network Layer Utilities	10, 11
IP Routing and Routing Protocols	3

> **NOTE**   The goal of self-assessment is to gauge your mastery of the topics in this chapter. If you do not know the answer to a question or are only partially sure of the answer, you should mark this question wrong for purposes of the self-assessment. Giving yourself credit for an answer that you correctly guess skews your self-assessment results and might provide you with a false sense of security.

1. Which of the following describes the functions of OSI Layer 3 protocols?

    a. Logical addressing

    b. Physical addressing

    c. Path selection

    d. Arbitration

    e. Error recovery

2. Imagine that PC1 needs to send some data to PC2, and PC1 and PC2 are separated by several routers. What are the largest entities that make it from PC1 to PC2?

    a. Frame

    b. Segment

    c. Packet

    d. L5PDU

    e. L3PDU

    f. L1PDU

3. Which of the following does a router normally use when making a decision about routing TCP/IP?

    a. Destination MAC address

    b. Source MAC address

    c. Destination IP address

    d. Source IP address

    e. Destination MAC and IP address

4. Imagine a network with two routers that are connected with a point-to-point HDLC serial link. Each router has an Ethernet, with PC1 sharing the Ethernet with Router1, and PC2 sharing an Ethernet with Router2. When PC1 sends data to PC2, which of the following is true?

    a. Router1 strips the Ethernet header and trailer off the frame received from PC1, never to be used again.

   b. Router1 encapsulates the Ethernet frame inside an HDLC header and sends the frame to Router2, which extracts the Ethernet frame for forwarding to PC2.

   c. Router1 strips the Ethernet header and trailer off the frame received from PC1, which is exactly re-created by R2 before forwarding data to PC2.

   d. Router1 removes the Ethernet, IP, and TCP headers, and rebuilds the appropriate headers before forwarding the packet to Router2.

5. Which of the following are valid Class C IP addresses?

   a. 1.1.1.1

   b. 200.1.1.1

   c. 128.128.128.128

   d. 224.1.1.1

   e. 223.223.223.255

6. What is the range for the values of the first octet for Class A IP networks?

   a. 0 to 127

   b. 0 to 126

   c. 1 to 127

   d. 1 to 126

   e. 128 to 191

   f. 128 to 192

7. PC1 and PC2 are on two different Ethernets that are separated by an IP router. PC1's IP address is 10.1.1.1, and no subnetting is used. Which of the following addresses could be used for PC2?

   a. 10.1.1.2

   b. 10.2.2.2

   c. 10.200.200.1

   d. 9.1.1.1

   e. 225.1.1.1

   f. 1.1.1.1

8. How many valid host IP addresses does each Class B network contain?

   a. 16,777,214

   b. 16,777,216

   c. 65,536

   d. 65,534

   e. 65,532

   f. 32,768

   g. 32,766

   h. 32,764

9. How many valid host IP addresses does each Class C network contain?

   a. 65,536

   b. 65,534

   c. 65,532

   d. 32,768

   e. 32,766

   f. 256

   g. 254

10. Which of the following protocols allows a client PC to discover the IP address of another computer, based on that other computer's name?

   a. ARP

   b. RARP

   c. DNS

   d. DHCP

   e. BOOTP

11. Which of the following protocols allow a client PC to request assignment of an IP address as well as learn its default gateway?

   a. ARP

   b. RARP

   c. DNS

   d. DHCP

12. Which term is defined by the following phrase: "the type of protocol that is being forwarded when routers perform routing."

    a. Routed protocol

    b. Routing protocol

    c. RIP

    d. IOS

    e. Route protocol

The answers to the "Do I Know This Already?" quiz are found in Appendix A, "Answers to the 'Do I Know This Already?' Quizzes and Q&A Sections." The suggested choices for your next step are as follows:

- **10 or less overall score**—Read the entire chapter. This includes the "Foundation Topics" and "Foundation Summary" sections and the "Q&A" section.

- **11 or 12 overall score**—If you want more review on these topics, skip to the "Foundation Summary" section and then go to the "Q&A" section. Otherwise, move to the next chapter.

Foundation Topics

OSI Layer 3–equivalent protocols use *routing* and *addressing* to accomplish their goals. The choices made by the people who made up addressing greatly affect how routing works, so the two topics are best described together.

This chapter begins with an overview of the functions of routing and network layer logical addressing. Following that, the text moves on to the basics of IP addressing, relating IP addressing to the OSI routing and addressing concepts covered in the first section. The chapter ends with an introduction to IP routing protocols.

Typical Features of OSI Layer 3

A protocol that defines routing and addressing is considered to be a network layer, or Layer 3, protocol. OSI does define a unique Layer 3 protocol called Connectionless Network Services (CLNS), but, as usual with OSI protocols, you rarely see it in networks today. However, you will see many other protocols that perform the OSI Layer 3 functions of routing and addressing, such as the Internet Protocol (IP), Novell Internetwork Packet Exchange (IPX), or AppleTalk Datagram Delivery Protocol (DDP).

The network layer protocols have many similarities, regardless of what Layer 3 protocol is used. In this section, network layer (Layer 3) addressing is covered in enough depth to describe IP, IPX, and AppleTalk addresses. Also, now that data link layer and network layer addresses have been covered in this book, this section undertakes a comparison between the two.

Routing (Path Selection)

Routing focuses on the end-to-end logic of forwarding data. Figure 5-1 shows a simple example of how routing works. The logic seen in the figure is relatively simple. For PC1 to send data to PC2, it must send something to R1, when sends it to R2, then on to R3, and finally to PC2. However, the logic used by each device along the path varies slightly.

PC1's Logic: Sending Data to a Nearby Router

In this example, PC1 has some data to send data to PC2. Because PC2 is not on the same Ethernet as PC1, PC1 needs to send the packet to a router that is attached to the same Ethernet as PC1. The sender sends a data-link frame across the medium to the nearby router; this frame includes the packet in the data portion of the frame. That frame uses data link layer (Layer 2) addressing in the data-link header to ensure that the nearby router receives the frame.

Figure 5-1   *Routing Logic: PC1 Sending to PC2*

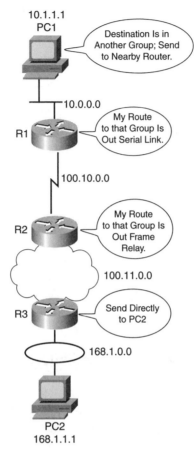

The main point here is that the originator of the data does not know much about the network—just how to get the data to some nearby router. In the post office analogy, it's like knowing how to get to the local post office, but nothing more. Likewise, PC1 needs to know only how to get the packet to R1.

R1 and R2's Logic: Routing Data Across the Network

R1 and R2 both use the same general process to route the packet. The *routing table* for any particular network layer protocol contains a list of network layer address *groupings*. Instead of a single entry in the routing table per individual destination address, there is one entry per group. The router compares the destination network layer address in the packet to the entries in the routing table, and a match is made. This matching entry in the routing table tells this router where to forward the packet next. The words in the bubbles in Figure 5-1 point out this basic logic.

The concept of network layer address grouping is similar to the U.S. ZIP code system. Everyone living in the same vicinity is in the same ZIP code, and the postal sorters just look for the ZIP codes, ignoring the rest of the address. Likewise, in Figure 5-1, everyone in this network whose IP address starts with 168.1 is on the Token Ring on which PC2 resides, so the routers can just have one routing table entry that means "all addresses that start with 168.1."

Any intervening routers repeat the same process. The destination network layer (Layer 3) address in the packet identifies the group in which the destination resides. The routing table is searched for a matching entry, which tells this router where to forward the packet next. Eventually, the packet is delivered to the router connected to the network or subnet of the destination host (R3), as previously shown in Figure 5-1.

R3's Logic: Delivering Data to the End Destination

The final router in the path, R3, uses almost the exact same logic as R1 and R2, but with one minor difference. R3 needs to forward the packet directly to PC2, not to some other router. On the surface, that difference seems insignificant. In the next section, when you read about how the network layer uses the data link layer, the significance of the difference will become obvious.

Network Layer Interaction with the Data Link Layer

In Figure 5-1, four different types of data links were used to deliver the data. When the network layer protocol is processing the packet, it decides to send the packet out the appropriate network interface. Before the actual bits can be placed onto that physical interface, the network layer must hand off the packet to the data link layer protocols, which, in turn, ask the physical layer to actually send the data. And as was described in Chapter 3, "Fundamentals of Ethernet LANs," the data link layer adds the appropriate header and trailer to the packet, creating a frame, before sending the frames over each physical network.

The routing process forwards the packet, and only the packet, from end-to-end through the network, discarding data link headers and trailers along the way. The network layer processes deliver the packet end-to-end, using successive data-link headers and trailers just to get the packet to the next router or host in the path. Each successive data link layer just gets the packet from one device to the next. Figure 5-2 shows the same diagram as Figure 5-1 but includes the concepts behind encapsulation.

Figure 5-2 *Network Layer and Data Link Layer Encapsulation*

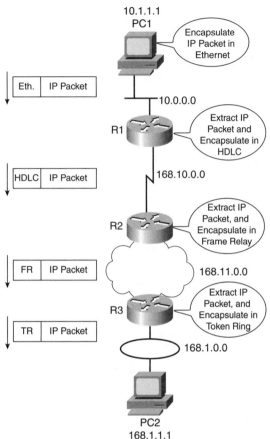

Because the routers build new data-link headers and trailers (trailers not shown in figure),and because the new headers contain data-link addresses, the PCs and routers must have some way to decide what data-link addresses to use. An example of how the router determines which data-link address to use is the IP Address Resolution Protocol (ARP). *ARP is used to dynamically learn the data-link address of an IP host connected to a LAN.* You will read more about ARP later in this chapter.

In short, the process of routing forwards Layer 3 packets, also called *Layer 3 protocol data units (L3 PDUs)*, based on the destination Layer 3 address in the packet. The process uses the data link layer to encapsulate the Layer 3 packets into Layer 2 frames for transmission across each successive data link.

Network Layer (Layer 3) Addressing

One key feature of network layer addresses is that they were designed to allow logical grouping of addresses. In other words, something about the numeric value of an address implies a group or set of addresses, all of which are considered to be in the same grouping. In TCP/IP, this group is called a *network* or a *subnet*. In IPX, it is called a *network*. In AppleTalk, the grouping is called a *cable range*. These groupings work just like U.S.P.S. ZIP codes, allowing the routers (mail sorters) to speedily route (sort) lots of packets (letters).

Just like postal street addresses, network layer addresses are grouped based on physical location in a network. The rules differ for some network layer protocols, but the grouping concept is identical for IP, IPX, and AppleTalk. In each of these network layer protocols, all devices on opposite sides of a router must be in a different Layer 3 group, just like in the examples earlier in this chapter.

Routing relies on the fact that Layer 3 addresses are grouped together. The routing tables for each network layer protocol can have one entry for the group, not one entry for each individual address. Imagine an Ethernet with 100 TCP/IP hosts. A router needing to forward packets to any of those hosts needs only one entry in its IP routing table. This basic fact is one of the key reasons that routers can scale to allow tens and hundreds of thousands of devices. It's very similar to the U.S.P.S. ZIP code system—it would be ridiculous to have people in the same ZIP code live somewhere far away from each other, or to have next-door neighbors be in different zip codes. The poor postman would spend all his time driving and flying around the country! Similarly, to make routing more efficient, network layer protocols group addresses together.

With that in mind, most network layer (Layer 3) addressing schemes were created with the following goals:

- The address space should be large enough to accommodate the largest network for which the designers imagined the protocol would be used.

- The addresses should allow for unique assignment.

- The address structure should have some grouping implied so that many addresses are considered to be in the same group.

- Dynamic address assignment for clients is desired.

The U.S. Postal Service analogy also works well as a comparison to how IP network numbers are assigned. Instead of getting involved with every small community's plans for what to name new streets, the post service simply has a nearby office with a ZIP code. If that local town wants to add streets, the rest of the post offices in the country already are prepared because they just forward letters based on the ZIP code, which they already know. The only postal employees who care about the new streets are the people in the local post office. It is the local postmaster's job to assign a mail carrier to deliver and pick up mail on any new streets.

Also, you can have duplicate local street addresses, as long as they are in different ZIP codes, and it all still works. There might be hundreds of Main streets in different ZIP codes, but as long as there is just one per ZIP code, the address is unique. Layer 3 network addresses follow the same concept—as long as the entire Layer 3 address is unique compared to the other Layer 3 addresses, all is well.

Example Layer 3 Address Structures

Each Layer 3 address structure contains at least two parts. One (or more) part at the beginning of the address works like the ZIP code and essentially identifies the grouping. All instances of addresses with the same value in these first bits of the address are considered to be in the same group—for example, the same IP subnet or IPX network or AppleTalk cable range. The last part of the address acts as a local address, uniquely identifying that device in that particular group. Table 5-2 outlines several Layer 3 address structures.

Table 5-2 *Layer 3 Address Structures*

Protocol	Size of Address in Bits	Name and Size of Grouping Field in Bits	Name and Size of Local Address Field in Bits
IP	32	Network or subnet (variable, between 8 and 30 bits)	Host (variable, between 2 and 24 bits)
IPX	80	Network (32)	Node (48)
AppleTalk	24	Network* (16)	Node (8)
OSI	Variable	Many formats, many sizes	Domain-specific part (DSP—typically 56, including NSAP)

*Consecutively numbered values in this field can be combined into one group, called a cable range.

Routing Protocols

Conveniently, the routing tables in the example based on Figure 5-2 had the correct routing information already in their routing tables. In most cases, these entries are built dynamically by use of a routing protocol. Routing protocols learn about all the locations of the network layer "groups" in a network and advertise the locations of the groups. As a result, each router can build a good routing table dynamically. Routing protocols define message formats and procedures, just like any other protocol. The end goal of each routing protocol is to fill the routing table with all known destination groups and with the best route to reach each group.

The terminology relating to routing protocols sometimes can get in the way. A *routing protocol* learns routes and puts those routes in a routing table. A *routed protocol* is the type of packet forwarded, or routed, through a network. In Figures 5-1 and 5-2, the figures represent how IP packets are routed, so IP would be the *routed protocol*. If the routers used the Routing Information Protocol (RIP) to learn the routes, then RIP would be the *routing protocol*.

Later in this chapter, the section titled "IP Routing Protocols" shows a detailed example of how routing protocols learn routes.

IP Addressing Fundamentals

No one reading this book should be shocked to hear that IP addressing is one of the most important topics for passing the the INTRO and ICND exams. In fact, IP addressing is the only major topic that is covered specifically on both the INTRO and ICND exams. Plus, you need a comfortable, confident understanding of IP addressing and subnetting for success on any Cisco certification. In other words, you had better know addressing and subnetting!

This section introduces IP addressing and subnetting, and also covers the concepts behind the structure of an IP address, including how it relates to IP routing. In Chapter 12, "IP Addressing and Subnetting," you will read about the math behind IP addressing and subnetting.

IP Addressing Definitions

If a device wants to communicate using TCP/IP, it needs an IP address. When the device has an IP address and the appropriate software and hardware, it can send and receive IP packets. Any device that can send and receive IP packets is called an *IP host*.

IP addresses consist of a 32-bit number, usually written in *dotted-decimal notation*. The "decimal" part of the term comes from the fact that each byte (8 bits) of the 32-bit IP address is converted to its decimal equivalent. The four resulting decimal numbers are written in sequence, with "dots," or decimal points, separating the numbers—hence the name *dotted-decimal*. For instance, 168.1.1.1 is an IP address written in dotted-decimal form, but the actual binary version is 10101000 00000001 00000001 00000001. (You almost never need to write down the binary version—but you will need to know how to convert between the two formats in Chapter 12, "IP Addressing and Subnetting.")

Each of the decimal numbers in an IP address is called an *octet*. The term *octet* is just a vendor-neutral term instead of *byte*. So, for an IP address of 168.1.1.1, the first octet is 168, the second octet is 1, and so on. The range of decimal numbers numbers in each octet is between 0 and 255, inclusive.

Finally, note that each network interface uses a unique IP address. Most people tend to think that their computer has an IP address, but actually their computer's network card has an IP address. If you put two Ethernet cards in a PC to forward IP packets through both cards, they both would need unique IP addresses. Similarly, routers, which typically have many network interfaces that forward IP packets, have an IP address for each interface.

Now that you have some idea about the basic terminology, the next section relates IP addressing to the routing concepts of OSI Layer 3.

How IP Addresses Are Grouped Together

To fully appreciate IP addressing, you first must understand the concepts behind the grouping of IP addresses. The first visions of what we call the Internet were for connecting research sites. A typical network diagram might have looked like Figure 5-3.

Figure 5-3 *Sample Network Using Class A, B, and C Network Numbers*

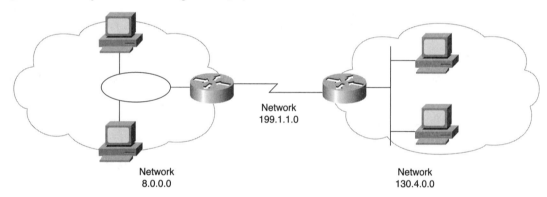

The conventions of IP addressing and IP address grouping make routing easy. For example, all IP addresses that begin with 8 are on the Token Ring on the left. Likewise, all IP addresses that begin with 130.4 are on the right. Along the same lines, 199.1.1 is the prefix on the serial link. By following this convention, the routers build a routing table with three entries, one for each prefix, or network number.

So, the general ideas about how IP address groupings can be summarized are as follows:

■ All IP addresses in the same group must not be separated by a router.

■ IP addresses separated by a router must be in different groups.

As mentioned earlier in this chapter, IP addressing behaves similarly to ZIP codes. Everyone living in my ZIP code lives in my town. If some members of my ZIP code were in California, some of my mail might be sent out there (I live in Georgia, by the way). Likewise, IP routing counts on the fact that all IP addresses in the same subnet are in the same general location, with the routers in the network forwarding traffic to addresses in my subnet to a router connected to my subnet.

Classes of Networks

In Figure 5-3 and the surrounding text, I claimed that the IP addresses of devices attached to the Token Ring all started with 8 and that the IP addresses of devices attached to the Ethernet all started with 130.4. Why only one number for the "prefix" on the Token Ring and two numbers on the Ethernet? Well, it all has to do with IP address classes.

RFC 790 defines the IP protocol, including multiple different classes of networks. IP defines three different network classes, called A, B, and C, from which individual hosts are assigned IP addresses. TCP/IP defines Class D (multicast) addresses and Class E (experimental) addresses as well.

By definition, all addresses in the same Class A, B, or C network have the same numeric value *network* portion of the addresses. The rest of the address is called the *host* portion of the address.

Using the post office example, the network part of an IP address acts like the ZIP code, and the host part acts like the street address. Just as a letter-sorting machine three states away from you cares only about the ZIP code on a letter addressed to you, a router three hops away from you cares only about the network number that your address resides in.

Class A, B, and C networks each have a different length for the part that identifies the network:

- Class A networks have a 1-byte-long network part. That leaves 3 bytes for the rest of the address, called the host part.

- Class B networks have a 2-byte-long network part, leaving 2 bytes for the host portion of the address.

- Class C networks have a 3-byte-long network part, leaving only 1 byte for the host part.

For instance, Figure 5-3 lists network 8.0.0.0 next to the Token Ring. Network 8.0.0.0 is a Class A network, which means that only 1 byte is used for the network part of the address. So, all hosts in network 8.0.0.0 begin with 8. Similarly, Class B network 130.4.0.0 is listed next to the Ethernet; because it is Class B, 2 bytes define the network part, and all addresses begin with those same two bytes. When written down, network numbers have all decimal 0s in the host part of the number. So, Class A network "8" is written 8.0.0.0, Class B network 130.4 is written 130.4.0.0, and so on.

Now consider the size of each class of network. Class A networks need 1 byte for the network part, leaving 3 bytes, or 24 bits, for the host part. There are 2^{24} different possible values in the host part of a Class A IP address. So, each Class A network can have 2^{24} IP addresses—except for two reserved host addresses in each network, as shown in the last column of Table 5-3. The table summarizes the characteristics of Class A, B, and C networks.

Table 5-3 *Sizes of Network and Host Parts of IP Addresses with No Subnetting*

Any Network of This Class	Number of Network Bytes (Bits)	Number of Host Bytes (Bits)	Number of Addresses per Network*
A	1 (8)	3 (24)	$2^{24} - 2$
B	2 (16)	2 (16)	$2^{16} - 2$
C	3 (24)	1 (8)	$2^{8} - 2$

*There are two reserved host addresses per network.

Network numbers look like actual addresses because they are in dotted-decimal format. However, network numbers are not actually IP addresses because they cannot be assigned to an interface as an IP address. Conceptually, network numbers represent the group of all IP addresses in the network, much like a ZIP code represents the group of all addresses in a community. Based on the three examples from Figure 5-3, Table 5-4 provides a closer look at the numerical version of the three network numbers: 8.0.0.0, 130.4.0.0, and 199.1.1.0.

Table 5-4 *Example Network Numbers, Decimal and Binary*

Network Number	Binary Representation, with Host Part Bold
8.0.0.0	00001000 **00000000 00000000 00000000**
130.4.0.0	10000010 00000100 **00000000 00000000**
199.1.1.0	11000111 00000001 00000001 **00000000**

Two numbers inside each Class A, B, or C network are reserved, as mentioned in Table 5-3. One of the two reserved values is the network number itself. For instance, each of the numbers in Table 5-4 is reserved. The other reserved value is the one with all binary 1s in the host part of the address—this number is called the *network broadcast* or *directed broadcast* address. Also, because the network number is the lowest numerical value inside that network and the broadcast address is the largest, all the numbers between the network number and the broadcast address are the valid, useful IP addresses that can be used to address interfaces in the network.

The Actual Class A, B, and C Network Numbers

Many different Class A, B, and C networks exist. If your firm connects to the Internet, it must use registered, unique network numbers. To that end, the Network Information Center (NIC) assigns network numbers so that all IP address are unique. By assigning one company a particular network number, and not assigning that same network number to any other company, all IP addresses can be unique throughout the Internet. Table 5-5 summarizes the possible network numbers, the total number of each type, and the number of hosts in each Class A, B, and C network.

Table 5-5 *List of All Possible Valid Network Numbers**

Class	First Octet Range	Valid Network Numbers	Total Number of This Class of Network	Number of Hosts per Network
A	1 to 126	1.0.0.0 to 126.0.0.0	$2^7 - 2$	$2^{24} - 2$
B	128 to 191	128.1.0.0 to 191.254.0.0	$2^{14} - 2$	$2^{16} - 2$
C	192 to 223	192.0.1.0 to 223.255.254.0	$2^{21} - 2$	$2^8 - 2$

*The Valid Network Numbers column shows actual network numbers. There are several reserved cases. For example, networks 0.0.0.0 (originally defined for use as a broadcast address) and 127.0.0.0 (still available for use as the loopback address) are reserved. Networks 128.0.0.0, 191.255.0.0, 192.0.0.0, and 223.255.255.0 also are reserved.

Memorizing the contents of Table 5-5 should be one of the first things you do in preparation for the CCNA exam(s). Engineers should be able to categorize a network as Class A, B, or C with ease. Also memorize the number of octets in the network part of Class A, B, and C addresses, as shown in Table 5-4.

IP Subnetting

One of the most important topics on both the INTRO and ICND exams is the topic of subnetting. You need to know how it works and how to "do the math" to figure out issues when subnetting is in use, both in real life and on the exam.

Chapter 12 covers the details of subnetting concepts, motivation, and math, but you should have a basic understanding of the concepts before covering the topics between here and Chapter 12. So, this section describes the basics.

IP subnetting creates vastly larger numbers of smaller groups of IP addresses, compared with simply using Class A, B, and C conventions. The Class A, B, and C rules still exist—but now, a single Class A, B, or C network can be subdivided into many smaller groups. Subnetting treats a subdivision of a single Class A, B, or C network as if it were a network itself. By doing so, a single Class A, B, or C network can be subdivided into many nonoverlapping subnets.

Comparing a single network topology using subnetting with the same topology without subnetting drives home the basic concept. Figure 5-4 shows such a network, without subnetting.

Figure 5-4   *Backdrop for Discussing Numbers of Different Networks/Subnetworks*

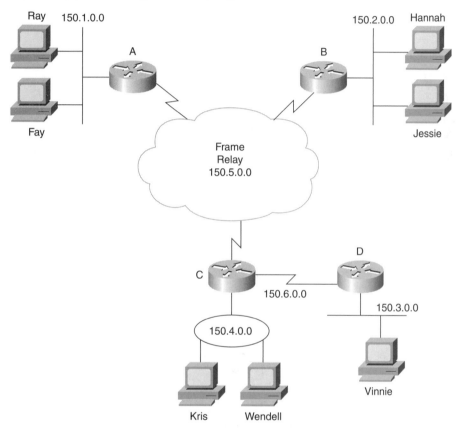

The design in Figure 5-4 requires six groups, each of which is a Class B network in this example. The four LANs each use a single Class B network. In other words, each of the LANs attached to routers A, B, C, and D is in a separate network. Additionally, the two serial interfaces composing the point-to-point serial link between routers C and D use the same network because these two interfaces are not separated by a router. Finally, the three router interfaces composing the Frame Relay network with routers A, B, and C are not separated by an IP router and would compose the sixth network.

Each Class B network has $2^{16} - 2$ hosts addresses in it—far more than you will ever need for each LAN and WAN link. In fact, this design would not be allowed if it were connected to the Internet. The NIC would not assign six separate registered Class B network numbers—

in fact, you probably would not even get one Class B network because most of the Class B addresses already are assigned. You more likely would get a couple of Class C networks, and the NIC would expect you to use subnetting.

Figure 5-5 illustrates a more realistic example that uses basic subnetting.

Figure 5-5 *Using Subnets*

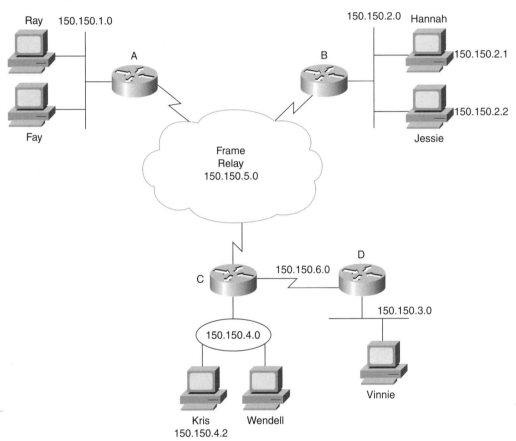

As in Figure 5-4, the design in Figure 5-5 requires six groups. Unlike Figure 5-5, this figure uses six subnets, each of which is a subnet of a single Class B network. This design subnets Class B network 150.150.0.0, which has been assigned by the NIC. To perform subnetting, the third octet (in this example) is used to identify unique subnets of network 150.150.0.0. Notice that each subnet number in the figure shows a different value in the third octet, representing each different subnet number. In other words, this design numbers or identifies each different subnet using the third octet.

When subnetting, a third part of an IP address appears between the network and host parts of the address—namely, the subnet part of the address. This field is created by "stealing" or "borrowing" bits from the host part of the address. The size of the network part of the address never shrinks—in other words, Class A, B, and C rules still apply when defining the size of the network part of an address. The host part of the address shrinks to make room for the subnet part of the address. Figure 5-6 shows the format of addresses when subnetting.

Figure 5-6 *Address Formats When Subnetting Is Used*

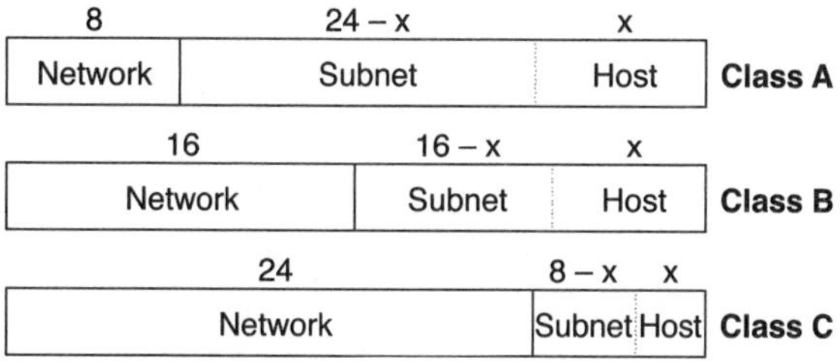

Now, instead of routing based on the network part of an address, routers can route based on the combined network and subnet parts. In fact, most people do not even bother distinguishing between the network part and the subnet part—they just call both fields together the subnet part of an address.

Finally, IP addressing with subnetting uses a concept called a *subnet mask*. A subnet mask helps define the structure of an IP address, as shown in Figure 5-6. Chapter 12 explains the details.

Network Layer Utilities

The TCP/IP network layer uses several utility protocols to help it complete its task. For instance, in the first section of this chapter, you read that the Address Resolution Protocol (ARP) could be used to discover the MAC address of another IP host. In this section, you will learn about some basic IP utilities, using other protocols beside IP that together help IP deliver packets end to end through an IP network.

Address Resolution Protocol and the Domain Name System

Network designers should try to make using the network as simple as possible. At most, users might want to remember the name of another computer with which they want to communicate, such as remembering the name of a web site. They certainly do not want to remember the IP address, nor do they want to try to remember any MAC addresses! So, TCP/

IP needs to have protocols that dynamically discover all the necessary information to allow communications, without the user knowing more than a name.

You might not even think that you need to know the name of another computer. For instance, when you open your browser, you probably have a default home page configured that the browser immediately downloads. You might not think of that URL string as a name, but the universal resource locator (URL) for the home page has a name embedded in it. For instance, in a URL such as www.skylinecomputer.com/Train_Welcome.asp, the www.skylinecomputer.com part is actually the name of the web server for the company that I work for. So, whether you type in the name of another networked computer or it is implied by what you see on your screen, the user typically identifies a remote computer by using a name.

So, TCP/IP needs a way to let a computer find the IP address of another computer based on its name. TCP/IP also needs a way to find MAC addresses associated with other computers on the same LAN subnet. Figure 5-7 outlines the problem.

Figure 5-7 *Hannah Knows Jessie's Name, Needs IP Address and MAC Address*

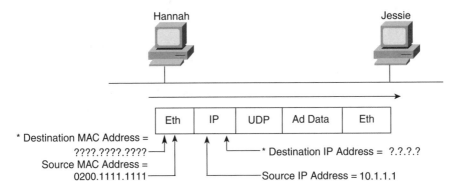

Hannah knows her own name, IP address, and MAC address because those things are configured in advance. *What Hannah does not know are Jessie's IP and MAC addresses.* To find the two missing facts, Hannah uses the Domain Name System (DNS) and the Address Resolution Protocol (ARP). Hannah knows the IP address of a DNS server because the address was preconfigured on Hannah's machine. Hannah now sends a *DNS request* to the DNS, asking for Jessie's IP address. The DNS replies with the address, 10.1.1.2. Figure 5-8 shows the simple process.

Figure 5-8 *DNS Request and Reply*

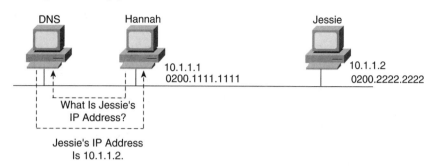

Hannah simply sends a DNS request to the server, supplying the name jessie, or
jessie.skylinecomputer.com, and the DNS replies with the IP address (10.1.1.2, in this case).
Effectively, the same thing happens when you surf the Internet and connect to any web site.
Your PC somehow knows the IP address of the DNS; that information can be preconfigured
or learned using Dynamic Host Configuration Protocol (DHCP), which is covered later in
this chapter. Your PC sends a request, just like Hannah's request for Jessie, asking the DNS
to resolve the name into an IP address. After that happens, your PC can start requesting that
the web page be sent.

Back to the example with Hannah. Hannah still needs to know the Ethernet MAC address
used by 10.1.1.2, so Hannah issues something called an *ARP broadcast*. An ARP broadcast
is sent to a broadcast Ethernet address, so everyone on the LAN receives it. Because Jessie is
on the LAN, Jessie receives the ARP broadcast. Because Jessie's IP address is 10.1.1.2 and the
ARP broadcast is looking for the MAC address associated with 10.1.1.2, Jessie replies with
her own MAC address. Figure 5-9 outlines the process.

Figure 5-9 *Sample ARP Process*

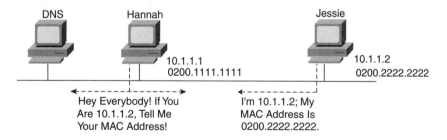

Now Hannah knows the destination IP and Ethernet addresses that she should use when
sending frames to Jessie, and the packet in Figure 5-7 can be sent successfully.

ICMP Echo and the ping Command

IP needs to have a way to test basic IP connectivity, without relying on any applications to be working. Hannah, being a great network troubleshooter (in spite of being my 2-year-old daughter), can test basic network connectivity using the **ping** command. **ping** (Packet INternet Groper) uses the *Internet Control Message Protocol (ICMP)*, sending a message called an *ICMP echo request* to another IP address. The computer with that IP address should reply with an *ICMP echo reply*. If that works, you successfully have tested the IP network. ICMP does not rely on any application, so it really just tests basic IP connectivity—Layers 1, 2, and 3 of the OSI model. Figure 5-10 outlines the basic process.

Figure 5-10   *Sample Network,* **ping** *Command*

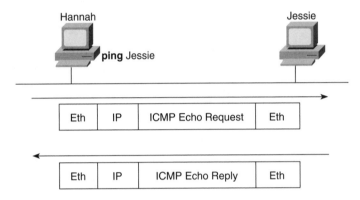

ICMP contains many features, which are discussed in detail in Chapter 13, "Basic Router Configuration and Operation."

RARP, BOOTP, and DHCP

Over the years, three protocols have been popular to allow a host computer to discover the IP address it should use:

■   Reverse ARP (RARP)

■   Boot Protocol (BOOTP)

■   Dynamic Host Configuration Protocol (DHCP)

RARP and BOOTP work using the same basic process. To use either protocol, a PC needs a LAN interface card. The computer sends a LAN broadcast frame announcing its own MAC address and requests that someone assign it an IP address. Figure 5-11 outlines the process for both RARP and BOOTP.

Figure 5-11 *RARP and BOOTP*

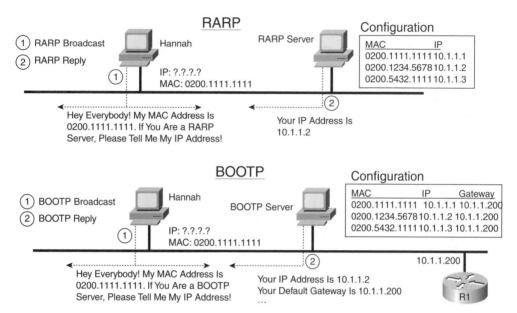

RARP and BOOTP requests sent to the LAN broadcast address simply ask for an IP address assignment. Both protocols allow for IP address assignment, but that is all that RARP can ask for—it can't even ask for the subnet mask used on the LAN. RARP is defined in RFC 903, whereas BOOTP was defined later in RFC 1542, including several improvements over RARP. So, BOOTP allows many more tidbits of information to be announced to a BOOTP client—its IP address, its subnet mask, its default gateway IP addresses, its other server IP addresses, and the name of a file that the computer should download.

Both RARP and BOOTP were created with the motivation to allow a diskless workstation to come up and start operating. With RARP, the creators of the protocol just wanted to get the machine an IP address so that a knowledgeable user could type in commands and copy the correct files from a server onto the diskless computer's RAM memory so that they could be used. The creators of BOOTP, anticipating a less sophisticated user in the future, wanted to automate as much of the process as possible—including the dynamic assignment of a default gateway (router) IP address.

BOOTP's name really comes from the feature in which BOOTP supplies the name of a file to the BOOTP client. Typically, the diskless workstations had enough permanent memory to boot a very simple operating system, with the expectation that the computer would use a simple protocol, such as the Trivial File Transfer Protocol (TFTP), to transfer a file containing a more sophisticated operating system into RAM. So, with the ultimate goal being to let a diskless computer complete the processing of initializing, or *booting*, a full operating system, BOOTP was aptly named.

Neither RARP nor BOOTP is used much today. (They are possible topics for the INTRO exam, though.) One of the problems with both RARP and BOOTP is that they required a computer to act as a server, and the server was required to know the MAC address of every computer and the corresponding configuration parameters that each computer should be told. So, administration in a network of any size was painful.

DHCP, which is very popular in real networks today, solves some of the scaling and configuration issues with RARP and BOOTP, while supplying the same types of information. The main protocols for DHCP are defined in RFC 2131, but a couple of dozen additional RFCs define extensions and applications of DHCP for a variety of other useful purposes.

Like BOOTP, DHCP uses the concept of the client making a request and the server supplying the IP address to the client, plus other information such as the default gateway, subnet mask, DNS IP address, and other information. The biggest advantage of DHCP compared to BOOTP and RARP is that DHCP does not require that the DHCP server be configured with all MAC addresses of all clients. DHCP defines a process by which the server knows the IP subnet in which the DHCP client resides, and it can assign an IP address from a pool of valid IP addresses in that subnet. So, the DHCP server does not need to know the MAC address ahead of time. Also, most of the other information that DHCP might supply, such as the default router IP address, is the same for all hosts in the same subnet, so DHCP servers simply can configure information per subnet rather than per host and save a lot of administrative hassle compared to BOOTP.

The basic DHCP messages for acquiring an IP address are shown in Figure 5-12.

Figure 5-12 *DHCP Messages to Acquire an IP Address*

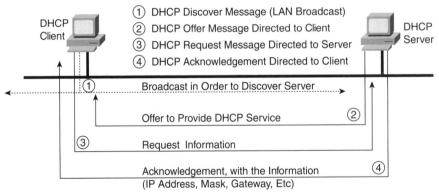

DHCP has become a very prolific protocol, with most end-user hosts on LANs in corporate networks getting their IP addresses and other basic configuration via DHCP.

IP Routing and Routing Protocols

In the first section of this chapter, you read about the basics of routing using a network with three routers and two PCs. Armed with more knowledge of IP addressing, you now can take a closer look at the process of routing IP. Figure 5-13 repeats the familiar network diagram, this time with subnets of network 150.150.0.0 used.

Figure 5-13   *Simple Routing Example, with IP Subnets*

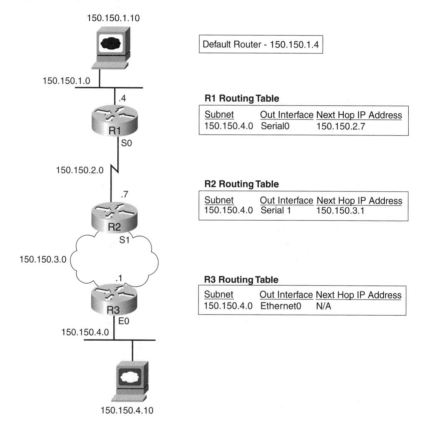

First, a few detail about the figure need to be explained. The subnet numbers are shown, with the whole third octet used for the subnet part of the addresses. The actual IP addressed for PC1 and PC2 are shown. However, the full IP addresses of the routers are not shown in the figure. Many times, to reduce clutter, only the host part of the address is listed in a figure. For instance, R2's IP address on the serial link to R1 is 150.150.2.7. The subnet is 150.150.2.0, and the .7 shown beside R2 in the figure represents the host part of the address, which is the fourth octet in this case.

A detailed examination of the routing logic used by PC1, R1, R2, and R3 is listed earlier in this chapter. That same logic is repeated here, using the more detailed information contained in the figure:

Step 1   **PC1 sends the packet to R1**—PC1 first builds the IP packet, with a destination address of PC2's IP address (150.150.4.10). PC1 needs to send the packet to R1 because it knows that its default router is 150.150.1.4. PC1 first checks its ARP cache, hoping to find R1's Ethernet MAC address. If it is not found, PC1 ARPs to learn R1's Ethernet MAC address. Then PC1 places the IP packet into an Ethernet frame, with a destination Ethernet address of R1's Ethernet address. PC1 sends the frame onto the Ethernet.

Step 2   **R1 processes the incoming frame and forwards the packet to R2**— Because the incoming Ethernet frame has a destination MAC of R1's Ethernet MAC, R1 copies the frame off the Ethernet for processing. If the FCS passes, meaning that the Ethernet frame did not have any errors in it, R1 looks at the Protocol Type field to discover that the packet inside the frame is an IP packet. R1 then discards the Ethernet header and trailer.

Next, R1 looks for the routing table entry that matches the destination address in the packet, 150.150.4.10. The routing table entry is listed in the figure—a route to subnet 150.150.4.0, with outgoing interface Serial0 to next-hop router R2 (150.150.2.7).

Now R1 just needs to build an HDLC frame and send it out its Serial0 interface to R2. As mentioned earlier, ARP is not needed on a point-to-point HDLC WAN link. R1 knows all the information necessary to out the packet inside an HDLC frame and send the frame.

Step 3   **R2 processes the incoming frame and forwards the packet to R3**—R2 repeats the same general process as R1 when it receives the HDLC frame. After stripping the HDLC header and trailer, R2 also needs to find the routing table entry that matches destination 150.150.4.10. R2's routing table has an entry for 150.150.4.0, outgoing interface serial1, to next-hop router 150.150.3.1, which is R3.

Before R2 can complete the task, the correct DLCI for the VC to R3 must be decided. The details of how R2 knows the right DLCI are covered in Chapter 11, "Frame Relay," of the *CCNA ICND Exam Certification Guide*. With that mapping information, R2 can complete the Frame Relay header and send the frame to R3.

Step 4   R3 processes the incoming frame and forwards the packet to PC2—
Like R1 and R2 before it, R3 checks the FCS in the data-link trailer,
looks at the type field to decide whether the packet inside the frame is
an IP packet, and then discards the Frame Relay header and trailer. The
routing table entry for 150.150.4.0 shows that the outgoing interface is
R3's Ethernet interface, but there is no next-hop router because R3 is
connected directly to subnet 150.150.4.0. All R3 has to do is
encapsulate the packet inside a Ethernet header and trailer, and forward
the frame. Before R3 can finish building the Ethernet header, an IP
ARP broadcast must be used to find PC2's MAC address (assuming that
R3 doesn't already have that information in its IP ARP cache).

The routing process relies on the rules relating to IP addressing. For instance, why did
150.150.1.10 (PC1) assume that 150.150.4.10 (PC2) was not on the same Ethernet? Well,
because 150.150.4.0, PC2's subnet, is different than 150.150.1.0, which is PC1's subnet.
Because IP addresses in different subnets must be separated by some router, PC1 needed to
send the packet to some router—and it did. Similarly, all three routers list a route to subnet
150.150.4.0, which, in this example, includes IP addresses 150.150.4.1 to 150.150.4.254.
What if someone tried to put PC2 somewhere else in the network, but still using
150.150.4.10? The routers then would forward packets to the wrong place. So, Layer 3
routing relies on the structure of Layer 3 addressing to route more efficiently.

IP Routing Protocols

IP routing protocols fill the IP routing table with valid, (hopefully) loop-free routes. Each
route includes a subnet number, the interface out which to forward packets so that they are
delivered to that subnet, and the IP address of the next router that should receive packets
destined for that subnet (if needed).

Before examining the underlying logic, you need to consider the goals of a routing protocol.
The goals described in the following list are common for any IP routing protocol, regardless
of its underlying logic type:

- To dynamically learn and fill the routing table with a route to all subnets in the network.

- If more than one route to a subnet is available, to place the best route in the routing table.

- To notice when routes in the table are no longer valid, and to remove those routes from
  the routing table.

- If a route is removed from the routing table and another route through another
  neighboring router is available, to add the route to the routing table. (Many people view
  this goal and the preceding one as a single goal.)

- To add new routes, or to replace lost routes, with the best currently available route as quickly as possible. The time between losing the route and finding a working replacement route is called *convergence* time.

- To prevent routing loops.

Routing protocols can become rather complicated, but the basic logic that they use is relatively simple. Routing protocols take the routes in a routing table and send a message to their neighbors telling them about the routes. After a while, everyone has heard about all the routes.

Figure 5-14 shows a sample network, with routing updates shown. Table 5-6 lists Router B's routing table before receiving the routing updates, and Table 5-7 lists Router B's routing table after receiving the routing updates.

Figure 5-14 *Router A Advertising Routes Learned from Router C*

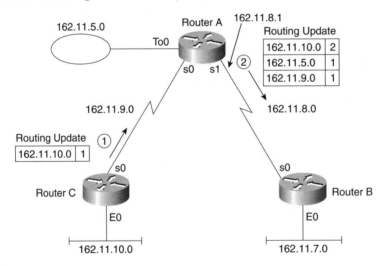

Table 5-6 *Router B Routing Table Before Receiving the Update Shown in Figure 5-14*

Group	Outgoing Interface	Next-Hop Router	Metric	Comments
162.11.7.0	E0	—	0	This is a directly connected route.
162.11.8.0	S0	—	0	This is a directly connected route.

Table 5-7 *Router B Routing Table After Receiving the Update Shown in Figure 5-14*

Group	Outgoing Interface	Next-Hop Router	Metric	Comments
162.11.5.0	S0	162.11.8.1	1	Learned from Router A, so next-hop is Router A.
162.11.7.0	E0	—	0	This is a directly connected route.
162.11.8.0	S0	—	0	This is a directly connected route.
162.11.9.0	S0	162.11.8.1	1	Learned from Router A, so next-hop is Router A.
162.11.10.0	S0	162.11.8.1	2	This one was learned from Router A, which learned it from Router C.

Router B adds routes for directly connected subnets when the interfaces first initialize. In fact, no routing protocols are needed for a router to learn routes to the directly connected subnets. So, before Router B receives any routing updates, it knows about only two routes—the two connected routes—as listed in Table 5-6.

After receiving the update from Router A, Router B has learned three more routes. Because Router B learned those routes from Router A, all three of B's routes point back to Router A as the next hop router. That makes sense because it is obvious from the figure that B's only path to the other subnets lies through Router A.

Router A learned about subnets 162.11.5.0 and 162.11.9.0 because A is connected directly to those subnets. Router A, in turn, learned about subnet 162.11.10.0, the subnet off Router C's Ethernet, from routing updates sent by Router C.

Foundation Summary

The "Foundation Summary" section of each chapter lists the most important facts from the chapter. Although this section does not list every fact from the chapter that will be on your CCNA exam, a well-prepared CCNA candidate should know, at a minimum, all the details in each "Foundation Summary" section before going to take the exam.

The routing process forwards the packet, and only the packet, from end to end through the network, discarding data-link headers and trailers along the way. The network layer processes deliver the packet end to end, using successive data-link headers and trailers just to get the packet to the next router or host in the path. Figure 5-15 shows the concepts behind encapsulation used by routers.

Figure 5-15 *Network Layer and Data Link Layer Encapsulation*

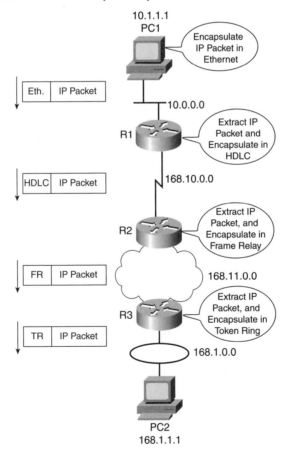

Table 5-8 outlines several Layer 3 address structures.

Table 5-8 *Layer 3 Address Structures*

Protocol	Size of Address in Bits	Name and Size of Grouping Field in Bits	Name and Size of Local Address Field in Bits
IP	32	Network or subnet (variable, between 8 and 30 bits)	Host (variable, between 2 and 24 bits)
IPX	80	Network (32)	Node (48)
AppleTalk	24	Network* (16)	Node (8)
OSI	Variable	Many formats, many sizes	Domain-specific part (DSP— typically 56, including NSAP)

*Consecutively numbered values in this field can be combined into one group, called a cable range.

The general ideas about how IP address groupings can be summarized as follows:

- All IP addresses in the same group must not be separated by a router.
- IP addresses separated by a router must be in different groups.

Table 5-9 summarizes the characteristics of Class A, B, and C networks.

Table 5-9 *Sizes of Network and Host Parts of IP Addresses with No Subnetting*

Any Network of This Class	Number of Network Bytes (Bits)	Number of Host Bytes (Bits)	Number of Addresses per Network*
A	1 (8)	3 (24)	$2^{24} - 2$
B	2 (16)	2 (16)	$2^{16} - 2$
C	3 (24)	1 (8)	$2^{8} - 2$

*There are two reserved host addresses per network.

Network numbers look like actual addresses because they are in dotted-decimal format. However, network numbers are not actually IP addresses because they cannot be assigned to an interface as an IP address.

Table 5-10 summarizes the possible network numbers, the total number of each type, and the number of hosts in each Class A, B, and C network.

Table 5-10   *List of All Possible Valid Network Numbers**

Class	First Octet Range	Valid Network Numbers*	Total Number of This Class of Network	Number of Hosts per Network
A	1 to 126	1.0.0.0 to 126.0.0.0	$2^7 - 2$	$2^{24} - 2$
B	128 to 191	128.1.0.0 to 191.254.0.0	$2^{14} - 2$	$2^{16} - 2$
C	192 to 223	192.0.1.0 to 223.255.254.0	$2^{21} - 2$	$2^8 - 2$

*The Valid Network Numbers column shows actual network numbers. There are several reserved cases. For example, networks 0.0.0.0 (originally defined for use as a broadcast address) and 127.0.0.0 (still available for use as the loopback address) are reserved. Networks 128.0.0.0, 191.255.0.0, 192.0.0.0, and 223.255.255.0 also are reserved.

When subnetting, the host part of the address shrinks to make room for the subnet part of the address. Figure 5-16 shows the format of addresses when subnetting.

Figure 5-16   *Address Formats When Subnetting Is Used*

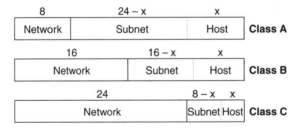

The goals described in the following list are common for any IP routing protocol, regardless of its underlying logic type:

- To dynamically learn and fill the routing table with a route to all subnets in the network.

- If more than one route to a subnet is available, to place the best route in the routing table.

- To notice when routes in the table are no longer valid, and to remove those routes from the routing table.

- If a route is removed from the routing table and another route through another neighboring router is available, to add the route to the routing table. (Many people view this goal and the preceding one as a single goal.)

- To add new routes, or to replace lost routes with the best currently available route, as quickly as possible. The time between losing the route and finding a working replacement route is called *convergence* time.

- To prevent routing loops.

Q&A

As mentioned in the introduction, you have two choices for review questions. The questions that follow give you a bigger challenge than the exam itself by using an open-ended question format. By reviewing now with this more difficult question format, you can exercise your memory better and prove your conceptual and factual knowledge of this chapter. The answers to these questions are found in Appendix A.

For more practice with exam-like question formats, including questions using a router simulator and multiple-choice questions, use the exam engine on the CD.

1. What are the two main functions of each OSI Layer 3–equivalent protocol?

2. Assume that PC1 sends data to PC2, and PC2 is separated from PC1 by at least one router. Are the IP addresses of the PCs in the same IP subnet? Explain your answer.

3. Assume that PC1 sends data to PC2, and PC2 is not separated from PC1 by at least one router. Are the IP, addresses of the PCs in the same IP subnet? Explain your answer.

4. How many bits are present in an IP address?

5. How many bits are present in an IPX address?

6. How many bits are present in an AppleTalk address?

7. Name the two main parts of an IPX address. Which part identifies which group this address is a member of?

8. Name the two main parts of an IP address. Which part identifies which group this address is a member of?

9. PC1 sends data to PC2 using TCP/IP. Three routers separate PC1 and PC2. Explain why the statement "PC1 sends an Ethernet frame to PC2" is true or false.

10. In IP addressing, how many octets are in 1 byte?

11. Describe the differences between a routed protocol and a routing protocol.

12. Name at least three routed protocols.

13. Name at least three IP routing protocols.

14. Imagine an IP host on an Ethernet, with a single router attached to the same segment. In which cases does an IP host choose to send a packet to this router instead of directly to the destination host, and how does this IP host know about that single router?

15. Name three items in an entry in any routing table.

16. Name the parts of an IP address when subnetting is used.

17. How many valid IP addresses exist in a Class A network? (You may refer to the formula if you do not know the exact number.)

18. How many valid IP addresses exist in a Class B network? (You may refer to the formula if you do not know the exact number.)

19. How many valid IP addresses exist in a Class C network? (You may refer to the formula if you do not know the exact number.)

20. What values can a Class A network have in the first octet?

21. What values can a Class B network have in the first octet?

22. What values can a Class C network have in the first octet?

23. When subnetting a Class B network, do you create the subnet field by taking bits from the network part of the address or the host part?

24. When subnetting a Class B network, using the entire third octet for the subnet part, describe the number of possible subnets created.

25. When subnetting a Class A network using the entire second octet for the subnet part, describe the number of hosts in each subnet.

26. When a router hears about multiple routes to the same subnet, how does it choose which route to use?

27. What is the primary purpose of a routing protocol?

28. True or false: "Routing protocols are required to learn routes of directly connected subnets."

29. Which IP routing protocols are Cisco proprietary?

30. List the similarities and differences between RARP and BOOTP.

31. List the similarities and differences between DHCP and BOOTP.

32. List the similarities and differences between ARP and DNS.

This chapter covers the following subjects:

■ Typical Features of OSI Layer 4

■ The Transmission Control Protocol

■ The User Datagram Protocol

CHAPTER 6

Fundamentals of TCP and UDP

The Transmission Control Protocol (TCP) and User Datagram Protocol (UDP) are the two most popular TCP/IP transport layer protocols. These TCP/IP protocols define a variety of functions considered to be OSI transport layer, or Layer 4, features. Some of the functions relate to things you see every day—for instance, when you open multiple web browsers on your PC, how does your PC know which browser to put the next web page in? When a web server sends you 500 IP packets containing the various parts of a web page, and 1 packet has errors, how does your PC recover the lost data? This chapter covers how TCP and UDP perform these two functions, along with the other functions performed by the transport layer.

"Do I Know This Already?" Quiz

The purpose of the "Do I Know This Already?" quiz is to help you decide whether you really need to read the entire chapter. If you already intend to read the entire chapter, you do not necessarily need to answer these questions now.

The ten-question quiz, derived from the major sections in "Foundation Topics" portion of the chapter, helps you determine how to spend your limited study time.

Table 6-1 outlines the major topics discussed in this chapter and the "Do I Know This Already?" quiz questions that correspond to those topics.

Table 6-1 *"Do I Know This Already?" Foundation Topics Section-to-Question Mapping*

Foundations Topics Section	Questions Covered in This Section
Typical Features of OSI Layer 4	4
The Transmission Control Protocol	1–3, 5–8, 10
The User Datagram Protocol	9

CAUTION The goal of self-assessment is to gauge your mastery of the topics in this chapter. If you do not know the answer to a question or are only partially sure of the answer, you should mark this question wrong for purposes of the self-assessment. Giving yourself credit for an answer that you correctly guess skews your self-assessment results and might provide you with a false sense of security.

1. Which of the following protocols are connection-oriented?

   a. Frame Relay

   b. TCP

   c. IP

   d. UDP

   e. Ethernet

2. Which of the following protocols are reliable?

   a. Frame Relay

   b. TCP

   c. IP

   d. UDP

   e. Ethernet

3. PC1 is using TCP, has a window of 4, and sends four segments numbered 2, 3, 4, and 5 to PC2. PC2 replies with an acknowledgment number 5. What should PC1 do next?

   a. Increase its window to five segments

   b. Increase its window by five more segments, for a total of nine

   c. Send segment 6

   d. Resend segment 5

   e. Resend segments 2 through 5

4. Which of the following are not features of a protocol that is considered to match OSI Layer 4?

   a. Error recovery

   b. Flow control

   c. Segmenting of application data

   d. Conversion from binary to ASCII

5. Which of the following flow-control methods let the receiver tell the sender how much data the sender is allowed to send before the sender must wait for an acknowledgment?

   a. Buffering

   b. Acknowledgments

   c. Windowing

   d. Congestion notification

   e. Congestion avoidance

6. Which of the following header fields identifies which TCP/IP application gets data received by the computer?

    a. Ethernet Type

    b. 802.3 DSAP

    c. SNAP Protocol Type

    d. IP Protocol Field

    e. TCP Port Number

    f. UDP Port Number

    g. Application ID

    h. Congestion Avoidance

7. Which of the TCP connection-establishment flows sets both the SYN and ACK flags in the TCP header?

    a. First segment

    b. Second segment

    c. Third segment

    d. Fourth segment

    e. Fifth segment

8. Which of the following is not a typical function of TCP?

    a. Windowing

    b. Error recovery

    c. Multiplexing

    d. Routing

    e. Encryption

    f. Ordered data transfer

9. Which of the following functions is performed by TCP and UDP?

    a. Windowing

    b. Error recovery

    c. Multiplexing

    d. Routing

    e. Encryption

    f. Ordered data transfer

10. Data that includes the Layer 4 protocol header, and data given to Layer 4 by the upper layers, not including any headers and trailers from Layers 1 to 3, is called what?

    a. Bits

    b. Chunk

    c. Segment

    d. Packet

    e. Frame

    f. L5PDU

    g. L4PDU

    h. L3PDU

    i. L2PDU

The answers to the "Do I Know This Already?" quiz are found in Appendix A, "Answers to the 'Do I Know This Already?' Quizzes and Q&A Sections." The suggested choices for your next step are as follows:

- **8 or less overall score**—Read the entire chapter. This includes the "Foundation Topics" and "Foundation Summary" sections and the Q&A section.

- **9 or 10 overall score**—If you want more review on these topics, skip to the "Foundation Summary" section and then go to the Q&A section. Otherwise, move to the next chapter.

Foundation Topics

As in the last two chapters, this chapter starts with a general discussion of the functions of an OSI layer—in this case, Layer 4, the transport layer. Two specific transport layer protocols—the Transmission Control Protocol (TCP) and the User Datagram Protocol (UDP) are covered later in the chapter. This chapter covers OSI Layer 4 concepts, but mostly through an examination of the TCP and UDP protocols. So, this chapter briefly introduces OSI transport layer details and then dives right into how TCP works.

Typical Features of OSI Layer 4

The transport layer (Layer 4) defines several functions, the most important of which are error recovery and flow control. Routers discard packets for many reasons, including bit errors, congestion and instances in which no correct routes are known. As you have read already, most data-link protocols notice errors but then discard frames that have errors. The OSI transport layer might provide for retransmission (error recovery) and help to avoid congestion (flow control)—or it might not. It really just depends on the particular protocol. However, if error recovery or flow control is performed with the more modern protocol suites, the functions typically are performed with a Layer 4 protocol.

OSI Layer 4 includes some other features as well. Table 6-2 summarizes the main features of the OSI transport layer. You will read about the specific implementation of these protocols in the sections about TCP and UDP.

Table 6-2 *OSI Transport Layer Features*

Feature	Explanation
Connection-oriented or connectionless	Defines whether the protocol establishes some correlation between two endpoints before any user data is allowed to be transferred (connection oriented), or not (connectionless).
Error recovery	The process of noticing errored or lost segments and causing them to be resent.
Reliability	Another term for error recovery.
Flow control	Processes that control the rates at which data is transferred between two endpoints.
Segmenting application data	Application layer protocols may need to send large chunks of data—much larger than can fit inside one IP packet. The transport layer is responsible for segmenting the larger data into pieces, called segments, that can fit inside a packet.

The Transmission Control Protocol

Each TCP/IP application typically chooses to use either TCP or UDP based on the application's requirements. For instance, TCP provides error recovery, but to do so, it consumes more bandwidth and uses more processing cycles. UDP does not do error recovery, but it takes less bandwidth and uses fewer processing cycles. Regardless of which of the two TCP/IP transport layer protocols the application chooses to use, you should understand the basics of how each of the protocols works.

TCP provides a variety of useful features, including error recovery. In fact, TCP is best known for its error-recovery feature—but it does more. TCP, defined in RFC 793, performs the following functions:

- Multiplexing using port numbers
- Error recovery (reliability)
- Flow control using windowing
- Connection establishment and termination
- End-to-end ordered data transfer
- Segmentation

TCP accomplishes these functions through mechanisms at the endpoint computers. TCP relies on IP for end-to-end delivery of the data, including routing issues. In other words, TCP performs only part of the functions necessary to deliver the data between applications, and the role that it plays is directed toward providing services for the applications that sit at the endpoint computers. Regardless of whether two computers are on the same Ethernet, or are separated by the entire Internet, TCP performs its functions the same way.

Figure 6-1 shows the fields in the TCP header. Not all the fields are described in this text, but several fields are referred to in this section. The Cisco Press book, *Internetworking Technologies Handbook*, Fourth Edition, lists the fields along with brief explanations.

Figure 6-1   *TCP Header Fields*

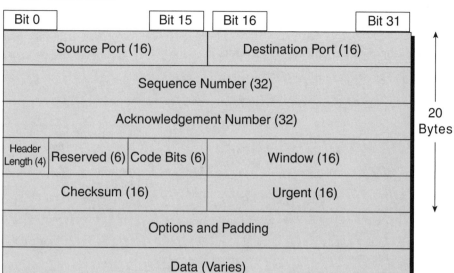

Multiplexing Using TCP Port Numbers

TCP provides a lot of features to applications, at the expense of requiring slightly more processing and overhead, as compared to UDP. However, TCP and UDP both use a concept called *multiplexing*. So, this section begins with an explanation of multiplexing with TCP and UDP. Afterward, the unique features of TCP and UDP are explored.

Multiplexing by TCP and UDP involves the process of how a computer thinks when receiving data. The computer might be running many applications, such as a web browser, an e-mail package, or an FTP client. TCP and UDP multiplexing enables the receiving computer to know which application to give the data to.

Some examples will help make the need for multiplexing obvious. The sample network consists of two PCs, labeled Hannah and Jessie. Hannah uses an application that she wrote to send advertisements that display on Jessie's screen. The application sends a new ad to Jessie every 10 seconds. Hannah uses a second application, a wire-transfer application, to send Jessie some money. Finally, Hannah uses a web browser to access the web server that runs on Jessie's PC. The ad application and wire-transfer application are imaginary, just for this example. The web application works just like it would in real life.

Figure 6-2 shows a figure of the example network, with Jessie running three applications:

■ A UDP-based ad application

■ A TCP-based wire-transfer application

■ A TCP web server application

Figure 6-2   *Hannah Sending Packets to Jessie, with Three Applications*

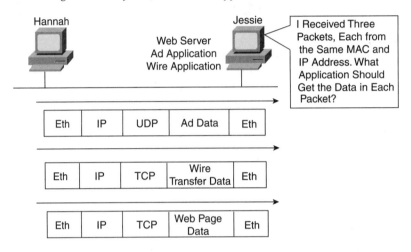

Jessie needs to know which application to give the data to, but all three packets are from the same Ethernet and IP address. You might think that Jessie could look at whether the packet contains a UDP or a TCP header, but, as you see in the figure, two applications (wire transfer and web) both are using TCP.

TCP and UDP solve this problem by using a port number field in the TCP or UDP header, respectively. Each of Hannah's TCP and UDP segments uses a different destination port number so that Jessie knows which application to give the data to. Figure 6-3 shows an example.

Multiplexing relies on the use of a concept called a *socket*. A socket consists of three things: an IP address, a transport protocol, and a port number. So, for a web server application on Jessie, the socket would be (10.1.1.2, TCP, port 80) because, by default, web servers use the well-known port 80. When Hannah's web browser connected to the web server, Hannah used a socket as well—possibly one like this: (10.1.1.1, TCP, 1030). Why 1030? Well, Hannah just needs a port number that is unique on Hannah, so Hannah saw that port 1030 was available and used it. In fact, hosts typically allocate dynamic port numbers starting at 1024 because the ports below 1024 are reserved for well-known applications, such as web services.

Figure 6-3 *Hannah Sending Packets to Jessie, with Three Applications Using Port Numbers to Multiplex*

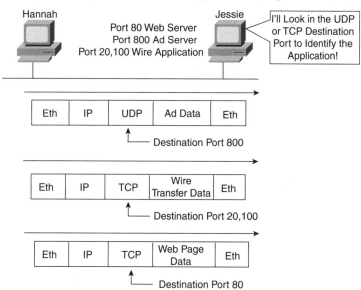

In Figure 6-3, Hannah and Jessie used three applications at the same time—hence, there were three socket connections open. Because a socket on a single computer should be unique, a connection between two sockets should identify a unique connection between two computers. The fact that each connection between two sockets is unique means that you can use multiple applications at the same time, talking to applications running on the same or different computers; multiplexing, based on sockets, ensures that the data is delivered to the correct applications. Figure 6-4 shows the three socket connections between Hannah and Jessie.

Figure 6-4 *Connections Between Sockets*

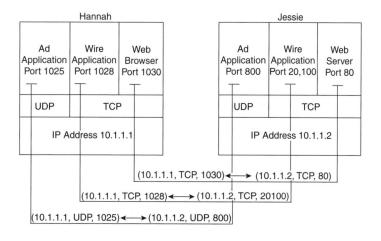

Port numbers are a vital part of the socket concept. Well-known port numbers are used by servers; other port numbers are used by clients. Applications that provide a service, such as FTP, Telnet, and web servers, open a socket using a well-known port and listen for connection requests. Because these connection requests from clients are required to include both the source and the destination port numbers, the port numbers used by the servers must be well known. Therefore, each server has a hard-coded, well-known port number, as defined in the well-known numbers RFC.

On client machines, where the requests originate, any unused port number can be allocated. The result is that each client on the same host uses a different port number, but a server uses the same port number for all connections. For example, 100 Telnet clients on the same host computer would each use a different port number, but the Telnet server with 100 clients connected to it would have only 1 socket and, therefore, only 1 port number. The combination of source and destination sockets allows all participating hosts to distinguish between the source and destination of the data. (Look to www.rfc-editor.org to find RFCs such as the well-known numbers RFC 1700.)

NOTE You can find all RFCs online at www.isi.edu/in-notes/rfc*xxxx*.txt, where *xxxx* is the number of the RFC. If you do not know the number of the RFC, you can try searching by topic at www.rfc-editor.org/rfcsearch.html.

Popular TCP/IP Applications

Throughout your preparation for the CCNA INTRO and ICND exams, you will come across a variety of TCP/IP applications. You should at least be aware of some of the applications that can be used to help manage and control a network.

The World Wide Web (WWW) application exists through web browsers accessing the content available on web servers, as mentioned earlier. While often thought of as an end-user application, you can actually use WWW to manage a router or switch by enabling a web server function in the router or switch, and using a browser to access the router or switch.

The Domain Name System (DNS) allows users to use names to refer to computers, with DNS being used to find the corresponding IP addresses. DNS also uses a client/server model, with DNS servers being controlled by networking personnel, and DNS client functions being part of most any device that uses TCP/IP today. The client simply asks the DNS server to supply the IP address that corresponds to a given name.

Simple Network Management Protocol (SNMP) is an application layer protocol used specifically for network device management. For instance, the Cisco Works network management software product can be used to query, compile, store, and display information about the operation of a network. In order to query the network devices, Cisco Works uses SNMP protocols.

Traditionally, in order to move files to and from a router or switch, Cisco used Trivial File Transfer Protocol (TFTP). TFTP defines a protocol for basic file transfer – hence the word "trivial" to start the name of the application. Alternately, routers and switches can use File Transfer Protocol (FTP), which is a much more functional protocol, for transferring files. Both work well for moving files into and out of Cisco devices. FTP allows many more features, making it a good choice for the general end-user population, whereas TFTP client and server applications are very simple, making them good tools as imbedded parts of networking devices.

Some of these applications use TCP, and some use UDP. As you will read later, TCP performs error recovery, whereas UDP does not. For instance, Simple Mail Transport Protocol (SMTP) and Post Office Protocol version 3 (POP3), both used for transferring mail, require guaranteed delivery, so they use TCP. Regardless of which transport layer protocol is used, applications use a well-known port number, so that clients know to which port to attempt to connect. Table 6-3 lists several popular applications and their well-known port numbers.

Table 6-3 *Popular Applications and Their Well-Known Port Numbers*

Port Number	Protocol	Application
20	TCP	FTP data
21	TCP	FTP control
23	TCP	Telnet
25	TCP	SMTP
53	UDP, TCP	DNS
67, 68	UDP	DHCP
69	UDP	TFTP
80	TCP	HTTP (WWW)
110	TCP	POP3
161	UDP	SNMP

Error Recovery (Reliability)

TCP provides for reliable data transfer, which is also called *reliability* or *error recovery*, depending on what document you read. To accomplish reliability, TCP numbers data bytes using the Sequence and Acknowledgment fields in the TCP header. TCP achieves reliability in both directions, using the Sequence Number field of one direction combined with the Acknowledgment field in the opposite direction. Figure 6-5 shows the basic operation.

In Figure 6-5, the Acknowledgment field in the TCP header sent by the web client (4000) implies the next byte to be received; this is called *forward acknowledgment*. The sequence number reflects the number of the first byte in the segment. In this case, each TCP segment is 1000 bytes in length; the Sequence and Acknowledgment fields count the number of bytes.

Figure 6-5 *TCP Acknowledgment Without Errors*

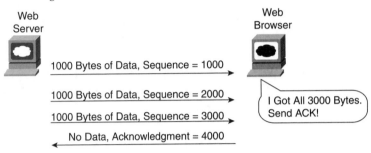

Figure 6-6 depicts the same scenario, but the second TCP segment was lost or was in error. The web client's reply has an ACK field equal to 2000, implying that the web client is expecting byte number 2000 next. The TCP function at the web server then could recover lost data by resending the second TCP segment. The TCP protocol allows for resending just that segment and then waiting, hoping that the web client will reply with an acknowledgment that equals 4000.

Figure 6-6 *TCP Acknowledgment with Errors*

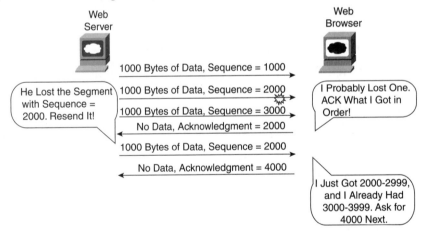

(Although not shown, the sender also sets a re-transmission timer, awaiting acknowledgment, just in case the acknowledgment is lost, or in case all transmitted segments are lost. If that timer expires, the TCP sender sends all segments again.)

Flow Control Using Windowing

TCP implements flow control by taking advantage of the Sequence and Acknowledgment fields in the TCP header, along with another field called the Window field. This Window field implies the maximum number of unacknowledged bytes allowed outstanding at any instant in time. The window starts small and then grows until errors occur. The window then "slides" up and down based on network performance, so it is sometimes called a *sliding window.* When the window is full, the sender will not send, which controls the flow of data. Figure 6-7 shows windowing with a current window size of 3000. Each TCP segment has 1000 bytes of data.

Figure 6-7   *TCP Windowing*

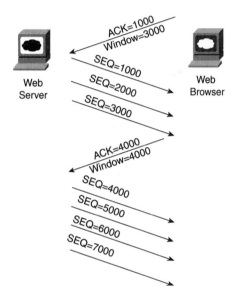

Notice that the web server must wait after sending the third segment because the window is exhausted. When the acknowledgment has been received, another window can be sent. Because there have been no errors, the web client grants a larger window to the server, so now 4000 bytes can be sent before an acknowledgment is received by the server. In other words, the Window field is used by the receiver to tell the sender how much data it can send before it must stop and wait for the next acknowledgment. As with other TCP features, windowing is symmetrical—both sides send and receive, and, in each case, the receiver grants a window to the sender using the Window field.

Windowing does not require that the sender stop sending in all cases. If an acknowledgment is received before the window is exhausted, a new window begins and the sender continues to send data until the current window is exhausted. (The term, *Positive Acknowledgement and Retransmission [PAR]*, is sometimes used to describe the error recovery and windowing processes used by TCP.)

Connection Establishment and Termination

TCP connection establishment occurs before any of the other TCP features can begin their work. Connection establishment refers to the process of initializing sequence and acknowledgment fields and agreeing to the port numbers used. Figure 6-8 shows an example of connection establishment flow.

Figure 6-8 *TCP Connection Establishment*

This three-way connection-establishment flow must complete before data transfer can begin. The connection exists between the two sockets, although there is no single socket field in the TCP header. Of the three parts of a socket, the IP addresses are implied based on the source and destination IP addresses in the IP header. TCP is implied because a TCP header is in use, as specified by the protocol field value in the IP header. Therefore, the only parts of the socket that need to be encoded in the TCP header are the port numbers.

TCP signals connection establishment using 2 bits inside the flag fields of the TCP header. Called the SYN and ACK flags, these bits have a particularly interesting meaning. SYN means "synchronize the sequence numbers," which is one necessary component in initialization for TCP. The ACK field means "the acknowledgment field is valid in this header." Until the sequence numbers are initialized, the acknowledgment field cannot be very useful. Also notice that in the initial TCP segment in Figure 6-8, no acknowledgment number is shown; this is because that number is not valid yet. Because the ACK field must be present in all the ensuing segments, the ACK bit continues to be set until the connection is terminated.

TCP initializes the Sequence Number and Acknowledgment Number fields to any number that fits into the 4-byte fields; the actual values shown in Figure 6-8 are simply example values. The initialization flows are each considered to have a single byte of data, as reflected in the Acknowledgment Number fields in the example.

Figure 6-9 shows TCP connection termination. This four-way termination sequence is straightforward and uses an additional flag, called the *FIN bit*. (FIN is short for "finished," as you might guess.) One interesting note: Before the device on the right sends the third TCP segment in the sequence, it notifies the application that the connection is coming down.

It then waits on an acknowledgment from the application before sending the third segment in the figure. Just in case the application takes some time to reply, the PC on the right sends the second flow in the figure, acknowledging that the other PC wants to take down the connection. Otherwise, the PC on the left might resend the first segment over and over.

Figure 6-9 *TCP Connection Termination*

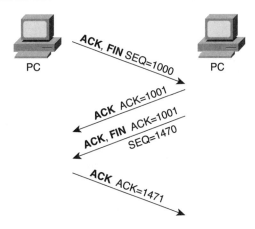

Connectionless and Connection-Oriented Protocols

The terms *connection-oriented* and *connectionless* have some relatively well-known connotations inside the world of networking protocols. The meaning of the terms is intertwined with error recovery and flow control, but they are not the same. So, first, some basic definitions are in order:

- **Connection-oriented protocol**—A protocol either that requires an exchange of messages before data transfer begins or that has a required pre-established correlation between two endpoints

- **Connectionless protocol**—A protocol that does not require an exchange of messages and that does not require a pre-established correlation between two endpoints

TCP is indeed connection oriented because of the set of three messages that establish a TCP connection. Likewise, Sequenced Packet Exchange (SPX), a transport layer protocol from Novell, is connection oriented. When using permanent virtual circuits (PVCs), Frame Relay does not require any messages to be sent ahead of time, but it does require predefinition in the Frame Relay switches, establishing a connection between two Frame Relay–attached devices. ATM PVCs are also connection oriented, for similar reasons.

> **NOTE** Some documentation refers to the terms *connected* and *connection-oriented*. These terms are used synonymously. You will most likely see the use of the term *connection-oriented* in Cisco documentation.

Many people confuse the real meaning of *connection-oriented* with the definition of a reliable, or error-recovering, protocol. TCP happens to do both, but just because a protocol is connection-oriented does not mean that it also performs error recovery. Table 6-4 lists some popular protocols and tells whether they are connected or reliable.

Table 6-4 *Protocol Characteristics: Recovery and Connections*

Connected?	Reliable?	Examples
Connection-oriented	Yes	LLC Type 2 (802.2), TCP, Novell SPX
Connection-oriented	No	Frame Relay VCs, ATM VCs, PPP
Connectionless	Yes	TFTP, NetWare NCP (no Packet Burst)
Connectionless	No	UDP, IP, most Layer 3 protocols

Data Segmentation and Ordered Data Transfer

Applications need to send data. Sometimes the data is small—in some cases, a single byte. In other cases, for instance, with a file transfer, the data might be millions of bytes.

Each different type of data link protocol typically has a limit on the *maximum transmission unit (MTU)* that can be sent. MTU refers to the size of the "data," according to the data link layer—in other words, the size of the Layer 3 packet that sits inside the data field of a frame. For many data link protocols, Ethernet included, the MTU is 1500 bytes.

TCP handles the fact that an application might give it millions of bytes to send by *segmenting* the data into smaller pieces, called *segments*. Because an IP packet can often be no more than 1500 bytes, and because IP and TCP headers are 20 bytes each, TCP typically segments large data into 1460 byte (or smaller) segments.

The TCP receiver performs reassembly when it receives the segments. To reassemble the data, TCP must recover lost segments, as was previously covered. However, the TCP receiver must also reorder segments that arrive out of sequence. Because IP routing can choose to balance traffic across multiple links, the actual segments may be delivered out of order. So, the TCP receiver also must perform *ordered data transfer* by reassembling the data into the original order. The process is not hard to imagine: If segments arrive with the sequence numbers 1000, 3000, and 2000, each with 1000 bytes of data, the receiver can reorder them and no retransmissions are required.

You should also be aware of some terminology related to TCP segmentation. The TCP header, along with the data field, together are called a *TCP segment*. This term is similar to a data link frame and an IP packet, in that the terms refer to the headers and trailers for the respective layers, plus the encapsulated data. The term *L4PDU* also can be used instead of the term *TCP segment* because TCP is a Layer 4 protocol.

TCP Function Summary

Table 6-5 summarizes TCP functions.

Table 6-5 *TCP Function Summary*

Function	Description
Multiplexing	Function that allows receiving hosts to decide the correct application for which the data is destined, based on the port number
Error recovery (reliability)	Process of numbering and acknowledging data with Sequence and Acknowledgment header fields
Flow control using windowing	Process that uses window sizes to protect buffer space and routing devices
Connection establishment and termination	Process used to initialize port numbers and Sequence and Acknowledgment fields
Ordered data transfer and data segmentation	Continuous stream of bytes from upper-layer process that is "segmented" for transmission and delivered to upper-layer processes at the receiving device, with the bytes in the same order

The User Datagram Protocol

UDP provides a service for applications to exchange messages. Unlike TCP, UDP is connectionless and provides no reliability, no windowing, and no reordering of the received data. However, UDP provides some functions of TCP, such as data transfer, segmentation, and multiplexing using port numbers, and it does so with fewer bytes of overhead and with less processing required.

UDP multiplexes using port numbers in an identical fashion to TCP. The only difference in UDP (compared to TCP) sockets is that, instead of designating TCP as the transport protocol, the transport protocol is UDP. An application could open identical port numbers on the same host but use TCP in one case and UDP in the other—that is not typical, but it certainly is allowed. If a particular service supports both TCP and UDP transport, it uses the same value for the TCP and UDP port numbers, as shown in the assigned numbers RFC (currently RFC 1700—see www.isi.edu/in-notes/rfc1700.txt).

UDP data transfer differs from TCP data transfer in that no reordering or recovery is accomplished. Applications that use UDP are tolerant of the lost data, or they have some application mechanism to recover lost data. For example, DNS requests use UDP because the user will retry an operation if the DNS resolution fails. The Network File System (NFS), a remote file system application, performs recovery with application layer code, so UDP features are acceptable to NFS.

Table 6-6 contrasts typical transport layer functions as performed (or not performed) by UDP or TCP.

Table 6-6 *TCP and UDP Functional Comparison*

Function	Description (TCP)	Description (UDP)
Ordered data transfer	This involves a continuous stream of ordered data.	Does not reorder received data.
Multiplexing using ports	Receiving hosts decide the correct application for which the data is destined, based on the port number.	Same as TCP.
Reliable transfer	Acknowledgment of data uses the Sequence and Acknowledgment fields in the TCP header.	This is not a feature of UDP.
Flow control	This process is used to protect buffer space and routing devices.	This is not a feature of UDP.
Connections	This process is used to initialize port numbers and other TCP header fields.	UDP is connectionless.

Figure 6-10 shows TCP and UDP header formats. Note the existence of both Source Port and Destination Port fields in the TCP and UDP headers, but the absence of Sequence Number and Acknowledgment Number fields in the UDP header. UDP does not need these fields because it makes no attempt to number the data for acknowledgments or resequencing.

Figure 6-10   *TCP and UDP Headers*

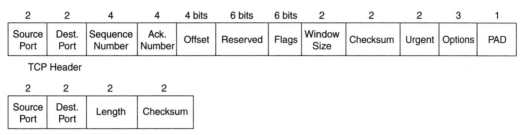

TCP Header

UDP Header

* Unless Specified, Lengths Shown
Are the Numbers of Bytes

UDP gains some advantages over TCP by not using the Sequence and Acknowledgment fields. The most obvious advantage of UDP over TCP is that there are fewer bytes of overhead. Not as obvious is the fact that UDP does not require waiting on acknowledgments or holding the data in memory until it is acknowledged. This means that UDP applications are not artificially slowed by the acknowledgment process, and memory is freed more quickly.

Foundation Summary

The "Foundation Summary" section of each chapter lists the most important facts from the chapter. Although this section does not list every fact from the chapter that will be on your CCNA exam, a well-prepared CCNA candidate should know, at a minimum, all the details in each "Foundation Summary" section before going to take the exam.

The terms *connection-oriented* and *connectionless* have some relatively well-known connotations inside the world of networking protocols. The meaning of the terms is intertwined with error recovery and flow control, but they are not the same. Some basic definitions are in order:

- **Connection-oriented protocol**—A protocol either that requires an exchange of messages before data transfer begins or that has a required pre-established correlation between two endpoints

- **Connectionless protocol**—A protocol that does not require an exchange of messages and that does not require a pre-established correlation between two endpoints

Figure 6-11 shows an example of windowing.

Figure 6-11 *TCP Windowing*

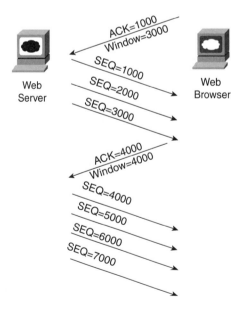

TCP and UDP multiplex between different applications using the port source and destination number fields. Figure 6-12 shows an example.

Figure 6-12   *Hannah Sending Packets to Jessie, with Three Applications Using Port Numbers to Multiplex*

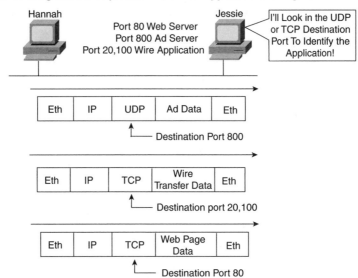

Figure 6-13 depicts TCP error recovery.

Figure 6-13   *TCP Acknowledgment with Errors*

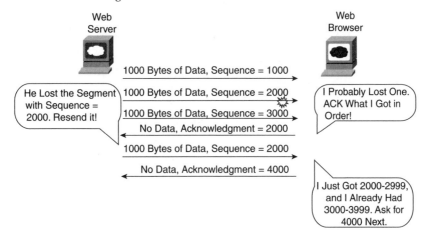

Figure 6-14 shows an example of a TCP connection-establishment flow.

Figure 6-14 *TCP Connection Establishment*

Table 6-7 contrasts typical transport layer functions as performed (or not performed) by UDP or TCP.

Table 6-7 *TCP and UDP Functional Comparison*

Function	Description (TCP)	Description (UDP)
Ordered data transfer	This involves a continuous stream of ordered data.	Does not reorder received data.
Multiplexing using ports	Receiving hosts decide the correct application for which the data is destined, based on the port number.	Same as TCP.
Reliable transfer	Acknowledgment of data uses the Sequence and Acknowledgment fields in the TCP header.	This is not a feature of UDP.
Flow control	This process is used to protect buffer space and routing devices.	This is not a feature of UDP.
Connections	This process is used to initialize port numbers and other TCP header fields.	UDP is connectionless.

Q&A

As mentioned in the introduction, you have two choices for review questions. The questions that follow give you a bigger challenge than the exam itself by using an open-ended question format. By reviewing now with this more difficult question format, you can exercise your memory better and prove your conceptual and factual knowledge of this chapter. The answers to these questions are found in Appendix A.

For more practice with exam-like question formats, including questions using a router simulator and multiple-choice questions, use the exam engine on the CD.

1. Describe the features required for a protocol to be considered connectionless.

2. Name at least three connectionless protocols.

3. Describe the features required for a protocol to be considered connection oriented.

4. In a particular error-recovering protocol, the sender sends three frames, labeled 2, 3, and 4. On its next sent frame, the receiver of these frames sets an Acknowledgment field to 4. What does this typically imply?

5. Name three connection-oriented protocols.

6. Describe how TCP performs error recovery. What role do the routers play?

7. How many TCP segments are exchanged to establish a TCP connection? How many are required to terminate a TCP connection?

8. Describe the purpose of the Port Number field in a TCP header. Give one example.

9. List the components of a TCP socket.

10. How many TCP segments must be sent to establish a TCP connection? How many are used with normal TCP connection termination?

11. How many UDP segments must be sent to establish a UDP connection? How many are used with normal UDP connection termination?

Cisco Published INTRO Exam Topics*
Covered in This Part:

1 Use a subset of Cisco IOS commands to analyze and report network problems

2 Use embedded layer 3 through layer 7 protocols to establish, test, suspend or disconnect connectivity to remote devices from the router console

4 Establish communication between a terminal device and the router IOS, and use IOS for system analysis

5 Manipulate system image and device configuration files

6 Perform an initial configuration on a router and save the resultant configuration file

7 Use commands incorporated within IOS to analyze and report network problems

8 Assign IP addresses

9 Describe and install the hardware and software required to be able to communicate via a network

10 Use embedded data link layer functionality to perform network neighbor discovery and analysis from the router console

18 Describe the purpose and fundamental operation of the internetwork operating system (IOS)

20 Identify the major internal and external components of a router, and describe the associated functionality

21 Identify and describe the stages of the router boot-up sequence

22 Describe how the configuration register and boot system commands modify the router boot-up sequence

37 Perform an initial configuration on a switch and save the resultant configuration file

* Always re-check www.cisco.com for the latest posted exam topics

PART II:
Operating Cisco Devices

This chapter covers the following subjects:

- The Cisco IOS Software Command-Line Interface

- Configuring Cisco IOS Software

- Upgrading Cisco IOS Software and the Cisco IOS Software Boot Process

CHAPTER 7

Operating Cisco Routers

To configure a Cisco router to route TCP/IP packets, you need to give each interface on the router an IP address and subnet mask. You also typically configure a dynamic routing protocol, which discovers the routes in a network. That's typically all the configuration that is required to make a Cisco router route IP packets.

However, Cisco covers many details of router operation on the INTRO exam beyond just configuring a few IP addresses and an IP routing protocol. So, before you even get into the details of configuring IP on a Cisco router, you need some background information on Cisco routers—this chapter covers those details. If you support Cisco routers as part of your job, most things in this chapter will be things that you do every day.

Some Cisco switches use a CLI such as Cisco IOS Software—for instance, the 1900 and 2950 series switches. This chapter covers the IOS CLI on a router, and Chapter 8, "Operating Cisco LAN Switches," covers some details of the IOS CLI on 2950 LAN switches.

"Do I Know This Already?" Quiz

The purpose of the "Do I Know This Already?" quiz is to help you decide whether you really need to read the entire chapter. If you already intend to read the entire chapter, you do not necessarily need to answer these questions now.

The ten-question quiz, derived from the major sections in the "Foundation Topics" portion of the chapter, helps you determine how to spend your limited study time.

Table 7-1 outlines the major topics discussed in this chapter and the "Do I Know This Already?" quiz questions that correspond to those topics.

Table 7-1 *"Do I Know This Already?" Foundation Topics Section-to-Question Mapping*

Foundations Topics Section	Questions Covered in This Section
The Cisco IOS Software Command-Line Interface	1, 2
Configuring Cisco IOS Software	3–6, 9–10
Upgrading Cisco IOS Software and the Cisco IOS Software Boot Process	7–8

> **CAUTION** The goal of self-assessment is to gauge your mastery of the topics in this chapter. If you do not know the answer to a question or are only partially sure of the answer, you should mark this question wrong for purposes of the self-assessment. Giving yourself credit for an answer that you correctly guess skews your self-assessment results and might provide you with a false sense of security.

1. In which of the following modes of the CLI could you configure a description of Ethernet0?

   a. User mode

   b. Enable mode

   c. Global configuration mode

   d. Setup mode

   e. Interface configuration mode

2. In which of the following modes of the CLI could you issue a command to reboot the router?

   a. User mode

   b. Enable mode

   c. Global configuration mode

   d. Interface configuration mode

3. What type of router memory is used to store the configuration used by the router when it is up and working?

   a. RAM

   b. ROM

   c. Flash

   d. NVRAM

   e. Bubble

4. What type of router memory is used to store the operating system used for low-level debugging and not for normal operation?

   a. RAM

   b. ROM

   c. Flash

   d. NVRAM

   e. Bubble

5. What command copies the configuration from RAM into NVRAM?

   a. copy running-config tftp

   b. copy tftp running-config

   c. copy running-config start-up-config

   d. copy start-up-config running-config

   e. copy startup-config running-config

   f. copy running-config startup-config

6. What mode prompts the user for basic configuration information?

   a. User mode

   b. Enable mode

   c. Global configuration mode

   d. Setup mode

   e. Interface configuration mode

7. Which of the following could cause a router to change the IOS that is loaded when the router boots?

   a. reload command

   b. boot exec command

   c. reboot exec command

   d. boot configuration command

   e. reboot configuration command

   f. configuration register

8. Which of the following hexadecimal values in the last nibble of the configuration register would cause a router to not look in Flash memory?

   a. 0

   b. 1

   c. 2

   d. 3

   e. 4

   f. 5

   g. 6

   h. F

9. Imagine that you have configured the **enable secret** command, followed by the **enable password** command, from the console. You log out of the router and log back in at the console. Which command defines the password that you had to type to access the router again from the console?

   a. **enable password**

   b. **enable secret**

   c. Neither **enable password** nor **enable secret**

10. Imagine that you have configured the **enable secret** command, followed by the **enable password** command, from the console. You log out of the router and log back in at the console. Which command defines the password that you had to type to access privileged mode?

    a. **enable password**

    b. **enable secret**

    c. Neither

    d. The **password** command, if configured

The answers to the "Do I Know This Already?" quiz are found in Appendix A, "Answers to the 'Do I Know This Already?' Quizzes and Q&A Sections." The suggested choices for your next step are as follows:

- **8 or less overall score**—Read the entire chapter. This includes the "Foundation Topics" and "Foundation Summary" sections and the Q&A section.

- **9 or 10 overall score**—If you want more review on these topics, skip to the "Foundation Summary" section and then go to the Q&A section. Otherwise, move to the next chapter.

Foundation Topics

The Cisco IOS Software Command-Line Interface

The majority of Cisco routers run Cisco IOS Software. IOS supplies several features, including basic connectivity for a variety of protocols, security features for those protocols, plus reliable and scalable network services. In short, IOS supplies network services to computers that use networked applications.

The exam topics covered in this section will become second nature to you as you work with Cisco routers more often. In this chapter, you will learn about the following three main features of Cisco IOS Software:

- You must know about the Cisco IOS Software command-line interface (CLI), which is the text-based user interface to a Cisco router.

- You need to understand the process of how to configure a router, even though you might not know all the commands that you can use to configure a router. (Later chapters cover a variety of configuration commands.)

- You need to know about upgrading Cisco IOS Software in a router; upgrading requires a reboot of the router, so you also need to know what happens during the boot process.

By the time you are finished with your CCNA study, the router CLI and configuration topics in this chapter will be second nature, for the most part.

Access to the CLI

Cisco uses the acronym CLI to refer to the terminal user command-line interface to the IOS. The term CLI implies that the user is typing commands at a terminal, a terminal emulator, or a Telnet connection.

To access the CLI, use one of three methods, as illustrated in Figure 7-1.

You access the router through the console, through a dialup device through a modem attached to the auxiliary port, or by using Telnet. The router has RJ-45 receptacles for both the console and the auxiliary port. The cable from the console to a PC requires a special eight-wire cable, called a *rollover cable*, in which pin 1 connects to pin 8 on the other end of the cable, pin 2 connects to pin 7, and so on. Figure 7-1 shows the cable pinouts. The modem connection from the auxiliary port uses a straight-through cable.

Figure 7-1 *CLI Access*

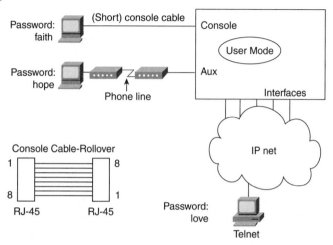

From any of the three methods of accessing the router, you enter *user exec mode* first. User exec mode, also sometimes called *user mode*, enables you to look around, but not break anything. The passwords shown in Figure 7-1 are not defaults—those passwords would be required if the configuration used in Table 7-2 were used. The console, auxiliary, and Telnet passwords all are set separately.

Table 7-2 *CLI Password Configuration*

Access From	Password Type	Configuration
Console	Console password	**line console** *0* **login** **password** *faith*
Auxiliary	Auxiliary password	**line aux** *0* **login** **password** *hope*
Telnet	vty password	**line vty** *0 4* **login** **password** *love*

Passwords are required for Telnet and auxiliary access as of Cisco IOS Software Release 12.0, and the exams are based on Cisco IOS Software Release 12.2. However, there are no preconfigured passwords—therefore, you must configure passwords for Telnet and auxiliary access from the console first.

All Cisco routers have a console port, and most have an auxiliary port. The console port is intended for local administrative access from an ASCII terminal or a computer using a terminal emulator. The auxiliary port, which is missing on a few models of Cisco routers, is intended for asynchronous dial access from an ASCII terminal or terminal emulator; the auxiliary port often is used for dial backup.

This chapter focuses on the process of using the CLI instead of a particular set of commands. However, if you see a command in this chapter, you probably should remember it. In the last column of Table 7-2, the first command in each configuration is a context-setting command, as described later in this chapter. But, as you see, the second and third commands would be ambiguous if you did not supply some additional information, such as whether the **password** command was for the console, aux, or Telnet. The **login** command actually tells the router to display a password prompt. The **password** commands specify the text password to be typed by the user to gain access. Sometimes network engineers choose to set all three passwords to the same value because they all let you get into user mode.

Several concurrent Telnet connections to a router are allowed. The **line vty** *0 4* command signifies that this configuration applies to vtys (virtual teletypes/terminals) 0 through 4. Originally, IOS allowed for only these five vtys, unless the router was also a dial access server, such as a Cisco AS5300. At IOS Version 12.2, 16 vtys are allowed by default on all models of routers. Regardless, all the configured vtys typically have the same password, which is handy because users connecting to the router through Telnet cannot choose which vty they get.

> **NOTE** On occasion, a network engineer might set the last vty to use a different password that no one else knows; that way, when all the other vtys are in use and that network engineer Telnets to the router, he can use the password only he knows—and always get access to the router.

User exec mode is one of two command exec modes in the IOS user interface. *Enable* mode (also known as *privileged* mode or *privileged exec* mode) is the other. Enable mode is so named because the **enable** command is used to reach this mode, as shown in Figure 7-2; privileged mode earns its name because powerful, or privileged, commands can be executed there.

Figure 7-2 *User and Privileged Modes*

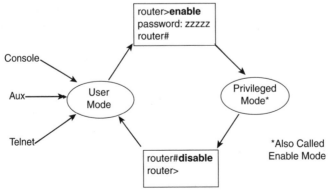

CLI Help Features

If you printed the IOS Command Reference documents, you would end up with a stack of paper several feet tall. No one should expect to memorize all the commands—and no one does in real life, either. Several very easy, convenient tools can be used to help you remember commands and then also save you time typing. As you progress through your Cisco certifications, the exams will cover progressively more commands. However, you should know the methods of getting command help.

Table 7-3 summarizes command-recall help options available at the CLI. Note that, in the first column, "Command" represents any command. Likewise, "parm" represents a command's parameter. For instance, the third row lists *command ?*, which means that commands such as **show ?** and **copy ?** would list help for the **show** and **copy** commands, respectively.

Table 7-3 *Cisco IOS Software Command Help*

What You Type	The Help You Get
?	Help for all commands available in this mode.
help	Text describing how to get help. No actual command help is given.
Command ?	Text help describing all the first parameter options for the command.
com?	A list of commands that start with "com."
command parm?	This style of help lists all parameters beginning with "parm." (Notice that no spaces exist between **parm** and the ?.)
command parm<Tab>	If you press the Tab key midword, the CLI either spells the rest of this parameter at the command line or does nothing. If the CLI does nothing, it means that this string of characters represents more than one possible next parameter, so the CLI does not know which to spell out.
command parm1 ?	If a space is inserted before the question mark, the CLI lists all the next parameters and gives a brief explanation of each.

When you type the **?**, IOS's CLI reacts immediately; that is, you don't need to press the Enter key or any other keys. The router also redisplays what you typed before the **?**, to save you some keystrokes. If you press Enter immediately after the **?**, IOS tries to execute the command with only the parameters that you have typed so far.

"command" represents any command, not the word *command*. Likewise, "parm" represents a command's parameter, not the word *parameter*.

The information supplied by using help depends on the CLI mode. For example, when **?** is typed in user mode, the commands allowed only in privileged exec mode are not displayed. Also, help is available in configuration mode; only configuration commands are displayed in that mode of operation.

IOS stores the commands that you type in a history buffer, storing ten commands by default. You can change the history size with the **terminal history size** *x* user exec command, where *x* is the number of commands for the CLI to recall; this can be set to a value between 0 and 256. You then can retrieve commands so that you do not have to retype the commands. Table 7-4 lists the commands used to manipulate previously typed commands.

Table 7-4   *Key Sequences for Command Edit and Recall*

Keyboard Command	What You Get
Up arrow or Ctrl-p	This displays the most recently used command. If it is pressed again, the next most recent command appears until the history buffer is exhausted. (The p stands for previous.)
Down arrow or Ctrl-n	If you have gone too far back into the history buffer, these keys will go forward to the more recently typed commands. (The n is for next.)
Left arrow or Ctrl-b	This moves the cursor backward in the currently displayed command without deleting characters. (The b stands for back.)
Right arrow or Ctrl-f	This moves the cursor forward in the currently displayed command without deleting characters. (The f stands for forward.)
Backspace	This moves the cursor backward in the currently displayed command, deleting characters.
Ctrl-a	This moves the cursor directly to the first character of the currently displayed command.
Ctrl-e	This moves the cursor directly to the end of the currently displayed command.
Esc-b	This moves the cursor back one word in the currently displayed command.
Esc-f	This moves the cursor forward one word in the currently displayed command.
Ctrl-r	This creates a new command prompt, followed by all the characters typed since the last command prompt was written. This is particularly useful if system messages confuse the screen and it is unclear what you have typed so far.

The key sequences in Table 7-4 are part of what Cisco calls *enhanced editing* mode. IOS enables enhanced editing mode by default and has for a long time. However, you can turn off these keystrokes with the **no terminal editing** exec command, and turn them back on with the **terminal editing** command. Why would you bother? Well, occasionally, you might be using a scripting language to run commands automatically on the router through a Telnet session, and enhanced editing mode sometimes can interfere with the scripts. For the exam, just remember that you can enable and disable enhanced editing mode.

The debug and show Commands

By far, the most popular single IOS command is the **show** command. The **show** command has a very large variety of options, and with those options, you can find the status of almost every feature of IOS. Essentially, the **show** command lists facts about the router's operational status that the router already knows.

Another less popular command is the **debug** command. The **debug** command actually tells the router to spend some CPU cycles to do things besides its normal functions, to provide the user with more information about what the router is doing. It requires more router CPU cycles, but it lets you watch what is happening in a router while it is happening.

When you use the **debug** command, IOS creates messages when different events occur and, by default, sends them to the console. These messages are called *syslog messages*. If you have used the console of a router for any length of time, you likely have noticed these messages—and when they are frequent, you probably became a little frustrated. You can view these same messages when you have Telnetted to a router by using the **terminal monitor** command.

Be aware that some **debug** options create so many messages that the IOS cannot process them all, possibly crashing the IOS. You might want to check the current router CPU utilization with the **show process** command before issuing any **debug** command. You also should know that the **no debug all** command disables all debugs. Before enabling an unfamiliar **debug** command option, issue a **no debug all** and then issue the debug that you want to use; then quickly retrieve the **no debug all** command using the up arrow or Ctrl-p key sequence. If the debug quickly degrades router performance, press Enter immediately, executing the **no debug all** command, to try to prevent the router from crashing.

Configuring Cisco IOS Software

You must understand how to configure a Cisco router to succeed on the exam—or to succeed in supporting Cisco routers. This section covers the basic configuration processes, including the concept of a configuration file and the locations in which the configuration files can be stored.

Configuration mode is another mode for the Cisco CLI, similar to user mode and privileged mode. User mode allows commands that are not disruptive to be issued, with some information being displayed to the user. Privileged mode supports a superset of commands compared to user mode, including commands that might harm the router. However, none of the commands in user or privileged mode changes the configuration of the router. Configuration mode is used to enter configuration commands into the router. Figure 7-3 illustrates the relationships among configuration mode, user exec mode, and privileged exec mode.

Figure 7-3 *CLI Configuration Mode Versus Exec Modes*

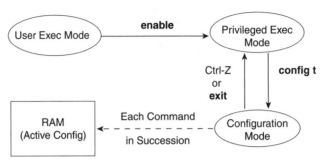

Commands typed in configuration mode update the active configuration file. *These changes to the configuration occur immediately each time you press the Enter key at the end of a command.* Be careful when you type in a configuration command!

Configuration mode itself contains a multitude of subcommand modes. Context-setting commands move you from one configuration subcommand mode to another. These context-setting commands tell the router the topic about which you will type the next few configuration commands. More important, they tell the router what commands to list when you ask for help. After all, the whole reason for these contexts is to make online help more convenient and clear for you. So, if you are confused now, hang on—the next sample will clarify what I mean.

> **NOTE** *Context setting* is not a Cisco term—it's just a term used here to help make sense of configuration mode.

The **interface** command is the most commonly used context-setting configuration command. As an example, the CLI user could enter interface configuration mode after typing the **interface ethernet 0** configuration command. Command help in Ethernet interface configuration mode displays only commands that are useful when configuring Ethernet interfaces. Commands used in this context are called *subcommands*—or, in this specific case, *interface subcommands*. If you have significant experience using the CLI in configuration mode, much of this will be second nature. From an INTRO exam perspective, recalling whether popular commands are global commands or subcommands will be useful, but you really should focus on the particular commands covered here. As a side effect, you will learn whether the commands are global configuration commands or subcommands.

No set rules exist for what commands are global commands or subcommands. Generally, however, when multiple instances of a parameter can be set in a single router, the command used to set the parameter is likely a configuration subcommand. Items that are set once for the entire router are likely global commands. For instance, the **hostname** command is a global command because there is only one host name per router. The **interface ethernet 0** command is a global configuration command because there is only one such interface in this router. Finally, the **ip address** command is an interface subcommand that sets the IP address on the interface; each interface has a different IP address.

Use Ctrl-z from any part of configuration mode (or use the **exit** command from global configuration mode) to exit configuration mode and return to privileged exec mode. The configuration mode **end** command also exits from any point in the configuration mode back to privileged exec mode. The **exit** command backs you out of configuration mode one sub-configuration mode at a time.

Example Configuration Process

Example 7-1 illustrates how the console password is defined; gives host name, prompt, and interface descriptions; and shows the finished configuration. The lines beginning with ! are comment lines that highlight significant processes or command lines within the example. The **show running-config** command output also includes comment lines with just a ! to make the output more readable—many comment lines in the examples in this book were added to explain the meaning of the configuration. You should remember the process as well as these particular commands for the INTRO exam.

Example 7-1 *Configuration Process Example*

```
User Access Verification

Password:
Router>enable
Password:
Router#configure terminal
Router(config)#enable password lu
Router(config)#line console 0
Router(config-line)#login
Router(config-line)#password cisco
Router(config-line)#hostname Critter
Critter(config)#prompt Emma
Emma(config)#interface serial 1
Emma(config-if)#description this is the link to Albuquerque
Emma(config-if)#exit
Emma(config)#exit
Emma#
Emma#show running-config
```

continues

Example 7-1 *Configuration Process Example (Continued)*

```
Building configuration...

Current configuration:
!
version 12.2   934 bytes
! Version of IOS on router, automatic command



service timestamps debug uptime
service timestamps log uptime
no service password-encryption
!
hostname Critter
prompt Emma
!
enable password lu
!
ip subnet-zero
no ip domain-lookup
!
interface Serial0
!
interface Serial1
 description this is the link to Albuquerque
!
interface Ethernet0
!
ip classless
no ip http server
line con 0
 password cisco
 login
!
line aux 0
line vty 0 4
!
end
```

The preceding example illustrates the differences between user and privileged modes and configuration mode. The **configure terminal** command is used to move from privileged mode into configuration mode. The command prompt changes when moving into configuration mode, and it also changes based on what you are doing in configuration mode. Plus, typing a ? in configuration mode gives you help just on configuration commands.

When you change from one configuration mode to another, the prompt changes. Example 7-2 repeats the same example as in Example 7-1, but with annotations for what is happening.

Example 7-2   *Configuration Process with Annotations*

```
User Access Verification

Password:
Router>enable
!In user mode, then you type the enable command
Password:
Router#configure terminal
!In privileged mode, using the configure terminal command to enter global
Router(config)#enable password lu
!The enable password command is a global command  so the prompt stays as a global
!command prompt
Router(config)#line console 0
!line console changes the context to console line configuration mode
Router(config-line)#login
!login is a console subcommand, so the prompt remains the same
Router(config-line)#password cisco
!password is also a console sub-command
Router(config-line)#hostname Critter
!hostname is a global command, so it is used, and the mode changes back to global  config mode
Critter(config)#prompt Emma
!prompt is a global command, so the prompt stays as a global command mode prompt
Emma(config)#interface serial 1
!interface changes contexts to interface subcommand mode
Emma(config-if)#description this is the link to Albuquerque
!description is a sub-command in interface config mode, so prompt stays the same
Emma(config-if)#exit
!exit backs up one mode towards global
Emma(config)#exit
!exit in global mode exits back to privileged mode
```

IOS also can change the contents of a configuration command that you type. For instance, if you type a command and set only default values, IOS typically does not add the command to the configuration file because it is not needed. Also, some commands include passwords that the router encrypts for display purposes, so the **show running-config** command lists only the encrypted form of the password. Example 11-3 shows a couple of examples of commands that show up differently in the **show running-config** output, as compared to the command typed in configuration mode.

Example 7-3 *Example Config Commands That IOS Changes*

```
Emma#configure terminal
Enter configuration commands, one per line.  End with CNTL/Z.
Emma(config)#enable secret cisco
Emma(config)#banner motd # This is banner line 1
Enter TEXT message.  End with the character '#'.
This is line 2
This is line 3, with an ending delimiter #
Emma(config)#^Z
Emma#show running-config
! Lines ommitted to save space
!
enable secret 5 $1$TRhO$BtwiiisUCcGYiM/oMjH6k0
!
! Lines ommitted to save space
!
banner motd ^C This is banner line 1
This is line 2
This is line 3, with an ending delimiter ^C
```

When moving from user mode to enable mode, you must type the **enable** command and supply a password. If the **enable password** command has been used to configure the password, you should type that password. If the **enable secret** command has been used, as in Example 7-3, you should use the enable secret password. If both are configured, you use the enable secret password.

IOS automatically encrypts the enable secret password, as seen in the output of the **show running-config** command in Example 7-3. The password set with the **enable password** command can be encrypted, but someone wrote a program to decrypt the password back to the original clear-text password. Technically, the algorithm used to change the enable secret password performs a one-way hash instead of simple encryption, which means that the password cannot be decrypted.

The **banner motd** command is the other command that IOS changes in Example 7-3. The **banner motd** (motd stands for "message of the day") command causes a text banner to display when someone accesses the router from the console, Telnet, or an auxiliary port. The banner can span many lines; to know when you stop typing the banner text, the command uses a delimiter character. In the example, the # character was used as a delimiter. At the end of the line, the Return key was pressed. Then the router added the line that says to keep typing the banner and end it with a #. Two more banner lines were added, with the last line ending in the delimiter character, telling the router that the **banner** command was finished.

The **show running-config** output confirms that a three-line banner was added to the configuration, but note that the delimeter has been set to ^C. ^C represents Control+c, which is an ASCII code that cannot be displayed. The router automatically changes the **banner** command to use ^C as the delimiter.

Router Memory, Processors, and Interfaces

The configuration file contains the configuration commands that you have typed, as well as some configuration commands entered by default by the router. The configuration file can be stored in a variety of places, including two inside a router. The router has a couple of other types of memory as well:

- **RAM**—Sometimes called DRAM for dynamic random-access memory, RAM is used by the router just as it is used by any other computer: for working storage. The running or active configuration file is stored here.

- **ROM**—This type of memory (read-only memory) stores a bootable IOS image, which typically is not used for normal operation. ROM contains the code that is used to boot the router until the router knows where to get the full IOS image or as a backup bootable image, in case there are problems.

- **Flash memory**—Either an EEPROM or a PCMCIA card, Flash memory stores fully functional IOS images and is the default location where the router gets its IOS at boot time. Flash memory also can be used to store any other files, including configuration files.

- **NVRAM**—Nonvolatile RAM stores the initial or startup configuration file.

All these types of memory, except RAM, are permanent memory. No hard disk or disk storage exists on Cisco routers. Figure 7-4 summarizes the use of memory in Cisco routers.

Figure 7-4   *Cisco Router Memory Types*

For the sake of consistency, Cisco IOS Software always uses the term *interfaces* to refer to the physical connections to a network. By being consistent, IOS commands familiar on one type of Cisco router will be familiar on another. Some nuances are involved in numbering the interfaces, however. In some smaller routers, the interface number is a single number. However, with some other families of routers, the interface is numbered first with the slot in which the card resides, followed by a slash and then the port number on that card. For example, port 3 on the card in slot 2 would be interface 2/3. Numbering starts with 0 for card slots and 0 for ports on any card. In some cases, the interface is defined by three numbers: first the card slot, then the daughter card (typically called a port adapter), and then a number for the physical interface on the port adapter.

Managing Configuration Files

IOS on a router uses a configuration file for the initial configuration at router startup and the active, running configuration file. The startup configuration file is in NVRAM; the other file, which is in RAM, is the one that the router uses during operation. When the router first comes up, the router copies the stored configuration file from NVRAM into RAM, so the running and startup configuration files are identical at that point. Also, exterior to the router, configuration files can be stored as ASCII text files anywhere using TFTP or FTP.

Example 7-4 demonstrates the basic interaction between the two files. In this example, the **show running-config** and **show startup-config** commands are used. These commands display the currently used, active, running configuration and the stored, startup configuration used when the router boots, respectively. The full command output is not shown; instead, you can see only a brief excerpt including the **host** command, which will be changed several times. (Notes are included inside the example that would not appear if you were doing these commands on a real router.)

Example 7-4 *Configuration Process Example*

```
hannah#show running-config
!… (lines omitted)
hostname hannah
!… (rest of lines omitted)

hannah#show startup-config
!… (lines omitted)
hostname hannah
!… (rest of lines omitted)
hannah#configure terminal
hannah(config)#hostname jessie
jessie(config)#exit
jessie#show running-config
!… (lines omitted)
hostname jessie
!… (rest of lines omitted - notice that the running configuration reflects the
!  changed hostname)
jessie# show startup-config
!… (lines omitted)
hostname hannah
!… (rest of lines omitted - notice that the changed configuration is not
!    shown in the startup config)
```

If you reload the router now, the host name would revert back to hannah. However, if you want to keep the changed host name of jessie, you would use the command **copy running-config startup-config,** which overwrites the current startup-config file with what is currently in the running configuration file.

The **copy** command can be used to copy files in a router, most typically a configuration file or a new version of the IOS Software. The most basic method for moving configuration files in and out of a router is to use the **copy** command to copy files between RAM or NVRAM on a router and a TFTP server. The files can be copied between any pair, as Figure 7-5 illustrates.

Figure 7-5 *Locations for Copying and Results from Copy Operations*

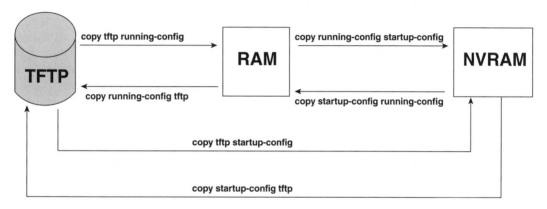

The commands can be summarized as follows:

```
copy {tftp | running-config | startup-config} {tftp | running-config | startup-config}
```

The first parameter is the "from" location; the next one is the "to" location. (Of course, choosing the same option for both parameters is not allowed.)

The **copy** command always replaces the existing file when the file is copied into NVRAM or into a TFTP server. In other words, it acts like the destination file was erased and the new file completely replaced the old one.

When the **copy** command copies a configuration file into RAM, the configuration file in RAM is not replaced. Effectively, any **copy** into RAM works just as if you typed the commands in the "from" configuration file in the order listed in the config file. In other words, it works as if the RAM configuration file and the newly copied files were merged.

So, who cares? Well, we do. If you change the running config and then decide that you want to revert to what's in the startup-config file, the only way to guarantee that is to issue the **reload** command, which reloads, or reboots, the router.

Three key commands can be used to erase the contents of NVRAM. The **write erase** and **erase startup-config** commands are older, whereas the **erase nvram:** command is the more recent, and recommended, command. All three commands simply erase the contents of the NVRAM configuration file. Of course, if the router is reloaded at this point, there is no initial configuration.

Viewing the Configuration and Old-Style Configuration Commands

Once upon a time, commands that were used to display and move configuration files among RAM, NVRAM, and TFTP did not use easy-to-recall parameters such as **startup-config** and **running-config**. In fact, most people could not remember the commands or got the different ones confused. Figure 7-6 shows both the old and the new commands used to view configurations.

Figure 7-6 *Configuration* show *Commands*

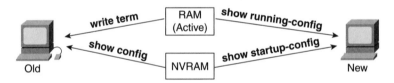

Initial Configuration (Setup Mode)

Setup mode leads a router administrator to a basic router configuration by using questions that prompt the administrator for basic configuration parameters. Instead of using setup mode, a Cisco router can be configured using the CLI in configuration mode. In fact, most networking personnel do not use setup at all, but new users sometimes like to use setup mode, particularly until they become more familiar with the CLI configuration mode.

Figure 7-7 and Example 7-5 describe the process used by setup mode. Setup mode is used most frequently when the router boots, and it has no configuration in NVRAM. Setup mode also can be entered by using the **setup** command from privileged mode.

Figure 7-7 *Getting into Setup Mode*

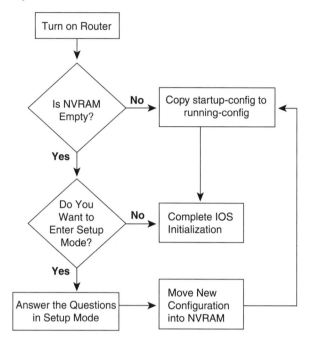

Example 7-5 shows a screen capture of using setup mode after booting a router with no configuration in NVRAM.

Example 7-5 *Router Setup Configuration Mode*

```
--- System Configuration Dialog ---

Would you like to enter the initial configuration dialog? [yes/no]: yes
At any point you may enter a question mark '?' for help.
Use ctrl-c to abort configuration dialog at any prompt.
Default settings are in square brackets '[]'.Basic management setup configures   only enough connectivity
for management of the system, extended setup will ask you
to configure each interface on the system

Would you like to enter basic management setup? [yes/no]: no
First, would you like to see the current interface summary? [yes]:
Any interface listed with OK? value "NO" does not have a valid configuration

Interface              IP-Address       OK? Method Status              Protocol
Ethernet0              unassigned       NO  unset  up                  down
Serial0                unassigned       NO  unset  down                down
Serial1                unassigned       NO  unset  down                down
```

continues

Example 7-5 *Router Setup Configuration Mode (Continued)*

```
Configuring global parameters:

 Enter host name [Router]: R1
     The enable secret is a password used to protect access to
     privileged EXEC and configuration modes. This password, after
     entered, becomes encrypted in the configuration.
     Enter enable secret: cisco
   The enable password is used when you do not specify an
     enable secret password, with some older software versions, and
     some boot images.
     Enter enable password: fred
   The virtual terminal password is used to protect
     access to the router over a network interface.
     Enter virtual terminal password: barney
   Configure SNMP Network Management? [yes]: no
   Configure bridging? [no]:
   Configure DECnet? [no]:
   Configure AppleTalk? [no]:
   Configure IPX? [no]:
   Configure IP? [yes]:
   Configure IGRP routing? [yes]:
   Your IGRP autonomous system number [1]:
   Configuring interface parameters:
   Do you want to configure Ethernet0  interface? [yes]:
   Configure IP on this interface? [yes]:
   IP address for this interface: 172.16.1.1
   Subnet mask for this interface [255.255.0.0] : 255.255.255.0
   Class B network is 172.16.0.0, 24 subnet bits; mask is /24
   Do you want to configure Serial0  interface? [yes]:
     Configure IP on this interface? [yes]:
   Configure IP unnumbered on this interface? [no]:
   IP address for this interface: 172.16.12.1
   Subnet mask for this interface [255.255.0.0] : 255.255.255.0
   Class B network is 172.16.0.0, 24 subnet bits; mask is /24
   Do you want to configure Serial1  interface? [yes]:
   Configure IP on this interface? [yes]:
   Configure IP unnumbered on this interface? [no]:
   IP address for this interface: 172.16.13.1
   Subnet mask for this interface [255.255.0.0] : 255.255.255.0
   Class B network is 172.16.0.0, 24 subnet bits; mask is /24


   The following configuration command script was created:

   hostname R1
   enable secret 5 $1$VOLh$pkIe0Xjx2sgjgZ/Y6Gt1s.
   enable password fred
```

Example 7-5 *Router Setup Configuration Mode (Continued)*

```
line vty 0 4
password barney
no snmp-server
!
no bridge 1
no decnet routing
no appletalk routing
no ipx routing
ip routing
 !
interface Ethernet0
ip address 172.16.1.1 255.255.255.0
no mop enabled
!
interface Serial0
ip address 172.16.12.1 255.255.255.0
no mop enabled
!
interface Serial1
ip address 172.16.13.1 255.255.255.0
no mop enabled
dialer-list 1 protocol ip permit
dialer-list 1 protocol ipx permit
!
router igrp 1
redistribute connected
network 172.16.0.0
!
end

[0] Go to the IOS command prompt without saving this config.
[1] Return back to the setup without saving this config.
[2] Save this configuration to nvram and exit.

Enter your selection [2]: 2
Building configuration...
[OK]Use the enabled mode 'configure' command to modify this configuration.
Press RETURN to get started!
```

Setup behaves like Example 7-5 illustrates, whether setup was reached by booting with an empty NVRAM or whether the **setup** privileged exec command was used. First, the router asks whether you want to enter the initial configuration dialog. Answering **y** or **yes** puts you in setup mode.

When you are finished with setup, you select one of three options for what to do next. Option 2 tells the router to save the configuration to NVRAM and exit; this option is used in Example 7-5. The router places the config in both NVRAM and RAM. This is the only operation in IOS that changes both configuration files to include the same contents based on a single action by the user. Options 0 and 1 tell the router to ignore the configuration that you just entered and to either exit to the command prompt (option 0) or start over again with setup (option 1). You can also abort the setup process before answering all the questions, and get to a CLI prompt by pressing CNTL-C.

Upgrading Cisco IOS Software and the Cisco IOS Software Boot Process

Engineers need to know how to upgrade the IOS to move to a later release. Typically, a router has one IOS image in Flash memory, and that is the IOS that is used. (The term *IOS image* simply refers to a file containing the IOS.) The upgrade process might include steps such as copying a newer IOS image into Flash memory, configuring the router to tell it which IOS image to use, and deleting the old one when you are confident that the new release works well.

A router decides what IOS image to use when the router boots. Also, to upgrade to a new IOS or back out to an older IOS, you must reload the router. So, it's a convenient time to cover the boot sequence and some of the related issues.

Upgrading a Cisco IOS Software Image into Flash Memory

IOS files typically are stored in Flash memory. Flash memory is rewriteable, permanent storage, which is ideal for storing files that need to be retained when the router loses power. Also, because there are no moving parts, there is a smaller chance of failure as compared with disk drives, which provides better availability. As you will read soon, IOS can be placed on an external TFTP server, but using an external server typically is done for testing—in production, practically every Cisco router loads an IOS stored in the only type of large, permanent memory in a Cisco router and that is Flash memory.

As Figure 7-8 illustrates, to upgrade an IOS image into Flash memory, you first must obtain the IOS image from Cisco. Then you must place the IOS image into the default directory of a TFTP server. Finally, you must issue the **copy** command from the router, copying the file into Flash memory. You also can use an FTP server, but the TFTP feature has been around a long time and is a more likely topic for the exam.

Figure 7-8 *Complete Cisco IOS Software Upgrade Process*

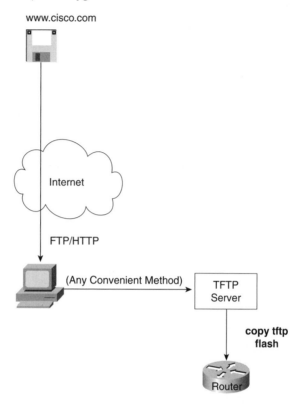

Example 7-6 provides an example of the final step, copying the IOS image into Flash memory.

Example 7-6 copy tftp flash *Command Copies the IOS Image to Flash Memory*

```
R1#copy tftp flash

System flash directory:
File   Length   Name/status
  1    7530760   c4500-d-mz.120-2.bin
[7530824 bytes used, 857784 available, 8388608 total]
Address or name of remote host [255.255.255.255]? 134.141.3.33
Source file name? c4500-d-mz.120-5.bin
Destination file name [c4500-d-mz.120-5.bin]?
Accessing file c4500-d-mz.120-5.bin ' on 134.141.3.33...
Loading c4500-d-mz.120-5.bin from 134.141.3.33 (via TokenRing0): ! [OK]

Erase flash device before writing? [confirm]
Flash contains files. Are you sure you want to erase? [confirm]
```

continues

Example 7-6 copy tftp flash *Command Copies the IOS Image to Flash Memory (Continued)*

```
Copy 'c4500-d-mz.120-5.bin ' from server
  as 'c4500-d-mz.120-5.bin ' into Flash WITH erase? [yes/no]y
Erasing device... eeeeeeeeeeeeeeeeeeeeeeeeeeeeeeeeeeee ...erased
Loading c4500-d-mz.120-5.bin  from 134.141.3.33 (via TokenRing0):
!!!!!!!!!!!!!!!!!!!!!!!!!!!!!!!!!!!!!!!!!!!!!!!!!!!!!!!!!!!!!!!!!!!!!!!!!!!!!!
!!!!!!!!!!!!!!!!!!!!!!!!!!!!!!!!!!!!!!!!!!!!!!!!!!!!!!!!!!!!!!!!!!!!!!! (leaving out lots of
exclamation points…)
[OK  7530760/8388608 bytes]

Verifying checksum...  OK (0xA93E)
Flash copy took 0:04:26 [hh:mm:ss]
R1#
```

During this process of copying the IOS image into Flash memory, the router needs to discover several important facts:

1. What is the IP address or host name of the TFTP server?

2. What is the name of the file?

3. Is space available for this file in Flash memory?

4. Does the server actually have a file by that name?

5. Do you want the router to erase the old files?

The router will prompt you for answers, as necessary. Afterward, the router erases Flash memory as needed, copies the file, and then verifies that the checksum for the file shows that no errors occurred in transmission. The **show flash** command then can be used to verify the contents of Flash memory (see Example 7-7). (The **show flash** output can vary among router families.) Before the new IOS image is used, however, the router must be reloaded.

Example 7-7 *Verifying Flash Memory Contents with the* **show flash** *Command*

```
fred#show flash

System flash directory:
File  Length   Name/status
  1   13305352  c2500-ds-l.122-1.bin
[13305416 bytes used, 3471800 available, 16777216 total]
16384K bytes of processor board System flash (Read ONLY)
```

In some cases, Flash memory can be in read-only mode. That is the case when a router loads only part of the IOS into RAM, to conserve RAM. Other parts of the IOS file are kept in Flash memory (Flash memory access time is much slower than RAM's). In this case, if Flash memory must be erased to make room for a new image, the IOS could not continue to run.

So, if the router is running from a portion of IOS in Flash memory, the router must must be booted using IOS in ROM. Then the Flash memory is in read/write mode and the erase and copy processes can be accomplished. The **copy tftp flash** command in later releases of the IOS actually performs the entire process for you. In earlier releases, you had to boot the router from ROM and then issue the **copy tftp flash** command.

When using the limited-function IOS in ROM, the router is in a mode called *Rxboot mode*. Routers cannot route packets while in Rxboot mode, but it can send and receive IP packets like an IP host. So, one of two things must be true for the router to be capable of sending packets to the TFTP server. First, the TFTP server could reside on the same subnet as one of the interfaces on the router. Alternately, you could configure a default route on the router, pointing to another router that is on one of the same subnets as the router in Rxboot mode.

The name of the IOS file identifies some basic information about that IOS image, so it is a good idea to keep the same filename when copying the file into flash. In particular, the first part of the name implies the router hardware platform. The second part identifies the feature set, with individual letters identifying different options—for instance, "j" means the IOS has the Enterprise feature set, which contains most features. Finally, the last few digits tell us some information about the run-time features—for instance, a "z" means that the file is compressed, and need decompression when being loaded. See www.cisco.com/warp/customer/620/1.html#5-1 for more information.

The Cisco IOS Software Boot Sequence

Cisco routers perform the same types of tasks that a typical computer performs when you power it on or reboot (reload) it. Of course, most of us do not think about these details very often. The router performs some somewhat obvious steps, with one of those being tricky—namely, the process of choosing the location of the software to load and use in the router. And that software might not be IOS.

The boot process follows this basic litany:

1. The router performs a power-on self-test (POST) to discover and verify the hardware.

2. The router loads and runs bootstrap code from ROM.

3. The router finds the IOS or other software and loads it.

4. The router finds the configuration file and loads it into running config.

All routers attempt all four steps each time that the router is powered on or reloaded. The POST code and functions cannot be changed by the router administrator. The location of the bootstrap code, the IOS to load, and the configuration file can be changed by the administrator—but you almost always use the default location for the bootstrap code

(ROM) and for the initial configuration (NVRAM). So, the location of IOS or other software is the only part that typically is changed.

Three categories of operating systems can be loaded into the router:

■ The full-function IOS image that you have already been introduced to in this chapter.

■ A limited-function IOS that resides in ROM.

■ A different non-IOS operating system that also is stored in ROM. This operating system, called ROM Monitor, or ROMMON, is used for two purposes—for low-level debugging and for password recovery. Unless you are performing password recovery, you seldom will use ROMMON mode.

Table 7-5 lists the three operating system categories and their main functions.

Table 7-5   *Three OS Categories for Routers*

Operating System	Typical Location Where It Is Stored	Purpose
Full-featured IOS	Flash	Full-featured, normal IOS used in production.
Limited-function IOS (RXBOOT mode)	ROM	Basic IP connectivity, used when Flash memory is broken and you need IP connectivity to copy a new IOS into Flash memory.
ROMMON	ROM	Low-level debugging, usually by the Cisco TAC and for password recovery.

You need to tell the router whether to use ROMMON, the limited-function IOS, or the full-featured IOS. Of course, most of the time you use the full-featured IOS in Flash memory. However, you might want to use IOS that resides on a TFTP server, or there could be multiple IOS images in Flash memory—and all of these options are configurable.

Two configuration tools tell the router what OS to load:

■ The configuration register

■ The **boot system** configuration command

First, the configuration register tells the router whether to use a full-featured IOS, ROMMON, or the limited-feature IOS, which also is called RXBOOT mode. The *configuration register* is a 16-bit software register in the router, and its value is set using the **config-register** global configuration command. (Some older routers had a hardware configuration register with jumpers on the processor card, to set bits to a value of 0 or 1.) On most Cisco routers, the default Configuration Register setting is hexadecimal 2102.

Figure 7-9 shows an example binary breakdown of the default value for the configuration register, which is hexadecimal 2102.

Figure 7-9   *Binary Version of Configuration Register, Value Hex 2102*

Bit Position, in Decimal	15	14	13	12	11	10	9	8	7	6	5	4	3	2	1	0
Default Binary Value	0	0	1	0	0	0	0	1	0	0	0	0	0	0	1	0

The boot field is the name of the low-order 4 bits of the configuration register. This field can be considered a 4-bit value, represented as a single hexadecimal digit. (Cisco represents hexadecimal values by preceding the hex digit[s] with 0x—for example, 0xA would mean a single hex digit A.) If the boot field is hex 0, ROMMON is loaded. If the boot field is hex 1, RXBOOT mode is used. For anything else, it loads a full-featured IOS. But which one?

The second method used to determine where the router tries to obtain an IOS image is through the use of the **boot system** configuration command. If the configuration register calls for a full-featured IOS (boot field 2-F), the router reads the startup-configuration file for **boot system** commands. If there are no boot system commands, the router takes the default action, which is to load the first file in Flash memory. Table 7-6 summarizes the use of the configuration register and the **boot system** command at initialization time, when the boot field's value implies that the router will look for **boot** commands.

Table 7-6   *Impact of the* **boot system** *Command on Choice of IOS: Boot Field Between 2 and F*

Boot System Commands	Result
No **boot** command	Tries loading the following (in order): first file in flash; broadcasts looking for TFTP server and a default filename; IOS in ROM; or uses ROM Monitor.
boot system ROM	IOS from ROM is loaded.
boot system flash	The first file from Flash memory is loaded.
boot system flash *filename*	IOS with the name *filename* is loaded from Flash memory.
boot system tftp *filename* **10.1.1.1**	IOS with the name *filename* is loaded from the TFTP server.
Multiple boot system commands, any variety	An attempt occurs to load IOS based on the first **boot** command the in configuration. If that fails, the second **boot** command is used, and so on, until one is successful.

Foundation Summary

The "Foundation Summary" section of each chapter lists the most important facts from the chapter. Although this section does not list every fact from the chapter that will be on your INTRO exam, a well-prepared CCNA candidate should know, at a minimum, all the details in each "Foundation Summary" section before going to take the exam.

The console, auxiliary, and Telnet passwords all are set separately, as shown in Table 7-7.

Table 7-7 *CLI Password Configuration*

Access From	Password Type	Configuration
Console	Console password	**line console** *0* **login** **password** *faith*
Auxiliary	Auxiliary password	**line aux** *0* **login** **password** *hope*
Telnet	vty password	**line vty** *0 4* **login** **password** *love*

Table 7-8 lists the commands used to manipulate previously typed commands.

Table 7-8 *Key Sequences for Command Edit and Recall*

Keyboard Command	What the User Gets
Up arrow or Ctrl-p	This displays the most recently used command.
Down arrow or Ctrl-n	After moving back into the histroy buffer of previously used commands, this key sequence moves you forward again.
Left arrow or Ctrl-b	This moves the cursor backward in the currently displayed command without deleting characters. (The b stands for back.)
Right arrow or Ctrl-f	This moves the cursor forward in the currently displayed command without deleting characters. (The f stands for forward.)

Table 7-8 *Key Sequences for Command Edit and Recall (Continued)*

Keyboard Command	What the User Gets
Backspace	This moves the cursor backward in the currently displayed command, deleting characters.
Ctrl-a	This moves the cursor directly to the first character of the currently displayed command.
Ctrl-e	This moves the cursor directly to the end of the currently displayed command.
Esc-b	This moves the cursor back one word in the currently displayed command.
Esc-f	This moves the cursor forward one word in the currently displayed command.
Ctrl-r	This creates a new command prompt, followed by all the characters typed since the last command prompt was written.

Figure 7-10 illustrates the relationships among configuration mode, user exec mode, and privileged exec mode.

Figure 7-10 *CLI Configuration Mode Versus Exec Modes*

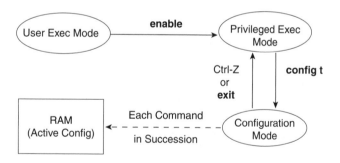

Routers have four types of memory:

■ **RAM**—Sometimes called DRAM for *dynamic* random-access memory, RAM is used by the router just as it is used by any other computer: for working storage. The *running* or *active configuration* file is stored here.

■ **ROM**—This type of memory (read-only memory) stores a bootable IOS image, which typically is not used for normal operation. ROM contains the code that is used to boot the router until the router knows where to get the full IOS image or as a backup bootable image, in case there are problems.

- **Flash memory**—Either an EEPROM or a PCMCIA card, Flash memory stores fully functional IOS images and is the default location where the router gets its IOS at boot time. Flash memory also can be used to store configuration files on some Cisco routers.

- **NVRAM**—Nonvolatile RAM stores the initial or startup configuration file.

The **copy** command is used to move configuration files among RAM, NVRAM, and a TFTP server. The files can be copied between any pair. The commands can be summarized as follows:

```
copy {tftp | running-config | startup-config} {tftp | running-config | startup-config}
```

The first parameter is the "from" location; the next one is the "to" location. (Of course, choosing the same option for both parameters is not allowed.)

Figure 7-11 shows both the old and the new commands used to view configurations.

Figure 7-11 *Configuration* **show** *Commands*

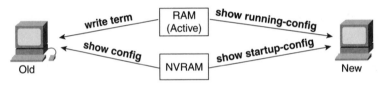

Figure 7-12 shows an example binary breakdown of the default value for the configuration register, which is hexadecimal 2102.

Figure 7-12 *Binary Version of Configuration Register, Value Hex 2102*

Bit Position, in Decimal	15	14	13	12	11	10	9	8	7	6	5	4	3	2	1	0
Default Binary Value	0	0	1	0	0	0	0	1	0	0	0	0	0	0	1	0

Table 7-9 summarizes the use of the configuration register and the **boot system** command at initialization time.

Table 7-9 boot system *Command*

Boot System Commands	Result
No **boot** command	Tries loading the following (in order): first file in flash; broadcasts looking for TFTP server and a default filename; IOS in ROM; or uses ROM Monitor.
boot system ROM	IOS from ROM is loaded.
boot system flash	The first file from Flash memory is loaded.
boot system flash *filename*	IOS with the name *filename* is loaded from Flash memory.
boot system tftp *filename* **10.1.1.1**	IOS with the name *filename* is loaded from the TFTP server.
Multiple boot system commands, any variety	An attempt occurs to load IOS based on the first **boot** command in the configuration. If that fails, the second **boot** command is used, and so on, until one is successful.

Q&A

As mentioned in the introduction, you have two choices for review questions. The questions that follow give you a bigger challenge than the exam itself by using an open-ended question format. By reviewing now with this more difficult question format, you can exercise your memory better and prove your conceptual and factual knowledge of this chapter. The answers to these questions are found in Appendix A.

For more practice with exam-like question formats, including questions using a router simulator and multiple-choice questions, use the exam engine on the CD.

1. What are the two names for the same CLI mode in a router, that when accessed, enables you to issue exec commands that could be disruptive to router operations?

2. What are three methods of logging on to a router?

3. What is the name of the user interface mode of operation used in which you cannot issue disruptive commands?

4. Can the auxiliary port be used for anything besides remote modem user access to a router? If so, what other purpose can it serve?

5. What command would you use to receive command help if you knew that a **show** command option begins with a c but you cannot recall the option?

6. While you are logged in to a router, you issue the command **copy ?** and get a response of "Unknown command, computer name, or host." Offer an explanation for why this error message appears.

7. Is the number of retrievable commands based on the number of characters in each command, or is it simply a number of commands, regardless of their size?

8. How can you retrieve a previously used command? (Name two ways.)

9. After typing **show ip route**, which is the only command that you typed since logging in to the router, you now want to issue the **show ip arp** command. What steps would you take to execute this command by using command-recall keystrokes?

10. After typing **show ip route 128.1.1.0**, you now want to issue the command **show ip route 128.1.4.0**. What steps would you take to do so, using command-recall and command-editing keystrokes?

11. What configuration command causes the router to require a password from a user at the console? What configuration mode context must you be in? (That is, what command[s] must be typed before this command after entering configuration mode?) List the commands in the order in which they must be typed while in config mode.

12. What configuration command is used to tell the router the password that is required at the console? What configuration mode context must you be in? (That is, what command[s] must you type before this command after entering configuration mode?) List the commands in the order in which they must be typed while in config mode.

13. What are the primary purposes of Flash memory in a Cisco router?

14. What is the intended purpose of NVRAM memory in a Cisco router?

15. What does the NV stand for in NVRAM?

16. What is the intended purpose of RAM in a Cisco router?

17. What is the main purpose of ROM in a Cisco router?

18. What configuration command would be needed to cause a router to use an IOS image named c2500-j-l.112-14.bin on TFTP server 128.1.1.1 when the router is reloaded? If you forgot the first parameter of this command, what steps must you take to learn the correct parameters and add the command to the configuration? (Assume that you are not logged in to the router when you start.)

19. What command sets the password that would be required after typing the **enable** command? Is that password encrypted by default?

20. To have the correct syntax, what must you add to the following configuration command?
```
banner This is Ivan Denisovich's Gorno Router--Do Not Use
```

21. Name two commands that affect the text used as the command prompt.

22. When using setup mode, you are prompted at the end of the process for whether you want to use the configuration parameters that you just typed in. Which type of memory is this configuration stored in if you type yes?

23. What two methods could a router administrator use to cause a router to load IOS stored in ROM?

24. What is the process used to update the contents of Flash memory so that a new IOS in a file called c4500-d-mz.120-5.bin on TFTP server 128.1.1.1 is copied into Flash memory?

25. Name three possible problems that could prevent the command **boot system tftp c2500-j-l.112-14.bin 128.1.1.1** from succeeding.

26. Two different IOS files are in a router's Flash memory: one called c2500-j-l.111-3.bin and one called c2500-j-l.112-14.bin. Which one does the router use when it boots up? How could you force the other IOS file to be used? Without looking at the router configuration, what command could be used to discover which file was used for the latest boot of the router?

27. Is the password required at the console the same one that is required when Telnet is used to access a router?

28. Which IP routing protocols could be enabled using setup?

29. Name two commands used to view the configuration to be used at the next reload of the router. Which one is a more recent addition to IOS?

30. Name two commands used to view the configuration that currently is used in a router. Which one is a more recent addition to IOS?

31. True or false: The **copy startup-config running-config** command always changes the currently used configuration for this router to exactly match what is in the startup configuration file. Explain.

This chapter covers the following subjects:

- Navigating Through a Cisco 2950 Switch

- Switch Initialization

- Configuring 2950 IOS Software

CHAPTER **8**

Operating Cisco LAN Switches

Cisco's LAN switch revenue surpassed router revenues about the time that the CCNA certification was first announced back in 1998, so there is little doubt about the importance of LAN switches to Cisco. Also, the vast majority of end-user devices connect to a network by connecting to a LAN switch. So, it's no surprise that the CCNA certification exams cover switching concepts extensively.

Cisco uses two major alternatives for LAN switch operating systems. Also, each model series of switches from Cisco has several differences in the commands used, as compared with other Cisco switches that even use the same operating system. Conversely, Cisco routers all use a single operating system, called Cisco IOS Software, and the commands work the same on every router. So, Cisco can easily cover router configuration on the CCNA exams, without having to force everyone studying for the CCNA certification to use a particular model of router. However, covering such a wide variety of switch product lines, each with its own quirks for configuration, makes testing about LAN switch configuration difficult.

This chapter covers the basics of configuring 2950 series LAN switches. The 2950 uses a CLI IOS-like, with several commands in common with router IOS. However, many commands differ, and a few of the processes of how to do things on the 2950 differ from a router. So, this chapter points out the similarities with routers, but only briefly because Chapter 7, "Operating Cisco Routers," already covered those details. Where 2950s act differently, this chapter goes into more depth.

> **NOTE** For those of you still working on the outdated 1900 series switches, the *ICND Exam Certification Guide*, Appendix E, contains coverage of the 1900 series switch CLI and commands.

"Do I Know This Already?" Quiz

The purpose of the "Do I Know This Already?" quiz is to help you decide whether you really need to read the entire chapter. If you already intend to read the entire chapter, you do not necessarily need to answer these questions now.

The eight-question quiz, derived from the major sections in the "Foundation Topics" portion of the chapter, helps you determine how to spend your limited study time.

Table 8-1 outlines the major topics discussed in this chapter and the "Do I Know This Already?" quiz questions that correspond to those topics.

Table 8-1 *Do I Know This Already?" Foundation Topics Section-to-Question Mapping*

Foundations Topics Section	Questions Covered in This Section
Navigating Through a Cisco 2950 Switch	2, 6
Switch Initialization	5, 7, 8
Configuring Cisco 2950 IOS Software	1, 3, 4

CAUTION The goal of self-assessment is to gauge your mastery of the topics in this chapter. If you do not know the answer to a question or are only partially sure of the answer, you should mark this question wrong for purposes of the self-assessment. Giving yourself credit for an answer that you correctly guess skews your self-assessment results and might provide you with a false sense of security.

1. In which of the following modes of the CLI could you configure the duplex setting for interface fastethernet 0/5?

   a. User mode

   b. Enable mode

   c. Global configuration mode

   d. Setup mode

   e. Interface configuration mode

2. In which of the following modes of the CLI could you issue a command to erase the initial configuration of the switch?

   a. User mode

   b. Enable mode

   c. Setup mode

   d. Global configuration mode

   e. Interface configuration mode

3. What type of switch memory is used to store the configuration used by the switch when the switch first comes up?

   a. RAM

   b. ROM

   c. Flash

   d. NVRAM

   e. Bubble

4. What command copies the configuration from RAM into NVRAM?

   a. copy running-config tftp

   b. copy tftp running-config

   c. copy running-config start-up-config

   d. copy start-up-config running-config

   e. copy startup-config running-config

   f. copy running-config startup-config

5. What mode prompts the user for basic configuration information?

   a. User mode

   b. Enable mode

   c. Global configuration mode

   d. Setup mode

   e. Interface configuration mode

6. Imagine that you had configured the **enable secret** command, followed by the **enable password** command, from the console. You log out of the switch and log back in at the console. Which command defined the password that you had to type to access privileged mode again from the console?

   a. enable password

   b. enable secret

   c. Neither **enable password** nor **enable secret**

   d. You cannot configure both **enable secret** and **enable password** at the same time.

7. In what LED mode does the switch use the per-port LEDs to show information about the current load on the switch?

    a. Duplex

    b. Util

    c. Speed

    d. Stat

8. Which of the following is not true of both a 2950 switch and Cisco routers?

    a. Accessible from a console and auxiliary port

    b. Can enter configuration mode using the **configure terminal** command

    c. Expects the **enable secret** password instead of the **enable** password if both are configured

    d. None of the above

The answers to the "Do I Know This Already?" quiz are found in Appendix A, "Answers to the 'Do I Know This Already?' Quizzes and Q&A Sections." The suggested choices for your next step are as follows:

- **6 or less overall score**—Read the entire chapter. This includes the "Foundation Topics" and "Foundation Summary" sections and the Q&A section.

- **7 or 8 overall score**—If you want more review on these topics, skip to the "Foundation Summary" section and then go to the Q&A section. Otherwise, move to the next chapter.

Foundation Topics

Navigating Through a Cisco 2950 Switch

You can buy a Cisco 2950 switch or any other model of Cisco switch, turn on the power, and plug in the Ethernet cables to your computers, and the LAN you just created typically works just fine. There is no need to ever perform any specific configuration on the switch. However, you will probably want to configure the switch and possibly investigate and troubleshoot problems when they occur. So, knowing how to configure and troubleshoot a switch can help you in almost any networking job.

The nice advantage when learning about the 2950 series of Cisco switches is that many of the details of how they operate are just like those of a router. Of course, a switch does things differently than a router, but the basics—how to access the switch, how to configure it, and so on—pretty much work like a router. So, this chapter covers the similarities with routers only briefly, but gives you more detail about anything unique to using the switches.

The first section of this chapter focuses on the features, functions, and processes used to install, configure, and operate a 2950 switch. It starts with the basic 2950 series of switches and how to perform some simple initial configuration. After that, you will learn how to access the switch command-line interface (CLI). When you are in the CLI, you can configure the switch, issue commands to find out how the switch is working, and update the software in the switch.

The second section of this chapter focuses on the basic commands used to configure and operate the 2950 series of switches.

2950 Series Features and Functions

Cisco produces a wide variety of switch families. Inside each family are several specific models of switches. Cisco positions the 2950 series of switches as a full-featured, low-cost wiring closet switch. That means that you would expect to use this switch as the connection point for end-user devices, with cabling running from desks to the wiring closet. You would also use a couple of Ethernet ports to connect to other switches to provide connectivity between the wiring closet and the rest of the network.

Figure 8-1 shows one model of a 2950 switch, the 2950-24-EI switch, which provides 24 10/100 Ethernet interfaces and two Gigabit interfaces.

Figure 8-1 *2950-24-EI Switch*

This particular model comes with 24 built-in 10/100 ports using RJ-45 connectors. Any of the ports can be used to connect to end-user devices or to other switches. This switch also includes two Gigabit Ethernet slots, on the right side of the figure, into which you can put the appropriate Gigabit Interface Converter (GBIC). You will read more about GBICs in Chapter 11, "LAN Cabling, Standards, and Topologies."

Switch commands refer to the the physical RJ-45 Ethernet connectors on a 2950 as *interfaces*. Each interface has a number in the style x/y, where x and y are two different numbers. On a 2950, the number before the / is always 0. The first interface is numbered 0/1, the second is 0/2, and so on.

2950 Switch Operating System

Cisco switch operating systems can be categorized into two types: Internetwork Operating System (IOS) switches, and Catalyst Operating System (Cat OS) switches. When Cisco first entered the LAN switching arena, it did so by acquiring Crescendo Communications, which at the time, sold a line of switches called Catalyst switches. At the time of acquisition, Cisco already had sold a lot of routers, and, not surprisingly, those routers had a different user interface compared to Crescendo's switches. So, Cisco was faced with a dilemma: Should it update all the Crescendo Catalyst switches to use a user interface like the routers? Should it just continue to use the Crescendo Catalyst OS, now typically called the Cat OS, and that alone, on all future switches? The answer: Some Cisco switches use the Cat OS CLI, and some use the IOS CLI.

Cisco IOS switches use the same CLI as the router IOS. Even though the switches have a similar look and feel to the router IOS, they do not actually run the same IOS as the routers because switches and routers do not share a lot of the same functions and features. For instance, Cisco calls the 2950 operating system the *2950 switch software* instead of IOS. However, because the look and feel of the user interface resembles the router IOS interface, most people simply call the 2950, and other switches that use the same CLI, *IOS-based switches*.

Accessing the Cisco 2950 Switch CLI

The 2950 CLI works just like the router IOS CLI. Some of the commands you use are different because switches perform different tasks than routers, but the process and the look and feel are the same. For instance:

- It uses user exec and priviledged (enable) exec modes.

- It uses the **enable** and **disable** commands to move between the two.

- It uses a console password and telnet (vty) password, configured just like a router.

- It uses an enable secret or just plain enable password, with the enable secret password taking precedence if both are configured.

- It uses the same editing keystrokes that allow you to retrieve previous commands and change the commands.

Only a few minor differences exist between 2950 switches and routers relating to how to access the switch and use the CLI. The first difference is that there is no auxiliary port on a switch. Figure 8-2 shows the two basic access methods—console and Telnet.

Figure 8-2   *2950 CLI Access*

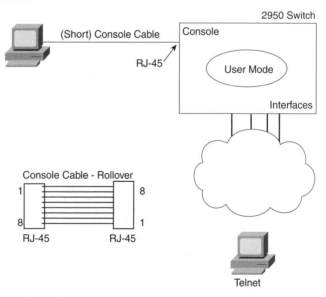

Notice that the same console cable (rollover cable) is used for the switch as well as the router.

The only other big difference between the CLI in a router and a 2950 switch is that the commands listed when you ask for help are different. The process is the same—type a ? whenever you need help, and commands and parameters are listed, depending on where you are when you type the ?.

Switch Initialization

A switch initializes when it is powered on. Like all computers, it performs some basic checks to discover what kind of hardware is installed, what is working, and what is not, and then it proceeds to load the operating system if enough of the hardware is in working order.

You should be aware of a couple of different things that can happen at switch initialization. First, you should at least know the basics of how a 2950 switch tells you its status during initialization by lighting the LEDs on the front panel of the switch. This process differs from what a router does at initialization. Second, you should be aware of the initial configuration dialogue, which works very similarly to the router initial configuration dialogue, with some minor differences.

Switch LEDs During POST

Power-On Self Test (POST) defines the series of steps that a device goes through to test the hardware and find out what is working before moving on to loading the operating system. POST processing is performed by boot code that is loaded into ROM.

Because a full operating system has not yet been loaded when the switch performs POST, it needs a way to tell the human user if POST worked well, if it failed partly, or if the switch is totally unusable. To communicate the status, the switch uses the light-emitting diodes (LEDs) on the front panel of the switch. During POST, these LEDs have one set of meanings; during normal operation, the LEDs are used for other purposes.

Figure 8-3 shows a representation of the front left part of a 2950 switch, with LEDs shown.

Figure 8-3 *2950 Front Panel and LEDs*

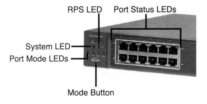

During POST, the switch varies the lights on the LEDs to imply what is happening. For instance, as do most devices, the switch starts by turning all the LEDs green for a moment, just so you can know whether the LEDs are working. On the 2950, if the system LED turns amber, the switch failed POST, meaning that it has a problem that prevents it from even bringing up the switch operating system. (Solid green on the system LED means all is well.)

The redundant power supply (RPS) LED identifies whether an RPS is installed, whether it is working, and so on. The 2950 does not have space inside the switch for an RPS, but it does allow the switch to connect to an external RPS. The LED color (green or amber), plus whether the LED is either on or flashing, tells you the status of an RPS.

Each physical port has a single LED associated with it. The meaning of those LEDs depends on which of the four port mode LEDs are lit—the stat, util, duplex, and speed LEDs. The mode button toggles the switch among the four settings, each time changing the mode from stat to util, or util to duplex, and so on. For instance, if the stat LED is on, each port LED shows a solid green light if the respective Ethernet links are working, and a flashing green when traffic is being sent across the links. If the duplex LED is lit, then the port LEDs are green if the port is using full duplex, and are not lit if using half duplex.

Table 8-2 lists the LEDs and some of their meanings.

Table 8-2 *2950 Switch LEDs and Meaning*

LED	Use and Meaning
System	OFF: Powered off GREEN: Up and working AMBER: POST failure
RPS	This signals the existence of RPS, the status of RPS, and the status of main power.
Port LEDs	Each port has a single LED, whose meaning is interpreted based on which of the four MODE leds is lit.
Mode button	When pressed, this button changes from one of four states: stat, util, duplex, and speed. The current mode is shown by the green LED beside only one of the four words stat, util, duplex, and speed.
Stat	When stat is green, each port LED shows the working status of the port. Green means functional, off means not functional, and flashing green shows link activity.
Util	This uses the combined port LEDs to give an indication of overall switch utilization. The more port LEDs are lit, the more switch utilization is occurring.
Duplex	The port LEDs show solid green if full duplex, and off if half duplex.
Speed	For 10/100 ports, the LED shows solid green if running 100 Mbps, and off if running 10 Mbps.

Initial Configuration Mode

The 2950 switch OS uses the same concepts of an initial configuration dialogue as does a router. When the switch initializes and finds no configuration file in NVRAM, it presents the console user with a question, asking whether to enter the initial configuration dialogue.

The only real difference between the router initial configuration dialogue and the 2950 switch initial configuration dialogue is in the things the switch lets you configure. Otherwise, the process is identical. Example 8-1 shows an example dialogue.

Example 8-1 *Innitial Configuration Dialogue Example*

```
            --- System Configuration Dialog ---

Would you like to enter the initial configuration dialog? [yes/no]: yes

At any point you may enter a question mark '?' for help.
Use ctrl-c to abort configuration dialog at any prompt.
Default settings are in square brackets '[]'.


Basic management setup configures only enough connectivity
for management of the system, extended setup will ask you
to configure each interface on the system

Would you like to enter basic management setup? [yes/no]: yes
Configuring global parameters:

  Enter host name [Switch]: fred

  The enable secret is a password used to protect access to
  privileged EXEC and configuration modes. This password, after
  entered, becomes encrypted in the configuration.
  Enter enable secret: cisco

  The enable password is used when you do not specify an
  enable secret password, with some older software versions, and
  some boot images.
  Enter enable password: notcisco

  The virtual terminal password is used to protect
  access to the router over a network interface.
  Enter virtual terminal password: wilma
  Configure SNMP Network Management? [no]:

Current interface summary

Any interface listed with OK? value "NO" does not have a valid configuration
```

Example 8-1   *Innitial Configuration Dialogue Example (Continued)*

```
Interface              IP-Address      OK? Method Status       Protocol
Vlan1                  unassigned      NO  unset  up           up
FastEthernet0/1        unassigned      YES unset  up           up
FastEthernet0/2        unassigned      YES unset  up           up
FastEthernet0/3        unassigned      YES unset  up           up
!
!Lines ommitted for brevity
!
GigabitEthernet0/1     unassigned      YES unset  down         down
GigabitEthernet0/2     unassigned      YES unset  down         down
Enter interface name used to connect to the
management network from the above interface summary: fastethernet0/5

Configuring interface FastEthernet0/5:
  Configure IP on this interface? [no]:
Would you like to enable as a cluster command switch? [yes/no]: no

The following configuration command script was created:

hostname fred
enable secret 5 $1$wNE7$4JSktD3uN1Af5FpctmPz11
enable password notcisco
line vty 0 15
password wilma
no snmp-server
!
!
interface Vlan1
shutdown
no ip address
!
interface FastEthernet0/1
!
interface FastEthernet0/2
!
interface FastEthernet0/3
!
interface FastEthernet0/4
!
interface FastEthernet0/5
no shutdown
no ip address
!
! Lines ommitted for brevity
!
interface GigabitEthernet0/1
!
```

continues

Example 8-1 *Innitial Configuration Dialogue Example (Continued)*

```
interface GigabitEthernet0/2
!
end


[0] Go to the IOS command prompt without saving this config.
[1] Return back to the setup without saving this config.
[2] Save this configuration to nvram and exit.

Enter your selection [2]: 2
Building configuration...
[OK]

Use the enabled mode 'configure' command to modify this configuration.
Press RETURN to get started!
```

As you can see from the example, the process works very much like router setup mode.

Configuring 2950 IOS Software

The configuration process and the configuration files used are identical when comparing the router IOS behavior and a 2950 switch. So there is nothing more to learn compared with the router IOS. In other words, the following are true:

- You use the **configure terminal** command from enable mode to enter configuration mode.

- Your configuration commands change the configuration of the switch the instant you press Enter at the end of each command.

- The help shown in configuration mode changes, depending on what configuration submode you are in.

- The **copy running-config startup-config** exec command saves the configuration to the permanent configuration file in NVRAM.

- The startup-config file is stored in NVRAM, and the switch OS is stored in Flash.

- All the variations of the **copy** command work just like they do on a router.

If you do not remember these details, just turn back to Chapter 7 and review the major heading titled, "Configuring Cisco IOS Software," for more information.

Foundation Summary

The "Foundation Summary" section of each chapter lists the most important facts from the chapter. Although this section does not list every fact from the chapter that will be on your INTRO exam, a well-prepared CCNA candidate should know, at a minimum, all the details in each "Foundation Summary" section before going to take the exam.

The 2950 CLI works just like the router IOS. Some of the commands that you use are different because switches perform different tasks than routers, but the process and the look and feel are the same. For instance:

- It uses user exec and priviledged (enable) exec modes.

- It uses the **enable** and **disable** commands to move between the two.

- It uses a console password and Telnet (vty) password, configured just like a router.

- It uses an enable secret or just plain enable password, with the enable secret password taking precedence if both are configured.

- It uses the same editing keystrokes that allow you to retrieve previous commands and change the commands.

Only a few minor differences exist between 2950 switches and routers relating to how to access the switch and use the CLI. The first difference is that there is no auxiliary port on a switch. The other is that the commands used on the switch can be different from those used on a router because switches perform different functions than do routers.

To access the 2950 switch CLI, you can use one of two methods, as illustrated in Figure 8-4.

Figure 8-4 *2950 CLI Access*

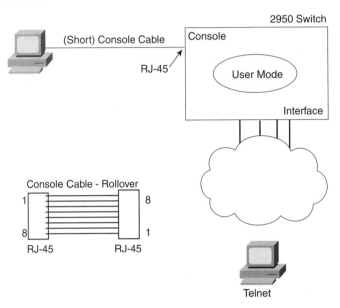

The configuration process and the configuration files used are identical when comparing the router IOS behavior and a 2950 switch. So there is nothing more to learn as compared with the router IOS. In other words, the following are true:

- You use the **configure terminal** command from enable mode to enter configuration mode.

- Your configuration commands change the configuration of the switch the instant you press Enter at the end of each command.

- The help shown in configuration mode changes, depending on what configuration submode you are in.

- The **copy running-config startup-config** command saves the configuration to the permanent configuration file in NVRAM.

- The startup-config file is stored in NVRAM, and the switch OS is stored in Flash.

- All the variations of the **copy** command work just like they do on a router.

Q&A

As mentioned in the introduction, you have two choices for review questions. The questions that follow next give you a bigger challenge than the exam itself by using an open-ended question format. By reviewing now with this more difficult question format, you can exercise your memory better, and prove your conceptual and factual knowledge of this chapter. The answers to these questions are found in Appendix A.

1. What are the two names for the switch's mode of operation that, when accessed, enables you to issue commands that could be disruptive to switch operations?

2. What are two methods of logging on to a switch?

3. What is the name of the user interface mode of operation used when you cannot issue disruptive commands?

4. What command would you use to receive command help if you knew that a **show** command option begins with a *c* but you cannot recall the option?

5. While you are logged in to a switch, you issue the command **copy ?** and get a response of "Unknown command, computer name, or host." Offer an explanation for why this error message appears.

6. How can you retrieve a previously used command? (Name two ways.)

7. What configuration command causes the switch to require a password from a user at the console? What configuration mode context must you be in? (That is, what command[s] must be typed before this command after entering configuration mode?) List the commands in the order in which they must be typed while in config mode.

8. What configuration command is used to tell the switch the password that is required at the console? What configuration mode context must you be in? (That is, what command[s] must you type before this command after entering configuration mode?) List the commands in the order in which they must be typed while in config mode.

9. What are the primary purposes of Flash memory in a Cisco switch?

10. What is the intended purpose of NVRAM memory in a Cisco 2950 switch?

11. What does the "NV" stand for in NVRAM?

12. What is the intended purpose of RAM in a Cisco switch?

13. What command sets the password that would be required after typing the **enable** command? Is that password encrypted by default?

14. Is the password required at the console the same one that is required when Telnet is used to access a switch?

15. Name two commands used to view the configuration to be used at the next reload of a 2950 switch. Which one is a more recent addition to IOS?

16. Name two commands used to view the configuration that is currently used in a 2950 switch. Which one is a more recent addition to IOS?

Cisco Published INTRO Exam Topics*
Covered in This Part:

1   Use a subset of Cisco IOS commands to analyze and report network problems

7   Use commands incorporated within IOS to analyze and report network problems

9   Describe and install the hardware and software required to be able to communicate via a network

15   Describe the physical, electrical and mechanical properties and standards associated with optical, wireless and copper media used in networks

16   Describe the topologies and physical issues associated with cabling common LANs

26   Compare and contrast collision and broadcast domains, and describe the process of network segmentation

27   Describe the principles and practice of switching in an Ethernet network

* Always re-check www.cisco.com for the latest posted exam topics

PART III: LAN Switching

This chapter covers the following subjects:

- The Case for Bridging and Switching

- Transparent Bridging

- LAN Switching

- LAN Segmentation

- The Need for Spanning Tree

CHAPTER 9

Cisco LAN Switching Basics

Cisco switches can perform the functions detailed in this chapter without any configuration. You can buy several switches, turn on the power, and cable the devices to the switch—and everything works! So, if the CCNA INTRO exam wanted to test you about only things you have to do to a switch to get it working, you would not even need this chapter.

Of course, Cisco wants you to know how switches work. Not only is that necessary for the CCNA exams, but it also helps you in a job as a network engineer. So, in this chapter, you will learn about bridges and switches and how they are both similar and different. You will learn how switches operate. You will also learn about a few related concepts, such as the Spanning Tree Protocol (STP), which is used to prevent Ethernet frames from looping around the network.

"Do I Know This Already?" Quiz

The purpose of the "Do I Know This Already?" quiz is to help you decide whether you really need to read the entire chapter. If you already intend to read the entire chapter, you do not necessarily need to answer these questions now.

The 12-question quiz, derived from the major sections in "Foundation Topics" portion of the chapter, helps you determine how to spend your limited study time.

Table 9-1 outlines the major topics discussed in this chapter and the "Do I Know This Already?" quiz questions that correspond to those topics.

Table 9-1 *"Do I Know This Already?" Foundation Topics Section-to-Question Mapping*

Foundations Topics Section	Questions Covered in This Section
Transparent Bridging	1–4
LAN Switching	5–8
LAN Segmentation	9–10
The Need for Spanning Tree	11–12

> **CAUTION** The goal of self-assessment is to gauge your mastery of the topics in this chapter. If you do not know the answer to a question or are only partially sure of the answer, you should mark this question wrong for purposes of the self-assessment. Giving yourself credit for an answer that you correctly guess skews your self-assessment results and might provide you with a false sense of security.

1. Which of the following statements describes part of the process of how a transparent bridge makes a decision to forward a frame destined to a unicast known MAC address?

   a. Compares unicast destination address to the bridging, or MAC address, table

   b. Compares unicast source address to the bridging, or MAC address, table

   c. Forwards out all interfaces in the same VLAN, except the incoming interface.

   d. Forwards based on the VLAN ID

   e. Compares the destination IP address to the destination MAC address

   f. Compares the incoming interface of the frame to the source MAC entry in the MAC address table

2. Which of the following statements describes part of the process of how a LAN switch makes a decision to forward a frame destined to a broadcast MAC address?

   a. Compares the unicast destination address to the bridging, or MAC address, table

   b. Compares the unicast source address to the bridging, or MAC address, table

   c. Forwards out all interfaces in the same VLAN, except the incoming interface.

   d. Forwards based on the VLAN ID

   e. Compares the destination IP address to the destination MAC address

   f. Compares the incoming interface of the frame to the source MAC entry in the MAC address table

3. Which of the following statements best describes what a transparent bridge does with a frame destined to an unknown unicast address?

   a. Forwards out all interfaces in the same VLAN, except the incoming interface.

   b. Forwards based on the VLAN ID

   c. Compares the destination IP address to the destination MAC address

   d. Compares the incoming interface of the frame to the source MAC entry in the MAC address table

4. Which of the following comparisons is made by a switch when deciding whether a new MAC address should be added to its bridging table?

   a. Compares the unicast destination address to the bridging, or MAC address, table

   b. Compares the unicast source address to the bridging, or MAC address, table

   c. Compares the VLAN ID to the bridging, or MAC address, table

   d. Compares the destination IP address's ARP cache entry to the bridging, or MAC address, table

5. Which of the following internal switching methods can start forwarding a frame before the entire frame has been received?

   a. Cisco Express Forwarding

   b. Fast Switching

   c. Fragment-free

   d. Cut-through

   e. Store-and-forward

6. Which of the following internal switching methods must wait to receive the entire frame before forwarding the frame?

   a. Cisco Express Forwarding

   b. Fast Switching

   c. Fragment-free

   d. Cut-through

   e. Store-and-forward

7. Which of the following features is determined during autonegotiation between a 10/100 Ethernet card and a switch?

   a. Speed (10 or 100)

   b. Power levels (half or full)

   c. Pins used for transmit

   d. Duplex (half or full)

8. Which of the following devices would be in the same collision domain as PC1 below?

   a. PC2, which is separated from PC1 by an Ethernet hub

   b. PC3, which is separated from PC1 by a transparent bridge

   c. PC4, which is separated from PC1 by an Ethernet switch

   d. PC5, which is separated from PC1 by a router

9. Which of the following devices would be in the same broadcast domain as PC1 below?

   a. PC2, which is separated from PC1 by an Ethernet hub

   b. PC3, which is separated from PC1 by a transparent bridge

   c. PC4, which is separated from PC1 by an Ethernet switch

   d. PC5, which is separated from PC1 by a router

10. A network currently has ten PCs, with five connected to hub1 and another five connected to hub2, with a cable between the two hubs. Fred wants to keep the PCs connected to their hubs but put a bridge between the two hubs. Barney wants to remove the hubs and connect all ten PCs to the same switch. Comparing Fred and Barney's solutions, which of the following is true?

   a. Barney's solution creates more bandwidth than Fred's.

   b. Barney's solution allows full duplex to the PCs, where Fred's does not.

   c. Barney's solution creates ten times more collision domains than Fred's.

   d. Barney's solution creates five times more collision domains than Fred's.

   e. Barney's solution creates ten times more broadcast domains than Fred's.

11. Imagine a network with three switches, each with an Ethernet segment connecting it to the other two switches. Each switch has some PCs attached to it as well. Which of the following frames would cause loops if the Spanning Tree Protocol were not running?

   a. Unicasts sent to the MAC address of a device that has never been turned on

   b. Unicasts sent to the MAC address of a device that has been turned on and is working

   c. Frames sent to the Ethernet broadcast address

   d. None of the above

12. Which of the following interface states could a switch interface settle into after STP has completed building a spanning tree?

   a. Listening

   b. Blocking

   c. Forwarding

   d. Learning

The answers to the "Do I Know This Already?" quiz are found in Appendix A, "Answers to the 'Do I Know This Already?' Quizzes and Q&A Sections." The suggested choices for your next step are as follows:

■ **10 or less overall score**—Read the entire chapter. This includes the "Foundation Topics" and "Foundation Summary" sections and the Q&A section.

■ **11 or 12 overall score**—If you want more review on these topics, skip to the "Foundation Summary" section and then go to the Q&A section. Otherwise, move to the next chapter.

Foundation Topics

The Case for Bridging and Switching

To appreciate the need for LAN switches and the logic behind LAN switches, you must learn about devices called transparent bridges. Vendors began offering transparent bridges in the marketplace long before switches. And because switches act like bridges in many ways, it helps your understanding of switches to first understand how bridges work and why they were created in the first place.

To appreciate the need for bridges, you must be reminded of the state of Ethernet networking before bridges came along. Once upon a time, there was no such thing as an Ethernet LAN. Then Ethernet was created, using a single electrical bus, and was cabled using coaxial cables between the Ethernet cards in the devices that needed to attach to the Ethernet.

As mentioned in Chapter 3, "Data Link Layer Fundamentals: Ethernet LANs," 10BASE-T was the next step in the development of Ethernet. 10BASE-T improved the availability of a LAN because a problem on a single cable did not affect the rest of the LAN, which did happen on 10BASE2 and 10BASE5 networks. 10BASE-T allowed the use of unshielded twisted-pair (UTP) cabling, which is much cheaper than coaxial cable. Also, many buildings already had UTP cabling installed for phone service, so 10BASE-T quickly became a popular alternative to 10BASE2 and 10BASE5 Ethernet networks.

Figure 9-1 depicts the typical topology for 10BASE2 and for 10BASE-T.

Figure 9-1 *10BASE2 and 10BASE-T Physical Topologies*

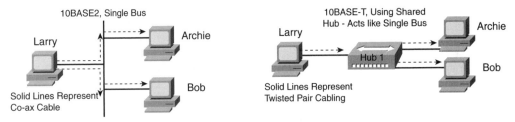

When transparent bridges first were introduced, Ethernet networks were either 10BASE5, 10BASE2, or 10BASE-T. Each of these three types of Ethernet had some common characteristics that drove the need for a bridging device:

- Any device sending a frame could have the frame collide with a frame sent by any other device attached to that LAN segment.

- Only one device could send a frame at a time, so the devices were sharing the 10-Mbps bandwidth.

- Broadcasts sent by one device would be heard by all other devices on the LAN.

When these three types of Ethernet first were introduced, a shared 10-Mbps of bandwidth was a huge amount of bandwidth! Before the introduction of LANs, people often used dumb terminals, with a 56-kbps WAN link being a really fast connection to the rest of the network—with that 56-kbps being shared among everyone in the building. So, getting to put your computer on a 10BASE-T Ethernet LAN was like getting a Gigabit Ethernet connection for your PC at your desk at work today—it was more bandwidth than you could imagine that you would need.

Over time, the performance of many Ethernet networks started to degrade. People developed applications to take advantage of the LAN bandwidth. More devices were added to each Ethernet. Eventually, an entire network became congested. The devices on the same Ethernet could not send (collectively) more than 10 Mbps of traffic because they were all sharing the 10 Mbps of bandwidth. However, with the increase in traffic volumes, collisions also increased. Long before the overall utilization approached 10 Mbps, Ethernet began to suffer because of increasing collisions.

Bridges solved the growing Ethernet congestion problem in two ways. First, they reduced the number of collisions that occur in a network. They also add bandwidth to the network. Figure 9-2 shows the basic premise behind an Ethernet transparent bridge.

The top part of the figure shows a 10BASE-T network before adding a bridge, and the lower part shows the network after it has been "segmented" using a bridge. The bridge creates two separate *collision domains*—two different sets of devices for which their frames can collide. For instance, Fred's frames can collide with Barney's, but they cannot collide with Wilma's or Betty's. If one LAN segment is busy, and the bridge needs to forward a frame, it simply holds the frame until the segment is no longer busy. By reducing collisions and assuming no significant change in the number of devices or the load on the network, network performance is greatly improved.

By adding a bridge between two hubs, the bridge really creates two separate 10BASE-T networks, one on the left and one on the right. So, the 10BASE-T network on the left has its own 10 Mbps to share, as does the network on the right. So, in this example, the total network bandwidth was doubled to 20 Mbps.

Figure 9-2   *Bridge Creates Two Collision Domains, Two Shared Ethernets*

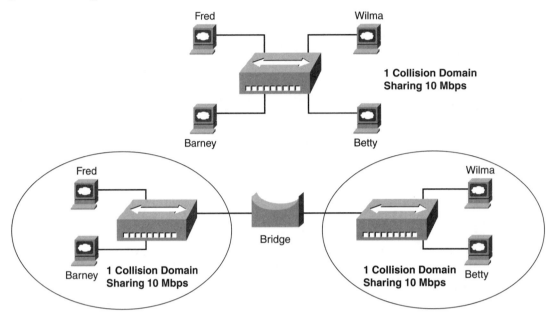

In summary, before bridges were created, 10BASE-T (and 10BASE2 and 10BASE5) network performance degraded as more stations and more traffic were introduced into the network. With the addition of bridges, an Ethernet network can add more capacity and increase performance.

Switches and bridges use the same core logic, as described in the next section of this chapter. Instead of using "bridges and switches" every time, I just refer to the devices as "bridges," but switches work the same way.

Transparent Bridging

Transparent bridges connect two or more Ethernet networks. By separating the network into multiple Ethernets, or multiple LAN segments, transparent bridges overcome some of the performance issues covered in the first section of this chapter.

Transparent bridging is called "transparent" because the endpoint devices do not need to know that the bridge(s) exist(s). In other words, the computers attached to the LAN do not behave any differently in the presence or absence of transparent bridges. Before diving into bridging and switching logic, a quick review of a couple of terms about MAC addresses is helpful. The following list defines three terms covered earlier in Chapter 3. These different types of MAC addresses can be treated differently by a bridge or switch.

The IEEE defines three general categories of MAC addresses on Ethernet:

- **Unicast addresses**—A MAC address that identifies a single LAN interface card. Today most cards use the MAC address that is burned in on the card.

- **Broadcast addresses**—The most often used of IEEE group MAC address, the broadcast address, has a value of FFFF.FFFF.FFFF (hexadecimal notation). The broadcast address implies that all devices on the LAN should process the frame.

- **Multicast addresses**—Multicast addresses are used to allow a subset of devices on a LAN to communicate. Some applications need to communicate with multiple other devices. By sending one frame, all the devices that care about receiving the data sent by that application can process the data, and the rest can ignore it. The IP protocol supports multicasting, and when IP multicasts over an Ethernet, the multicast MAC addresses used by IP follow this format: 0100.5e*xx.xxxx*, where any value can be used in the last half of the addresses.

Transparent bridges forward frames when necessary and do not forward when there is no need to do so, thus reducing overhead. To accomplish this, transparent bridges perform three actions:

1. Learning MAC addresses by examining the source MAC address of each frame received by the bridge

2. Deciding when to forward a frame or when to filter (not forward) a frame, based on the destination MAC address

3. Creating a loop-free environment with other bridges by using the Spanning Tree Protocol

The Forward Versus Filter Decision

Transparent bridges reduce collisions by forwarding traffic from one segment to the other only when necessary. To decide whether to forward a frame, the bridge uses a dynamically built table, called a *bridge table*. The bridge examines the bridging table to decide whether it should forward a frame. For example, consider the simple network shown in Figure 9-3, with Fred first sending a frame to Barney and then one to Wilma.

Figure 9-3 *Example Transparent Bridging Forwarding and Filtering Decision*

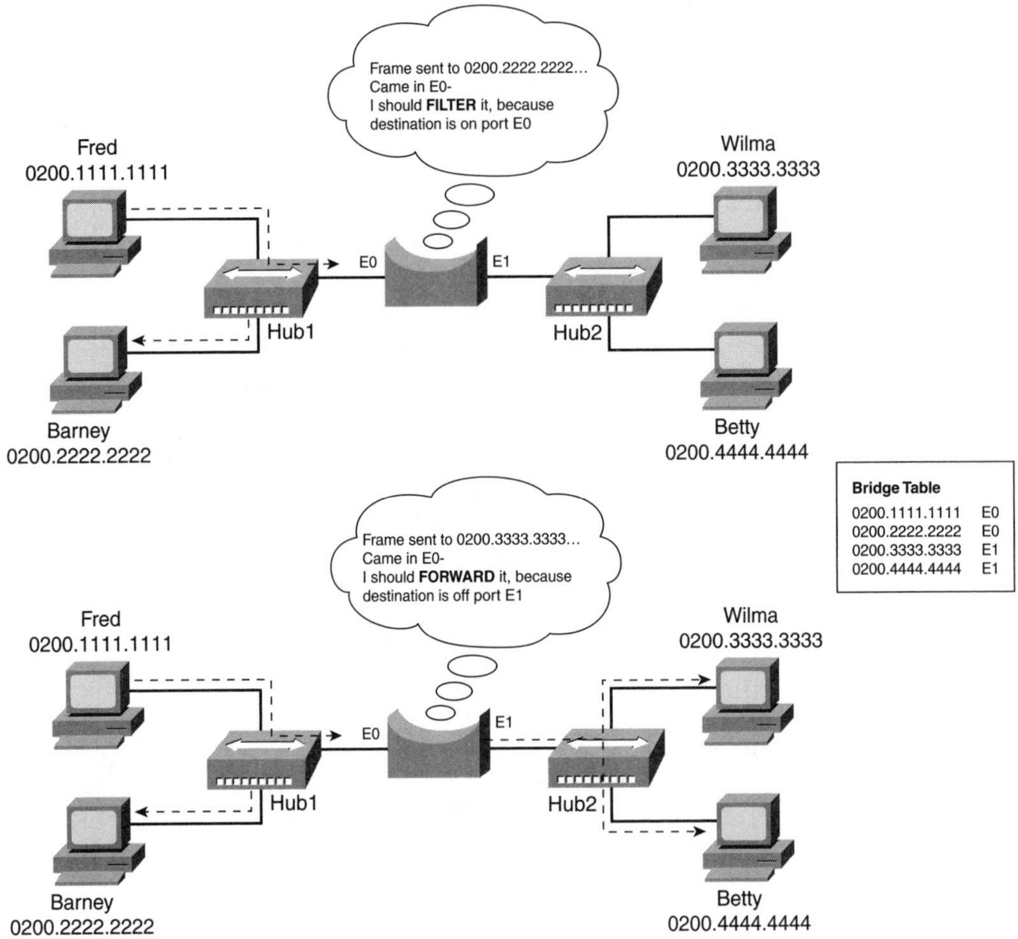

The bridge decides to filter (not forward) the frame that Fred sends to Barney. Fred sends a frame with the destination MAC address of 0200.2222.2222, which is Barney's MAC address. The bridge overhears the frame because it is attached to Hub1. The bridge then decides what common sense tells you from looking at the figure—it should not forward the frame because Barney, attached to Hub1 as well, already will have received the frame. But how does the bridge know to make that decision? The bridge decides to filter—in other words, not forward—the frame because it received the frame on port E0, and it knows that Barney's MAC also is located out E0.

Conversely, the bridge decides to forward the frame that Fred sends to Wilma in the lower part of the figure. The frame enters the bridge's E0 interface, and the bridge knows that the destination address, 0200.3333.3333, is located somewhere out its E1 interface. So, the bridge forwards the frame.

The rules for hub behavior have not changed—whenever a frame is sent toward a hub, the hub repeats the frame out every other port.

How Bridges Learn MAC Addresses

Bridges perform three main functions, as mentioned earlier. One of those key functions is to learn the MAC addresses in the network to build its bridging table. With a full, accurate bridging table, the bridge can make accurate forwarding and filtering decisions.

Bridges build the bridge table by listening to incoming frames and examining the source MAC address in the frame. If a frame enters the bridge and the source MAC address is not in the bridge table, the bridge creates an entry in the table. The MAC address is placed into the table, along with the interface in which the frame arrived. Bridge learning logic is that simple.

Figure 9-4 depicts the same network as Figure 9-3, but before the bridge has built any bridge table entries. In the figure, the first two frames sent in this network are shown—first a frame from Fred, addressed to Barney, followed by Barney's response, addressed to Fred.

Figure 9-4 *Bridge Learning: Empty Table and Adding Two Entries*

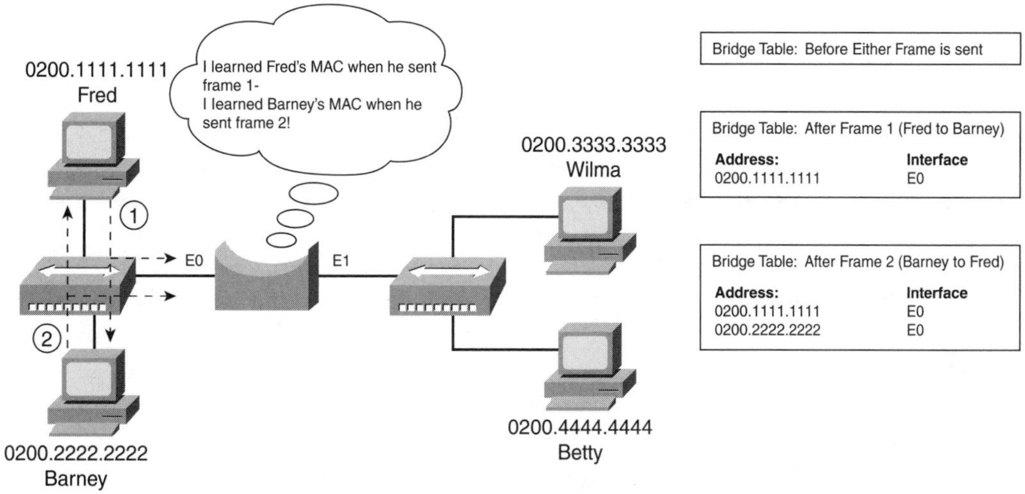

As seen in the figure, after Fred sends his first frame to Barney, the bridge has an entry for 0200.1111.1111, Fred's MAC address, associated with interface E0. When Barney replies at Step 2, the bridge adds a second entry, this one for 0200.2222.2222, Barney's MAC address. Learning always occurs by looking at the source MAC address in the frame.

Forwarding Unknown Unicasts and Broadcasts

What do you suppose the bridge did with Fred's first frame in Figure 9-4, the one that occurred when there were no entries in the bridging table? As it turns out, when there is no matching entry in the table, bridges forward the frame out all interfaces. Bridges were designed to forward what are called *unknown unicast frames* (frames whose destination MAC addresses are not yet in the bridging table), with the hope that the unknown device will be on some other Ethernet segment and will reply, and the bridge will build a correct entry in the bridging table. For instance, in Figure 9-4, the bridge forwards the first frame over to the right-side Ethernet, even though Barney is not on the right side of the bridge. Later, the bridge will filter a frame sent from Fred to Barney because the bridge would have an entry in the bridging table telling the bridge that Barney is also off port E0.

Bridges also forward LAN broadcasts. LAN broadcasts, by definition, need to be received by all devices on the same LAN. So, the bridge simply forwards broadcasts. Generally, bridges also forward LAN multicast frames out all ports, just like they do for broadcasts. However, a few multicast features in switches limit the flooding of multicasts, such as Internet Group Management Protocol (IGMP) snooping. Bridges never forward traffic out the same interface it came in—so, broadcast, multicast, and unkown unicast frames are actually sent out all interfaces except the incoming interface.

LAN Switching

Before bridges were created, a 10BASE-T network might have begun to suffer from performance problems. As described in the previous section, to improve performance, you might have added a two-port bridge, created two LAN segments, doubled the bandwidth, reduced collisions, and improved performance.

Now take a step back and think about what might happen to that network with the bridge 6 months later. More devices have been added to the segments on each side of the bridge. More bandwidth-hungry applications have been added. Eventually, both LAN segments might become as congested as the original single Ethernet segment was 6 months earlier.

What's the solution? What about a four-port bridge? The engineer adds the four-port bridge, converting the two segments to four segments, again doubling bandwidth, and again reducing collisions. A few months later, the number of devices has increased, more bandwidth-hungry applications have been added, and you need an eight-port bridge! You can see a vicious cycle beginning to occur.

From one perspective, switches are bridges with lots of ports. Switches behave identically to transparent bridges in terms of forwarding and learning, but switches typically have many more ports and much faster internal processing. So, if a campus network needed to be broken into 100 different segments, you could use a switch with 100 ports in it. It would break the

Ethernet into 100 different collision domains, or segments, and create 100 different sets of 10-Mbps bandwidth (or more, if Fast Ethernet or Gigabit Ethernet were used). It again would reduce collisions, just like bridges. In short, switches do the same thing as bridges, only faster and better. In fact, an old saying says it best: "Switches are bridges on steroids."

So, if bridges and switches do the same things the same way, why have two names? There were many reasons, none of which matters for the CCNA exams. Today you do not even have to choose between buying a bridge or a switch—vendors sell only switches.

The following list provides a quick review of the basic forwarding logic used by a switch or bridge:

1. A frame is received.

2. If the destination is a broadcast or multicast, forward on all ports except the port in which the frame was received.

3. If the destination is a unicast and the address is not in the address table, forward on all ports except the port in which the frame was received.

4. If the destination is a unicast and the address is in the address table, and if the associated interface is not the interface in which the frame arrived, forward the frame out the one correct port.

5. Otherwise, filter (do not forward) the frame.

For instance, in Figure 9-5, the network has been migrated to use a switch. The switch's bridging table already has been populated with all the MAC addresses in the network. Fred sends another frame to Barney. The switch knows that Barney is located off his E1 port, so the switch forwards the frame out E1.

Figure 9-5 *Example: Forwarding Logic for a Switch*

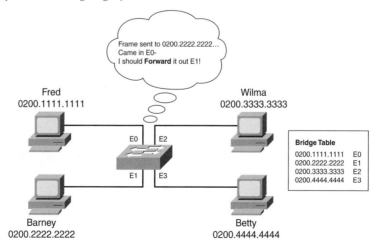

Although the basic operation of bridges and switches is identical, switches do differ from transparent bridges in some regards. Some of the differences exist just because newer features were introduced to the market around the same time that switches became popular. Other features, such as the optimized internal processing on switches, do create a significant advantage to switches over bridges. Practically, the differences do not really matter because vendors continue to improve and develop features for switches, whereas it is hard to find vendors that offer products called bridges anymore.

Full-Duplex Ethernet

Full-duplex Ethernet was explained back in Chapter 3. Briefly, when a switch port has only a single device attached to it, no collisions could possibly occur because there is only one connected device. So, the device cabled to that switch port disables its NIC loopback logic, allowing the device to both send a frame and receive a frame at the same time.

If a hub with multiple devices is connected to a switch port, collisions still can occur, so half-duplex operation must be used. Figure 9-6 summarizes the concept.

Figure 9-6 *Full Duplex and Half Duplex*

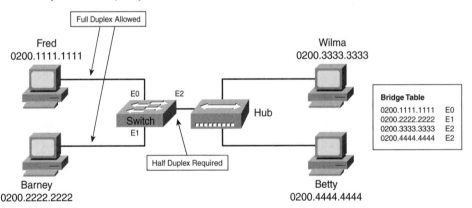

Internal Processing on Cisco Switches

Switches use a couple of different types of internal processing variations. Almost of the more recently released switches use store-and-forward processing, but all three types of switching are supported in at least one type of currently available Cisco switch.

Some switches, and transparent bridges in general, use *store-and-forward processing*. With store-and-forward, the entire frame is received by the switch before the first bit of the frame is forwarded. However, Cisco also offers two other internal processing methods for switches, called cut-through and fragment-free.

With store-and-forward processing, the switch must wait for the entire frame to be received. However, because the forwarding/filtering logic is based on the destination address, which is inside the header, the switch can make the forwarding decision before the entire frame has been received. With cut-through processing, the switch starts sending the frame out the output port before the whole frame has been received. In other words, as soon as the incoming switch port receives enough of the frame to see the destination MAC address, the forwarding decision is made and the frame is transmitted out the appropriate outgoing port to the destination device. So, each frame might experience slightly less latency.

Cut-through processing reduces latency, but it also propagates errors. Because the frame check sequence (FCS) is in the Ethernet trailer, a cut-through forwarded frame might have bit errors in it that the switch will not notice before sending most of the frame.

Fragment-free processing works similarly to cut-through, but it tries to reduce the number of errored frames that it forwards. One interesting fact about Ethernet CSMA/CD logic is that collisions should be detected within the first 64 bytes of a frame. Fragment-free processing works like cut-through logic, but it waits to receive the first 64 bytes before forwarding a frame. The frames experience less latency than with store-and-forward logic and slightly more latency than cut-through—but frames that have errors as a result of collisions are not forwarded.

With many links to the desktop running at 100 Mbps, uplinks at 1 Gbps, and faster ASICs, today's switches typically use store-and-forward processing.

The internal processing algorithms used by switches vary among models and vendors; regardless, the internal processing can be categorized as one of the methods listed in Table 9-2.

Table 9-2 *Switch Internal Processing*

Switching Method	Description
Store-and-forward	The switch fully receives all bits in the frame (store) before forwarding the frame (forward). This allows the switch to check the FCS before forwarding the frame. (The FCS is in the Ethernet trailer.)
Cut-through	The switch performs the address table lookup as soon as the destination address field in the header is received. The first bits in the frame can be sent out the outbound port before the final bits in the incoming frame are received. This does not allow the switch to discard frames that fail the FCS check. (FCS is in the Ethernet trailer.)
Fragment-free	This performs like cut-through switching, but the switch waits for 64 bytes to be received before forwarding the first bytes of the outgoing frame. According to Ethernet specifications, collisions should be detected during the first 64 bytes of the frame, so frames in error because of a collision will not be forwarded.

Speed and Autonegotiation

Ethernet autonegotiation uses a process by which a switch and an Ethernet NIC together determine the best combination of parameters for that particular link. To support autonegotiation, the switch and the NIC must support multiple speeds, and they also probably support both half and full duplex. So, a 10/100 card connected to a switch can negotiate to use full-duplex 100 Mbps. If the next switch port is connected to a 10-Mbps-only card that does not even support autonegotiation, the switch will use 10 Mbps, half duplex.

Interestingly, a minor debate still pops up in the networking trade press occasionally about how reliable the Ethernet autonegotiation process really works. Many people recommend that you set the speed and duplex settings on any switch port for which you know the settings desired by the device on the other end of the cable. You should understand autonegotiation, but in real life, you should consider statically configuring these parameters for switch ports connected to servers, switches, and routers.

Summary: Bridges and Switches

Table 9-3 summarizes the similarities and differences between transparent bridges and switches.

Table 9-3 *Switch Internal Processing*

Fact/Feature	Transparent Bridge	Switch
Unicast forwarding	Based on bridge table and destination MAC	Same as Bridge
Broadcast forwarding	All broadcasts forwarded	Same as bridge
Learning the bridge table	Examining source MAC of all received frames	Same as bridge
Loop avoidance	Uses Spanning Tree Protocol	Same as bridge
Popular in the market today	No	Yes
Supports dozens or hundreds of physical ports	No	Yes
Allows full duplex when appropriate	No	Yes
Uses specialized hardware (ASICs) for faster processing	No	Yes
Allows cut-through internal processing, as well as store-and-forward processing	No	Yes

LAN Segmentation

LAN segmentation simply means breaking one LAN into parts, with each part called a *segment*. The term *LAN segment* comes from the original use of a physical bus with 10BASE2 and 10BASE5. A single Ethernet segment consisted of the devices connected serially with coaxial cable. When 10BASE-T came along, the term segment still was used, this time to identify a hub with multiple devices connected to it.

Figure 9-7 repeats an earlier figure, but with the term segment noted on the figure.

Figure 9-7   *Segments and Segmentation with a Bridge*

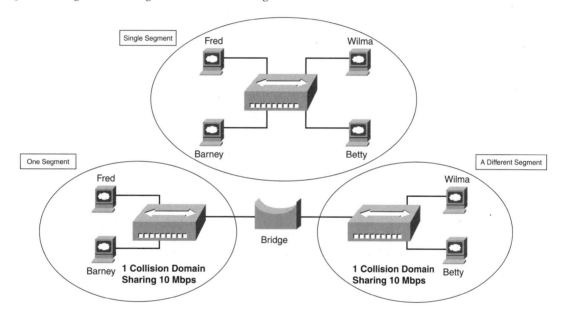

With a single hub, or multiple hubs but no bridges, switches, or routers, you have a single segment. When you separate the network with a bridge, switch, or router, you create multiple segments. So, in Figure 9-7, you can say that the bridge separates the network into two separate segments. Many people use the term *Ethernet segment* very loosely, but for the CCNA exams, you can think of segment as meaning the same thing as collision domain.

As mentioned earlier, a *collision domain* is the set of LAN interfaces whose frames could collide with each other, but not with any other devices in the network. The bridge in Figure 9-7 creates two separate Ethernet segments, and each is a separate collision domain. Figure 9-8 shows a typical example of the definition of collision domains.

Figure 9-8 *Collision Domains*

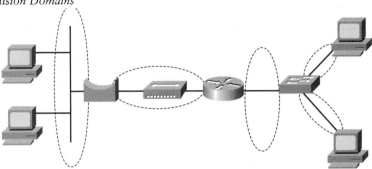

Each separate segment, or collision domain, is shown with a dashed-line circle in the figure. The switch on the right has a separate collision domain for each port. The hub near the center of the network does not create multiple collision domains because it repeats all frames out all ports. Routers also separate LANs into separate collision domains (although that was not covered earlier in this chapter.)

Just like the concept of a collision domain relates to where a frame can be sent and where it can cause collisions, the concept of a broadcast domain relates to where broadcasts can be forwarded. Bridges and switches forward broadcasts and multicasts on all ports. Because broadcast frames are sent out all ports, a bridge or switch creates only a single broadcast domain. A *broadcast domain* is the set of devices for which, when one of the devices sends a broadcast, all the other devices receive a copy of the broadcast.

Only routers stop the flow of broadcasts. Figure 9-9 provides the broadcast domains for the same network depicted in Figure 9-8.

Broadcasts sent by a device in one broadcast domain are not forwarded to devices in another broadcast domain. In this example, there are two broadcast domains. For instance, the router will not forward a LAN broadcast sent by a PC on the left to the segment on the right. In the old days, the term *broadcast firewall* described the fact that routers did not forward LAN broadcasts.

Figure 9-9 *Broadcast Domains*

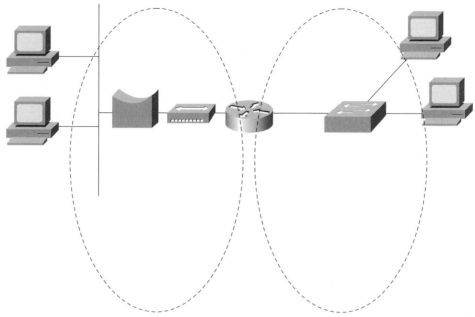

General definitions for a collision domain and a broadcast domain are as follows:

- A *collision domain* is a set of network interface cards (NICs) for which a frame sent by one NIC could result in a collision with a frame sent by any other NIC in the same collision domain.

- A *broadcast domain* is a set of NICs for which a broadcast frame sent by one NIC will be received by all other NICs in the same broadcast domain.

In short, hubs do not actually segment an Ethernet into multiple segments. Bridges and switches do segment an Ethernet into different collision domains, and routers segment an Ethernet into different collision and broadcast domains.

The INTRO exam actually might phrase questions in terms of the benefits of LAN segmentation instead of just asking for the facts related to collision domains and broadcast domains. Table 9-4 lists some of the key benefits. The features in the table should be interpreted within the following context: "If I migrated from a single Ethernet segment to a network with two segments separated by a bridge/switch/router, and if traffic loads and destinations stayed constant, the result would be _____."

Table 9-4 *Benefits When Moving from One Ethernet Segment to Multiple Segments Using Bridges, Switches, and Routers*

Feature	Bridging	Switching	Routing
Greater cabling distances allowed	Yes	Yes	Yes
Decrease in collisions	Yes	Yes	Yes
Decreased adverse impact of broadcasts	No	No	Yes
Decreased adverse impact of multicasts	No	No*	Yes
Increase in bandwidth	Yes	Yes	Yes

*Switches today support several methods to optimize multicast forwarding, such as Internet Group Management Protocol (IGMP) snooping

The Need for Spanning Tree

Without the Spanning Tree Protocol (STP), frames would loop for an indefinite period of time in networks with physically redundant links. To prevent looping frames, STP blocks some ports from forwarding frames so that only one active path exists between any pair of LAN segments (collision domains). The result of STP is good: Frames do not loop infinitely, which makes the LAN usable. However, the network uses some redundant links in case of a failure, but not for balancing traffic.

To avoid loops, all bridging devices, including switches, use STP. STP causes each interface on a bridging device to settle into a blocking state or a forwarding state. *Blocking* means that the interface cannot forward or receive data frames. *Forwarding* means that the interface can send and receive data frames. By having a correct subset of the interfaces blocked, a single currently active logical path will exist between each pair of LANs.

STP behaves identically for a transparent bridge and a switch. So, the terms *bridge, switch,* and *bridging device* all are used interchangeably when discussing STP.

A simple example makes the need for STP more obvious. Remember, switches forward frames sent to both unknown unicast MAC addresses and the broadcast address, out all interfaces (except the incoming interface). Figure 9-10 shows that a single frame, sent by Larry to Bob, loops forever because the network has redundancy but no STP.

Figure 9-10   *Network with Redundant Links but Without STP: Frame Loops Forever*

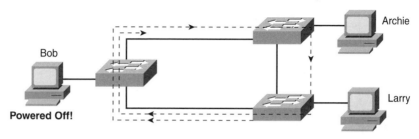

Larry sends a single unicast frame to Bob's MAC address, but Bob is powered off, so none of the switches has learned Bob's MAC address yet. Bob's MAC address would be an unknown unicast address at this point in time. Therefore, frames addressed to Bob's MAC address will be forwarded by each switch out every port. These frames will loop forever—or at least until time is no more! Because the switches never learn Bob's MAC address (remember, he's powered off and can send no frames), they keep forwarding the frame out all ports, and copies of the frame go around and around.

Similarly, bridges and switches forward broadcasts on all interfaces, so if any of the PCs sent a broadcast, the broadcast would loop indefinitely as well.

One way to solve this problem is to design the LAN with no redundant links. However, most network engineers will not design a multiswitch campus LAN without physical redundancy between the switches, similar to the network in Figure 9-10. Eventually, a switch or a link will fail, and you want the network to still be available. The right solution includes bridged/switched networks with physical redundancy, using STP to dynamically block some interface(s) so that only one active path exists between two endpoints at any instant in time.

How Spanning Tree Works

The Spanning Tree Algorithm places each bridge or switch port into either a forwarding state or a blocking state. All the ports in the forwarding state are considered to be in the current spanning tree. The collective set of forwarding ports creates a single path over which frames are sent between Ethernet segments. Switches can forward frames out ports and receive frames in ports that are in a forwarding state; switches do not forward frames out ports and receive frames in ports that are in a blocking state.

Figure 9-11 shows a simple STP tree with one port on SW3 in a blocking state.

Figure 9-11 *Network with Redundant Links, with STP*

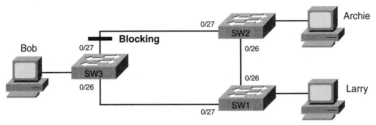

Now when Larry sends a frame to Bob's MAC address, the frame does not loop. SW1 sends a copy to SW3, but SW3 does not forward the frame to SW2 out its port 0/27 because that interface is blocking. STP's job is to figure out how to put the correct interfaces into blocking and forwarding states to prevent loops but allow frames to be sent between every segment. The process itself is not too difficult. First, STP uses *Hello messages*, also called *Bridge Protocol Data Units (BPDUs)*. Each switch and bridge claims to be the root bridge, and the one with the lowest bridge ID is elected root. The 8-byte bridge ID is the combination of a priority (2-byte) and a MAC address on the switch (6-byte). STP places all ports on the root switch into a forwarding state. In Figure 9-11, SW1 became the root switch.

The root bridge continually sends Hello BPDUs. Each nonroot switch receives the Hellos, changes a few fields, and forwards out all ports. One of the fields that is changed is called *cost*. This cost field, in which each switch increments before forwarding the Hello message, helps the nonroot bridges decide how good a particular path is to the root bridge. A switch that receives a Hello that has been forwarded by ten other switches probably has a higher cost than a Hello received directly from the root switch, for instance.

Each switch decides which of its interfaces is this switch's root port. The root port of each switch is placed into a forwarding state. To decide which port is the root port, the switch compares the cost value in all the Hello messages that it receives via different physical paths to the root bridge. The interface that received the least-cost Hello message is that switch's *root port*. In Figure 9-11, SW2's 0/26 interface and SW3's 0/26 interface became their respective root ports.

Finally, each LAN segment has an STP designated bridge on that segment. Many switches can attach to the same Ethernet segment. The switch with the lowest administrative cost from itself to the root bridge, as compared to the other bridges attached to the same segment, is the designated bridge for that segment. The interface that the switch uses to connect to that segment is called the *designated port* for that segment; that port is placed into a forwarding state. In Figure 9-11, SW2's 0/27 interface became the designated port on the segment between SW2 and SW3.

STP places all other ports into a blocking state. In Figure 9-11, the only port that had not been placed into a forwarding state was SW3's 0/27 interface, so it was placed into a blocking state.

Table 9-5 summarizes the reasons why STP places a port in forwarding or blocking state.

Table 9-5 *STP: Reasons for Forwarding State*

Characterization of Port	Explanation
All root bridge's ports	The root bridge is always the designated bridge on all connected segments.
Each nonroot bridge's root port	The root port is the port that receives the lowest-cost BPDU from the root.
Each LAN's designated port	The bridge that forwards the lowest-cost BPDU onto the segment is the designated bridge for that segment.
All other ports	All ports that do not meet the other criteria are placed into a blocking state.

STP uses a couple of port states besides forwarding and blocking.

- **Listening**—Listens to incoming Hello messages to ensure that there are no loops, but does not forward traffic or learn MAC addresses on the interface. This is an interim state between blocking and forwarding.

- **Learning**—Still listens to BPDUs, plus learns MAC addresses from incoming frames. It does not forward traffic. This is an interim state between blocking and forwarding.

- **Disabled**—Administratively down.

Under normal operation, when a port needs to change from blocking to forwarding, it first transitions to listening, then learning, and then forwarding. This process, with default timers, takes around 50 seconds.

STP might seem a bit overwhelming at this point. You should key on the general concepts, and the interface states, for the INTRO exam. Refer to Chapter 2, "Spanning Tree Protocol," of the *CCNA ICND Exam Certification Guide* for a detailed discussion on STP.

Foundation Summary

The "Foundation Summary" section of each chapter lists the most important facts from the chapter. Although this section does not list every fact from the chapter that will be on your CCNA exam, a well-prepared CCNA candidate should know, at a minimum, all the details in each "Foundation Summary" section before going to take the exam.

Transparent bridges forward frames when necessary and do not forward when there is no need to do so, thus reducing overhead. To accomplish this, transparent bridges perform three actions:

1. Learning MAC addresses by examining the source MAC address of each frame received by the bridge

2. Deciding when to forward a frame or when to filter (not forward) a frame, based on the destination MAC address

3. Creating a loop-free environment with other bridges by using the Spanning Tree Protocol

The following list provides a quick review of the basic logic used by a switch or bridge:

1. A frame is received.

2. If the destination is a broadcast or multicast, forward on all ports except the port in which the frame was received.

3. If the destination is a unicast and the address is not in the address table, forward on all ports except the port in which the frame was received.

4. If the destination is a unicast and the address is in the address table, and if the associated interface is not the interface in which the frame arrived, forward the frame out the one correct port.

5. Otherwise, filter (do not forward) the frame.

The internal processing algorithms used by switches vary among models and vendors; regardless, the internal processing can be categorized as one of the methods listed in Table 9-6.

Table 9-6 *Switch Internal Processing*

Switching Method	Description
Store-and-forward	The switch fully receives all bits in the frame (store) before forwarding the frame (forward). This allows the switch to check the FCS before forwarding the frame. (The FCS is in the Ethernet trailer.)
Cut-through	The switch performs the address table lookup as soon as the destination address field in the header is received. The first bits in the frame can be sent out the outbound port before the final bits in the incoming frame are received. This does not allow the switch to discard frames that fail the FCS check. (The FCS is in the Ethernet trailer.)
Fragment-free	This performs like cut-through switching, but the switch waits for 64 bytes to be received before forwarding the first bytes of the outgoing frame. According to Ethernet specifications, collisions should be detected during the first 64 bytes of the frame, so frames in error because of a collision will not be forwarded.

General definitions for a collision domain and a broadcast domain are as follows:

- A *collision domain* is a set of network interface cards (NICs) for which a frame sent by one NIC could result in a collision with a frame sent by any other NIC in the same collision domain.

- A *broadcast domain* is a set of NICs for which a broadcast frame sent by one NIC will be received by all other NICs in the same broadcast domain.

Figure 9-12 shows a typical example of the definition of collision domains, while Figure 9-13 shows broadcast domains in the same network.

Figure 9-12 *Collision Domains*

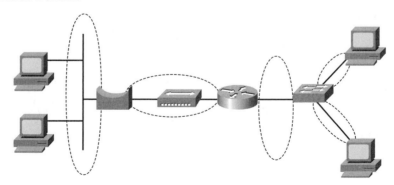

Figure 9-13 *Broadcast Domains*

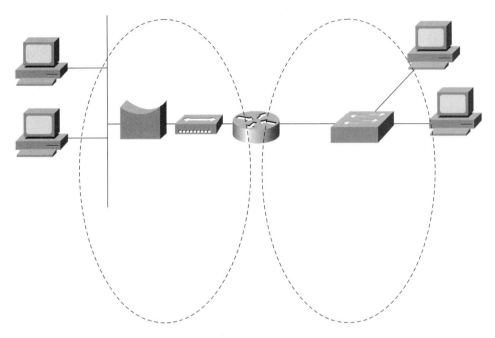

Table 9-7 summarizes the reasons STP places a port in forwarding or blocking state.

Table 9-7 *STP: Reasons for Forwarding State*

Characterization of Port	Explanation
All root bridge's ports	The root bridge is always the designated bridge on all connected segments.
Each nonroot bridge's root port	The root port is the port that receives the lowest-cost BPDU from the root.
Each LAN's designated port	The bridge that forwards the lowest-cost BPDU onto the segment is the designated bridge for that segment.
All other ports	All ports that do not meet the other criteria are placed into a blocking state.

Q&A

As mentioned in the introduction, you have two choices for review questions. The questions that follow give you a bigger challenge than the exam itself by using an open-ended question format. By reviewing now with this more difficult question format, you can exercise your memory better and prove your conceptual and factual knowledge of this chapter. The answers to these questions are found in Appendix A.

For more practice with exam-like question formats, including questions using a router simulator and multiple-choice questions, use the exam engine on the CD.

1. Name two of the methods of internal switching on typical switches today. Which provides less latency for an individual frame?

2. Describe how a transparent bridge decides whether it should forward a frame, and tell how it chooses the output interface.

3. Define the term collision domain.

4. Name two benefits of LAN segmentation using transparent bridges.

5. What routing protocol does a transparent bridge use to learn about Layer 3 addressing groupings?

6. If a Fast Ethernet NIC currently is receiving a frame, can it begin sending a frame?

7. Why did Ethernet networks' performance improve with the advent of bridges?

8. Why did Ethernet networks' performance improve with the advent of switches?

9. What are two key differences between a 10-Mbps NIC and a 10/100 NIC?

10. Assume that a building has 100 devices attached to the same Ethernet. These users then are migrated onto two separate shared Ethernet segments, each with 50 devices, with a transparent bridge between them. List two benefits that would be derived for a typical user.

11. Assume that a building has 100 devices attached to the same Ethernet. These devices are migrated to two different shared Ethernet segments, each with 50 devices. The two segments are connected to a Cisco LAN switch to allow communication between the two sets of users. List two benefits that would be derived for a typical user.

12. How fast is Fast Ethernet?

13. How does a transparent bridge build its address table?

14. How many bytes long is a MAC address?

15. Does a bridge or switch examine just the incoming frame's source MAC, the destination MAC, or both? Why does it examine the one(s) that it examines?

16. Define the term broadcast domain.

17. Describe the benefits of creating 3 VLANs of 25 ports each, versus a single VLAN of 75 ports, in each case using a single switch. Assume that all ports are switched ports (each port is a different collision domain).

18. Explain the function of the loopback and collision-detection features of an Ethernet NIC in relation to half-duplex and full-duplex operations.

19. Describe the benefit of the Spanning Tree Protocol as used by transparent bridges and switches.

20. Name the three reasons why a port is placed in forwarding state as a result of spanning tree.

21. Name the three interface states that the Spanning Tree Protocol uses other than forwarding. Which of these states is transitory?

This chapter covers the following subjects:

- Virtual LAN Concepts

- Trunking with ISL and 802.1Q

- Passing Traffic Between VLANs

CHAPTER 10

Virtual LANs and Trunking

It's hard to be a networker today and not work with virtual LANs (VLANs) and VLAN trunking. Almost every campus LAN uses VLANs, and almost every campus LAN with more than one switch uses trunking. In short, you have to know these topics.

VLANs allow a switch to separate different physical ports into different groups so that traffic from devices in one group never gets forwarded to the other group. This allows engineers to build networks that meet their design requirements, without having to buy a different switch for each group. Also, multiple switches can be connected together, with traffic from multiple VLANs crossing the same Ethernet links, using a feature called trunking.

"Do I Know This Already?" Quiz

The purpose of the "Do I Know This Already?" quiz is to help you decide whether you really need to read the entire chapter. If you already intend to read the entire chapter, you do not necessarily need to answer these questions now.

The eight-question quiz, derived from the major sections in "Foundation Topics" portion of the chapter, helps you determine how to spend your limited study time.

Table 10-1 outlines the major topics discussed in this chapter and the "Do I Know This Already?" quiz questions that correspond to those topics.

Table 10-1 *"Do I Know This Already?" Foundation Topics Section-to-Question Mapping*

Foundations Topics Section	Questions Covered in This Section
Virtual LAN Concepts	1, 7, 8
Trunking with ISL and 802.1q	3, 4,
Passing Traffic Between VLANs	2, 5, 6

> **CAUTION** The goal of self-assessment is to gauge your mastery of the topics in this chapter. If you do not know the answer to a question or are only partially sure of the answer, you should mark this question wrong for purposes of the self-assessment. Giving yourself credit for an answer that you correctly guess skews your self-assessment results and might provide you with a false sense of security.

1. In a LAN, which of the following terms best equates to the term *VLAN*?

    a. Collision domain

    b. Broadcast domain

    c. Subnet domain

    d. Single switch

    e. Trunk

2. Imagine a switch with three configured VLANs. How many IP subnets would be required, assuming that all hosts in all VLANs want to use TCP/IP?

    a. 0

    b. 1

    c. 2

    d. 3

    e. Can't tell from the information provided

3. Which of the following fully encapsulates the original Ethernet frame in a trunking header?

    a. VTP

    b. ISL

    c. 802.1q

    d. Both ISL and 802.1q

    e. None of the above

4. Which of the following allows a spanning tree instance per VLAN?

  a. VTP

  b. ISL

  c. 802.1q

  d. Both ISL and 802.1q

  e. None of the above

5. Imagine a Layer 2 switch with three configured VLANs, using an external router for inter-VLAN traffic. What is the least number of router Fast Ethernet interfaces required to forward traffic between VLANs?

  a. 0

  b. 1

  c. 2

  d. 3

  e. Can't tell from the information provided

6. Which of the following terms refers to a function that can forward traffic between two different VLANs?

  a. Layer 2 switching

  b. Layer 3 switching

  c. Layer 4 switching

  d. All of the above

7. Imagine a small campus network with three VLANs spread across two switches. Which of the following would you expect to also have a quantity of 3?

  a. Collision domains

  b. IP subnets

  c. Broadcast domains

  d. All of the above

  e. None of the above

8. Which of the following are considered to be ways of configuring VLANs?

   a. By statically assigning a switch port to a VLAN

   b. By assigning a MAC address to a particular VLAN

   c. By allowing DHCP to dynamically assign a PC to a particular VLAN

   d. By using the DVTP protocol

The answers to the "Do I Know This Already?" quiz are found in Appendix A, "Answers to the 'Do I Know This Already?' Quizzes and Q&A Sections." The suggested choices for your next step are as follows:

■ **6 or less overall score**—Read the entire chapter. This includes the "Foundation Topics" and "Foundation Summary" sections and the Q&A section.

■ **7 or 8 overall score**—If you want more review on these topics, skip to the "Foundation Summary" section and then go to the Q&A section. Otherwise, move to the next chapter.

Foundation Topics

Virtual LAN Concepts

Before understanding VLANs, you must first have a very specific understanding of the definition of a LAN. Although you can think about LANs from many perspectives, one perspective in particular will help you with understanding VLANs:

A LAN includes all devices in the same broadcast domain.

As described in Chapter 9, "Cisco LAN Switching Basics," a broadcast domain includes the set of all LAN connected devices that can send a broadcast frame, and all the other devices in the same LAN get a copy of the frame. So, you can think of a LAN and a broadcast domain as being basically the same thing.

Without VLANs, a switch treats all interfaces on the switch as being in the same broadcast domain—in others words, all connected devices are in the same LAN. With VLANs, a switch can put some interfaces into one broadcast domain and some into another. Essentially, the switch creates multiple broadcast domains. These individual broadcast domains created by the switch are called virtual LANs.

This chapter focuses on VLANs and the concepts and configuration required to implement VLANs on Cisco switches. This chapter covers VLAN concepts, including VLAN trunking. Also, you will read about what types of devices can be used to forward traffic between different VLANs.

VLAN Basics

A *virtual LAN* (*VLAN*) is a broadcast domain created by one or more switches. The switch creates a VLAN simply by putting some interfaces in one VLAN and some in another. So, instead of all ports on a switch forming a single broadcast domain, the switch separates them into many, based on configuration. It's really that simple.

The first two figures in this chapter compare two networks. First, before VLANs existed, if a design specified two separate broadcast domains, two switches would be used—one for each broadcast domain, as shown in Figure 10-1.

Figure 10-1 *Example Network with Two Broadcast Domains and No VLANs*

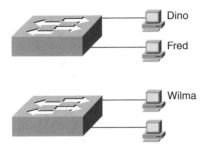

Alternately, you can create multiple broadcast domains using a single switch. Figure 10-2 shows the same two broadcast domains as in Figure 10-1, now implemented as two different VLANs on a single switch.

Figure 10-2 *Example Network with Two VLANs Using One Switch*

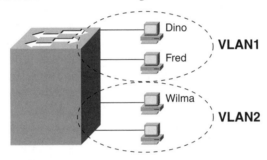

In a network as small as the one in Figure 10-2, you might not really need to use VLANs. However, there are many motivations for using VLANs, including these:

- To group users by department, or by groups that work together, instead of by physical location

- To reduce overhead by limiting the size of each broadcast domain

- To enforce better security by keeping sensitive devices on a separate VLAN

- To separate specialized traffic from mainstream traffic—for example, putting IP telephones on a separate VLAN from user PCs

Creating VLANs

Switches normally define VLANs in terms of which ports are in each VLAN. You literally configure something as simply as "interface 0/1 is in VLAN 1" and "interface 0/2 is in VLAN 33." Port-based VLANs, the typical choice for configuring VLANs in a switch, can be done very easily, without needing to know the MAC address of the device. However, you need good documentation to make sure that you cable the right devices into the right switch port, thereby putting them in the right VLANs.

A rarely used alternative for creating VLANs is to group devices into a VLAN based on MAC address. The engineer would discover all the MAC addresses of all the devices and then would configure the MAC addresses in the various switches, associating each MAC address with a VLAN. When a device moves to a different switch port and sends a frame, the device stays in the same VLAN. This allows devices to move around more easily. However, the administrative overhead of configuring the MAC address of the devices can be a large administrative chore, so this option is seldom used.

Trunking with ISL and 802.1q

When using VLANs in networks that have multiple interconnected switches, you need to use VLAN trunking between the switches. When sending a frame to another switch, the switches need a way to identify the VLAN from which the frame was sent. With VLAN trunking, the switches tag each frame sent between switches so that the receiving switch knows which VLAN the frame belongs to. Figure 10-3 outlines the basic idea.

Figure 10-3 *VLAN Trunking Between Two Switches*

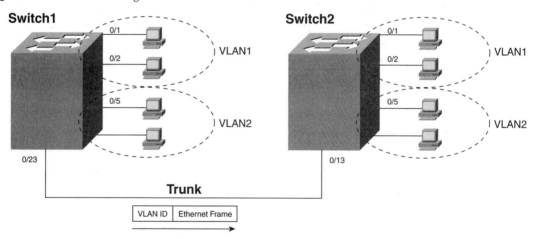

With trunking, you can support multiple VLANs that have members on more than one switch. For instance, when Switch1 receives a broadcast from a device in VLAN1, it needs to forward the broadcast to Switch2. Before sending the frame, Switch1 adds another header to the original Ethernet frame; that new header has the VLAN number in it. When Switch2 receives the frame, it sees that the frame was from a device in VLAN1, so Switch2 knows that it should forward the broadcast only out its own interfaces in VLAN1.

Cisco switches support two different trunking protocols, Inter-Switch Link (ISL) and IEEE 802.1q. They both provide basic trunking, as shown in Figure 10-3. They do have some differences, as will be covered next.

Cisco ISL

Cisco created ISL before the IEEE standardized a trunking protocol. Because ISL is Cisco proprietary, it can be used only between two Cisco switches. ISL fully encapsulates each original Ethernet frame in an ISL header and trailer, with the encapsulated original Ethernet frame being unchanged. Figure 10-4 shows the framing for ISL.

Figure 10-4   *ISL Header*

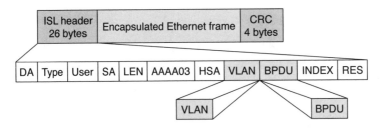

The ISL header includes several fields, but most important, the ISL header VLAN field provides a place to encode the VLAN number. By tagging a frame with the correct VLAN number inside the header, the sending switch can ensure that the receiving switch knows which VLAN the encapsulated frame belongs to. Also, the source and destination addresses in the ISL header use MAC addresses of the sending and receiving switch, as opposed to the devices that actually sent the original frame. Other than that, the details of the ISL header are not that important.

IEEE 802.1q

The IEEE standardizes many of the protocols relating to LANs today, and VLAN trunking is no exception. Years after Cisco created ISL, the IEEE completed work on the 802.1q standard, which defines a different way to do trunking.

802.1q uses a different style of header than does ISL for tagging frames with a VLAN number. In fact, 802.1q does not actually encapsulate the original frame—instead, it adds an extra 4-byte header to the middle of the original Ethernet header. That additional header includes a field with which to identify the VLAN number. Because the original header is now longer, 802.1q encapsulation forces a recalculation of the original FCS field in the Ethernet trailer because the FCS is based on the contents of the entire frame. Figure 10-5 shows the 802.1q header and framing of the revised Ethernet header.

Figure 10-5   *802.1q Trunking Header*

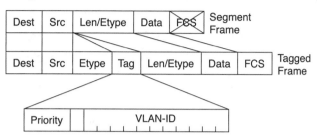

ISL and 802.1q Compared

Both ISL and 802.1q provide trunking. The header used by each varies, and only ISL actually encapsulates the original frame, but both allow the use of a 12-bit-long VLAN ID field. So, either works fine and supports the same number of VLANs as a result of both using a 12-bit VLAN Number field.

ISL and 802.1q both support a separate instance of spanning tree for each VLAN. ISL supported this feature much earlier than did 802.1q, so in years past, one of the stated differences between the two trunking protocols was that 802.1q did not support multiple spanning trees. To appreciate the benefits of multiple spanning trees, examine Figure 10-6, which shows a simple network, with two VLANs and three interconnected switches.

Figure 10-6   *ISL Per VLAN Spanning Tree (PVST)*

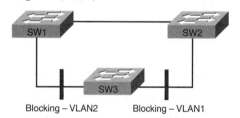

You can tune STP parameters in each VLAN so that when all links are up, different interfaces block for different VLANs. In the figure, only one of the six switch interfaces connecting the switches needs to block to prevent loops. STP can be configured so that VLAN 1 and VLAN 2 block different interfaces on SW3. So, SW3 actually uses the available bandwidth on each of its links to the other switches because, on SW3, traffic in VLAN 1 uses the link to SW1, and traffic in VLAN 2 uses the link to SW2. Of course, if a link fails, both STP instances can converge so that a path is still available.

Passing Traffic Between VLANs

At the beginning of this chapter, a VLAN was defined as a broadcast domain. To take that concept a bit further, the same devices that comprise a VLAN are also in the same TCP/IP subnet. So, devices in the same VLAN are in the same subnet, and devices in different VLANs must be in different IP subnets. Although the concept of a VLAN and a subnet are indeed different concepts, they have a one-to-one relationship.

This section covers some of the terminology regarding possibilities for passing packets between devices in different VLANs.

Layer 2 Switching

The term *Layer 2 switching (L2 switching)* refers to the typical switch-processing logic covered in Chapter 9. A switch receives a frame and looks at the destination MAC address. If the MAC table has an entry for that destination, it forwards the frame; if not, or if the frame is a broadcast, it forwards the frame out all ports, except the port in which the frame entered the switch.

When VLANs are used, an L2 switch uses the same logic, but per VLAN. So, there is a MAC address table for each VLAN. Because the MAC address tables are separate, unicasts sent inside one VLAN cannot be forwarded out ports in another VLAN. Likewise, broadcasts in one VLAN cannot be forwarded out ports in another VLAN.

In short, L2 switches cannot forward traffic between VLANs. The last few pages of this chapter cover a few alternatives for how you can forward traffic between VLANs.

Layer 3 Forwarding Using a Router

Switches do not forward frames between different VLANs. So, when you have multiple VLANs, what do you do when the hosts in each VLAN want to communicate with each other? Well, you use a router. Figure 10-7 outlines the general idea in a network with one switch and three VLANs.

Although the switch cannot forward frames between two VLANs, a router can. First, notice that three VLANs are shown, and each VLAN corresponds to a different subnet. The router needs an interface in each subnet to forward traffic between the subnets—that is true even without VLANs being used. So, in this case, the router has three interfaces, each cabled to the switch. The switch configures the corresponding interfaces to be in VLAN1, VLAN2, and VLAN3. Hosts in VLAN1, when they want to send packets to hosts in VLAN2 or VLAN3, send their packets to the router, which then forwards the packets out another interface into the other VLAN.

Figure 10-7   *Routing Between VLANs*

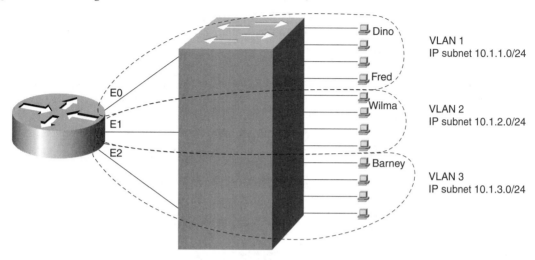

You might be thinking that using three interfaces on the router in Figure 10-7 seems wasteful—and it is. Alternately, you can use a router with a Fast Ethernet port that supports trunking and use a single physical connection from the router to the switch (trunking is not supported on 10 Mbps Ethernet interfaces). Figure 10-8 shows the same network as Figure 10-7, but with a trunk between the router and the switch.

Figure 10-8   *Example of a Router Forwarding Between VLANs over a Trunk*

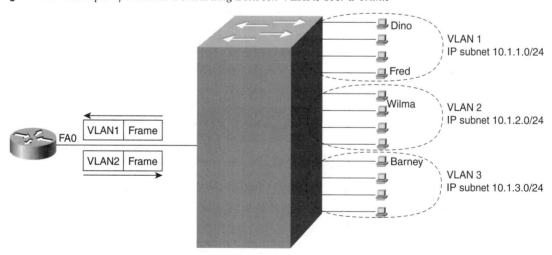

Chapter 8, "Advanced TCP/IP Topics" in the *CCNA ICND Exam Certification Guide* shows an example configuration for the router in this example. The process works the same as in Figure 10-7, except that the actual frames go to the router and leave the router over the same cable.

Layer 3 Forwarding Using a Layer 3 Switch

The term *Layer 3 switch (L3 switch)* refers to a switch that also has routing features. So, instead of requiring a router external to the switch, as in Figure 10-8, the router internal to the switch performs the same routing function.

The only difference between routing using a router, as in Figure 10-8, and using a Layer 3 switch lies in the internal processing. Outwardly, nothing is different. For instance, Figure 10-9 shows routing and L3 switching between two interfaces in two different VLANs. If you were to put a LAN analysis tool at the points shown in each of the two topologies and compare the packets being forwarded between the two, you would see no difference.

Figure 10-9 *Analysis Points Showing No Difference Between L3 Switching and Routing*

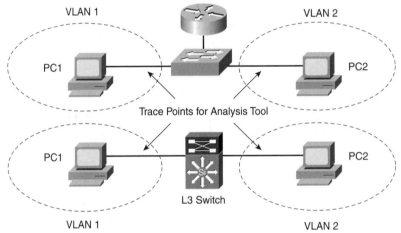

By tracing the two similar networks at the points shown, you can confirm that there are no differences to the effect of the external router versus the L3 switch. The L3 switch runs routing protocols and builds an IP routing table, and the switch makes the forwarding decision based on destination IP address. The L3 switch even discards the only Ethernet data link header and builds a new one, as described in Chapter 5, "Fundamentals of IP."

The differences between the two options relates to what happens inside the L3 switch. L3 switches used specialized hardware to make the forwarding process run very fast. The switch ASICs (Application Specific Integrated Circuits) on an L3 switch have been built so that the normal, very fast L2 forwarding path can also be caused to perform the forwarding for Layer 3. In other words, the actual receipt, changing of headers, and forwarding of the packets uses the same high-speed internal processing of the L2 switch. The L3 switch also includes the software used to run other processes, such as routing protocols, which are used to populate the tables used by the specialized forwarding hardware. You do not need to know the specifics of how any one single L3 switch works internally; just know that the difference between L3 switching and routing is based on what happens inside the L3 switch.

Layer 4 Switching

The term *Layer 4 switches* (*L4 switches*) refers to a type of switching in which the switch considers the information in the Layer 4 headers when forwarding the packet. In some cases, the forwarding decision is based upon information inside the Layer 4 headers. In other cases, L3 forwarding is used, but the switch does accounting based on the Layer 4 headers. Both are considered to be Layer 4 switching.

The key to understanding L4 switching is to remember the function of TCP and UDP port numbers, as covered in Chapter 6, "Fundamentals of TCP and UDP." Port numbers identify the application process of the sender and the receiver of a packet. An L4 switch can make the decision of where to forward the packet based on the information in the TCP or UDP header, typically the port numbers. Alternately, it can also simply keep track of the numbers of packets and bytes sent per TCP port number, while still performing Layer 3 forwarding.

Figure 10-10 shows an example with an L4 switch making its forwarding decisions based on the TCP port number. The figure shows a server farm, with two servers that have replicated web content, meaning that either server can be used to server any user. The third server processes all FTP traffic—so when a user of the web server clicks something to start an FTP download, the download comes from SVR-3.

Figure 10-10   *L4 Switching Based on TCP Port Numbers*

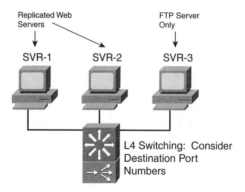

All requests for the web servers or for FTP services would be directed to the server farm via a single IP address that represents all three servers. Upon seeing the first packet in a new TCP connection going to the web destination port (port 80), the L4 switch would pick either SVR-1 or SVR-2. After this choice, all packets for that individual TCP connection would be switched to that same server. Similarly, when a new TCP connection was requested, with destination port 21 (FTP), the switch would know to just forward the request to SVR-3.

To perform L4 switching, the switch must keep track of every individual Layer 4 flow. If you had 1000 concurrent TCP connections into the server farm, you would now need 1000 entries in the L4 forwarding table. Comparing that to L3 switching, you would need only one route in the L3 routing table to support forwarding packets to the subnet of the server farm. So, L4 switching does require more switching capacity than does the equivalent with L3 switching.

Finally, L4 switching does not always imply a change in how packets are forwarded. A switch can perform accounting to track the volumes of traffic per TCP and UDP port number but still make the decisions based on L3 switching logic. With Cisco switches, you can enable a feature called *NetFlow switching*, which performs the accounting based on Layer 4 information while forwarding traffic like a Layer 3 switch.

Layer 5–7 Switching

The TCP/IP application layer closely correlates to OSI Layers 5 through 7. In the last several years, the terms *Layer 5–7 switching*, *Layer 7 switching*, and *application layer switching* have all become common terms, meaning basically the same thing. A switch could look past the Layer 4 header, into the application layer headers, to make switching decisions—and that is what an L5-L7 switch does. Layer 5-7 switching typically falls into a category of features and products that Cisco calls Content Delivery Networks (CDN).

Multilayer Switching

A switch does not have to just perform switching at one layer or another. For instance, for traffic between ports in the same VLAN, L2 switching is needed. For traffic between two different VLANs, L3 switching is needed. So, often a switch performs switching at multiple layers. These switches are called *multilayer switches*. Most of the time today, when you hear of a Layer 3 switch, it is really a multilayer switch because it almost always is also a Layer 2 switch.

Table 10-2 summarizes the key points about each type of switching.

Table 10-2 *Comparison of Multilayer Switching Options*

Type	Description
Layer 2 switching*	The process of forwarding frames based on their MAC addresses.
External router, connected to L2 switch	Router forwards like always, based on destination IP address.
Layer 3 switch	Switch's forwarding logic forwards based on destination IP address for traffic destined for another VLAN.
Layer 4 switch	Can forward based on Layer 4 information, typically port numbers, but can also just do accounting based on L4 information.
Layer 5–7 switch	Forwards based on application layer information; typically considered a CDN feature.
Multilayer switch	A switch that concurrently performs switching based on multiple layers. For instance, most L3 switches also perform L2 switching inside a VLAN, and L3 switching for traffic between VLANs.

*L2 switching is the only option in the table that does not allow forwarding from one VLAN to another.

Foundation Summary

The "Foundation Summary" section of each chapter lists the most important facts from the chapter. Although this section does not list every fact from the chapter that will be on your CCNA exam, a well-prepared CCNA candidate should know, at a minimum, all the details in each "Foundation Summary" section before going to take the exam.

Figure 10-11 shows the general idea of a VLAN, showing two different VLANs/broadcast domains.

Figure 10-11 *Example Network with Two VLANs Using One Switch*

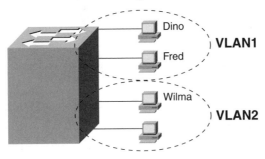

With VLAN trunking, the switches tag each frame sent between switches so that the receiving switch knows what VLAN the frame belongs to. Figure 10-12 outlines the basic idea.

Figure 10-12 *VLAN Trunking Between Two Switches*

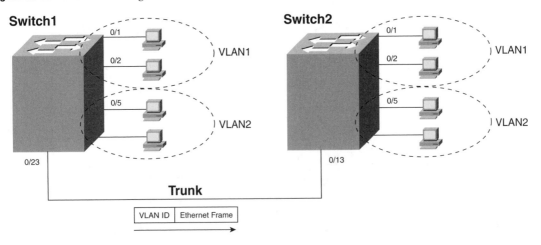

Figure 10-13 shows the benefit of using multiple VLANs, each with a separate spanning tree.

Figure 10-13 *ISL Per VLAN Spanning Tree (PVST)*

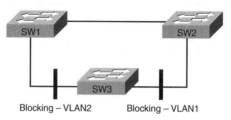

Blocking – VLAN2   Blocking – VLAN1

Table 10-3 summarizes the key points about each type of switching.

Table 10-3 *Comparison of Multilayer Switching Options*

Type	Description
Layer 2 switching*	The process of forwarding frames based on their MAC addresses.
External router, connected to L2 switch	Router forwards like always, based on destination IP address.
Layer 3 switch	Switch's forwarding logic forwards based on destination IP address for traffic destined for another VLAN.
Layer 4 switch	Can forward based on Layer 4 information, typically port numbers, but can also just do accounting based on L4 information.
Layer 5–7 switch	Forwards based on application layer information; typically considered a CDN feature.
Multilayer switch	A switch that concurrently performs switching based on multiple layers. For instance, most L3 switches also perform L2 switching inside a VLAN, and L3 switching for traffic between VLANs.

*L2 switching is the only option in the table that does not allow forwarding from one VLAN to another.

Q&A

As mentioned in the introduction, you have two choices for review questions. The questions that follow give you a bigger challenge than the exam itself by using an open-ended question format. By reviewing now with this more difficult question format, you can exercise your memory better and prove your conceptual and factual knowledge of this chapter. The answers to these questions are found in Appendix A.

For more practice with exam-like question formats, including questions using a router simulator and multiple-choice questions, use the exam engine on the CD.

1. Define the term collision domain.

2. Define the term broadcast domain.

3. Define the term VLAN.

4. If two Cisco LAN switches are connected using Fast Ethernet, what VLAN trunking protocols could be used? If only one VLAN spanned both switches, is a VLAN trunking protocol needed?

5. Must all members of the same VLAN be in the same collision domain, the same broadcast domain, or both?

6. What is the acronym and complete name of Cisco's proprietary trunking protocol over Ethernet?

7. Consider the phrase "A VLAN is a broadcast domain is an IP subnet." Do you agree or disagree? State your reasons.

8. What fields are added or changed in an Ethernet header when using 802.1q? Where is the VLAN ID in those fields?

9. Compare and contrast the use of a Layer 3 switch versus an external router connected to a Layer 2 switch using a trunk for forwarding between VLANs.

10. Compare and contrast a Layer 3 switch with a multilayer switch. Describe in what cases the terms could be used synonymously.

This chapter covers the following subjects:

- Network Topologies

- Cabling and Connectors

- Ethernet Standards

- Wireless Communications

CHAPTER 11

LAN Cabling, Standards, and Topologies

This chapter completes the Ethernet puzzle for this book, in relation to the requirements of the INTRO exam. Ethernet was covered in several other chapters of this book—specifically, Chapter 3, "Data Link Layer Fundamentals: Ethernet LANs," Chapter 9, "Cisco LAN Switching Basics," and Chapter 10, "Virtual LANs and Trunking." The topics in those chapters laid the foundation of a relatively broad knowledge of Ethernet. However, to keep those chapters flowing and not get bogged down in some long tangents (in some cases, relatively unimportant tangents), those earlier chapters did not cover all the details of Ethernet that might be on the INTRO exam.

For those of you studying for the CCNA exam—in other words, the single-exam method of getting your CCNA certification—you are probably following the reading plan outlined in the introduction. For you, after this chapter, you should move on to the first three chapters of *CCNA ICND Exam Certification Guide*.

> **AUTHOR'S NOTE** While they may be on the CCNA exam, the topics in this chapter are less likely to be on the CCNA exam than most other topics in this book. For those of you that are planning to take the CCNA exam, instead of taking both the INTRO and ICND exams, you might consider skipping this chapter. Refer to the introduction to this book for more perspectives on the CCNA exam topics.

"Do I Know This Already?" Quiz

The purpose of the "Do I Know This Already?" quiz is to help you decide whether you really need to read the entire chapter. If you already intend to read the entire chapter, you do not necessarily need to answer these questions now.

The eight-question quiz, derived from the major sections in "Foundation Topics" portion of the chapter, helps you determine how to spend your limited study time.

Table 11-1 outlines the major topics discussed in this chapter and the "Do I Know This Already?" quiz questions that correspond to those topics.

Table 11-1 *"Do I Know This Already?" Foundation Topics Section-to-Question Mapping*

Foundations Topics Section	Questions Covered in This Section
Network Topologies	1–2
Cabling and Connectors	3–5
Ethernet Standards	6–7
Wireless Communications	8

CAUTION The goal of self-assessment is to gauge your mastery of the topics in this chapter. If you do not know the answer to a question or are only partially sure of the answer, you should mark this question wrong for purposes of the self-assessment. Giving yourself credit for an answer that you correctly guess skews your self-assessment results and might provide you with a false sense of security.

1. Which of the following network topologies is characterized by attachments from many devices to a single linear cable?

   a. Bus

   b. Star

   c. Extended star

   d. Full mesh

   e. Partial mesh

2. Which of the following types of networks is considered to be a logical bus topology?

   a. 10BASE5

   b. PCs connected to a hub using 10BASE-T

   c. PCs connected to a switch using 10BASE-T

   d. Five routers, each with a PVC connecting it to all the others, over Frame Relay

3. Which pins typically are used on an RJ-45 connector by an Ethernet card to support Fast Ethernet over UTP cabling?

   a. 1, 2, 3, 4

   b. 1, 2, 4, 5

   c. 1, 2, 3, 6

  d. 1, 2, 7, 8

  e. 5, 6, 7, 8

4. Which part of an optical cable reflects the light back into the cable as a result of a different refractive index?

  a. Cladding

  b. Core

  c. Jacket

  d. Plastic shield

  e. Kevlar shield

5. Which of the following UTP cable types support Gigabit Ethernet?

  a. CAT3

  b. CAT4

  c. CAT5

  d. CAT5E

  e. CAT6

6. Which of the following Ethernet standards call for the use of 802.3 MAC and 802.2 LLC standards?

  a. 802.3u

  b. 802.3z

  c. 802.3ab

  d. 802.3ae

  e. All of the above

7. Which of the following Ethernet standards refer to Gigabit Ethernet?

  a. 802.3u

  b. 802.3z

  c. 802.3ab

  d. 802.3ae

  e. All of the above

8. Which of the following IEEE standards define framing used when transmitting wireless LAN traffic?

   a. IEEE 802.2

   b. IEEE 802.3

   c. IEEE 802.1d

   d. IEEE 802.11

   e. None of the above

The answers to the "Do I Know This Already?" quiz are found in Appendix A, "Answers to the 'Do I Know This Already?' Quizzes and Q&A Sections." The suggested choices for your next step are as follows:

■ **6 or less overall score**—Read the entire chapter. This includes the "Foundation Topics" and "Foundation Summary" sections and the Q&A section.

■ **7 or 8 overall score**—If you want more review on these topics, skip to the "Foundation Summary" section and then go to the Q&A section. Otherwise, move to the next chapter.

Foundation Topics

This chapter begins with a description of different topologies that you might find in different types of networks, including Ethernets, but also including other types of networks. Next, Ethernet standards and cabling options are detailed. Finally, the chapter closes with a brief description of wireless technology and wireless LANs.

Network Topologies

You already have been introduced to several different network topologies as you have read through this book. For instance, 10BASE2 networks use a physical bus topology, whereas 10BASE-T networks use a physical star topology. This section introduces you to several other types of network topologies.

Figure 11-1 shows the different types of Ethernet topologies covered earlier in the book, with some specific terms used to describe the topology for each design.

Figure 11-1   *Different Types of Network Topologies for Ethernet So Far in This Book*

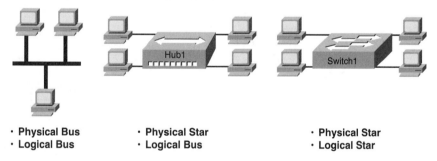

- **Physical Bus**   - **Physical Star**   - **Physical Star**
- **Logical Bus**   - **Logical Bus**   - **Logical Star**

The figure shows a 10BASE5 network, a 10BASE-T network using a shared hub, and a switch with 10/100 links. Physically, the topologies with the hub and the switch look a little like how a child might draw a star, or the sun, with a center (the hub or switch) and with beams of light pointing outward (like the Ethernet cables to the PCs in the figure). Star topologies also are called *hub-and-spoke topologies*.

Physical bus topologies transmit the electrical signal from one end of a cable to the other, with the signal being picked up at each connection point.

The term *logical topology* refers to how the network behaves. For instance, from Chapter 3, you know that a 10BASE-T hub repeats an incoming signal out every other port on the hub.

So, logically, it also causes the electrical signals to be sent to every connection on the network—more like a bus in logic. So, people might describe a network using a hub as a physical star, but a logical bus. The logical topology for the switch network is a star because, unlike a hub, a switch does not repeat the signal out every port, but just to the appropriate device.

Figure 11-2 shows three other types of network topologies, which could be used for interconnecting Ethernet hubs and switches.

Figure 11-2   *Extended Star, Full Mesh, and Partial Mesh*

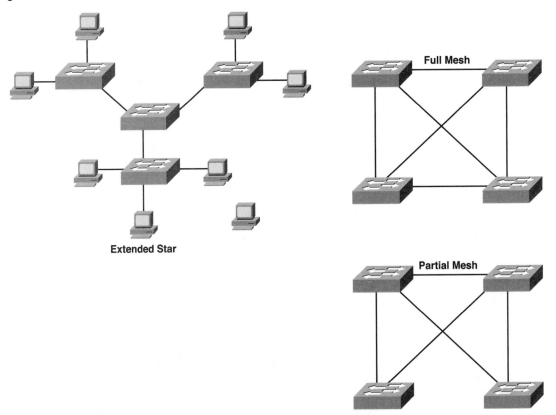

The extended star is characterized by parts of the topology that look like a star, which, in turn, are connected in star fashion to some other node. For instance, the three switches with PC attached, taken alone, form a star topology. By connecting to another switch in the middle, another star is formed, so this topology would be characterized as an extended star. Extended star topologies are rare for Ethernets.

If you pursue your CCDA certification, you will come across many designs in which you see the full mesh and partial mesh topologies shown in the figure. A full mesh is typical of switches that collectively form the core and distribution layers of a campus LAN design that includes Layer 3 switching. The partial mesh design often is found between distribution layer and access layer switches. If you want to learn more about LAN design concepts, pick up the *CCDA Exam Certification Guide* and read more. For our purposes, you should just know that a full mesh means that all the respective nodes in the network have a direct connection. A partial mesh means that some of the nodes in a network have a direct connection, but others do not.

Frame Relay networks often are described as being full mesh or partial mesh. For instance, consider Figure 11-3, with a Frame Relay network.

Figure 11-3   *Physical Star, with Full and Partial Mesh*

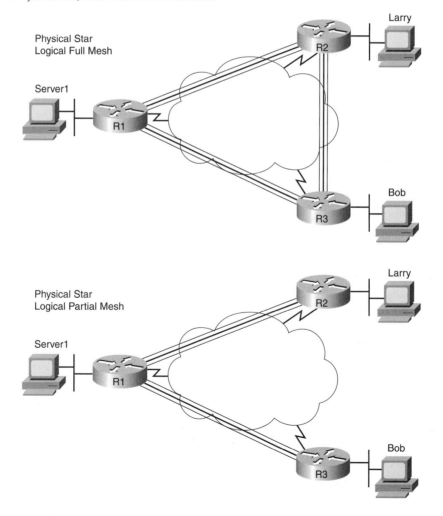

Frame Relay networks use a physical star topology because each Frame Relay DTE device connects to a central Frame Relay network. However, depending on which sites have VCs connecting them, the logical design is either full mesh or partial mesh. When you study for the ICND exam, you will see many Frame Relay examples with full- and partial-mesh designs. Practically, no one really refers to Frame Relay as using a physical star design, but many people do refer to a Frame Relay design as either full mesh or partial mesh.

Figure 11-4 shows the final topology covered here—the ring topology.

Figure 11-4   *Single-Ring and Dual-Ring Topologies*

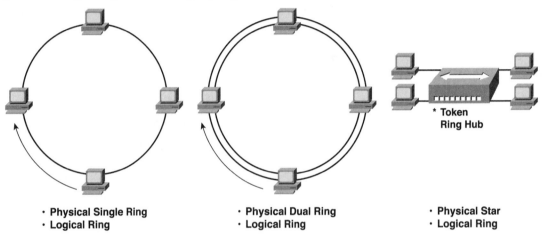

- **Physical Single Ring**
- **Logical Ring**

- **Physical Dual Ring**
- **Logical Ring**

- **Physical Star**
- **Logical Ring**

The left-most figure depicts a concept in which each device is cabled to the next, with the signal transmitted in a single direction. By doing so, the signal starts with one device, and eventually, the signal makes it all the way back to the original sender of the data. With one physical path, the topology is called a single ring, and with two physical paths, the topology is called a dual ring.

Dual rings are useful for failover. With dual rings, one ring is used to transmit data under normal operations, with the second ring for failover. If the physical path between two adjacent devices fails, the two devices on either side of the problem simply can loop the signal on one ring onto the other—and another physical loop has been created. This dual-ring topology was used with the now outdated Token Ring and Fiber Distributed Data Interface (FDDI) LANs. The same concept is used in optical networking today.

Finally, on the right side of Figure 11-4, you see an example of how Token Ring was cabled—back when anyone cared. Each device had a cable connecting it to a hub, with a transmit wire and a receive wire inside the cable. The electrical signal was sent down each wire and was repeated back up the wire to the hub; then the hub repeated the process with the next device, and so on. Electrically, a single ring was created, so Token Ring uses a logical ring topology, but physically, it uses a star topology.

Table 11-2 summarizes the types of physical topology covered in this chapter.

Table 11-2 *Physical Topology Types*

Term	Definition
Bus	This is a linear topology, with all devices connected to the cable.
Star	Each device is connected to a central point. Sometimes called hub-and-spoke.
Extended star	A star topology is in the center, but instead of each point being a single device, it can be the center of another star topology.
Full mesh	Each device has a direct connection to each other device.
Partial mesh	Each device does not have a direct connection to each other device.
Single ring	Each device is connected directly to two others so that the signal is repeated in one direction, creating a ring or loop.
Dual ring	Two rings go through the same set of devices, allowing loops to be made upon failure, which continues the operation of a ring.

Cabling and Connectors

Practically every other Cisco certification exam ignores the topic of cabling; those exams just assume that you can read the manuals and figure out what cables are needed. Interestingly, a well-designed cabling plan, with the right cables, can be a big component of making a LAN more manageable and available. So, cabling is indeed important in real networks.

The cables themselves contain different components inside the cable—you just have to cut one open to look inside to see internal components. Also, each type of cable might allow for a variety of connectors at the end of the cable. So, in this section, you will read about the types of cables, what's inside them, and what connectors can be used to terminate them.

General Features of Metallic Cabling

The term *cable* refers to a combination of plastics, metal wires, optical fibers, possibly rubber, and other materials molded into a cord of varying lengths. Well, that's at least a formal definition. People see cables every day. The power cords that go from the electrical wall socket to each of your electrically powered appliances and lamps at home are all cables. There are cables protruding from the back of your PC. And for networking, the phone cord stretching from the wall outlet to your phone is actually a networking cable.

Most networking cables use either copper wires inside the cable to transfer an electrical signal, or glass fiber inside the cable to transfer optical light signals. So, many people refer to cabling as *wiring* just because the vast majority of networking cables are actually copper wire cables. The wire cables also sometimes are called *copper cabling*, just because the most popular metal to use in the cable is copper.

When sending an electrical signal over a cable, the signal introduces a magnetic field and also introduces radio frequency interference. Translation: When the cable is in use, it emits radiation that can interfere with other signals in other wires or signals that pass through the air. When one wire affects another in this manner, it is commonly referred to as *crosstalk*. So, the various national governments tend to regulate how much of these unwanted physics effects are allowed. These metallic wire cables are designed to reduce the effects of the radiation and interference.

The wires can be affected by outside interference as well. Nearby cables can interfere with the transmission on the cable, actually changing the electrical signal and causing bit errors. So, electrical cables create their own emissions and are susceptible to problems from the emissions from other sources, particularly nearby cables.

The most popular way today to reduce the effects of emissions is to transmit over a pair of wires and twist those two wires together. By using an opposite current on each wire, each wire produces an identical magnetic field, but in an opposite direction. It's sort of like having two equal-power magnets of the same polarity, both trying to pull things toward them. If you put a paper clip between them at equal distances, with equal strength for the magnets, the paper clip should not move. If only one magnet were there, it would attract the paper clip. Essentially, twisting the wires has a similar effect—the two magnetic fields cancel each other out.

Twisted-pair wiring is used in today's most popular electrical (wire) networking cables.

The other popular way to reduce the emissions of copper cabling is to shield the wires. That means that the wires have some material placed around them, using a material that blocks most of the electromagnetic radiation. The concept is similar to when you need to get an x-ray, and the person taking the x-ray leaves the room or stands behind a screen made of lead—the x-rays (which are a form of electromagnetic radiation) do not pass through the lead screen. Similarly, by shielding the cables, the cables emit less radiation.

Unfortunately, shielding the wires makes the cable more expensive and less flexible. The need to add more materials to a cable to shield the cable increases materials and manufacturing costs for the cables. You need a lot of cables to build a typical enterprise network, so the extra cost does add up. If the cable does not bend easily, you might not be able to run it in tight spaces behind walls, in ceilings, into where the wall plate sits behind the wall, and so on. So, inflexible cabling could require you to open walls in the building to make a new space for the cables to run—costing time and money.

Unshielded Twisted-Pair and Shielded Twisted-Pair Cabling and Connectors

The Telecommunications Information Associatation (TIA) defines standards for LAN cabling. For copper-wire LAN cabling, two main branches have been defined:

■ Unshielded twisted pair (UTP)

■ Shielded twisted pair (STP)

Figure 11-5 shows a conceptual diagram of each type of cable. The figure shows a side view of each cable and a straight-on view of a UTP cable. All the parts of the figure show the cable cut open so that you can see the internal components of the cables.

Figure 11-5 *UTP and STP Cable Components*

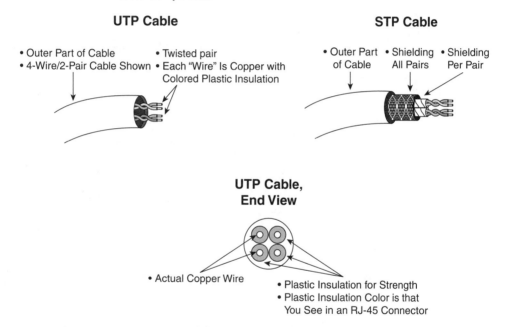

The figure shows most of the pertinent details of both types of cables. Working from the outside in, the UTP cable has an outer jacket—its main purpose is to hold all the interior cabling together. Inside, you have some number of twisted pairs of cables. From the lowest part of the figure, looking straight at the end of the cable, you can see that each wire does not simply sit inside the outer jacket—instead, each wire has some colored plastic insulation attached to it. Copper, when spun to such a small diameter, would break very easily without some support. So, the thin plastic insulation provides some strength for each individual wire.

Each wire's thin plastic insulation also is colored differently, either a solid color or a stripe against a white background. The colors help when making individual cables by cutting a length of cable off a large cable spool and adding connectors, such as an RJ-45 connector, on the end of a cable. Each wire can be identified by the color of the plastic insulation at each end of the cable. Also, each twisted pair uses the same color—one wire with the solid color and one striped.

The STP cable diagram on the right of Figure 11-5 just shows the additional components of an STP cable as compared with an UTP cable. Each pair is covered with insulating material, with another insulator covering all pairs combined. The extra materials cause the relative lack of flexibility in the cable and, of course, add the benefit of less interference.

UTP Standards

The TIA defines several standards for UTP cabling. The UTP cable types are defined in different categories—but no one would really use the term *UTP category* in normal speech—instead, you would say something like "Are you using CAT5 cables?" Table 11-3 lists the characteristics of the different categories of UTP cable as defined by the TIA.

Table 11-3 *UTP Cable Categories/Characterisics*

UTP Category	Max Speed Rating	Description
1	—	Used for telephones but not for data.
2	4 Mbps	Originally intended to support Token Ring over UTP.
3	10 Mbps	Can be used for telephones as well. Popular option for Ethernet in years past, if CAT3 cabling for phones was already in place.
4	16 Mbps	Intended for the fast Token Ring speed option.
5	1 Gbps	Very popular for cabling to the desktop.
5e	1 Gbps	Lower emissions, more expensive than CAT5, but better for Gigabit Ethernet.
6	1 Gbps+	Intended as a replacement for CAT5e, with capabilities to support multigigabit speeds when standards are created.

UTP Connectors

UTP cables use Registered Jack 45 (RJ-45) connectors. Some cables need only two twisted pairs, typically using pairs 2 and 3, as specified by the TIA. Figure 11-6 shows a picture of an RJ-45 connector, with some details of the eight pins on the connector. Figure 11-7 shows the pinouts on a typical four-pair UTP cable using an RJ-45 connector, according to the TIA specifications.

Figure 11-6   *RJ-45 Connector*

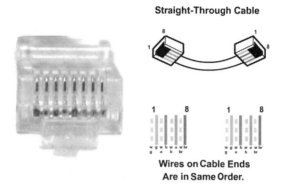

Straight-Through Cable

Wires on Cable Ends
Are in Same Order.

Figure 11-7   *Four-Pair UTP Cable: Pinouts Using RJ-45*

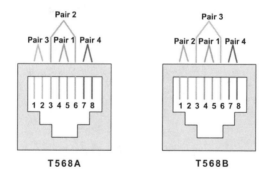

T568A   T568B

The wiring diagram shows four-pair cabling that uses all eight pins on an RJ-45 connector. Some Ethernet standards require only two pairs and typically use the pair on pins 1 and 2 and the pair on pins 3 and 6.

Coaxial Cabling

Coaxial cabling was used for 10BASE2 and 10BASE5 Ethernet in years past. 10BASE5 was referred to as *thicknet*, and 10BASE2 was referred to as *thinnet* because 10BASE5 used thicker coaxial cable.

Even 10 years ago, newly installed Ethernet networks most often were not 10BASE2 or 10BASE5 networks, but rather were 10BASE-T. I personally have not seen a 10BASE2 or 10BASE5 Ethernet NIC available for sale from a vendor for at least 5 years. So, the relative importance of remembering the details of coaxial cabling for your job is pretty small.

Coaxial cables are shielded. They have a single copper wire in the center, with plastic insulation and copper shielding surrounding the copper wire.

For 10BASE5, the network consisted of a length of coaxial cable of up to 500 m in length. In fact, the "5" in 10BASE5 represents the maximum length of a single cable segment. To connect to the segment, a *vampire tap* was used. The *vampire tap* is a piece of metal in the shape of a cylinder when closed. By closing the tap around the cable, the tap actually pushed through the shielding to let the metal in the vampire tap touch the copper wire inside the cable. I'm sure it is now obvious where the name vampire tap came from! From the vampire tap, a short cable, called an *Attachment Unit Interface (AUI) cable*, connected the tap to the Ethernet card on the PC.

Running individual shielded, heavy, relatively inflexible coaxial cable for 500 m for a long 10BASE5 network was, to say the least, a lot of work. For 10BASE2, which was developed after 10BASE5, instead of a single length of cable, the bus was created by a series of cables. 10BASE2 used thinner, more flexible coax cabling as well. The cables used a British Naval Connector (BNC) connector, which was a lot easier to work with than the vampire taps. To connect a computer, a T-connector was used, with one end plugged into the Ethernet card, another into a cable from the upstream cable, and another cable connecting to the next device downstream. Figure 11-8 shows a picture of the BNC connector, and Figure 11-9 shows the typical cabling options for 10BASE2 and 10BASE5.

Figure 11-8   *BNC Connector on a Coaxial Cable*

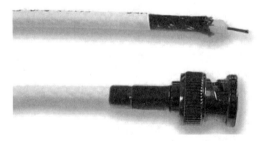

The one component shown in Figure 11-9 that was not already discussed is the term *transceiver*. This term was created by melding the terms transmitter and receiver. Instead of having the Ethernet card itself include the electronics that sent and received the signal on the Ethernet cable, the original Ethernet designs used an external device to actually encode the bits. The concept is not terribly different from having an external CSU/DSU on a WAN circuit, as covered in Chapter 4, "Fundamentals of WANs."

Figure 11-9 *10BASE5 and 10BASE2 Connectors*

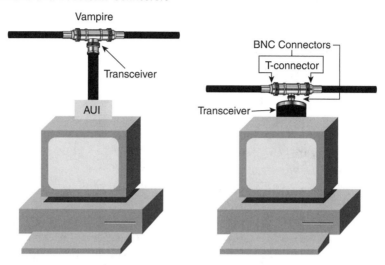

For the purposes of networking, coaxial cable has some advantages. It allows for longer network segments—500 m, with longer distances allowed using repeaters. However, the cons of coaxial cabling include the fact that it is more expensive, heavier, larger (takes up more room in conduits), and relatively inflexible. Also, when used for Ethernet, a single break in the cable takes down the entire Ethernet segment! All of these factors add up to some of the reasons that coaxial cabling is not a popular option for network cabling today.

Fiber-Optic Cabling and Connectors for Ethernet

Fiber cabling, also called *optical cabling* or *fiber optics*, provides another option for cabling Ethernet. The main differences, in terms of function, between optical cabling for Ethernet and electrical cabling are as follows:

- Longer distances supported by optical cabling
- Greater monetary cost
- Less magnetic interference, making it slightly more secure
- Only type of cabling supported by 10 Gig Ethernet

For instance, network engineers might choose to use optical interfaces and cabling for Ethernet when building a campus LAN when the buildings happen to be a few miles apart because optical cables allow longer cables to be used. If the company has the right of way, it can run optical cable between the sites and still build a campus LAN.

Also, if you want to use Ethernet between two buildings that are a few miles apart but you do not have the right of way, you might be able to lease what is called *dark fiber* from a service provider. Dark fiber is just optical cabling run by the service provider, which it can do because it owns the right to run the cable under the streets. The service provider typically runs a lot of different optical fibers and then just leases to you the number of optical fibers you need.

In other cases, you might choose to use optical cabling to help protect highly sensitive traffic. Because of the emissions coming from electrical cabling, with the right tools, you actually can tell what signals are being sent across a cable. So, when an Ethernet cable might become accessible to someone who wants to listen in, the use of optical cabling can thrwart that person's efforts, because unlike electrical cabling, optical cabling does not emit electromagnetic radiation.

The key component of optical cabling is the fiberglass center of the cable. The devices on the end of the cable, such as Ethernet switches, generate an optical light signal. The signal travels down the optical fiber in the center of the cable. No electricity is used across the cable—just light is used.

Optical cabling can be divided into two general categories:

■ Multimode (MM)

■ Single-mode (SM)

SM fiber uses a very small-diameter optical fiber, with MM fiber using a larger size. SM cables require more precision in the manufacturing process and more precision by the hardware that generates the light that crosses the cable, so SM cables and cards tend to be more expensive. However, SM cables typically allow for much longer distances and data rate than does MM fiber. MM cable still allows longer distances than copper cabling.

Often Ethernet cards use light-emitting diodes (LEDs) to generate light for MM cable, and other more expensive interfaces use a laser to generate the light for SM cables. The LEDs actually generate more than one wavelength of light, which, in part, is where the name multimode comes from. The actual terms *multimode* and *single-mode* refer to the fact that LEDs generate multiple wavelengths of light, whereas lasers generate a single specific wavelength.

Figure 11-10 shows a side view of an optical cable, including a view of the optical fiber itself.

Figure 11-10   *Components of a Fiber-Optic Cable*

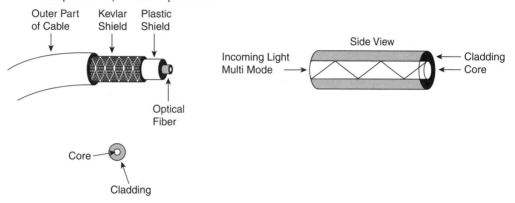

Yes, the center of the cable is made from glass, so it is fragile—but it is sturdy enough to work with the cable without worrying every second that you will break it. First, it is fiberglass, which does not break as easily as the glass in the windows of your house. The plastic adds some strength to the fiberglass. Most important for strength, a Kevlar coating is applied— Kevlar is the stuff that most bullet-proof vests are made from today.

The right side of the figure shows an example of how the light signal actually bounces off the interior walls of the glass fiber. The fiber has an inner part, called the *core*, and an outer part, called the *cladding*. The cladding has a different *refractive index* than the core, meaning that when the light hits the outer wall of the core, which is also the inner wall of the cladding, the light is reflected back into the core. This might be a bit oversimplified, but it's like having a mirror on the inside wall of the cladding so that the light keeps getting reflected back into the core—the light eventaully makes it to the other end of the cable.

Optical Connectors for Ethernet

To transmit data over a fiber cable, you need a single *strand* of fiber. The term *strand* refers to the center of the cable, the glass part, as shown in Figure 11-10. To transmit data in both directions, you need a pair of strands—one for each direction of data transmission. However, because there are no emissions to speak of, there is no need to twist the strands together. So, to connect two devices using fiber cabling, you just need two strands, or fibers, and the correct connector on each end.

A variety of connectors can be used for terminating optical cable when used for Ethernet. One type, called an ST connector, terminates each fiber strand with a barrel connector, much like a BNC connector. You place the connector onto a cylindrical male connector on the Ethernet interface (typically a switch) and twist to make the connector secure. Figure 11-11 shows another type of connector, called an SC connector.

Figure 11-11 *Fiber-Optic SC Connector*

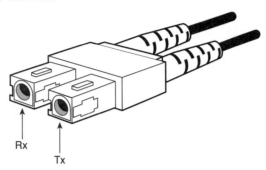

Rx

Tx

The figure shows two cables, each of which has a single fiber strand inside, attaching into a single connctor. Upon close examination, you can see that each strand terminates into a piece of plastic, with a larger, rectangular piece of plastic holding the two together. The larger piece of plastic holds the two internal connectors the the same distance from each other as the two receptacles on a card on a switch so that you can plug the whole connector into an Ethernet port at the same time. So, you have either both fibers connected or neither.

A newer type of connector, called an MT-RJ connector, has become more popular in recent years. The MT-RJ connector uses the same plastic mold as an RJ-45 connector, which makes it easy to install. Two fibers connect into the single connector, similar in concept to an SC connector. Figure 11-12 shows an MT-RJ connector.

Figure 11-12 *MT-RJ Connector*

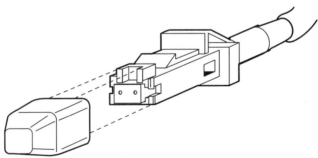

Optical cabling costs more than copper cabling, and the Ethernet cards that can use optical cabling also cost more. However, there are several advantages to using optical cabling for Ethernet. You can have Ethernet segments that stretch over 10 km in length and have Ethernet speeds up to 10 Gbps, with little conduit space consumed due to the small diameter of the cable. Also, fiber cabling is more secure than copper wiring, because of the absence of emissions.

Summary: Ethernet Cabling

Ethernet networks can be built with a variety of cabling types, as covered in this chapter. Table 11-4 summarizes the types of cable and main features, with some comments about disadvantages and advantages of each.

Table 11-4 *Summary of Ethernet Cabling Types*

	Maximum Length, Single Segment	Maximum Speed for Ethernet	Relative Cost	Advantages	Disadvantages
UTP	100 m	1 Gbps	Low	Easy to install, commonly available, popular	Susceptible to interference, limited distance
STP	100 m	100 Mbps	Medium	Low emissions, less susceptible to interference	Difficult to work with, limited distance
Coaxial	500 m (thicknet) 185 m (thinnet)	100 Mbps	Medium	Least susceptible to interference of all copper media	Difficult to work with (thicknet), single cable problem fails whole network
Fiber	10 km+ (SM) 2 km+ (MM)	100 Gbps (SM) 10 Gbps (MM)	High	More secure, long distances, not susceptible to EMI, highest speeds	Difficult to terminate when attaching connectors

Ethernet Standards

Back in Chapter 3, this book introduced you to the most important Ethernet standards. Those included the IEEE 802.3 standard, including the Media Access Control (MAC) sublayer, which defines the 6-byte Ethernet addresses. Ethernet also uses IEEE 802.2, which defines a sublayer called Logical Link Control (LLC). 802.2 includes the DSAP field, which identifies the type of packet held in an Ethernet frame. Also in that chapter, you learned the main IEEE standards for Fast Ethernet (802.3u) and Gigabit Ethernet (802.3z and 802.3ab).

This short section describes several other Ethernet standards and summarizes all the salient points of the various Ethernet standards.

Ethernet Framing

All types of Ethernet use either the IEEE-defined framing or the older Ethernet Version 2 framing that predated the standardization of Ethernet by the IEEE. With 802.3 Ethernet, there are two main variations of framing—one without the use of a SNAP header and one with the use of a SNAP header. Figure 11-13 shows the three variations of headers.

Figure 11-13   *Ethernet Framing*

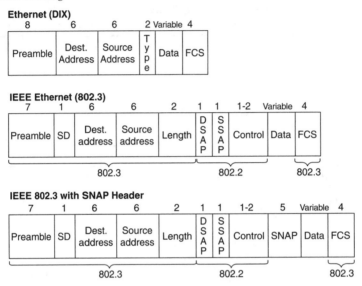

One of Ethernet's greatest strengths is that each newly defined Ethernet standard has used the same MAC and LLC headers and trailers, including the same address formats. So, when a new type of Ethernet is developed, engineers have very little new information to learn before supporting the new type.

Ethernet Cabling Standards

Each IEEE Ethernet standard defines the details for supporting a particular speed over a particular type of cabling. Also, each of these definitions specifies the maximum cable length and the required features of the cabling. Tables 11-5, 11-6, and 11-7 list the pertinent details of the standards, and the cabling.

Table 11-5   *Ethernet 802.3 Cabling Standards*

Standard	Cabling	Maximum Length
10BASE5	Thick coaxial	500 m
10BASE2	Thin coaxial	185 m
10BASE-T	UTP CAT3, 4, 5, 5e, 6	100 m

Table 11-6 *Fast Ethernet 802.3u Cabling Standards*

Standard	Cabling	Maximum Length
100BASE-FX	Two strands, multimode	400 m
100BASE-T	UTP CAT3, 4, 5, 5e, 6, two-pair	100 m
100BASE-T4	UTP CAT3, 4, 5, 5e, 6, 4-pair	100 m
100BASE-TX	UTP CAT3, 4, 5, 5e, 6, or STP, two-pair	100 m

Table 11-7 *Gigabit 802.3z (Optical) and 802.3ab (Electrical) Cabling Standards*

Standard	Cabling	Maximum Length
1000BASE-LX	Long-wavelength laser, MM or SM fiber	10 km (SM) 3 km (MM)
1000BASE-SX	Short-wavelength laser, MM fiber	220 m with 62.5-micron fiber; 550 m with 50-micron fiber
1000BASE-ZX	Extended wavelength, SM fiber	100 km
1000BASE-CS	STP, two-pair	25 m
1000BASE-T	UTP CAT5, 5e, 6, four-pair	100 m

10-Gigabit Ethernet

Tens years ago, compared to when I was writing this chapter in April 2003, Ethernet technology was just getting to the point that 10BASE-T networks were becoming common. Those networks shared 10 Mbps between all devices. On the horizon at that time was the promise of Ethernet switching, with which you could actually have 10 Mbps on each port of the switch.

Ethernet has gone from being one of many competing LAN technologies, with several competitors, to the king of the LAN in 10 years. With "10 Gig E," as it is commonly called, Ethernet has increased its speed a thousandfold in 10 years and has won the war in terms of LAN technologies. Just as the last 10 years have seen the emergence of TCP/IP as the most prolific Layer 3 protocol, Ethernet has become the most prolific Layer 1 and Layer 2 LAN standard.

10 Gig Ethernet, defined in IEEE 802.3ae, runs at 10 Gbps—it would be poorly named if not! It uses the same 802.3 MAC and 802.2 LLC as the other types of Ethernet. But it does have some differences with the other types:

- It allows only a point-to-point topology because it is intended for connectivity between switching devices.

- It allows only full-duplex communication.

- It specifies only optical fiber—no copper cabling. (Support for copper wiring might be added later.)

It will be a while before 10 Gig E becomes a cost-effective alternative for the wiring closet, but it is becoming a part of high-speed core enterprise networks already. Also, 10 Gig E has some very interesting applications for service providers as a trunking mechanism between switching locations. And with support for 10 Gig E using SM fiber for up to 40 km, 10 Gig E might help Ethernet continue its movement from a LAN technology into the WAN arena.

Wireless Communications

Wireless LANs enable users to communicate without any cabling. However, devices on these wireless LANs need to communicate with the devices on the "wired LANs," so this seemed like an appropriate place to cover the basics of wireless LANs.

Wireless communication happens all around us—literally. Cordless phones are relatively common, with commmunications between the phone and the base unit happening using radio waves. Similarly, mobile phones use radio waves to communicate to a transmitter and receiver on a cell tower nearby. Your TV remote control even performs some basic wireless communication using infrared waves.

Wireless communication uses some form of electromagnetic energy that passes through space. The energy propagates through the air at varying wavelengths. Depending on the wavelength of the energy, the energy might be visible or not. Given the large number of applications for wireless in the world, different wavelengths of energy are given different names, such as infrared for one range, radio frequency for another, and so on.

Electromagnetic energy actually can pass through matter, but often the matter reflects the energy to some degree and absorbs part of the energy as well. Some wavelengths require a line-of-sight for communication to happen because the wavelengths do not pass through matter well. For instance, a TV remote control using infrared typically requires a line-of-sight. Others, such as the wavelengths used for your cell phone, do not require line-of-sight but are affected to some degree by the number, thickness, and materials in the obstructions the phone and the cell tower. Many of you have probably walked around a building trying to find a place with good reception for your mobile phone—the problems are caused in part to the building absorbing and reflecting some of the energy.

Wireless LANs have become hugely popular in companies as well as in the home. The beauty of all wireless communication, including wireless LANs, is the lack of wires. No cables are required, and there's no need to open up walls, get a ladder to get up in the ceiling, or pay $100 plus per cable to get new cables run. The downsides relate to the speeds (generally less than those of wired LANs today), security risks (anyone nearby can attempt to eavesdrop), and the extra engineering effort to make sure you have enough coverage in the area in which you allow people to roam with their wireless devices.

IEEE 802.11 Wireless LANs

The most popular type of wireless LAN today is based on the IEEE 802.11 standard, which is known informally as *Wi-Fi*. The 802.11 specification defines what happens on the wireless network to let two or more devices send and receive data.

Wireless LAN communication is really a shared LAN because only one station effectively can transmit at one time, at least in a particular constrained geography. 802.11 signals effectively might reach another device as far as 300 feet away. So, you can have lots of people around the planet using the airwaves for 802.11 at any one point in time, but only one device can send at a time when within range of the wireless signals.

Wireless LANs typically include one or more computers that have a wireless 802.11 LAN card, plus one or more wireless *access points (APs)*. Access points bridge or route traffic from the wireless LAN to the "wired" LAN and vice versa. Figure 11-14 depicts the general idea.

Figure 11-14 *Wireless Access Point and 802.11 Framing*

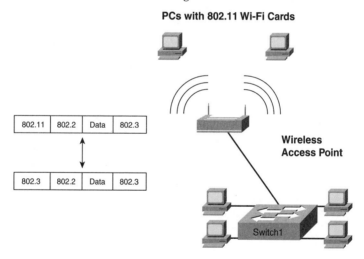

The AP shows two antennae protruding from the corners—indeed, a component of wireless communications is the antennae used to receive and transmit wireless radio signals. The two PCs at the top of the figure also have antennae, typically connected to the end of the 802.11 LAN card and protruding out from the PC.

Note that 802.11 calls for the use of IEEE 802.2 LLC, as well as the same format of addresses defined in 802.3. 802.11 does use a different MAC header than 802.3, however. So, to bridge the traffic, the access point simply swaps an 802.11 header for an 802.3 header, and vice versa, using the same MAC addresses. Some wireless APs route traffic from the wireless network to the wired network.

802.11 includes several standards. 802.11b transmits at 11 Mbps using the 2.4 GHz frequency band, but it is shared, with the maximum throughput capped at about 7 Mbps. 802.11a, which runs in the 5 Ghz frequency band, now can run at speeds up to 54 Mbps, as can 802.11g, which uses the 2.4 Ghz band, like 802.11b. When this book was published, there was still debate in the industry as to which of the higher-speed wireless standards would emerge as the more popular technology in the marketplace.

Foundation Summary

The "Foundation Summary" section of each chapter lists the most important facts from the chapter. Although this section does not list every fact from the chapter that will be on your CCNA exam, a well-prepared CCNA candidate should know, at a minimum, all the details in each "Foundation Summary" section before going to take the exam.

Table 11-8 summarizes the type of physical topology covered in this chapter.

Table 11-8   *Physical Topology Types*

Term	Definition
Bus	This is a linear topology, with all devices connected to the cable.
Star	Each device is connected to a central point. Sometimes called hub-and-spoke.
Extended star	A star topology is in the center, but instead of each point being a single device, it can be the center of another star topology.
Full mesh	Each device has a direction connection to each other device.
Partial mesh	Each device does not have a direct connection to each other device.
Single ring	Each device is connected connected to two others so that the signal is repeated in one direction, causing a ring or loop.
Dual ring	Two rings go through the same set of devices, allowing loops to be made upon failure, which continues the operation of a ring.

Figure 11-15 shows a conceptual diagram of UTP and STP cabling.

Figure 11-15 *UTP and STP Cable Components*

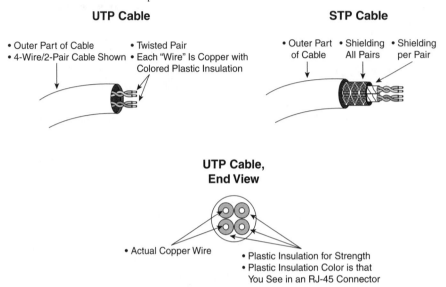

Table 11-9 outlines the types of UTP cabling.

Table 11-9 *UTP Cable Categories/Characteristics*

UTP Category	Max Speed Rating	Description
1	—	Used for telephones but not for data.
2	4 Mbps	Originally intended to support Token Ring over UTP.
3	10 Mbps	Can be used for telephones as well. Popular option for Ethernet in years past, if CAT3 cabling for phones already was in place.
4	16 Mbps	Intended for the fast Token Ring speed option.
5	1 Gbps	Very popular for cabling to the desktop.
5e	1 Gbps	Lower emissions, more expensive than CAT5, but better for Gigabit Ethernet.
6	1 Gbps+	Intended as a replacement for CAT5e, with capabilities to support multigigabit speeds when standards are created.

Figure 11-16 shows the pinouts on a typical four-pair UTP cable using an RJ-45 connector.

Figure 11-16   *Four-Pair UTP Cable: Pinouts Using RJ-45*

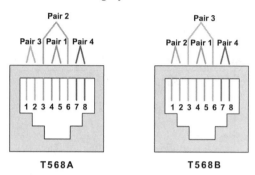

Figure 11-17 shows a side view of an optical cable, including a view of the optical fiber itself.

Figure 11-17   *Components of a Fiber-Optic Cable*

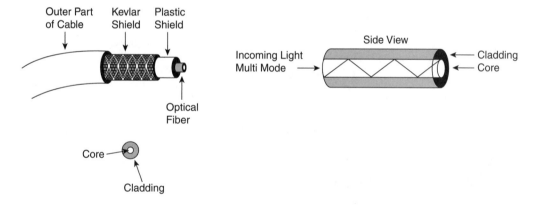

Table 11-10 summarizes the types of cable and main features, with some comments about disadvantages and advantages of each.

Table 11-10 *Summary of Ethernet Cabling Types*

	Maximum Length, Single Segment	Maximum Speed for Ethernet	Relative Cost	Advantages	Disadvantages
UTP	100 m	1 Gbps	Low	Easy to install, commonly available, popular	Susceptible to interference, limited distance
STP	100 m	100 Mbps	Medium	Low emissions, less susceptible to interference	Difficult to work with, limited distance
Coaxial	500 m (thicknet) 185 m (thinnet)	100 Mbps	Medium	Least susceptible to interference of all copper media	Difficult to work with (thicknet), single cable problem fails whole network
Fiber	10 km+ (SM) 2 km+ (MM)	100 Gbps (SM) 10 Gbps (MM)	High	More secure, long distances, not susceptible to EMI, highest speeds	Difficult to terminate when attaching connectors

Tables 11-11, 11-12, and 11-13 list the pertinent details of the standards and the cabling.

Table 11-11 *Ethernet 802.3 Cabling Standards*

Standard	Cabling	Maximum Length
10BASE5	Thick coaxial	500 m
10BASE2	Thin coaxial	185 m
10BASE-T	UTP CAT3, 4, 5, 5e, 6	100 m

Table 11-12 *FastEthernet 802.3u Cabling Standards*

Standard	Cabling	Maximum Length
100BASE-FX	Two strands, multimode	400 m
100BASE-T	UTP CAT3, 4, 5, 5e, 6, two-pair	100 m
100BASE-T4	UTP CAT3, 4, 5, 5e, 6, four-pair	100 m
100BASE-TX	UTP CAT3, 4, 5, 5e, 6, or STP, two-pair	100 m

Table 11-13 *Gigabit 802.3z (Optical) and 802.3ab (Electrical) Cabling Standards*

Standard	Cabling	Maximum Length
1000BASE-LX	Long-wavelength laser, MM or SM fiber	10 km (SM) 3 km (MM)
1000BASE-SX	Short-wavelength laaser, MM fiber	220 m with 62.5-micron fiber; 550 m with 50-micron fiber
1000BASE-ZX	Extended wavelength, SM fiber	100 km
1000BASE-CS	STP, two-pair	25 m
1000BASE-T	UTP CAT5, 5e, 6, four-pair	100 m

Q&A

As mentioned in the introduction, you have two choices for review questions. The questions that follow give you a bigger challenge than the exam itself by using an open-ended question format. By reviewing now with this more difficult question format, you can exercise your memory better and prove your conceptual and factual knowledge of this chapter. The answers to these questions are found in Appendix A.

For more practice with exam-like question formats, including questions using a router simulator and multiple-choice questions, use the exam engine on the CD.

1. Describe why a 10BASE-T network using a hub is considered to be a logical bus topology.

2. Compare and contrast full-mesh versus partial-mesh topologies, in relation to physical topologies.

3. Compare and contrast full-mesh versus partial-mesh topologies, in relation to logical topologies.

4. What is the main motivation for using a dual-ring physical topology versus a single ring? Why?

5. What two methods are used to reduce the amount of electromagnetic emissions emanating from copper Ethernet cabling? Why do they help reduce emissions?

6. Which wires are used by a typical Ethernet CAT5 cable? Which ones are used for transmit, and which ones are used to receive, by an Ethernet card?

7. Which TIA standards for UTP cabling support 10BASE-T?

8. What are the maximum lengths for coaxial cables as used by 10BASE5? 10BASE2?

9. What are key differences between multimode and single-mode optical cabling?

10. What types of cabling are least susceptible to having someone eavesdrop and somehow discover what is being transmitted over the cable?

11. What are the IEEE standards for 10BASE-T, Fast Ethernet, Gigabit Ethernet, and 10-Gigabit Ethernet?

12. Which variations on the Fast Ethernet standard, which use names like "10BASE-something," specifically state the need for four pairs of wires in the cable? What about for Gigabit Ethernet?

13. Which variations on the Fast Ethernet and Gigabit standard use IEEE 802.3 MAC and 802.2 LLC framing?

14. What were some of the differences between 10-Gigabit Ethernet, as compared with other types of Ethernet, as outlined in this chapter?

15. What IEEE standards are used by an 802.11 access point?

16. What does the term line-of-sight mean in relation to wireless communications?

Cisco Published INTRO Exam Topics*
Covered in This Part:

1   Use a subset of Cisco IOS commands to analyze and report network problems

3   Determine IP addresses

7   Use commands incorporated within IOS to analyze and report network problems

8   Assign IP addresses

9   Describe and install the hardware and software required to be able to communicate via a network

10   Use embedded data link layer functionality to perform network neighbor discovery and analysis from the router console

11   Use embedded layer 3 through layer 7 protocols to establish, test, suspend or disconnect connectivity to remote devices from the router console

12   Demonstrate the mathematical skills required to work seamlessly with integer decimal, binary and hexadecimal numbers and simple binary logic (AND)

23   Describe the concepts associated with routing, and the different methods and protocols used to achieve it

24   Describe how an IP address is associated with a device interface, and the association between physical and logical addressing

25   Employ IP addressing techniques

30   Describe how the protocols associated with TCP/IP allow host communication to occur

31   Describe the operation of the Internet Control Message Protocol (ICMP) and identify the reasons, types and format of associated error and control messages

32   Describe the principles and practice of packet switching utilizing the Internet Protocol (IP)

* Always re-check www.cisco.com for the latest posted exam topics

PART IV: TCP/IP

This chapter covers the following subjects:

- IP Addressing Review

- Analyzing and Interpreting IP Addresses and Subnets

- Scaling the IP Address Space for the Internet

CHAPTER 12

IP Addressing and Subnetting

In Chapter 5, "Fundamentals of IP," you learned about the basic concepts and terminology relating to IP addressing. These concepts were introduced early in the book because your understanding of many basic networking concepts depends on a base knowledge of IP addressing.

In this chapter, you will learn about the concepts and mathematics that let you analyze IP addresses and subnets. IP addressing is the only major topic that happens to get coverage on both of the INTRO and ICND exams. To answer questions on either CCNA exam, you will need to discover the structure of IP addresses, list the addresses in the same subnet, list the other subnets of that same network, identify the numbers of hosts in a subnet, and identify other information about addresses and subnets. This chapter describes the math and processes used to answer these questions.

This chapter also happens to cover a few topics related IP address scalability issues related to Internet growth.

"Do I Know This Already?" Quiz

The purpose of the "Do I Know This Already?" quiz is to help you decide whether you really need to read the entire chapter. If you already intend to read the entire chapter, you do not necessarily need to answer these questions now.

The 14-question quiz, derived from the major sections in the "Foundation Topics" portion of the chapter, helps you determine how to spend your limited study time.

Table 12-1 outlines the major topics discussed in this chapter and the "Do I Know This Already?" quiz questions that correspond to those topics.

Table 12-1 *"Do I Know This Already?" Foundation Topics Section-to-Question Mapping*

Foundations Topics Section	Questions Covered in This Section
Analyzing and Interpreting IP Addresses and Subnets	1–10
Scaling the IP Address Space for the Internet	11–14

> **CAUTION** The goal of self-assessment is to gauge your mastery of the topics in this chapter. If you do not know the answer to a question or are only partially sure of the answer, you should mark this question wrong for purposes of the self-assessment. Giving yourself credit for an answer that you correctly guess skews your self-assessment results and might provide you with a false sense of security.

1. Which of the following is the result of a Boolean AND between IP address 150.150.4.100, mask 255.255.192.0?

   a. 1001 0110 1001 0110 0000 0100 0110 0100

   b. 1001 0110 1001 0110 0000 0000 0000 0000

   c. 1001 0110 1001 0110 0000 0100 0000 0000

   d. 1001 0110 0000 0000 0000 0000 0000 0000

2. If mask 255.255.255.128 were used with a Class B network, how many subnets could exist, with how many hosts per subnet, respectively?

   a. 256 and 256

   b. 254 and 254

   c. 62 and 1022

   d. 1022 and 62

   e. 510 and 126

   f. 126 and 510

3. If mask 255.255.255.240 were used with a Class C network, how many subnets could exist, with how many hosts per subnet, respectively?

   a. 16 and 16

   b. 14 and 14

   c. 12 and 12

   d. 8 and 32

   e. 32 and 8

   f. 6 and 30

   g. 30 and 6

4. Which of the following IP addresses would not be in the same subnet as 190.4.80.80, mask 255.255.255.0?

   a. 190.4.80.1

   b. 190.4.80.50

   c. 190.4.80.100

   d. 190.4.80.200

   e. 190.4.90.1

   f. 10.1.1.1

5. Which of the following IP addresses would not be in the same subnet as 190.4.80.80, mask 255.255.240.0?

   a. 190.4.80.1

   b. 190.4.80.50

   c. 190.4.80.100

   d. 190.4.80.200

   e. 190.4.90.1

   f. 10.1.1.1

6. Which of the following IP addresses would not be in the same subnet as 190.4.80.80, mask 255.255.255.128?

   a. 190.4.80.1

   b. 190.4.80.50

   c. 190.4.80.100

   d. 190.4.80.200

   e. 190.4.90.1

   f. 10.1.1.1

7. Which of the following subnet masks would allow a Class B network to allow subnets
    to have up to 150 hosts and allow for up to 164 subnets?

    a. 255.0.0.0

    b. 255.255.0.0

    c. 255.255.255.0

    d. 255.255.192.0

    e. 255.255.240.0

    f. 255.255.252.0

    g. 255.255.255.192

    h. 255.255.255.240

8. Which of the following subnet masks would allow a Class A network to allow subnets
    to have up to 150 hosts and would allow for up to 164 subnets?

    a. 255.0.0.0

    b. 255.255.0.0

    c. 255.255.255.0

    d. 255.255.192.0

    e. 255.255.240.0

    f. 255.255.252.0

    g. 255.255.255.192

    h. 255.255.255.240

9. Which of the following are valid subnet numbers in network 180.1.0.0, when using
    mask 255.255.248.0?

    a. 180.1.2.0

    b. 180.1.4.0

    c. 180.1.8.0

    d. 180.1.16.0

    e. 180.1.32.0

    f. 180.1.40.0

10. Which of the following are valid subnet numbers in network 180.1.0.0, when using mask 255.255.255.0?

   a. 180.1.2.0

   b. 180.1.4.0

   c. 180.1.8.0

   d. 180.1.16.0

   e. 180.1.32.0

   f. 180.1.40.0

11. Which of the following best describes a feature of CIDR?

   a. Grouping a large number of Class C networks into a single group, and putting a single entry for that group in an Internet router, to reduce the overall size of the IP routing table

   b. To represent hundreds or thousands of client TCP or UDP connections from different hosts as that same number of connections, but making it appear as if all connections are from one host

   c. The use network 10.0.0.0 in an Enterprise network

   d. The use of addresses such as 0000:0000:0000:0000:0000:FFFF:FFFF:0A01:0101

12. The phrase "to represent hundreds or thousands of client TCP or UDP connections from different hosts as that same number of connections, but making it appear as if all connections are from one host" best describes which of the following tools?

   a. Private addressing

   b. CIDR

   c. NAT

   d. IPv6

13. The phrase "grouping a large number of Class C networks into a single group, and putting a single entry for that group in an Internet router, to reduce the overall size of the IP routing table " best describes which of the following tools?

   a. Private addressing

   b. CIDR

   c. NAT

   d. IPv6

14. The phrase "the use network 10.0.0.0 in an enterprise network" best describes which of the following tools?

  a. Private addressing

  b. CIDR

  c. NAT

  d. IPv6

The answers to the "Do I Know This Already?" quiz are found in Appendix A, "Answers to the 'Do I Know This Already?' Quizzes and Q&A Sections." The suggested choices for your next step are as follows:

- **11 or less overall score**—Read the entire chapter. This includes the "Foundation Topics" and "Foundation Summary" sections and the Q&A section.

- **12, 13, or 14 overall score**—If you want more review on these topics, skip to the "Foundation Summary" section and then go to the Q&A section. Otherwise, move to the next chapter.

Foundation Topics

This chapter begins with a brief review of IP addressing and subnetting. Following that, the text takes a thorough look at several types of IP addressing questions and the math you can use to find the answers.

IP Addressing Review

Chapter 5 explained the concepts behind IP addressing; Class A, B, and C networks; and subnetting. Before looking at the math behind IP addressing, a quick review will be helpful.

Many different Class A, B, and C networks exist. Table 12-2 summarizes the possible network numbers, the total number of each type, and the number of hosts in each Class A, B, and C network.

Table 12-2   *List of All Possible Valid Network Numbers**

	Class A	Class B	Class C
First Octet Range	1 to 126	128 to 191	192 to 223
Valid Network Numbers	1.0.0.0 to 126.0.0.0	128.1.0.0 to 191.254.0.0	192.0.1.0 to 223.255.254.0
Number of Networks of This Class	$2^7 - 2$	$2^{14} - 2$	$2^{21} - 2$
Number of Hosts per Network	$2^{24} - 2$	$2^{16} - 2$	$2^8 - 2$
Size of Network Part of Address (bytes)	1	2	3
Size of Host Part of Address (bytes)	3	2	1

*The "Valid Network Numbers" row shows actual network numbers. There are several reserved cases. For example, networks 0.0.0.0 (originally defined for use as a broadcast address) and 127.0.0.0 (still available for use as the loopback address) are reserved. Networks 128.0.0.0, 191.255.0.0, 192.0.0.0, and 223.255.255.0 also are reserved.

Without subnetting, a different IP network must be used for each physical network. For example, Figure 12-1 shows three example IP addresses, each from a different network. One address is in a Class A network, one is in a Class B network, and one is in a Class C network.

Figure 12-1 *Example Class A, B, and C IP Addresses and Their Formats*

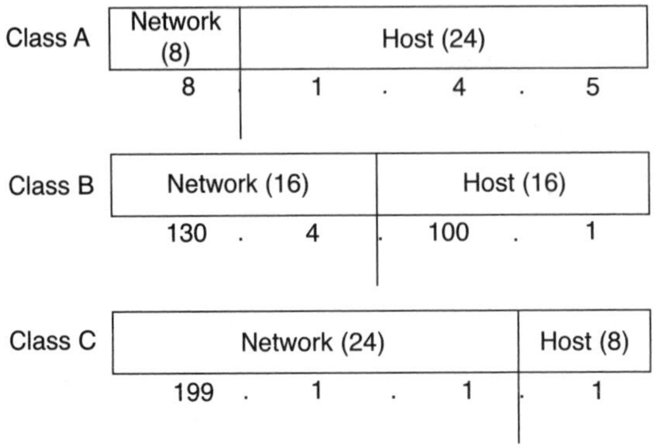

By definition, an IP address that begins with 8 in the first octet is in a Class A network, so the network part of the address is the first byte, or first octet. An address that begins with 130 is in a Class B network; by definition, Class B addresses have a 2-byte network part, as shown. Finally, any address that begins with 199 is in a Class C network, which has a 3-byte network part. Also by definition, a Class A address has a 1-byte host part, Class B has a 2-byte host part, and Class C has a 1-byte host part.

Humans simply can remember the numbers in Table 12-2 and the concepts in Figure 12-1 and then quickly determine the network and host part of an IP address. Computers, however, use a mask to define the size of the network and host parts of an address. The logic behind the mask results in the same conventions of Class A, B, and C networks that you already know, but the computer can deal with it better as a binary math problem. The mask is a 32-bit binary number, usually written in dotted-decimal format. The purpose of the mask is to define the structure of an IP address. In short, the mask defines the size of the host parts of an IP address, representing the host part of the IP address with binary 0s in the mask. Class A mask has its last 24 bits as binary 0, which means that the last three octets of the mask are 0s. Table 12-3 summarizes the default masks and reflects the sizes of the two parts of an IP address.

Table 12-3 *Class A, B, and C Networks—Network and Host Parts and Default Masks*

Class of Address	Size of Network Part of Address, in Bits	Size of Host Part of Address, in Bits	Default Mask for Each Class of Network
A	8	24	255.0.0.0
B	16	16	255.255.0.0
C	24	8	255.255.255.0

IP Subnetting

IP subnetting creates vastly larger numbers of smaller groups of IP addresses, compared with simply using Class A, B, and C conventions. The Class A, B, and C rules still exist—but now a single Class A, B, or C network can be subdivided into many smaller groups. Subnetting treats a subdivision of a single Class A, B, or C network as if it were a network itself. By doing so, a single Class A, B, or C network can be subdivided into many nonoverlapping subnets.

Figures 12-2 and 12-3 show the basic differences between a network that does not use subnetting and one that does use subneting. First, look at Figure 12-2, which uses six different IP networks.

Figure 12-2 *Network Topology Using Six IP Networks*

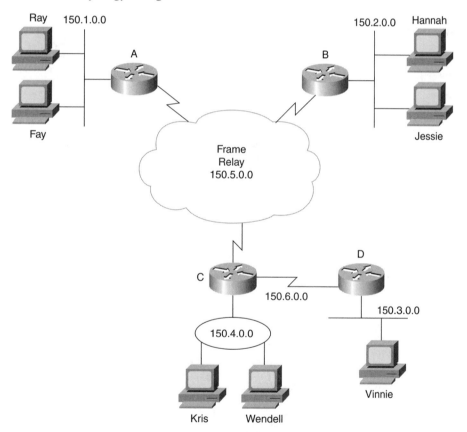

The design in Figure 12-2 requires six groups, each of which is a Class B network. The four LANs each use a single Class B network. In other words, the LANs attached to Routers A, B, C, and D are each a separate network. Additionally, the two serial interfaces composing the point-to-point serial link between Routers C and D use the same network because these two interfaces are not separated by a router. Finally, the three router interfaces composing the Frame Relay network with Routers A, B, and C are not separated by an IP router and would compose the sixth network.

CAUTION Other Frame Relay IP addressing options would require one or two more IP network numbers for this physical network.

As in Figure 12-2, the design in Figure 12-3 requires six groups. Unlike Figure 12-2, Figure 12-3 uses six subnets, each of which is a subnet of a single Class B network.

Figure 12-3 *Same Network Topology, Using One IP Network, with Six Subnets*

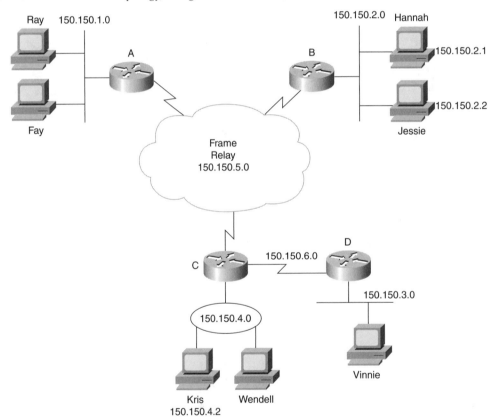

This design subnets Class B network 150.150.0.0. The IP network designer has chosen a mask of 255.255.255.0, the last octet of which implies 8 host bits. Because it is a Class B network, there are 16 network bits. Therefore, there are 8 subnet bits, which happen to be bits 17 through 24—in other words, the third octet.

Note that the network part (the first two octets in this example) all begin with 150.150, meaning that each of the six subnets is a subnet of Class B network 150.150.0.0.

When subnetting, a third part of an IP address appears in the middle of the address—namely, the subnet part of the address. This field is created by "stealing" or "borrowing" bits from the host part of the address. The size of the network part of the address never shrinks—in other words, Class A, B, and C rules still apply when defining the size of the network part of an address. However, the host part of the address shrinks to make room for the subnet part of the address. Figure 12-4 shows the format of addresses when subnetting.

Figure 12-4 *Address Formats When Subnetting Is Used*

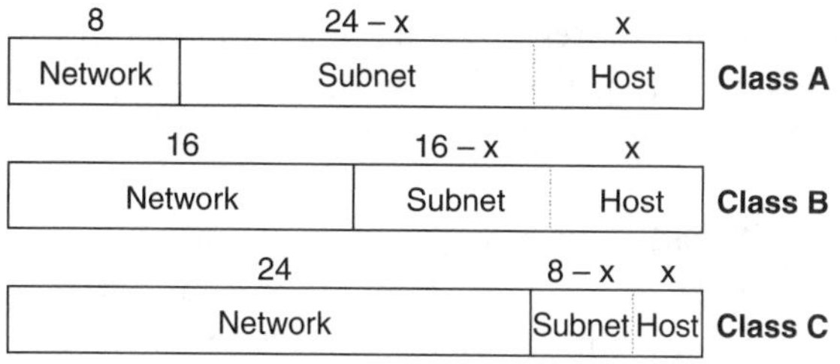

8	24 – x	x	
Network	Subnet	Host	**Class A**

16	16 – x	x	
Network	Subnet	Host	**Class B**

24	8 – x	x	
Network	Subnet	Host	**Class C**

Analyzing and Interpreting IP Addresses and Subnets

No one reading this book should be shocked to hear that IP addressing is one of the most important topics on both exams. You need a comfortable, confident understanding of IP addressing and subnetting for success on any Cisco certification. You should be prepared to answer questions about the following:

- An interpretation of an address
- Its network number
- Its subnet number
- The other IP addresses in the same subnet
- The broadcast address
- The other subnets that could be used if the same mask were in use

In other words, you had better know IP addressing and subnetting!

Besides just answering questions on the CCNA exams, network engineers need to understand subnetting very well to do their jobs. Engineers who work with multiple networks must decipher IP addresses quickly, without running off to use a subnet calculator tool. For example, someone with a problem might call and tell you his IP address. After finding out the mask that's used, you do a **show ip route** command on a router, but that typically lists subnets—so you need to be able to easily figure out the subnet of which the address is a member. And not all networks will be using nice, easy subnet masks.

No matter how useful this book is in helping you with a real networking job, the primary goal of this book is to help you pass the exam. So, the rest of this chapter is geared toward helping you understand how to interpret and analyze IP addresses.

Math Operations Used to Answer Subnetting Questions

Computers, especially routers, do not think about IP addresses in terms of the conventions shown in Table 12-2. They think in terms of 32-bit binary numbers, which is fine because, technically, that's what IP addresses really are. Also, computers use a mask to define the structure of these binary IP addresses. A full understanding of what that means is not too difficult. However, getting accustomed to doing the binary math in your head is challenging for most of us, particularly if you don't do it every day.

In this section, you will read about two key math operations that will be used throughout the discussion of answering CCNA addressing and subnetting questions. One operation converts IP addresses from decimal to binary and then back to decimal. The other operation performs a binary math operation called a *Boolean AND*.

Converting IP Addresses from Decimal to Binary, and Back Again

If you already know how binary works, how binary-to-decimal and decimal-to-binary conversion works, and how to convert IP addresses from decimal to binary and back, skip to the next section, "The Boolean AND Operation."

IP addresses are 32-bit binary numbers, written as a series of decimal numbers, separated by periods. To examine an address in its true form, binary, you need to convert from decimal to binary. To put a 32-bit binary number in the decimal form that is needed when configuring a router, you need to convert the 32-bit number back to decimal, 8 bits at a time.

One key to the conversion process for IP addresses is remembering these facts:

When converting from one format to the other, each decimal number represents 8 bits.

When converting from decimal to binary, each decimal number converts to an 8-bit number.

When converting from binary to decimal, each set of 8 consecutive bits converts to one decimal number.

Consider the conversion of IP address 150.150.2.1 to binary for a moment. The number 150, when converted to its 8-bit binary equivalent, is 10010110. How do you know that? For now, look in the conversion chart in Appendix B, "Binary to Decimal Conversion Chart. The next byte, another decimal 150, is converted to 10010110. The third byte, decimal 2, is converted to 00000010; finally, the fourth byte, decimal 1, is converted to 00000001. The combined series of 8-bit numbers is the 32-bit IP address—in this case, 10010110 10010110 00000010 00000001.

If you start with the binary version of the IP address, you first separate it into four sets of eight digits. Then you convert each set of eight binary digits to its decimal equivalent. For example, writing an IP address as follows is correct but not very useful:

10010110100101100000001000000001

To convert this number to a more convenient decimal form, first separate it into four sets of eight digits:

10010110 10010110 00000010 00000001

Then look in the conversion chart in Appendix B and find that the first 8-bit number converts to 150, and so does the second set. The third set of 8 bits converts to 2, and the fourth converts to 1—giving you 150.150.2.1.

Using the chart in Appendix B makes this much easier—but you will not have the chart on the exam, of course! So you can do a couple of things. First, you can learn how to do the conversion. The book does not cover it, but a couple of web sites referenced at the end of this section can help. The other alternative is to use the chart when studying, and study the examples that show you how to manipulate IP addresses and find the right answers to the test questions without doing any binary math. If that works for you, you actually do not need to be speedy and proficient at doing binary-to-decimal and decimal-to-binary conversions.

One last important fact: When subnetting, the subnet and host parts of the address might span only part of a byte of the IP address. But when converting from binary to decimal and decimal to binary, the rule of always converting an 8-bit binary number to a decimal number is always true. However, when thinking about subnetting, you will need to ignore byte boundaries and think about IP addresses as 32-bit numbers without specific byte boundaries. But that is explained more later in the section titled "Finding the Subnet Number."

Interestingly, you should actually be prepared to do basic binary, decimal, and hexadecimal conversions if taking the INTRO exam. While the shortcuts that can help you perform subnetting quickly are still very valuable, make sure you can convert numbers between all three types. Some sites that might help you if you want more information are as follows:

■ For basic information on base 10, base 2 (binary), and conversion practice, visit www.ibilce.unesp.br/courseware/datas/numbers.htm#mark2.

■ For a description of the conversion process, try doit.ort.org/course/inforep/135.htm.

- For another description of the conversion process, try www.goshen.edu/compsci/ mis200/decbinary.htm.

- For some free video classes that cover binary, conversion, and subnetting, go to www.learntosubnet.com.

The Boolean AND Operation

George Boole, a mathemetician who lived in the 1800s, created a branch of mathematics that came to be called Boolean math, after the name of its creator. Boolean math has many applications in computing theory. In fact, you can find subnet numbers, given an IP address and subnet mask, but using a Boolean AND.

A Boolean AND is a math operation performed to a pair of one-digit binary numbers. The result is another one-digit binary number. The actual math is even simpler than those first two sentences! The following list shows the four possible inputs to a Boolean AND and the result:

- 0 AND 0 yields a 0.

- 0 AND 1 yields a 0.

- 1 AND 0 yields a 0.

- 1 AND 1 yields a 1.

In other words, the input to the equation consists of two one-digit binary numbers, and the output of the equation is one single-digit binary number. *The only time the result is a binary 1 is when both input numbers are also binary 1; otherwise, the result of a Boolean AND is a 0.*

You can perform a Boolean AND on longer binary numbers, but you are really just performing an AND on each pair of numbers. For instance, if you wanted to AND together two four-digit numbers 0110 and 0011, then you would perform an AND of the first digit of each number and write down the answer. Then you would perform an AND on the second digit of each number, and so on, through the four digits. Table 12-4 shows the general idea.

Table 12-4 *Bitwise Boolean AND Between Two Four-Digit Numbers*

	Four-Digit Binary	First Digit	Second Digit	Third Digit	Fourth Digit
First number	0110	0	1	1	0
Second number	0011	0	0	1	1
Boolean AND result	0010	0	0	1	0

The table separates the four digits of each original number to make the point more obvious. Look at the column holding the first digit's values. The first digit of the first number is 0, and the first digit of the second number is also 0. 0 AND 0 yields a binary 0, which is listed as the Boolean AND result in that same column. Similarly, the second digits of the two original numbers are 1 and 0, respectively, so the Boolean AND result in the second digit column shows a 0. For the third digit, the two original numbers' third digits were 1 and 1, so the AND result this time shows a binary 1. Finally, the fourth digits of the two original numbers were 0 and 1, so the Boolean AND result is 0 for that column in the table.

When you Boolean AND two longer binary numbers together, you actually perform what is called a *bitwise Boolean AND*. This term simply means that you do what the previous example showed: You AND together the first digits from each of the two original numbers, then the second digits, and then the third, and so on, until the each pair of single-digit binary numbers has been ANDed.

IP subnetting math frequently uses a Boolean AND between two 32-bit binary numbers. The actual operation works just like the example in Table 12-4, except that it is longer.

To discover the subnet number in which a particular IP address resides, you perform a bitwise AND between the IP address and the subnet mask. Humans sometimes can look at an IP address and mask in decimal and derive the subnet number, but routers and other computers use a Boolean AND between the IP address and the subnet mask to find the subnet number, so you should understand the process. In this chapter, you also will read about a process by which you can find the subnet number without using any binary conversion or Boolean ANDs.

An example of the derivation of a subnet number is shown in Table 12-5.

NOTE Appendix B has a binary-to-decimal conversion chart.

Table 12-5 *Bitwise Boolean AND Example*

	Decimal	**Binary**
Address	150.150.2.1	1001 0110 1001 0110 0000 0010 **0000 0001**
Mask	255.255.255.0	1111 1111 1111 1111 1111 1111 **0000 0000**
Result of AND	150.150.2.0	1001 0110 1001 0110 0000 0010 **0000 0000**

First, focus only on the third column of the table. The binary version of the IP address 150.150.2.1 is listed first. The next row shows the 32-binary version of the subnet mask (255.255.255.0). The last row shows the results of a bitwise AND of the two numbers—in other words, the first bit in each number is ANDed, then the second bit in each number, then the third pair, and so on, until all 32 bits in the first number have been ANDed with the bit in the same position in the second number.

The resulting 32-bit number is the subnet number in which 150.150.2.1 resides. All you have to do is convert the 32-bit number back to decimal, 8 bits at a time. So, the subnet number in this case is 150.150.2.0.

If you understand the basic idea but would like additional examples to make it more clear, read on. In the next section, you will use Boolean ANDs to answer basic questions about IP subnetting. Also, on the CD, look for the chapter titled "Subnetting Practice: 25 Subnetting Questions," where 25 IP addressing practice questions are available, each with the binary math worked out for performing the Boolean AND.

Prefix Notation

Finally, any Cisco-oriented IP addressing coverage would be incomplete without a discussion of prefix notation.

In this chapter, you will get more comfortable using subnet masks. The masks can be written in decimal form, or they can be written as a 32-bit binary number. However, there is a third alternative, called *prefix notation,* which allows a router to display mask information more succinctly.

To understand prefix notation, it is important to know that all subnet masks have some number of consecutive binary 1s, followed by binary 0s. In other words, a subnet mask cannot have 1s and 0s interspersed throughout the mask—the mask always has some number of binary 1s, followed only by binary 0s.

Prefix notation simply denotes the number of binary 1s in a mask, preceded by a /. In other words, for subnet mask 255.255.255.0, whose binary equivalent is 11111111 11111111 11111111 00000000, the equivalent prefix notation would be /24 because there are 24 consecutive binary 1s in the mask. When talking about subnets, you can say things like "That subnet uses a *slash 24 prefix*" or "That subnet has a 24-bit prefix" instead of saying something like "That subnet uses a mask of 255.255.255.0."

Prefix notation makes talking about subnet masks a little easier, and it makes the information displayed by the router a little briefer as well. For instance, just try saying "255.255.255.0" out loud a few times, and imagine that the network is down while you're saying it, and you will hear the benefit.

Now that the basic math tools have been covered, the specifics on how to use them to find the right answers to subnetting questions are covered next.

How Many Hosts, and How Many Subnets?

You also should know how to figure out how many network, subnet, and host bits are used with that subnetting scheme. From those facts, you easily can figure out how many hosts exist in the subnet and how many subnets you can create in that network using that subnet mask.

You already have learned that Class A, B, and C networks have either 8, 16, or 24 bits in their network fields, respectively. Those rules do not change. You also already have read that, without subnetting, Class A, B, and C addresses have 24, 16, or 8 bits in their host fields, respectively. With subnetting, the network part of the address does not shrink or change, but the host field shrinks to make room for the subnet field. So, the key to answering these types of questions is to figure out how many host bits remain after applying subnetting, which then can tell you the size of the subnet field. The rest of the answers follow from those two facts.

The following facts tell you how to find the sizes of the network, subnet, and host parts of an IP address:

- The network part of the address always is defined by class rules.

- The host part of the address always is defined by the mask; binary 0s in the mask mean that the corresponding address bits are part of the host field.

- The subnet part of the address is what's left over in the 32-bit address.

Table 12-6 lists these three key facts along with the first example. If you have forgotten the ranges of values in the first octet for addresses in Class A, B, and C networks, refer to Table 12-2 earlier in the chapter.

Table 12-6 *First Example, with Rules for Learning Network, Subnet, and Host Part Sizes*

Step	Example	Rules to Remember
Address	8.1.4.5	—
Mask	255.255.0.0	—
Number of network bits	8	Always defined by Class A, B, C
Number of host bits	16	Always defined as number of binary 0s in mask
Number of subnet bits	8	32 – (network size + host size)

In this example, there are 8 network bits because the address is in a Class A network, 8.0.0.0. There are 16 host bits because, when you convert 255.255.0.0 to binary, there are 16 binary 0s—the last 16 bits in the mask. (If you do not believe me, look at Appendix B, in the binary-to-decimal conversion chart. 255 decimal is eight binary 1s, and 0 decimal is eight binary 0s.) The size of the subnet part of the address is what's left over, or 8 bits.

Two other examples with easy-to-convert masks might help your understanding. Consider address 130.4.102.1, with mask 255.255.255.0. First, 130.4.102.1 is in a Class B network, so there are 16 network bits. A subnet mask of 255.255.255.0 has only eight binary 0s, implying 8 host bits, which leaves 8 subnet bits in this case.

For another example, consider 199.1.1.100, with mask 255.255.255.0. In fact, this example does not even use subnetting. 199.1.1.100 is in a Class C network, which means that there are 24 network bits. The mask has eight binary 0s, yielding 8 host bits, with no bits remaining for the subnet part of the address. In fact, if you remembered that the default mask for Class C networks is 255.255.255.0, you might have realized already that no subnetting was being used in this example.

Most of us can calculate the number of host bits easily if the mask uses only decimal 255s and 0s because it is easy to remember that decimal 255 represents 8 binary 1s, and decimal 0 represents 8 binary 0s. So, for every decimal 0 in the mask, there are 8 host bits. However, when the mask uses other decimal values besides 0 and 255, deciphering the number of host bits is more difficult. Examining the subnet masks in binary helps overcome the challenge. Consider the following addresses and masks, along with the binary version of the masks, as shown in Table 12-7.

Table 12-7 *Two Examples Using More Challenging Masks*

Mask in Decimal	Mask in Binary
130.4.102.1, mask 255.255.252.0	1111 1111 1111 1111 1111 1100 0000 0000
199.1.1.100, mask 255.255.255.224	1111 1111 1111 1111 1111 1111 1110 0000

The number of host bits implied by a mask becomes more apparent after converting the mask to binary. In the first mask, 255.255.252.0, there are ten binary 0s, implying a 10-bit host field. Because that mask is used with a Class B address (130.4.102.1), implying 16 network bits, there are 6 remaining subnet bits. In the second example, the mask has only five binary 0s, for 5 host bits. Because the mask is used with a Class C address, there are 24 network bits, leaving only 3 subnet bits. The process so far is straightforward:

- The class rules define the network part.
- The mask binary 0s define the host part.
- What's left over defines the size of the subnet part.

The only big problem occurs when the mask is tricky, which is true in the last two examples. When the mask is tricky, you have two alternatives for deciding how many host bits are defined:

- Convert the mask to binary, using any method for conversion at your disposal, and count the number of zeros.

- Convert the mask to binary after memorizing the nine decimal and binary values in Table 12-8. These are the only nine valid decimal values used in a subnet mask. Converting a mask to binary without having to convert from decimal to binary will be much faster.

Table 12-8 lists the only valid decimal values in a mask and their binary equivalents. Memorizing these values will help you convert masks from between their decimal and binary forms more quickly on the exam.

Table 12-8   *Decimal and Binary Values in a Single Octet of a Valid Subnet Mask*

Decimal	Binary
0	0000 0000
128	1000 0000
192	1100 0000
224	1110 0000
240	1111 0000
248	1111 1000
252	1111 1100
254	1111 1110
255	1111 1111

Without the use of a calculator, PC, or decimal-to-binary conversion chart, binary conversion of a subnet mask becomes easy after memorizing this chart. The binary equivalents of 255 and decimal 0 are obvious. The other seven values are not. But notice the values in succession: Each value has an additional binary 1 and one less binary 0. Each mask value, in succession, shows a mask value that reduces the number of host bits by 1 and adds 1 to the size of the subnet field. If you simply memorize each decimal value and its binary equivalent, converting masks from decimal to binary will be a breeze. In fact, you could sit down to take the exam, and before starting, go ahead and write down the information in the table so you could easily refer to it during the exam.

So far, the book has not told you how to answer a question like this:

> Given an address and mask, how many subnets are there? And how many hosts are there in a single subnet?

Well, two simple formulas provide the answers, and the formulas are based on the information that you just learned how to derive:

$$\text{Number of subnets} = 2^{\text{number-of-subnet-bits}} - 2$$
$$\text{Number of hosts per subnet} = 2^{\text{number-of-host-bits}} - 2$$

The formulas calculate the number of things that can be numbered using a binary number and then subtract 2 for two special cases. IP addressing conventions define that two subnets per network should not be used and that two hosts per subnet should not be used.

One reserved subnet, the subnet that has all binary 0s in the subnet field, is called the *zero subnet*. The subnet with all binary 1s in the subnet field is called the *broadcast subnet*—and it also is reserved. (Well, in fact, you can use both these subnets on a Cisco router, but it is recommended that you avoid using them. On the exam, the "right" answer is that you do not use them—hence the "minus 2" part of the $2^{\text{number-of-subnet-bits}} - 2$ formula.) In fact, the courses upon which CCNA is based now use the term *discouraged* instead of *reserved*, meaning that although those two subnets can be used, you should avoid it.

IP addressing conventions also reserve two IP addresses per subnet: the first (all binary 0s in the host field) and last (all binary 1s in the host field) addresses. No tricks exist to make these two addresses usable—they are indeed always reserved.

Table 12-9 summarizes the five examples used so far in this chapter.

Table 12-9 *Five Example Addresses/Masks, with Number of Network, Subnet, and Host Bits*

Address	8.1.4.5/16	130.4.102.1/24	199.1.1.100/24	130.4.102.1/22	199.1.1.100/27
Mask	255.255.0.0	255.255.255.0	255.255.255.0	255.255.252.0	255.255.255.224
Number of network bits	8	16	24	16	24
Number of host bits	16	8	8	10	5
Number of subnet bits	8	8	0	6	3
Number of hosts per subnet	$2^{16} - 2$, or 65,534	$2^8 - 2$, or 254	$2^8 - 2$, or 254	$2^{10} - 2$, or 1022	$2^5 - 2$, or 30
Number of subnets	$2^8 - 2$, or 254	$2^8 - 2$, or 254	0	$2^6 - 2$, or 62	$2^3 - 2$, or 6

The details of the algorithm used to answer subnetting questions about the number of hosts and subnets are summarized in the following list:

Step 1   Identify the structure of the IP address.

Step 2   Identify the size of the network part of the address, based on Class A, B, and C rules.

Step 3   Identify the size of the host part of the address, based on the number of binary 0s in the mask. If the mask is tricky, use the chart of typical mask values to convert the mask to binary more quickly.

Step 4   The size of the subnet part is what's "left over"; mathematically, it is $32 - $ (number of network + host bits).

Step 5   Declare the number of subnets, which is $2^{\text{number-of-subnet-bits}} - 2$.

Step 6   Declare the number of hosts per subnet, which is $2^{\text{number-of-host-bits}} - 2$.

What Is the Subnet Number, and What Are the IP Addresses in the Subnet?

One of the most common things you need to figure out is that after you know an IP address and subnet mask, you must answer questions about them. The question might be straightforward, such as "What is the subnet number?", or it might be more subtle, such as "Which of the following IP addresses are in the same subnet as the stated address?" In either case, if you can dissect an IP address as described in this chapter, you can answer any variation of this type of question.

In the next several sections, you will learn how to derive the subnet number and the subnet broadcast address. After deriving these two values, you easily can find the range of valid IP addresses in the subnet.

Finding the Subnet Number

Earlier, you learned that computers perform a Boolean AND of the address and mask to find the subnet number. The following tables (Tables 12-10 through 12-14) show the Boolean AND process for the five examples used in the previous section of this chapter:

Table 12-10   *Boolean AND Calculation for Subnet, Address 8.1.4.5, Mask 255.255.0.0*

Address	8.1.4.5	0000 1000 0000 0001 0000 0100 0000 0101
Mask	255.255.0.0	1111 1111 1111 1111 **0000 0000 0000 0000**
AND result	8.1.0.0	0000 1000 0000 0001 0000 0000 0000 0000

Table 12-11   *Boolean AND Calculation for Subnet, Address 130.1.102.4, Mask 255.255.255.0*

Address	130.4.102.1	1000 0010 0000 0100 0110 0110 0000 0001
Mask	255.255.255.0	1111 1111 1111 1111 1111 1111 **0000 0000**
AND result	130.4.102.0	1000 0010 0000 0100 0110 0110 0000 0000

Table 12-12   *Boolean AND Calculation for Subnet, Address 199.1.1.100, Mask 255.255.255.0*

Address	199.1.1.100	1100 0111 0000 0001 0000 0001 0110 0100
Mask	255.255.255.0	1111 1111 1111 1111 1111 1111 **0000 0000**
AND result	199.1.1.0	1100 0111 0000 0001 0000 0001 0000 0000

Table 12-13   *Boolean AND Calculation for Subnet, Address 130.4.102.1, Mask 255.255.252.0*

Address	130.4.102.1	1000 0010 0000 0100 0110 0110 0000 0001
Mask	255.255.252.0	1111 1111 1111 1111 1111 1100 **0000 0000**
AND result	130.4.100.0	1000 0010 0000 0100 0110 0100 0000 0000

Table 12-14   *Boolean AND Calculation for Subnet, Address 199.1.1.100, Mask 255.255.255.224*

Address	199.1.1.100	1100 0111 0000 0001 0000 0001 0110 0100
Mask	255.255.255.224	1111 1111 1111 1111 1111 1111 **1110 0000**
AND result	199.1.1.96	1100 0111 0000 0001 0000 0001 0110 0000

Although the tables show the answers, they do not show the process. The steps taken to complete the tables are as follows:

Step 1   To begin, you start with a decimal address and mask stated in the question.

Step 2   Then you must convert the two numbers to binary, as seen in all five examples.

Step 3   Next, each bit is ANDed with the bit in the same position in the other number (in other words, a bitwise Boolean AND), giving the result of the Boolean AND.

Step 4   Finally, the Boolean AND result must be converted back to decimal.

The last step in this process, conversion of the binary number back to decimal, is the step that causes most of the problems for people new to subnetting. In some cases, the conversion is simple. For instance, in the first example, the subnet mask is 255.255.0.0. Because the mask has only 255s or 0s in decimal, the boundary between the subnet and host fields is on a byte boundary as well—between the second and third bytes, in this case. So, the conversion from binary back to decimal for the result of the Boolean AND—0000 1000 0000 0001 0000 0000 0000 0000—typically does not pose a problem.

The confusion typically arises when the boundary between the subnet and host part of the address is in the middle of a byte, which occurs when the subnet mask has some value besides

0 or 255 decimal. For example, with 130.4.102.1, mask 255.255.252.0, the first 6 bits of the third octet comprise the subnet field, and the last 2 bits of the third octet, plus the entire fourth octet, comprise the host field. The problem that some people experience is that they try to convert the 6-bit subnet part from binary to decimal, and the 10-bit host part to decimal. However, when converting binary to decimal to find the dotted decimal IP address, you always convert the entire octet—even if part of the octet is in the subnet part of the address and part is in the host part of the address.

So, in this example, the subnet number (130.4.100.0), in binary, is 1000 0010 0000 0100 **0110 0100** 0000 0000. The entire third octet is shown in bold, which converts to 100 in decimal. When converting, each set of 8 bits is converted to decimal, giving 130.4.100.0.

Finding the Subnet Broadcast Address

The subnet broadcast address, sometimes called the *directed broadcast address*, can be used to send a packet to every device in a single subnet. However, few tools and protocols use the subnet broadcast address anymore. However, by calculating the subnet broadcast address, you easily can calculate the largest valid IP address in the subnet, which is an important part of answering subnetting questions.

There is a binary math operation to calculate the subnet broadcast address. However, there is a much easier process, especially if you already have the subnet number in binary:

Change all the host bit values in the subnet number to binary 1s.

You can examine this simple math behind calculating the subnet broadcast address in the five tables (Tables 12-15 through 12-19) that follow. The host parts of the addresses, masks, subnet numbers, and broadcast addresses are in bold.

Table 12-15 *Calculating Broadcast Address, Address 8.1.4.5, Mask 255.255.0.0*

Address	8.1.4.5	0000 1000 0000 0001 **0000 0100 0000 0101**
Mask	255.255.0.0	1111 1111 1111 1111 **0000 0000 0000 0000**
AND result	8.1.0.0	0000 1000 0000 0001 **0000 0000 0000 0000**
Broadcast	8.1.255.255	0000 1000 0000 0001 **1111 1111 1111 1111**

Table 12-16 *Calculating Broadcast Address, Address 130.4.102.1, Mask 255.255.255.0*

Address	130.4.102.1	1000 0010 0000 0100 0110 0110 **0000 0001**
Mask	255.255.255.0	1111 1111 1111 1111 1111 1111 **0000 0000**
AND result	130.4.102.0	1000 0010 0000 0100 0110 0110 **0000 0000**
Broadcast	130.4.102.255	1000 0010 0000 0100 0110 0110 **1111 1111**

Table 12-17 *Calculating Broadcast Address, Address 199.1.1.100, Mask 255.255.255.0*

Address	199.1.1.100	1100 0111 0000 0001 0000 0001 **0110 0100**
Mask	255.255.255.0	1111 1111 1111 1111 1111 1111 **0000 0000**
AND result	199.1.1.0	1100 0111 0000 0001 0000 0001 **0000 0000**
Broadcast	199.1.1.255	1100 0111 0000 0001 0000 0001 **1111 1111**

Table 12-18 *Calculating Broadcast Address, Address 130.4.102.1, Mask 255.255.252.0*

Address	130.4.102.1	1000 0010 0000 0100 0110 01**10 0000 0001**
Mask	255.255.252.0	1111 1111 1111 1111 1111 11**00 0000 0000**
AND result	130.4.100.0	1000 0010 0000 0100 0110 01**00 0000 0000**
Broadcast	130.4.103.255	1000 0010 0000 0100 0110 01**11 1111 1111**

Table 12-19 *Calculating Broadcast Address, Address 199.1.1.100, Mask 255.255.255.224*

Address	199.1.1.100	1100 0111 0000 0001 0000 0001 0110 **0100**
Mask	255.255.255.224	1111 1111 1111 1111 1111 1111 1110 **0000**
AND result	199.1.1.96	1100 0111 0000 0001 0000 0001 0110 **0000**
Broadcast	199.1.1.127	1100 0111 0000 0001 0000 0001 0111 **1111**

Simply by examining the subnet broadcast addresses in binary, you can see that they are identical to the subnet numbers, except that all host bits have a value of binary 1 instead of binary 0. (Look for the bold digits in the examples.)

NOTE For those of you who just want to know, to derive the broadcast address using Boolean math, first start with the subnet number and mask, in binary. Invert the mask ("invert" means change all 1s to 0s, and all 0s to 1s). Then do a bitwise Boolean OR between the two 32-bit numbers. (An OR yields a 0 when both bits are 0 and yields a 1 in any other case.) The result is the subnet broadcast address.

Finding the Range of Valid IP Addresses in a Subnet

You also need to be able to figure out which IP addresses are in a particular subnet and which are not. You already know how to do the hard part of finding that answer. You know that in any subnet, two numbers are reserved. The two reserved numbers are the subnet number itself and the subnet broadcast address. The subnet number is the numerically smallest number in the subnet, and the broadcast address is the numerically largest number. So, the range of valid IP addresses starts with one more than the subnet number and ends with the address that is one less than the broadcast address. It's that simple!

A formal definition of the "algorithm" to find the first and last IP addresses in a subnet after the subnet number and broadcast addresses are known is as follows:

■ For the first valid IP address: Copy the subnet number, but add 1 to the fourth octet.

■ For the last valid IP address: Copy the subnet broadcast address, but subtract 1 from the fourth octet.

■ The range of valid IP addresses starts with the first number and ends with the last.

Tables 12-20 through 12-24 summarize the answers for the five examples used in this section.

Table 12-20 *Subnet Chart—130.4.102.1/255.255.255.0*

Octet	1	2	3	4
Address	130	4	102	1
Mask	255	255	255	0
Subnet number	130	4	102	0
First address	130	4	102	1
Broadcast	130	4	102	255
Last address	130	4	102	254

Table 12-21 *Subnet Chart—130.4.102.1/255.255.252.0*

Octet	1	2	3	4
Address	130	4	102	1
Mask	255	255	252	0
Subnet number	130	4	100	0
First address	130	4	100	1
Broadcast	130	4	103	255
Last address	130	4	103	254

Table 12-22 *Subnet Chart—8.1.4.5/255.255.0.0*

Octet	1	2	3	4
Address	8	1	4	5
Mask	255	255	0	0
Subnet number	8	1	0	0
First address	8	1	0	1
Broadcast	8	1	255	255
Last address	8	1	255	254

Table 12-23   *Subnet Chart—199.1.1.100/255.255.255.0*

Octet	1	2	3	4
Address	199	1	1	100
Mask	255	255	255	0
Subnet number	199	1	1	0
First address	199	1	1	1
Broadcast	199	1	1	255
Last address	199	1	1	254

Table 12-24   *Subnet Chart—199.1.1.100/255.255.255.224*

Octet	1	2	3	4
Address	199	1	1	100
Mask	255	255	255	224
Subnet number	199	1	1	96
First address	199	1	1	97
Broadcast	199	1	1	127
Last address	199	1	1	126

Finding the Answers Without Using Binary

You actually can derive the subnet number and broadcast addresses without ever converting to and from binary, or performing Boolean math. Using the binary math required to find the subnet number and broadcast address really does help you understand subnetting to some degree. To get the correct answers faster on the exam, you might want to avoid all the conversions and binary math.

If you can find the subnet number and broadcast address, you easily can find the range of valid addresses in the subnet. So, the easy math described in this section focuses on helping you find the subnet number and broadcast address.

Easier Math with Easy Masks

Of all the possible subnet masks, three masks, 255.0.0.0, 255.255.0.0, and 255.255.255.0, use only 255s and 0s. I call these masks "easy" masks because you can find the subnet number and broadcast address easily, without any real math tricks. In fact, some of you might have realized already how to find the answers when an easy mask is used—if so, go ahead and skip to the section titled "Easier Math with Difficult Masks."

In fact, of these three easy masks, 255.0.0.0 does not actually cause any subnetting. So, this section worries about only how to use the two easy masks that can be used for subnetting— 255.255.0.0 and 255.255.255.0.

The process is simple. To find the subnet number, when given an IP address and a mask of 255.255.0.0 or 255.255.255.0, do the following:

Step 1   Copy the first two (mask 255.255.0.0) or first three (mask 255.255.255.0) octets from the original IP address.

Step 2   Write down 0s in the last two octets (mask 255.255.0.0) or the last octet (mask 255.255.255.0).

Yep, it's that easy! Finding the subnet broadcast address is just as easy:

> Do the same thing that you did for finding the subnet, but instead of writing down 0s in the last octet or two, write down 255s.

When you know the subnet number and broadcast address, you easily can find the first and last IP addresses in the subnet, using the same simple logic covered earlier:

■   To find the first valid IP address in the subnet, copy the subnet number, but add 1 to the fourth octet.

■   To find the last valid IP address in the subnet, copy the broadcast address, but subtract 1 from the fourth octet.

Easier Math with Difficult Masks

When the subnet mask is not 255.255.0.0 or 255.255.255.0, I consider the mask to be a difficult mask. Why is it difficult? Most people cannot easily derive the subnet number and broadcast address without using binary math. You can use the same binary processes exactly the same way, whether the mask is easy or difficult. However, these binary processes take time to do when you cannot use a calculator. So, a quicker method for finding the same answers can help.

The following process helps you find the subnet number and broadcast address without binary math when using a difficult mask. You also can find 25 more problems with solutions on the CD chapter titled, "Subnetting Practice: 25 Subnetting Questions." The process uses something I call a subnet chart, as shown in Table 12-25.

Table 12-25   *Subnet Chart—Generic*

Octet	1	2	3	4
Address				
Mask				
Subnet number				
First address				
Broadcast				
Last address				

With the type of question this shortcut is helping you to answer, the question supplies the address and subnet mask. So, you would simply record the IP address and mask in the table, putting each octet in a different column.

The unusual part of this shortcut begins when you draw a box around the "interesting" octet in the table. I call a mask octet that's not a 255 or a 0 the interesting octet because it is the octet that gives everyone heartburn when first learning subnetting. The box draws attention to the tricky part of the logic used in this shortcut.

For example, consider 130.4.102.1, with mask 255.255.252.0. Because the third octet of the mask is not a 0 or a 255, the third octet is where the interesting part of the shortcut takes place. So, you would create a subnet chart, fill in the address and mask, and draw a box around the third octet, as shown in Table 12-26.

Table 12-26   *Subnet Chart—130.4.102.1/255.255.252.0, After Drawing a Box Around the Interesting Octet*

Octet	1	2	3	4
Address	130	4	102	1
Mask	255	255	252	0
Subnet number				
First address				
Broadcast				
Last address				

Next, you should complete the chart for everything to the left of the box. To complete the chart, look at the original IP address octets to the left of the box, and copy those into the subnet, first valid address, broadcast, and last valid address fields. Note that only octets fully to the left of the box should be copied—the interesting octet, which is inside the box, should not be copied. Table 12-27 shows the same example, after this step.

Table 12-27 *Subnet Chart—130.4.102.1/255.255.252.0, After Copying Octets to the Left*

Octet	1	2	3	4
Address	130	4	102	1
Mask	255	255	252	0
Subnet number	130	4		
First address	130	4		
Broadcast	130	4		
Last address	130	4		

To find the subnet number, you have a couple of steps. The first step is easy. In the subnet number, for any octets fully to the right of the box, write down a 0. That should leave you with one octet of the subnet number missing—the interesting octet.

Next comes the tricky part of this shortcut, which gives you the value of the subnet number in the interesting octet. First, you find what I will call the *magic number*—which is 256 minus the *mask's interesting octet*. In this case, you have 256 – 252, or a magic number of 4. Then you find the multiple of the magic number that is the closest to the *address's interesting octet*, but less than or equal to it. In this example, 100 is a multiple of the magic number (4 * 25), and this multiple is less than or equal to 102. The next-higher multiple of the magic number, which is 104, is, of course, more than 102, so that's not the right number. The multiple of the magic number closest to but not more than the address's interesting octet is the subnet's interesting octet value. The following items summarize this important step:

Step 1 Find the magic number, which is 256 minus the value of the mask's interesting octet.

Step 2 Find the multiple of the magic number that is closest to, but not greater than, the address's interesting octet.

Step 3 Write down that multiple of the magic number as the value of the subnet number's interesting octet.

In this example, simply plug in 100 for the third octet of the subnet number in Table 12-27.

When you know the subnet number, you easily can find the first valid IP address in the subnet:

> To find the first valid IP address in the subnet, copy the subnet number, but add 1 to the fourth octet.

That's all! Table 12-28 shows the same example, but with the subnet number and first valid IP address shown

Table 12-28 *Subnet Chart—130.4.102.1/255.255.252.0, with Subnet and First IP Address*

Octet	1	2	3	4	Comments
Address	130	4	102	1	
Mask	255	255	252	0	
Subnet number	130	4	100	0	Magic = 256 – 252 = 4; 4 * 25 = 100, closest multiple < 102.
First address	130	4	100	1	Add 1 to subnet's last octet
Broadcast	130	4			
Last address	130	4			

To review, in Table 12-28, the first two octets of the subnet number and first valid address already were filled in because they are to the left of the box around the third octet—the interesting octet, in this case. In the subnet number, the last octet is 0 because it is to the right of the box. To find the interesting octet value, compare the IP address's interesting octet to find the closest multiple of the magic number that's not larger, which is 100 in this case. To get the first valid address, just add 1 to the last octet of the subnet number, giving you 130.4.100.1.

The final step in the shortcut finds the broadcast address, from which you easily can find the last valid address in the subnet. First, in the broadcast address, write down a decimal 255 for all octets to the right of the line or the box. Do not write down a 255 in the octet inside the box. Remember, the octets to the left of the box in the subnet chart already should have been filled in, leaving a single octet with no value—the interesting octet. To fill in the interesting octet of the broadcast address, you again use the magic number. The magic number is 256 minus the mask's interesting octet. In this case, you have 256 – 252, or a magic number of 4. Then you add the magic number to the interesting octet value of the subnet number and subtract 1. The result is the broadcast address's value in the interesting octet. In this case, the value is as follows:

100 + 4 (magic number) – 1 = 103

When you know the broadcast address, you easily can find the last valid IP address in the subnet:

> To find the last valid IP address in the subnet, copy the broadcast address, but subtract 1 from the fourth octet.

To summarize the tricky part of this shortcut algorithm:

> To find the broadcast address's interesting octet value, take the subnet number's interesting octet value, add the magic number, and subtract 1.

Table 12-29 shows the completed answers, with annotations.

Table 12-29 *Subnet Chart—130.4.102.1/255.255.252.0, Complete*

Octet	1	2	3	4	Comments
Address	130	4	102	1	
Mask	255	255	252	0	
Subnet number	130	4	100	0	Magic = 256 – 252 = 100; 25 × 4 = 100, closest multiple < 102
First address	130	4	100	1	Add 1 to fourth octet of subnet
Broadcast	130	4	103	255	Subnet-interesting-octet + magic – 1 (100 + 4 – 1)
Last address	130	4	103	254	Subtract 1 from fourth octet

The entire process for dissecting IP addresses that use difficult masks is now complete. The following list summarizes the tasks in each step:

Step 1   Create and complete the easy parts of a subnet chart.

- Create a generic subnet chart.
- Write down the IP address and subnet mask in the first two rows of the chart.
- Draw a box around the column of the interesting octet.
- Copy the address octets to the left of the line or the box into the final four rows of the chart.

Step 2   Derive the subnet number and the first valid IP address.

- Write down 0s in the subnet number for the octets to the right of the box.
- Find the magic number, which is 256 minus the value of the mask's interesting octet.
- Find the multiple of the magic number that is closest to but not greater than the address's interesting octet.

- Write down that multiple of the magic number as the value of the subnet number's interesting octet.

- To find the first valid IP address in the subnet, copy the subnet number, but add 1 to the fourth octet.

Step 3   Derive the broadcast address and the last valid IP address.

- Write down 255s in the broadcast address octets to the right of the line or the box.

- To find the broadcast address's interesting octet value, take the subnet number's interesting octet value, add the magic number, and subtract 1.

- To find the last valid IP address in the subnet, copy the broadcast address, but subtract 1 from the fourth octet.

Becoming proficient at this shortcut will take some practice. To make sure you have the process down, review the examples in the CD chapter, "Subnetting Practice: 25 Subnetting Questions," which has 25 different examples, including the Boolean AND and shortcut methods of finding the subnet number.

What Subnet Masks Meet the Stated Design Requirements?

So far in this chapter, the text has explained how to answer questions that provide the subnet number. However, some questions do not supply the subnet number, but instead ask you to choose the "correct" subnet mask, given a set of requirements. The most common of these questions reads something like this:

> You are using Class B network X, and you need to have 200 subnets, with at most 200 hosts per subnet. Which of the following subnet masks can be used? (followed by some subnet masks that you can pick from for the answer)

The find the correct answers to these types of questions, you first need to decide how many subnet bits and host bits you need to meet the requirements. Basically, the number of hosts per subnet is $2^x - 2$, where x is the number of host bits in the address. Likewise, the number of subnets of a network, assuming that the same subnet mask is used all over the network, is also $2^x - 2$, but with x being the number of subnet bits. When you know how many subnet bits and host bits are required, you can figure out what mask, or masks, meet the stated design goals in the question.

Examples certainly help; the first example question reads like this:

> Your network can use Class B network 130.1.0.0. What subnet masks meet the requirement that you plan to allow at most 200 subnets, with at most 200 hosts per subnet?

First, you need to figure out how many subnet bits allow for 200 subnets. You simply can use the formula $2^x - 2$ and plug in values for x, until one of the numbers is at least 200. In this case, x turns out to be 8—in other words, you need at least 8 subnet bits to allow for 200 subnets.

If you do not want to keep plugging in values into the $2^x - 2$ formula, you can instead memorize Table 12-30.

Table 12-30 *Maximum Number of Subnets/Hosts*

Number of Bits in the Host or Subnet Field	Maximum Number of Hosts or Subnets ($2^x - 2$)
1	0
2	2
3	6
4	14
5	30
6	62
7	126
8	254
9	510
10	1022
11	2046
12	4094
13	8190
14	16,382

As you can see, if you already have the powers of 2 memorized, you really do not need to memorize the table—just remember the formula.

As for the first example question, 7 subnet bits are not enough because that allows for only 126 subnets. You need 8 subnet bits. Similarly, because you need up to 200 hosts per subnet, you need 8 host bits.

Finally, you need to decide somehow what mask(s) to use, knowing that you have a Class B network and that you must have at least 8 subnet bits and 8 host bits. Using the letter N to represent network bits, the letter S to represent subnet bits, and the letter H to represent host bits, the following text shows the sizes of the various fields:

NNNNNNNN NNNNNNNN SSSSSSSS HHHHHHHH

All that is left is to derive the actual subnet mask. Because you need 8 bits for the subnet field and 8 for the host field, and the network field takes up 16 bits, you already have allocated all 32 bits of the address structure. So, only one possible subnet mask works. To figure out the mask, you need to write down the 32-bit subnet mask, applying the following fact and subnet masks:

> The network and subnet bits in a subnet mask are, by definition, all binary 1s. Similarly, the host bits in a subnet mask are, by definition, all binary 0s.

So, the only valid subnet mask, in binary, is this:

> 11111111 11111111 11111111 00000000

When converted to decimal, this is 255.255.255.0.

A second example shows how the requirements stated in the question might allow for multiple possible subnet masks. For instance:

> Your network can use Class B network 130.1.0.0. What subnet masks meet the requirement that you plan to allow at most 50 subnets, with at most 200 hosts per subnet?

For this design, you still need at least 8 host bits, but now you need only at least 6 subnet bits. Six subnet bits would allow for $2^6 - 2$, or 62, subnets. Following the same convention as before, but now using an x for bits that can be either subnet or host bits, the format of the address struture would be as follows:

> NNNNNNNN NNNNNNNN SSSSSS**XX** HHHHHHHH

In other words, the addresses will have 16 network bits, at least 6 subnet bits, and at least 8 host bits. This example actually allows for three valid subnet masks, whose strcuture are as follows:

> NNNNNNNN NNNNNNNN SSSSSSSS HHHHHHHH—8 subnet, 8 host
> NNNNNNNN NNNNNNNN SSSSSSS**H** HHHHHHHH—7 subnet, 9 host
> NNNNNNNN NNNNNNNN SSSSSS**HH** HHHHHHHH—6 subnet, 10 host

So, based on the requirements in the question, three different valid subnet masks meet the requirements. The three values are as follows:

> 11111111 11111111 1111111**1** 00000000 255.255.255.0
> 11111111 11111111 1111111**0** 00000000 255.255.254.0
> 11111111 11111111 111111**00** 00000000 255.255.252.0

The 2 bits that could be subnet bits or host bits, based on the requirements, are shown in bold.

What Are the Other Subnet Numbers?

The final general type of IP addresing and subnetting question covered in this chapter asks you to list all the subnets of a particular network. You could use a long process, which requires you to count in binary and convert many numbers from binary to decimal. However, because most people would either learn the shortcut or use a subnet calculator in their normal jobs, I decided to just show you the shortcut method for this particular type of question.

First, the question needs a better definition—or, at least, a more complete one. The question might be better stated like this:

> If the same subnet mask is used for all subnets of this Class A, B, or C network, what are the valid subnets?

IP design conventions do not require the engineer to use the same mask for every subnet. Unless specifically stated, the question "What are all the subnets?" probably assumes that the same mask is used for all subnets, unless the question specifically states that different masks can be used on different subnets.

The following easy decimal process lists all the valid subnets, given the network number, and the only mask used on that network. This three-step process assumes that the size of the subnet part of the address is, at most, 8 bits in length. The same general process can be expanded to work when the size of the subnet part of the address is more than 8 bits, but that expanded process is not described here.

The three-step process uses a chart that I call the *subnet list chart*. I made up the name just for this book, simply as another tool to use. Table 12-31 presents a generic version of the subnet list chart.

Table 12-31   *Three-Step Process Generic Subnet List Chart*

Octet	1	2	3	4
Network number				
Mask				
Subnet zero				
First subnet				
Next subnet				
Last subnet				
Broadcast subnet				

You list the known network number and subnet mask as the first step in the process. If the question gives you an IP address and mask instead of the network number and mask, just write down the network number of which that IP address is a member. (Remember, this three-step process assumes that the subnet part of the addresses is 8 bits or less.)

For the second of the three steps, copy the network number into the row labeled "Subnet Zero." *Subnet zero*, or the *zero subnet*, is numerically the first subnet, and it is one of the two reserved subnet numbers in a network. (You can use the zero subnet on a Cisco router if you configure the global configuration command **ip zero-subnet**.) Interestingly, a network's zero subnet has the exact same numeric value as the network itself—which is one of the reasons that it should not be used. For the purposes of answering questions on the exam about the number of valid subnets in a network, consider the zero subnet unusable unless the question tells you that using it is ok. In real life, do not use the zero subnet if you do not have to.

The third step in the process will be covered after Tables 12-32 and 12-33, which list two familiar examples, with the first two steps completed.

Table 12-32 *Subnet List Chart—130.4.0.0/24*

Octet	1	2	3	4
Network number	130	4	0	0
Mask	255	255	255	0
Subnet zero	130	4	0	0

Table 12-33 *Subnet List Chart—130.4.0.0/22*

Octet	1	2	3	4
Network number	130	4	0	0
Mask	255	255	252	0
Subnet zero	130	4	0	0

The last step in this process, Step 3, is repeated many times. This last step uses the magic number, which is 256 minus the mask octet value in the interesting octet. With this process of finding all the subnet numbers, the interesting octet is the octet that contains *all* of the subnet part of the addresses. (Remember, the process assumes 8 or fewer subnet bits!) In both Tables 11-32 and 11-33, the interesting octet is the third octet.

The third and final step in the process to find all the subnet numbers goes like this: Starting with the last row that's completed in the table, do the following:

a. Because this process assumes 1 byte or less in the subnet part of the addresses, on the next row of the table, copy down the three octets that are not part of the subnet field. Call the octet that is not copied down the "subnet octet" or "interesting octet."

b. Add the magic number to the previous subnet octet, and write that down as the value of the subnet octet.

c. Repeat the last two tasks until the next number that you would write down in the subnet octet is 256. (Don't write that one down—it's not valid.)

The idea behind the process of finding all the subnets becomes apparent by reviewing the same two examples used earlier. First, Table 12-34 lists the example with the easy mask. Note that the magic number is 256 – 255 = 1 in this case, and that the third octet is the interesting subnet octet.

Table 12-34 *Subnet List Chart—130.4.0.0/255.255.255.0 Completed*

Octet	1	2	3	4
Network number	130	4	0	0
Mask	255	255	255	0
Subnet zero	130	4	0	0
First subnet	130	4	1	0
Next subnet	130	4	2	0
Next subnet	130	4	3	0
Next subnet	130	4	4	0
(Skipping a bunch)	130	4	X	0
Last subnet	130	4	254	0
Broadcast subnet	130	4	255	0

The logic behind how the process works might be better understood by looking at the first few entries and then the last few entries. The zero subnet is found easily because it's the same number as the network number. The magic number is 256 – 255 = 1, in this case. Essentially, you increment the third octet (in this case) by the magic number for each successive subnet number.

In the middle of the table, one row is labeled "Skipping a Bunch." Instead of making the book even bigger, I left out several entries but included enough that you could see that the subnet number's third octet just gets bigger by 1, in this case, for each successive subnet number.

Looking at the end of the table, the last entry lists 255 in the third octet. 256 decimal is never a valid value in any IP address, and the directions said to not write down a subnet with 256 in it, so the last number in the table is 130.4.255.0. *The last subnet is the broadcast subnet, which is the other reserved subnet number. The subnet before the broadcast subnet is the highest, or last, valid subnet number.*

With a simple subnet mask, the process of answering this type of question is very simple. In fact, many people might even refer to these subnets using just the third octet. If all subnets of a particular organization were in network 130.4.0.0, with mask 255.255.255.0, you might say simply "subnet five" when referring to subnet 130.4.5.0.

The process works the same with difficult subnet masks, even though the answers are not as intuitive. Table 12-35 lists the answers for the second example, using a mask of 255.255.252.0 The third octet is again the interesting subnet octet, but this time the magic number is 256 − 252 = 4.

Table 12-35 *Subnet List Chart—130.4.0.0/255.255.252.0*

Octet	1	2	3	4
Network number	130	4	0	0
Mask	255	255	252	0
Subnet zero	130	4	0	0
First subnet	130	4	4	0
Next valid subnet	130	4	8	0
Skip a lot	130	4	X	0
Last subnet	130	4	248	0
Broadcast subnet	130	4	252	0

The first subnet number numerically, the zero subnet, starts the list. By adding the magic number in the interesting octet, you find the rest of the subnet numbers. Like the previous example, to save space in the book, many subnet numbers were skipped.

Most of us would not guess that 130.4.252.0 was the broadcast subnet for this latest example. However, adding the magic number 4 to 252 would give you 256 as the next subnet number, which is not valid—so, 130.4.252.0 is indeed the broadcast subnet.

The three-step process to find all the subnet numbers of a network is shown here:

1. Write down the network number and subnet mask in the first two rows of the subnet list chart.

2. Write down the network number in the third row. This is the zero subnet, which is one of the two reserved subnets.

3.   Do the following two tasks, stopping when the next number that you would write down in the interesting column is 256. (Don't write that one down—it's not valid.)

a.   Copy all three noninteresting octets from the previous line.

b.   Add the magic number to the previous interesting octet, and write that down as the value of the interesting octet.

Scaling the IP Address Space for the Internet

The original design for the Internet required every organization to ask for and receive one or more registered IP network numbers. The people administering the program ensured that none of the IP network numbers was used by multiple companies or organizations. As long as every organization used only IP addresses inside their own registered network numbers, then IP addresses would never be duplicated and IP routing could work well.

Connecting to the Internet using only a registered network number or several registered network numbers worked very well for a while. In the early and mid-1990s, it became apparent that the Internet was growing so fast that all IP network numbers would be assigned by the mid-1990s. Concern arose that all the network numbers would be assigned, so some organizations would not be capable of connecting to the Internet. It would have been the equivalent of calling the local phone company to ask for a new phone line to be installed and being told that the company ran out of numbers; you would have to wait until someone didn't want a phone number any more!

This last section covers several features that together have allowed the Internet to grow, without letting us run out of IP addresses. Network Address Translation (NAT), along with a feature called *private addressing*, allows organizations to use unregistered IP network numbers internally and still communicate well with the Internet. Classless Interdomain Routing (CIDR) allows Internet service providers (ISPs) to reduce the wasting of IP addresses, by assigning a company a subset of a network number instead of the entire network. CIDR also reduces the size of Internet routing tables, allowing the Internet to grow. Also, a new version of IP, IP Version 6, uses much larger addresses, 128-bit long addresses, which allow for (hopefully) enough IP addresses so that we will never possibly run out again.

CIDR

CIDR is a convention defined in RFC 1817 (www.ietf.org/rfc/rfc1817.txt) that calls for aggregating multiple network numbers into a single routing entity. CIDR actually was created to help the scalability of Internet routers—imagine a router in the Internet with a route to every Class A, B, and C network on the planet! There are actually a little more than two million Class C networks alone! By aggregating the routes, Internet routers have a significantly smaller number of routes in their routing tables.

Figure 12-5 shows a typical case of how CIDR might be used to consolidate routes to multiple Class C networks into a single route.

Figure 12-5 *Typical Use of CIDR*

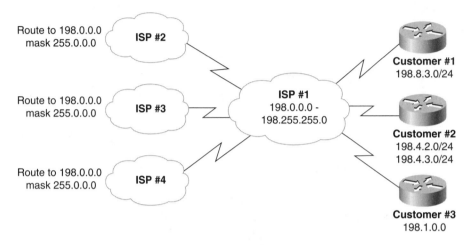

Imagine that ISP 1 owns Class C networks 198.0.0.0 through 198.255.255.0 (they might look funny, but they are valid Class C network numbers). Without CIDR, all other ISPs' routing tables would have a separate route to each of the 2^{16} Class C networks that begin with 198. With CIDR, as the illustration shows, the other ISPs' routers will have a single route to 198.0.0.0/8—in other words, a route to all hosts whose IP address begins with 198. More than two million Class C networks alone exist, but CIDR has helped Internet routers reduce their routing tables to a more manageable size, in the range of 120,000 routes by mid-2003.

By using a routing protocol that exchanges the mask as well as the subnet/network number, a classless view of the number can be attained. In other words, routers treat the grouping as a math problem, ignoring the Class A, B, and C rules. For instance, 198.0.0.0/8 (198.0.0.0, mask 255.0.0.0) defines a set of addresses whose first 8 bits are equal to decimal 198. This route is advertised by ISP 1 to the other ISPs, which need a route only to 198.0.0.0/8. In its routers, ISP 1 knows which Class C networks are at which customer sites. This is how CIDR gives Internet routers a much more scalable routing table, by reducing the number of entries in the tables.

For CIDR to work as shown in Figure 12-5, ISPs need to be in control of consecutive network numbers. Today IP networks are allocated by administrative authorities for various regions of the world, which, in turn, allocate consecutive ranges of network numbers to particular ISPs in those regions. This allows summarization of multiple networks into a single route, as shown in Figure 12-5.

CIDR also helps to reduce the chance that we will run out of IP addresses for new companies connecting to the Internet. CIDR also allows an ISP to allocate a subset of a Class A, B, or C network to a single customer. For instance, imagine that ISP 1's Customer 1 needs only 10 IP addresses and that Customer 3 needs 25 IP addresses. So, ISP 1 does something like this: It assigns IP subnet 198.8.3.16/28, with assignable addresses 198.8.17 to 198.8.30, to Customer 1. For Customer 3, ISP 1 suggests 198.8.3.32/27, with 30 assignable addresses (198.8.3.33 to 198.8.3.62). (Feel free to check the math with the IP addressing algorithms listed earlier.)

CIDR helps prevent the wasting of IP addresses, thereby reducing the need for registered IP network numbers. Instead of the two customers consuming two whole Class C networks, each consumes a small portion of a single Class C network. At the same time, CIDR, along with the intelligent administration of consecutive network numbers to each ISP, allows the Internet routing table to support a much smaller routing table in Internet routers than otherwise would be required.

Private Addressing

Some computers will never be connected to the Internet. These computers' IP addresses could be duplicates of registered IP addresses in the Internet. So, when designing the IP addressing convention for such a network, an organization could pick and use any network number(s) that it wanted, and all would be well. For instance, you can buy a few routers, connect them together in your office, and configure IP addresses in network 1.0.0.0 and make it work. The IP addresses that you use might be duplicates of real IP addresses in the Internet, but if all you want to do is learn on the lab in your office, all is well.

When building a private network that will have no Internet connectivity, you also can use IP network numbers called *private internets*, as defined in RFC 1918, "Address Allocation for Private Internets" (www.ietf.org/rfc/rfc1918.txt). This RFC defines a set of networks that never will be assigned to any organization as a registered network number. Instead of using someone else's registered network numbers, you can use numbers in a range that are not used by anyone in the public Internet. Table 12-36 shows the private address space defined by RFC 1918.

Table 12-36 *RFC 1918 Private Address Space*

Range of IP Addresses	Class of Networks	Number of Networks
10.0.0.0 to 10.255.255.255	A	1
172.16.0.0 to 172.31.255.255	B	16
192.168.0.0 to 192.168.255.255	C	256

In other words, any organization can use these network numbers. However, no organization is allowed to advertise these networks using a routing protocol on the Internet.

Many of you might be wondering, "Why bother reseverving special private network numbers when it doesn't matter whether the addresses are duplicates?" Well, as it turns out, you can use private addressing in a network and use the Internet at the same time, as long as you use the next feature covered in this chapter—Network Address Translation (NAT).

Network Address Translation

NAT, defined in RFC 1631, allows a host that does not have a valid registered IP address to communicate with other hosts through the Internet. Of course, if you do not have to use a registered IP address, you can help avoid the day when we run out of available IP addresses! NAT allows these addresses that are not Internet-ready to continue to be used but still allows communication with hosts across the Internet. The ICND exam covers NAT in more detail, including configuration.

To conserve addresses, NAT uses an additional feature called Port Address Translation (PAT). PAT takes advantage of the fact that a server really does not care whether it has one connection each to three different hosts, or three connections to a single host IP address. So, to support lots of private IP addresses with only one or a few publicly registered IP addresses, NAT/PAT translates the private IP address into a valid public address as the packet exits the private IP network. However, instead of just translating the IP address, it also translates the port number. Figure 12-6 outlines the logic.

Figure 12-6   *NAT Overload Using PAT*

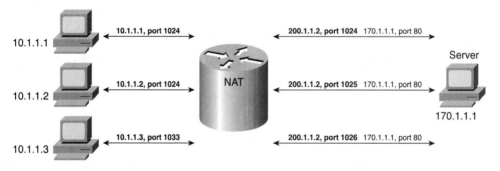

Dynamic NAT Table, With Overloading

Inside Local	Inside Global
10.1.1.1:1024	200.1.1.2:1024
10.1.1.2:1024	200.1.1.2:1025
10.1.1.3:1033	200.1.1.2:1026

The NAT router keeps a NAT table entry for every unique combination of private IP address and port, with translation to the public IP address and a unique port number associated with the public IP address. Because the port number field has 16 bits, NAT/PAT can support more than 64,000 connections using one public IP address, which helps the IP address space scale.

IP Version 6 Addressing

The short-term solution to the problem of depleting the entire IPv4 address space included NAT and private addressing. CIDR provider a short-term solution to the growing size of IP routing tables. The long-term solution to both problems, at least according to some, is to use a new version of the IP protocol—Version 6 (IPv6). (The version discussed in this book is Version 4. Version 5 was defined for experimental reasons and never was deployed.)

IPv6 calls for a much larger address structure so that the convention of all organizations using unique groupings (networks) of IP addresses still would be reasonable—the numbers of IPv6-style networks would reach into the trillions and beyond. That solution is still technically viable and possibly one day will be used. However, many people believe that the short-term solutions have made IPv4 viable for a long time, and they see no reason to upgrade. Others think that IPv6 is inevitable. Cisco simply supports both options, so whatever happens, it will still be able to sell products.

IPv6 uses a 128-bit IP address written in hexadecimal notation, with colons between each quartet of symbols. How many addresses can you possibly have with a 128-bit number? The only answer that matters in real life is "more than you can possibly ever need." The number is around 3.4×10^{38}—yes, that's a 39-digit decimal number. It's huge! You could have a million IP addresses per every person who ever has lived and still not have run out. So, a migration to IPv6 certainly looks like it solves the IP address scalability problem—the only question is whether the other short-term solutions, such as NAT and CIDR, have solved IPv4's problems so well that no one wants to migrate to IPv6.

Table 12-37 summarizes some of the pertinent information comparing IPv4 addresses with IPv6.

Table 12-37 *IPv4 Versus IPv6*

Feature	IPv4	IPv6
Size of address (bits or bytes per octets)	32 bits, 4 octets	128 bits, 16 octets
Example address	10.1.1.1	0000:0000:0000:0000:0000:FFFF:FFFF:0A01:0101
Number of possible addresses, ignoring reserved values	2^{32}, (roughly 4 billion)	2^{128}, or roughly $3.4 * 10^{38}$

Foundation Summary

The "Foundation Summary" section of each chapter lists the most important facts from the chapter. Although this section does not list every fact from the chapter that will be on your CCNA exam(s), a well-prepared CCNA candidate should know, at a minimum, all the details in each "Foundation Summary" section before going to take the exam.

The thought process used to answer questions about the number of hosts and subnets in a network, based on a network number and a subnet mask, is summarized in the following list:

Step 1   Identify the structure of the IP address.

Step 2   Identify the size of the network part of the address, based on Class A, B, and C rules.

Step 3   Identify the size of the host part of the address, based on the number of binary 0s in the mask.

Step 4   The size of the subnet part is what's left over; mathematically, it is 32 – (number of network + host bits).

Step 5   Declare the number of subnets, which is $2^{number\text{-}of\text{-}subnet\text{-}bits} - 2$.

Step 6   Declare the number of hosts per subnet, which is $2^{number\text{-}of\text{-}host\text{-}bits} - 2$.

A formal definition of the "algorithm" to find the first and last IP addresses in a subnet when the subnet number and broadcast addresses are known is as follows:

■   For the first valid IP address: Copy the subnet number, but add 1 to the fourth octet.

■   For the last valid IP address: Copy the broadcast address, but subtract 1 from the fourth octet.

■   The range of valid IP addresses starts with the first number and ends with the last.

To find the subnet number, perform a Boolean AND between the address and the subnet mask. For example, see Table 12-38.

Table 12-38   *Bitwise Boolean AND Example*

	Decimal	Binary
Address	150.150.2.1	1001 0110 1001 0110 0000 0010 0000 0001
Mask	255.255.255.0	1111 1111 1111 1111 1111 1111 0000 0000
Result of AND	150.150.2.0	1001 0110 1001 0110 0000 0010 0000 0000

To find the subnet broadcast address, take the subnet number in binary and change all the host bits to binary 1s.

The following three-step process lists all the subnet numbers of a network. The process refers to the chart that follows the three-step list:

Step 1   Write down the network number and subnet mask in the first two rows of the subnet list chart.

Step 2   Write down the network number in the third row. This is the zero subnet, which is one of the two reserved subnets.

Step 3   Do the following two tasks, stopping when the next number that you would write down in the interesting column is 256. (Don't write that one down—it's not valid.)

    a.   Copy all three noninteresting octets from the previous line.

    b.   Add the magic number to the previous interesting octet, and write that down as the value of the interesting octet. (See Table 12-39).

Table 12-39 *Subnet List Chart*

Octet	1	2	3	4
Network number				
Mask				
Subnet zero				
First subnet				
Next subnet				
Skip a lot				
Last subnet				
Broadcast subnet				

Q&A

As mentioned in the introduction, you have two choices for review questions. The questions that follow give you a bigger challenge than the exam itself by using an open-ended question format. By reviewing now with this more difficult question format, you can exercise your memory better and prove your conceptual and factual knowledge of this chapter. The answers to these questions are found in Appendix A.

For those of you who want more questions and practice with subnetting, you have a couple of options. You can look at the appendix on the CD titled "Subnetting Practice: 25 Subnetting Questions." Also, if you bought the two-book set and you already own the *CCNA ICND Exam Certification Guide*, you can look at the questions at the end of Chapter 4 of that book. Chapter 4 of the other book repeats what is inside this chapter, for readers who buy just that book. However, more than half of the questions at the end of that chapter are different than the ones in this chapter, so you can get some more practice.

For more practice with exam-like question formats, including questions using a router simulator and multiple-choice questions, use the exam engine on the CD.

1. Name the parts of an IP address.

2. Define the term subnet mask. What do the bits in the mask whose values are binary 0 tell you about the corresponding IP address(es)?

3. Given the IP address 134.141.7.11 and the mask 255.255.255.0, what is the subnet number?

4. Given the IP address 193.193.7.7 and the mask 255.255.255.0, what is the subnet number?

5. Given the IP address 200.1.1.130 and the mask 255.255.255.224, what is the subnet number?

6. Given the IP address 220.8.7.100 and the mask 255.255.255.240, what is the subnet number?

7. Given the IP address 134.141.7.11 and the mask 255.255.255.0, what is the subnet broadcast address?

8. Given the IP address 193.193.7.7 and the mask 255.255.255.0, what is the broadcast address?

9. Given the IP address 200.1.1.130 and the mask 255.255.255.224, what is the broadcast address?

10.   Given the IP address 220.8.7.100 and the mask 255.255.255.240, what is the broadcast address?

11.   Given the IP address 134.141.7.11 and the mask 255.255.255.0, what are the assignable IP addresses in this subnet?

12.   Given the IP address 193.193.7.7 and the mask 255.255.255.0, what are the assignable IP addresses in this subnet?

13.   Given the IP address 200.1.1.130 and the mask 255.255.255.224, what are the assignable IP addresses in this subnet?

14.   Given the IP address 220.8.7.100 and the mask 255.255.255.240, what are the assignable IP addresses in this subnet?

15.   Given the IP address 134.141.7.7 and the mask 255.255.255.0, what are all the subnet numbers if the same (static) mask is used for all subnets in this network?

16.   Given the IP address 220.8.7.100 and the mask 255.255.255.240, what are all the subnet numbers if the same (static) mask is used for all subnets in this network?

17.   How many IP addresses could be assigned in each subnet of 134.141.0.0, assuming that a mask of 255.255.255.0 is used? If the same (static) mask is used for all subnets, how many subnets are there?

18.   How many IP addresses could be assigned in each subnet of 220.8.7.0, assuming that a mask of 255.255.255.240 is used? If the same (static) mask is used for all subnets, how many subnets are there?

19.   You design a network for a customer, and the customer insists that you use the same subnet mask on every subnet. The customer will use network 10.0.0.0 and needs 200 subnets, each with 200 hosts maximum. What subnet mask would you use to allow the largest amount of growth in subnets? Which mask would work and would allow for the most growth in the number of hosts per subnet?

20. Referring to Figure 12-7, Fred has been configured with IP address 10.1.1.1, Router A's Ethernet has been configured with 10.1.1.100, Router A's Serial interface uses 10.1.1.101, Router B's serial uses 10.1.1.102, Router B's Ethernet uses 10.1.1.200, and the web server uses 10.1.1.201. Mask 255.255.255.192 is used in all cases. Is anything wrong with this network? What is the easiest thing that could be done to fix it? You can assume any working interior routing protocol.

Figure 12-7 *Example Network for Subnetting Questions*

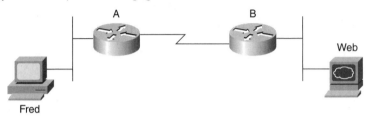

21. Referring to Figure 12-7, Fred has been configured with IP address 10.1.1.1, mask 255.255.255.0; Router A's Ethernet has been configured with 10.1.1.100, mask 255.255.255.224; Router A's serial interface uses 10.1.1.129, mask 255.255.255.252; Router B's serial uses 10.1.1.130, mask 255.255.255.252; Router B's Ethernet uses 10.1.1.200, mask 255.255.255.224; and the web server uses 10.1.1.201, mask 255.255.255.224. Is anything wrong with this network? What is the easiest thing that could be done to fix it? You can assume any working interior routing protocol.

22. Referring to Figure 12-7, Fred has been configured with IP address 10.1.1.1, mask 255.255.255.240; Router A's Ethernet has been configured with 10.1.1.2, mask 255.255.255.240; Router A's Serial interface uses 10.1.1.129, mask 255.255.255.252; Router B's serial uses 10.1.1.130, mask 255.255.255.252; Router B's Ethernet uses 10.1.1.200, mask 255.255.255.128; and the web server uses 10.1.1.201, mask 255.255.255.128. Is anything wrong with this network? What is the easiest thing that could be done to fix it? You can assume any working interior routing protocol.

23. What are the valid private IP network numbers, according to RFC 1918?

24. How large are IPv6 addresses?

25. How does CIDR help reduce the size of Internet routing tables?

This chapter covers the following subjects:

■ Configuring IP Addresses

■ IP Troubleshooting Features

CHAPTER 13

Basic Router Configuration and Operation

To configure a Cisco router to route TCP/IP packets, you typically configure an IP address and subnet mask on each interface. You also typically configure a dynamic routing protocol, which discovers the routes in a network. That's all the configuration that is required to make a Cisco router route IP packets.

In this chapter, you will read about the basic commands to configure IP addresses and IP routing on a Cisco router. You also will read about a variety of commands that you can use to discover how the router is working. By the end of this chapter, you will know how to configure Cisco routers to implement a simple IP network—with the exception that you will not yet have seen how to configure IP routing protocols. Chapter 14, "Introduction to Dynamic Routing Protocols," covers many of the concepts behind routing protocols, and chapters in the *CCNA ICND Exam Certification Guide* will show you how to configure several routing protocols.

"Do I Know This Already?" Quiz

The purpose of the "Do I Know This Already?" quiz is to help you decide whether you really need to read the entire chapter. If you already intend to read the entire chapter, you do not necessarily need to answer these questions now.

The ten-question quiz, derived from the major sections in "Foundation Topics" portion of the chapter, helps you determine how to spend your limited study time.

Table 13-1 outlines the major topics discussed in this chapter and the "Do I Know This Already?" quiz questions that correspond to those topics.

Table 13-1 *"Do I Know This Already?" Foundation Topics Section-to-Question Mapping*

Foundations Topics Section	Questions Covered in This Section
Configuring IP Addresses	1–4
IP Troubleshooting Features	5–10

> **CAUTION** The goal of self-assessment is to gauge your mastery of the topics in this chapter. If you do not know the answer to a question or are only partially sure of the answer, you should mark this question wrong for purposes of the self-assessment. Giving yourself credit for an answer that you correctly guess skews your self-assessment results and might provide you with a false sense of security.

1. Which of the following commands is valid for the configuration of IP address 10.1.1.1, mask 255.255.255.0?

   a. ip address 10.1.1.1

   b. ip address 10.1.1.1 mask 255.255.255.0

   c. ip address 10.1.1.1 255.255.255.0

   d. ip address 10.1.1.1 prefix /24

   e. ip address 10.1.1.1 /24

2. Which of the following must be true before Cisco IOS Software adds a connected route to the routing table?

   a. IP address must be configured on an interface.

   b. A router must receive a routing update from a neighboring router.

   c. The **ip route** command must be added to the configuration.

   d. The **ip address** command must use the **special** keyword.

   e. The interface status must be up and up.

3. Which of the following represents the same ideas as mask 255.255.240.0?

   a. /16

   b. /18

   c. /20

   d. /22

   e. /24

   f. /26

   g. /192

   h. /224

   i. /240

4. What command brings up an interface that previously was administratively disabled?

   a. no shutdown

   b. shutdown

   c. enable

   d. up

   e. no disable

   f. disable

5. Imagine that a PC is attached to the same Ethernet as a router. The PC makes a DNS request for host name Fred, and the PC gets a reply showing IP address 10.1.1.1. What command could be issued on the router to list the information learned in that DNS request and reply?

   a. show hosts

   b. show ip hosts

   c. show names

   d. None of the above

6. Imagine that a neighboring router's host name is Hannah. Which of these commands could tell you information about the IOS version on Hannah, without Telnetting to Hannah?

   a. show neighbor

   b. show neighbor Hannah

   c. show cdp

   d. show cdp Hannah

   e. show cdp interface

   f. show cdp neighbor

   g. show cdp neighbor Hannah

   h. show cdp entry hannah

   i. show cdp neighbor detail

7. What CDP command(s) could identify the model of hardware of a neighbor?

a. show neighbors

b. show neighbors Hannah

c. show cdp

d. show cdp Hannah

e. show cdp interface

f. show cdp neighbors

g. show cdp entry hannah

h. show cdp neighbors detail

8. Imagine that you used a **ping** command successfully. What messages would have been sent by the **ping** command?

a. ICMP ping

b. ICMP echo request

c. ICMP echo management

d. ICMP query

9. Imagine that you just erased all the configuration on a router and reloaded it. To configure the router to use a DNS at IP address 10.1.1.1, which of the following commands is required?

a. ip name-server 10.1.1.1

b. ip dns 10.1.1.1

c. ip domain-lookup

d. ip dns-lookup

10. Imagine that you just logged in to the console of router R1 and then Telnetted to R2. What must you type to suspend your Telnet connection, going back to R1?

a. suspend

b. Ctrl-z

c. Ctrl-Shift-6, then x

d. quit

The answers to the "Do I Know This Already?" quiz are found in Appendix A, "Answers to the 'Do I Know This Already?' Quizzes and Q&A Sections." The suggested choices for your next step are as follows:

- **8 or less overall score**—Read the entire chapter. This includes the "Foundation Topics" and "Foundation Summary" sections and the Q&A section.

- **9 or 10 overall score**—If you want more review on these topics, skip to the "Foundation Summary" section and then go to the Q&A section. Otherwise, move to the next chapter.

Foundation Topics

Configuring IP Addresses

You easily can configure a Cisco router to forward IP traffic when you understand IP addressing and the IOS configuration process described in Chapter 7, "Operating Cisco Routers." This chapter shows you examples of a variety of commands used to configure and troubleshoot the routing of IP packets in a Cisco router. Tables 13-2 and 13-3 summarize many of the most common commands used for IP configuration and verification.

You can refer to other sources for more information about basic IP configuration on Cisco routers. The Cisco IOS documentation is an excellent reference for additional IP commands (see www.cisco.com/univercd/home/home.htm). Also, the Cisco Press book *Interconnecting Cisco Network Devices* is an excellent reference, particularly if you are not able to attend the instructor-led version of the class. This chapter focuses on the most common commands—the ones most likely to be on the CCNA exams.

Table 13-2 *IP Configuration Commands*

Command	Configuration Mode
ip address *ip-address mask* [**secondary**]	Interface mode
ip host *name* [*tcp-port-number*] *address1* [*address2...address8*]	Global
ip route *network-number network-mask* {*ip-address* | *interface*} [*distance*] [**name** *name*]	Global
ip name-server *server-address1* [[*server-address2*]...*server-address6*]	Global
ip domain-lookup	Global
ip routing	Global
hostname *name*	Global
login	Line configuration mode
password *value*	Line configuration mode
enable password [**level** *level*] {*password* | [*encryption-type*] *encrypted-password*}	Global
enable secret [**level** *level*] {*password* | [*encryption-type*] *encrypted-password*}	Global
keepalive [*seconds*]	Interface subcommand
exec-timeout *minutes* [*seconds*]	Line subcommand
logging synchronous	Line subcommand

Table 13-3 *IP EXEC Commands*

Command	Function
show hosts	Lists all host names and corresponding IP addresses
show interfaces [*type number*]	Lists interface statistics, including IP address
show ip interface [*type number*]	Provides a detailed view of IP parameter settings per interface
show ip interface brief	Provides a summary of all interfaces and their IP addresses
show ip route [*ip-address* [*mask*] [**longer-prefixes**]]	[*protocol* [*process-id*]]	Shows entire routing table or a subset if other parameters are entered
show ip arp [*ip-address*] [*host-name*] [*mac-address*] [*type number*]	Displays IP ARP cache
debug ip packet	Issues log messages for each IP packet
terminal ip netmask-format {bitcount I decimal I hexadecimal}	Sets type of display for subnet masks in **show** commands
ping [*protocol* I **tag**] {*host-name* I *system-address*}	Sends and receives ICMP echo messages to verify connectivity
trace [*protocol*] [*destination*]	Sends a series of UDP packets with increasing TTL values to verify the current route to a host

Most of the examples in this chapter refer to the routers in Figure 13-1. The figure shows a simple network with three routers, with each pair of routers having a serial link to the other two routers and a local Ethernet.

Figure 13-1 *Sample Network with Three Routers, with Point-to-Point Serial Links*

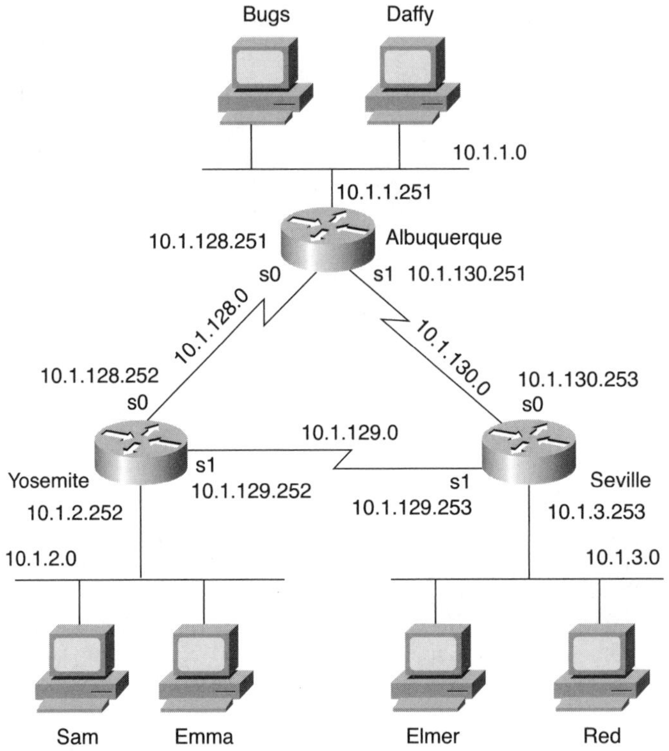

Basic Administrative Configuration

Chapter 7 focused on the configuration process more than the actual configuration commands that happened to be in the chapter. Before you configure IP, this short section reviews some of the basic commands you typically will configure on any router.

On most routers, you would configure at least the following:

- A host name for the router
- Reference to a DNS so that commands typed on the router can refer to host names instead of IP addresses
- Set a password on the console port
- Set a password for those Telnetting to the router
- Set the enable secret password to protect access to privileged mode
- Create a banner stating an appropriate warning, depending on the security practices at that company

Example 13-1 shows the output of the **show running-config** command on Albuquerque. The functions described in the list have been configured using the commands that are highlighted in the example.

Example 13-1   *Basic Adminsitrative Settings on Albuquerque Router*

```
Albuquerque#show running-config
Building configuration...

Current configuration : 872 bytes
!
version 12.2
service timestamps debug uptime
service timestamps log uptime
no service password-encryption
!
hostname Albuquerque
!
enable secret 5 $1$J3Fz$QaEYNIiI2aMu.3Ar.q0Xm.
!
!
ip name-server 10.1.1.100
ip name-server 10.1.2.100
!
interface Serial0
!
interface Serial1
!
interface Ethernet0
!
no ip http server

banner motd ^C
   Should've taken a left turn here! This is Albuquerque...  ^C
!
line con 0
 password cisco
 login
 exec timeout 00
line aux 0
line vty 0 4
 password cisco
 login
loggiing synchronous
```

None of the commands highlighted in Example 13-1 is required for the router to route IP, but the commands are generally useful in real networks. Of note, to make the router ask for a password at the console, you need the **login** console subcommand; the **password** console subcommand tells the router what password is required at the console. Similar logic applies to the **login** and **password** vty subcommands. And although you do not have to refer to a name server, when you do, you typically refer to at least two because most networks have at least two name servers for redundancy and availability.

When configuring the **enable secret** command, you type the password just like you want the user to type it when logging in to the router; however, the IOS changes the value that is saved in the configuration. For instance, for Example 13-1, I typed **enable secret cisco**, and the router changed cisco to a hashed value that cannot be converted back to cisco.

Two other things that you might want to configure habitually on routers are the console timeout and the synchronization of unsolicited messages. In some cases, you want the router to exit the user from the console after a period of inactivity. In other cases, you do not want the console disabled at all because of inactivity. The **exec timeout** *minutes seconds* command sets the inactivity timeout. Also, unsolicited informational messages and output from the IOS **debug** command both show up at the console by default. These same messages can be seen at the aux port or when Telnetting into a router by using the **terminal monitor** command. The **logging synchronous** line subcommand tells the router not to interrupt the output of a **show** command with these unsolicited messages, letting you read the output of the command that you typed before the router displays the other messages. **logging synchronous** can make your life a lot easier when using a router.

Configuring IP Addresses

Before you configure IP addresses, you first must decide what IP addresses to configure. Figure 13-1 not only outlined the network diagram, but it also listed the IP addresses chosen for the network. In this case, network 10.0.0.0 hs been subnetted with six subnets and a mask of 255.255.255.0.

After you have chosen the IP addresses and masks, configuration is simple. Examples 13-2, 13-3, and 13-4 show the IP configuration details for the three routers in Figure 13-1. The full configuration for Albuquerque is shown in Example 13-2, with a briefer version of the configs of the other two routers in Examples 13-3 and 13-4.

Example 13-2 *Albuquerque Router Configuration and Exec Commands*

```
Albuquerque#configure terminal
Enter configuration commands, one per line.  End with CNTL/Z.
Albuquerque(config)#interface serial 0
Albuquerque(config-if)#ip address 10.1.128.251 255.255.255.0
Albuquerque(config)#interface serial 1
Albuquerque(config-if)#ip address 10.1.130.251 255.255.255.0
Albuquerque(config)#interface ethernet 0
Albuquerque(config-if)#ip address 10.1.1.251 255.255.255.0
```

Example 13-2 *Albuquerque Router Configuration and Exec Commands (Continued)*

```
Albuquerque#show running-config
Building configuration...

Current configuration : 872 bytes
!
version 12.2
service timestamps debug uptime
service timestamps log uptime
no service password-encryption
!
hostname Albuquerque
!
enable secret 5 $1$J3Fz$QaEYNIiI2aMu.3Ar.q0Xm.
!
!
ip name-server 10.1.1.100
ip name-server 10.1.2.100
!
interface Serial0
 ip address 10.1.128.251 255.255.255.0
!
interface Serial1
 ip address 10.1.130.251 255.255.255.0
!
interface Ethernet0
 ip address 10.1.1.251 255.255.255.0
!
no ip http server

banner motd ^C
  Should've taken a left turn here! This is Albuquerque...  ^C
!
line con 0
 password cisco
 login
line aux 0
line vty 0 4
 password cisco
 login
!
end

Albuquerque#show ip route
Codes: C - connected, S - static, I - IGRP, R - RIP, M - mobile, B - BGP
       D - EIGRP, EX - EIGRP external, O - OSPF, IA - OSPF inter area
       N1 - OSPF NSSA external type 1, N2 - OSPF NSSA external type 2
```

continues

Example 13-2   *Albuquerque Router Configuration and Exec Commands (Continued)*

```
          E1 - OSPF external type 1, E2 - OSPF external type 2, E - EGP
          i - IS-IS, L1 - IS-IS level-1, L2 - IS-IS level-2, ia - IS-IS inter area
          * - candidate default, U - per-user static route, o - ODR
          P - periodic downloaded static route

Gateway of last resort is not set

     10.0.0.0/24 is subnetted, 3 subnets
C        10.1.1.0 is directly connected, Ethernet0
C        10.1.130.0 is directly connected, Serial1
C        10.1.128.0 is directly connected, Serial0

Albuquerque#terminal ip netmask-format decimal
Albuquerque#show ip route
Codes: C - connected, S - static, I - IGRP, R - RIP, M - mobile, B - BGP
          D - EIGRP, EX - EIGRP external, O - OSPF, IA - OSPF inter area
          N1 - OSPF NSSA external type 1, N2 - OSPF NSSA external type 2
          E1 - OSPF external type 1, E2 - OSPF external type 2, E - EGP
          i - IS-IS, L1 - IS-IS level-1, L2 - IS-IS level-2, ia - IS-IS inter area
          * - candidate default, U - per-user static route, o - ODR
          P - periodic downloaded static route

Gateway of last resort is not set

     10.0.0.0 255.255.255.0 is subnetted, 3 subnets
C        10.1.1.0 is directly connected, Ethernet0
C        10.1.130.0 is directly connected, Serial1

C        10.1.128.0 is directly connected, Serial0
```

Example 13-3   *Yosemite Router Configuration and Exec Commands*

```
Yosemite#show running-config
Building configuration...

! Lines ommitted for brevity
!
interface Serial0
 ip address 10.1.128.252 255.255.255.0
!
interface Serial1
 ip address 10.1.129.252 255.255.255.0
!
interface Ethernet0
 ip address 10.1.2.252 255.255.255.0
!
! lines ommitted for brevity
```

Example 13-4 *Seville Router Configuration and Exec Commands*

```
Seville#show running-config
! Lines ommitted for brevity
!
!
interface Serial0
 ip address 10.1.130.253 255.255.255.0
!
interface Serial1
 ip address 10.1.129.253 255.255.255.0
!
Ethernet0
 ip address 10.1.3.253 255.255.255.0
!
! Lines ommitted for brevity
```

The **ip address** interface subcommand configures the IP address for each interface, as seen in the highlighted portions of the examples. Because each interface has an IP address, the **interface** configuration command precedes each **ip address** command, identifying to IOS the interface to which the IP address should be assigned. It's that simple!

Prefix Notation

At the end of Example 13-2 (Albuquerque), you also see the results of the **show ip route** command. The output of the command lists the network (10.0.0.0), followed by the notation of /24. This notation, called *prefix notation*, denotes the subnet mask in terms of the number of 1 bits in the subnet mask. The number of bits of value binary 1 in the mask is considered to be the prefix. For instance, mask 255.255.255.0, used in the examples, translates to a prefix of /24 because 255.255.255.0 has 24 binary 1s. Prefix notation is simply a shorter way to write the mask.

If you prefer to see the subnet masks instead of the prefix, simply use the **terminal ip netmask-format decimal** exec command, as shown at the end of Example 13-2. Note that the **show ip route** command issued after the **terminal** command shows the subnet mask instead of the prefix.

Seeding the Routing Table with Connected IP Routes

The Cisco IOS routes IP packets by default—in other words, you do not need to type any commands to tell the router to enable IP routing. Before the router will route packets in or out an interface, the interface must have an IP address, as shown in the earlier examples. So, as configured, each of the three routers can route packets on three different interfaces.

The problem with the configurations shown so far is that the routers do not know routes to all the subnets in the network. The ultimate solution to this problem is to configure a dynamic routing protocol. However, in this chapter, you will learn about how the router learns some routes by virtue of the configuration of IP addresses on the interface. Chapter 14 introduces the different IP routing protocols, and the *CCNA ICND Exam Certification Guide* covers the detailed concepts and configuration for several IP routing protocols.

Routers add routes to their routing tables for the subnets associated with their own physical interfaces. To get a better appreciation of this fact, examine Example 13-5, which shows several commands from the Seville router.

Example 13-5 *Seville Router Routing Table and Interface Status Commands*

```
Seville#show ip route
Codes: C - connected, S - static, I - IGRP, R - RIP, M - mobile, B - BGP
       D - EIGRP, EX - EIGRP external, O - OSPF, IA - OSPF inter area
       N1 - OSPF NSSA external type 1, N2 - OSPF NSSA external type 2
       E1 - OSPF external type 1, E2 - OSPF external type 2, E - EGP
       i - IS-IS, L1 - IS-IS level-1, L2 - IS-IS level-2, ia - IS-IS inter area
       * - candidate default, U - per-user static route, o - ODR
       P - periodic downloaded static route
Gateway of last resort is not set


10.0.0.0/24 is subnetted, 3 subnets
C       10.1.3.0 is directly connected, Ethernet0
C       10.1.130.0 is directly connected, Serial0
C       10.1.129.0 is directly connected, Serial1


Seville#show ip interface brief
Interface          IP-Address      OK? Method Status            Protocol
Serial0            10.1.130.253    YES manual up                up
Serial1            10.1.129.253    YES manual up                up
Ethernet0          10.1.3.253      YES manual up                up


Seville#show interface serial 0
Serial0 is up, line protocol is up
  Hardware is HD64570
  Internet address is 10.1.130.253/24
  MTU 1500 bytes, BW 1544 Kbit, DLY 20000 usec,
     reliability 255/255, txload 1/255, rxload 1/255
  Encapsulation HDLC, loopback not set
  Keepalive set (10 sec)
  Last input never, output never, output hang never
  Last clearing of "show interface" counters never
  Input queue: 0/75/0/0 (size/max/drops/flushes); Total output drops: 0
  Queueing strategy: weighted fair
  Output queue: 0/1000/64/0 (size/max total/threshold/drops)
     Conversations  0/0/256 (active/max active/max total)
```

Example 13-5 *Seville Router Routing Table and Interface Status Commands (Continued)*

```
      Reserved Conversations 0/0 (allocated/max allocated)
      Available Bandwidth 1158 kilobits/sec
  5 minute input rate 0 bits/sec, 0 packets/sec
  5 minute output rate 0 bits/sec, 0 packets/sec
      0 packets input, 0 bytes, 0 no buffer
      Received 0 broadcasts, 0 runts, 0 giants, 0 throttles
      0 input errors, 0 CRC, 0 frame, 0 overrun, 0 ignored, 0 abort
      0 packets output, 0 bytes, 0 underruns
      0 output errors, 0 collisions, 1 interface resets
      0 output buffer failures, 0 output buffers swapped out
      0 carrier transitions
      DCD=up  DSR=up  DTR=up  RTS=up  CTS=up


Seville#show ip interface serial 1
Serial1 is up, line protocol is up
  Internet address is 10.1.129.253/24
  Broadcast address is 255.255.255.255
  Address determined by non-volatile memory
  MTU is 1500 bytes
  Helper address is not set
  Directed broadcast forwarding is disabled
  Outgoing access list is not set
  Inbound  access list is not set
  Proxy ARP is enabled
  Security level is default
  Split horizon is disabled
  ICMP redirects are always sent
  ICMP unreachables are always sent
  ICMP mask replies are never sent
  IP fast switching is enabled
  IP fast switching on the same interface is enabled
  IP Flow switching is disabled
  IP Feature Fast switching turbo vector
  IP multicast fast switching is disabled
  IP multicast distributed fast switching is disabled
  IP route-cache flags are Fast
  Router Discovery is disabled
  IP output packet accounting is disabled
  IP access violation accounting is disabled
  TCP/IP header compression is disabled
  RTP/IP header compression is disabled
  Probe proxy name replies are disabled
  Policy routing is disabled
  Network address translation is disabled
  WCCP Redirect outbound is disabled
  WCCP Redirect inbound is disabled
  WCCP Redirect exclude is disabled
  BGP Policy Mapping is disabled
```

First, here is a quick introduction to the four commands in the example. The **show ip route** command lists routes to the three subnets connected to the Seville router, namely 10.1.130.0, 10.1.129.0, and 10.1.3.0, all with mask 255.255.255.0 (prefix /24). The output from the command lists a C in the first column, which, according to the notes at the beginning of the command output, means "connected." In other words, this router is connected directly to these subnets.

Following the **show ip route** command, the example contains three commands that list information about the interfaces in the router. The **show ip interface brief** command lists one line per interface, with IP address information and interface status. Next, the **show interface serial 0** command lists more details about a single interface, with most of those details about the interface itself. Finally, the **show ip interface serial 1** command shows detailed information about the IP protocol running over interface serial 1.

IOS adds connected routes to the routing table that meet the following requirements:

■ The interface has been configured with a valid IP address.

■ The interface is in an up and up status according to the various interface-oriented **show** commands.

All three of the **show** commands in Example 13-5 that list interface status information use two designations of up and up. The first status keyword (the first of the two ups in this case) generally refers to OSI Layer 1 status. For instance, if there is no cable plugged in, the first status word would be down instead of up. The second status word generally refers to the status of OSI Layer 2. For instance, if Seville defaulted to use HDLC on serial 0, but Albuquerque configured PPP as the data-link protocol on its serial 1 interface on the other end of the link, the interface status on each end would show up and down.

Another instance in which a router might put an interface in status up and down is when the router does not receive keepalive messages on a regular basis. Cisco routers send, and expect to receive, proprietary keepalive messages on each interface. The purpose of the keepalives is to know whether the interface is usable. For instance, on a point-to-point link between Albuquerque and Yosemite, each router sends a keepalive every 10 seconds. As long as they each receive a keepalive every 10 seconds, they think the link is up and up. If Yosemite did not hear a keepalive for three times the keepalive interval (default 10-second interval, for a total of 30 seconds), Yosemite would put the interface into an up and down status. You can disable keepalives with the **no keepalive** interface subcommand, or you can change the timer with the **keepalive** *interval* interface subcommand.

Those comments aside, as long as an interface status is up and up, the router believes that the interface is usable, so the router can add the associated connected IP route to the routing table.

In some cases, you want an interface to be down for administrative reasons, but you do not want to have to unconfigure it or pull out the cable to keep the interface from being up and up. To bring down an interface for administrative reasons and, as a side effect, remove the connected route from the routing table, you can use the **shutdown** interface subcommand, as shown in Example 13-6.

Example 13-6   *Using the* shutdown *Command*

```
Seville#configure terminal
Enter configuration commands, one per line.  End with CNTL/Z.
Seville(config)#interface serial 1
Seville(config-if)#shutdown
Seville(config-if)#^Z
Seville#show ip route
Codes: C - connected, S - static, I - IGRP, R - RIP, M - mobile, B - BGP
       D - EIGRP, EX - EIGRP external, O - OSPF, IA - OSPF inter area
       N1 - OSPF NSSA external type 1, N2 - OSPF NSSA external type 2
       E1 - OSPF external type 1, E2 - OSPF external type 2, E - EGP
       i - IS-IS, L1 - IS-IS level-1, L2 - IS-IS level-2, ia - IS-IS inter area
       * - candidate default, U - per-user static route, o - ODR
       P - periodic downloaded static route
Gateway of last resort is not set


10.0.0.0/24 is subnetted, 2 subnets
C        10.1.3.0 is directly connected, Ethernet0
C        10.1.130.0 is directly connected, Serial0

Seville#show ip interface brief
Interface            IP-Address      OK? Method Status                Protocol
Serial0              10.1.130.253    YES manual up                    up
Serial1              10.1.129.253    YES manual Administratively down down
Ethernet0            10.1.3.253      YES manual up                    up

Seville#configure terminal
Enter configuration commands, one per line.  End with CNTL/Z.
Seville(config)#interface serial 1
Seville(config-if)#no shutdown
Seville(config-if)#^Z
```

In the example, after the **shutdown** command under **interface serial 1,** the route connected to serial 1 (10.1.129.0, mask 255.255.255.0) was removed from the routing table, leaving only two entries. Also, the output of the **show ip interface brief** command lists a status of administratively down and down. (The **show ip interface** and **show interface** commands would show the same status for serial 1.) At the end of the example, the **no shutdown** command brings the interface back up.

Bandwidth, Clock Rate, and Serial Lines in the Lab

As mentioned back in Chapter 4, "Fundamentals of WANs," you can build a WAN link in a lab without using a CSU/DSU. The lab network that I used to build the examples in this chapter used three "back-to-back" serial cables, essentially a DTE and DCE cable pair connected together.

To use a back-to-back WAN connection, one router must supply the clocking. Example 13-7 shows an example configuration for Seville, with a couple of important commands related to WAN links.

Example 13-7 *Seville Router Configuration with* clock rate *Command*

```
Seville#show running-config
! Lines ommitted for brevity
!
interface Serial0
 ip address 10.1.130.253 255.255.255.0
 clock rate 128000
!
interface Serial1
 ip address 10.1.129.253 255.255.255.0
 clock rate 128000
 bandwidth 128
!
Ethernet0
 ip address 10.1.3.253 255.255.255.0
!
! Lines ommitted for brevity

Seville#show controllers serial 0/0
Interface Serial0
Hardware is PowerQUICC MPC860
DCE V.35, clock rate 128000
idb at 0x8169BB20, driver data structure at 0x816A35E4
! Lines ommitted for brevity
```

The **clock rate** command sets the rate in bits per second on the router that has the DCE cable plugged into it. In this case, Seville was supplying clocking on both serial interfaces. If no cable has been plugged in, the IOS accepts the command. If a DTE cable has been plugged in, IOS rejects the command. If you do not know which router has the DCE cable in it, you can find out by using the **show controllers** command, as shown at the end of the example. In the example, you can see that the output identifies the type of serial cable.

Also notice the **bandwidth 128** command on serial 1. The **bandwidth** command tells IOS the speed of the link, in kilobits per second, regardless of whether the router is supplying clocking. The bandwidth setting does not change anything that the router does at Layer 1; instead, this setting is used by IOS software for other purposes. For instance, IGRP and EIGRP both use bandwidth to calculate a metric for routing protocols; they use the bandwidth setting on the interfaces. **bandwidth** defaults to T1 speed on serial interfaces. There is no default for **clock rate**, even with a DCE cable plugged in—it must be configured.

IP Troubleshooting Features

Cisco includes coverage of basic troubleshooting commands and concepts on the CCNA exams. These commands are contained in several places in this book, as well as in the *CCNA ICND Exam Certification Guide*. This section covers some of the tools and commands specific to troubleshooting IP.

Internet Control Message Protocol

Earlier in this chapter, you read about how to configure IP addresses and how to perform some basic troubleshooting. For troubleshooting, you have seen how to look at the routing table with the **show ip route** command, how to look at interface status with several options on the **show interfaces** command, and how to use standard and extended **ping** commands for basic troubleshooting.

TCP/IP includes a protocol specifically to help manage and control the operation of a TCP/IP network, called the Internet Control Message Protocol (ICMP). The ICMP protocol provides a wide variety of information about the health and operational status of a network. *Control Message* is the most descriptive part of the name—ICMP defines messages that helps control and manage the work of IP and, therefore, is considered to be part of TCP/IP's network layer. Because ICMP helps control IP, it can provide useful troubleshooting information. In fact, the ICMP messages sit inside an IP packet, with no transport layer header at all–so it is truly just an extension of the TCP/IP network layer.

RFC 792 defines ICMP and includes the following excerpt, which describes the protocol well:

> Occasionally a gateway (router) or destination host will communicate with a source host, for example, to report an error in datagram processing. For such purposes, this protocol, the Internet Control Message Protocol (ICMP), is used. ICMP uses the basic support of IP as if it were a higher level protocol; however, ICMP is actually an integral part of IP and must be implemented by every IP module.

ICMP uses messages to accomplish its tasks. Many of these messages are used in even the smallest IP network. Table 13-4 lists several ICMP messages.

Table 13-4 *ICMP Message Types*

Message	Purpose
Destination unreachable	This tells the source host that there is a problem delivering a packet.
Time exceeded	The time that it takes a packet to be delivered has expired; the packet has been discarded.
Redirect	The router sending this message has received some packet for which another router would have had a better route; the message tells the sender to use the better route.
Echo	This is used by the **ping** command to verify connectivity.

ICMP Echo Request and Echo Reply

The ICMP echo request and echo reply messages are sent and received by the **ping** command. In fact, when people say that they "sent a ping packet," they really mean that they sent an ICMP echo request. These two messages are very self-explanatory. The echo request simply means that the host to which it is addressed should reply to the packet. The echo reply is the ICMP message type that should be used in the reply. The echo request includes some data that can be specified by the **ping** command; whatever data is sent in the echo request is sent back in the echo reply.

Example 13-8 shows two **ping** commands testing IP connectivity from Albuquerque to Yosemite. Figure 13-2 precedes the example, as a reminder of the topology and IP addresses in the network.

Figure 13-2   *Sample Network Used for* ping *Example*

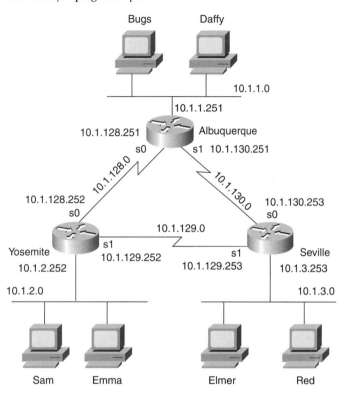

Example 13-8   *Example with One Working* ping, *and One Failing* ping

```
Albuquerque#show ip route
Codes: C - connected, S - static, I - IGRP, R - RIP, M - mobile, B - BGP
       D - EIGRP, EX - EIGRP external, O - OSPF, IA - OSPF inter area
       N1 - OSPF NSSA external type 1, N2 - OSPF NSSA external type 2
       E1 - OSPF external type 1, E2 - OSPF external type 2, E - EGP
       i - IS-IS, L1 - IS-IS level-1, L2 - IS-IS level-2, ia - IS-IS inter area
       * - candidate default, U - per-user static route, o - ODR
       P - periodic downloaded static route

Gateway of last resort is not set

     10.0.0.0/24 is subnetted, 3 subnets

C       10.1.1.0 is directly connected, Ethernet0
C       10.1.130.0 is directly connected, Serial1
C       10.1.128.0 is directly connected, Serial0
Albuquerque#ping 10.1.128.252
Type escape sequence to abort.
```

continues

Example 13-8   *Example with One Working* ping, *and One Failing* ping

```
Sending 5, 100-byte ICMP Echos to 10.1.128.252, timeout is 2 seconds:
!!!!!
Success rate is 100 percent (5/5), round-trip min/avg/max = 4/4/8 ms

Albuquerque#ping 10.1.2.252
Type escape sequence to abort.
Sending 5, 100-byte ICMP Echos to 10.1.2.252, timeout is 2 seconds:
.....
Success rate is 0 percent (0/5)
```

The **ping** command sends a packet to the stated destination address. The TCP/IP software at the destination then replies to the ping packet with a similar packet. The **ping** command sends the first packet and waits on the response. If a response is received, the command displays an exclamation mark (!). If no response is received within the default timeout of 2 seconds, the **ping** command displays a period (.). The IOS **ping** command sends five of these packets by default.

In Example 13-8, the **ping 10.1.128.2** command works, but the **ping 10.1.2.252** command does not. The first **ping** command works because Albuquerque has a route to the subnet in which 10.1.128.2 resides (subnet 10.1.128.0). However, the second **ping** to 10.1.2.252 does not work because the subnet in which 10.1.2.252 resides, subnet 10.1.2.0, is not connected to Albuquerque, so Albuquerque does not have a route to that subnet. So, none of the five ping packets works, resulting in five periods in the output of the **ping** command. (The ping would have worked if a routing protocol had been implemented successfully in this network.) Had these routers been using a routing protocol, the correct routes would have been known, and the second **ping** would have worked.

The **ping** command itself supplies many creative ways to use echo requests and replies. For instance, the **ping** command enables you to specify the length as well as the source and destination addresses, and it also enables you to set other fields in the IP header.

Destination Unreachable ICMP Message

The ICMP Destination Unreachable message is sent when a message cannot be delivered completely to the application at the destination host. Because packet delivery can fail for many reasons, there are five separate unreachable functions (codes) using this single ICMP unreachable message. All five code types pertain directly to an IP, TCP, or UDP feature. The network shown in Figure 13-3 helps you understand them.

Figure 13-3   *Sample Network for Discussing ICMP Unreachable Codes*

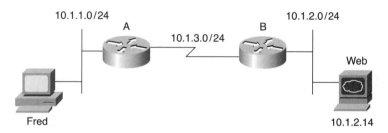

Assume that Fred is trying to connect to the web server, called Web. (Web uses HTTP, which in turn uses TCP as the transport layer protocol.) Three of the ICMP unreachable codes can possibly be used by Routers A and B. The other two codes are used by the web server. These ICMP codes are sent to Fred as a result of the packet originally sent by Fred.

Table 13-5 summarizes the more common ICMP unreachable codes. After the table, the text explains how each ICMP code might be needed for the network in Figure 13-3.

Table 13-5   *ICMP Unreachable Codes*

Unreachable Code	When It Is Used	What It Typically Is Sent By
Network unreachable	There is no match in a routing table for the packet's destination.	Router
Host unreachable	The packet can be routed to a router connected to the destination subnet, but the host is not responding.	Router
Can't fragment	The packet has the Don't Fragment bit set, and a router must fragment to forward the packet.	Router

continues

Table 13-5 *ICMP Unreachable Codes (Continued)*

Unreachable Code	When It Is Used	What It Typically Is Sent By
Protocol unreachable	The packet is delivered to the destination host, but the transport layer protocol is not available on that host.	Endpoint host
Port unreachable	The packet is delivered to the destination host, but the destination port has not been opened by an application.	Endpoint host

The following list explains each code in Table 8-8 in greater detail using the network in Figure 13-3 as an example:

- **Network unreachable**—Router A uses this code if it does not have a route telling it where to forward the packet. In this case, Router A needs a route to subnet 10.1.2.0. Router A sends Fred the ICMP Destination Unreachable message with the code "network unreachable" in response to Fred's packet destined for 10.1.2.14.

- **Host unreachable**—This code implies that the single destination host is unavailable. If Router A has a route to 10.1.2.0, the packet is delivered to Router B. However, if the web server is down, Router B does not get an ARP reply from the web server. Router B sends Fred the ICMP Destination Unreachable message with the code "host unreachable" in response to Fred's packet destined for 10.1.2.14.

- **Can't fragment**—This code is the last of the three ICMP unreachable codes that a router might send. Fragmentation defines the process in which a router needs to forward a packet, but the outgoing interface allows only packets that are smaller than the forwarded packet. The router can break the packet into pieces. However, if Router A or B needs to fragment the packet but the Do Not Fragment bit is set in the IP header, the router discards the packet. Router A or B sends Fred the ICMP Destination Unreachable message with the code "can't fragment" in response to Fred's packet destined for 10.1.2.14.

- **Protocol unreachable**—If the packet successfully arrives at the web server, two other unreachable codes are possible. One implies that the protocol above IP, typically TCP or UDP, is not running on that host. This is highly unlikely, because most operating systems that use TCP/IP use a single software package that provides IP, TCP, and UDP functions. But if the host receives the IP packet and TCP or UDP is unavailable, the web server host sends Fred the ICMP Destination Unreachable message with the code "protocol unreachable" in response to Fred's packet destined for 10.1.2.14.

■ **Port unreachable**—The final code field value is more likely today. If the server is up but the web server software is not running, the packet can get to the server but cannot be delivered to the web server software. The web server host sends Fred the ICMP Destination Unreachable message with the code "port unreachable" in response to Fred's packet destined for 10.1.2.14.

One key to troubleshooting with the **ping** command is understanding the various codes the command uses to signify the various responses it can receive. Table 13-6 lists the various codes that the Cisco IOS software **ping** command can supply.

Table 13-6 *Codes That the* **ping** *Command Receives in Response to Its ICMP Echo Request*

ping Command Code	Description
!	ICMP Echo Reply received
.	Nothing was received before the **ping** command timed out
U	ICMP unreachable (destination) received
N	ICMP unreachable (network) received
P	ICMP unreachable (port) received
Q	ICMP source quench received
M	ICMP Can't Fragment message received
?	Unknown packet received

IP Naming Commands

When using the IOS CLI, you will want to refer to names instead of IP addresses. Particularly for the **trace**, **ping**, and **telnet** commands, the IP address or host name must be supplied. This section describes the use of host names on an IOS-based device. Along the way, some nuances of the use of Telnet are covered.

IOS can use statically configured names as well as refer to one or more DNSs. Example 13-9 shows some names statically configured, with configuration pointing to two different DNSs.

Example 13-9 *IP Naming Configuration and* **show host** *Command*

```
hostname Cooperstown
!
ip host Mays 10.1.1.1
ip host Aaron 10.2.2.2
ip host Mantle 10.3.3.3
!
ip domain-name gileadfoundation.org
ip name-server 10.1.1.200  10.2.2.200
ip domain-lookup
```

continues

Example 13-9 *IP Naming Configuration and* **show host** *Command (Continued)*

```
Cooperstown#show hosts
Default domain is gileadoundation.org
Name/address lookup uses static mappings

Host                    Flags      Age Type   Address(es)
Mays                    (perm, OK) 0   IP     10.1.1.1
Aaron                   (perm, OK) 0   IP     10.2.2.2
Mantle                  (perm, OK) 0   IP     10.3.3.3
Cooperstown#
```

Router Cooperstown will use any of the three statically configured host name–to–IP address mappings. Three names are configured statically in this case—Mays, Aaron, and Mantle. Any command referring to Mays, Aaron, or Mantle will resolve into the IP addresses shown in the **ip host** command.

Router Cooperstown also will ask a DNS for name resolution if it does not know the name and IP address already. The DNS configuration is shown toward the end of the configuration. The IP addresses of the name servers are shown in the **ip name-server** command. Up to six DNSs can be listed; they are searched for each request sequentially, based on the order in the command. Finally, the **ip domain-lookup** command enables IOS to ask a name server. IP domain lookup is the default; **no ip domain-lookup** disables the DNS client function. For names that do not include the full domain name, the **ip domain-name** command defines the domain name that should be assumed by the router.

The **show ip host** command lists the static entries, in addition to any entries learned from a DNS request. Only the three static entries were in the table, in this case. The term **perm** in the output implies that the entry is static. Also note that when short names are used—in other words, the name does not include the DNS domain name—the router adds the domain name of gileadfoundation.org, as configured in the **ip domain-name gileadfoundation.org** command.

Table 13-7 summarizes the key naming commands in IOS.

Table 13-7 *IP Naming Commands*

Function	Command Options
Tell IOS to use a DNS	Configure the **ip domain-lookup** global configuration command.
Configure IP addresses of name servers	Configure the **ip name-server** *svr1 svr2...* global configuration command.
Configure static host names	Use the **ip host** *name address* command.
List current host name information	Use the **show hosts** exec command.

Telnet and Suspend

The **telnet** IOS exec command enables you to Telnet from one Cisco device to another; in practical use, it is typically to another Cisco device. One of the most important features of the **telnet** command is the suspend feature. To understand the suspend function, you should to refer to the network diagram in Figure 13-4.

Figure 13-4 *Telnet Suspension*

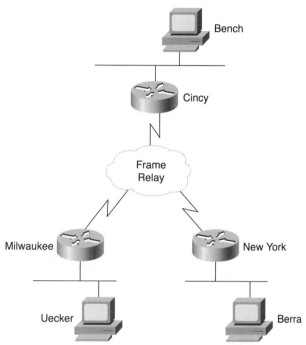

In the figure, the router administrator is using Bench to Telnet into the Cincy router. When in Cincy, the user Telnets to Milwaukee. When in Milwaukee, the user suspends the Telnet by pressing Ctrl-Shift-6, followed by pressing the letter x. The user then Telnets to New York and again suspends the connection. The example begins with Bench already logged into Cincy. Example 13-10 shows example output, with annotations to the side.

Example 13-10 *Telnet Suspensions*

```
Cincy#telnet milwaukee              (User issues command to Telnet to Milwaukee)
Trying Milwaukee (10.1.4.252)... Open


User Access Verification

Password:             (User plugs in password, can type commands at Milwaukee)
```

continues

Example 13-10 *Telnet Suspensions (Continued)*

```
Milwaukee>
Milwaukee>
Milwaukee>
                          (Note: User pressed Ctrl-Shift-6 and then x)
Cincy#telnet NewYork            (User back at Cincy because Telnet was suspended)
Trying NewYork (10.1.6.253)... Open
                  (User is getting into New York now, based on telnet NewYork command)


User Access Verification

Password:
NewYork>                              (User can now type commands on New York)
NewYork>
NewYork>
NewYork>
                              (Note: User pressed Ctrl-Shift-6 and then x)

Cincy#show sessions            (This command lists suspended Telnet sessions)
Conn Host              Address           Byte  Idle Conn Name
   1 Milwaukee         10.1.4.252           0     0 Milwaukee
*  2 NewYork           10.1.6.253           0     0 NewYork

Cincy#where                  (where does the same thing)
Conn Host              Address           Byte  Idle Conn Name
   1 Milwaukee         10.1.4.252           0     0 Milwaukee
*  2 NewYork           10.1.6.253           0     0 NewYork

Cincy#resume 1       (Resume connection 1 (see show session) to Milwaukee)
[Resuming connection 1 to milwaukee ... ]

Milwaukee>                      (User can type commands on Milwaukee)
Milwaukee>
Milwaukee>
(Note: User pressed Ctrl-Shift-6 and then x)    (User wants to go back to Cincy)
Cincy#         (WOW! User just pressed Enter and resumes the last Telnet)
 [Resuming connection 1 to milwaukee ... ]

Milwaukee>
Milwaukee>
Milwaukee>
                            (Note: User pressed Ctrl-Shift-6 and then x)
                       (Tired of Milwaukee again  can't imagine why!)
Cincy#disconnect 1         (No more need to use Milwaukee  Telnet terminated!)
Closing connection to milwaukee [confirm]        (User presses Enter to confirm)
Cincy#
[Resuming connection 2 to NewYork ... ]
```

Example 13-10   *Telnet Suspensions (Continued)*

```
                        (Pressing Enter resumes most recently suspended active Telnet)

NewYork>
NewYork>
NewYork>
                                    (Note: User pressed Ctrl-Shift-6 and then x)
Cincy#disconnect 2                   (Done with New York, terminate Telnet)
Closing connection to NewYork [confirm]       (Just press Enter to confirm)
Cincy#
```

The play-by-play notes in the example explain most of the details. Example 13-10 begins with the Cincy command prompt that would be seen in Bench's Telnet window because the user at Bench Telnetted into Cincy first. After Telnetting to Milwaukee, the Telnet connection was suspended. Then, after Telnetting to New York, that connection was suspended. The two connections can be suspended or resumed easily. The **resume** command can be used to resume either connection; however, the **resume** command requires a connection ID, which is shown in the **show sessions** command. (The **where** command provides the same output.) Also, instead of using the **resume** command, you can just use the session number as a command. For instance, just typing the command **2** does the same thing as typing the command **resume 2**.

The interesting and potentially dangerous nuance here is that if a Telnet session is suspended and you simply press Enter, Cisco IOS Software resumes the connection to the most recently suspended Telnet connection. That is fine, until you realize how much you tend to press the Enter key occasionally to clear some of the clutter from the screen. With a suspended Telnet connection, you also just happened to reconnect to another router. This is particularly dangerous when you are changing the configuration or using potentially damaging exec commands—be careful about what router you are actually using when you have suspended Telnet connections.

If you want to know which session has been suspended most recently, look for the session listed in the **show sessions** command that has an asterisk to the left of the entry. That session was the most recently suspended session.

Table 13-8 summarizes the commands related to Telnet.

Table 13-8 *Telnet Command Options*

Function	Command Options
Telnet to another device	Use the **telnet** exec command. Just type the host name or IP address from exec mode.
Suspend a Telnet session	Press the key sequence Ctrl-Shift-6, then x.
Discover currently suspended Telnet session	Use the **where** exec command. Use the **show sessions** exec command.
Resume a suspended Telnet session	Use the **resume** command, with no parameter, to reconnect to the most recently suspended Telnet. Use the **resume** *x* command, where *x* is the number of the suspended Telnet session based on the output of **show sessions**. Just press Enter in exec mode to resume to the most recently suspended Telnet session.
Terminate a suspended telnet	Resume connection, and log out using the **quit** command. Use the **disconnect** command on the router you Telnetted from.

Cisco Discovery Protocol

The Cisco Discovery Protocol (CDP) discovers basic information about neighboring routers and switches, without needing to know the passwords for the neighboring devices. CDP supports any LAN, HDLC, Frame Relay, and ATM interface—in fact, it supports any interface that supports the use of SNAP headers. The router or switch can discover Layer 2 and Layer 3 addressing details of neighboring routers without even configuring that Layer 3 protocol—this is because CDP is not dependent on any particular Layer 3 protocol.

When Cisco first developed the proprietary CDP, it was used mainly between routers. Today most Cisco products support CDP, including Cisco switches and Cisco IP Phones.

Devices that support CDP advertise their own information and learn information about others by listening for their advertisements. On media that support multicasts at the data link layer, CDP uses multicast; on other media, CDP sends a copy of the CDP update to any known data-link addresses. So, any CDP-supporting device that shares a physical medium with another CDP-supporting device can learn about the other device.

CDP discovers several useful details from the neighboring device:

- **Device identifier**—Typically the host name
- **Address list**—Network and data-link addresses
- **Port identifier**—Text that identifies the port, which is another name for an interface
- **Capabilities list**—Information on what type of device it is—for instance, a router or a switch
- **Platform**—The model and OS level running in the device

CDP is enabled in the configuration by default. The **no cdp run** global command disables CDP for the entire device, and the **cdp run** global command re-enables CDP. Likewise, the **no cdp enable** interface subcommand disables CDP just on that interface, and the **cdp enable** command switches back to the default state of CDP being enabled.

A variety of **show cdp** command options are available. Example 13-11 lists the output of the commands, with some commentary following.

Example 13-11   show cdp *Command Options*

```
Seville#show cdp ?
  entry      Information for specific neighbor entry
  interface  CDP interface status and configuration
  neighbors  CDP neighbor entries
  traffic    CDP statistics
  |          Output modifiers
  <cr>
Seville#show cdp neighbor
Capability Codes: R - Router, T - Trans Bridge, B - Source Route Bridge
                  S - Switch, H - Host, I - IGMP, r - Repeater

Device ID        Local Intrfce     Holdtme    Capability  Platform  Port ID
fred             Ser 1             172          R          2500      Ser 1
Yosemite         Ser 0.2          161          R          2500      Ser 0.2
Switch           Eth 0            123          S I         WS-C3550-2Fas 0/4

Seville#show cdp entry fred
-------------------------
Device ID: fred
Entry address(es):
  IP address: 163.5.8.3
Platform: cisco 2500,  Capabilities: Router
Interface: Serial1,  Port ID (outgoing port): Serial1
Holdtime : 168 sec

Version :
Cisco Internetwork Operating System Software
IOS (tm) 2500 Software (C2500-DS-L), Version 12.2(3), RELEASE SOFTWARE (fc1)
```

continues

Example 13-11 show cdp *Command Options (Continued)*

```
Copyright  1986-2001 by cisco Systems, Inc.
Compiled Wed 18-Jul-01 21:10 by pwade


advertisement version: 2


Seville#show cdp neighbor detail
------------------------
Device ID: fred
Entry address(es):
  IP address: 163.5.8.3
Platform: cisco 2500,  Capabilities: Router
Interface: Serial1,  Port ID (outgoing port): Serial1
Holdtime : 164 sec


Version :
Cisco Internetwork Operating System Software
IOS (tm) 2500 Software (C2500-DS-L), Version 12.2(3), RELEASE SOFTWARE (fc1)
Copyright  1986-2001 by cisco Systems, Inc.
Compiled Wed 18-Jul-01 21:10 by pwade


advertisement version: 2


------------------------
Device ID: Yosemite
Entry address(es):
  IP address: 10.1.5.252
Platform: cisco 2500,  Capabilities: Router
Interface: Serial0.2,  Port ID (outgoing port): Serial0.2
Holdtime : 146 sec


Version :
Cisco Internetwork Operating System Software
IOS (tm) 2500 Software (C2500-DS-L), Version 12.2(3), RELEASE SOFTWARE (fc1)
Copyright  1986-2001 by cisco Systems, Inc.
Compiled Wed 18-Jul-01 21:10 by pwade


advertisement version: 2


------------------------
Device ID: Switch
Entry address(es):
Platform: cisco WS-C3550-24,  Capabilities: Switch IGMP
Interface:    Ethernet0,    Port ID (outgoing port): FastEthernet0/4
Holdtime : 160 sec


Version :
Cisco Internetwork Operating System Software
```

Example 13-11   show cdp *Command Options (Continued)*

```
IOS (tm) C3550 Software (C3550-I5Q3L2-M), Version 12.1(11)EA1, RELEASE SOFTWARE
(fc1)
Copyright  1986-2002 by cisco Systems, Inc.
Compiled Wed 28-Aug-02 10:03 by antonino

advertisement version: 2
Protocol Hello:  OUI=0x00000C, Protocol ID=0x0112; payload len=27, value=0000000
0FFFFFFFF010231FF000000000000000AB7DCB780FF0000
VTP Management Domain: ''
Native VLAN: 1
Duplex: half
Seville#show cdp interface
Ethernet0 is up, line protocol is down
  Encapsulation ARPA
  Sending CDP packets every 60 seconds
  Holdtime is 180 seconds
Serial0.2 is up, line protocol is up
  Encapsulation FRAME-RELAY
  Sending CDP packets every 60 seconds
  Holdtime is 180 seconds
Serial1 is up, line protocol is up
  Encapsulation HDLC
  Sending CDP packets every 60 seconds
  Holdtime is 180 seconds

Seville#show cdp traffic
CDP counters :
        Total packets output: 31, Input: 41
        Hdr syntax: 0, Chksum error: 0, Encaps failed: 9
        No memory: 0, Invalid packet: 0, Fragmented: 0
        CDP version 1 advertisements output: 0, Input: 0
        CDP version 2 advertisements output: 31, Input: 41
```

The commands provide information about both the neighbors and the behavior of the CDP protocol itself. The **show cdp** command has four options, as shown at the beginning of the example. For instance, the **show cdp neighbor** command lists each neighbor, with one line of output per neighbor. Notice that Seville has two router neighbors, denoted by the R, and one switch, in this case a 3550, denoted with an S.

Next in the example, you see two commands that list details per neighbor. The **show cdp entry fred** command lists the details learned by CDP about the neighbor whose host name is fred. (Before using the command, you would just use the **show cdp neighbor** command to find the host names of any neighbors that CDP already has found.) Another command that lists the detailed information is the **show cdp neighbor detail** command, which is in the same format as **show cdp** entry but lists the information for every neighbor.

You actually can draw a network diagram by using CDP, exercising a little patience, and issuing the right commands on all the devices in a network. Whether you are using the briefer output of **show cdp neighbor** or the more complete output of **show cdp neighbor detail** or **show cdp entry,** the output lists both the local interface and the port ID. The port ID is the interface number, as designated by the other device. For instance, the switch uses port 0/4 to connect to this device. So, you literally could piece together the network diagram from the CDP output.

Foundation Summary

The "Foundation Summary" section of each chapter lists the most important facts from the chapter. Although this section does not list every fact from the chapter that will be on your CCNA exam, a well-prepared CCNA candidate should know, at a minimum, all the details in each "Foundation Summary" before going to take the exam.

The **ip address** interface subcommand assigns an IP address and mask to an interface. If the associated interface is also in an up and up status, the router adds a connected route to the routing table for the subnet connected to that interface. Example 13-12 shows an example configuration with the resulting connected routes.

Example 13-12 *Albuquerque Router Configuration and Connected Routes*

```
Albuquerque#configure terminal
Enter configuration commands, one per line.  End with CNTL/Z.
Albuquerque(config)#interface serial 0
Albuquerque(config-if)#ip address 10.1.128.251 255.255.255.0
Albuquerque(config)#interface serial 1
Albuquerque(config-if)#ip address 10.1.130.251 255.255.255.0
Albuquerque(config)#interface ethernet 0
Albuquerque(config-if)#ip address 10.1.1.251 255.255.255.0

Albuquerque#show ip route
Codes: C - connected, S - static, I - IGRP, R - RIP, M - mobile, B - BGP
       D - EIGRP, EX - EIGRP external, O - OSPF, IA - OSPF inter area
       N1 - OSPF NSSA external type 1, N2 - OSPF NSSA external type 2
       E1 - OSPF external type 1, E2 - OSPF external type 2, E - EGP
       i - IS-IS, L1 - IS-IS level-1, L2 - IS-IS level-2, ia - IS-IS inter area
       * - candidate default, U - per-user static route, o - ODR
       P - periodic downloaded static route

Gateway of last resort is not set

     10.0.0.0/24 is subnetted, 3 subnets
C       10.1.1.0 is directly connected, Ethernet0
C       10.1.130.0 is directly connected, Serial1
C       10.1.128.0 is directly connected, Serial0
```

Table 13-9 summarizes the key naming commands in IOS.

Table 13-9 *IP Naming Commands*

Function	Command Options
Tell IOS to use a DNS	Configure the **ip domain-lookup** global configuration command.
Configure IP addresses of name servers	Configure the **ip name-server** *svr1 svr2...* global configuration command.
Configure static host names	Use the **ip host** *name address* command.
List current host name information	Use the **show hosts** exec command.

Table 13-10 summarizes the commands related to Telnet.

Table 13-10 *Telnet Command Options*

Function	Command Options
Telnet to another device	Use the **telnet** exec command. Just type the host name or IP address from exec mode.
Suspend a Telnet session	Press the key sequence Ctrl-Shift-6, then x.
Discover currently suspended Telnet session	Use the **where** exec command. Use the **show sessions** exec command.
Resume a suspended Telnet session	Use the **resume** command, with no parameter, to reconnect to the most recently suspended Telnet session. Use the **resume** *x* command, where *x* is the number of the suspended Telnet session based on the output of **show sessions**. Just press Enter in exec mode to resume to the most recently suspended Telnet session.
Terminate a suspended Telnet session	Resume connection, and log out using the **quit** command. Use the **disconnect** command on the router you Telnetted from.

CDP discovers several useful details from neighboring networking devices, including the following. You also should review the actual CDP commands in the chapter and memorize which commands provide which details.

- **Device identifier**—Typically the host name
- **Address list**—Network and data-link addresses
- **Port identifier**—Text that identifies the port, which is another name for an interface
- **Capabilities list**—Information on what type of device it is—for instance, a router or a switch
- **Platform**—The model and OS level running in the device

Q&A

As mentioned in the introduction, you have two choices for review questions. The questions that follow give you a bigger challenge than the exam itself by using an open-ended question format. By reviewing now with this more difficult question format, you can exercise your memory better and prove your conceptual and factual knowledge of this chapter. The answers to these questions are found in Appendix A.

For more practice with exam-like question formats, including questions using a router simulator and multiple-choice questions, use the exam engine on the CD.

1. Create a minimal configuration enabling IP on each interface on a 2501 router (two serial, one Ethernet). The NIC assigned you network 8.0.0.0. Your boss says that you need, at most, 200 hosts per subnet. You decide against using VLSM. Your boss also says to plan your subnets so that you can have as many subnets as possible rather than allow for larger subnets later. When choosing the actual IP address values and subnet numbers, you decide to start with the lowest numerical values. Assume that point-to-point serial links will be attached to this router.

2. In the previous question, what would be the IP subnet of the link attached to serial 0? If another user wanted to answer the same question but did not have the enable password, what command(s) might provide this router's addresses and subnets?

3. What must be done to make the output of the **show ip route** command list subnet masks in decimal format instead of prefixes? In what mode would you use the command?

4. What are the differences between the **clock rate** and **bandwidth** commands?

5. Compare and contrast the commands used to set the enable, console, and telnet passwords on a router.

6. In the output of **show ip route,** when a C shows up in the left side of the output on a line for a particular route, what does that mean?

7. Define the term prefix notation. Give two examples.

8. What does ICMP stand for? To which OSI layer would you consider this protocol to apply most closely?

9. Identify two methods to tell a router to ask for name resolution from two different name servers.

10. What keyboard sequence suspends a Telnet session in a Cisco router?

11. What two commands, and what part the command output, tells you which suspended Telnet connection will be reconnected if you just press the Enter key, without any characters typed on the command line?

12. Imagine that you typed a **ping** command and got 5 "!" back. What type of messages were sent through the network? Be as specific as possible.

13. How do you make a router not ask for DNS resolution from a name server?

14. Imagine that you are just logged in at the console of R1, and you Telnet to routers R2, R3, and R4 in succession, but you suspended your Telnet connection each time—in other words, all three Telnet connections go from R1 to the other three routers, respectively. What options do you have for reconnecting to R2?

15. Imagine that you are just logged in at the console of R1, and you Telnet to routers R2, R3, and R4 in succession, but you suspended your Telnet connection each time—in other words, all three Telnet connections go from R1 to the other three routers, respectively. What options do you have for reconnecting to R4?

16. List the five key pieces of information that can be gathered using CDP, as mentioned in the chapter.

17. Imagine a network with Switch1, connected to Router1, with a point-to-point serial link to Router2, which, in turn, is connected to Switch2. Assuming that you are logged into R1, what commands could be used to find the IP addresses of Router2 and Switch1 without logging in to either device?

18. Imagine that a network with Switch1 is connected to Router1, with a point-to-point serial link to Router2, which, in turn, is connected to Switch2. You can log in only to Switch1. Which of the other devices could Switch1 learn about using CDP? Why?

19. What command lists a brief one-line description of CDP information about each neighbor?

This chapter covers the following subjects:

- Routing Protocol Overview

CHAPTER 14

Introduction to Dynamic Routing Protocols

The United States Postal Service routes a huge number of letters and packages each day. To do so, the postal sorting machines run fast, sorting lots of letters. Then the letters are placed in the correct container and onto the correct truck or plane to reach the final destination. However, if no one programs the letter-sorting machines to know where letters to each ZIP code should be sent, the sorter can't do its job. Similarly, Cisco routers can route many packets, but if the router doesn't know any routes, it can't do its job.

This chapter introduces the basic concepts behind IP routing protocols and lists some of the key features of each of the IP routing protocols covered on the INTRO exam. Cisco expects CCNAs to demonstrate a comfortable understanding of the logic behind the routing of packets and the different but related logic behind routing protocols—the protocols used to discover routes. To fully appreciate the nuances of routing protocols, you need a thorough understanding of routing—the process of forwarding packets. You might even want to review the section "IP Routing and Routing Protocols," in Chapter 5, "Fundamentals of IP," for a review of routing, before proceeding with this chapter.

For those of you studying for the CCNA exam, if you are following the reading plan outlined in the introduction, you will move to the *CCNA ICND Exam Certification Guide* after this chapter. For those of you studying just for the INTRO exam, this chapter completes the coverage of topics related to IP and IP routing.

"Do I Know This Already?" Quiz

The purpose of the "Do I Know This Already?" quiz is to help you decide whether you really need to read the entire chapter. If you already intend to read the entire chapter, you do not necessarily need to answer these questions now.

The eight-question quiz, derived from the major sections in the "Foundation Topics" portion of the chapter, helps you determine how to spend your limited study time.

Table 14-1 outlines the major topics discussed in this chapter and the "Do I Know This Already?" quiz questions that correspond to those topics.

Table 14-1 *"Do I Know This Already?" Foundation Topics Section-to-Question Mapping*

Foundations Topics Section	Questions Covered in This Section
Routing Protocol Overview	1–8

> **CAUTION** The goal of self-assessment is to gauge your mastery of the topics in this chapter. If you do not know the answer to a question or are only partially sure of the answer, you should mark this question wrong for purposes of the self-assessment. Giving yourself credit for an answer that you correctly guess skews your self-assessment results and might provide you with a false sense of security.

1. Which of the following routing protocols are considered to use distance vector logic?

    a. RIP

    b. IGRP

    c. EIGRP

    d. OSPF

    e. BGP

2. Which of the following routing protocols are considered to use link-state logic?

    a. RIP V1

    b. RIP V2

    c. IGRP

    d. EIGRP

    e. OSPF

    f. BGP

    g. Integrated IS-IS

3. Which of the following routing protocols use a metric that is, by default, at least partially affected by link bandwidth?

    a. RIP V1

    b. RIP V2

    c. IGRP

    d. EIGRP

    e. OSPF

    f. BGP

    g. Integrated IS-IS

4. Which of the following interior routing protocols support VLSM?

    a. RIP V1

    b. RIP V2

    c. IGRP

    d. EIGRP

    e. OSPF

    f. Integrated IS-IS

5. Which of the following situations would cause RIP to remove all the routes learned from a particular neighboring router?

    a. Keepalive failure

    b. No longer receiving updates from that neighbor

    c. Updates received 5 or more seconds after the last update was sent to that neighbor

    d. Updates from that neighbor have the global "route bad" flag

6. Which of the following interior routing protocols are considered to be capable of converging quickly?

    a. RIP V1

    b. RIP V2

    c. IGRP

    d. EIGRP

    e. OSPF

    f. Integrated IS-IS

7. Which of the following interior routing protocols use hop count as their metric?

   a. RIP V1

   b. RIP V2

   c. IGRP

   d. EIGRP

   e. OSPF

   f. Integrated IS-IS

8. What update timer is used by IGRP?

   a. 5 seconds

   b. 10 seconds

   c. 30 seconds

   d. 60 seconds

   e. 90 seconds

   f. None of the above

The answers to the "Do I Know This Already?" quiz are found in Appendix A, "Answers to the 'Do I Know This Already?' Quizzes and Q&A Sections." The suggested choices for your next step are as follows:

- **6 or less overall score**—Read the entire chapter. This includes the "Foundation Topics" and "Foundation Summary" sections and the Q&A section.

- **7 or 8 overall score**—If you want more review on these topics, skip to the "Foundation Summary" section and then go to the Q&A section. Otherwise, move to the next chapter.

Foundation Topics

To pass the INTRO exam, you need to know some basic information about several IP routing protocols. For the ICND exam, you will need to know distance vector concepts, as well as how to configure two distance vector IP routing protocols—the Routing Information Protocol (RIP) and the Interior Gateway Routing Protocol (IGRP). You will also need to know the concepts behind Enhanced IGRP (EIGRP), as well as Open Shortest Path First (OSPF)—two other IP routing protocols.

This chapter provides overview of routing protocols and the underlying logic used by these protocols.

Routing Protocol Overview

IP routing protocols have one primary goal—to fill the IP routing table with the current best routes it can find. The goal is simple, but the process and options can be complicated.

Terminology can get in the way when you're learning about routing protocols. This book's terminology relating to routing and routing protocols is consistent with the authorized Cisco courses, as well as with most Cisco documentation. So, just to make sure you have the terminology straight before diving into the details, a quick review of a few related terms might be helpful:

- A *routing protocol* fills the routing table with routing information. Examples include RIP and IGRP.

- A *routed protocol* is a protocol with OSI Layer 3 characteristics that define logical addressing and routing. The packets defined by the network layer (Layer 3) portion of these protocols can be routed. Examples of routed protocols include IP and IPX.

- The term *routing type* has been used in other Cisco courses, so you should also know this term. It refers to the type of routing protocol, such as link-state or distance vector.

IP routing protocols fill the IP routing table with valid, (hopefully) loop-free routes. Although the primary goal is to build a routing table, each routing protocol has a very important secondary goal of preventing loops. The routes added to the routing table include a subnet number, the interface out which to forward packets so that they are delivered to that subnet, and the IP address of the next router that should receive packets destined for that subnet (if needed).

An analogy about routing protocols can help. Imagine that a stubborn man is taking a trip to somewhere he has never been. He might look for a road sign referring to the destination town and pointing him to the next turn. By repeating the process at each intersection, he eventually should make it to the correct town. Of course, if a routing loop occurs (in other words, he's lost!) and he stubbornly never asks for directions, he could drive around forever—or at least until he runs out of gas. In this analogy, the guy in the car is like a routed protocol—it travels through the network from the source to the destination. The *routing protocol* is like the fellow whose job it is to decide what to paint on the various road signs. As long as all the road signs have correct information, the guy in the car should make it to the right town just by reading the road signs. Likewise, as long as the routing protocol puts the right routes in the various routing tables, the routers should deliver packets successfully.

All routing protocols have several general goals, as summarized in the following list:

■ To dynamically learn and fill the routing table with a route to all subnets in the network.

■ If more than one route to a subnet is available, to place the best route in the routing table.

■ To notice when routes in the table are no longer valid, and to remove those routes from the routing table.

■ If a route is removed from the routing table and another route through another neighboring router is available, to add the route to the routing table. (Many people view this goal and the preceding one as a single goal.)

■ To add new routes, or to replace lost routes with the best currently available route, as quickly as possible. The time between losing the route and finding a working replacement route is called *convergence time*.

■ To prevent routing loops.

So, all routing protocols have the same general goals. Cisco IOS Software supports a large variety of IP routing protocols. IP's long history and continued popularity have resulted in the specification and creation of several different competing routing protocol options. So, classifying IP routing protocols based on their differences is useful.

Comparing and Contrasting IP Routing Protocols

Routing protocols can be categorized in several ways. One distinction is whether the protocol is more useful between two companies or inside a single company. Only one IP routing protocol that is popular today, the Border Gateway Protocol (BGP), is designed specifically for use between two different organizations. In fact, BGP distributes routing information between ISPs worldwide today and between ISPs and their customers as need be.

Routing protocols that are best used to distribute routes between companies and organizations, such as BGP, are called *exterior routing protocols*. Routing protocols designed to distribute routing information inside a single organization are called *interior* routing protocols. The comparison is like the U.S. Department of Transportation (DOT) versus the local government's transportation department. The U.S. DOT plans the large interstate highways, but it could care less that someone just sold a farm to a developer and the local government has given the developer the approval to pave a new street so that he can build some houses. The U.S. DOT could be compared to exterior routing protocols—they care about overall worldwide connectivity, but they could care less when a single company adds a new LAN and a new subnet. However, the interior routing protocols do care, so when the packet gets to the company, all the routers will have learned about any new subnets, and the packet can be delivered successfully.

This section focuses on how to compare the interior IP routing protocols because there are several on the INTRO exam and there are many points of comparison. Table 14-2 lists some of the major comparison points.

Table 14-2   *Major Comparison Points Between Interior Routing Protocols*

Point of Comparison	Description
Type of routing protocol	Each interior routing protocol covered in this chapter can be characterized based on the underlying logic used by the routing protocol. This underlying logic often is referred to as the type of routing protocol. The three types are distance vector, link-state, and hybrid.
Full/partial updates	Some interior routing protocols send their entire routing tables regularly, which are called *full routing updates*. Other routing protocols send only a subset of the routing table in updates, typically just the information about any changed routes. This subset is referred to as *partial routing updates*. Partial routing updates require less overhead in the network.
Convergence	Convergence refers to the time required for routers to react to changes (for example, link failures and router failures) in the network, removing bad routes and adding new, better routes so that the current best routes are in all the routers' routing tables.
Metric	The metric refers to the numeric value that describes how good a particular route is. The lower the value is, the better the route is. Some metrics provide a more realistic perspective on which routes are truly the best routes.
Support for VLSM	*Variable-length subnet masking (VLSM)* means that, in a single Class A, B, or C network, multiple subnet masks can be used. The advantage of VLSM is that it enables you to vary the size of each subnet, based on the needs of that subnet. For instance, a point-to-point serial link needs only two IP addresses, so a subnet mask of 255.255.255.252, which allows only two valid IP addresses, meets the requirements but does not waste IP addresses. A mask allowing a much larger number of IP addresses then can be used on each LAN-based subnet. Some routing protocols support VLSM, and some do not.
Classless or classful	*Classless routing protocols* transmit the subnet mask along with each route in the routing updates sent by that protocol. *Classful routing protocols* do not transmit mask information. So only classless routing protocols support VLSM. To say that a routing protocol is classless is to say that it supports VLSM, and vice versa.

The next few sections take you through the basics of each of the types of interior routing protocols, as well as give you a short description of each routing protocol.

Routing Through the Internet with the Border Gateway Protocol

ISPs use BGP today to exchange routing information between themselves and other ISPs and customers. Whereas interior routing protocols might be concerned about advertising all subnets inside a single organization, with a large network having a few thousand routes in the IP routing table, exterior routing protocols try to make sure that advertising routes reach every organization's network. Exterior routing protocols also deal with routing tables that, with a lot of work done to keep the size down, still exceed 100,000 routes.

BGP advertises only routing information to specifically defined peers using TCP. By using TCP, a router knows that any routing updates will be re-sent if they happen to get lost in transit.

BGP uses a concept called autonomous systems when describing each route. An *autonomous system (AS)* is a group of devices under the control of a single organization—in other words, that organization has autonomy from the other interconnected parts of the Internet. An AS number (ASN) is assigned to each AS, uniquely identifying each AS in the Internet. BGP includes the ASNs in the routing updates to prevent loops. Figure 14-1 shows the general idea.

Figure 14-1 *BGP Uses ASNs to Prevent Routing Loops*

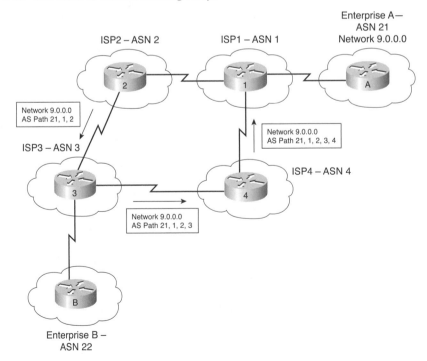

Notice that in the figure, the BGP updates sent to each successive AS show the ASNs in the route. When R1 receives the BGP update from R4, it notices that its own ASN in found inside the AS path and ignores that particular route.

BGP does not use a metric like internal routing protocols. Because BGP expects to be used between different ISPs and between ISPs and customers, BGP allows for a very robust set of alternatives for deciding what route to use; these alternatives are called policies. Routing policy can be based on the fact that an ISP might have a better business relationship with a particular ISP. For instance, in Figure 14-1, packets from Enterprise B toward Enterprise A can take the "high" route (from ASN 3, to ASN 2, and then to ASN 1) if ISP3 has a better business relationship with ISP2, as compared with ISP4.

In the next section, you will learn about interior routing protocols and how they use some more obvious metrics.

Distance Vector Protocols: RIP and IGRP

Distance vector protocols advertise routing information by sending messages, called *routing updates*, out the interfaces on a router. These updates contain a series of entries, with each entry representing a subnet and a metric. The metric represents how good the route is from that router's perspective, with a smaller number being a better route.

Any routers that receive a copy of a distance vector routing update receive that information and possibly add some routes to their routing table. The receiving router adds the routes only if the routing update described a route to a subnet that it did not already know about or if it described a route that already was known, but the newly learned route has a better (lower) metric.

Figure 14-2 depicts the basic process.

Figure 14-2   *Basic Distance Vector Routing Update, with Resulting Learned Route*

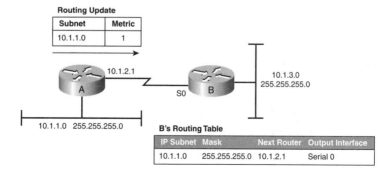

Note that Router A advertises the route to its LAN subnet to Router B. The update includes only the subnet number and a metric. Router B then adds a route to its routing table, but the route has more information in it than did the routing update itself. When B received the update, it came in interface Serial0, so Router B considers Serial0 to be the correct outgoing interface. The update came from IP address 10.1.2.1, so Router B considers that IP address to be the next-hop IP address. Also, if the distance vector update does not include the subnet mask, as in the figure, Router B assumes that Router A uses the same mask that it does. As it turns out, these routers would not support VLSM because if Router A used a different subnet mask than Router B, B would make a wrong assumption about the mask. The fact that the routing protocol in this example does not transmit mask information also makes it a classful routing protocol. For these examples, assume that all routers are using the same subnet mask in this network—specifically, 255.255.255.0.

If it seems simple, then you understand it well—distance vector protocols first were created about 20 years ago, when the processor in a routing device was probably less powerful than the processor in your cell phone today. It had to be simple so as not to overburden the router's processor, and also not to overload the network with overhead traffic.

The following list formalizes the basic distance vector logic and introduces a few important concepts that are explained over the next several pages:

- Routers add directly connected subnets to their routing tables, even without a routing protocol.
- Routers send routing updates out their interfaces to advertise the routes that this router already knows. These routes include directly connected routes as well as routes learned from other routers.
- Routers listen for routing updates from their neighbors so that they can learn new routes.
- The routing information includes the subnet number and a metric. The metric defines how good the route is; lower metric routes are considered better routes.
- When possible, routers use broadcasts or multicasts to send routing updates. By using a broadcast or multicast packet, all neighbors on a LAN can receive the same routing information in a single update.
- If a router learns multiple routes to the same subnet, the router chooses the best route based on the metric. (If the metrics tie, there are a variety of options, which are described in Chapter 6, "OSPF and EIGRP Concepts and Configuration," of the *CCNA ICND Exam Certification Guide*.)
- Routers send periodic full updates and expect to receive periodic updates from neighboring routers.
- Failure to receive updates from a neighbor in a timely manner results in the removal of the routes previously learned from that neighbor.
- A router assumes that, for a route advertised by Router X, the next-hop router in that route is Router X.

Routing Information Protocol Version 1

RIP Version 1 (RIP-1) has been around for a long time—longer than 15 years for use with IP networks. It has many shortcomings compared to some of the relatively newer IP routing protocols, but it does work and is an easy tool to use for comparison with the other routing protocols.

RIP uses hop count for a metric. That means that, from an individual router's perspective, if there are two routers between itself and a subnet, its metric for that subnet is 2. Figure 14-3 outlines the concept.

Figure 14-3   *RIP's Use of Hop Count as Metric*

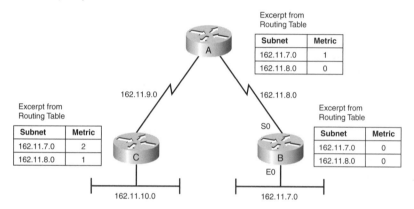

Only a part of the routing table for each router is shown in the figure, but from those shown, you can see what is meant by the hop count. Router B's metrics for its locally attached subnets are both 0 because there are no routers between B and those subnets. Similarly, Router A's metric for 162.11.8.0 is 0. Because Router B separates Router A from subnet 162.11.7.0, Router A's metric for subnet 162.11.7.0 is 1. Finally, Router C's metric for subnet 162.11.7.0 is 2 because two routers separate it from that subnet.

You will learn much more about RIP and the underlying distance vector logic used by RIP as you prepare for the ICND exam. For now, this short list of RIP-1 features can help you compare RIP-1 to some of the other IP routing protocols covered in this overview:

■   Based on distance vector Logic

■   Uses hop count for the metric

■   Sends periodic full routing updates every 30 seconds

■   Converges slowly, often taking 3 to 5 minutes

■   Does not support VLSM, also making it a classful routing protocol

RIP Version 2

RIP Version 2 (RIP-2), as currently defined in RFC 2453, defines several enhancements to the original RIP protocol. RIP-2 uses distance vector logic; uses hop count for the metric; sends full, periodic updates; and still converges relatively slowly.

RIP-2 does add support for VLSM, as compared with RIP-1, making it a classless routing protocol, with RIP-2 including the subnet mask for each subnet in the routing updates. Table 14-3 outlines the improvements made to RIP with the creation of RIP-2.

Table 14-3 *Improvements Made to RIP by RIP V2*

Feature	Description
Transmits subnet mask with route	This feature allows VLSM by passing the mask along with each route so that the subnet is defined exactly. It allows VLSM, making RIP-2 a classless routing protocol.
Provides authentication	Both clear text (RFC-defined) and MD5 encryption (Cisco-added feature) can be used to authenticate the source of a routing update.
Includes a next-hop router IP address in its routing update	A router can advertise a route but direct any listeners to a different router on that same subnet.
Uses external route tags	RIP can pass information about routes learned from an external source and redistributed into RIP. Another router then can pass these external tags to that same routing protocol in a difference part of the network, effectively helping that other routing protocol pass information.
Uses multicast routing updates	Instead of broadcasting updates to 255.255.255.255 like RIP-1, the destination IP address is 224.0.0.9, an IP multicast address. 224.0.0.9 is reserved specifically for use by RIP-2. This reduces the amount of processing required on non–RIP-speaking hosts on a common subnet.

The most important feature comparing the two is that RIP-2 supports VLSM. Today, when choosing a routing protocol, RIP-1 would not be the best choice—in fact, the RIP-1 RFC has been designated for historic status. Both protocols work well, but RIP-2 is more functional. If you want a routing protocol that uses a public standard and you want to avoid the complexity of link-state protocols, RIP-2 is your best choice.

Interior Gateway Routing Protocol

IGRP is a Cisco-proprietary IP routing protocol created by Cisco more than 10 years ago. Cisco created IGRP to provide a better distance vector protocol to its customers, as compared with RIP-1.

The most obvious difference between RIP-1 and IGRP is the metric. IGRP advertises up to five parameters that describe the metric for each route, although, practically, only two ever are used—bandwidth and delay. The bandwidth part of this more complex metric describes the constrained link speed. For instance, if a route to a subnet contained all Fast Ethernet links, the bandwidth in the update would be 100 Mbps; however, if a single 56-kbps link were in the path, the bandwidth would be listed as 56 kbps. The delay component includes a cumulative number—for instance, a route going over ten Fast Ethernet links would have its delay part of the metric ten times bigger than a route with a single 100-Mbps link in the path.

IGRP calculates the metric based on a mathematical formula that you do not really need to know for the exam. The formula uses bandwidth and delay as input and results in an integer value, the metric, between 1 and 4,294,967,295.

Figure 14-4 shows the benefit of this better metric.

Figure 14-4 *RIP and IGRP Metrics Compared*

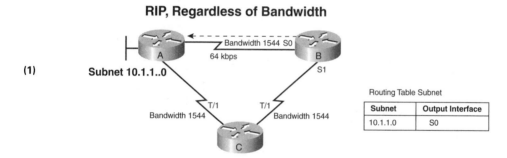

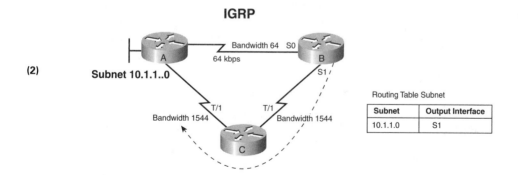

As shown in the figure, Router B's route to 10.1.1.0 points through Router A because that route has a lower hop count (1) than the route through Router C (2). However, Router B will choose the two-hop route through Router C when using IGRP because the bandwidths of the two links in the route are much higher than that of the single-hop route. In the top trio of routers, the engineer let the **bandwidth** command default to 1544 on each link because RIP does not consider the bandwidth. On the bottom trio, the engineer correctly configured **bandwidth** to match the actual link speeds, thereby allowing IGRP to choose the faster route. (The **bandwidth interface** subcommand does not change the actual physical speed of the interface–it just tells the IOS what speed to assume the interface is using.)

IGRP and RIP-1 were the main options for routing protocols back in the early 1990s. RIP-2 came later, but only after two better alternatives, OSPF and EIGRP, had become better options for most networks. Table 14-4 summarizes some of the key comparison points between these three protocols.

Table 14-4 *Distance Vector Protocols Compared*

Feature	RIP-1	RIP-2	IGRP
Update timer for full routing updates	30 seconds	30 seconds	90 seconds
Metric	Hop count	Hop count	Function of bandwidth and delay (the default). Can include reliability, load, and MTU.
Supports VLSM	No	Yes	No
Infinite-metric value	16	16	4,294,967,295
Convergence	Slow	Slow	Slow

Link-State Protocols: OSPF and Integrated IS-IS

Link-state and distance vectors share a common goal—to fill the routing tables with the current best routes. They differ significantly in how they each accomplish the task. The largest difference between the two is that distance vector protocols advertise sparse information; in fact, distance vector protocols know only that other routers exist if the other router broadcasts a routing update to them. When a distance vector protocol in a router hears a routing update, the update says nothing about the routers beyond that neighboring router that sent the update. Conversely, link-state protocols advertise a large amount of topological information about the network, and the routers perform some CPU-intensive computation on the topological data. They even discover their neighbors before bothering to exchange routing information.

To figure out the current best routes, a router processes the link-state topology database using an algorithm called the Dijkstra *Shortest Path First (SPF) algorithm.* This detailed topology information, along with the Dijkstra algorithm, helps link-state protocols avoid loops and converge quickly.

Link-state protocols prevent loops from occurring easily because each router essentially has a complete map of the network. If you take a trip in your car and you have a map, you are a lot less likely to get lost than someone else who is just reading the signs by the side of the road. Likewise, the detailed topological information helps link-state protocols easily avoid loops. As you will read later, the main reasons that distance vector protocols converge slowly are related to the loop-avoidance features. With link-state protocols, those same loop-avoidance features are not needed, allowing for fast convergence—often in less than 10 seconds.

Open Shortest Path First

OSPF is the most popular link-state IP routing protocol today and is likely to be the most popular one for some time. It works well, is widely deployed, and includes a wide variety of features that have been added over the years to accommodate new requirements.

The basic operation of OSPF differs from that of the distance vector protocols. For the ICND exam, you will need to know a few more details, of course, but for now, a brief look at how OSPF works will help you compare it with distance vector protocols.

One difference relates to how and when OSPF actually sends routing information. A router does not send routing information with OSPF until it discovers other OSPF-speaking routers on a common subnet. The following list gives you some idea of the process:

1. Each router discovers its neighbors on each interface. The list of neighbors is kept in a neighbor table.

2. Each router uses a reliable protocol to exchange topology information with its neighbors.

3. Each router places the learned topology information into its topology database.

4. Each router runs the SPF algorithm against its own topology database to calculate the best routes to each subnet in the database.

5. Each router places the best route to each subnet into the IP routing table.

Link-state protocols do require more work by the routers, but the work is typically worth the effort. A router running a link-state protocol uses more memory and more processing cycles than do distance vector protocols. The topology updates require a large number of bytes to describe the details of every subnet, every router, and which routers are connected to which subnets. However, because OSPF does not send full updates on a regular short interval (like RIP), the overall number of bytes sent for routing information is typically smaller. Also, OSPF converges much more quickly than do distance vector protocols—and fast convergence is one of the most important features of a routing protocol.

OSPF uses a concept called *cost* for the metric. Each link is considered to have a cost; a route's cost is the sum of the cost for each link. By default, Cisco derives the cost value for a link from the bandwidth, so you can think of the metric as being based on cumulative link bandwidth. (IGRP's metric is based on delay and bandwidth, but it does not treat bandwidth as a cumulative value; it considers only the slowest link in a path.)

The following list points out some of the key features of OSPF:

- Converges very quickly—from the point of recognizing a failure, it often can converge in less than 10 seconds.

- Supports VLSM.

- Uses short Hello messages on a short regular interval (the Hello interval), with the absence of Hello messages indicating that a neighbor is no longer reachable.

- Sends partial updates when link status changes, and floods full updates every 30 minutes. The flooding, however, does not happen all at once, so the overhead is minimal.

- Uses cost for the metric.

Integrated IS-IS

Once upon a time, the world of networking consisted of proprietary networking protocols from the various computer vendors. For companies that bought computers from only that one vendor, there was no problem. However, when you used multiple vendor's computers, networking became more problematic.

One solution to the problem was the development of a standardized networking protocol, such as TCP/IP. Skipping a few dozen years of history, you get to today's networking environment, where a computer vendor couldn't sell a computer without it also supporting TCP/IP. Problem solved!

Well, before TCP/IP became the networking protocol standard solving all these problems, the International Organization for Standardization (ISO) worked hard on a set of protocols that together fit into an architecture called Open System Interconnection (OSI). As you recall from Chapter 2, "The TCP/IP and OSI Networking Models," OSI defined its own protocols for Layers 3 through 7, relying on other standards for Layers 1 and 2, much like TCP/IP does today. OSI did not become commercially viable, whereas TCP/IP did—the victory going to the nimbler, more flexible TCP/IP.

So, why bother telling you all this now? Well, OSI defines a network layer protocol called the Connectionless Network Protocol (CLNP). It also defines a routing protocol—a routing protocol used to advertise CLNP routes, called Intermediate System-to-Intermediate System (IS-IS). IS-IS advertises CLNP routes between "intermediate systems," which is what OSI calls routers.

Later in life, IS-IS was updated to include the capability to advertise IP routes as well as CLNP routes. To distinguish it from the older IS-IS, this new updated IS-IS is called *Integrated IS-IS*. The word integrated identifies the fact that the routing protocol can exchange routing information for multiple Layer 3 routed protocols.

Integrated IS-IS has an advantage over OSPF because it supports both CLNP and IP route advertisement, but most installations could not care less about CLNP. Table 14-5 outlines the key comparison points with all Interior routing protocols for both Integrated IS-IS and OSPF.

Table 14-5   *IP Link-State Protocols Compared*

Feature	OSPF	Integrated IS-IS
Period for individual reflooding of routing information	30 minutes	15 minutes
Metric	Cost	Metric
Supports VLSM	Yes	Yes
Convergence	Fast	Fast

Balanced Hybrid Protocols: Enhanced IGRP

EIGRP does not use distance vector or link-state logic, but instead it uses a whole new category of routing protocol. This new category has some features similar to link-state protocols, others similar to distance vector protocols, and yet others unlike either of the two. Cisco sometimes categorizes EIGRP as a *balanced hybrid protocol*, so you should remember the term.

The internal workings of EIGRP depend on an algorithm called the *Diffusing Update Algorithm (DUAL)*. DUAL exchanges more topology information than a distance vector routing protocol, but it does not transmit full topology information like a link-state protocol. Also, the computations used by DUAL require far less processing than the computation-intensive Dijkstra SPF algorithm.

DUAL defines a method for each router not only to calculate the best current route to each subnet, but also to calculate alternative routes that could be used if the current route fails. An alternative route, using what DUAL calls a *feasible successor route*, is guaranteed to be loop-free. So, if the current best route fails, the router immediately can start using the feasible successor route instead so that convergence can happen very quickly.

The following list points out some of the key similarities to some of the other protocols covered in this introduction:

■ Like OSPF and Integrated IS-IS, it converges quickly, often in less than 3 seconds after a failure is recognized.

■ Like OSPF, EIGRP discovers neighbors before sending them routing information.

■ Like RIP and IGRP, EIGRP requires very little design effort. (Link-state protocols require some design work in medium to larger networks).

■ Like IGRP, EIGRP is Cisco proprietary.

■ Like IGRP, EIGRP uses a metric based on bandwidth and delay. EIGRP uses the same metric as IGRP, except that EIGRP scales the metric by multiplying by 256.

■ Like link-state protocols, EIGRP does not send full updates on a periodic interval, but rather sends partial updates only as links or routers go up and down.

■ Like link-state protocols, EIGRP builds some topology tables in addition to the IP routing table.

Summary of Interior Routing Protocols

Before finishing your study for the ICND or CCNA exam, you will learn a lot more about RIP-1, IGRP, EIGRP, and OSPF. This chapter has introduced you to some of the key terms and points of comparison for these routing protocols, as well as a few others. Table 14-6 summarizes the most important points of comparison between the interior routing protocols, and Table 14-7 lists some of the key terminology.

Table 14-6 *Interior IP Routing Protocols Compared: Summary*

Routing Protocol	Metric	Convergence Speed	Supports VLSM and Is a Classless Routing Protocol	Default Period for Full Routing Updates
RIP-1	Hop count	Slow	No	30 seconds
RIP-2	Hop count	Slow	Yes	30 seconds
IGRP	Calculated based on constraining bandwidth and cumulative delay	Slow	No	90 seconds
EIGRP	Same as IGRP, except multiplied by 256	Very fast	Yes	N/A
OSPF	Cost, as derived from bandwidth by default	Fast	Yes	N/A
Integrated IS-IS	Metric	Fast	Yes	N/A

Table 14-7   *Routing Protocol Terminology*

Term	Definition
Routing protocol	A protocol whose purpose is to learn the available routes, place the best routes into the routing table, and remove routes when they are no longer valid.
Exterior routing protocol	A routing protocol designed for use between two different organizations. These typically are used between ISPs or between a company and an ISP. For example, a company would run BGP, an exterior routing protocol, between one of its routers and a router inside an ISP.
Interior routing protocol	A routing protocol designed for use within a single organization. For example, an entire company might choose the IGRP routing protocol, which is an interior routing protocol.
Distance vector	The logic behind the behavior of some interior routing protocols, such as RIP and IGRP.
Link state	The logic behind the behavior of some interior routing protocols, such as OSPF.
Balanced hybrid	The logic behind the behavior of EIGRP, which is more like distance vector than link state but is different from these other two types of routing protocols.
Dijkstra Shortest Path First (SPF) algorithm	Magic math used by link-state protocols, such as OSPF, when the routing table is calculated.
Diffusing Update Algorithm (DUAL)	The process by which EIGRP routers collectively calculate the routes to place into the routing tables.
Convergence	The time required for routers to react to changes in the network, removing bad routes and adding new, better routes so that the current best routes are in all the routers' routing tables.
Metric	The numeric value that describes how good a particular route is. The lower the value is, the better the route is.

Foundation Summary

The "Foundation Summary" section of each chapter lists the most important facts from the chapter. Although this section does not list every fact from the chapter that will be on your CCNA exam, a well-prepared CCNA candidate should know, at a minimum, all the details in each "Foundation Summary" section before going to take the exam.

All routing protocols have several general goals, as summarized in the following list:

- To dynamically learn and fill the routing table with a route to all subnets in the network.

- If more than one route to a subnet is available, to place the best route in the routing table.

- To notice when routes in the table are no longer valid, and to remove those routes from the routing table.

- If a route is removed from the routing table and another route through another neighboring router is available, to add the route to the routing table. (Many people view this goal and the preceding one as a single goal.)

- To add new routes, or to replace lost routes with the best currently available route, as quickly as possible. The time between losing the route and finding a working replacement route is called *convergence time.*

- To prevent routing loops.

The following list summarizes a few very important terms related to routing and routing protocols:

- A *routing protocol* fills the routing table with routing information. Examples include RIP and IGRP.

- A *routed protocol* is a protocol with OSI Layer 3 characteristics that define logical addressing and routing. The packets defined by the network layer (Layer 3) portion of these protocols can be routed. Examples of protocols include IP and IPX.

- The term *routing type* has been used in other Cisco courses, so you also should know this term. It refers to the type of routing protocol, such as link-state or distance vector.

Table 14-8 lists some of the major comparison points between interior routing protocols.

Table 14-8 *Major Comparison Points Between Interior Routing Protocols*

Point of Comparison	Description
Type of routing protocol	Each interior routing protocol covered in this chapter can be characterized based on the underlying logic used by the routing protocol. This underlying logic often is referred to as the type of routing protocol. The three types are distance vector, link state, and hybrid.
Full/partial updates	Some interior routing protocols send their entire routing tables regularly, which is called *full routing updates*. Other routing protocols send only a subset of the routing table in updates, typically just the information about any changed routes. This is called *partial routing updates*. Partial updates require less overhead in the network.
Convergence	Convergence refers to the time required for routers to react to changes (for example, link failures and router failures) in the network, removing bad routes and adding new, better routes so that the current best routes are in all the routers' routing tables.
Metric	The numeric value that describes how good a particular route is. The lower the value is, the better the route is. Some metrics provide a more realistic perspective on which routes are truly the best routes.
Support for VLSM	*Variable-length subnet masking (VLSM)* means that, in a single Class A, B, or C network, multiple subnet masks can be used. The advantage of VLSM is that it enables you to vary the size of each subnet, based on the needs of that subnet. For instance, a point-to-point serial link needs only two IP addresses, so a subnet mask of 255.255.255.252, which allows only two valid IP addresses, meets the requirements but does not waste IP addresses. A mask allowing a much larger number of IP addresses then can be used on each LAN-based subnet. Some routing protocols support VLSM, and some do not.
Classless or classful	*Classless routing protocols* transmit the subnet mask along with each route in the routing updates sent by that protocol. *Classful routing protocols* do not transmit mask information. So only classless routing protocols support VLSM. To say that a routing protocol is classless is to say that it does support VLSM, and vice versa.

Table 14-9 summarizes the most important points of comparison between the interior routing protocols.

Table 14-9   *Interior IP Routing Protocols Compared—Summary*

Routing Protocol	Metric	Convergence Speed	Supports VLSM, and Is a Classless Routing Protocol	Period for Full routing Updates
RIP-1	Hop count	Slow	No	30 seconds
RIP-2	Hop count	Slow	Yes	30 seconds
IGRP	Calculated based on constraining bandwidth and cumulative delay	Slow	No	90 seconds
EIGRP	Same as IGRP, except multiplied by 256	Very fast	Yes	N/A
OSPF	Cost, as derived from bandwidth by default	Fast	Yes	N/A
Integrated IS-IS	Metric	Fast	Yes	N/A

Table 14-10 outlines some of the key comparison points between RIP and IGRP.

Table 14-10   *RIP and IGRP Feature Comparison*

Feature	RIP (Default)	IGRP (Default)
Update timer	30 seconds	90 seconds
Metric	Hop count	Function of bandwidth and delay (the default). Can include reliability, load, and MTU.
Hold-down timer	180	280
Flash (triggered) updates	Yes	Yes
Mask sent in update	No	No
Infinite-metric value	16	4,294,967,295

Q&A

As mentioned in the introduction, you have two choices for review questions. The questions that follow give you a bigger challenge than the exam itself by using an open-ended question format. By reviewing now with this more difficult question format, you can exercise your memory better and prove your conceptual and factual knowledge of this chapter. The answers to these questions are found in Appendix A.

For more practice with exam like question formats, including questions using a router simulator and multiple-choice questions, use the exam engine on the CD.

1. Which interior IP routing protocols covered in this chapter support VLSM?

2. Which IP routing protocols covered in this chapter use distance vector logic?

3. Which interior IP routing protocols covered in this chapter are considered to converge quickly?

4. Compare distance vector and link-state protocols in terms of what information is sent in routing updates.

5. List three similarities between EIGRP's balanced hybrid logic and link-state logic.

6. Explain the basic concept behind why some routing protocols support VLSM and some do not.

7. Explain the difference between interior and exterior routing protocols.

8. Explain the difference between full and partial routing updates.

9. Define the term balanced hybrid in relation to the terms distance vector and link state.

10. Compare and contrast the types of information sent in distance vector routing updates versus link-state routing updates.

11. What term describes the underlying logic behind the OSPF routing protocol?

Cisco Published INTRO Exam Topics*
Covered in This Part:

* Always re-check www.cisco.com for the latest posted exam topics

PART V: Wide-Area Networking

Chapter 15: Remote Access Technologies

This chapter covers the following subjects:

- Perspectives on the PSTN

- Analog Modems

- Integrated Services Digital Network

- Digital Subscriber Line

- Cable Modems

- Comparison of Remote Access Technologies

Remote Access Technologies

Earlier in this book, you learned about Ethernet LANs, point-to-point WAN links, and Frame Relay. All of these technologies can be used to connect a corporate site to the Internet. However, none of these options is cost-effective for connecting the typical home-based user to the Internet.

In this chapter, you will learn about several different technologies used for Internet access from the home. Some of these same technologies can be used to remotely access corporate networks as well. This chapter covers the most common remote access technologies—namely, analog modems, DSL, ISDN, and cable.

> **AUTHOR'S NOTE** While they may be on the CCNA exam, the topics in this chapter are less likely to be on the CCNA exam than most other topics in this book. For those of you that are planning to take the CCNA exam, instead of taking both the INTRO and ICND exams, you might consider skipping this chapter. Refer to the introduction to this book for more perspectives on the CCNA exam topics.

"Do I Know This Already?" Quiz

The purpose of the "Do I Know This Already?" quiz is to help you decide whether you really need to read the entire chapter. If you already intend to read the entire chapter, you do not necessarily need to answer these questions now.

The 15-question quiz, derived from the major sections in the "Foundation Topics" portion of the chapter, helps you determine how to spend your limited study time.

Table 15-1 outlines the major topics discussed in this chapter and the "Do I Know This Already?" quiz questions that correspond to those topics.

Table 15-1 *"Do I Know This Already?" Foundation Topics Section-to-Question Mapping*

Foundations Topics Section	Questions Covered in This Section
Perspectives on the PSTN	1—2
Analog Modems	3—4
ISDN	5—7
DSL	8—10
Cable Modems	11—12
Comparisons of Remote Access Technologies	13—15

CAUTION The goal of self-assessment is to gauge your mastery of the topics in this chapter. If you do not know the answer to a question or are only partially sure of the answer, you should mark this question wrong for purposes of the self-assessment. Giving yourself credit for an answer that you correctly guess skews your self-assessment results and might provide you with a false sense of security.

1. Which of the following acronyms identifies a voice codec used to encode analog voice signals into a 64-kbps digital data stream?

    a. PSTN

    b. MCNS

    c. ADSL

    d. PCM

    e. AS-CELP

2. How many DS0 channels are in a DS1 in the United States?

    a. 1

    b. 2

    c. 8

    d. 16

    e. 24

    f. 28

    g. 32

3. Which of the following best describes the function of demodulation by a modem?

   a. Encoding an incoming analog signal as a digital signal

   b. Decoding an incoming digital signal into an analog signal

   c. Encoding a set of binary digits as an analog electrical signal

   d. Decoding an incoming analog electrical signal into a set of binary digits

   e. Encoding a set of binary digits as a digital electrical signal

   f. Decoding an incoming digital electrical signal into a set of binary digits

4. Which of the following modem standards do not support 56-kbps speeds downstream?

   a. V.22

   b. V.22bis

   c. V.42

   d. V.90

   e. V.92

   f. V.32

   g. V.32bis

   h. V.34

5. Which of the following terms best describes features of an ISDN PRI in Europe?

   a. B+D

   b. 2B+D

   c. 23B+D

   d. 24B+D

   e. 30B+D

   f. 31B+D

   g. 32B+D

6. Imagine that you plug an analog phone into an ISDN modem and call a friend at her house, where she uses an analog phone using plain-old telephone service (POTS). At which of the following points in a network will a voice codec be used?

   a. Your friend's telephone

   b. The phone switch into which your friend's local line is connected

   c. The phone switch into which your ISDN BRI line is connected

   d. Your ISDN modem

   e. Your telephone

7. What does the letter B stand for in the ISDN term *B channel*?

   a. Bearer

   b. Broadband

   c. Binary

   d. Best

8. Which of the following DSL standards has a limit of 18,000 feet for the length of the local loop?

   a. IDSL

   b. DSL

   c. ADSL

   d. VDSL

   e. HDSL

9. Imagine a local phone line from a house to a local telco CO. When the customer at that house requests DSL service, what type of device does the telco move the CO end of the local line to?

   a. DSLAM

   b. DSL router

   c. DSL modem

   d. Class 5 switch

   e. Voice switch

   f. Head end

10. Which of the following protocols are used by DSL modem and routers for data link layer functions?

    a. PPP

    b. IEEE 802.3

    c. ATM

    d. IEEE 802.1Q

    e. MCNS MAC

11. Which of the following protocols is used by cable modems for data link layer functions?

    a. PPP

    b. IEEE 802.3

    c. ATM

    d. IEEE 802.1Q

    e. MCNS MAC

12. Which of the following protocols are used by a cable modem for the upstream data?

    a. PCM

    b. QAM-16

    c. QAM-64

    d. QAM-256

    e. QPSK

13. Which of the following remote access technologies uses ATM, Ethernet, and PPP as data-link protocols?

    a. Analog modems

    b. ISDN

    c. DSL

    d. Cable modems

14. Which of the following remote access technologies support specifications that allow both symmetric speeds and asymmetric speeds?

    a. Analog modems

    b. ISDN

    c. DSL

    d. Cable modems

15. Which of the following remote access technologies, when used to connect to an ISP, is considered to be an "always on" service?

    a. Analog modems

    b. ISDN

    c. DSL

    d. Cable modems

The answers to the "Do I Know This Already?" quiz are found in Appendix A, "Answers to the 'Do I Know This Already?' Quizzes and Q&A Sections." The suggested choices for your next step are as follows:

- **12 or less overall score**—Read the entire chapter. This includes the "Foundation Topics" and "Foundation Summary" sections and the Q&A section.

- **13-15 overall score**—If you want more review on these topics, skip to the "Foundation Summary" section and then go to the Q&A section. Otherwise, move to the next chapter.

Foundation Topics

Many companies like the idea of letting workers telecommute, working out of their houses. To gain access to applications residing at the corporate site, companies can support various types of dynamic access to the corporate network for the home user. For instance, a home-based worker might use a modem to dial into the corporate site.

At the same time, most corporations today connect to the Internet using a leased WAN connection of some kind, typically one or more T1 circuits, or possibly even T3 circuits. If their home-based users have access to the Internet, the users could be allowed to access the necessary corporate applications and data through their Internet connection. Depending on the geography, fees for Internet access, and other factors, allowing access through the Internet might be cheaper than providing the capability for users to connect directly into the corporate network.

This chapter begins by covering some background information about the Public Switched Telephone Network (PSTN). Most remote access technologies use the PSTN for basic physical access. The chapter continues with coverage of each of the four types of remote access technologies—modems, ISDN, DSL, and cable.

Perspectives on the PSTN

The Public Switched Telephone Network (PSTN) was built to support traffic between telephones—in other words, voice traffic. Three of the four access technologies covered in this chapter happen to use the PSTN, so a basic understanding of the PSTN can help you appreciate how modems, ISDN, and DSL work. If you already know a fair amount about the PSTN, feel free to jump ahead to the section titled "Analog Modems."

Sound waves travel through the air by vibrating the air. The human ear hears the sound because the ear vibrates as a result of the air inside the ear moving, which, in turn, causes the brain to process the sounds that were heard by the ear.

The PSTN, however, cannot forward sound waves. Instead, a telephone includes a microphone, which simply converts the sound waves into an analog electrical signal. The PSTN can send the electrical signal between one phone and another. On the receiving side, the phone converts the electrical signal back to sound waves using a speaker that is inside the part of the phone that you put next to your ear.

The analog electrical signals used to represent sound can be shown on a graph, as in Figure 15-1.

Figure 15-1   *Analog Electrical Signal: Frequency, Amplitude, and Phase*

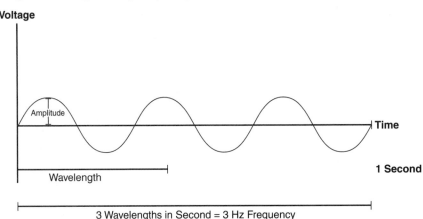

The graph represents the three main components of the signal:

- **Frequency**—Frequency is defined as how many times the signal would repeat itself, from peak to peak, in 1 second (assuming that the sound didn't change for a whole second.) The figure shows a frequency of 3 Hertz (Hz). The greater the frequency of the electrical signal is, the higher the pitch is of the sound being represented.

- **Amplitude**—The amplitude represents how strong the signal is; a higher amplitude peak represents a louder sound.

- **Phase**—Phase refers to where the signal is at a point in time—at the top, going down, at the bottom, going up, and so on.

The goal of the original PSTN was to create a circuit between any two phones. Each circuit consisted of an electrical path between two phones, which, in turn, supported the sending of an analog electrical signal in each direction, allowing the people on the circuit to have a conversation. Remember, the original PSTN, built by Alexander Graham Bell's new company, predated the first vacuum tube computers, so the concept of support data communication between computers wasn't a consideration for the original PSTN. It just wanted to get these analog electrical signals, which represented sounds, from one place to the other.

To set up a circuit, when the PSTN first got started, you picked up your phone. A flashing light at a switchboard at the local phone company office told the operator to pick up the phone, and then you told the operator who you wanted to talk to. If it was a local call, the operator completed the circuit literally by patching the cable at the end of the phone line connected to your house to the end of the phone line connected to the house of the person you were calling. Figure 15-2 depicts the basic concept.

Figure 15-2   *Human Operator Setting Up a Circuit at a Switchboard*

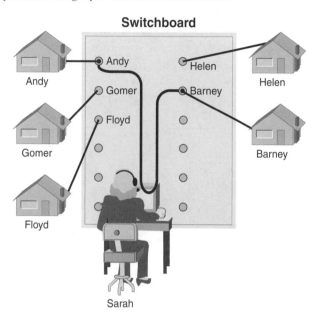

In the figure, Sarah, the operator, picks up the phone when she sees a light flashing telling her that someone at Andy's house has picked up the phone. Andy might say something like, "Sarah, I want to talk to Barney." Because Andy, Sarah, and Barney probably all knew each other, that was enough. In a larger town, Andy might simply say, "Please ring phone number 555-1212," and Sarah would connect the call. In fact, patching the call on the switchboard is where we got the old American saying "patch me through."

Over the years, the signaling to set up a circuit got more sophisticated. Phones evolved to have a rotary dial on them, so you could just pick up the phone and dial the number you wanted to call. Later, 12-digit keypads replaced the dial so that you could simply press the numbers. For those of you who do not remember phones with dials on them, it would have taken you 20 seconds to dial a number that had lots of 8s, 9s, and 0s in them, so a keypad was a big timesaver!

The PSTN also evolved to use digital signals instead of analog signals inside the core of the PSTN. By using digital signals instead of analog, the PSTN could send more voice calls over the same physical cables, which, in turn, allowed it to grow while reducing the per-call-minute cost.

So, what is a digital signal? Digital signals represent binary numbers. Electrically, digital signals use a defined set of both positive and negative voltages, which, in turn, represent either a binary 0 or a binary 1. *Encoding schemes* define the rules as to which electrical signals mean a binary 0 and which ones mean a binary 1. The simplest encoding scheme might be to represent a binary 1 with +5V and a binary 0 with —5V; much more sophisticated encoding schemes are used today. Figure 15-3 shows an example of a graph of a digital signal over time, using the basic encoding scheme that was just described.

Figure 15-3   *Example of a Digital Signal with a Simple Encoding Scheme*

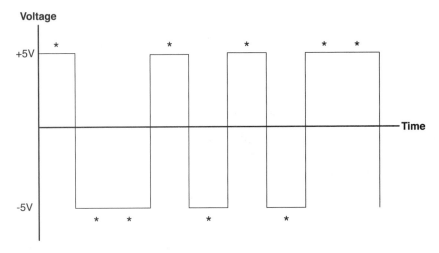

The sender of the digital signal simply varies the signal based on the encoding scheme. The receiver interprets the incoming signal according to the same encoding scheme, re-creating the digits. In the figure, if the receiver examined the signal at each point with an asterisk, the binary code would be 100101011.

So, if a device wanted to somehow send a set of binary digits to another device and there was a digital circuit between the two, it could send the appropriate digital signals over the circuit. To achieve a particular bit rate, the sender would make sure that the voltage level was at the right level at regular intervals, and the receiver would sample the incoming signal at the same rate. For instance, to achieve 28 kbps, the sender would change (as necessary) the voltage level every 1/28,000th of a second. The receiver would sample the incoming digital signal every 1/28,000th of a second as well.

Converting Analog Voice to Digital Voice

The last step in understanding how the PSTN supports voice across a digital PSTN relates to how the PSTN converts the analog electrical signals to digital signals, and vice versa. To see the need for the conversion, examine Figure 15-4.

Figure 15-4 *Analog Voice Calls Through a Digital PSTN*

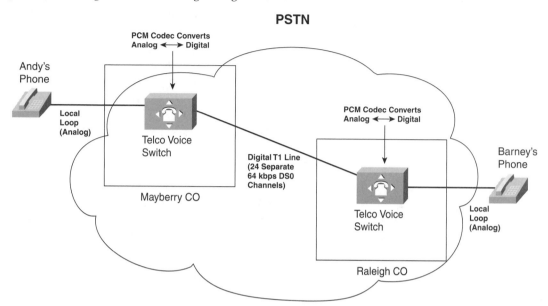

When Andy calls Barney in Raleigh, the circuit is set up by the telco. (Yes, Barney moved to Raleigh since the last example.) And it works! It works because the phone company switch in the Central Office (CO) in Mayberry performs analog-to-digital (A/D) conversion of Andy's incoming voice. When the switch in Raleigh gets the digital signal, before sending it out the analog line to Barney's house, it reverses the process, converting the digital signal back to analog. The analog signal going over the local line to Barney's house is roughly the same analog signal that Andy's phone sent over his local line.

The original standard for converting analog voice to a digital signal is called *pulse-code modulation (PCM)*. PCM defines that an incoming analog voice signal should be sampled 8000 times per second by the analog-to-digital (A/D) converter. A/D converters that are used specifically for processing voice are called *codecs* (meaning encoder/decoder). For each sample, the codec measures the frequency, amplitude, and phase of the analog signal. PCM defines a table of possible values for frequency/amplitude/phase. The codec finds the table entry that most closely matches the measured values. Along with each entry is an 8-bit binary code, which tells the codec what bits to use to represent that single sample. So PCM, sampling at 8000 times per second finds the best match of frequency/amplitude/phase in the table, finds the matching 8-bit code, and sends those 8 bits as a digital signal.

The PCM codec converts from digital to analog by reversing the process. The decoding process re-creates the analog signal, but not quite exactly. For instance, if the original frequency was 2139.3, the decoded frequency might be 2140. For normal speech, the quality is great. If you were trying to listen to DVD-quality sounds over the telephone, it probably wouldn't sound as good as it would if you were actually there, but it's pretty close.

If you do the math, you will notice that a single voice call requires 64 kbps of bandwidth in the digital part of the PSTN. PCM says that you need to sample the analog signal 8000 times per second, and each sample needs 8 bits to represent it. A bright fellow at Bell Labs, Nyquist, did some research that showed this sampling rate was needed for digitized voice. He noticed that the human voice could create sounds between 300 Hz and 3300 Hz, and that the sampling rate needed to be twice that of the highest frequency. So, to overcome some other physics problems, Nyquist and the team at Bell Labs decided to round that range of frequencies for the human voice to 0 Hz to 4000 Hz. So, because Nyquist's theorem states that you need twice the number of samples as the highest frequency, you need 8000 samples. To make sure the voice sounded good after being decoded, they decided to use 256 different binary values, each representing a different combination of amplitude, frequency, and phase. To represent the 256 values, they needed 8 bits; for 8000 samples per second, 64 kbps is needed for a PCM-encoded voice call.

Because a single call needs 64 kbps, the digital PSTN first was built on a basic transmission speed of 64 kbps. A single 64-kbps channel was dubbed a Digital Signal Level 0—or DS0. In the United States, the phone company (American Telephone and Telegraph [AT&T] by that point in its history) decided to create hardware that could multiplex 24 DS0s onto a single line, so it called that type of line a Digital Signal Level 1—or DS1. The more popular name for a DS1 today, of course, is T1. Some parts of the world followed AT&T's lead for DS1 with 24 DS0 channels, and other parts of the world, mainly Europe and Australia, chose instead to combine 32 different 64-kbps DS0 channels onto a single line, which is the basis for today's E1s. As you might imagine, even faster digital facilities are defined as well, such as a T3-line, which has 28 T1s in it.

Finally, this small history lesson comes to an end. Most of the work on modems and ISDN, and some of the work for DSL, occurred with the expectation that these technologies needed to work over the PSTN.

In summary:

- The telco switch in the CO expects to send and receive analog voice over the physical line to a typical home (the *local loop*).
- The telco converts the received analog voice to the digital equivalent using a codec.
- The telco converts the digital voice back to the analog equivalent for transmission over the local loop at the destination.
- The voice call, with PCM in use, uses 64 kbps through the digital part of the PSTN.

Analog Modems

Analog modems allow two computers to send and receive a serial stream of bits, with no physical changes required on the typical analog local loop between a residence and the telco CO. Because the switch in the CO expects to send and receive analog voice signals over the local loop, modems simply send an analog signal to the PSTN and expect to receive an analog signal from the PSTN. However, that analog signal represents some bits that the computer needs to send to another computer, instead of voice created by a human speaker. Similar in concept to a phone converting sound waves into an analog electrical signal, a modem converts a string of binary digits on a computer into a representative analog electrical signal.

Modems encode a binary 0 or 1 onto the analog signal by varying the frequency, amplitude, or phase. Changing the analog signal is referred to as modulation. For instance, one of the earliest standards called for a modem to send an analog signal of 2250 Hz for a binary 1, and 2100 Hz for binary 0. A modem would modulate, or change, between the two frequency levels to imply a binary 1 or 0.

To achieve a particular bit rate, the sending modem would modulate the signal at that rate. For instance, to send 9600 bps, the sending modem would change the signal (as necessary) every 1/9600th of a second. Similarly, the receiving modem would sample the incoming analog signal every 1/9600th of a second, interpreting the signal as a binary 1 or 0. (The process of the receiving end is called *demodulation*. The term *modem* is a shortened version of the combination of the two words *modulation* and *demodulation*.)

Modems must work over the existing PSTN. Figure 15-5 outlines the basic process.

Figure 15-5 *Basic Operation of Modems over PSTN*

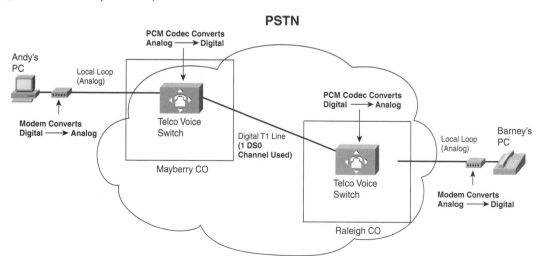

First, a circuit (call) must be established. One modem signals the phone number for the call in the same way that a telephone does today, by sending the tones associated with the keys on a telephone keypad. The CO switch interprets these tones, called dual-tone multifrequency (DTMF) tones, just like it would for a voice call.

When the circuit has been established by the telco, the two modems must agree to what modem standard they will use. As long as the two modems use the same rules for how they perform modulation and demodulation, the modems can communicate. Many modem standards exist, and many modems support several standards. Modems can probe and negotiate to find the best modem standard that both endpoint modems support. These standards are explained briefly and listed later in the chapter.

Note that the PSTN still converts the analog signals to and from PCM using a codec. In effect, the data ping-pongs between different states as it passes through the network:

1. The bits start out stored in digital form on a computer.

2. The bits are converted to an analog signal by the modem.

3. The analog signal is converted into a different digital format by a switch in the PSTN, using a PCM codec.

4. The CO switch near the receiving end using a PCM codec to convert back to an analog signal.

5. The receiving modem converts the incoming analog signal to the correct set of bits.

Modems work well and have been around for a long time, so the conversion steps do not pose a problem.

Modulation and Demodulation

Most people can fully appreciate the concept of the speed of a dialed circuit in terms of bits per second. However, another term, baud, often is used to describe the speed of a modem. In fact, some people say things like "That modem runs at 33 kilo baud per second," really meaning 33 kilobits per second (kbps), thinking that "bits per second" and "baud per second" are the same thing. But the two terms are not synonymous, as you will read shortly.

Modems create an analog signal when sending data. As mentioned earlier, analog electrical signals can be analyzed in terms of frequency, amplitude, and phase. So, modem standards define that particular values for these three parts of the signal imply a 1 or a 0. To appreciate what that means, consider the two parts of Figure 15-6.

Figure 15-6   *Amplitude, Frequency, and Phase Modulation*

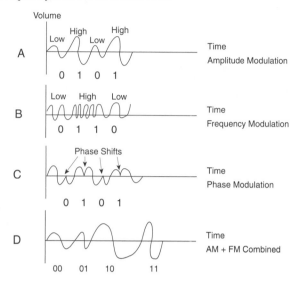

The figure depicts some very simple ways that a modem could be used to create an analog signal that can be interpreted by the receiver as a set of binary digits. In Graph A, a low amplitude means a binary 0, and a high amplitude means a binary 1. All the sending modem has to do is modulate (change) the amplitude of the signal to imply a 1 or a 0. For instance, if the modem was running at 28 kbps, then every 1/28,000th of a second, it would make the amplitude of the signal low or high, to encode a binary 0 or 1.

The process of changing, or modulating, the amplitude is called *amplitude modulation.* Modulation, as defined by www.dictionary.com, is "the variation of a property of an electromagnetic wave or signal, such as its amplitude, frequency, or phase," which is exactly what amplitude modulation does, specifically for the amplitude.

Graph B in Figure 15-6 depicts *frequency modulation.* In this simple example, the higher frequency (the part with the curved lines closer together) means 0, and the lower frequency means 1. Notice that the amplitude stays the same in that case, so this modem standard simply changes the frequency to imply a 1 or a 0. So, if the modems are running at 28 kbps, then every 1/28,000th of a second, the modem would make the frequency high or low to encode a binary 0 or 1.

Graph C in Figure 15-6 depicts *phase modulation.* Phase modulation changes the phase of the signal—instead of the signal following its normal pattern of rising to the highest positive voltage, gradually lowering to the lowest voltage and back again, the signal changes directions—which changes the phase. Modems can modulate the phase to imply a binary 0 or 1 as well.

Finally, Graph D in Figure 15-6 shows a combination of frequency modulation and amplitude modulation. With this final scheme, each signal represents 2 bits. For instance, a low-amplitude and low-frequency signal might mean 00, whereas a low-amplitude but high-frequency signal might mean 01. Table 15-2 lists the four combinations possible with this example combined modulation scheme.

Table 15-2   *Combinations of Bits with FM and AM Together*

Amplitude	Frequency	Used for This Binary Code
Low	Low	00
Low	High	01
High	Low	10
High	High	11

The modulation scheme in Graph D of Figure 15-6 provides a good context from which to understand the term *baud*. To achieve higher bit rates, modems tend to use modulation techniques that encode more than 1 bit in the signal, as in this example. For instance, to achieve 28 kbps with this last modulation scheme, the modems would need to change (sender) or sample (receiver) the analog signal only every 1/14,000th of a second, because each sample represents 2 bits.

The term *baud* refers to a single encoded energy signal that can represent 1 or more bits. In this final example, a baud happens to represent 2 bits. Baud is not an acronym; it is taken from the name of the inventor (Baudot) of one of the first modulation schemes that implied more than 1 bit. So, the modem running at 28,000 bps, with a modulation scheme that sends/receives 2 bits per baud, is running at 14,000 baud per second.

Point-to-Point Protocol Features with Modems

Most computers today use PPP as the data-link protocol when using modems. Modems essentially provide an OSI Layer 1 service, supporting the transmission and reception of a serial bit stream. In fact, a dialed circuit between two modems creates a physical network that has a lot of similarities with a leased point-to-point circuit. Also, analog modems typically transmit traffic asynchronously. PPP supports both synchronous communication, as typically is done over leased point-to-point lines, as well as asynchronous communication, which typically is done over dialed circuits using modems. So, PPP is the logical choice for a data-link protocol when using modems today.

PPP includes some features that are important when using modems to dial into an ISP. PPP includes the capability of dynamically assigning an IP address to a device on the other end of the PPP link. So, when you dial into an ISP, the ISP dynamically assigns an IP address to your computer. Also, PPP supports that Challenge Handshake Authentication Protocol (CHAP), which popularly is used to allow the dial-in user to supply a username and password to gain access to the ISP network. (CHAP is covered in the *CCNA ICND Exam Certification Guide*.)

Modem Installation and Cabling

PC modems can be located internally or externally. Internal modems are placed inside the PC itself, whereas external modems are external to the PC. Laptops might come with a modem built in or simply might use a convenient type of internal modem called a PCMCIA card, or simply PC card. PC cards are roughly the size of a credit card and easily can be inserted and removed from a PC.

Most PC hardware comes with either a serial communications port, called a COM port, or a Universal Serial Bus (USB) port. Both USB and COM ports are intended to support external devices that communicate using a serial bit stream. So, External modems can be connected to a PC using either a COM port or a USB port. Figure 15-7 depicts the typical topology.

Figure 15-7   *Modem Installation Options and Concepts*

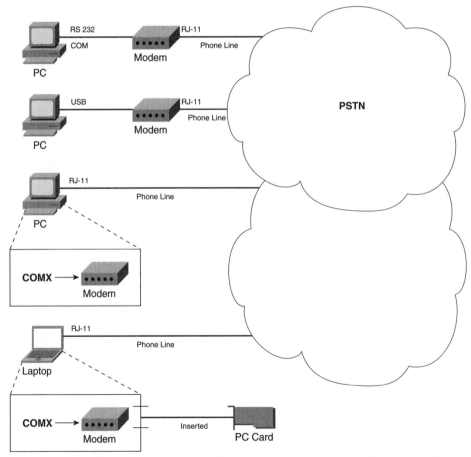

COM ports usually consist of either a female RS-232 connector, which is a D-shell connector with 25 pins, or a DB-9 connector, which uses 9 pins. USB ports are rectangular female connectors about one quarter inch by 1 inch long. In either case, the computer sends a serial bit stream to the external modem over the cable, expecting the modem to send the data. At the same time, the modem forwards bits received from the phone line back to the PC.

Internal modems do not require the use of an RS-232, DB-9, or USB cable—they simply connect directly to the phone line. In the United States, that means using the same type of cable that is used to connect to an analog phone, with an RJ-11 connector. However, the installation of an internal modem still uses the logical concept of a COM port. That is true of internal modems that are installed in an expansion card slot and of PCMCIA modems that simply can be inserted into the convenient PC card slot in the side of a laptop computer. The operating system in the computer still uses the concept of sending data serially, but instead of it physically being sent over a cable to an external modem, it simply goes to the internal modem card.

Modem Standards

Modems have been around for more than 30 years, so as you might imagine, a lot of standards have evolved. Table 15-3 summarizes some of the modem standards.

Table 15-3 *Modem Standards*

Standard	Speed	Comments
V.22	1200 bps (600 baud)	Mainly used outside the United States
V.22bis*	2400 bps (600 baud)	First widely deployed worldwide standard
V.32	4800/9600 (2400 baud)	Adjusts speed based on line quality
V.32bis*	14.4kbps (2400 baud)	Backward compatible with V.32
V.34	28.8 kbps	Backward compatible with V.32bis and V.32
V.42	28.8 kbps	Same speed as V.34, but with error-correction features
V.90	56 kbps (downstream), 33 kbps (upstream)	Created from two earlier competing standards, X2 and K56Flex
V.92	56 kbps/33 kbps (downstream/ upstream) or 48 kbps (each direction)	Connects and finds correct speed more quickly than V.90; allows "modem-on-hold"

*"bis" simply means "version 2."

Note that for some standards, the speed differs depending on the direction of transmission. Most applications today cause a lot more data to be sent toward the client side of the connection. For instance, when you sit at a PC and browse a web page, the web server sends many more bytes to you than you send to it. By using modem standards that use asymmetric rates, the maximum rate can be increased for the direction of data that needs the additional bandwidth.

V.92, the latest of these standards, has some very interesting features. You can configure it to transfer data at symmetric (48-kbps) rates or asymmetric rates equivalent to V.90's 56 kbps downstream and 33 kbps upstream. It also allows the modem to recognize "call waiting" signals from the telco, letting you take or make a call while keeping your modem connection up for a short time. Technically, you are not sending data and talking at the same time because data transmission is put "on hold," but it is a very convenient feature.

Analog Modem Summary

Modems have the great advantage of being the most pervasively available remote access technology. The history of modems is long, with modems growing to be a very reliable choice for remote access. Speeds have improved over the years, with compression technology increasing the effective throughput to beyond 100 kbps.

Modems provide a Layer 1 service of delivering a bit stream between the two endpoints on the dialed circuit. To pass IP traffic, an appropriate data-link protocol must be used, typically PPP.

The biggest negatives about using modems include their relatively low speed and the fact that you cannot use the phone at the same time as you send data.

Integrated Services Digital Network

Integrated Services Digital Network (ISDN) provides switched (dialed) digital WAN services in increments of 64 kbps. Before ISDN, the only widely-available method to dial a circuit for data communication between two computers was to use analog modems. When ISDN was created, analog modem speeds typically did not even exceed 9600 bps. The phone companies of the world wanted to have a dialed service that not only allowed faster transmission rates, but also was pervasive as a simple analog line used for voice.

Today one could argue that the collective phone companies of the world were ultimately successful with this goal, but not *totally* successful. ISDN is widely available. It is still a popular technology for dial backup between business sites when a point-to-point or Frame Relay link fails. ISDN was created more than 20 years ago, and it began being widely deployed in the United States by the early 1990s. However, competing technologies, such as DSL and cable, have usurped ISDN in the marketplace for home access to ISPs. However, ISDN remains a popular choice for dial backup.

ISDN requires that the two endpoint computers have the ISDN equivalent of an analog modem. There are many variations of these ISDN devices, mainly as a result of the fact that ISDN was created as a worldwide standard, so many options were needed to meet the differing needs of the telcos in different parts of the world. Figure 15-8 shows the required ISDN hardware for a typical connection.

Figure 15-8 *ISDN Local Loops and Equipment*

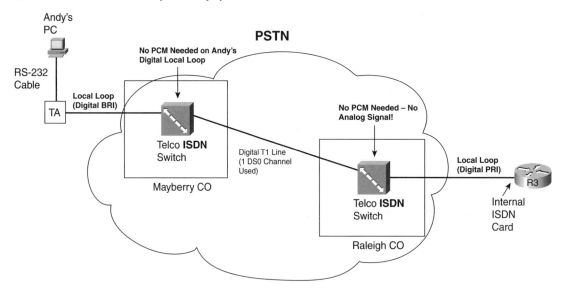

Notice that both the home PCs and the router at the ISP use ISDN gear. Routers often use ISDN cards that can be connected directly to the ISDN circuit supplied by the telco. PCs typically use an ISDN device called an ISDN terminal adapter (TA), which often is called an ISDN modem. Because ISDN uses digital signals across the local loop, it does not actually do any modulation or demodulation. However, the term *ISDN modem* emerged because it was cabled and installed similarly to an external analog modem. So, for the consumer marketplace, the marketing people started calling TAs by the technically wrong but easy-to-understand term ISDN modem.

Note that the local loop from the home and the CO now connects to a device called an ISDN switch. Local phone lines typically connect to a voice switch in the CO. ISDN uses digitial signals, so the telco actually must terminate the line from your house in a telco switch that expects digitial signals that conform to ISDN specifications.

ISDN Channels

ISDN includes two types of lines: Basic Rate Interface (BRI) and Primary Rate Interface (PRI). Both BRI and PRI provide multiple digital bearer channels (B channels) over which data can be sent and received. Because both BRI and PRI have multiple B channels, a single BRI or PRI line can have concurrent digital dial circuits to multiple sites. Alternately, you can create multiple circuits to the same remote site to increase available bandwidth to that site.

B channels transport data. They operate at speeds of up to 64 kbps, although the speed might be lower, depending on the service provider, or might be based on standards in some parts of the world. For instance, some national standards outside the United States call for 56-kbps B channels.

ISDN uses another channel inside the same single physical line to ask the telco to set up and tear down circuits. The signaling channel, called the *D channel*, signals new data calls. When a router wants to create a B-channel call to another device using a BRI or PRI, it sends the phone number that it wants to connect to inside a message sent across the D channel. The phone company's switch receives the message and sets up the circuit. Signaling a new call over the D channel is effectively the same thing as when you pick up the phone and dial a number to create a voice call.

The different types of ISDN lines often are described with a phrase that implies the number of each type of channel. For instance, BRIs are referred to as 2B+D, meaning two B channels, and one D channel. PRIs based on T1 framing, as in the United States, are referred to as 23B+D, and PRIs based on E1 framing, typically found in Europe, are referred to as 30B+D. E1s have 32 DS0 channels, with 1 reserved for framing and 1 used for the D channel when used as a PRI—that leaves 30 DS0 channels as B channels. Table 15-4 lists the number of channels for each type of ISDN line and the terminology used to describe them.

Table 15-4   *BRI and PRI B and D Channels*

Type of Interface	Number of Bearer Channels (B Channels)	Number of Signaling Channels (D Channels)	Descriptive Term
BRI	2	1 (16 kbps)	2B+D
PRI (T1)	23	1 (64 kbps)	23B+D
PRI (E1)	30	1 (64 kbps)	30B+D

ISDN Call Setup and Data Link Protocols

Call setup differs between ISDN and modems. With a telephone call and with analog modems, DTMF tones are sent across the analog local loop to the telco. The telco switch at the local CO interprets the dialed digits and sets up the call. However, with ISDN, there is no analog local loop over which the analog DTMF tones can be sent.

ISDN devices send and receive signaling messages to and from the local ISDN switch to which it is connected. In telco terminology, *signaling* refers to any type of request to establish a circuit. So, punching keys on your telephone is considered signaling to set up a circuit over an analog local line. Instead of DTMF tones, ISDN defines a set of messages that are sent over the D channel to the local CO. As a result, the PSTN sets up a circuit to the ISDN device whose phone number was put inside the signaling message. Figure 15-9 outlines the process and the result.

Figure 15-9   *D Channel Call Setup Signaling and Resulting B-Channel Call*

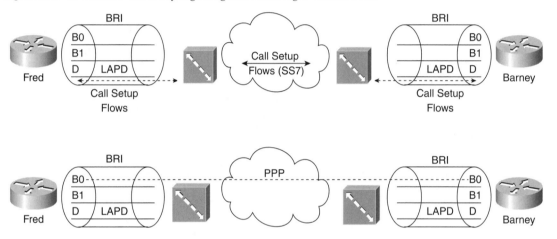

The service provider can use anything it wants to set up the call inside its network. ITU Q.931 messages are used for signaling between the ISDN device and the CO; typically, Signaling System 7 (SS7) is used between the two telco switches—the same protocol used inside phone company networks to set up circuits for phone calls.

When the call is established, a 64-kbps circuit exists between a B channel on each of the two routers in the figure. The routers can use High-Level Data Link Control (HDLC), but they typically use PPP as the data-link protocol on the B channel from end to end. As on leased lines and dialed circuits using modems, the switches in the phone company do not interpret the bits sent inside this circuit—they just help create a serial bit stream in each direction.

The D channel remains up all the time so that new signaling messages can be sent and received. Because the signals are sent outside the channel used for data, this is called *out-of-band signaling*.

Typical Uses of ISDN

Routers frequently use ISDN to create a backup link when their primary leased line or Frame Relay connection is lost. Although the leased line or Frame Relay access link seldom fails, when it does, a remote site might be completely cut off from the rest of the network. Depending on the business goals of the network, long outages might not be acceptable, so ISDN could be used to dial back to the main site.

The ICND exam covers ISDN as well, including the features and configuration used by routers. The scenarios in Figure 15-10 show some of the typical situations in which ISDN can be used, described as follows:

- Case 1 shows dial-on-demand routing (DDR). Logic is configured in the routers to trigger the dial when the user sends traffic that needs to get to another site.

- Case 2 shows a typical telecommuting environment.

- Case 3 shows a typical dial-backup topology. The leased line fails, so an ISDN call is established between the same two routers.

- Case 4 shows where an ISDN BRI can be used to dial directly to another router to replace a Frame Relay access link or a failed virtual circuit (VC).

Figure 15-10 *Typical Occasional Connections Between Routers*

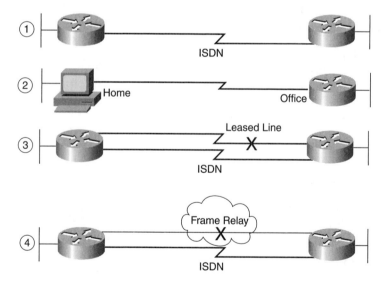

PRIs allow for larger-scale ISDN because they support far more B channels on a single physical line. Imagine an ISP that supports ISDN, with 1000 customers. If that ISP wanted to support up to 230 concurrent ISDN customers, each using a single B channel, that ISP would need 10 PRIs (assuming that it was in the United States). Also, each user might want to use both B channels at the same time, doubling the speed to the Internet; to support 2 B channels each for 230 concurrent users, that ISP would need 460 B channels, or the equivalent of 20 PRIs. However, if it just used BRI lines, it would need 230 different physical BRI lines, which probably would be much more expensive, would require more equipment, and would be a cabling hassle.

ISDN supports voice as well as data circuits. ISDN BRI circuits do not support analog voice, but they do support digital voice. You might recall that a single PCM voice call requires 64 kbps and that a single B channel provides 64 kbps. So, ISDN devices, like a terminal adapter, perform the PCM encoding and decoding features and send the voice traffic over a B channel. In fact, most ISDN modems have two RJ-11 ports that can be used to connect a normal analog phone. Figure 15-11 depicts the cabling and some important concepts about how it all works.

Figure 15-11 *ISDN Support for Voice*

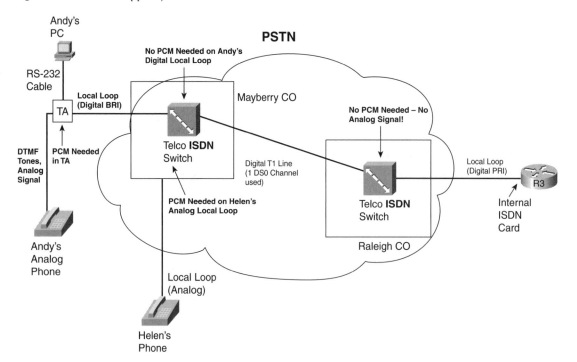

The analog phone works just like it normally works. You pick it up and punch in some digits, generating DTMF tones. The ISDN TA can't send the tones, so it interprets the tones and generates a signaling message over the D channel. After the telco sets up a circuit over one of the B channels, the TA begins using its PCM codec to convert the incoming analog voice from the phone into PCM digits, sending them across the B channel. In the Figure 15-11 example, the other phone is an analog phone connected to the PSTN at Helen's house. So, the voice switch connected to Helen's phone line converts the incoming digital signal from the back to analog voice using a PCM codec, just like it normally does for a call between two analog phone.

Finally, ISDN supports multiple concurrent data bearer channels. For instance, you can use your PC to dial two different sites at the same time. You can make two calls to the same ISP, increasing the speed. You also can use one B channel for data and make a voice call using the other B channel.

ISDN Installation and Cabling

ISDN installation for a home-based PC works much like it does for modems. The most popular option uses an external ISDN modem, or terminal adapter. Figure 15-12 depicts the typical cabling.

Figure 15-12   *Cabling a PC to an ISDN TA*

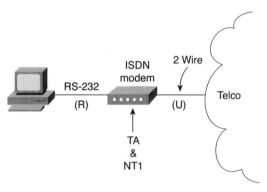

In this case, a COM port (shown) or a USB port (not shown) connects to the TA. The TA terminates the ISDN cable from the telco.

The cable from the telco uses an RJ-45 connector, the same type used for Ethernet cables. However, the pins used inside the cable are different than those for Ethernet, so do not just grab any old cable with an RJ-45 connector. Piins 3 and 6 are used for transmit and pins 4 and 5 used for receive.

ISDN Summary

ISDN supports a BRI service with 2 B channels, and a PRI service with either 23 (T1) or 30 (E1) B channels. Signaling for call setup and teardown occurs over an out-of-band D channel.

After a circuit has been established over a B channel, ISDN provides a Layer 1 service, delivering a serial bit stream between the two endpoints of the circuit.

ISDN's advantages include the capability to support voice calls concurrently with a data call. Also, ISDN can be used over the local telco loop, with no significant distance limitations. And it provides more bandwidth than do modems, particularly with both B channels dialed to the same remote site.

ISDN does have a few disadvantages, with the biggest disadvantage being the lower speeds than DSL or cable.

Digital Subscriber Line

Any two computers using compatible modems could communicate with each other. Those computers might just be two PCs, a PC dialing into a router or access server at one of the business offices, or a PC dialing into a router or access server at an ISP. As long as both endpoints have a compatible modem, the two can communicate.

By the time DSL came around in the mid- to late 1990s, the main goal for remote access was not the capability to connect to any site anywhere, but to connect to either the Internet or a corporate IP network. In years past, modems were used to dial a large variety of different computers, which was useful. Today you can think of the Internet like you think of the electric company, the gas company, and so on—it's a utility that provides IP connectivity to the rest of the world.

Because most people today just want access to the utility—in other words, the Internet—DSL can be defined a little differently. In fact, DSL was designed to provide high-speed access between a home or business and the local CO. By removing the requirement to allow connection between any two endpoints, DSL can be defined to reach much higher speeds.

Because DSL really just defines how to transmit data between a customer site and the local CO, the expectation with DSL is that the data would not flow through DS0 channels inside the PSTN. Instead, it would be forwarded through some IP network. By removing the need to be compatible with the entirety of the core of the PSTN, DSL can be defined to provide some nice services and better transmission speeds.

DSL's basic services have some similarities, as well as differences, when compared to analog modems and ISDN lines. Some of the key features are as follows:

- DSL allows analog voice signals and digital data signals to be sent over the same local loop wiring.

- Similar to ISDN, the local loop must be connected to something besides a traditional voice switch at the local CO: a device called a DSL access multiplexer (DSLAM).

- DSL allows for a concurrent voice call to be up at the same time as the data connection.

- Unlike modems and ISDN, DSL's data component is always on—in other words, you don't have to signal to set up a data circuit.

DSL really does provide some great benefits—you can use the same old phones that you already have, you can keep the same phone number, and you can just sit down at your PC at home and start using the Internet. Figure 15-13 shows some of the details of a typical DSL connection.

Figure 15-13 *DSL Connection from the Home*

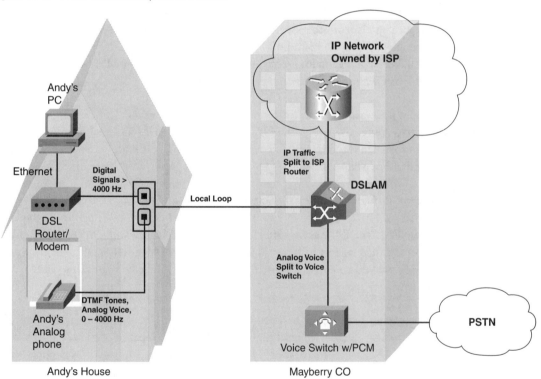

In the home, a DSL modem or DSL-capable router is connected to the phone line (the local loop) using a typical telephone cable. The cable uses RJ-11 connectors, as is typical for a cable for an analog phone or a modem, with pin 3 for transmit and pin 4 for receive. The DSL modem understands the Layer 1 encoding details for DSL and encodes the data correctly. DSL routers might include the DSL modem feature, as well as providing other features, such as IP routing, allowing the home user to connect multiple PCs in the home to the Internet at the same time.

DSL allows a concurrent voice call at the same time as allowing an always-on Internet connection. The figure shows an analog phone and a DSL modem connected to a single wall plate with two receptacles. Physically, you connect your DSL modem to a wall socket just like any of the phones in your house. The phone generates an analog signal at frequency ranges between 0 and 4000 Hz; the DSL modem uses frequencies higher than 4000 Hz so that they do not interfere with each other very much. You typically need to put a filter between each phone and the wall socket (not shown) to prevent interference.

The same wiring can be used in the local loop as was used for normal telephone service, but now the CO connects the local loop wiring to a device called a DSLAM. The DSLAM splits the data and voice signals from the local loop. The DSLAM gives the analog voice signal— the frequency range between 0 Hz and 4000 Hz—to a voice switch. The voice switch treats that signal just like any other analog voice line—the switch listens for DTMF tones, creates a circuit, and does PCM encoding to convert the analog signal.

The DSLAM does not pass the data traffic into the PSTN, however. The DSLAM forwards the data traffic to a router owned by the ISP providing the service in this figure. Alternately, the DSLAM can forward the data traffic over an IP network, ultimately reaching a router inside a corporate network.

Notice that the ISP's router actually is depicted as being resident in the local telco's CO—that is true in many cases. However, many people use an ISP that does not happen to be the local telco. To support DSL, the ISP works with the local telco to install some of the ISP's gear in the CO—a process called *co-location*, or *co-lo* for short. The local telco DSLAM forwards and receives the IP packets to and from the ISP router, while the telco maintains control over the local voice traffic.

Typically, the consumer requests high-speed Internet access using DSL from an ISP; the ISP charges the customer for the service, and then the ISP pays the local telco some cut of the fee.

DSL Standards

DSL comes in many flavors to meet different needs. For instance, DSL has limits on how long the local loop can be (the length of the local loop is simply the length of the combined cables that stretch from a house to the CO). Some DSL variants allow the local loop to be much longer, while others allow for only a shorter local loop. For the standards with a shorter local loop, the transmission rates tend to be much higher—a simple design trade-off. ADSL and SDSL tend to be the most popular option in the United States today.

Another architectural difference among the different specifications is that some DSL variants use asymmetric transmission rates, while others use symmetric rates.

Table 15-5 lists the major DSL variants, the standard defining that variant, the speeds, the distance limitations, and encoding.

Table 15-5 *DSL Technologies Standards Comparison*

DSL Type	Standards	Modulation/Encoding Technique	Speed	Distance Limit
Full-rate ADSL/ G.DMT	ANSI T1.413 Issue 2	Discrete multitone (DMT) or carrierless amplitude phase (CAP)	Downstream speed of 384 to 8 Mbps; upstream speed slower, up to 1.024 Mbps	18,000 feet
G.Lite	ITU-T G.992.1, ITU-T G.992.2	DMT	Downstream speed up to 1.544 Mbps to 6 Mbps; upstream speed up to 640 kbps	18,000 feet
Very-high-data-rate DSL (VDSL)	ETSI and ANSI in process	DMT/single-carrier modulation (SCM)	12.96 Mbps to 52.8 Mbps for both upstream and downstream speed	4500 feet
ISDN DSL (IDSL)	ANSI ETR 080	Two binary one quaternary (2B1Q)	144 kbps for both upstream and downstream speed	18,000 feet
Symmetric DSL (SDSL)	None	2B1Q	768 kbps for both upstream and downstream speed	22,000 feet
High-data-rate DSL (HDSL	ITU G.991.1, ANSI TR 28	2B1Q	1.544 or 2.048 Mbps for both upstream and downstream speed	12,000 feet
G.SHDSL	ITU G.991.2	Trellis-coded pulse amplitude modulation (TC PAM)	192 kbps to 2.360 Mbps for both upstream and downstream speed	28,000 feet

A wide variety of standards bodies and vendor consortiums helped develop these standards. As you might imagine, with so many standards, many different organizations pushed for standards that best met their needs. Over time, the number of differing standards will stabilize.

The following organizations are among the key players in the development of DSL:

- American National Standards Institute (ANSI)

- Institute of Electrical and Electronics Engineers (IEEE)

- International Telecommunications Union (ITU)

- European Telecommunications Standards Institute (ETSI)

- DSL Forum

DSL Protocols

DSL itself provides a Layer 1 transmission path between two endpoints, in some ways like the Layer 1 service that analog modems and ISDN modems provide. However, DSL uses some additional protocols to support data transfer. For instance, DSL uses ATM as the Layer 2 protocol between the DSL router or DSL modem in the home and the ISP router. Additionally, DSL uses a protocol called PPP over ATM (PPPoA). PPP and ATM are both data-link protocols, but they serve different purposes. PPP provides dynamic address assignment by the ISP for the DSL modem and some basic authentication with Challenge Handshake Authentication Protocol (CHAP). (CHAP is covered in the CCNA ICND Exam Certification Guide and the ICND exam.) Also, depending on the gear installed at a site, DSL might require PPP over Ethernet (PPPoE) for traffic between a PC in the home and the DSL modem/router in the home.

Figure 15-14 shows a typical installation using an ADSL router, like the Cisco 827H series. The 827H acts as both a router and a DSL modem.

Figure 15-14   *Protocols Used with a DSL Router*

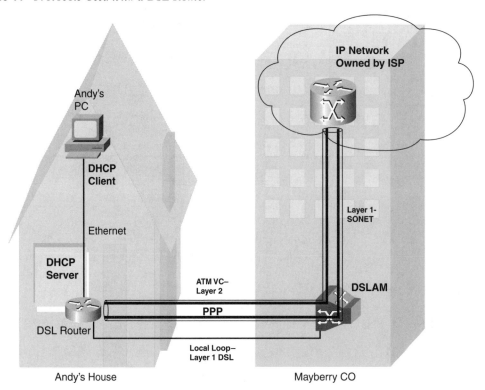

Any PCs at the home can connect to the DSL router using Ethernet. In fact, as is common with many DSL routers, the Cisco 827H DSL router includes a four-port Ethernet hub built into the router, so you can just cable a PC directly to the 827H. Alternately, you can create an Ethernet any way you want, as long as there is Ethernet connectivity from the PC to the DSL router. A straight-through Ethernet cable would be used to connect the PC directly to the DSL router.

The PC can be configured just like it would be on any other Ethernet, thinking of the DSL router like any other router. The PC would point to the DSL router's Ethernet IP address as its default gateway. The PC even can use DHCP to acquire an IP address, with the DSL router providing the DHCP server feature.

DSL provides the Layer 1 encoding features for high-speed transmission over the local loop, but it also references ATM as the data-link protocol to use over the DSL link. Back in Chapter 4, "Fundamentals of WANs," you read about the basic features of ATM and SONET, and how ATM sends and receives ATM cells at Layer 2, with SONET providing the Layer 1 transmission details. DSL defines how you can use ATM cells over DSL lines, instead of over SONET, with the ATM cells being forwarded over the DSL connecting from the home to the DSLAM.

The ISP's router needs to receive the data traffic, not the DSLAM in the local CO. So, the DSLAM forwards the ATM cells over the link to the ISP router, probably using an optical cable and Sonet at Layer 1. The receiving ISP router can reassemble the cells and extract the IP packet.

DSL Summary

DSL provides OSI Layer 1 and Layer 2 services to the home. The goal of DSL is to deliver IP packets from the remote user to a router—a router owned by an ISP, or a router resident inside a corporate network. To do so, DSL provides a digital Layer 1 service—serial bit streams in each direction—between the remote site and the local CO. On top of that, DSL uses a combination of ATM, Ethernet, and PPP to help deliver IP packets between the home and a router at an ISP.

DSL brings high-speed remote access capabilities to the home. Depending on the distance to the local CO and the DSL standard supported by the local telco, DSL can support over 1 Mbps. It supports concurrent voice and data, with the data service always being turned on— no dialing is required. And the service speed does not degrade when more users are added to the network.

DSL has some obvious drawbacks. DSL simply will not be available to some people, particular those in rural areas, based on the distance from the home to the CO. The local telco must have DSL equipment in the CO before it, or any ISP, can offer DSL services. Also, even when the home is close enough to the CO, sites farther from the CO might run slower than sites closer to the CO.

Cable Modems

Of all the access technologies covered in this chapter, cable modems are the only one not using a phone line from the local telco for physical connectivity. Many homes also have a cable TV service supplied by an analog electrical signal entering the home over a coaxial cable—in other words, over the cable TV cabling. Cable modems provide an always-on Internet access service, while allowing you to surf the Internet over the cable and make all the phone calls you want over your telephone line—and you can watch TV at the same time!

Cable modems use some of the bandwidth that otherwise might have been allocated for new TV channels, using those frequency bands for transferring data. It's a little like having an "Internet" channel to go along with CNN, TBS, ESPN, The Cartoon Network, and all your other favorite cable channels.

To appreciate how cable modems work, you need a little perspective on some cable TV terminology. Cable TV traditionally has been a one-way service—the cable provider sends electrical signals down the cable for all the channels. All you have to do, after the physical installation is complete, is choose the channel you want to watch. While you are watching The Cartoon Network, the electrical signals for CNN still are coming into your house over the cable—your TV is just ignoring that part of the signal. If you have two TVs in your house, you can watch two different channels because the signals for all the channels are being sent down the cable.

Cable TV technology has its own set of terminology, just like most of the other access technologies covered in this chapter. Figure 15-15 outlines some of the key terms.

The *cable head-end site* is a main site that receives the programming. Programming typically is received via a satellite receiver dish. The head end converts the signals to match the correct encoding and frequencies used on the cable and transmits the signals. It also might scramble channels that require an extra fee from subscribers so that you have to get a descrambler—typically called a *set-top box*—from the CATV company.

Figure 15-15 *Cable TV Terminology*

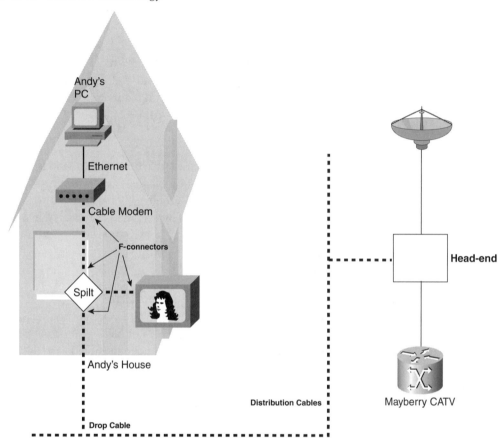

Essentially, the CATV signal is broadcast over the rest of the cable plant, being amplified along the way. A *drop cable* taps into the *distibution cable* that runs near your house and then enters your home and connects to the back of a wall plate near your TV. You just need to run the short coax cable from the back of your TV to the wall plug, and the cabling is complete.

Because most people will want to watch TV as well, possibly multiple TVs, the drop cable must be split. Splitting does not mean literally taking the wire out of the cable and cutting it in half—instead, it means that you use a small device that passively lets the signal coming in from the street pass through to other cables in your house. You can use the same kind of line splitter when using a cable modem that you use when you connect two TVs to the cable TV line at the same time. In the figure, the splitter connects to the drop cable, as well as the two cables connecting to the cable modem and the TV. The splitter just takes the incoming signal from the drop cable and passes it out both of the other lines. Note that the connector, the round connector common on most CATV cabling, is called an *f-connector*.

When using a cable modem, the CATV company becomes your ISP. Everything between your house and the router at the head end is a single physical and data link. The PC in your home uses a router owned by the cable company, housed at the head-end site, as its default gateway. In fact, the PC typically uses DHCP to discover its IP address and the IP address of its default gateway; the DHCP server would be inside the cable company's IP network, typically at the head-end site.

Conceptually, what happens between the home and the cable head end is similar to a single LAN segment. The details, of course, are different, but the cable installation provides a combination of Layer 1 and Layer 2 protocols to let a PC deliver IP packets to a router inside the cable network. So, as you read about the details of what happens between the home and the router at the head end, keep in mind that the goal is simply to deliver IP packets between the home and the head-end router, and vice versa.

Layer 1 and Layer 2 between the Home and the Head End

Cable TV systems originally were built to send TV video and audio signals to lots of places, with no need to receive a signal back. In other words, the idea of having someone's TV send some information back to the cable company was not even under consideration. Because the original CATV architecture allowed for sending signals from the head end outward, and the capability for two-way communication was added later, data over cable standards treats data going toward the home differently than data coming from the home. In fact, CATV terminology refers to the data going toward the home as *downstream data*, and data from the home as *upstream data*.

Downstream data uses standards that are consistent with some of the standards for sending digital video over cable. In fact, you can think of the downstream data as being sent over another TV channel. For downstream data, the data over cable standards takes advantage of the fact that the signals are broadcast to all subscribers in a section of the cable plant. Just like the TV channels' signals go to every home, the signals for the downstream data go to every home. In many ways, the concepts are similar to an Ethernet broadcast domain: When a broadcast Ethernet frame is sent, everyone in the broadcast domain receives the frame. With downstream cable transmissions, not just broadcast frames, but all data, is broadcast to all receivers. Yes, the data that you receive over the web actually could be captured with a network analysis tool by one of your neighbors.

Because every home in a part of the cable network receives the same data channel, some form of addresses must be used so that only the correct device tries to process incoming data. For instance, your PC does not need to process any data being sent to your neighbor's PC. So, CATV standards call for the use of a data-link protocol called Multimedia Cable Network Systems (MCNS) MAC. (You might remember that MAC stands for Media Access Control.) MCNS is similar to Ethernet's MAC, as defined in the IEEE 802.3 specification, including the use of Ethernet MAC addresses. So, although all downstream data is sent to all drops in the cable system, only those with a cable modem know that data has been received, and only the PCs with the correct MAC address process the data.

MCNS also defines the physical encoding details. MCNS calls for the use of a modulation method called quadrature amplitude modulation (QAM). Two options can be used for downstream data, one called QAM-64 and the other called QAM-256. QAM-64 represents 6 bits per baud, and QAM-256 represents 8 bits per baud.

Table 15-6 summarizes some of the key reference information about downstream data over cable.

Table 15-6 *Downstream Data over Cable: Interesting Facts*

	Downstream Rate
OSI Layer 1	QAM-64 and QAM-256 encoding
OSI Layer 2	MCNS MAC and IEEE 802.2 LLC
Multiplexing used	Frequency-division multiplexing
Speed	30 to 40 Mbps

Upstream Data

The upstream data channel uses a totally separate frequency range than the downstream channel, so no collisions occur between downstream and upstream data. However, all upstream data from multiple cable subscribers does share the same frequency range—the same channel, essentially—so collisions can occur between data sent toward the Internet by the different home users.

Noticing that a collision has occurred in an upstream cable channel is much more difficult than with an Ethernet. Cables inside the CATV cable plant might be miles long, which means that a device would have to wait longer for the electrical signal from a collision to return. So, the CSMA/CD algorithm used by Ethernet does not work well on the upstream channel. Instead, MCNS defines the use of a multiplexing method called time-division multiple access (TDMA), in which each home user is granted regular time periods during which to send upstream data. These time slots happen multiple times per second. By using TDMA, most collisions can be avoided.

The upstream channel uses the same data-link protocols as the downstream channel, with MAC addressing, but it uses different modulation schemes. The upstream channel uses quaternary phase-shift keying (QPSK) or QAM-16. QPSK modulates the signal using phase shifts, while QAM uses amplitude modulation.

Both the downstream and upstream channels compete with other users for the use of the channel. So, as more subscribers are added, the actual throughput of the connection actually can slow down.

Table 15-7 summarizes some of the key points about the upstream data channel.

Table 15-7 *Upstream Data over Cable: Interesting Facts*

	Downstream Rate
OSI Layer 1	QPSK and QAM-16
OSI Layer 2	MCNS MAC and IEEE 802.2 LLC
Multiplexing used	Time-division multiple access (TDMA)
Speed	320 kbps to 10 Mbps

Cable Modem Summary

Like DSL, cable modems bring high-speed remote access capabilities to the home. The speeds might seem astounding—30 to 40 Mbps downstream is indeed impressive. In fact, I had a cable modem a few years ago and was one of the first people in my neighborhood to get it. I surfed the web much faster from home than I did from the local Cisco Systems office! The data service is always on, even when someone is watching TV. Because it doesn't use the telephone line at all, you also can use the phone at the same time.

Cable modems do have a few drawbacks. The per-user data rates degrade as more users are added to the network. Also, because the network broadcasts all downstream traffic, anyone can put a network-analysis tool in their home and get a copy of what their neighbor is receiving.

Comparison of Remote Access Technologies

This chapter scratches the surface of how modems, ISDN, cable, and DSL work. Consumers choose between these options for Internet access all the time, and network engineers choose between these options for supporting their work-at-home users as well. So, it seems appropriate to close the chapter by listing some of the key comparison points for these options.

The remote access technologies in this chapter provide services at Layer 1, and possibly Layer 2, of the OSI reference model. TCP/IP and all the associated higher-layer protocols (TCP, UDP, HTTP, FTP, Telnet, DNS, DHCP, and so on) can run over any of these access technologies; the differences lie in what is done at Layers 1 and 2. Figure 15-16 outlines the protocols used by each.

Figure 15-16 *The OSI Reference Model and Remote Access Technologies*

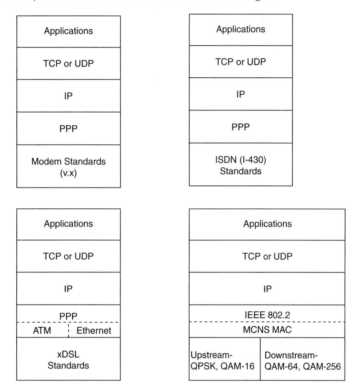

Table 15-8 lists some of the main points for comparison of these technologies.

Table 15-8 *Comparison of Modems, ISDN, DSL, and Cable*

	Analog Modems	**ISDN**	**DSL**	**Cable Modems**
Transport	Telco line	Telco line	Telco line	CATV cable
Supports symmetric speeds?	Yes	Yes	Yes	No
Supports asymmetric speeds?	Yes	No	Yes	Yes
Speed ranges	56 kbps and lower	64 kbps per B channel	56 kbps to 2 Mbps	320 kbps to 40 Mbps

continues

Table 15-8   *Comparison of Modems, ISDN, DSL, and Cable (Continued)*

	Analog Modems	ISDN	DSL	Cable Modems
Degrades under higher loads?	No	No	No	Yes
Supports IP and associated higher-layer protocols?	Yes	Yes	Yes	Yes
Allows concurrent voice and data?	No	Yes	Yes	Yes
Always on?	No	No	Yes	Yes
Local loop distance issues	No	No	Yes; distance varies	No

Foundation Summary

The "Foundation Summary" section of each chapter lists the most important facts from the chapter. Although this section does not list every fact from the chapter that will be on your CCNA exam, a well-prepared CCNA candidate should know, at a minimum, all the details in each "Foundation Summary" section before going to take the exam.

Figure 15-17 depicts the PSTN and how it supports analog voice through a digital T1 core.

Figure 15-17 *Analog Voice Calls Through a Digital PSTN*

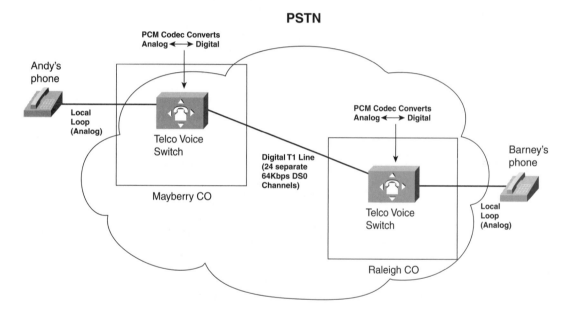

Table 15-9 lists some of the key modem standards.

Table 15-9 *Modem Standards*

Standard	Speed	Comments
V.22	1200 bps (600 baud)	Mainly used outside the United States
V.22bis*	2400 bps (600 baud)	First widely deployed worldwide standard
V.32	4800/9600 (2400 baud)	Adjusts speed based on line quality
V.32bis*	14.4kbps (2400 baud)	Backward compatible with V.32

continues

Table 15-9 *Modem Standards (Continued)*

Standard	Speed	Comments
V.34	28.8 kbps	Backward compatible with V.32bis and V.32
V.42	28.8 kbps	Same speed as V.34, but with error-correction features
V.90	56 kbps (downstream), 33 kbps (upstream)	Created from two earlier competing standards, X2 and K56Flex
V.92	56 kbps/33 kbps (downstream/upstream) or 48 kbps (each direction)	Connects and finds correct speed more quickly than V.90; allows "modem-on-hold"

*"bis" simply means "version 2."

Figure 15-18 shows the typical topology with ISDN in use for access to an ISP.

Figure 15-18 *ISDN Local Loops and Equipment*

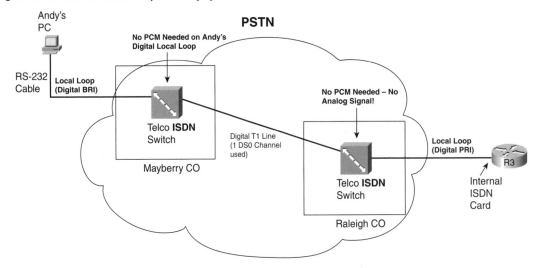

Table 15-10 lists the number of channels for each type of ISDN line and the terminology used to describe them.

Table 15-10 *BRI and PRI B and D Channels*

Type of Interface	Number of Bearer Channels (B Channels)	Number of Signaling Channels (D Channels)	Descriptive Term
BRI	2	1 (16 kbps)	2B+D
PRI (T1)	23	1 (64 kbps)	23B+D
PRI (E1)	30	1 (64 kbps)	30B+D

Figure 15-19 shows some of the detail of a typical DSL connection.

Figure 15-19 *DSL Connection from the Home*

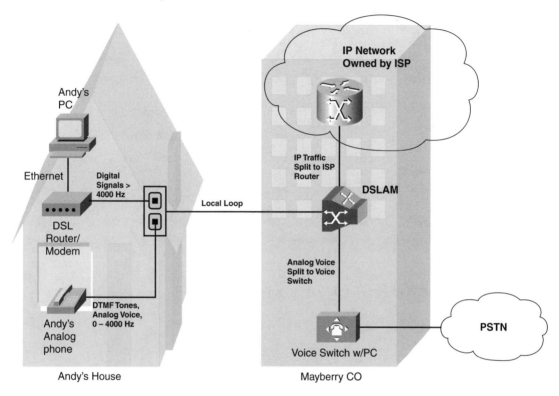

Table 15-11 lists the major DSL variants, the standard defining that variant, the modulation/encoding technique, speed, and distance limitations.

Table 15-11 *DSL Technologies Standards Comparison*

DSL Type	Standards	Modulation/Encoding Technique	Speed	Distance Limit
Full-rate ADSL/G.DMT	ANSI T1.413 Issue 2	Discrete multitone (DMT) or carrierless amplitude phase (CAP)	Downstream speed of 384 to 8 Mbps; upstream speed slower, up to 1.024 Mbps	18,000 feet
G.Lite	ITU-T G.992.1, ITU-T G.992.2	DMT	Downstream speed up to 1.544 Mbps to 6 Mbps; upstream speed up to 640 kbps	18,000 feet

continues

Table 15-11   *DSL Technologies Standards Comparison (Continued)*

DSL Type	Standards	Modulation/Encoding Technique	Speed	Distance Limit
Very-high-data-rate DSL (VDSL)	ETSI and ANSI in process	DMT/single-carrier modulation (SCM)	12.96 Mbps to 52.8 Mbps for both upstream and downstream speed	4500 feet
ISDN DSL (IDSL)	ANSI ETR 080	Two binary one quaternary (2B1Q)	144 kbps for both upstream and downstream speed	18,000 feet
Symmetric DSL (SDSL)	None	2B1Q	768 kbps for both upstream and downstream speed	22,000 feet
High-data-rate DSL (HDSL	ITU G.991.1, ANSI TR 28	2B1Q	1.544 or 2.048 Mbps for both upstream and downstream speed	12,000 feet
G.SHDSL	ITU G.991.2	Trellis-coded pulse amplitude modulation (TC PAM)	192 kbps to 2.360 Mbps for both upstream and downstream speed	28,000 feet

Figure 15-20 outlines some of the key terms used with CATV.

Figure 15-20 *Cable TV Terminology*

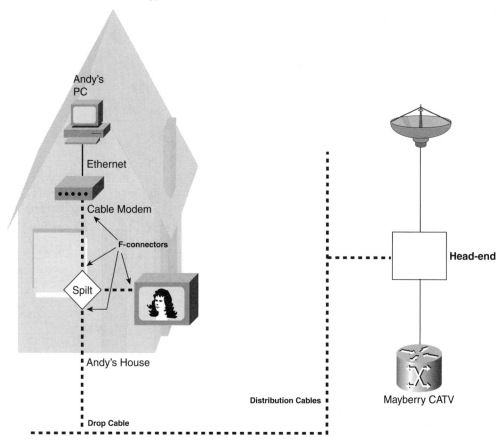

Table 15-12 summarizes some of the key reference information about downstream CATV data over cable.

Table 15-12 *Downstream Data over Cable: Interesting Facts*

	Downstream Rate
OSI Layer 1	QAM-64 and QAM-256 encoding
OSI Layer 2	MCNS MAC and IEEE 802.2 LLC
Multiplexing used	Frequency-division multiplexing
Speed	30 to 40 Mbps

Table 15-13 summarizes some of the key points about the upstream CATV data channel.

Table 15-13   *Upstream Data over Cable: Interesting Facts*

	Downstream Rate
OSI Layer 1	QPSK and QAM-16
OSI Layer 2	MCNS MAC and IEEE 802.2 LLC
Multiplexing used	Time-division multiple access (TDMA)
Speed	320 kbps to 10 Mbps

The remote access technologies in this chapter provide services at Layer 1, and possibly Layer 2, of the OSI model. TCP/IP and all the associated higher-layer protocols (TCP, UDP, HTTP, FTP, Telnet, DNS, DHCP, and so on) can run over any of these access technologies; the differences lie in what is done at Layers 1 and 2. Figure 15-21 outlines the protocols used by each.

Figure 15-21   *The OSI Model and Remote Access Technologies*

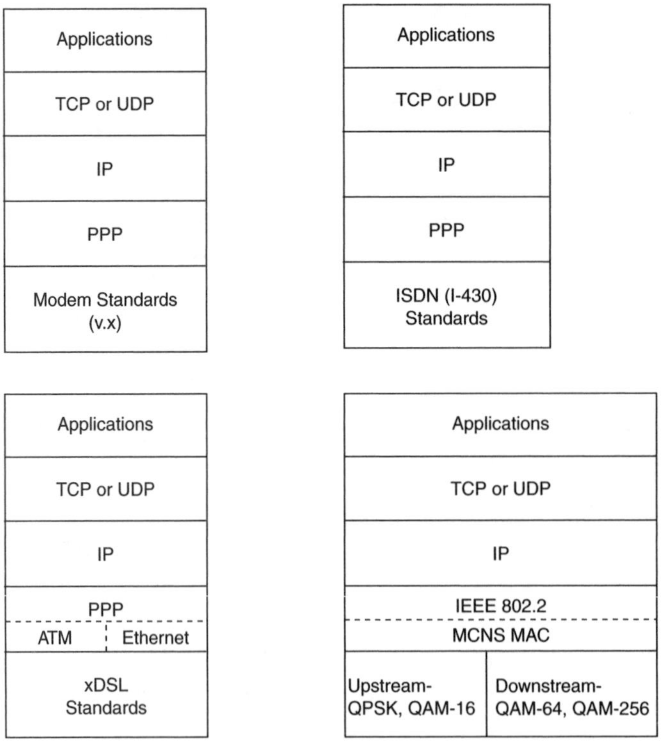

Table 15-14 lists some of the main points for comparison of these technologies. Comparison points are always good material for exam questions.

Table 15-14 *Comparison of Modems, ISDN, DSL, and Cable*

	Analog Modems	**ISDN**	**DSL**	**Cable Modems**
Transport	Telco line	Telco line	Telco line	CATV cable
Supports symetric speeds?	Yes	Yes	Yes	No
Supports asymmetric speeds?	Yes	No	Yes	Yes
Speed ranges	Less than 56 kbps	64 kbps per B channel	56 kbps to 2 Mbps	320 kbps to 40 Mbps
Degrades under higher loads?	No	No	No	Yes
Supports IP and associated higher-layer protocols?	Yes	Yes	Yes	Yes
Allows concurrent voice and data?	No	Yes	Yes	Yes
Always on?	No	No	Yes	Yes
Local loop distance issues	No	No	Yes; distance varies	No

Q&A

As mentioned in the introduction, you have two choices for review questions. The questions that follow give you a bigger challenge than the exam itself by using an open-ended question format. By reviewing now with this more difficult question format, you can exercise your memory better and prove your conceptual and factual knowledge of this chapter. The answers to these questions are found in Appendix A.

For more practice with exam-like question formats, including questions using a router simulator and multiple-choice questions, use the exam engine on the CD.

1. What do ISDN, BRI, and PRI stand for?

2. How many bearer channels are in a BRI? What about a PRI in North America? What about a PRI in Europe?

3. Define what a voice codec does, and explain why a PCM codec needs 64 kbps for a single voice call.

4. Two terms were shortened and combined to first create the word modem. Identify those two words and describe what each word means.

5. Define what the terms symmetric and asymmetric mean in relation to modem specifications. Also explain why asymmetric might be a better option.

6. Compare the V.90 and V.92 modem specifications.

7. Compare analog modems, ISDN BRIs, DSL, and cable modems in terms of concurrent support for voice and data.

8. Compare analog modems, ISDN BRIs, DSL, and cable modems in terms of whether the data service is always on.

9. List some of the pros and cons regarding the use of analog modems for remote access.

10. List some of the pros and cons regarding the use of ISDN for remote access.

11. List some of the pros and cons regarding the use of DSL for remote access.

12. Define what the acronym DSLAM stands for, and explain the concept behind how a DSLAM allows voice and data to flow over the same local loop phone line.

13. Which of the DSL standards is the most common in the United States today? What is the range of upstream and downstream speeds for that type of DSL, as well as the maximum distance of the local loop?

14. What protocols are used by DSL at the data link layer?

15. Imagine that Andy and Barney are neighbors, and they both use cable modems. Describe the type of traffic that they could generate that could cause collisions, and tell what is done to help prevent those collisions.

16. Name the four different Layer 1 encoding methods defined for use by cable modems. For each one, list whether it is used for upstream data, downstream data, or both.

17. Which of the four different remote access technologies support IP, TCP, UDP, and the rest of the higher-layer TCP/IP protocols?

18. Compare and contrast the cabling used by an analog modem and a DSL router/modem when connecting to the local phone company line. Identify the purpose of each pin on the connector.

19. Compare and contrast the cabling used by an ISDN modem and a cable modem when connecting to the local phone company line or cable drop line. Identify the purpose of each pin on the connector.

20. List four standards bodies that have been involved in the development of DSL standards.

PART VI: Final Preparation

Chapter 16: Final Preparation

Final Preparation

So, you have made it through most of the book, and you have probably either scheduled your INTRO exam or CCNA exam, or at least thought about when you want to try to take it. Congratulations for getting this far! You will soon have finished your first step toward building your networking career résumé.

This chapter provides some tips on your final preparation for the exam. It also provides an example scenario, which helps you to pull many of the hands-on skills together into a single review section.

Suggestions for Final Preparation

Everyone has their own study habits, and you should know what works well for you. However, here are a few suggestions you can try in the week or two before you take the exam:

- Reread the "Foundation Summary" sections of each chapter.

- When reviewing tables and definitions, you should cover up portions of summary tables with a piece of paper, forcing yourself to try to remember the details instead of just glancing at them.

- Answer all the questions from inside the book again. You should strive to master these questions so that you can answer the questions quickly.

- If you are still slow in answering subnetting questions, practice until you can find the subnet number and broadcast address when the mask is "difficult" within 1 minute. You can use the CD-based chapter with 25 subnetting practice questions for this exercise.

- Before using the CD for general questions, use the mode that lets you perform a simulated exam. This will help you prepare for the exam experience.

- Repeat answering all the questions on the CD until you can answer most of them almost automatically.

- Using a real set of routers and switches, or using a simulation product (such as Netsim, which is included on the accompanying CD), practice these basic skills:
  - — Accessing a switch and a router
  - — Configuring basic administrative settings (passwords, host name, IP addresses)
  - — Practice configuring IP, static routes, and RIP
  - — Refer to Appendix C for a list of labs from this book that can be performed using the NetSim simulator that is included on the accompanying CD.

Preparing for the Actual Exam Experience

For some of you, either the INTRO exam or the CCNA exam will be your first experience with a proctored computer-based exam for Cisco certification. Do not be alarmed—it's not terribly different than using the exam software on the CD that came with the book. However, you should go into the exam day with the following in mind:

- You typically need two forms of ID, at least one of which is a picture ID. A driver's license, a passport, and a military ID are all valid.

- The testing center is probably just an extra room inside the offices of a company that does something else for its primary business. Often training companies are also testing centers. The proctor usually has other responsibilities besides monitoring the exams. The proctor seldom enters the testing room, other than to bring in another person who has an exam scheduled. So, do not worry about someone staring at you and making you nervous. However, most testing centers do have video cameras for monitoring—just because you cannot see them, it does not mean that they are not watching.

- You will need to turn off all electronics that you bring with you—phone, pager, and secret decoder rings. I typically just leave them in the car. They may ask you to leave your pager or phone at the front desk as well.

- You cannot bring any of your own paper into the room, either. The proctor will give you something to write on, either paper or a dry-erase board and marker. In either case, you should return these to the proctor when you are done.

- You will take the exam using a PC. The proctor will start the software for you; all you have to do is follow the instructions. You will not be forced to start the exam the instant that you sit down because you will typically be allowed to take a four- to five-question practice test. The practice exam asks you questions in different formats about a totally unrelated topic, just to let you get used to the interface. Cisco often adds an optional survey before the exam as well, just to gather demographic information about who is taking the exam. If you've never taken a Cisco exam, take the extra few minutes to take the practice test, just to get completely comfortable with the environment.

- You can actually write on your scratch paper before the exam begins, if you like. For instance, some people like to write down the list of all the valid subnet masks, the corresponding prefixes, and possibly even the binary equivalents for the decimal numbers used inside subnet masks. I've heard of some people writing down hard-to-memorize information that they were cramming for in the lobby of the testing center! Personally, I do not find it helpful to write down the hard-to-memorize things right before the exam begins, but for some people, it does help. Many people find it helpful to write down the subnetting information just mentioned.

- The exam engine does not let you go back and change an earlier answer. So, read each question thoroughly and read every answer thoroughly. When you move on to the next question, you can't go back.

- Some questions require that you drag and drop the answers into the correct slots in an answer area. Exam question writers like to use this type of question for lists or sequences in particular. Like all questions, you can answer and then change the answer, as long as you have not moved on to the next question yet. For drag-and-drop questions, many people benefit from moving the answers they are confident about into the (presumably) correct place, and then they fit in the others in; a lot of times, that helps complete the answers correctly. Just don't forget, when you move on to the next question, you can't go back!

- For simulated lab questions, you should go back and confirm that any new configurations are working. For instance, if the question asks that you configure RIP, but you do not see any routes when you use a **show ip route** command, then you have not finished the question correctly. The simulator used on the exam does work so that the **show** commands reflect what should actually be happening. Many of the simulated lab questions require that you configure something, but it will also be helpful if you know the pertinent **show** commands to verify the correct operation. Also, just for good measure, save your configuration unless the question tells you not to.

That's a long list, but hopefully it will help you prepare for taking the exam. The most important tip is to simply relax. A good night's rest is better than a night full of cramming for most people.

The following list gives a short reminder of the things you might want to keep in mind as you prepare to walk in the door at the testing center:

- Bring two pens.
- Bring two IDs, one with a picture.
- Turn off your electronics before going to the exam room.
- Relax!

A Final Lab Scenario

The current CCNA exams include simulated lab questions. The best way to prepare for those is to work with live networks using Cisco routers and switches. You should also make sure to do all the questions in the testing engine on the CD, as it contains a large number of simulated lab questions. You can also use the NetSim network simulator on the CD, or rent time via online labs.

Regardless of how much time and effort you spend with hands-on practice, the following lab scenario can help you with your final preparation if you simply read through the scenario. Throughout the book, the portions that covered how to do something on a switch or a router focused on the specific topics covered in that chapter. The scenario in this chapter touches on many of the topics in this book that are in some way related to configuration or operation of a router or switch. So, you can use this scenario as part of your strategy for final preparation for the exam.

If you have enough time, review all the parts of the scenario. If you have time, try to perform all the tasks outlined in Steps A, B, and C. However, if you have limited time, you might want to review the problem statements and then review the answers for each of the three parts. At least you will get a good review of some of the more important commands that could be on the exam.

If you are reading this chapter as your final review before taking the exam, let me take this opportunity to wish you success. Hopefully, you will be relaxed and confident for your exam—and hopefully, this book will have helped you build your knowledge and confidence.

Scenario, Part A: Planning

This scenario has three parts, listed as Parts A, B, and C. Part A begins with some planning guidelines that mainly consist of planning an IP addressing scheme for a network. After you complete Part A, Part B of the scenario asks you to configure the three routers and one switch to implement the planned design. Finally, Part C asks you to examine router command output and answer questions about the details of current operation of the network. Part C also lists some questions related to the user interface and protocol specifications.

Your job is to deploy a new network with three sites, as shown in Figure 16-1. The decision to use point-to-point serial links has already been made, and the products have been chosen. For Part A of this scenario, perform the following tasks:

1. Plan the IP addressing and subnets used in this network. Class B network 163.1.0.0 has been assigned by the NIC. The maximum number of hosts per subnet is 100.

2. Assign IP addresses to the PCs as well.

3. Assign addresses for the switches near R1 for management purposes.

Assume that a single VLAN is used on the switches near Router 1 (R1).

Tables 16-1 and 16-2 are provided as a convenient place to record your IP subnets and IP addresses when performing the planning tasks for this scenario.

Figure 16-1 *Scenario Network Diagram*

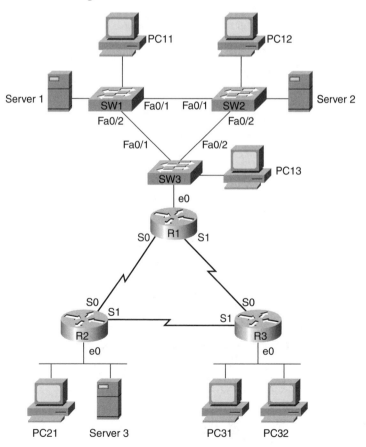

Table 16-1 *Part A: IP Subnet and IP Address Planning Chart*

Location of Subnet/Network Geographically	Subnet Mask	Subnet Number
R1 Ethernet		
R2 Ethernet		
R3 Ethernet		
Serial between R1 and R2		
Serial between R1 and R3		
Serial between R2 and R3		

Table 16-2 *Part A: IP Address Planning Chart*

Host	Address
PC11	
PC12	
PC13	
PC21	
PC31	
PC32	
SW1	
SW2	
SW3	
R1–E0	
R1–S0	
R1–S1	
R2–E0	
R2–S0	
R2–S1	
R3–E0	
R3–S0	
R3–S1	
Server 1	
Server 2	
Server 3	

Solutions to Part A: Planning

It's a good idea to keep the design as simple as possible, without making it so simple that it will not be useful as the network evolves. In this case, any subnet mask with at least 7 host bits would work, including the easy mask of 255.255.255.0. Any choice of mask between 255.255.224.0 and 255.255.255.128 would have allowed for 6 subnets and 100 hosts per subnet.

Table 16-3 shows one solution for the subnet numbers chosen, using mask 255.255.255.128, with Table 16-4 showing some sample IP address assignments.

Table 16-3 *Part A: The Completed IP Subnet Planning Chart*

Location of Subnet/Network Geographically	Subnet Mask	Subnet Number
R1 Ethernet	255.255.255.128	163.1.1.128
R2 Ethernet	255.255.255.128	163.1.2.128
R3 Ethernet	255.255.255.128	163.1.3.128
Serial between R1 and R2	255.255.255.128	163.1.12.128
Serial between R1 and R3	255.255.255.128	163.1.13.128
Serial between R2 and R3	255.255.255.128	163.1.23.128

Table 16-4 *Part A: The Completed IP Address Planning Chart*

Host	Address
PC11	163.1.1.211
PC12	163.1.1.212
PC13	163.1.1.213
PC21	163.1.2.221
PC31	163.1.3.231
PC32	163.1.3.232
SW1	163.1.1.211
SW2	163.1.1.212
SW3	163.1.1.213
R1–E0	163.1.1.201
R1–S0	163.1.12.201
R1–S1	163.1.13.201
R2–E0	163.1.2.202
R2–S0	163.1.12.202

continues

Table 16-4 *Part A: The Completed IP Address Planning Chart (Continued)*

Host	Address
R2–S1	163.1.23.202
R3–E0	163.1.3.203
R3–S0	163.1.13.203
R3–S1	163.1.23.203
Server 1	163.1.1.241
Server 2	163.1.1.242
Server 3	163.1.2.243

As long as the numbers are in the right subnet, the actual IP addresses that you chose for your answer are fine. I just picked numbers between 200 and 209 for the last octet for router addresses, and between 210 and 239 for the switches and PCs. In real networks, you might reserve particular ranges of last octet values in each subnet for network overhead devices. For instance, all of your routers' LAN interface IP addresses might always be between 1 and 5.

Scenario Part B: Configuration

The next step in your job is to deploy the network designed in Part A. Perform the following tasks:

1. Configure IP addresses based on the design from Part A.

2. Although this book did not cover RIP configuration, assume that someone else who knows how to configure RIP will configure the routers to support RIP.

3. Use PPP as the data-link protocol on the link between R2 and R3. Use the default serial encapsulation elsewhere.

4. Configure basic administrative settings for SW3, assuming that it is a 2950 series switch. Set the host name, IP address, default gateway, enable password, telnet password, and console password. Save the configuration as well.

Solutions to Part B: Configuration

Examples 16-1, 16-2, 16-3, and 16-4 show the configurations for Part B.

Example 16-1 *R1 Configuration*

```
hostname R1
!
interface Serial0
```

Example 16-1 *R1 Configuration (Continued)*

```
 ip address 163.1.12.201 255.255.255.128
 !
interface Serial1
 ip address 163.1.13.201 255.255.255.128
 !
Ethernet0
 ip address 163.1.1.201 255.255.255.128
 !
router rip
network 163.1.0.0
```

Example 16-2 *R2 Configuration*

```
hostname R2
 !
interface Serial0
 ip address 163.1.12.202 255.255.255.128
 !
interface Serial1
 encapsulation ppp
 ip address 163.1.23.202 255.255.255.128
 !
Ethernet0
 ip address 163.1.2.202 255.255.255.128
 !
! the following 2 commands configure RIP.
 !
router rip
network 163.1.0.0
```

Example 16-3 *R3 Configuration*

```
hostname R3
 !
interface Serial0
 ip address 163.1.13.203 255.255.255.128
 !
interface Serial1
 encapsulation ppp
 ip address 163.1.23.203 255.255.255.128
 !
Ethernet0
 ip address 163.1.3.203 255.255.255.128
 !
router rip
network 163.1.0.0
```

Example 16-4 *SW3 Configuration*

```
Switch>enable
Switch#configure terminal
Enter configuration commands, one per line.  End with CNTL/Z.
Switch(config)#hostname SW3
SW3(config)#enable secret cisco
SW3(config)#line vty 0 15
SW3(config-line)#password cisco
SW3(config-line)#login
SW3(config-line)#line con 0
SW3(config-line)#login
% Login disabled on line 0, until 'password' is set
SW3(config-line)#password cisco
SW3(config-line)#interface vlan 1
SW3(config-if)#ip address 163.1.1.213 255.255.255.128
SW3(config-if)#no shutdown
SW3(config-if)#exit
SW3(config)#ip default-gateway 163.1.1.201
SW3(config)#interface fastEthernet 0/1
SW3(config-if)#description trunk to SW1
SW3(config-if)#interface fastethernet 0/2
SW3(config-if)#description trunk to SW2
SW3(config-if)#^Z
SW3#
SW3#copy running-config startup-config
Destination filename [startup-config]?
Building configuration...
[OK]
SW3#
```

Scenario Part C: Verification and Questions

The INTRO exam tests you on your memory of the kinds of information you can find in the output of various **show** commands. Using Examples 16-5, 16-6, and 16-7 as references, answer the questions following the examples.

> **NOTE** In the network from which these commands were captured, several administrative settings not mentioned in the scenario were configured. For example, the enable password was configured. So, the configurations might contain additional items not specifically mentioned in the instructions, but none of those impact the actual behavior of the features discussed in the scenario.

Example 16-5 *Scenario Part C: R1* **show** *and* **debug** *Output*

```
R1#show ip interface brief
Interface          IP-Address      OK? Method Status           Protocol
Serial0            163.1.12.201    YES NVRAM  up               up
Serial1            163.1.13.201    YES NVRAM  up               up
Ethernet0          163.1.1.201     YES NVRAM  up               up
R1#show access-lists
Standard IP access list 83
    deny   163.1.3.0, wildcard bits 0.0.0.127
    permit any
R1#
```

Example 16-6 *Part C: R2* **show** *and* **debug** *Output*

```
R2#show interface
Serial0 is up, line protocol is up
  Hardware is HD64570
  Internet address is 163.1.12.202/25
  MTU 1500 bytes, BW 1544 Kbit, DLY 20000 usec,
      reliability 255/255, txload 1/255, rxload 1/255
  Encapsulation HDLC, loopback not set
  Keepalive set (10 sec)
  Last input never, output never, output hang never
  Last clearing of "show interface" counters never
  Input queue: 0/75/0/0 (size/max/drops/flushes); Total output drops: 0
  Queueing strategy: weighted fair
  Output queue: 0/1000/64/0 (size/max total/threshold/drops)
      Conversations  0/0/256 (active/max active/max total)
      Reserved Conversations 0/0 (allocated/max allocated)
      Available Bandwidth 1158 kilobits/sec
  5 minute input rate 0 bits/sec, 0 packets/sec
  5 minute output rate 0 bits/sec, 0 packets/sec
      1242 packets input, 98477 bytes, 0 no buffer
      Received 898 broadcasts, 0 runts, 0 giants, 0 throttles
      0 input errors, 0 CRC, 0 frame, 0 overrun, 0 ignored, 0 abort
      1249 packets output, 91395 bytes, 0 underruns
      0 output errors, 0 collisions, 2 interface resets
      0 output buffer failures, 0 output buffers swapped out
      12 carrier transitions
      DCD=up  DSR=up  DTR=up  RTS=up  CTS=up
Serial1 is up, line protocol is up
  Hardware is HD64570
  Internet address is 163.1.23.202/25
    MTU 1500 bytes, BW 1544 Kbit, DLY 20000 usec,
        reliability 255/255, txload 1/255, rxload 1/255
    Encapsulation PPP, loopback not set
    Keepalive set (10 sec)
    LCP Open
```

continues

Example 16-6 *Part C: R2* show *and* debug *Output (Continued)*

```
   Open: IPCP, CDPCP
   Last input 00:00:03, output 00:00:03, output hang never
   Last clearing of "show interface" counters 00:00:15
   Input queue: 0/75/0/0 (size/max/drops/flushes); Total output drops: 0
   Queueing strategy: weighted fair
   Output queue: 0/1000/64/0 (size/max total/threshold/drops)
      Conversations  0/1/256 (active/max active/max total)
      Reserved Conversations 0/0 (allocated/max allocated)
      Available Bandwidth 1158 kilobits/sec
 5 minute input rate 0 bits/sec, 0 packets/sec
 5 minute output rate 0 bits/sec, 0 packets/sec
    1654 packets input, 90385 bytes, 0 no buffer
    Received 1644 broadcasts, 0 runts, 0 giants, 0 throttles
    0 input errors, 0 CRC, 0 frame, 0 overrun, 0 ignored, 0 abort
    1674 packets output, 96130 bytes, 0 underruns
    0 output errors, 0 collisions, 8 interface resets
    0 output buffer failures, 0 output buffers swapped out
    13 carrier transitions
    DCD=up  DSR=up  DTR=up  RTS=up  CTS=up
Ethernet0 is up, line protocol is up
  Hardware is MCI Ethernet, address is 0000.0c89.b170 (bia 0000.0c89.b170)
  Internet address is 163.1.2.202, subnet mask is 255.255.255.128
    MTU 1500 bytes, BW 10000 Kbit, DLY 1000 usec,
    reliability 255/255, txload 1/255, rxload 1/255
  Encapsulation ARPA, loopback not set, keepalive set (10 sec)
  ARP type: ARPA, ARP Timeout 4:00:00
Last input 00:00:00, output 00:00:04, output hang never
  Last clearing of "show interface" counters never
  Queuing strategy: fifo
  Output queue 0/40, 0 drops; input queue 0/75, 0 drops
  5 minute input rate 0 bits/sec, 0 packets/sec
  5 minute output rate 0 bits/sec, 0 packets/sec
    2274 packets input, 112381 bytes, 0 no buffer
    Received 1913 broadcasts, 0 runts, 0 giants, 0 throttles
    0 input errors, 0 CRC, 0 frame, 0 overrun, 0 ignored, 0 abort
    863 packets output, 110146 bytes, 0 underruns
    0 output errors, 0 collisions, 2 interface resets
    0 output buffer failures, 0 output buffers swapped out
    6 transitions

R2#show ip protocol
Routing Protocol is "rip"
  Sending updates every 30 seconds, next due in 6 seconds
  Invalid after 180 seconds, hold down 180, flushed after 240
  Outgoing update filter list for all interfaces is not set
  Incoming update filter list for all interfaces is not set
  Redistributing: rip
```

Example 16-6 *Part C: R2* **show** *and* **debug** *Output (Continued)*

```
   Default version control: send version 1, receive any version
    Interface        Send  Recv   Key-chain
    Serial0            1    1 2
    Serial1            1    1 2
    Ethernet0          1    1 2
  Automatic network summarization is in effect
  Maximum path: 4
Routing for Networks:
    163.1.0.0
  Routing Information Sources:
    Gateway          Distance      Last Update
    163.1.13.201          120      00:00:02
    163.1.23.202          120      00:00:09
  Distance: (default is 120)
```

Example 16-7 *Part C: R3* **show** *and* **debug** *Output*

```
R3#show running-config
Building configuration...

Current configuration : 888 bytes
!
version 12.2
service timestamps debug uptime
service timestamps log uptime
no service password-encryption
!
hostname R3
!
enable secret 5 $1$J3Fz$QaEYNIiI2aMu.3Ar.q0Xm.
!
ip subnet-zero
no ip domain-lookup
!
interface Serial0
 ip address 163.1.13.203 255.255.255.128
 no fair-queue
!
interface Serial1
 ip address 163.1.23.203 255.255.255.128
 encapsulation ppp
!
interface Ethernet0
 ip address 163.1.3.203 255.255.255.128


!
router rip
```

continues

Example 16-7 *Part C: R3* show *and* debug *Output* *(Continued)*

```
 network 163.1.0.0
 !
 ip classless
 no ip http server
 !
 !
 !
 !
 line con 0
  password cisco
  login
 line aux 0
 line vty 0 4
  password cisco
  login
 !
 end

 R3#show ip arp
 Protocol  Address          Age (min)  Hardware Addr   Type    Interface
 Internet  163.1.3.203           -      0000.0c89.b1b0  SNAP    Ethernet0

 R3#show ip route
 Codes: C - connected, S - static, I - IGRP, R - RIP, M - mobile, B - BGP
        D - EIGRP, EX - EIGRP external, O - OSPF, IA - OSPF inter area
        N1 - OSPF NSSA external type 1, N2 - OSPF NSSA external type 2
        E1 - OSPF external type 1, E2 - OSPF external type 2, E - EGP
        i - IS-IS, L1 - IS-IS level-1, L2 - IS-IS level-2, ia - IS-IS inter area
        * - candidate default, U - per-user static route, o - ODR
        P - periodic downloaded static route

 Gateway of last resort is not set

      163.1.0.0/16 is variably subnetted, 7 subnets, 2 masks
 R       163.1.2.128/25 [120/1] via 163.1.23.202, 00:00:22, Serial1
 C       163.1.3.128/25 is directly connected, Ethernet0
 R       163.1.1.128/25 [120/1] via 163.1.13.201, 00:00:28, Serial0
 R       163.1.12.128/25 [120/1] via 163.1.13.201, 00:00:28, Serial0
                         [120/1] via 163.1.23.202, 00:00:22, Serial1
 C       163.1.13.128/25 is directly connected, Serial0
 C       163.1.23.128/25 is directly connected, Serial1
 C       163.1.23.202/32 is directly connected, Serial1

 R3#trace 163.1.13.203


 Type escape sequence to abort.
```

Example 16-7 *Part C: R3* **show** *and* **debug** *Output (Continued)*

```
Tracing the route to 163.1.13.203

  1 163.1.13.201 16 msec 16 msec 16 msec
  2 163.1.13.203 44 msec *   32 msec

R3#ping 163.1.13.203

Type escape sequence to abort.
Sending 5, 100-byte ICMP Echos to 163.1.13.203, timeout is 2 seconds:
!!!!!
Success rate is 100 percent (5/5), round-trip min/avg/max = 64/66/68 ms
```

Answer the following questions. Use Examples 16-5, 16-6, and 16-7 as references:

1. What command tells you the contents of the ARP cache?

2. What command is used to find the path a packet would take from R3 to 163.1.1.1?

3. Imagine that R3's E0 interface needs to use a new IP address and mask (10.1.1.1, 255.255.255.0). If the user is in user mode, what steps are necessary to change the IP address?

4. If an exec command that you cannot recall begins with the letter C, how can you get Help to list all commands that start with C? List the steps, assuming that you are in privileged mode.

5. Name the two commands to list the currently used configuration in a router.

6. Name the two commands to list the configuration that will be used the next time the router is reloaded.

7. What does CDP stand for?

Solutions to Part C: Verification and Questions

The answers to the questions for Part C are as follows:

1. The **show ip arp** command (refer to Example 16-7) contains MAC and IP addresses.

2. The **trace 163.1.1.1** command could be used to find the path that a packet would take from R3 to 163.1.1.1 (refer to Example 16-7).

3. To change the IP address on an interface, use the following steps:

```
R3> enable
password: password
R3#configure terminal
R3(config)#interface ethernet 0
```

```
R3(config-if)#ip address 10.1.1.1 255.255.255.0
R3(config)#Ctrl-Z
R3#
```

4. To find all commands that start with the letter C, do the following:

```
R3#c?
clear   clock   configure   connect   copy

R3#c
```

5. The two commands that list the currently used configuration in a router are **show running-config** and **write terminal**.

6. The two commands that list the configuration that will be used the next time the router is reloaded are **show startup-config** and **show config**.

7. CDP stands for Cisco Discovery Protocol.

PART VII: Appendixes

Answers to the "Do I Know This Already?" Quizzes and Q&A Sections

Chapter 2

"Do I Know This Already?" Quiz

1. Which of the following protocols are examples of TCP/IP transport layer protocols?

   Answer: D and F

2. Which of the following protocols are examples of TCP/IP network interface layer protocols?

   Answer: A and G

3. Which OSI layer defines the functions of logical network-wide addressing and routing?

   Answer: C

4. Which OSI layer defines the standards for cabling and connectors?

   Answer: A

5. Which OSI layer defines the standards for data formats and encryption?

   Answer: F

6. Which of the following terms are not valid terms for the names of the seven OSI layers?

   Answer: C and E

7. The process of HTTP asking TCP to send some data and make sure that it is received correctly is an example of what?

   Answer: B

8. The process of TCP on one computer marking a segment as segment 1, and the receiving computer then acknowledging the receipt of segment 1, is an example of what?

Answer: B

9. The process of a web server adding a HTTP header to a web page, followed by adding a TCP header, then an IP header, and then data link header and trailer is an example of what?

Answer: A

10. Which of the following terms is used specifically to identify the entity that is created when encapsulating data inside data-link headers and trailers?

Answer: D

Q&A

1. Name the seven layers of the OSI model.

Answer: Application (Layer 7), presentation (Layer 6), session (Layer 5), transport (Layer 4), network (Layer 3), data link (Layer 2), and physical (Layer 1). Some mnemonics to help you recall the names of the layers are: All People Seem To Need Data Processing (Layers 7 to 1), Please Do Not Take Sausage Pizzas Away (Layers 1 to 7), and the ever-popular Pew! Dead Ninja Turtles Smell Particularly Awful (Layers 1 to 7).

2. What is the main purpose(s) of Layer 7?

Answer: Layer 7 (the application layer) provides standardized services to applications. The definition for this layer is typically ambiguous because it varies. The key is that it does not define a user interface, but instead it is a sort of toolbox used by application developers. For example, a web browser is an application that uses HTTP, as defined as a TCP/IP application layer protocol, to transfer the contents of web page between a server and client.

3. What is the main purpose(s) of Layer 6?

Answer: Layer 6 (the presentation layer) defines data formats, compression, and possibly encryption.

4. What is the main purpose(s) of Layer 5?

Answer: Layer 5 (the session layer) controls the conversation between two endpoints. Although the term used is session, the term conversation more accurately describes what is accomplished. The session layer ensures that not only communication, but also useful sets of communication between endpoints is accomplished.

5. What is the main purpose(s) of Layer 4?

Answer: Layer 4 (the transport layer) provides end-to-end error recovery, if requested.

6. What is the main purpose(s) of Layer 3?

Answer: Layer 3 (the network layer) defines logical addressing and routing as a means of delivering data across an entire network. IP and IPX are two examples of Layer 3–equivalent protocols.

7. What is the main purpose(s) of Layer 2?

Answer: The data link layer defines addressing specific to a particular medium as part of the means of providing delivery of data across that medium. It also includes the protocols used to determine what device(s) accesses the media at any point in time.

8. What is the main purpose(s) of Layer 1?

Answer: Layer 1 (physical layer) is responsible for encoding energy signals onto the medium and interpreting a received energy signal. Layer 1 also defines the connector and cabling details.

9. Describe the process of data encapsulation as data is processed from creation until it exits a physical interface to a network. Use the OSI model as an example.

Answer: Data encapsulation represents the process of a layer adding a header (and possibly a trailer) to the data as it is processed by progressively lower layers in the protocol specification. In the context of OSI, each layer could add a header so that—other than the true application data—there would be six other headers (Layers 2 to 7) and a trailer for Layer 2, with this L2PDU being encoded by the physical layer onto the network media.

10. Name three benefits to layering networking protocol specifications.

Answer: Some examples of benefits to layering networking protocol specifications include reduced complexity, standardized interfaces, modular engineering, interoperable technology, accelerated evolution, and simplified teaching and learning. Questions such as this on the exam require some subjective interpretation of the wording on your part.

11. What header or trailer does a router discard as a side effect of routing?

Answer: A router discards the data-link header and trailer as a side effect of routing. This is because the network layer, where routing is defined, is interested in delivering the network layer (Layer 3) PDU from end to end. Routing uses intermediate data links

(Layer 2) to transport the data to the next routers and eventually to the true destination. The data-link header and trailer are useful only to deliver the data to the next router or host, so the header and trailer are discarded by each router.

12.   What OSI layer typically encapsulates using both a header and a trailer?

Answer: The data link layer typically encapsulates using both a header and a trailer. The trailer typically includes a frame check sequence (FCS), which is used to perform error detection.

13.   What terms are used to describe the contents of the data encapsulated by the data link, network, and transport layers, respectively?

Answer: Frame, packet, and segment, respectively.

14.   Explain the meaning of the term L5PDU.

Answer: PDU stands for protocol data unit. A PDU is the entity that includes the headers and trailers created by a particular networking layer, plus any encapsulated data. For instance, an L5PDU includes Layer 5 headers and the encapsulated data.

15.   Explain how Layer x on one computer communicates with Layer x on another computer.

Answer: Each layer of a networking model works with the same layer on another computer with which it wants to communicate. The protocol defined by each layer uses a header that is transmitted between the computers to communicate what each computer wants to do.

16.   List the terms behind the acronym TCP/IP.

Answer: Transmission Control Protocol and Internet Protocol.

17.   List the terms behind the acronym OSI.

Answer: Open Systems Interconnection.

Chapter 3

"Do I Know This Already?" Quiz

1.   Which of the following best describes the main function of OSI Layer 1 protocols?

Answer: B

2. Which of the following are part of the functions of OSI Layer 2 protocols?

   Answer: A

3. Which of the following is true about Ethernet crossover cables?

   Answer: B

4. Which of the following are true about the format of Ethernet addresses?

   Answer: B, C, and E

5. Which of the following is true about the Ethernet FCS field?

   Answer: C

6. Which of the following fields can be used by Ethernet as a "type" field, to define the type of data held in the "data" portion of the Ethernet frame?

   Answer: C and D

7. Which of the following are true about the CSMA/CD algorithm?

   Answer: B

8. Which of the following would be a collision domain?

   Answer: A

9. Which terms describe Ethernet addresses that can be used to communicate with more than one device at a time?

   Answer: C and D

10. With autonegotiation on a 10/100 card, what characteristics are negotiated if the device on the other end does not perform negotiation at all?

    Answer: C

Q&A

1. What is the main purpose(s) of Layer 2?

   Answer: The data link layer defines addressing specific to a particular medium as part of the means of providing delivery of data across that medium. It also includes the protocols used to determine what device(s) accesses the media at any point in time.

2. What is the main purpose(s) of Layer 1?

Answer: Layer 1 (the physical layer) is responsible for encoding energy signals onto the medium and interpreting a received energy signal. Layer 1 also defines the connector and cabling details.

3. What does MAC stand for?

Answer: MAC stands for Media Access Control.

4. Name three terms popularly used as a synonym for *MAC address*.

Answer: NIC address, card address, LAN address, hardware address, Ethernet address, Token Ring address, FDDI address, and burned-in address are all synonymous with MAC address. All of these names are used casually and in formal documents, and they refer to the same 6-byte MAC address concept as defined by IEEE.

5. What portion of a MAC address encodes an identifier representing the manufacturer of the card?

Answer: The first 3 bytes, called the Organizationally Unique Identified (OUI), comprise the portion of a MAC address that encodes an identifier representing the manufacturer of the card.

6. Are MAC addresses defined by a Layer 2 or Layer 3 protocol?

Answer: MAC addresses are defined by a Layer 2 protocol. Ethernet and Token Ring MAC addresses are defined in the 802.3 and 802.5 specifications.

7. How many bits are present in a MAC address?

Answer: MAC addresses have 48 bits. The first 24 bits for burned-in addresses represent a code that identifies the manufacturer.

8. Name the two main parts of a MAC address. Which part identifies which "group" this address is a member of?

Answer: There are no parts, and nothing defines a grouping concept in a MAC address. This is a trick question. Although you might have guessed that the MAC address has two parts—the first part dictated to the manufacturer, and the second part made up by the manufacturer—there is no grouping concept.

9. What OSI layer typically encapsulates using both a header and a trailer?

Answer: The data link layer typically encapsulates using both a header and a trailer. The trailer typically includes a frame check sequence (FCS), which is used to perform error detection.

10. If a Fast Ethernet NIC currently is receiving a frame, can it begin sending a frame?

Answer: Yes, if the NIC is operating in full-duplex mode.

11. What are the two key differences between a 10-Mbps NIC and a 10/100 NIC?

Answer: The obvious benefit is that the 10/100 NIC can run at 100 Mbps. The other benefit is that 10/100 NICs can autonegotiate both speed and duplex between itself and the device that it is cabled to, typically a LAN switch.

12. What is the distance limitation of a single cable for 10BASE-T? For 100 BASE-TX?

Answer: 10BASE-T allows 100 m between the device and the hub or switch, as does 100 BASE-TX.

13. How fast is Fast Ethernet?

Answer: 100 million bits per second (100 Mbps).

14. How many bytes long is a MAC address?

Answer: 6 bytes long, or 48 bits.

15. Define the difference between broadcast and multicast MAC addresses.

Answer: Both identify more than one device on the LAN. Broadcast always implies all devices on the LAN, whereas multicast implies some subset of all devices. Multicast is not allowed on Token Ring; broadcast is allowed on all LAN types. Devices that intend to receive frames addressed to a particular multicast address must be aware of the particular multicast address(es) that they should process. These addresses are dependent on the applications used. Read RFC 1112, "The Internet Group Message Protocol (IGMP)," for related information about the use of Ethernet multicast in conjunction with IP multicast. For example, the broadcast address is FFFF.FFFF.FFFF, and one sample multicast address is 0100.5e00.0001.

16. Explain the function of the loopback and collision-detection features of an Ethernet NIC in relation to half-duplex and full-duplex operations.

Answer: The loopback feature copies the transmitted frame back onto the receive pin on the NIC interface. The collision-detection logic compares the received frame to the transmitted frame during transmission; if the signals do not match, a collision is occurring. With full-duplex operation, collisions cannot occur, so the loopback and collision-detection features are purposefully disabled, and concurrent transmission and reception is allowed.

Chapter 4

"Do I Know This Already?" Quiz

1. Which of the following best describes the main function of OSI Layer 1 protocols?

    Answer: B

2. Which of the following typically connects to a four-wire line provided by a telco?

    Answer: B

3. Which of the following typically connects to a V.35 or RS-232 end of a cable when cabling a leased line?

    Answer: B

4. Which of the following functions of OSI Layer 2 is specified by the protocol standard for PPP, but is implemented with a Cisco proprietary header field for HDLC?

    Answer: E

5. Which of the following WAN data link protocols on Cisco routers support multiple Layer 3 protocols by virtue of having some form of Protocol Type field?

    Answer: A, B, and C

6. On a point-to-point WAN link between two routers, what device(s) are considered to be the DTE devices?

    Answer: A

7. Imagine that Router1 has three point-to-point serial links, one link each to three remote routers. Which of the following is true about the required HDLC addressing at Router1?

    Answer: E

8. What is the name of the Frame Relay field used to identify Frame Relay Virtual Circuits?

    Answer: A

9. Which of the following is true about Frame Relay virtual circuits?

    Answer: B

10. Which of the following defines a SONET link speed around 155 Mbps?

    Answer: E

Q&A

1. Are DLCI addresses defined by a Layer 2 or Layer 3 protocol?

Answer: DLCI addresses are defined by a Layer 2 protocol. Although they are not covered specifically in this chapter, Frame Relay protocols do not define a logical addressing structure that can usefully exist outside a Frame Relay network; by definition, the addresses would be OSI Layer 2–equivalent.

2. What OSI layer typically encapsulates using both a header and a trailer?

Answer: The data link layer typically encapsulates using both a header and a trailer. The trailer typically includes a frame check sequence (FCS), which is used to perform error detection.

3. Define the terms DCE and DTE in the context of the physical layer and a point-to-point serial link.

Answer: At the physical layer, DTE refers to the device that looks for clocking from the device on the other end of the cable on a link. The DCE supplies that clocking. For example, the computer is typically the DTE, and the modem or CSU/DSU is the DCE. At the data link layer, both X.25 and Frame Relay define a logical DTE and DCE. In this case, the customer premises equipment (CPE), such as a router and a CSU/DSU, is the logical DTE, and the service provider equipment (the Frame Relay switch and the CSU/DSU) is the DCE.

4. Which layer or layers of OSI are most closely related to the functions of Frame Relay? Why?

Answer: OSI Layers 1 and 2. Frame Relay refers to well-known physical layer specifications. Frame Relay does define headers for delivery across the Frame Relay cloud, making it a Layer 2 protocol. Frame Relay does not include any routing or logical addressing specifications, so it is not a Layer 3 protocol.

5. What is the name of the field that identifies, or addresses, a Frame Relay virtual circuit?

Answer: The data-link connection identifier (DLCI) is used to identify a VC.

6. True or False: "A leased line between two routers provides a constant amount of bandwidth—never more and never less." Defend your answer.

Answer: True. A leased line creates the cabling equivalent of having a cable between the two routers, with the speed (clock rate) defined by the telco. Even when the routers have no data to send, the full bandwidth is available to be used.

7. True or False: "Frame Relay VCs provide a constant amount of bandwidth between two devices, typically routers—never more and never less." Defend your answer.

   Answer: False. The provider assigns a guaranteed bandwidth, or CIR, for a VC, but the routers on either end of the VC can send more than the CIR of data. As long as the service provider has enough capacity to support it, the frames are forwarded over the VC.

8. Explain how many DS0 channels fit into a T1, and why the total does not add up to the purported speed of a T1, which is 1.544 Mbps.

   Answer: Each DS0 channel runs at 64 kbps. With 24 in a T1, the T1 speed seemingly would be 24 * 64 kbps, or 1.536 Mbps. T1 also includes 8 kbps for management, which, when added to the 1.536 Mbps total, gives you the full T1 rate—1.544 Mbps.

9. Define the term synchronous.

   Answer: The imposition of time ordering on a bit stream. Practically, a device will try to use the same speed as another device on the other end of a serial link. By examining transitions between voltage states on the link, the device can notice slight variations in the speed on each end and can adjust its speed accordingly.

10. Imagine a drawing with two routers, each connected to an external CSU/DSU, which each is connected with a four-wire circuit, as seen in this chapter. Describe the role of the devices in relation to clocking and synchronization.

    Answer: The routers receive clocking from their respective CSU/DSUs. One of the two CSU/DSUs is configured as the master. The other CSU/DSU, as the slave, adjusts its clock to match the speed of the master CSU/DSU.

11. Imagine a drawing with two routers, each connected to an external CSU/DSU, which each is connected with a four-wire circuit, as seen in this chapter. List the words behind the acronyms DTE and DCE, and describe which devices in this imagined network are DTE and which are DCE.

    Answer: DTE stands for data terminal equipment, and DCE stands for data communications equipment. The routers are DTEs, and the CSU/DSUs are DCEs.

12. Imagine a drawing with two routers, each connected to a Frame Relay switch over a local access link. Describe which devices in this imagined network are Frame Relay DTEs and which are Frame Relay DCEs.

    Answer: The routers are DTEs, and the Frame Relay switches are DCEs.

13. Do HDLC and PPP, as implemented by Cisco routers, support protocol type fields and error detection? Explain your answer.

    Answer: Both protocols support a protocol type field and an FCS field to perform error detection. PPP has both fields based on the protocol specification; Cisco added the protocol type field to the standard HDLC header.

14. Imagine a point-to-point leased line between two routers, with PPP in use. What are the names of the protocols inside PPP that would be used on this link? What are their main functions?

    Answer: The PPP Link Control Protocol (LCP) controls and manages the link. The IP Control Protocol (IPCP) also would be used because you need a CP for each Layer 3 protocol. IPCP can assign IP addresses to devices on the other end of a link.

15. What are some of the main similarities between Frame Relay and ATM?

    Answer: Both use an access link to access the service provider. Both use the concept of a virtual circuit between DTE devices. And both allow multiple VCs to cross a single access link.

16. Compare and contrast ATM and SONET in terms of the OSI model.

    Answer: SONET defines the Layer 1 details of passing traffic over optical cabling, whereas ATM provides the Layer 2 functionality, including link-specific addressing, framing, and error detection.

17. Besides HDLC and PPP, list the other four serial point-to-point data-link protocols covered in this chapter.

    Answer: SDLC, LAPB, LAPD, and LAPF.

18. List the speeds of a T1 line, E1, OC-3, and OC-12.

    Answer: 1.544 Mbps, 2.048 Mbps, 155 Mbps, and 622 Mbps.

Chapter 5

"Do I Know This Already?" Quiz

1. Which of the following describes the functions of OSI Layer 3 protocols?

    Answer: A and C

2. Imagine that PC1 needs to send some data to PC2, and PC1 and PC2 are separated by several routers. What are the largest entities that make it from PC1 to PC2?

   Answer: C and E

3. Which of the following does a router normally use when making a decision about routing TCP/IP?

   Answer: C

4. Imagine a network with two routers that are connected with a point-to-point HDLC serial link. Each router has an Ethernet, with PC1 sharing the Ethernet with Router1, and PC2 sharing an Ethernet with Router2. When PC1 sends data to PC2, which of the following is true?

   Answer: A

5. Which of the following are valid Class C IP addresses?

   Answer: B

6. What is the range for the values of the first octet for Class A IP networks?

   Answer: D

7. PC1 and PC2 are on two different Ethernets that are separated by an IP router. PC1's IP address is 10.1.1.1, and no subnetting is used. Which of the following addresses could be used for PC2?

   Answer: D and F

8. How many valid host IP addresses does each Class B network contain?

   Answer: D

9. How many valid host IP addresses does each Class C network contain?

   Answer: G

10. Which of the following protocols allows a client PC to discover the IP address of another computer, based on that other computer's name?

    Answer: C

11. Which of the following protocols allow a client PC to request assignment of an IP address as well as learn its default gateway?

Answer: D

12. Which term is defined by the following phrase: "the type of protocol that is being forwarded when routers perform routing."

Answer: A

Q&A

1. What are the two main functions of each OSI Layer 3–equivalent protocol?

Answer: Path selection, which is also called routing, and logical addressing.

2. Assume that PC1 sends data to PC2, and PC2 is separated from PC1 by at least one router. Are the IP addresses of the PCs in the same IP subnet? Explain your answer.

Answer: They must be in different subnets. IP addressing rules require that IP hosts separated by a router be in different subnets.

3. Assume that PC1 sends data to PC2, and PC2 is not separated from PC1 by at least one router. Are the IP, addresses of the PCs in the same IP subnet? Explain your answer.

Answer: They must be in the same subnet. IP addressing rules require that IP hosts not separated by a router be in the same subnet.

4. How many bits are present in an IP address?

Answer: IP addresses have 32 bits: a variable number in the network portion, and the rest of the 32 in the host portion. IP Version 6 uses a 128-bit address!

5. How many bits are present in an IPX address?

Answer: IPX addresses have 80 bits: 32 bits in the network portion and 48 bits in the node portion.

6. How many bits are present in an AppleTalk address?

Answer: AppleTalk addresses have 24 bits: 16 in the cable-range portion and 8 bits in the node portion.

7. Name the two main parts of an IPX address. Which part identifies which group this address is a member of?

Answer: Network number and node number are the two main parts of an IPX address. Addresses with the same network number are in the same group. On LAN interfaces, the node number is made to have the same value as the LAN MAC address.

8. Name the two main parts of an IP address. Which part identifies which group this address is a member of?

Answer: Network and host are the two main parts of an IP address. As described in Chapter 5, technically there are three portions of the IP address: network, subnet, and host. However, because most people think of the network and subnet portions as one portion, another correct answer to this question, using popular terminology, would be subnet and host. In short, without subnetting, the network part identifies the group; with subnetting, the network and subnet part together identifies the group.

9. PC1 sends data to PC2 using TCP/IP. Three routers separate PC1 and PC2. Explain why the statement "PC1 sends an Ethernet frame to PC2" is true or false.

Answer: False. Packets are delivered from end to end across a network, whereas frames simply pass between devices on each common physical network. The intervening routers discard the original Ethernet header, replacing it with other data-link headers as needed. A truer statement would be "PC1 sends an IP packet to PC2."

10. In IP addressing, how many octets are in 1 byte?

Answer: One. Octet is a generic word to describe a single byte. Each IP address is 4 bytes, or four octets, long.

11. Describe the differences between a routed protocol and a routing protocol.

Answer: The routed protocol defines the addressing and Layer 3 header in the packet that actually is forwarded by a router. The routing protocol defines the process of routers exchanging topology data so that the routers know how to forward the data. A router uses the routing table created by the routing protocol when choosing where to route a packet.

12. Name at least three routed protocols.

Answer: TCP/IP (IP), Novell (IPX), OSI (CLNP), DECnet (CLNP), AppleTalk (DDP), and VINES are some examples of routed protocols.

13. Name at least three IP routing protocols.

Answer: IP RIP, IP IGRP, IP/IPX/AppleTalk EIGRP, IP OSPF, OSI NLSP, and OSI IS-IS are some examples of routing protocols.

14. Imagine an IP host on an Ethernet, with a single router attached to the same segment. In which cases does an IP host choose to send a packet to this router instead of directly to the destination host, and how does this IP host know about that single router?

Answer: Typically an IP host knows to what router to send a packet based on its configured default router. If the destination of the packet is in another subnet, the host sends the packet to the default router. Otherwise, the host sends the packet directly to the destination host because it is in the same subnet and, by definition, must be on the same data link.

15. Name three items in an entry in any routing table.

Answer: A number that identifies a group of addresses, the interface out which to forward the packet, and the Layer 3 address of the next router to send this packet to are three items that you will always find in a routing table entry. For instance, IP routes contain subnet numbers, the outgoing interface, and the IP address of the next-hop router.

16. Name the parts of an IP address when subnetting is used.

Answer: Network, subnet, and host are the three parts of an IP address. However, many people commonly treat the network and subnet parts of an address as a single part, leaving only two parts, the subnet and host parts. On the exam, the multiple-choice format should provide extra clues as to which terminology is used.

17. How many valid IP addresses exist in a Class A network? (You may refer to the formula if you do not know the exact number.)

Answer: 16,777,214, derived by the formula $2^{24} - 2$.

18. How many valid IP addresses exist in a Class B network? (You may refer to the formula if you do not know the exact number.)

Answer: 65,534, derived by the formula $2^{16} - 2$.

19. How many valid IP addresses exist in a Class C network? (You may refer to the formula if you do not know the exact number.)

Answer: 254, derived by the formula $2^8 - 2$.

20. What values can a Class A network have in the first octet?

Answer: 1 through 126, inclusive.

21. What values can a Class B network have in the first octet?

Answer: 128 through 191, inclusive.

22. What values can a Class C network have in the first octet?

    Answer: 192 through 223, inclusive.

23. When subnetting a Class B network, do you create the subnet field by taking bits from the network part of the address or the host part?

    Answer: Host part.

24. When subnetting a Class B network, using the entire third octet for the subnet part, describe the number of possible subnets created.

    Answer: The subnet part consists of a full octet, which is 8 bits long. You can number 2^8 things with 8 bits, or 256. However, 2 subnet numbers are reserved, leaving 254 subnets.

25. When subnetting a Class A network using the entire second octet for the subnet part, describe the number of hosts in each subnet.

    Answer: The host part consists of two entire octets in this case, which is 16 bits long. You can number 2^{16} things with 16 bits, or 65,536. However, 2 host addresses are reserved, leaving 65,534 hosts per subnet.

26. When a router hears about multiple routes to the same subnet, how does it choose which route to use?

    Answer: Routing protocols use a metric to describe how good each route is. The lower the metric is, the better the route is.

27. What is the primary purpose of a routing protocol?

    Answer: Routing protocols discover the routes in network and build routing tables.

28. True or false: "Routing protocols are required to learn routes of directly connected subnets."

    Answer: False. Routers add routes to directly connected subnets when the interfaces initialize. No routing protocols are needed.

29. Which IP routing protocols are Cisco proprietary?

    Answer: IGRP and EIGRP.

30. List the similarities and differences between RARP and BOOTP.

Answer: Both protocols send broadcasts looking for a server, and they hope to have the server assign them an IP address. BOOTP also can be used to assign other parameters, such as the subnet mask, default gateway, DNS address, and filenames for downloading an operating system.

31. List the similarities and differences between DHCP and BOOTP.

Answer: Both protocols send broadcasts looking for a server, and they hope to have the server assign them an IP address. Both can be used to assign a large variety of parameters, such as the subnet mask, default gateway, DNS address, and filenames for downloading an operating system. DHCP does not require that the server be preconfigured with the MAC addresses of all the DHCP client PCs, making it much more scalable.

32. List the similarities and differences between ARP and DNS.

Answer: Both protocols send messages with one bit of information, hoping to learn another bit of information. The similarities do not go beyond that fact. DNS requests are unicast IP packets sent specifically to the DNS server, whereas ARP uses a LAN broadcast frame. DNS queries supply a name, expecting to hear the corresponding IP address back from the server. ARP requests supply an IP address, hoping to hear a corresponding MAC address not from a server, but from the host that uses that IP address.

Chapter 6

"Do I Know This Already?" Quiz

1. Which of the following protocols are connection-oriented?

Answer: A and B

2. Which of the following protocols are reliable?

Answer: B

3. PC1 is using TCP, has a window of 4, and sends four segments numbered 2, 3, 4, and 5 to PC2. PC2 replies with an acknowledgment number 5. What should PC1 do next?

Answer: D

4. Which of the following are not features of a protocol that is considered to match OSI Layer 4?

   Answer: D

5. Which of the following flow-control methods let the receiver tell the sender how much data the sender is allowed to send before the sender must wait for an acknowledgment?

   Answer: C

6. Which of the following header fields identifies which TCP/IP application gets data received by the computer?

   Answer: E and F

7. Which of the TCP connection-establishment flows sets both the SYN and ACK flags in the TCP header?

   Answer: B

8. Which of the following is not a typical function of TCP?

   Answer: D and E

9. Which of the following functions is performed by TCP and UDP?

   Answer: C

10. Data that includes the Layer 4 protocol header, and data given to Layer 4 by the upper layers, not including any headers and trailers from Layers 1 to 3, is called what?

    Answer: C and G

Q&A

1. Describe the features required for a protocol to be considered connectionless.

   Answer: Unordered low-overhead delivery of data from one host to another is the service provided in most connectionless protocol services.

2. Name at least three connectionless protocols.

   Answer: LLC Type 1, UDP, IPX, and IP are some examples of connectionless protocols. Remember, Frame Relay, X.25, and ATM are connection oriented, regardless of whether they define error recovery.

3. Describe the features required for a protocol to be considered connection oriented.

   Answer: Either the protocol must exchange messages with another device before data is allowed to be sent, or some pre-established correlation between the two endpoints must be defined. TCP is an example of a connection-oriented protocol that exchanges messages before data can be sent; Frame Relay is a connection-oriented protocol for which a pre-established correlation between endpoints is defined.

4. In a particular error-recovering protocol, the sender sends three frames, labeled 2, 3, and 4. On its next sent frame, the receiver of these frames sets an Acknowledgment field to 4. What does this typically imply?

   Answer: Frames through number 3 were received successfully. The receiver might have not received Frame 4, or Frame 4 might not have passed the FCS check.

5. Name three connection-oriented protocols.

   Answer: TCP, SPX, LLC Type 2, and X.25 are some examples of connection-oriented protocols that provide error recovery. ATM and Frame Relay are also connection oriented, but without error recovery.

6. Describe how TCP performs error recovery. What role do the routers play?

   Answer: TCP numbers the first byte in each segment with a sequence number. The receiving host uses the Acknowledgment field in segments that it sends back to acknowledge receipt of the data. If the receiver sends an acknowledgment number that is a smaller number than the sender expected, the sender believes that the intervening bytes were lost, so the sender resends them. The router plays no role unless the TCP connection ends in the router—for example, a Telnet into a router. A full explanation is provided in the section "Error Recovery (Reliability)."

7. How many TCP segments are exchanged to establish a TCP connection? How many are required to terminate a TCP connection?

   Answer: A three-way connection-establishment sequence is used, and a four-way connection-termination sequence is used.

8. Describe the purpose of the Port Number field in a TCP header. Give one example.

   Answer: The port numbers are used to help computers multiplex received data. For instance, a PC with two web browsers open can receive an IP packet. The destination TCP port number identifies which of the two browsers should receive the data.

9. List the components of a TCP socket.

Answer: A socket consists of three things: an IP address, a transport layer protocol (TCP or UDP), and the TCP or UDP port number.

10. How many TCP segments must be sent to establish a TCP connection? How many are used with normal TCP connection termination?

Answer: Three TCP segments are needed to establish the connection, and four are needed to tear it down under normal operation.

11. How many UDP segments must be sent to establish a UDP connection? How many are used with normal UDP connection termination?

Answer: UDP does not establish connections because it is not connection oriented.

Chapter 7

"Do I Know This Already?" Quiz

1. In which of the following modes of the CLI could you configure a description of Ethernet0?

Answer: E. The description command is an interface subcommand.

2. In which of the following modes of the CLI could you issue a command to reboot the router?

Answer: B. The reload command is an exec command, so it cannot be issued from any configuration mode. User mode does not allow the use of the reload command.

3. What type of router memory is used to store the configuration used by the router when it is up and working?

Answer: A. The IOS loads the config from NVRAM into RAM during the boot sequence; therefore, the router uses the configuration in RAM for normal operations.

4. What type of router memory is used to store the operating system used for low-level debugging and not for normal operation?

Answer: B. The ROMMON operating system is stored in ROM.

5. What command copies the configuration from RAM into NVRAM?

Answer: F. The first parameter identifies the source of the config, and the last parameter identifies the destination.

6. What mode prompts the user for basic configuration information?

    Answer: D

7. Which of the following could cause a router to change the IOS that is loaded when the router boots?

    Answer: D and F. The boot command is a configuration command that identifies the source and possibly the name of the IOS to load. The configuration register tells the router the source from which to find the file containing the IOS.

8. Which of the following hexadecimal values in the last nibble of the configuration register would cause a router to not look in Flash memory?

    Answer: A and B. A 0 makes the router load ROMMON code; a 1 makes the router load the RXBOOT IOS image.

9. Imagine that you have configured the **enable secret** command, followed by the **enable password** command, from the console. You log out of the router and log back in at the console. Which command defines the password that you had to type to access the router again from the console?

    Answer: C. The password subcommand, under the line console 0 command, sets the console password.

10. Imagine that you have configured the **enable secret** command, followed by the **enable password** command, from the console. You log out of the router and log back in at the console. Which command defines the password that you had to type to access privileged mode?

    Answer: B. If both are configured, the enable secret password is required to gain access to privileged mode.

Q&A

1. What are the two names for the same CLI mode in a router, that when accessed, enables you to issue exec commands that could be disruptive to router operations?

    Answer: Enable mode and privileged mode. Both names are commonly used and are found in Cisco documentation.

2. What are three methods of logging on to a router?

    Answer: Console, auxiliary port, and Telnet. All three cause the user to enter user exec mode.

3. What is the name of the user interface mode of operation used in which you cannot issue disruptive commands?

   Answer: User exec mode.

4. Can the auxiliary port be used for anything besides remote modem user access to a router? If so, what other purpose can it serve?

   Answer: Yes. For direct attachment of a terminal, and dial for the purpose of routing packets. Although it originally was created to support remote administration access, many customers use an auxiliary port for dial backup, particularly when analog lines are desired or when that is all that is available.

5. What command would you use to receive command help if you knew that a **show** command option begins with a c but you cannot recall the option?

   Answer: show c?. Help would appear immediately after you typed the ? symbol. You would not need to press Enter after the ?. If you did so, the router would try to execute the command with only the parameters that you had typed after the ?.

6. While you are logged in to a router, you issue the command **copy ?** and get a response of "Unknown command, computer name, or host." Offer an explanation for why this error message appears.

   Answer: You were in user mode. You must be in enable/privileged mode to use the copy command. When in user mode, the router does not provide help for privileged commands, and it treats the request for help as if there is no such command.

7. Is the number of retrievable commands based on the number of characters in each command, or is it simply a number of commands, regardless of their size?

   Answer: The number of commands. The length (that is, the number of characters) of each command does not affect the command history buffer.

8. How can you retrieve a previously used command? (Name two ways.)

   Answer: Ctrl-p and up arrow (literally the up arrow key on the keyboard). Not all terminal emulators support Ctrl-p or the up arrow, so recalling both methods is useful.

9. After typing **show ip route,** which is the only command that you typed since logging in to the router, you now want to issue the **show ip arp** command. What steps would you take to execute this command by using command-recall keystrokes?

   Answer: Press the up arrow, press Backspace five times, and type arp. The up arrow key retrieves the show ip route command. Backspace moves the cursor backward and erases the character. Typing inserts the characters into the line.

10. After typing **show ip route 128.1.1.0,** you now want to issue the command **show ip route 128.1.4.0.** What steps would you take to do so, using command-recall and command-editing keystrokes?

    Answer: Press the up arrow or Ctrl-p, then press Ctrl-b (or the left arrow) twice, and press Backspace once; and type 4. The Ctrl-b and left arrow keys back up one character in the line, without deleting the character. The Backspace key deletes the 1, in this case. And newly typed characters appear where the cursor sits in the command line.

11. What configuration command causes the router to require a password from a user at the console? What configuration mode context must you be in? (That is, what command[s] must be typed before this command after entering configuration mode?) List the commands in the order in which they must be typed while in config mode.

    ```
    line console 0
    login
    ```

    Answer: The line console 0 command is a context-setting command; it adds no information to the configuration. The command can be typed from any part of configuration mode. The login command, which follows the line console 0 command, tells IOS that a password prompt is desired at the console.

12. What configuration command is used to tell the router the password that is required at the console? What configuration mode context must you be in? (That is, what command[s] must you type before this command after entering configuration mode?) List the commands in the order in which they must be typed while in config mode.

    ```
    line console 0
    password xxxxxxx
    ```

    Answer: The password command tells IOS the value that should be typed when a user wants access from the console. This value is requested by IOS because of the login command. The password *xxxxxxx* must be typed while in console configuration mode, which is reached by typing line console 0.

13. What are the primary purposes of Flash memory in a Cisco router?

    Answer: To store IOS and microcode files. In most routers, only IOS is stored in flash. If microcode is upgraded, the files also reside in Flash memory.

14. What is the intended purpose of NVRAM memory in a Cisco router?

    Answer: To store a single configuration file, used at router load time. NVRAM does not support multiple files.

15. What does the NV stand for in NVRAM?

Answer: Nonvolatile. NVRAM is battery powered if it is really RAM. In some routers, Cisco has (sneakily) used a small portion of Flash memory for the purpose of NVRAM, but Cisco would not ask such trivia on the test.

16. What is the intended purpose of RAM in a Cisco router?

Answer: RAM is used as IOS working memory (storing such things as routing tables or packets) and for IOS code storage. (In some router models, not all IOS is copied into RAM. Some of IOS is left in Flash memory so that more RAM is available for working memory.) It also holds the currently-in-use configuration file called running-config.

17. What is the main purpose of ROM in a Cisco router?

Answer: To store a small, limited-function version of IOS and to store bootstrap code. Typically, this type of IOS is used only during maintenance or emergencies.

18. What configuration command would be needed to cause a router to use an IOS image named c2500-j-l.112-14.bin on TFTP server 128.1.1.1 when the router is reloaded? If you forgot the first parameter of this command, what steps must you take to learn the correct parameters and add the command to the configuration? (Assume that you are not logged in to the router when you start.)

```
boot system tftp c2500-j-1.112-14.bin 128.1.1.1
```

Answer: As for the second part of the question: Log in from con/aux/telnet, type the enable command, type the enable password, type the configure terminal command, and type boot ?. Help appears for the first parameter of the boot command.

19. What command sets the password that would be required after typing the **enable** command? Is that password encrypted by default?

Answer: enable password or enable secret. The password in the enable command is not encrypted, by default. The enable secret password is encrypted using MD5.

20. To have the correct syntax, what must you add to the following configuration command?

```
banner This is Ivan Denisovich's Gorno Router--Do Not Use
```

Answer: This command does not use a delimiter character at the beginning and end of the text. The correct syntax follows:

```
banner # This is Ivan.... Do Not Use #
```

Answer: As typed, IOS would think that the letter T was the delimiter character, so the banner actually would be "his is Ivan Denisovich's Gorno Rou". The motd parameter is not shown because it is not required. An alternate correct command would be this:

```
banner motd # This is Ivan.... Do Not Use #
```

21. Name two commands that affect the text used as the command prompt.

    Answer: hostname and prompt.

22. When using setup mode, you are prompted at the end of the process for whether you want to use the configuration parameters that you just typed in. Which type of memory is this configuration stored in if you type yes?

    Answer: Both NVRAM and RAM. Setup is the only IOS feature that modifies both the active and the startup configuration files as the result of one action by the user.

23. What two methods could a router administrator use to cause a router to load IOS stored in ROM?

    Answer: Setting the configuration register boot field to binary 0001, or adding boot system rom to the configuration file and copying it to the startup configuration file. To set the configuration register to hex 2101, which would yield binary 0001 in the boot field, the config-register 0x2101 global configuration command would be used. A third method, not mentioned in the chapter, includes removing the Flash memory in a router and then reloading.

24. What is the process used to update the contents of Flash memory so that a new IOS in a file called c4500-d-mz.120-5.bin on TFTP server 128.1.1.1 is copied into Flash memory?

    Answer: copy tftp flash. The other details—namely, the IP address of the TFTP server and the filename—are requested through prompts to the user.

25. Name three possible problems that could prevent the command **boot system tftp c2500-j-l.112-14.bin 128.1.1.1** from succeeding.

    Answer: The possible reasons include: 128.1.1.1 is not accessible through the network, there is no TFTP server on 128.1.1.1, the file is not in the TFTP default directory, the file is corrupted, a different boot command could precede this boot command in the configuration file, meaning that the IOS referenced in the first boot command would be used instead.

26. Two different IOS files are in a router's Flash memory: one called c2500-j-l.111-3.bin and one called c2500-j-l.112-14.bin. Which one does the router use when it boots up? How could you force the other IOS file to be used? Without looking at the router configuration, what command could be used to discover which file was used for the latest boot of the router?

    Answer: The first IOS file listed in the show flash command is the one used at reload time, unless a boot system command is configured. The configuration command boot system flash c2500-j-l.112-14.bin would override the IOS's decision to look for files in order in Flash memory. show version is the command used to display the filename of IOS

for the latest reload of a router. The show version output tells you the version as well as the name of the file that was used at last reload time. It is particularly difficult to find in the output of the command.

27. Is the password required at the console the same one that is required when Telnet is used to access a router?

    Answer: No. The Telnet (virtual terminal) password is not the same password, although many installations use the same value.

28. Which IP routing protocols could be enabled using setup?

    Answer: RIP and IGRP.

29. Name two commands used to view the configuration to be used at the next reload of the router. Which one is a more recent addition to IOS?

    Answer: show config and show startup-config. show startup-config is the newer one and, hopefully, is easier to remember.

30. Name two commands used to view the configuration that currently is used in a router. Which one is a more recent addition to IOS?

    Answer: write terminal and show running-config. show running-config is the newer command and, hopefully, is easier to remember.

31. True or false: The **copy startup-config running-config** command always changes the currently used configuration for this router to exactly match what is in the startup configuration file. Explain.

    Answer: False. Some configuration commands do not replace an existing command but simply are added to a list of related commands. If such a list exists, the copy startup-config running-config command simply adds those to the end of the list. Many of these lists in a router configuration are order dependent.

Chapter 8

"Do I Know This Already?" Quiz

1. In which of the following modes of the CLI could you configure the duplex setting for interface fastethernet 0/5?

    Answer: E. The duplex command is an interface subcommand.

2. In which of the following modes of the CLI could you issue a command to erase the initial configuration of the switch?

    Answer: B. The erase command is an exec command, so it cannot be issued from any configuration mode. User mode does not allow the use of the erase command.

3. What type of switch memory is used to store the configuration used by the switch when the switch first comes up?

    Answer: D. IOS loads the config from NVRAM into RAM during the boot sequence.

4. What command copies the configuration from RAM into NVRAM?

    Answer: F. The first parameter identifies the source of the config, and the last parameter identifies the destination.

5. What mode prompts the user for basic configuration information?

    Answer: D

6. Imagine that you had configured the **enable secret** command, followed by the **enable password** command, from the console. You log out of the switch and log back in at the console. Which command defined the password that you had to type to access privileged mode again from the console?

    Answer: B. When both are configured, the enable secret password takes precedence over the enable password.

7. In what LED mode does the switch use the per-port LEDs to show information about the current load on the switch?

    Answer: B

8. Which of the following is not true of both a 2950 switch and Cisco routers?

    Answer: A. 2950 switches do not have auxiliary ports.

Q&A

1. What are the two names for the switch's mode of operation that, when accessed, enables you to issue commands that could be disruptive to switch operations?

    Answer: Enable mode and privileged mode. Both names are commonly used and found in Cisco documentation.

2. What are two methods of logging on to a switch?

   Answer: Console and Telnet. Both cause the user to enter user exec mode.

3. What is the name of the user interface mode of operation used when you cannot issue disruptive commands?

   Answer: User exec mode.

4. What command would you use to receive command help if you knew that a **show** command option begins with a *c* but you cannot recall the option?

   Answer: show c?. Help would appear immediately after you typed the ? symbol. You would not need to press Enter after the ?. If you did so, the switch would try to execute the command with only the parameters that you had typed after the ?.

5. While you are logged in to a switch, you issue the command **copy ?** and get a response of "Unknown command, computer name, or host." Offer an explanation for why this error message appears.

   Answer: You were in user mode. You must be in enable/privileged mode to use the copy command. When in user mode, the switch does not provide help for privileged commands, and it treats the request for help as if there is no such command.

6. How can you retrieve a previously used command? (Name two ways.)

   Answer: Use Ctrl-p and the up arrow (literally the up arrow key on the keyboard). Not all terminal emulators support Ctrl-p or the up arrow, so recalling both methods is useful.

7. What configuration command causes the switch to require a password from a user at the console? What configuration mode context must you be in? (That is, what command[s] must be typed before this command after entering configuration mode?) List the commands in the order in which they must be typed while in config mode.

   ```
   line console 0
   login
   ```

   Answer: The line console 0 command is a context-setting command; it adds no information to the configuration. The command can be typed from any part of configuration mode. The login command, which follows the line console 0 command, tells IOS that a password prompt is desired at the console.

8. What configuration command is used to tell the switch the password that is required at the console? What configuration mode context must you be in? (That is, what command[s] must you type before this command after entering configuration mode?) List the commands in the order in which they must be typed while in config mode.

```
line console 0
password xxxxxxx
```

Answer: The password command tells IOS the value that should be typed when a user wants access from the console. This value is requested by IOS because of the login command. The password xxxxxxx must be typed while in console configuration mode, which is reached by typing line console 0.

9. What are the primary purposes of Flash memory in a Cisco switch?

Answer: To store IOS and microcode files. In most switches, only IOS is stored in flash. If microcode is upgraded, the files also reside in Flash memory.

10. What is the intended purpose of NVRAM memory in a Cisco 2950 switch?

Answer: To store a single configuration file, used at switch load time. NVRAM does not support multiple files.

11. What does the "NV" stand for in NVRAM?

Answer: Nonvolatile. NVRAM is battery powered if it is really RAM. In some switches, Cisco has (sneakily) used a small portion of Flash memory for the purpose of NVRAM, but Cisco would not ask such trivia on the test.

12. What is the intended purpose of RAM in a Cisco 2950 switch?

Answer: RAM is used as IOS working memory (storing such things as MAC address tables and frames) and for IOS code storage.

13. What command sets the password that would be required after typing the enable command? Is that password encrypted by default?

Answer: enable password or enable secret. The password in the enable command is not encrypted, by default. The enable secret password is encrypted using MD5.

14. Is the password required at the console the same one that is required when Telnet is used to access a switch?

    Answer: No. The Telnet ("virtual terminal") password is not the same password, although many installations use the same value.

15. Name two commands used to view the configuration to be used at the next reload of a 2950 switch. Which one is a more recent addition to IOS?

    Answer: show config and show startup-config. show startup-config is the newer one and, hopefully, is easier to remember.

16. Name two commands used to view the configuration that is currently used in a 2950 switch. Which one is a more recent addition to IOS?

    Answer: write terminal and show running-config. show running-config is the newer command and, hopefully, is easier to remember.

Chapter 9

"Do I Know This Already?" Quiz

1. Which of the following statements describes part of the process of how a transparent bridge makes a decision to forward a frame destined to a unicast known MAC address?

    Answer: A

2. Which of the following statements describes part of the process of how a LAN switch makes a decision to forward a frame destined to a broadcast MAC address?

    Answer: C

3. Which of the following statements best describes what a transparent bridge does with a frame destined to an unknown unicast address?

    Answer: A

4. Which of the following comparisons is made by a switch when deciding whether a new MAC address should be added to its bridging table?

    Answer: B

5. Which of the following internal switching methods can start forwarding a frame before the entire frame has been received?

    Answer: C and D

6. Which of the following internal switching methods must wait to receive the entire frame before forwarding the frame?

    Answer: E

7. Which of the following features is determined during autonegotiation between a 10/100 Ethernet card and a switch?

    Answer: A and D

8. Which of the following devices would be in the same collision domain as PC1 below?

    Answer: A

9. Which of the following devices would be in the same broadcast domain as PC1 below?

    Answer: A, B, and C

10. A network currently has ten PCs, with five connected to hub1 and another five connected to hub2, with a cable between the two hubs. Fred wants to keep the PCs connected to their hubs but put a bridge between the two hubs. Barney wants to remove the hubs and connect all ten PCs to the same switch. Comparing Fred and Barney's solutions, which of the following is true?

    Answer: A, B, and D

11. Imagine a network with three switches, each with an Ethernet segment connecting it to the other two switches. Each switch has some PCs attached to it as well. Which of the following frames would cause loops if the Spanning Tree Protocol were not running?

    Answer: A and C. Without STP, any frame that a switch would forward out all ports would loop for an indefinitely long period of time. Switches always forward broadcasts out all ports. Likewise, unicast frames to MAC addresses that are not in the MAC address table are flooded out all ports.

12. Which of the following interface states could a switch interface settle into after STP has completed building a spanning tree?

    Answer: B and C

Q&A

1. Name two of the methods of internal switching on typical switches today. Which provides less latency for an individual frame?

   Answer: Store-and-forward, cut-through, and Fragment Free switching. Cut-through switching has less latency per frame but does not check for bit errors in the frame, including errors caused by collisions. Store-and-forward switching stores the entire received frame, verifies that the FCS is correct, and then sends the frame. Cut-through switching sends out the first bytes of the frame before the last bytes of the incoming frame have been received. Fragment Free switching is similar to cut-through switching in that the frame can be sent before the incoming frame is totally received; however, Fragment Free processing waits to receive the first 64 bytes, to ensure no collisions, before beginning to forward the frame.

2. Describe how a transparent bridge decides whether it should forward a frame, and tell how it chooses the output interface.

   Answer: The bridge examines the destination MAC address of a frame and looks for the address in its bridge (or address) table. If found, the matching entry tells the bridge which output interface to use to forward the frame. If not found, the bridge forwards the frame out all other interfaces (except for interfaces blocked by spanning tree and the interface in which the frame was received). The bridge table is built by examining incoming frames' source MAC addresses.

3. Define the term collision domain.

   Answer: A collision domain is a set of Ethernet devices for which concurrent transmission of a frame by any two of them will result in a collision. Bridges, switches, and routers separate LAN segments into different collision domains. Repeaters and shared hubs do not separate segments into different collision domains.

4. Name two benefits of LAN segmentation using transparent bridges.

   Answer: The main benefits are reduced collisions and more cumulative bandwidth. Multiple 10- or 100- Mbps Ethernet segments are created, and unicasts between devices on the same segment are not forwarded by the bridge, which reduces overhead. Because frames can be sent over each segment at the same time, it increases the overall bandwidth available in the network.

5. What routing protocol does a transparent bridge use to learn about Layer 3 addressing groupings?

   Answer: None. Bridges do not use routing protocols. Transparent bridges do not care about Layer 3 address groupings. Devices on either side of a transparent bridge are in the same Layer 3 group—in other words, the same IP subnet or IPX network.

6. If a Fast Ethernet NIC currently is receiving a frame, can it begin sending a frame?

Answer: **Yes, if the NIC is operating in full-duplex mode.**

7. Why did Ethernet networks' performance improve with the advent of bridges?

Answer: **Before bridges and switches existed, all devices were cabled to the same shared Ethernet. The CSMA/CD algorithm was used to determine who got to send across the Ethernet. As the amount of traffic increased, collisions and waiting (because CSMA/CD) increased, so frames took longer to send. Bridges separated the network into multiple collision domains, reducing collisions and allowing devices on opposite sides of the bridge to send concurrently.**

8. Why did Ethernet networks' performance improve with the advent of switches?

Answer: **Before bridges and switches existed, all devices were cabled to the same shared Ethernet. The CSMA/CD algorithm was used to determine who got to send across the Ethernet. As the amount of traffic increased, collisions and waiting (because of CSMA/CD) increased, so frames took longer to send. Switches separated the network into multiple collision domains, typically one per port, reducing collisions and allowing devices on opposite sides of the bridge to send concurrently.**

9. What are two key differences between a 10-Mbps NIC and a 10/100 NIC?

Answer: **The obvious benefit is that the 10/100 NIC can run at 100 Mbps. The other benefit is that 10/100 NICs can autonegotiate both speed and duplex between themselves and the device that they are cabled to—typically a LAN switch.**

10. Assume that a building has 100 devices attached to the same Ethernet. These users then are migrated onto two separate shared Ethernet segments, each with 50 devices, with a transparent bridge between them. List two benefits that would be derived for a typical user.

Answer: **Fewer collisions due to having two collision domains. Also, less waiting should occur because twice as much capacity exists.**

11. Assume that a building has 100 devices attached to the same Ethernet. These devices are migrated to two different shared Ethernet segments, each with 50 devices. The two segments are connected to a Cisco LAN switch to allow communication between the two sets of users. List two benefits that would be derived for a typical user.

Answer: **Two switch ports are used, which reduces the possibility of collisions. Also, each segment has its own 10- or 100-Mbps capacity, allowing more throughput and reducing the likelihood of collisions. Furthermore, some Cisco switches can reduce the flow of multicasts using the Cisco Group Message Protocol (CGMP) and IGMP snooping.**

12. How fast is Fast Ethernet?

Answer: 100 million bits per second (100 Mbps).

13. How does a transparent bridge build its address table?

Answer: The bridge listens for incoming frames and examines the source MAC address. If it is not in the table, the source address is added, along with the port (interface) by which the frame entered the bridge. The bridge also marks an entry for freshness so that entries can be removed after a period of disuse. This reduces table size and allows for easier table changes in case a spanning tree change forces more significant changes in the bridge (address) table.

14. How many bytes long is a MAC address?

Answer: 6 bytes long, or 48 bits.

15. Does a bridge or switch examine just the incoming frame's source MAC, the destination MAC, or both? Why does it examine the one(s) that it examines?

Answer: The bridge or switch examines both MAC addresses. The source is examined so that entries can be added to the bridge/address table. The destination address is examined to determine the interface out which to forward the frame. Table lookup is required for both addresses for any frame that enters an interface. That is one of the reasons that LAN switches, which have a much larger number of interfaces than traditional bridges, need to have optimized hardware and logic to perform table lookup quickly.

16. Define the term broadcast domain.

Answer: A broadcast domain is a set of Ethernet devices for which a broadcast sent by any one of them should be received by all others in the group. Unlike routers, bridges and switches do not stop the flow of broadcasts. Two segments separated by a router each would be in different broadcast domains. A switch can create multiple broadcast domains by creating multiple VLANs, but a router must be used to route packets between the VLANs.

17. Describe the benefits of creating 3 VLANs of 25 ports each, versus a single VLAN of 75 ports, in each case using a single switch. Assume that all ports are switched ports (each port is a different collision domain).

     Answer: Three different broadcast domains are created with three VLANs, so the devices' CPU utilization should decrease because of decreased broadcast traffic. Traffic between devices in different VLANs will pass through some routing function, which can add some latency for those packets. Better management and control are gained by including a router in the path for those packets.

18. Explain the function of the loopback and collision-detection features of an Ethernet NIC in relation to half-duplex and full-duplex operations.

     Answer: The loopback feature copies the transmitted frame back onto the receive pin on the NIC interface. The collision-detection logic compares the received frame to the transmitted frame during transmission; if the signals do not match, a collision is occurring. With full-duplex operation, collisions cannot occur, so the loopback and collision-detection features are purposefully disabled, and concurrent transmission and reception is allowed.

19. Describe the benefit of the Spanning Tree Protocol as used by transparent bridges and switches.

     Answer: Physically redundant paths in the network are allowed to exist and be used when other paths fail. Also, loops in the bridged network are avoided. Loops are particularly bad because bridging uses LAN headers, which do not provide a mechanism to mark a frame so that its lifetime can be limited; in other words, the frame can loop forever.

20. Name the three reasons why a port is placed in forwarding state as a result of spanning tree.

     Answer: First, all ports on the root bridge are placed in forwarding state. Second, one port on each bridge is considered its root port, which is placed in forwarding state. Finally, on each LAN segment, one bridge is considered to be the designated bridge on that LAN; that designated bridge's interface on the LAN is placed in a forwarding state.

21. Name the three interface states that the Spanning Tree Protocol uses other than forwarding. Which of these states is transitory?

     Answer: Blocking, Layer 2 listening, and learning. Blocking is the only stable state; the other two are transitory between blocking and forwarding.

Chapter 10

"Do I Know This Already?" Quiz

1. 1.In a LAN, which of the following terms best equates to the term VLAN?

    Answer: B. By definition, a VLAN includes all devices in the same LAN broadcast domain.

2. Imagine a switch with three configured VLANs. How many IP subnets would be required, assuming that all hosts in all VLANs want to use TCP/IP?

    Answer: D. The hosts in each VLAN must be in different subnets.

3. Which of the following fully encapsulates the original Ethernet frame in a trunking header?

    Answer: B. ISL fully encapsulates the original frame, whereas 802.1q simply adds an additional header inside the original Ethernet frame.

4. Which of the following allows a spanning tree instance per VLAN?

    Answer: D

5. Imagine a Layer 2 switch with three configured VLANs, using an external router for inter-VLAN traffic. What is the least number of router Fast Ethernet interfaces required to forward traffic between VLANs?

    Answer: B. You can use one Fast Ethernet interface and use trunking between the router and the switch. A router is required to forward traffic between the VLANs.

6. Which of the following terms refers to a function that can forward traffic between two different VLANs?

   Answer: B and C. Layer 2 switching forwards frames only inside a single VLAN. Layer 3 switching and Layer 4 switching forward traffic between VLANs, either based on the Layer 3 destination address (Layer 3 switching) or the Layer 4 port numbers (Layer 4 switching).

7. Imagine a small campus network with three VLANs spread across two switches. Which of the following would you expect to also have a quantity of 3?

   Answer: B and C. By definition, a VLAN is a set of devices in the same broadcast domain. An IP subnet on a LAN is typically comprised of devices in the same VLAN.

8. Which of the following are considered to be ways of configuring VLANs?

   Answer: A and B.

Q&A

1. Define the term collision domain.

   Answer: A collision domain is a set of Ethernet devices for which concurrent transmission of a frame by any two of them will result in a collision. Bridges, switches, and routers separate LAN segments into different collision domains. Repeaters and shared hubs do not separate segments into different collision domains.

2. Define the term broadcast domain.

   Answer: A broadcast domain is a set of Ethernet devices for which a broadcast sent by any one of them should be received by all others in the group. Unlike routers, bridges and switches do not stop the flow of broadcasts. Two segments separated by a router would each be in a different broadcast domain. A switch can create multiple broadcast domains by creating multiple VLANs, but a router must be used to route packets between the VLANs.

3. Define the term VLAN.

   Answer: Virtual LAN (VLAN) refers to the process of treating one subset of a switch's interfaces as one broadcast domain. Broadcasts from one VLAN are not forwarded to other VLANs; unicasts between VLANs must use a router. Advanced methods, such as Layer 3 switching, can be used to allow the LAN switch to forward traffic between VLANs without each individual frame being routed by a router.

4. If two Cisco LAN switches are connected using Fast Ethernet, what VLAN trunking protocols could be used? If only one VLAN spanned both switches, is a VLAN trunking protocol needed?

   Answer: ISL and 802.1q are the trunking protocols used by Cisco over Fast Ethernet. If only one VLAN spans the two switches, a trunking protocol is not needed. Trunking or tagging protocols are used to tag a frame as being in a particular VLAN; if only one VLAN is used, tagging is unnecessary.

5. Must all members of the same VLAN be in the same collision domain, the same broadcast domain, or both?

   Answer: By definition, members of the same VLAN are all part of the same broadcast domain. They might all be in the same collision domain, but only if all devices in the VLAN are connected to hubs.

6. What is the acronym and complete name of Cisco's proprietary trunking protocol over Ethernet?

   Answer: Inter-Switch Link (ISL).

7. Consider the phrase "A VLAN is a broadcast domain is an IP subnet." Do you agree or disagree? State your reasons.

   Answer: From one perspective, the statement is false because an IP subnet is a Layer 3 protocol concept, and a broadcast domain and VLAN are Layer 2 concepts. However, the devices in one broadcast domain comprise the exact same set of devices that would be in the same VLAN and in the same IP subnet.

8. What fields are added or changed in an Ethernet header when using 802.1q? Where is the VLAN ID in those fields?

   Answer: A new 4-byte 802.1q header, which includes the VLAN ID, is added after the source MAC address field. The original FCS field in the Ethernet trailer is modified because the value must be recalculated as a result of changing the header.

9. Compare and contrast the use of a Layer 3 switch versus an external router connected to a Layer 2 switch using a trunk for forwarding between VLANs.

   Answer: Functionally, the end result of each process is identical. However, L3 switches optimize the internal processing of the switch, using a very fast forwarding path, typically using ASICs. The end result is that L3 switches forward traffic between VLANs at much higher speeds than do externally attached routers.

10. Compare and contrast a Layer 3 switch with a multilayer switch. Describe in what cases the terms could be used synonymously.

    Answer: A Layer 3 switch forwards packets based on their destination IP address, much like a router, but with the forwarding logic performed quickly inside hardware in the switch. A multilayer switch performs switching at multiple layers. Many Layer 3 switches also perform Layer 2 switching for frames destined to another device in the same VLAN, and Layer 3 switching for packets destined to another subnet/VLAN. The terms are often used synonymously because many people assume that a LAN switch can always perform L2 switching, with L3 switching being an additional function.

Chapter 11

"Do I Know This Already?" Quiz

1. Which of the following network topologies is characterized by attachments from many devices to a single linear cable?

    Answer: A

2. Which of the following types of networks is considered to be a logical bus topology?

    Answer: A and B. 10BASE5 is a physical bus, and it behaves like a bus, making it a logical bus topology. Because a 10BASE-T hub repeats incoming transmissions out all other ports, effectively creating a bus, it is considered to be a logical bus topology.

3. Which pins typically are used on an RJ-45 connector by an Ethernet card to support Fast Ethernet over UTP cabling?

    Answer: C

4. Which part of an optical cable reflects the light back into the cable as a result of a different refractive index?

    Answer: A

5. Which of the following UTP cable types support Gigabit Ethernet?

    Answer: C, D, and E.

6. Which of the following Ethernet standards call for the use of 802.3 MAC and 802.2 LLC standards?

    Answer: E. All the Ethernet standards call for the use of 802.3 framing, including the 802.3 MAC and 802.2 LLC sublayers.

7. Which of the following Ethernet standards refer to Gigabit Ethernet?

   Answer: B and C. 802.3z refers to Gigabit over optical, and 802.3ab refers to Gigabit over copper cabling.

8. Which of the following IEEE standards define framing used when transmitting wireless LAN traffic?

   Answer: A and D. Wireless LANs use the IEEE 802.11 standard instead of 802.3 for the MAC sublayer header, and also use IEEE 802.2 for the LLC sublayer header.

Q&A

1. Describe why a 10BASE-T network using a hub is considered to be a logical bus topology.

   Answer: A physical bus causes the transmitted electrical signal to be propagated to all devices connected to the bus. A 10BASE-T hub repeats a signal entering one port out all the other ports, ensuring that all devices receive the same signal. Hubs do not have any logic to prevent some frames from being sent out ports (all signals are repeated), creating a single collision domain, just like a physical bus.

2. Compare and contrast full-mesh versus partial-mesh topologies, in relation to physical topologies.

   Answer: In a full mesh, for a particular set of networking devices, a direct cable connects each pair of devices. For a partial mesh, some pairs of devices are not directly connected.

3. Compare and contrast full-mesh versus partial-mesh topologies, in relation to logical topologies.

   Answer: Regardless of the physical topology, a topology is considered a logical full mesh if each pair of devices can communicate directly, and is considered a partial mesh if some pairs cannot communicate directly. A Frame Relay network uses a star physical topology. Depending on what VCs have been defined, it might use a logical full mesh or a logical partial mesh.

4. What is the main motivation for using a dual-ring physical topology versus a single ring? Why?

   Answer: For better network availability. With dual rings, if a cable or a device fails, the devices near the failure can loop the signals from the two different cables together, thereby creating a single phyiscal path that loops to each node.

5. What two methods are used to reduce the amount of electromagnetic emissions emanating from copper Ethernet cabling? Why do they help reduce emissions?

    Answer: By using two pairs of wires for transmission, with differing currents, and twisting the wires, the magnetic fields generated when the electrical current flows are cancelled. The other method is to put insulating material around the wires, which shields the emissions to a great degree.

6. Which wires are used by a typical Ethernet CAT5 cable? Which ones are used for transmit, and which ones are used to receive, by an Ethernet card?

    Answer: Ethernet cards transmit on the pair using pins 1 and 2, and receive on the pair at pins 3 and 6.

7. Which TIA standards for UTP cabling support 10BASE-T?

    Answer: CAT3, 5, 5e, and 6.

8. What are the maximum lengths for coaxial cables as used by 10BASE5? 10BASE2?

    Answer: 500 m and 185 m, respectively.

9. What are key differences between multimode and single-mode optical cabling?

    Answer: Multimode cabling typically supports shorter distances than single-mode. Single-mode uses a much smaller diameter for the glass fiber, which allows for the greater distances.

10. What types of cabling are least susceptible to having someone eavesdrop and somehow discover what is being transmitted over the cable?

    Answer: Optical cables do not emit any EM radiation outside the cable, as do metallic copper cables. So, you cannot simply sense what signal is crossing over an optical cable without physically breaking into the cable, which makes the cable unusable.

11. What are the IEEE standards for 10BASE-T, Fast Ethernet, Gigabit Ethernet, and 10-Gigabit Ethernet?

    Answer: 802.3, 802.3u (Fast Ethernet), 802.3z and 802.3ab (Gigabit Ethernet), and 802.3ae (10 Gigabit).

12. Which variations on the Fast Ethernet standard, which use names like "10BASE-something," specifically state the need for four pairs of wires in the cable? What about for Gigabit Ethernet?

    Answer: 100BASE-T4 for Fast Ethernet, and 1000BASE-T for Gigabit Ethernet.

13. Which variations on the Fast Ethernet and Gigabit standard use IEEE 802.3 MAC and 802.2 LLC framing?

    Answer: All of them.

14. What were some of the differences between 10-Gigabit Ethernet, as compared with other types of Ethernet, as outlined in this chapter?

    Answer: The speed, of course, is the obvious difference. Additionally, 10-Gigabit Ethernet is allowed to be used in a point-to-point topology only, it supports full-duplex only, and today it supports only optical cabling.

15. What IEEE standards are used by an 802.11 access point?

    Answer: The access point uses 802.11 standards for communication across the wireless LAN, including 802.2 LLC. It also connects to a wired LAN, so it uses 802.3 for its wired Ethernet.

16. What does the term line-of-sight mean in relation to wireless communications?

    Answer: Line-of-sight means that you could stand beside one device, and see the other device. Some wireless technologies require a line-of-sight, and others do not.

Chapter 12

"Do I Know This Already?" Quiz

1. Which of the following is the result of a Boolean AND between IP address 150.150.4.100, mask 255.255.192.0?

   Answer: B

2. If mask 255.255.255.128 were used with a Class B network, how many subnets could exist, with how many hosts per subnet, respectively?

   Answer: E. Class B networks imply 16 network bits; the mask implies 7 host bits (7 binary 0s in the mask), leaving 9 subnet bits. $2^9 - 2$ yields 510 subnets, and $2^7 - 2$ yields 126 hosts per subnet.

3. If mask 255.255.255.240 were used with a Class C network, how many subnets could exist, with how many hosts per subnet, respectively?

   Answer: B. Class C networks imply 24 network bits; the mask implies 4 host bits (4 binary 0s in the mask), leaving 4 subnet bits. $2^4 - 2$ yields 14 subnets, and $2^4 - 2$ yields 14 hosts per subnet.

4. Which of the following IP addresses would not be in the same subnet as 190.4.80.80, mask 255.255.255.0?

   Answer: E and F are correct.

5. Which of the following IP addresses would not be in the same subnet as 190.4.80.80, mask 255.255.240.0?

   Answer: F. 190.4.80.80, mask 255.255.240.0, is in subnet 190.4.80.0, broadcast address 190.4.95.255, with a range of valid addresses of 190.4.80.1 through 190.4.95.254.

6. Which of the following IP addresses would not be in the same subnet as 190.4.80.80, mask 255.255.255.128?

   Answer: D, E, and F. 190.4.80.80, mask 255.255.255.128, is in subnet 190.4.80.0, broadcast address 190.4.80.127, with a range of valid addresses of 190.4.80.1 through 190.4.80.126.

7. Which of the following subnet masks would allow a Class B network to allow subnets to have up to 150 hosts and allow for up to 164 subnets?

   Answer: C. You need 8 bits to number up to 150 hosts because $2^7 - 2$ is less than 150, but $2^8 - 2$ is greater than 150. Similarly, you need 8 subnet bits. The only valid Class B subnet mask with 8 host and 8 subnet bits is 255.255.255.0.

8. Which of the following subnet masks would allow a Class A network to allow subnets to have up to 150 hosts and would allow for up to 164 subnets?

   Answer: B, C, D, E, and F are correct.

9. Which of the following are valid subnet numbers in network 180.1.0.0, when using mask 255.255.248.0?

    Answer: C, D, E, and F. In this case, the subnet numbers begin with 180.1.0.0 (subnet zero), and then 180.1.8.0, 180.1.16.0, 180.1.24.0, and so on, increasing by 8 in the third octet, up to 180.1.240.0 (last valid subnet) and 180.1.248.0 (broadcast subnet).

10. Which of the following are valid subnet numbers in network 180.1.0.0, when using mask 255.255.255.0?

    Answer: A, B, C, D, E, and F. In this case, the subnet numbers begin with 180.1.0.0 (subnet zero), and then 180.1.1.0, 180.1.2.0, 180.1.3.0, and so on, increasing by 1 in the third octet, up to 180.1.254.0 (last valid subnet) and 180.1.255.0 (broadcast subnet).

11. Which of the following best describes a feature of CIDR?

    Answer: A

12. The phrase "to represent hundreds or thousands of client TCP or UDP connections from different hosts as that same number of connections, but making it appear as if all connections are from one host" best describes which of the following tools?

    Answer: C

13. The phrase "grouping a large number of Class C networks into a single group, and putting a single entry for that group in an Internet router, to reduce the overall size of the IP routing table " best describes which of the following tools?

    Answer: B

14. The phrase "the use network 10.0.0.0 in an enterprise network" best describes which of the following tools?

    Answer: A

Q&A

1. Name the parts of an IP address.

    Answer: Network, subnet, and host are the three parts of an IP address. However, many people commonly treat the network and subnet parts of an address as a single part, leaving only two parts, the subnet and host parts. On the exam, the multiple-choice format should provide extra clues as to which terminology is used.

2. Define the term subnet mask. What do the bits in the mask whose values are binary 0 tell you about the corresponding IP address(es)?

    Answer: A subnet mask defines the number of host bits in an address. The bits of value 0 define which bits in the address are host bits. The mask is an important ingredient in the formula to dissect an IP address; along with knowledge of the number of network bits implied for Class A, B, and C networks, the mask provides a clear definition of the size of the network, subnet, and host parts of an address.

3. Given the IP address 134.141.7.11 and the mask 255.255.255.0, what is the subnet number?

    Answer: The subnet is 134.141.7.0. The binary algorithm is shown in the table that follows.

Address	134.141.7.11	1000 0110 1000 1101 **0000 0111** 0000 1011
Mask	255.255.255.0	1111 1111 1111 1111 **1111 1111** 0000 0000
Result	134.141.7.0	1000 0110 1000 1101 **0000 0111** 0000 0000

4. Given the IP address 193.193.7.7 and the mask 255.255.255.0, what is the subnet number?

    Answer: The network number is 193.193.7.0. Because this is a Class C address and the mask used is 255.255.255.0 (the default), no subnetting is in use. The binary algorithm is shown in the table that follows.

Address	193.193.7.7	1100 0001 1100 0001 0000 0111 0000 0111
Mask	255.255.255.0	1111 1111 1111 1111 1111 1111 0000 0000
Result	193.193.7.0	1100 0001 1100 0001 0000 0111 0000 0000

5. Given the IP address 200.1.1.130 and the mask 255.255.255.224, what is the subnet number?

   Answer: The answer is 200.1.1.128. The table that follows shows the subnet chart to help you learn the way to calculate the subnet number without binary math. The magic number is 256 – 224 = 32.

Octet	1	2	3	4	Comments
Address	200	1	1	130	—
Mask	255	255	255	224	Interesting octet is the fourth octet (magic = 256 – 224 = 32).
Subnet number	200	1	1	128	128 is the closest multiple of the magic number not greater than 130.
First address	200	1	1	129	Add 1 to the last octet of the subnet number.
Broadcast	200	1	1	159	Subnet + magic – 1.
Last address	200	1	1	158	Subtract 1 from broadcast.

6. Given the IP address 220.8.7.100 and the mask 255.255.255.240, what is the subnet number?

   Answer: The answer is 220.8.7.96. The table that follows shows the subnet chart to help you learn the way to calculate the subnet number without binary math. The magic number is 256–240=16.

Octet	1	2	3	4	Comments
Address	220	8	7	100	—
Mask	255	255	255	240	Interesting octet is the fourth octet.
Subnet number	220	8	7	96	96 is the closest multiple of the magic number not greater than 100.
First address	220	8	7	97	Add 1 to the last octet.
Broadcast	220	8	7	111	Subnet + magic – 1.
Last address	220	8	7	110	Subtract 1 from broadcast.

7.   Given the IP address 134.141.7.11 and the mask 255.255.255.0, what is the subnet broadcast address?

Answer: The broadcast address is 134.141.7.255. The binary algorithm is shown in the table that follows.

Address	134.141.7.11	1000 0110 1000 1101 0000 0111 0000 1011
Mask	255.255.255.0	1111 1111 1111 1111 1111 1111 0000 0000
Result	134.141.7.0	1000 0110 1000 1101 0000 0111 0000 0000
Broadcast address	134.141.7.255	1000 0110 1000 1101 0000 0111 **1111 1111**

8.   Given the IP address 193.193.7.7 and the mask 255.255.255.0, what is the broadcast address?

Answer: The broadcast address is 193.193.7.255. Because this is a Class C address and the mask used is 255.255.255.0 (the default), no subnetting is in use. The binary algorithm is shown in the table that follows.

Address	193.193.7.7	1100 0001 1100 0001 0000 0111 0000 0111
Mask	255.255.255.0	1111 1111 1111 1111 1111 1111 0000 0000
Result	193.193.7.0	1100 0001 1100 0001 0000 0111 0000 0000
Broadcast address	193.193.7.255	1100 0001 1100 0001 0000 0111 **1111 1111**

9.   Given the IP address 200.1.1.130 and the mask 255.255.255.224, what is the broadcast address?

Answer: The broadcast address is 200.1.1.159. The binary algorithm math is shown in the table that follows. The easy decimal algorithm is shown in the answer to an earlier question.

Address	200.1.1.130	1100 1000 0000 0001 0000 0001 1000 0010
Mask	255.255.255.224	1111 1111 1111 1111 1111 1111 1110 0000
Result	200.1.1.128	1100 1000 0000 0001 0000 0001 1000 0000
Broadcast address	200.1.1.159	1100 1000 0000 0001 0000 0001 100**1 1111**

10. Given the IP address 220.8.7.100 and the mask 255.255.255.240, what is the broadcast address?

Answer: The broadcast address is 220.8.7.111. The binary algorithm is shown in the table that follows.

Address	**220.8.7.100**	1101 1100 0000 1000 0000 0111 0110 0100
Mask	**255.255.255.240**	1111 1111 1111 1111 1111 1111 1111 0000
Result	**220.8.7.96**	1101 1100 0000 1000 0000 0111 0110 0000
Broadcast address	**220.8.7.111**	1101 1100 0000 1000 0000 0111 0110 **1111**

11. Given the IP address 134.141.7.11 and the mask 255.255.255.0, what are the assignable IP addresses in this subnet?

Answer: The subnet number is 134.141.7.0, and the subnet broadcast address is 134.141.7.255. The assignable addresses are all the addresses between the subnet and broadcast addresses, namely 134.141.7.1 to 134.141.7.254.

12. Given the IP address 193.193.7.7 and the mask 255.255.255.0, what are the assignable IP addresses in this subnet?

Answer: The subnet number is 193.193.7.0, and the network broadcast address is 193.193.7.255. The assignable addresses are all the addresses between the network and broadcast addresses, namely 193.193.7.1 to 193.193.7.254.

13. Given the IP address 200.1.1.130 and the mask 255.255.255.224, what are the assignable IP addresses in this subnet?

Answer: The subnet number is 200.1.1.128, and the subnet broadcast address is 200.1.1.159. The assignable addresses are all the addresses between the subnet and broadcast addresses, namely 200.1.1.129 to 200.1.1.158.

14. Given the IP address 220.8.7.100 and the mask 255.255.255.240, what are the assignable IP addresses in this subnet?

Answer: The subnet number is 220.8.7.96, and the subnet broadcast address is 220.8.7.111. The assignable addresses are all the addresses between the subnet and broadcast addresses, namely 220.8.7.97 to 220.8.7.110.

15. Given the IP address 134.141.7.7 and the mask 255.255.255.0, what are all the subnet numbers if the same (static) mask is used for all subnets in this network?

Answer: The answer is 134.141.1.0, 134.141.2.0, 134.141.3.0, and so on, up to 134.141.254.0. 134.141.0.0 is the zero subnet, and 134.141.255.0 is the broadcast subnet.

16. Given the IP address 220.8.7.100 and the mask 255.255.255.240, what are all the subnet numbers if the same (static) mask is used for all subnets in this network?

Answer: The answer is not as obvious in this question. The Class C network number is 220.8.7.0. The mask implies that bits 25 through 28, which are the first 4 bits in the fourth octet, comprise the subnet field. The answer is 220.8.7.16, 220.8.7.32, 220.8.7.48, and so on, through 220.8.7.224. 220.8.7.0 is the zero subnet, and 220.8.7.240 is the broadcast subnet. The following table outlines the easy decimal algorithm to figure out the subnet numbers.

Octet	1	2	3	4	Comments
Network number	220	8	7	0	—
Mask	255	255	255	240	The last octet is interesting; the magic number is 256 − 240 = 16.
Subnet zero	220	8	7	0	Copy the network number; it's the zero subnet.
First subnet	220	8	7	16	Add magic to the last subnet number's interesting octet.
Next subnet	220	8	7	32	Add magic to the previous one.
Last subnet	220	8	7	224	You eventually get her...
Broadcast subnet	220	8	7	240	...and then here, the broadcast subnet, because the next one is 256, which is invalid.

17. How many IP addresses could be assigned in each subnet of 134.141.0.0, assuming that a mask of 255.255.255.0 is used? If the same (static) mask is used for all subnets, how many subnets are there?

Answer: There will be $2^{hostbits}$, or 2^8 hosts per subnet, minus two special cases. The number of subnets will be $2^{subnetbits}$, or 2^8, minus two special cases.

Network and Mask	Number of Network Bits	Number of Host Bits	Number of Subnet Bits	Number of Hosts per Subnet	Number of Subnets
134.141.0.0, 255.255.255.0	16	8	8	254	254

18. How many IP addresses could be assigned in each subnet of 220.8.7.0, assuming that a mask of 255.255.255.240 is used? If the same (static) mask is used for all subnets, how many subnets are there?

    Answer: There will be $2^{hostbits}$, or 2^4 hosts per subnet, minus two special cases. The number of subnets will be $2^{subnetbits}$, or 2^4, minus two special cases.

Network and Mask	Number of Network Bits	Number of Host Bits	Number of Subnet Bits	Number of Hosts per Subnet	Number of Subnets
220.8.7.0, 255.255.255. 240	24	4	4	14	14

19. You design a network for a customer, and the customer insists that you use the same subnet mask on every subnet. The customer will use network 10.0.0.0 and needs 200 subnets, each with 200 hosts maximum. What subnet mask would you use to allow the largest amount of growth in subnets? Which mask would work and would allow for the most growth in the number of hosts per subnet?

    Answer: Network 10.0.0.0 is a Class A network, so you have 24 host bits with no subnetting. To number 200 subnets, you will need at least 8 subnet bits because 2^8 is 256. Likewise, to number 200 hosts per subnet, you will need 8 host bits. So, you need to pick a mask with at least 8 subnet bits and 8 host bits. 255.255.0.0 is a mask with 8 subnet bits and 16 host bits. That would allow for the 200 subnets and 200 hosts, while allowing the number of hosts per subnet to grow to $2^{16} - 2$, quite a large number. Similarly, a mask of 255.255.255.0 gives you 16 subnet bits, allowing $2^{16} - 2$ subnets, each with $2^8 - 2$ hosts per subnet.

20. Referring to Figure A-1, Fred has been configured with IP address 10.1.1.1, Router A's Ethernet has been configured with 10.1.1.100, Router A's Serial interface uses 10.1.1.101, Router B's serial uses 10.1.1.102, Router B's Ethernet uses 10.1.1.200, and the web server uses 10.1.1.201. Mask 255.255.255.192 is used in all cases. Is anything wrong with this network? What is the easiest thing that could be done to fix it? You can assume any working interior routing protocol.

Figure A-1 *Example Network for Subnetting Questions*

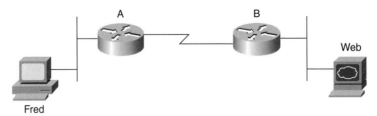

Answer: Router A's Ethernet interface and Fred's Ethernet should be in the same subnet, but they are not. Fred's configuration implies a subnet with IP addresses ranging from 10.1.1.1 through 10.1.1.62; Router A's Ethernet configuration implies a subnet with addresses between 10.1.1.65 and 10.1.1.126. Also, Router A's two interfaces must be in different subnets; as configured, they would be in the same subnet. So, the solution is to change Router A's Ethernet IP address to something between 10.1.1.1 and 10.1.1.62, making it be in the same subnet as Fred.

21. Referring to Figure A-1, Fred has been configured with IP address 10.1.1.1, mask 255.255.255.0; Router A's Ethernet has been configured with 10.1.1.100, mask 255.255.255.224; Router A's serial interface uses 10.1.1.129, mask 255.255.255.252; Router B's serial uses 10.1.1.130, mask 255.255.255.252; Router B's Ethernet uses 10.1.1.200, mask 255.255.255.224; and the web server uses 10.1.1.201, mask 255.255.255.224. Is anything wrong with this network? What is the easiest thing that could be done to fix it? You can assume any working interior routing protocol.

Answer: Fred's configuration implies a subnet with a range of addresses from 10.1.1.1 through 10.1.1.254, so he thinks that Router A's Ethernet interface is in the same subnet. However, Router A's configuration implies a subnet with addresses from 10.1.1.97 through 10.1.1.126, so Router A does not think that Fred is on the same subnet as Router A's Ethernet. Several options exist for fixing the problem. You could change the mask used by Fred and Router A's Ethernet to 255.255.255.128, which makes them both reside in the same subnet.

22. Referring to Figure A-1, Fred has been configured with IP address 10.1.1.1, mask 255.255.255.240; Router A's Ethernet has been configured with 10.1.1.2, mask 255.255.255.240; Router A's Serial interface uses 10.1.1.129, mask 255.255.255.252; Router B's serial uses 10.1.1.130, mask 255.255.255.252; Router B's Ethernet uses 10.1.1.200, mask 255.255.255.128; and the web server uses 10.1.1.201, mask 255.255.255.128. Is anything wrong with this network? What is the easiest thing that could be done to fix it? You can assume any working interior routing protocol.

Answer: Router B's configuration implies a subnet with a range of addresses from 10.1.1.129 to 10.1.1.130 on the serial link, and 10.1.1.129 to 10.1.1.254 on the Ethernet. So, the subnets overlap. One solution would be to configure Router B and the web server's masks to 255.255.255.192, which would change the subnet so that the valid addresses would be between 10.1.1.193 and 10.1.1.254.

23. What are the valid private IP network numbers, according to RFC 1918?

Answer: Network 10.0.0.0, Class B networks that from 172.16.0.0 through 172.31.0.0, and Class C networks beginning with 192.168.

24. How large are IPv6 addresses?

Answer: 128 bits long.

25. How does CIDR help reduce the size of Internet routing tables?

Answer: By using a routing protocol that exchanges the mask as well as the subnet/ network number, a classless view of the number can be attained. By advertising many networks as a single route, the routing table can be shortened. For instance, 198.0.0.0/8 (198.0.0.0, mask 255.0.0.0) defines a set of addresses whose first 8 bits are equal to decimal 198. Instead of the more than 65,000 routes needed to list a route for each class C network that starts with 198, CIDR allows those routes to be represented by a single route.

Chapter 13

"Do I Know This Already?" Quiz

1. Which of the following commands is valid for the configuration of IP address 10.1.1.1, mask 255.255.255.0?

Answer: C

2. Which of the following must be true before Cisco IOS Software adds a connected route to the routing table?

Answer: A and E. The router adds the subnet number of the directly connected interface to the routing table after the IP address is configured. The interface must be operational before the route is added.

3. Which of the following represents the same ideas as mask 255.255.240.0?

Answer: C. The answers all use prefix notation, which represents the subnet mask by stating the number of binary 1s in the mask.

4. What command brings up an interface that previously was administratively disabled?

Answer: A. shutdown disables the interface, and no shutdown brings it back up.

5. Imagine that a PC is attached to the same Ethernet as a router. The PC makes a DNS request for host name Fred, and the PC gets a reply showing IP address 10.1.1.1. What command could be issued on the router to list the information learned in that DNS request and reply?

Answer: D. The show hosts command lists the host name configured in the router or names learned by the router from the DNS as a result of a command on the router using the name. The router does not learn about names as a result of DNS requests from an end user.

6. Imagine that a neighboring router's host name is Hannah. Which of these commands could tell you information about the IOS version on Hannah, without Telnetting to Hannah?

Answer: H and I. CDP discovers information about neighbors. show cdp gives you several options that display more or less information, depending on the parameters used.

7. What CDP command(s) could identify the model of hardware of a neighbor?

Answer: F, G, and H

8. Imagine that you used a **ping** command successfully. What messages would have been sent by the **ping** command?

Answer: B

9. Imagine that you just erased all the configuration on a router and reloaded it. To configure the router to use a DNS at IP address 10.1.1.1, which of the following commands is required?

Answer: A

10. Imagine that you just logged in to the console of router R1 and then Telnetted to R2. What must you type to suspend your Telnet connection, going back to R1?

Answer: C

Q&A

1. Create a minimal configuration enabling IP on each interface on a 2501 router (two serial, one Ethernet). The NIC assigned you network 8.0.0.0. Your boss says that you need, at most, 200 hosts per subnet. You decide against using VLSM. Your boss also says to plan your subnets so that you can have as many subnets as possible rather than allow

for larger subnets later. When choosing the actual IP address values and subnet numbers, you decide to start with the lowest numerical values. Assume that point-to-point serial links will be attached to this router.

```
interface ethernet 0
ip address 8.0.1.1 255.255.255.0
interface serial 0
ip address 8.0.2.1 255.255.255.0
interface serial 1
ip address 8.0.3.1 255.255.255.0
```

Answer: The zero subnet was not used in this solution. If desired, the ip subnet-zero global command could have been used, enabling subnet 8.0.0.0/24 as well as subnets 8.0.1.0/24 and 8.0.2.0/24 to be used as the three subnets in the configuration.

2. In the previous question, what would be the IP subnet of the link attached to serial 0? If another user wanted to answer the same question but did not have the enable password, what command(s) might provide this router's addresses and subnets?

   Answer: The attached subnet is 8.0.2.0, 255.255.255.0. The show interface, show ip interface, and show ip interface brief commands would supply this information, as would show ip route. The show ip route command would show the actual subnet number instead of the address of the interface.

3. What must be done to make the output of the **show ip route** command list subnet masks in decimal format instead of prefixes? In what mode would you use the command?

   Answer: You must use the terminal ip netmask-format decimal command in enable mode.

4. What are the differences between the **clock rate** and **bandwidth** commands?

   Answer: clock rate sets the physical (Layer 1) actual transmission rate, in bits per second, and only when a DCE cable has been plugged into that interface. The bandwidth command, with units of kbps, does not affect Layer 1 transmission rates. Instead, it is used by Cisco IOS Software as its understanding of the Layer 1 rate, for purposes such as calculation of routing protocol metrics.

5. Compare and contrast the commands used to set the enable, console, and telnet passwords on a router.

   Answer: The password command sets the console and telnet password. When used as a line console 0 subcommand, it sets the console password; under line vty 0 4, it sets the telnet password. The enable password can be set with the enable password or enable secret commands, with the enable secret password taking precedence if both are configured.

6. In the output of **show ip route**, when a C shows up in the left side of the output on a line for a particular route, what does that mean?

Answer: C means "connected." This means that the route was learned by this router because it has an operational interface that is connected directly to that subnet.

7. Define the term prefix notation. Give two examples.

Answer: The representation of a subnet mask with a slash character (/), followed by a number that represents the number of binary 1s in the mask. For example, /16 means the same thing as 255.255.0.0, and /22 means the same thing as 255.255.252.0.

8. What does ICMP stand for? To which OSI layer would you consider this protocol to apply most closely?

Answer: Internet Control Message Protocol. ICMP is considered a Layer 3 protocol because it is used for control and management of IP.

9. Identify two methods to tell a router to ask for name resolution from two different name servers.

ip name-server 1.1.1.1 2.2.2.2

or

ip name-server 1.1.1.1

ip name-server 2.2.2.2

Answer: Both methods tell the router to first try the name server at 1.1.1.1 and then try the name server at 2.2.2.2.

10. What keyboard sequence suspends a Telnet session in a Cisco router?

Answer: Ctrl-Shift-6, followed by x.

11. What two commands, and what part the command output, tells you which suspended Telnet connection will be reconnected if you just press the Enter key, without any characters typed on the command line?

Answer: show sessions and where. Both commands supply the same information. The suspended session with an asterisk in the left side of the output line designates the session to which you would be connected if you just pressed Return, with no characters on the command line.

12. Imagine that you typed a **ping** command and got 5 "!" back. What type of messages were sent through the network? Be as specific as possible.

Answer: ICMP echo request messages were sent by the ping command, with the remote host replying with five ICMP echo reply messages.

13. How do you make a router not ask for DNS resolution from a name server?

Answer: By using the no ip domain-lookup global configuration command.

14. Imagine that you are just logged in at the console of R1, and you Telnet to routers R2, R3, and R4 in succession, but you suspended your Telnet connection each time—in other words, all three Telnet connections go from R1 to the other three routers, respectively. What options do you have for reconnecting to R2?

Answer: You can use the resume 1 command or just use the 1 command.

15. Imagine that you are just logged in at the console of R1, and you Telnet to routers R2, R3, and R4 in succession, but you suspended your Telnet connection each time—in other words, all three Telnet connections go from R1 to the other three routers, respectively. What options do you have for reconnecting to R4?

Answer: You can use the resume 3 command or just use the 3 command. Or, you can simply press Enter, which resumes your connection to the last suspended Telnet connection—in this case, R4.

16. List the five key pieces of information that can be gathered using CDP, as mentioned in the chapter.

Answer: Device identifier, address list, port identifier, capabilities list, and platform.

17. Imagine a network with Switch1, connected to Router1, with a point-to-point serial link to Router2, which, in turn, is connected to Switch2. Assuming that you are logged into R1, what commands could be used to find the IP addresses of Router2 and Switch1 without logging in to either device?

Answer: On Router1, you could use either the show cdp neighbor detail command or the show cdp entry command. Both commands list IP addresses of the neighboring devices, assuming that CDP is up and working.

18. Imagine that a network with Switch1 is connected to Router1, with a point-to-point serial link to Router2, which, in turn, is connected to Switch2. You can log in only to Switch1. Which of the other devices could Switch1 learn about using CDP? Why?

Answer: Switch1 could learn about only Router1 because CDP learns information about only devices that are connected to the same data link.

19. What command lists a brief one-line description of CDP information about each neighbor?

Answer: The show cdp neighbor command.

Chapter 14

"Do I Know This Already?" Quiz

1. Which of the following routing protocols are considered to use distance vector logic?

Answer: A and B

2. Which of the following routing protocols are considered to use link-state logic?

Answer: E and G

3. Which of the following routing protocols use a metric that is, by default, at least partially affected by link bandwidth?

Answer: C, D, and E

4. Which of the following interior routing protocols support VLSM?

Answer: B, D, E, and F

5. Which of the following situations would cause RIP to remove all the routes learned from a particular neighboring router?

Answer: B. Distance vector protocols rely on regular receipt of routing updates from their neighbors to continue believing that the routes through that neighbor are still valid.

6. Which of the following interior routing protocols are considered to be capable of converging quickly?

Answer: D, E, and F

7. Which of the following interior routing protocols use hop count as their metric?

Answer: A and B

8. What update timer is used by IGRP?

Answer: E

Q&A

1. Which interior IP routing protocols covered in this chapter support VLSM?

Answer: RIP-2, EIGRP, OSPF, Integrated IS-IS, and BGP.

2. Which IP routing protocols covered in this chapter use distance vector logic?

Answer: RIP-1, RIP-2, and IGRP.

3. Which interior IP routing protocols covered in this chapter are considered to converge quickly?

Answer: EIGRP, OSPF, and Integrated IS-IS.

4. Compare distance vector and link-state protocols in terms of what information is sent in routing updates.

Answer: Distance vector protocols send sparse information, typically describing a subnet and a metric for each route. Link-state protocols send much more detailed topology information, describing each router and each link so that every router knows a full conceptual picture of the network.

5. List three similarities between EIGRP's balanced hybrid logic and link-state logic.

Answer: Fast convergence, neighbor discovery before sending routing information, not sending of full updates on a regular period, some topology tables built in addition to the IP routing table.

6. Explain the basic concept behind why some routing protocols support VLSM and some do not.

   Answer: VLSM implies that different subnet masks are used for different subnets of the same network. To advertise subnets that have different sizes, the routing protocol must include the subnet mask information for each subnet in the routing updates. Routing protocols that do not support VLSM do not include the mask in the routing updates.

7. Explain the difference between interior and exterior routing protocols.

   Answer: Interior routing protocols are designed to advertise detailed routing information about each subnet, typically inside a single company or organization. Exterior routing protocols are designed to advertise information about how to reach different organizations' networks through the Internet, and they purposefully try to reduce the detailed routing information to reduce the number of routes in Internet routers' routing tables.

8. Explain the difference between full and partial routing updates.

   Answer: Full routing updates include information about each subnet during each update interval. Partial updates just include changed routes, such as newly learned subnets and subnets whose routes have failed.

9. Define the term balanced hybrid in relation to the terms distance vector and link state.

   Answer: Balanced hybrid is a term used to refer to the logic used by EIGRP. The logic can be viewed as a combination of features like those of distance vector protocols and link-state protocols.

10. Compare and contrast the types of information sent in distance vector routing updates versus link-state routing updates.

    Answer: Distance vector routing updates contain a subnet number and a metric for each route. Link-state updates define much more detailed information, such as the identity of each router and which subnets each router is connected to. Therefore, the information in link-state updates is much more detailed than the equivalent information with distance vector updates. The more detailed information allows a link-state protocol to build a mathematical representation of the network topology, whereas distance vector protocols simply know that subnets exist and where to send packets to reach those subnets.

11. What term describes the underlying logic behind the OSPF routing protocol?

    Answer: Link state.

Chapter 15

"Do I Know This Already?" Quiz

1. Which of the following acronyms identifies a voice codec used to encode analog voice signals into a 64-kbps digital data stream?

Answer: D

2. How many DS0 channels are in a DS1 in the United States?

Answer: E

3. Which of the following best describes the function of demodulation by a modem?

Answer: D. Modems demodulate an analog signal sent by the phone company. The goal is to re-create the original bits sent by the other modem, so the demodulation function converts the analog signal into the bits that it was intended to represent.

4. Which of the following modem standards do not support 56-kbps speeds downstream?

Answer: A, B, C, F, G, and H

5. Which of the following terms best describes features of an ISDN PRI in Europe?

Answer: E. PRIs in Europe are based on E1 circuits, which have 32 DS0 channels. One channel is reserved for framing, and one channel is used for a D channel, leaving 30 B channels.

6. Imagine that you plug an analog phone into an ISDN modem and call a friend at her house, where she uses an analog phone using plain-old telephone service (POTS). At which of the following points in a network will a voice codec be used?

Answer: B and D. Because the ISDN modem sends only digital signals over the local loop, it must convert the analog voice from the phone connected to it into digital voice using a voice codec.

7. What does the letter B stand for in the ISDN term *B channel*?

Answer: A

8. Which of the following DSL standards has a limit of 18,000 feet for the length of the local loop?

Answer: C

9.   Imagine a local phone line from a house to a local telco CO. When the customer at that house requests DSL service, what type of device does the telco move the CO end of the local line to?

Answer: A. The CO uses a DSLAM to terminate local loops that use DSL. A DSL router or DSL modem is connected to the local loop at the subscriber (home) location.

10. Which of the following protocols are used by DSL modem and routers for data link layer functions?

Answer: A, B, and C. DSL calls for the use of PPP over ATM (PPPoA) over the DSL part of the network. PPP can extend to the PCs at the home location using PPP over Ethernet (PPPoE).

11. Which of the following protocols is used by cable modems for data link layer functions?

Answer: E. Multimedia Cable Network Services (MCNS) defines a MAC layer that also uses IEEE 802.2 as part of the data link layer.

12. Which of the following protocols are used by a cable modem for the upstream data?

Answer: B and E

13. Which of the following remote access technologies uses ATM, Ethernet, and PPP as data-link protocols?

Answer: C

14. Which of the following remote access technologies support specifications that allow both symmetric speeds and asymmetric speeds?

Answer: A and C. ISDN always uses symmetric speeds, and cable modems always use asymmetric speeds.

15. Which of the following remote access technologies, when used to connect to an ISP, is considered to be an "always on" service?

Answer: C and D. Analog modems and ISDN lines must signal or dial to set up a circuit before any data can be passed, whereas DSL and cable modems do not do this.

Q&A

1.   What do ISDN, BRI, and PRI stand for?

Answer: ISDN stands for Integrated Services Digital Network. BRI stands for Basic Rate Interface. PRI stands for Primary Rate Interface.

2. How many bearer channels are in a BRI? What about a PRI in North America? What about a PRI in Europe?

   Answer: BRI uses two bearer channels and one signaling channel (2B+D). PRI uses 23B+D in North America and 30B+D in Europe. The signaling channel on BRI is a 16-kbps channel; on PRI, it is a 64-kbps channel.

3. Define what a voice codec does, and explain why a PCM codec needs 64 kbps for a single voice call.

   Answer: Voice codecs code and decode voice signals, converting from analog to digital, and digital to analog. A PCM codec samples the analog signal 8000 times per second, generating an 8-bit code to represent each sample. So, 64,000 bits are needed for a single second of voice.

4. Two terms were shortened and combined to first create the word modem. Identify those two words and describe what each word means.

   Answer: The term modem is formed as a combination of the words modulation and demodulation. Modulation means to vary or change a wave form to encode information. A modem varies an analog electrical signal to encode information, representing binary digits, onto an analog signal. Modulation refers to the creation of the analog signal based on a string of bits, and demodulation simply refers to a modem performing the reverse process upon receiving the analog signal.

5. Define what the terms symmetric and asymmetric mean in relation to modem specifications. Also explain why asymmetric might be a better option.

   Answer: Symmetric means that the speed in each direction of flow is the same, whereas asymmetric means that the speed in one direction is faster than the other. Asymmetric speeds might be a good choice because typical traffic flows require a much greater amount of data to flow in one direction, typically from a server to a client. Asymmetric speeds allow the speed in one direction to be faster than it could be with symmetric speeds, accommodating the need for more bandwidth in one direction.

6. Compare the V.90 and V.92 modem specifications.

   Answer: Based on this chapter, V.92 is an improvement over the V.90 standard. V.92 supports symmetric and asymmetric speeds, whereas V.90 supports only asymmetric speeds. The upstream speed has been increased from 33 kbps up to 48 kbps. It supports modem-on-hold, which allows the user to accept a voice call in response to a call-waiting signal, putting the modem connection on hold. It also senses the correct operational speed more quickly than V.90.

7. Compare analog modems, ISDN BRIs, DSL, and cable modems in terms of concurrent support for voice and data.

Answer: Analog modems do not support concurrent voice and data transmission. ISDN and DSL both support simultaneous voice and data over the same local loop (local phone line). Cable allows simultaneous data, voice, and TV reception.

8. Compare analog modems, ISDN BRIs, DSL, and cable modems in terms of whether the data service is always on.

Answer: Analog modems and ISDN BRIs must signal to set up a circuit, so any data capabilities, such as Internet connectivity, are not "always on." DSL and cable do not require any signaling to set up a circuit—in fact, no circuit is needed in the PSTN to support these technologies, so these services are "always on."

9. List some of the pros and cons regarding the use of analog modems for remote access.

Answer: Modems have the great advantage of being the most pervasively available remote access technology. The history of modems is long, with modems growing to be a very reliable choice for remote access. Speeds have improved over the years, with compression technology increasing the effective throughput to beyond 100 kbps. The biggest negatives about using modems include their relatively low speed and the fact that you cannot use the phone at the same time as you send data.

10. List some of the pros and cons regarding the use of ISDN for remote access.

Answer: ISDN's advantages include the capability to support voice calls concurrently with a data call. Also, ISDN can be used over the local telco loop, with no significant distance limitations. And it provides more bandwidth than do modems, particularly with both B channels dialed to the same remote site. ISDN does have a few disadvantages, with the biggest disadvantage being the lower speeds than DSL or cable.

11. List some of the pros and cons regarding the use of DSL for remote access.

Answer: DSL provides high-speed Internet access to the home, exceeding downstream speeds of 1 Mbps. It supports concurrent voice and data, with the data service always being turned on—no dialing is required. And the service speed does not degrade when more users are added to the network. However, DSL simply will not be available to some people, based on the distance to the local CO or the availability of DSL services from the local telco. Also, even when the home is close enough to the CO, sites farther from the CO might run slower than sites closer to the CO.

12. Define what the acronym DSLAM stands for, and explain the concept behind how a DSLAM allows voice and data to flow over the same local loop phone line.

Answer: DSLAM stands for DSL access multiplexer, with DSL meaning digital subscriber line. The DSLAM is connected to the local loop, splitting off the voice frequencies (0 to 4000 Hz) for the voice switch in the CO. It also interprets the higher frequencies as encoded digital signals, receiving the ATM cells sent over that digital signal, and forwards those ATM cells to the appropriate router.

13. Which of the DSL standards is the most common in the United States today? What is the range of upstream and downstream speeds for that type of DSL, as well as the maximum distance of the local loop?

Answer: ADSL, meaning asynchronous DSL, is the most popular. The downstream speeds range from 1.5 to 8 Mbps, with upstream speeds from 64 to 800 kbps. The maximum distance is 18,000 feet (approximately 5500 meters).

14. What protocols are used by DSL at the data link layer?

Answer: ATM, Ethernet, and PPP.

15. Imagine that Andy and Barney are neighbors, and they both use cable modems. Describe the type of traffic that they could generate that could cause collisions, and tell what is done to help prevent those collisions.

Answer: Downstream data never can cause a collision with upstream data because the two are sent in different frequency ranges. Because only the head end sends downstream data, no collisions can occur. Upstream data from all subscribers uses the same frequency range, so data sent to the head end by Andy and Barney could collide. Cable standards use a feature called time-division multiple access (TDMA) to assign time slots to each subscriber. This prevents most collisions so no collisions should occur.

16. Name the four different Layer 1 encoding methods defined for use by cable modems. For each one, list whether it is used for upstream data, downstream data, or both.

Answer: QAM-64 and QAM-256 are both available for use as downstream encoding methods. QAM-16 and QPSK are both available for upstream encoding.

17. Which of the four different remote access technologies support IP, TCP, UDP, and the rest of the higher-layer TCP/IP protocols?

Answer: All of them!

18. Compare and contrast the cabling used by an analog modem and a DSL router/modem when connecting to the local phone company line. Identify the purpose of each pin on the connector.

    Answer: Both use a cable with two wires, using an RJ-11 connector. Pin 3 is used for transmit; pin 4 is used for receive.

19. Compare and contrast the cabling used by an ISDN modem and a cable modem when connecting to the local phone company line or cable drop line. Identify the purpose of each pin on the connector.

    Answer: ISDN uses a four-wire cable using an RJ-45 connector. The pinouts: pins 3 and 6 for transmit, and pins 4 and 5 for receive. Cable modems use coaxial cable with a single conductor, so there are no pins. The round connector on the end of the cable is called an f-connector.

20. List four standards bodies that have been involved in the development of DSL standards.

    Answer: ANSI, IEEE, ETSI, ITU.

Decimal to Binary Conversion Table

Decimal Value	Binary Value	Decimal Value	Binary Value
0	0000 0000	23	0001 0111
1	0000 0001	24	0001 1000
2	0000 0010	25	0001 1001
3	0000 0011	26	0001 1010
4	0000 0100	27	0001 1011
5	0000 0101	28	0001 1100
6	0000 0110	29	0001 1101
7	0000 0111	30	0001 1110
8	0000 1000	31	0001 1111
9	0000 1001	32	0010 0000
10	0000 1010	33	0010 0001
11	0000 1011	34	0010 0010
12	0000 1100	35	0010 0011
13	0000 1101	36	0010 0100
14	0000 1110	37	0010 0101
15	0000 1111	38	0010 0110
16	0001 0000	39	0010 0111
17	0001 0001	40	0010 1000
18	0001 0010	41	0010 1001
19	0001 0011	42	0010 1010
20	0001 0100	43	0010 1011
21	0001 0101	44	0010 1100
22	0001 0110	45	0010 1101

continues

Decimal Value	Binary Value	Decimal Value	Binary Value
46	0010 1110	76	0100 1100
47	0010 1111	77	0100 1101
48	0011 0000	78	0100 1110
49	0011 0001	79	0100 1111
50	0011 0010	80	0101 0000
51	0011 0011	81	0101 0001
52	0011 0100	82	0101 0010
53	0011 0101	83	0101 0011
54	0011 0110	84	0101 0100
55	0011 0111	85	0101 0101
56	0011 1000	86	0101 0110
57	0011 1001	87	0101 0111
58	0011 1010	88	0101 1000
59	0011 1011	89	0101 1001
60	0011 1100	90	0101 1010
61	0011 1101	91	0101 1011
62	0011 1110	92	0101 1100
63	0011 1111	93	0101 1101
64	0100 0000	94	0101 1110
65	0100 0001	95	0101 1111
66	0100 0010	96	0110 0000
67	0100 0011	97	0110 0001
68	0100 0100	98	0110 0010
69	0100 0101	99	0110 0011
70	0100 0110	100	0110 0100
71	0100 0111	101	0110 0101
72	0100 1000	102	0110 0110
73	0100 1001	103	0110 0111
74	0100 1010	104	0110 1000
75	0100 1011	105	0110 1001

Decimal Value	Binary Value	Decimal Value	Binary Value
106	0110 1010	136	1000 1000
107	0110 1011	137	1000 1001
108	0110 1100	138	1000 1010
109	0110 1101	139	1000 1011
110	0110 1110	140	1000 1100
111	0110 1111	141	1000 1101
112	0111 0000	142	1000 1110
113	0111 0001	143	1000 1111
114	0111 0010	144	1001 0000
115	0111 0011	145	1001 0001
116	0111 0100	146	1001 0010
117	0111 0101	147	1001 0011
118	0111 0110	148	1001 0100
119	0111 0111	149	1001 0101
120	0111 1000	150	1001 0110
121	0111 1001	151	1001 0111
122	0111 1010	152	1001 1000
123	0111 1011	153	1001 1001
124	0111 1100	154	1001 1010
125	0111 1101	155	1001 1011
126	0111 1110	156	1001 1100
127	0111 1111	157	1001 1101
128	1000 0000	158	1001 1110
129	1000 0001	159	1001 1111
130	1000 0010	160	1010 0000
131	1000 0011	161	1010 0001
132	1000 0100	162	1010 0010
133	1000 0101	163	1010 0011
134	1000 0110	164	1010 0100
135	1000 0111	165	1010 0101

continues

Decimal Value	Binary Value	Decimal Value	Binary Value
166	1010 0110	196	1100 0100
167	1010 0111	197	1100 0101
168	1010 1000	198	1100 0110
169	1010 1001	199	1100 0111
170	1010 1010	200	1100 1000
171	1010 1011	201	1100 1001
172	1010 1100	202	1100 1010
173	1010 1101	203	1100 1011
174	1010 1110	204	1100 1100
175	1010 1111	205	1100 1101
176	1011 0000	206	1100 1110
177	1011 0001	207	1100 1111
178	1011 0010	208	1101 0000
179	1011 0011	209	1101 0001
180	1011 0100	210	1101 0010
181	1011 0101	211	1101 0011
182	1011 0110	212	1101 0100
183	1011 0111	213	1101 0101
184	1011 1000	214	1101 0110
185	1011 1001	215	1101 0111
186	1011 1010	216	1101 1000
187	1011 1011	217	1101 1001
188	1011 1100	218	1101 1010
189	1011 1101	219	1101 1011
190	1011 1110	220	1101 1100
191	1011 1111	221	1101 1101
192	1100 0000	222	1101 1110
193	1100 0001	223	1101 1111
194	1100 0010	224	1110 0000
195	1100 0011	225	1110 0001

Decimal Value	Binary Value	Decimal Value	Binary Value
226	1110 0010		
227	1110 0011		
228	1110 0100		
229	1110 0101		
230	1110 0110		
231	1110 0111		
232	1110 1000		
233	1110 1001		
234	1110 1010		
235	1110 1011		
236	1110 1100		
237	1110 1101		
238	1110 1110		
239	1110 1111		
240	1111 0000		
241	1111 0001		
242	1111 0010		
243	1111 0011		
244	1111 0100		
245	1111 0101		
246	1111 0110		
247	1111 0111		
248	1111 1000		
249	1111 1001		
250	1111 1010		
251	1111 1011		
252	1111 1100		
253	1111 1101		
254	1111 1110		
255	1111 1111		

Using the Simulation Software for the Hands-on Exercises

One of the most important skills required for passing the INTRO, ICND, and CCNA exams is the ability to configure Cisco routers and switches with confidence. In fact, one of the reasons that this book is relatively long is the effort put into explaining the commands, the output of **show** commands, and how the commands work together. Many CCNA candidates simply do not get a lot of hands-on experience, so this book is designed to help those who do not have real gear.

Another way to practice and develop hands-on skills is to use a simulator. A company called Boson Software, Inc. (www.boson.com) produces a network simulation product called the Boson NetSim™. The full NetSim product, available over the Internet from Boson, contains a large number of lab exercises and support for a large number of devices. You can even design your own network topology from scratch! It is a very impressive product.

The CD-ROM included with this book has a version of NetSim built specifically for this book. This version of NetSim includes support for several lab exercises and lab scenarios that were written just for this book. Although the software lets you work through these exercises, it is a limited-feature demo version of the actual NetSim software, which requires paid registration for full functionality. The full-feature version of NetSim includes a large set of other labs, including labs appropriate for the CCNP exams. You can also build a network topology with the full version of the product, so you can try any of the examples in this book or to experiment with networks.

This short appendix explains the following:

- How to get to the NetSim user interface on the CD-ROM
- What hands-on exercises in the book can be performed using this special edition of NetSim

Accessing NetSim from the CD

Accessing NetSim from the CD is relatively simple. Put the CD in the CD drive, and the software on the CD starts. (If it doesn't, run the command **autorun.exe** that is on the CD's root directory.) After logging in, select the Hands-on Practice Exercises and NetSim Demo Software link in the main menu. Another menu opens that allows you to view the CD-only appendixes of labs and to start the NetSim software.

NetSim lets you pick which lab topology to load. You pick a lab topology, and you next see the NetSim user interface.

You can think of what you see next as a real lab, with real routers and switches. The cabling topology and interface numbers match the labs and scenarios in this book. So you can access the devices and start entering commands!

The NetSim software includes the NetSim user guide, which helps you figure out how to navigate and use the NetSim product. (Just select "help" and "User guide" from NetSim.) However, the user manual does not tell you anything about the hands-on exercises you can do with this special version of NetSim! You can always just experiment using NetSim, trying all the commands you can think of, but remember that this is a limited-use version of the software, so not all commands are enabled. If you want some instructions on good things to try to do with the simulator, read the next section. It lists all the labs and scenarios in this book that can be performed using NetSim!

Hands-on Exercises Available with NetSim

This book includes two main types of exercises that can be duplicated using real gear or the special NetSim network simulator—scenarios and labs. You can improve your hands-on skills whether you perform these exercises using real gear, perform them using NetSim, or just read through the exercises.

Scenarios

In this Cisco Press Exam Certification Guide series, scenarios include some form of a problem statement, asking you to solve the problem. Then a suggested solution is shown, with an explanation of some of the pitfalls you might have encountered with your answer. Many of these scenarios include configuration and EXEC commands, but some do not. These scenarios are designed so that if you don't have access to real hardware, you can still learn more about the commands on routers and switches. These same scenarios can also be performed using NetSim!

Labs

This book also includes lab exercises, which follow a format typical of labs used in networking courses. These labs give you more guidance than do the scenarios. For instance, the scenarios simply state a goal, such as "Configure these three routers to support a full mesh of PVCs," whereas a lab gives you instructions for each step you need to take to configure the network. You simply read the lab instructions, and the lab guides you through the steps required to configure a network based on a stated set of requirements.

As with the scenarios, you can perform these labs on real gear or using the special NetSim build included with the CD that comes with this book. You can also just read through the labs and their solutions if your time is limited, but you might want to at least try to write down the solution before looking at the answer!

Listing of the Hands-on Exercises

To best use NetSim, you should first pick a particular lab or scenario. You might even want to print a copy if the lab or scenario is in one of the CD-only appendixes. Then you can bring up NetSim and select the corresponding NetSim lab topology that matches the lab or scenario. NetSim creates a simulated network that matches the lab or scenario, so all you have to do is start entering commands, just as if it were a real network with real gear!

The scenarios and labs are located in a couple different places. First, Chapter 18, "Final Preparation," includes one scenario. It covers a lot of different topics from the book. The CD contains a scenarios appendix (CD-only Appendix B, "Scenarios") and a lab appendix (CD-only Appendix C, "Hands-on Lab Exercises"). These scenarios and labs focus on a more specific set of topics. If you plan to use NetSim frequently, you should probably print the CD-only Appendixes B and C.

In CD-only Appendix B, the scenarios are numbered in a way to help remind you of the corresponding chapter in the book. For instance, Scenario 1 reinforces topics covered in Chapter 7, "Operating Cisco Routers," and Scenario 3 covers the same commands covered in Chapter 8, "Operating Cisco LAN Switches."

Table C-1 lists the different scenarios and labs from this book that can be performed using NetSim. Note that some of the scenarios in CD-only Appendix B cannot be performed on the simulator, mainly because those scenarios do not ask you to implement anything on a network, making the simulator unnecessary. So Table C-1 lists the scenarios and labs that can be performed using NetSim.

Table C-1 *Scenarios and Labs That Can Be Performed Using NetSim*

Scenario or Lab	Location	Topic	NetSim Lab Number
Scenario 1*	Chapter 16	Comprehensive scenario for topics in this book	1
Scenario 3	CD-only Appendix B	LAN switch basic configuration	2
Scenario 6	CD-only Appendix B	Subnet design with a Class B network	3
Lab 1*	CD-only Appendix C	Router command-line interface familiarization	4
Lab 2*	CD-only Appendix C	2950 series switch command-line interface familiarization	5
Lab 3*	CD-only Appendix C	Basic router IP configuration and management navigation	6

* Labs with an asterisk can be performed with the limited-function version of NetSim included with this book. To perform the other lab scenarios, you will need to purchase the full version of NetSim.

How You Should Proceed with NetSim

You can bring up NetSim and dive right in. However, here a a few suggestions before you are ready to do all the labs:

- Bring up NetSim now, and make sure you can at least get to a router command prompt, using the PC you will most likely use when studying. That way, when you are ready to do your first lab or scenario, you know you have worked out any installation issues.

- If you intend to do most of the labs and scenarios, you might want to print CD-only Appendixes B and C.

- Decide if you prefer to do the labs and scenarios after reading the book or as you go along.

- If you want to do the labs as you progress through the book, refer to Table C-2 for my suggestions on the best time to do the labs and scenarios.

Table C-2 *The Best Time to Do Each Lab or Scenario Using NetSim*

Scenario or Lab	Location	Topic	After Reading Which Chapter
Scenario: Chapter 16 of this book	Chapter 16	Comprehensive scenario for topics in this book	16
Scenario 3	CD-only Appendix B	LAN switch basic configuration	8
Scenario 6	CD-only Appendix B	Subnet design with a Class B network	12
Lab 1	CD-only Appendix C	Router command-line interface familiarization	7
Lab 2	CD-only Appendix C	2950 series switch command-line interface familiarization	8
Lab 3	CD-only Appendix C	Basic router IP configuration and management navigation	13

Considerations When Using NetSim

NetSim is a wonderful product, and you can certainly get a lot of good hands-on experience using the NetSim product that is included with the book. However, like any simulator product, it does not mimic a network with 100% accuracy. Some situations are difficult to simulate. For instance, it is very challenging to simulate the output of **debug** commands, because the simulator is not actually running IOS. If you intend to use NetSim, please download the latest list of hints, tips, and caveats from www.ciscopress.com/1587200945.

10BASE-T   The 10-Mbps baseband Ethernet specification using two pairs of twisted-pair cabling (Categories 3, 4, or 5): One pair transmits data and the other receives data. 10BASE-T, which is part of the IEEE 802.3 specification, has a distance limit of approximately 100 m (328 feet) per segment.

802.1Q   The IEEE standardized protocol for VLAN trunking.

AAA   Authentication, Authorization, and Accounting. Authentication confirms the identity of the user or device. Authorization determines what the user or device is allowed to do. Accounting records information about access attempts, including inappropriate request.

accounting   In security, the recording of access attempts. *See* AAA.

ADSL   Asymmetric digital subscriber line. One of many DSL technologies, ADSL is designed to deliver more bandwidth downstream (from the central office to the customer site) than upstream.

AppleTalk DDP   The AppleTalk Data Delivery Protocol (DDP) is the AppleTalk equivalent of the IP protocol. It defines a 24-bit address, with 16 bits defining the network and 8 bits defining the node.

ARP   Address Resolution Protocol. An Internet protocol used to map an IP address to a MAC address. Defined in RFC 826.

asynchronous   The lack of an imposed time ordering on a bit stream. Practically, both sides agree to the same speed, but there is no check or adjustment of the rates if they are slightly different. However, because only 1 byte per transfer is sent, slight differences in clock speed are not an issue. A start bit is used to signal the beginning of a byte.

ATM   Asynchronous Transfer Mode. The international standard for cell relay in which multiple service types (such as voice, video, or data) are conveyed in fixed-length (53-byte) cells. Fixed-length cells allow cell processing to occur in hardware, thereby reducing transit delays. ATM is designed to take advantage of high-speed transmission media, such as E3, SONET, and T3.

authentication   In security, the verification of the identity of a person or a process. *See* AAA.

authorization   In security, the determination of a user or devices rights in a network. *See* AAA.

auxiliary port   A physical connector on a router that is designed to be used to allow a remote terminal, or PC with a terminal emulator, to access a router using an analog modem.

balanced hybrid   A term that refers to a third general type of routing protocol algorithm, the other two being distance vector and link state. EIGRP is the only routing protocol that Cisco classifies as using a balanced hybrid algorithm.

Boolean AND   A math operation performed to a pair of one-digit binary numbers. The result is another one-digit binary number. 1 AND 1 yields 1; all other combinations yield a 0.

BRI   Basic Rate Interface. An ISDN interface composed of two bearer (B) channels and one data (D) channel for circuit-switched communication of voice, video, and data.

broadcast address   An IP address in each subnet is considered to be the broadcast address for that subnet. It is the highest numerical value in the range of numbers for the subnet; the broadcast address cannot be assigned as an IP address to a computer. Packets sent to this address are delivered to all hosts in the subnet.

broadcast domain   A set of all devices that receive broadcast frames originating from any device within the set. Devices in the same VLAN are in the same broadcast domain.

broadcast subnet   When subnetting a Class A, B, or C network, two subnet numbers are "discouraged" from use; one of those two subnets is the broadcast subnet. It is the subnet number for which the subnet bits all have a value of binary 1.

bus   A common physical signal path composed of wires or other media across which signals can be sent from one part of a computer to another. Also called a *highway*.

CDP   Cisco Discovery Protocol. A media- and protocol-independent device-discovery protocol that runs on all Cisco-manufactured equipment, including routers, access servers, bridges, and switches. Using CDP, a device can advertise its existence to other devices and receive information about other devices on the same LAN or on the remote side of a WAN. Runs on all media that support SNAP headers, including LANs, Frame Relay, and ATM media.

CHAP   Challenge Handshake Authentication Protocol. A security feature supported on lines using PPP encapsulation that prevents unauthorized access. CHAP does not itself prevent unauthorized access; it merely identifies the remote end. The router or access server then determines whether that user is allowed access.

CLI   Command-line interface. An interface that enables the user to interact with the operating system by entering commands and optional arguments.

clock source   The device to which the other devices on the link adjust their speed when using synchronous links.

codec   Coder-decoder. An integrated circuit device that transforms analog voice signals into a digital bit stream and then transforms digital signals back into analog voice signals.

collision domain   A set of network interface cards (NICs) for which a frame sent by one NIC could result in a collision with a frame sent by any other NIC in the same collision domain.

configuration mode   Inside the Cisco IOS Software CLI, a user can move among various modes. Configuration mode enables the user to enter configuration commands but not any EXEC commands—for instance, the user can configure an IP address, but cannot show the status of any router features.

configuration register   In Cisco routers, a 16-bit, user-configurable value that determines how the router functions during initialization. In software, the bit position is set by specifying a hexadecimal value using configuration commands.

console port   A component of a router or switch through which commands are entered into a host.

convergence   The time required for routers to react to changes in the network, removing bad routes and adding new, better routes so that the current best routes are in all the routers' routing tables.

CPE   Customer premises equipment. Any equipment related to communications that is located at the customer site, as opposed to inside the telephone company's network.

CSMA/CD   Carrier sense multiple access collision detect. A media-access mechanism in which devices ready to transmit data first check the channel for a carrier. If no carrier is sensed for a specific period of time, a device can transmit. If two devices transmit at once, a collision occurs and is detected by all colliding devices. This collision subsequently delays retransmissions from those devices for some random length of time.

CSU/DSU   Data service unit/channel service unit. Used on digital links as an interface to the telephone company in the United States. Routers typically use a short cable from a serial interface to a DSU/CSU, which is attached to the line from the telco with a similar configuration at the other router on the other end of the link.

demarc   The demarcation or separation point between carrier equipment and CPE.

Diffusing Update Algorithm (DUAL)   The process by which EIGRP routers collectively calculate the routes to place into the routing tables.

Dijkstra Shortest Path First (SPF) algorithm   Magic math used by link-state protocols, such as OSPF, when the routing table is calculated.

directed broadcast address   Same thing as broadcast address.

distance vector   The logic behind the behavior of some interior routing protocols, such as RIP and IGRP. Distance vector routing algorithms call for each router to send its entire routing table in each update, but only to its neighbors. Distance vector routing algorithms can be prone to routing loops but are computationally simpler than link-state routing algorithms. Also called *Bellman-Ford routing algorithm*.

DNS   Domain Name System. A system used on the Internet for translating names of network nodes into addresses.

DSL   Digital subscriber line. Public network technology that delivers high bandwidth over conventional copper wiring at limited distances. The most common types of DSL are ADSL, HDSL, SDSL, and VDSL. Because most DSL technologies do not use the complete bandwidth of the twisted pair, there is room remaining for a voice channel.

E1   Similar to a T1, but used in Europe. It uses a rate of 2.048 Mbps and 32 64-kbps channels.

enable mode   Inside the Cisco IOS Software CLI, a user can move among various modes. Enable mode, also called enable EXEC mode, allows the user to use the most powerful and potentially disruptive commands on a router.

encapsulation   The wrapping of data in a particular protocol header. For example, an IP packet could be encapsulated in an Ethernet header and trailer before being sent over an Ethernet.

encryption   Applying a specific algorithm to data to alter the appearance of the data, making it incomprehensible to those who are not authorized to see the information.

error recovery   The process of noticing when some transmitted data was not successfully received and resending the data until it is successfully received.

Ethernet   A baseband LAN specification invented by Xerox Corporation and developed jointly by Xerox, Intel, and Digital Equipment Corporation. Ethernet networks use CSMA/CD and run over a variety of cable types.

exterior routing protocol   A routing protocol designed for use between two different organizations. These typically are used between ISPs or between a company and an ISP. For example, a company would run BGP, an exterior routing protocol, between one of its routers and a router inside an ISP.

FCIP   Fibre Channel over IP. A protocol for sending Fibre Channel protocols over an IP network.

Fibre Channel   A technology for transmitting data between computer devices at data rates from 100 MBps to 400 MBps over optical fiber or copper. Fibre Channel is optimized for connecting servers to shared storage devices and for interconnecting storage controllers and drives.

filter   Generally, a process or a device that screens network traffic for certain characteristics, such as source address, destination address, or protocol, and determines whether to forward or discard that traffic based on the established criteria.

firewall   A device or a software package that separates more secure network components from less secure components, protecting the more secure network from inappropriate access.

Flash   A type of permanent memory, implemented either with a EEPROM chip or with a PC card that can be easily removed. Routers use flash instead of disk drives for storing large files, particularly the IOS.

flow control   The process of regulating the amount of data sent by a sending computer towards a receiving computer. Several flow control mechanisms exist, including TCP flow control which uses windowing.

forward   To send a frame received in one interface out another interface, toward its ultimate destination.

four-wire circuit   A line from the telco with four wires, composed of two twisted-pair wires. Each pair is used to send in one direction, so a four-wire circuit allows full-duplex communication.

Frame Relay   An industry-standard, switched data link layer protocol that handles multiple virtual circuits using LAPF encapsulation between connected devices. Frame Relay is more efficient than X.25, the protocol for which it generally is considered a replacement.

frame   A logical grouping of information sent as a data link layer unit over a transmission medium. Can also be called an *L2PDU*.

full mesh   A term describing a network in which devices are organized in a mesh topology, with each network node having either a physical circuit or a virtual circuit connecting it to every other network node. A full mesh provides a great deal of redundancy, but because it can be prohibitively expensive to implement, it usually is reserved for network backbones.

hash   A mathematical formula applied to some input value for which it is difficult to recreate the input value even if you know the results of the formula. Hashes are useful for transmission of passwords because, even if intercepted, the hashed representation of a password cannot easily be used to find the original password.

HDLC   High-Level Data Link Control. A bit-oriented synchronous data link layer protocol that specifies a data encapsulation method on synchronous serial links using frame characters and checksums.

head end   The upstream, transmit end of a CATV installation.

holddown   A state into which a route is placed so that routers neither advertise the route nor accept advertisements about the route for a specific length of time (the holddown period). Holddown is used to flush bad information about a route from all routers in the network. A route typically is placed in holddown when a link in that route fails.

host address   The IP address assigned to a network card on a computer.

host   A computer system on a network. Similar to a node, except that host usually implies a computer system, whereas node generally applies to any networked system, including access servers and routers.

HTML   Hypertext Markup Language. A simple hypertext document-formatting language that uses tags to indicate how a given part of a document should be interpreted by a viewing application, such as a web browser.

HTTP   Hypertext Transfer Protocol. The protocol used by web browsers and web servers to transfer files, such as text and graphic files.

ICMP   Internet Control Message Protocol. A network layer Internet protocol that reports errors and provides other information relevant to IP packet processing. Documented in RFC 792.

IEEE 802.2   An IEEE LAN protocol that specifies an implementation of the LLC sublayer of the data link layer. IEEE 802.2 handles errors, framing, flow control, and the network layer (Layer 3) service interface. Used in IEEE 802.3 and IEEE 802.5 LANs.

IEEE 802.3   An IEEE LAN protocol that specifies an implementation of the physical layer and the MAC sublayer of the data link layer. IEEE 802.3 uses CSMA/CD access at a variety of speeds over a variety of physical media.

IEEE   Institute of Electrical and Electronics Engineers. A professional organization that develops communications and network standards, among other activities.

IGRP   Interior Gateway Routing Protocol. Interior Gateway Protocol (IGP) developed by Cisco to address the issues associated with routing in large networks.

interior routing protocol   A routing protocol designed for use within a single organization. For example, an entire company might choose the IGRP routing protocol, which is an interior routing protocol.

IOS   Cisco operating system software that provides common functionality, scalability, and security for all Cisco products. Cisco IOS Software allows centralized, integrated, and automated installation and management of internetworks while ensuring support for a wide variety of protocols, media, services, and platforms.

IP   Internet Protocol. The network layer protocol in the TCP/IP stack offering a connectionless internetwork service.

IP address   A 32-bit address assigned to hosts using TCP/IP. Each address consists of a network number, an optional subnetwork number, and a host number. The network and subnetwork numbers together are used for routing, and the host number is used to address an individual host within the network or subnetwork.

IPX   Internetwork Packet Exchange. A Novell NetWare network layer (Layer 3) protocol used for transferring data from servers to workstations. IPX is similar to IP and XNS.

iSCSI   IP SCSI. A protocol for sending and receiving SCSI commands over an IP network, providing file-level access to shared storage devices.

ISDN   Integrated Services Digital Network. A service offered by telephone companies that permits telephone networks to carry data, voice, and other source traffic.

ISL   Inter-Switch Link. The Cisco proprietary VLAN trunking protocol.

ISO   International Organization for Standardization. An international organization that is responsible for a wide range of standards, including those relevant to networking. The ISO developed the OSI reference model, a popular networking reference model.

L4PDU   The data compiled by a Layer 4 protocol, including Layer 4 headers and encapsulated high-layer data, but not including lower-layer headers and trailers.

Layer 3 protocol   A protocol that it has characteristics like OSI Layer 3, which defines logical addressing and routing. IP, IPX, and AppleTalk DDP are all Layer 3 protocols.

learn   The process of discovering MAC addresses, and their relative location by looking at the source MAC address of all frames received by a bridge or switch.

link-state   A type of routing protocol which sends full topology information about the network to all routers, so they all have a consistent view of the network topology and status. Link-state algorithms create a consistent view of the network and, therefore, are not prone to routing loops; however, they achieve this at the cost of relatively greater computational difficulty and more widespread traffic.

LLC   Logical Link Control. The higher of the two data link layer sublayers defined by the IEEE. Synonymous with IEEE 802.2.

local loop   A line from the premises of a telephone subscriber to the telephone company CO.

MAC Media Access Control. The lower of the two sublayers of the data link layer defined by the IEEE. Synonymous with IEEE 802.3 for Ethernet LANs.

MAC address A standardized data link layer address that is required for every device that connects to a LAN. Ethernet MAC addresses are 6 bytes long and are controlled by the IEEE. Also known as a *hardware address*, a *MAC layer address*, and a *physical address*.

metric A unit of measure used by routing protocol algorithms to determine the best pathway for traffic to use to reach a particular destination.

modem Modulator-demodulator. A device that converts digital and analog signals for the purpose of communicating over analog telephone lines. At the source, a modem converts digital signals to a form suitable for transmission over analog communication facilities. At the destination, the analog signals are returned to their digital form. Modems allow data to be transmitted over voice-grade telephone lines.

multimode A type of fiber-optic cabling with a larger core than single-mode cabling, allowing light to enter at multiple angles. Such cabling has lower bandwidth than single-mode fiber but requires a typically cheaper light source, such as an LED.

name server A server connected to a network that resolves network names into network addresses.

network A collection of computers, printers, routers, switches, and other devices that can communicate with each other over some transmission medium.

network number A number that uses dotted-decimal notation like IP addresses, but the number itself represents all hosts in a single Class A, B, or C IP network.

NVRAM Nonvolatile RAM. A type of random-access memory (RAM) that retains its contents when a unit is powered off.

OSI Open System Interconnection reference model. A network architectural model developed by the ISO. The model consists of seven layers, each of which specifies particular network functions, such as addressing, flow control, error control, encapsulation, and reliable message transfer. The OSI reference model is used universally as a method for teaching and understanding network functionality.

packet A logical grouping of information that includes the network layer header and encapsulated data.

PAP Password Authentication Protocol. An authentication protocol that allows Point-to-Point Protocol (PPP) peers to authenticate one another. Unlike the Challenge Handshake Authentication Protocol (CHAP), PAP passes the password and the host name or username in the clear (unencrypted).

partial mesh A network in which devices are organized in a mesh topology, with some network nodes organized in a full mesh but others that are connected only to one or two other nodes in the network. A partial mesh does not provide the level of redundancy of a full-mesh topology but is less expensive to implement. Partial-mesh topologies generally are used in the peripheral networks that connect to a fully meshed backbone.

PCM Pulse code modulation. A technique of encoding analog voice into a 64-kbps data stream by sampling with 8-bit resolution at a rate of 8000 times per second.

PDU Protocol data unit. An OSI term to refer generically to a grouping of information by a particular layer of the OSI mode. More specifically, an LxPDU would imply the data and headers as defined by Layer x.

ping Packet Internet groper. An Internet Control Message Protocol (ICMP) echo message and its reply; ping often is used in IP networks to test the reachability of a network device.

port number A field in a TCP or UDP header that identifies the application that either sent (source port) or should receive (destination port) the data inside the data segment.

PPP Point-to-Point Protocol. A protocol that provides router-to-router and host-to-network connections over synchronous and asynchronous circuits.

prefix notation A shorter way to write a subnet mask in which the number of binary 1s in the mask is simply written in decimal. For instance, /24 denotes the subnet mask with 24 binary 1 bits in the subnet mask. The number of bits of value binary 1 in the mask is considered to be the prefix.

PRI Primary Rate Interface. An Integrated Services Digital Network (ISDN) interface to primary rate access. Primary rate access consists of a single 64-kbps D channel plus 23 (T1) or 30 (E1) B channels for voice or data.

Protocol Type field A field in a LAN header that identifies the type of header that follows the LAN header. Includes the DIX Ethernet Type field, the IEEE 802.2 DSAP field, and the SNAP protocol Type field.

PSTN Public Switched Telephone Network. A general term referring to the variety of telephone networks and services in place worldwide. Sometimes called *POTS*.

PTT Post, telephone, and telegraph. A government agency that provides telephone services. PTTs exist in most areas outside of North America and provide both local and long-distance telephone services.

RAM Random-access memory. A type of volatile memory that can be read and written by a microprocessor.

RFC Request For Comments. A document used as the primary means for communicating information about the TCP/IP protocols. Some RFCs are designated by the Internet Architecture Board (IAB) as Internet standards, and others are informational. RFCs are available online from numerous sources, including www.rfc-editor.org/.

RIP Routing Information Protocol. An Interior Gateway Protocol (IGP) supplied with UNIX Berkeley Standard Distribution (BSD) systems. RIP is the most common IGP in the Internet and uses hop count as a routing metric.

RJ-45 A popular type of cabling connector used for Ethernet cabling. It is similar to the RJ-11 connector used for telephone wiring in homes in the United States. RJ-45 allows the connection of eight wires.

ROM Read-only memory. A type of nonvolatile memory that can be read but not written by the microprocessor.

routed protocol A protocol that can be routed by a router. A router must be capable of interpreting the logical internetwork as specified by that routed protocol. Examples of routed protocols include AppleTalk, DECnet, and IP.

routing protocol A protocol that accomplishes routing through the implementation of a specific routing algorithm. Examples of routing protocols include the Interior Gateway Routing Protocol (IGRP), the Open Shortest Path First (OSPF) protocol, and the Routing Information Protocol (RIP).

segment A term used in the TCP specification to describe a single transport layer unit of information. Can instead be called an *L4PDU*.

segmentation The process of breaking a large piece of data from an application into pieces appropriate in size to be sent through the network.

single-mode A type of fiber-optic cabling with a narrow core that allows light to enter only at a single angle. Such cabling has a higher bandwidth than multimode fiber but requires a light source with a narrow spectral width (such as a laser).

socket A software structure operating as a communications endpoint within a network device.

SONET Synchronous Optical Network. A standard format for transporting a wide range of digital telecommunications services over optical fiber. SONET is characterized by standard line rates, optical interfaces, and signal formats. SONET is a high-speed (up to 2.5 Gbps) synchronous network specification developed by Bellcore and designed to run on optical fiber. STS-1 is the basic building block of SONET. It was approved as an international standard in 1988.

star A method of connecting devices in which endpoints on a network are connected to a common central switch by point-to-point links.

storage router A device that sits between an IP network and storage devices, translating between disk IO protocols as they pass through non-IP and IP networks.

STP Shielded twisted pair. A two-pair wiring medium used in a variety of network implementations. Shielded twisted-pair cabling has a layer of shielded insulation to reduce electromagnetic interference (EMI). Can also refer to Spanning Tree Protocol, which is used to prevent bridging/switching loops.

subnet broadcast address Same thing as broadcast address.

subnet mask A 32-bit address mask used indicate the bits of an IP address that are being used for the subnet part of the address. Sometimes referred to simply as the mask.

subnet Subnets are subdivisions of a Class A, B, or C network, as configured by a network administrator. Subnets allow a single Class A, B, or C network to be used instead of multiple networks, and still allow for a large number of groups of IP addresses, as is required for efficient IP routing.

subnetting The process of subdividing a Class A, B, or C network and into smaller portions called subnets.

switch A network device that filters, forwards, and floods frames based on the destination address of each frame. The switch operates at the data link layer of the Open System Interconnections (OSI) reference model.

synchronous The imposition of time ordering on a bit stream. Practically, a device will try to use the same speed as another device on the other end of a serial link. However, by examining transitions between voltage states on the link, the device can notice slight variations in the speed on each end and can adjust its speed accordingly.

T1   A line from the telco that allows transmission of data at 1.544 Mbps.

TCP   Transmission Control Protocol. A connection-oriented transport layer TCP/IP protocol that provides reliable data transmission.

TCP/IP   Transmission Control Protocol/Internet Protocol. A common name for the suite of protocols developed by the U.S. Department of Defense in the 1970s to support the construction of worldwide internetworks. TCP and IP are the two best-known protocols in the suite.

telco   A common abbreviation for telephone company.

Telnet   The standard terminal emulation protocol in the TCP/IP protocol stack. Telnet is used for remote terminal connection, enabling users to log in to remote systems and use resources as if they were connected to a local system. Telnet is defined in RFC 854.

trace   Short for traceroute. A program available on many systems that traces the path that a packet takes to a destination. It is used mostly to debug routing problems between hosts. A traceroute protocol also is defined in RFC 1393.

transparent bridge   A device that forwards frames between LAN segments based on the destination MAC address. Transparent bridging is so named because the presence of bridges is transparent to network end nodes.

trunking   Also called *VLAN trunking*. A method (using either Cisco's ISL protocol or the IEEE 802.1q protocol) to support multiple VLANs that have members on more than one switch.

twisted pair   Transmission medium consisting of two insulated wires arranged in a regular spiral pattern. The wires can be shielded or unshielded. Twisted pair is common in telephony applications and in data networks.

UDP   User Datagram Protocol. Connectionless transport layer protocol in the TCP/IP protocol stack. UDP is a simple protocol that exchanges datagrams without acknowledgments or guaranteed delivery.

update timer   A timer used by a router to indicate when to send the next routing update.

user mode   A mode of the user interface to a router or switch in which the user can type only nondisruptive EXEC commands, generally just to look at the current status, but not to change any operational settings.

UTP   Unshielded twisted pair. A four-pair wire medium used in a variety of networks. UTP does not require the fixed spacing between connections that is necessary with coaxial-type connections. Five types of UTP cabling are commonly used: Category 1 through Category 5 cabling.

VLAN   A group of devices on one or more LANs that are configured (using management software) so that they can communicate as if they were attached to the same wire, when, in fact, they are located on a number of different LAN segments. Because VLANs are based on logical instead of physical connections, they are extremely flexible.

VoIP   Voice over IP. The capability to carry voice over an IP-based Internet. VoIP enables a router to carry voice traffic (for example, telephone calls and faxes) over an IP network.

well-known port   A port number reserved for use by a particular application. The use of well-known ports allows a client to send a TCP or UDP segment to a server, to the correct destination port for that application.

windowing   The term window represents the number of bytes that can be sent without receiving an acknowledgment. Windowing is the dynamic raising and lowering of the window to control the flow of data in a network.

WWW   World Wide Web. A large client/server network of Internet servers providing hypertext and other services (based on HTML and HTTP) to terminals running client applications, such as a browser.

zero subnet   When subnetting a Class A, B, or C network, two subnet numbers are "discouraged" from use; the zero subnet is one of these two subnets. It is the subnet number for which the subnet bits all have a value of binary 0.

Index

Symbols & Numerics

? (question mark), CLI help system, 179

10Base2, **53–54, 60**
    LAN switching, 60–63
    repeaters, 55
10Base5, **53–54, 60**
    LAN switching, 60–63
    repeaters, 55
10BaseT
    full-duplex, 71
    half-duplex, 59
    LAN switching, 60–63
10 Gigabit Ethernet, 299–300
10-Mbps Ethernet, 53–56, 60–61
    cabling, 57–58
    hubs, 59–60
    switching, 60–63
802.11 WLANs, 301–302
802.1q trunking, 266–267

A

access links, 97
access lists, 486–487
accessing CLI, 176–177, 214, 221
    multiple Telnet connections, 178
    on Cisco 2950 switches, 215
    passwords, 177
ACK field, TCP connection
    establishment, 158
active configuration, 188
adding connected routes to routing tables,
    376–379
address classes, 122–124, 319–320

addresses, 51
    addressing schemes, 118
    AppleTalk addresses
        grouping, 118
        structure, 119, 139
    burned-in addresses, 65
    group addresses, 64
    IP addresses
        Class A networks, 122
        Class B networks, 122
        Class C networks, 122
        grouping, 118
        hostnames, displaying, 369
        interfaces, displaying, 369
        structure, 119, 139
    IPX addresses
        grouping, 118
        structure, 119, 139
    MAC addresses, 64
        BIAs, 64
        broadcast addresses, 64, 237
        components, 64
        LAN card addressing, 64, 237
        multicast addresses, 65, 237
        OUI, 64
        unicast, 64
    network layer, 118–119
amplitude modulation, 443
analog modems
    baud, 444
    installing, 445–446
    modulation, 442–444
    PPP, 444
    standards, 446–447
analog signals, 436
    converting to digital, 438–439
    Nyquist's theorem, 440

K-L

Cisco Press

Learning is serious business.

Invest wisely.

learn

NOW
I HAVE THE POWER TO MAKE
YOU MORE PRODUCTIVE ON THE JOB.
I CAN PREPARE YOU TO MEET
NEW CHALLENGES.

I AM A CISCO CAREER CERTIFICATION.
ADD ME TO YOUR TOOLBOX WITH
AUTHORIZED TRAINING FROM
CISCO LEARNING PARTNERS...
PAY EASILY WITH CISCO
LEARNING CREDITS.

It is the power to acquire new skillsets, and expand your capabilities. Only Cisco Learning Partners can put you ahead of the curve. Visit **www.cisco.com/go/learningpartners**.

THIS IS THE POWER OF THE NETWORK. now.

CISCO SYSTEMS

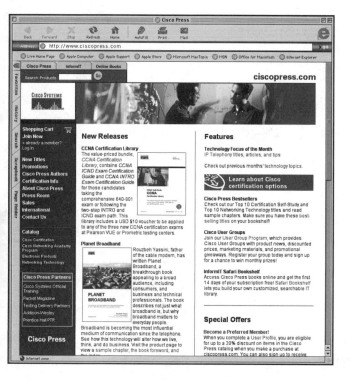

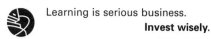

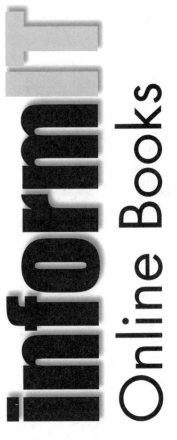